Footprint story

It was 1921

Ireland had just been partitioned, the British miners were striking for more pay and the federation of British industry had an idea. Exports were booming in South America – how about a handbook for businessmen trading in that far away continent? The Anglo-South American Handbook was born that year, written by W Koebel, the most prolific writer on Latin America of his day.

1924

Two editions later the book was 'privatized' and in 1924, in the hands of Royal Mail, the steamship company for South America, it became The South American Handbook, subtitled 'South America in a nutshell'. This annual publication became the 'bible' for generations of travellers to South America and remains so to this day. In the early days travel was by sea and the Handbook gave all the details needed for the long voyage from Europe. What to wear for dinner; how to arrange a cricket match with the Cable & Wireless staff on the Cape Verde Islands and a full account of the journey from Liverpool up the Amazon to Manaus: 5898 miles without changing cabin!

1939

As the continent opened up, the South American Handbook reported the new Pan Am flying boat services, and the fortnightly airship service from Rio to Europe on the Graf Zeppelin. For reasons still unclear but with extraordinary determination, the annual editions continued through the Second World War.

1970s

Many more people discovered South America and the backpacking trail started to develop. All the while the Handbook was gathering fans, including literary vagabonds such as Paul Theroux and Graham Greene (who once sent some updates addressed to "The publishers of the best travel guide in the world, Bath, England").

1990s

During the 1990s the company set about developing a new travel guide series using this legendary title as the flagship. By 1997 there were over a dozen guides in the series and the Footprint imprint was launched.

2000s

The series grew quickly and there were soon Footprint travel guides covering more than 150 countries. In 2004, Footprint launched its first thematic guide: Surfing Europe, packed with colour photographs, maps and charts. This was followed by further thematic guides such as Diving the World, Snowboarding the World, Body and Soul escapes, Travel with Kids and European City Breaks.

2011

Today we continue the traditions of the last 90 years that have served legions of travellers so well. We believe that these help to make Footprint guides different. Our policy is to use authors who are genuine experts who write for independent travellers; people possessing a spirit of adventure, looking to get off the beaten track.

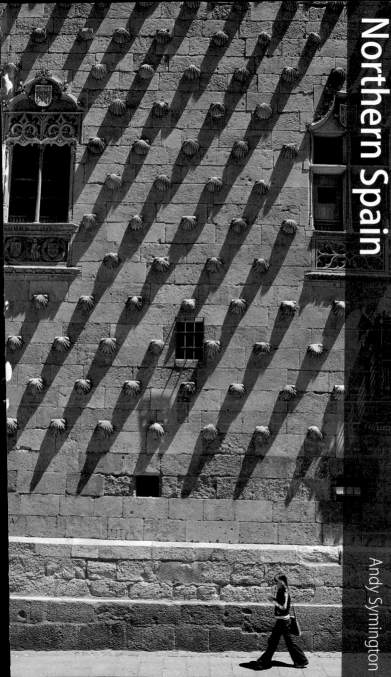

Northern Spain

Andy Symington

Spain began in its north. Say that to the Asturians and they'll puff up with pride, for when the Moorish wave swept rapidly across the peninsula in the eighth century, the small mountain kingdom stood indomitable. It was from here that the long process of Christian reconquest began, laying the foundations of modern Spain. It wasn't necessarily subtle, and the culturally sophisticated Moors must have wondered where they had gone wrong, but the tide turned. The Asturians erected beautiful churches in the eighth century, León had 24 kings before Castilla had laws, and Castilla was a muscly European kingdom centuries before Madrid was heard of. Aragón ruled the western Mediterranean and half of Italy, and progressive Navarra briefly united the whole of Christian Spain in days when Vikings still prowled the seas.

Fascinatingly, these ancient kingdoms still exist, and not just in terms of modern administrative boundaries. Travel between the Basque country and neighbouring Burgos and you're crossing a sociocultural border that's immediately evident in every way: how people eat, dress, earn a living and even what language they speak. The same goes for Asturias, for Aragón, for Galicia; and the cities of the plain in Castilla seem like little autonomous kingdoms. One common aspect is the region's immense architectural wealth. Even the most forgotten of villages may flaunt city walls, a majestic church and a handful of imposing stone palacios unchanged by the passage of time. On the natural side is a series of fabulous protected parks and reserves backed by a network of excellent rural accommodation.

Tourism in the north is is a world away from the crowded colonies of the southern coasts. It's the original Spain, or more accurately Spains, and whether you're admiring Gothic vaulting, nosing wine in the Rioja, surfing Basque waves or pacing the pilgrim road to Santiago, it's a vital, vivid and engaging place.

This page The coast of Asturias, near Llanes.
Previous page The Casa de las Conchas, Salamanca.

Highlights

Atlantic Ocean

A Coruña • Ferrol

12

Avilés • Gijón **10**

Oviedo •

Llanes

Santiago de Compostela

Lugo •

11

ASTURIAS

Torrecerredo (2684m)

Cordillera Cantábrica

Picos de Europa **9**

GALICIA

Ponferrada

Montes de León

6 León

Pontevedra •

Monforte •

Cabeza de Manzaneda (1778m)

Astorga

Camino de Santiago

Vigo •

Ourense •

Moncalvo (2044m)

CASTILLA Y LEON

Benavente •

Medina de Rioseco

Palencia •

PORTUGAL

Zamora •

Valladolid •

Toro •

Tordesillas

Medina del Campo

Salamanca •

8

① There's heavenly bar food and a fabulous beach at San Sebastián, the gourmet capital of the region. ❯❯ page 58.

② Bilbao is a masterclass on urban regeneration; the Guggenheim's just part of it. ❯❯ page 90.

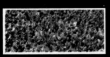

③ Pamplona goes mad for nine days of bull-running and wine-swilling at the Fiesta de San Fermín. ❯❯ page 132.

④ The Aragonese Pyrenees are the most magnificent part of this breathtakingly splendid mountain range. ❯❯ page 190.

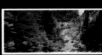

⑤ Catacomb-style bodegas and striking modern wineries are on show in medieval Rioja Alavesa and Rioja Alta. ❯❯ page 221.

⑥ León's Gothic cathedral has an inspiring assemblage of stained glass. ❯❯ page 264.

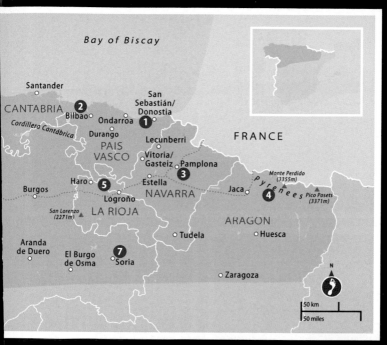

Bay of Biscay

Santander
CANTABRIA
Cordillera Cantábrica
Bilbao **2**
Ondarroa
Durango
1 San Sebastián/Donostia
PAIS VASCO
Lecunberri
Vitoria/Gasteiz
Pamplona
Estella
3
FRANCE
Monte Perdido (3355m)
Pyrenees
Jaca
4
Pico Posets (3371m)
Haro **5**
Burgos
Logroño
NAVARRA
San Lorenzo (2271m)
LA RIOJA
Aranda de Duero
El Burgo de Osma
7 Soria
Tudela
ARAGON
Huesca
Zaragoza

N

50 km
50 miles

7 Charming, church-filled Soria is one of Spain's smallest, least visited provincial capitals. ▶▶ page 286.

8 Possibly Spain's most beautiful town, Salamanca has an utterly harmonious Plaza Mayor. ▶▶ page 326.

9 There's excellent walking among the deservedly eulogized limestone massifs of the Picos de Europa. ▶▶ page 360.

10 Celtic Gijón and the Asturian coast offer free-flowing cider, delicious seafood, bagpipes and rustic cheer. ▶▶ page 394.

11 Each year, magical, granite Santiago de Compostela is destination for 100,000 pilgrims. ▶▶ page 431.

12 There's superb setting, fine architecture, great beach and unforgettable octopus bars in A Coruña. ▶▶ page 453.

Clockwise from top
Salamanca.
A Coruña.
San Sébastián.
León.

Opposite page top Picos de Europa.
Opposite page bottom Bilbao.

Camino de Santiago

The revival of the medieval pilgrim route to Santiago's magnificent cathedral has been striking. Today's *peregrinos* come from all backgrounds; some seek spiritual redemption, others time to think, and yet others just a good long walk. It's a fantastic way to see Northern Spain; the route crosses the whole region, taking in the Pyrenees, verdant Galicia, historic Castilla and many of the area's most picturesque villages and interesting towns. There's a huge variety of routes to choose from. The full route from Roncesvalles to Santiago is some 800 km, which translates to a walk of four to five weeks or a cycle ride of a fortnight. Many pilgrims do the journey in stages, a week each year, or just do the last bit, from León or Ponferrada.

The most travelled route, and the one with the most pilgrim facilities, is the Camino Francés. Originating in the French town of St Jean Pied-de-Port in the Pyrenees, it crosses a pass to Roncesvalles, then descends the Navarran valley to Pamplona. Heading southwest, it passes through Puente la Reina and Estella, near which is a tap dispensing red wine! Then it goes through Viana to Logroño, capital of the Rioja region. The next stages take in Nájera and Santo Domingo de la Calzada, where the chickens in the church are part of the Camino's rich folk history.

Once out of La Rioja, the *meseta* plain kicks in. The next major stop is Burgos, then it's more villages, all bursting with Romanesque architecture.

León province follows, through Sahagún and to the capital itself, a good rest stop normally reached by walkers 17-20 days into the journey. The pilgrims continue to Astorga, then Ponferrada via the enchanting village of Molinaseca.

From Ponferrada, the last, long climb begins into the Galician mountains. This ascent to the Piedrafita pass is one of the prettiest sections of the route.

From there, it's up and down over the rolling hills of central Galicia to the granite towers of the cathedral in Santiago. Some pilgrims continue on to Finisterre, but take a photocopy of your *credencial*, which you've probably handed over in Santiago.

The Camino Aragonés is also popular, differing only initially as it crosses into Spain in a more spectacular section of the Pyrenees, and descends the Canfranc Valley to the lively town of Jaca. It joins the Camino Francés at the town of Puente la Reina in Navarra.

A less used route, the Camino del Norte, follows the north coast and is arguably the most scenic, while the Ruta de la Plata, taken by people coming from the south of Spain, passes through Salamanca and Zamora. The Camino Primitivo starts from a village near Lugo, the Camino Portugués starts from Porto and heads north, and the Camino Inglés starts at A Coruña (where English pilgrims arriving by boat traditionally disembarked) and tracks south. These alternative routes have the benefit of far lower numbers of high-season pilgrims. The Confraternity of Saint James, www.csj.org.uk, is a useful organization that issues Pilgrim Passports and sells guides to the pilgrim routes. The website is also helpful for further information on the Camino. For practical information, see page 22 and relevant sections throughout the book.

Santiago de Compostela,
the end of the road.

Contents

CANTABRIA
& THE
PICOS DE
EUROPA

ASTURIAS

GALICIA

PAIS
VASCO

NAVARRA

CASTILLA Y LEON

LA RIOJA

NORTHERN
ARAGON

Contents

Footprint features

Essentials

Planning your trip

Where to go

In such a large and diverse region as Northern Spain, where you choose to go is largely a matter of what you're intrigued by, as well as the length of time you've got and where your point of entry is. Northern Spain is composed of several distinct regions, all of which offer a very different travel experience.

The green, fertile País Vasco has traditionally been a base of both agriculture and heavy industry and is homeland of the Basques, independent in outlook and spirit. It fascinates on many levels: the scenic coast and rugged interior, the leisured gourmet paradise of San Sebastián reclining languidly around its sumptuous bay, and the tangibly energetic dynamo that is Bilbao, still confident about its urban regeneration of which the spectacularly fluid Guggenheim Museum is only a part.

The genteel port of Santander is many ferryboating visitors' first point of contact with the north, and a fine spot it is too, with marvellous beaches and charismatic taverns. Its province, Cantabria, has important prehistoric caves, noble stone-built villages such as Liérganes or Santillana del Mar, and the awesome scenery plus inspiring walking of the lofty Picos de Europa, whose mountainscapes leave an indelible impression at any time of year.

These mountains are shared with Asturias, a wonderful enclave of green valleys, character-packed fishing towns and convivial cider culture that will have you staying longer than you planned. Its capital, Oviedo, is a noble, staid sort of place, while larger Gijón backs a magnificent town beach with a hard-working heritage and an appetite for fun.

West of here, Galicia faces the Atlantic with the gruff melancholy of a fisherman riding out a storm. It's a land of Celtic roots, with corners of its interior being among the peninsula's least explored areas. Its impossibly tortuous coast is an obvious draw too, but it's the region's cities – from rugged maritime Vigo to bonhomie-filled Lugo and magnificent A Coruña, not to mention the granite marvel that is Santiago de Compostela – that have a special magic.

Northern Spain's inland regions are in the main more traditionally 'Spanish'; Castilla y León is replete with villages, towns, and cities fortified for ongoing battles between Christians and Moors and endowed with numerous churches in various styles. French influence brought both the soft arches and curious capitals of the Romanesque – prevalent along the Pilgrim Route to Santiago and in out-of- the-way cities like Zamora and Soria – and the lofty, gravity-defying Gothic, whose soaring testaments to faith include such wonders as the cathedrals of Léon and Burgos. Plateresque was a more specifically home-grown style, evident in numerous ornate monasteries and palaces across the region as well as in the university in Salamanca, perhaps Spain's most beautiful city. Castles stud the landscape throughout, from the desolate hilltop of Gormaz to the Templar fortress in the centre of busy Ponferrada. Cold in winter and baking hot in summer, the almost treeless *meseta* exercises a mesmeric pull. Here, the cuisine is hearty and no-nonsense, best drunk with a red wine from the fabled Ribera del Duero region. Wine, too, is the main focus in neighbouring La Rioja, whose vineyards stretch out from perfectly formed little towns gracing the hilltops.

In the east of the region, neighbouring Navarra and Aragón have similar geographies, rising from the hot plains of the south – where Zaragoza is a seldom-visited but appealing

Packing for Northern Spain

Spain is a modern European country, and you can buy almost everything you'll need here.

Be prepared for all weather; Northern Spain can be very cold outside summer, and the coast sees rain all year round.

Unless you're going to the beach or staying in hostels, you can leave the towel at home; even the most modest *pensión* will provide one with the room. Take an adaptor for electrical goods (see page 45).

city – through foothills – where the town of Pamplona hosts its world-famous *encierro*, or Running of the Bulls – to the Pyrenees. This spectacular, soaring mountain range offers superb walking and good skiing, and numerous valleys to delve down in search of pockets of distinctive local culture and delicious artisanal cheeses.

Itineraries

One week

If you're on a short break from Britain, an obvious option is to spend it in the Basque country; there are budget flights from London to Bilbao, the distances are short, and there's an excellent variety of attractions for all tastes. Bilbao itself shouldn't be missed, and the superb Guggenheim museum is only part of the story. San Sebastián is languidly attractive, the coast very beautiful, the food and company excellent, the Basque mountains green and wild, and La Rioja wine country is within easy reach, too. It's also one of the few regions that are easy to get around without your own transport.

Another appealing option would be to take a budget flight to Asturias and spend the break exploring the Gijón, Oviedo and Avilés triangle, with great seafood and cheery cider bars bolstering the fine old towns and crashing surf, or to take a flight into Asturias and out of Santiago, following the region's jagged coastline and Celtic culture while munching barnacles and octopus and savouring the aromas of Albariño white wines.

Two weeks

With more time at your disposal the main decision is colour: whether to go for the green hills of the north coast, or the fascinating towns of the thirsty brown *meseta*. A top fortnight could see you flying into Bilbao and heading west, exploring coastal towns such as Castro Urdiales, Santillana del Mar and Cudillero, as well as the cities of Santander, Oviedo and Gijón. The Picos de Europa mountains are within easy reach, too. Once in Galicia, head to A Coruña, one of the most pleasant cities of Northern Spain, then to Santiago before heading back, perhaps taking in one of the inland cities, such as lovely León. This itinerary is suitable for driving, but another excellent coastal option is the slow, but scenic FEVE train that runs from Bilbao west through Cantabria and Asturias and into Galicia.

Exploring Castilla is another good way to spend a couple of weeks. Fly into Valladolid (or Madrid) and investigate that city's wealth of historical associations, before tracking west to Salamanca, one of Europe's most attractive towns. Next take a circle through Zamora, León, Palencia, Burgos and Soria, then head back along the Duero river via towns such as Burgo de Osma and Peñafiel, capital of one of Spain's best wine regions, before returning to Valladolid.

If architecture is your thing, following the Camino de Santiago is a very rewarding experience, whether on foot or bike on the pilgrim trail, or by car or public transport.

The route takes in many of the finest cathedrals of the north at León, Burgos, Jaca and Santiago itself, as well as a superb series of Romanesque churches in places like Estella and Frómista. A side trip could take you up to Asturias to investigate the pre-Romanesque buildings there. If you're a castle fan, the Duero valley is full of them: Peñafiel, Gormaz and Berlanga are impressive. Navarra and Aragón also have several, including superb Loarre, near Huesca. If you like beautiful brick, a *mudéjar* kick could take you around Zaragoza, Tarazona and Sahagún.

For the great outdoors, the Pyrenees are an obvious attraction; you could easily spend a week or fortnight exploring the area in northern Navarra and Aragón. Not far away, Alquézar will appeal to canyoning fans. The Picos de Europa are smaller but equally picturesque. For a more out-of-the-way experience, explore the Asturian forests in places like the Somiedo or Muniellos natural parks.

If wine is a passion, start in Bilbao and head east along the coast to gourmet San Sebastián through *txakolí* country before tracking south past Vitoria to the Basque Rioja. Stay in Laguardia for a couple of days, then explore the wineries around Haro and Logroño. If you've got time, travel eastwards to Estella to investigate the Navarran wines, then southwest to Peñafiel to sample the superb Ribera del Duero reds. From here head west to Valladolid for its nearby Rueda whites, then northwest to Galicia via Toro, whose reds are making waves, and Ponferrada, centre of the Bierzo wine region. Stay in Ourense drinking Ribeiros, then continue west to the Rías Baixas for their superb Albariños. And then? Well, don't say we told you, but the port lodges of Porto are only a short hop south ...

For a varied fortnight in July, head to Navarra to spend four days at the riotous Sanfermines fiestas in Pamplona, a couple of days in the south and west around beautiful Estella, Viana and Olite, and then head for the peaceful beauty of the Pyrenean valleys to unwind.

Three weeks/one month
With three or four weeks to spare, you can combine a couple of the above itineraries. A good month's trip would start in the Basque country, go west along the coast, taking in the Picos de Europa on the way, and then explore Galicia. From here, head across to León, and then south to Zamora and Salamanca. Make your way east along the Duero Valley to Soria, then cut into Aragón and head for the Pyrenees for some fresh air after the heat of the *meseta*.

When to go

The whole of Spain is busy in July and August and, while the north isn't ridiculously crowded, you'll need to reserve rooms in advance, for which you'll be paying slightly higher prices, and significantly higher on the coast. That said, it's an enjoyable time to be in the country as there are dozens of fiestas, and everything happens outdoors. It'll be pleasantly warm on the coast and in the mountains (although you're likely to see rain in both areas), and very hot in Castilla and La Rioja – expect days in the mid to high 30s, if not higher.

June is a good time too, with milder weather and far fewer crowds, as Spanish holidays haven't started. Spring (apart from Easter week) is also quiet, and not too hot, although expect coastal showers if not serious rain. In the mountains, some routes may still be snowbound. Autumn is a good all-round time. Prices on the coast are slashed (although many hotels shut), and there are few tourists. The weather is unpredictable at this time: cool, crisp days in the mountains are likely, but on the coast you could get a week of warm sun or a fortnight of unrelenting drizzle. The cities of the interior are likely to be dry but cold – temperatures can drop below zero at night as early as October in places like Burgos and León. A bonus is that flights are cheap at these times.

In winter, temperatures are mild on the coast and cold inland. Accommodation is cheap, but many places in the mountains and on the coast are closed. Skiing starts in earnest in late January.

What to do

Archaeology

A trip along the north coast of Spain can easily be focused on the region's prehistory. The cave paintings at Altamira in Cantabria are well known, but there are several other caves around here and in Asturias that also offer an intriguing glimpse into our ancestry.

Bronze Age dolmens are common throughout the north, particularly in Alava and Galicia, while Celtic culture is also very evident in the form of *castros*, attractive hilltop settlements composed of tightly packed roundhouses and a wall. These have a high concentration in Asturias and Galicia. A detour south to Burgos will take you to Atapuerca, the site where Europe's oldest known human remains have been found.

While the peninsula has some excellent Roman ruins, few of them are in the north. The cities of Clunia and the former Iberian settlement of Numancia are large, but there's little to see; the villas in Palencia province – La Olmeda, in particular – are better, and Zaragoza has several spots where you can see the Roman foundations under the new city. Lugo's walls, though heavily modified, are the most impressive structure from this period. See page 51 for specialist tour operators.

Birdwatching

Northern Spain is a good place for birding, and where you go is largely determined by what birds you wish to observe. The Pyrenees and the Picos de Europa shelter large numbers of birds of prey, including the lammergeyer (*quebrantahuesos*) and golden eagle (*águila dorada*); other sought-after sights are the capercaillie (*urogallo*) and the wallcreeper (*treparriscos*). Spain is also an important staging-post on the migration routes between Africa and Northern Europe/Arctic. Navarra, Aragón and Alava have some worthwhile spots, mostly lakes where vast flocks stop in for refreshment. The coast, particularly around Galicia's rías, is a haven for waterbird-spotting. Some of the most enjoyable birdwatching, however, is to be done in the towns of Castilla in summer, as graceful storks circle their massive nests in the evening air (see box, page 531). **Contact** www.spainbirds.com for information on birding and nature tours.

Cycling

Many organizations run cycling trips around Northern Spain. Apart from the dusty Castilian plains, the region offers very good cycling, and it's a popular weekend activity in Navarra and Euskadi. The valleys of the Pyrenees and its foothills here and in Aragón make for demanding but spectacular excursions. In towns, cyclists are not well catered for, but the situation is slowly improving, with cycle lanes popping up in several cities; free bike stands for citizens to borrow a pair of wheels will also increase awareness of the need for more facilities.

Road cycling is a popular spectator sport, with the **Vuelta a España** in Sep being one of the sport's three prime European events. It's particularly followed in the Basque country, where the hilly terrain lends itself to strong thighs. The Euskaltel team has promoted

the País Vasco on the world cycling stage, while 5-times Tour de France winner Miguel Indurain is a hero in his home region of Navarra. At time of research, the last 3 winners of the Tour were Spanish.
Contact Real Federación de Ciclismo en España, www.rfec.com.

Fishing

Northern Spain has some superb trout and salmon fishing, as immortalized by Hemingway in *Fiesta/The Sun Also Rises*. It's all regulated and you'll need a permit (*permiso de pesca*), usually obtainable from the local Ayuntamiento and valid for 2 weeks.
Contact Federación Española de Pesca, Navas de Tolosa 3, Madrid, T915 328 353, www.fepyc.es, is a good starting point.

Football

The sports daily, *Marca*, is a thick publication dedicated mostly to football, and it's the most widely read paper in Spain. Not far behind comes *As*, also devoted to the game. The conclusion to be drawn is that Spaniards are big on sport, and football is king.

While none of Spain's biggest clubs are in Northern Spain, the region has held its own: **Athletic Bilbao**, **Real Sociedad** and **Deportivo La Coruña** have all won the championship, while **Real Zaragoza** have won 2 European titles, and no team relishes an away trip to Santander or Gijón. Going to a game is an excellent experience; crowds are enthusiastic but well behaved, and it's much more of a family affair than in the UK, for example. Games usually take place on a Sunday evening (most at 1700) although there are a couple of Saturday fixtures, and tickets are relatively easy to come by for most games. The *taquillas* (ticket booths) are normally open at the ground for 2 days before the match and for the couple of hours before kick-off. Watching the game in a bar is a Sun ritual for many people, and also good fun.

Golf

Northern Spain doesn't have the concentration of golf courses that you find in Andalucía and the southeast coast, but there are enough quality spots to keep any golfer interested, and the higher rainfall on the north coast makes for a guilt-free swing. You'll need a green card (insurance) and handicap certificate to play most of Northern Spain's courses.
Contact www.golfspain.com has good course information in English.

Skiing

There are 13 ski resorts in the area covered by this guide, the best and most popular of which are in the Aragonese Pyrenees. **Candanchú** and **Formigal** offer the greatest variety of runs. The resorts are fairly priced by European standards but the snow quality is variable. The season runs from Christmas to Apr, with Feb likely to be the best month. Skiing packages are on offer in travel agents, but don't necessarily save a great deal of money. Most resorts have a ski-school and a range of accommodation, although budget options should be booked well in advance.
Contact ATUDEM, T913 591 557, www.esquiespana.org, is the Spanish ski-tourism agency. Check the web pages of the individual resorts, or see the Spanish tourist board's skiing pages at www.spain.info.

Spas

The glorious days of taking the waters are back with us, and spas (*balnearios*) have returned with a bang in Spain. Not the grim institutional places where the sore-of-joint are sent on state-subsidized rest cures, but upbeat modern places. Some of these offer holistic health packages for an all-round wellness experience while others are upmarket boutique hotels with bubbles and massages to add to the relaxation. They are dotted all over the region; some of the best are at **Arnedillo** in La Rioja,

Basque sports

The best-known Basque sport is **pelota**, www.euskalpilota.com, sometimes called *jai alai*, played on a three-sided court known as a *frontón*. In the most common version, two teams of two hit the ball with their hands against the walls seeking, like squash, to prevent the other team from returning it. The ball is far from soft; after a long career players' hands resemble winning entries in a root-vegetable show. Variations of the game are *pelota a pala*, using bats, and *cesta punta*, using a wickerwork glove that can propel the ball at frightening speeds. Most courts have matches on Saturday and Sunday evenings. Confusingly, the seasons vary from town to town, but there's always something on somewhere. Other traditional Basque sports tend to be unreconstructed tests of strength, such as **wood-chopping**, or the alarming **stone-lifting**, in which stocky *harrijasotzaileak* dead-lift weights in excess of 300 kg. The best places to see these sports are at village fiestas.

Puente Viesgo in Cantabria, El Convento near Zamora, the wine spa at **Marqués de Riscal** in Elciego, in the País Vasco part of the Rioja region, and up in the Pyrenees at **Benasque**. **Contact** The national spa association website, www.anbal.es, has a map of some, but by no means all, of the spa facilities in Spain.

Surfing and other watersports

There are good surf beaches right along the coast and the sport is growing in popularity in Spain. There's a big scene around **Zarautz** and **Mundaka** in Euskadi, and places west of Santander, such as Suances, are also popular destinations. Asturias has good waves throughout, but particularly in the west around Tapia de Casariego. The north and northwest coast of Galicia is also a worthwhile destination. Many of the best surf beaches are listed in the text of this guide; check out Footprint's *Surfing Europe* for more detailed information.

The north coast is the obvious choice for watersports, with many companies arranging activities in Euskadi, Cantabria and Asturias. The **Río Sella** in Asturias is a popular choice for canoeing and rafting, while windsurfers generally head for the **Rías Baixas** in Galicia. There's some reasonable diving on the **Guipúzcoan Coast** too.

Walking and climbing

As well as the Camino de Santiago, Northern Spain offers some fantastic walking, mostly in its mountainous and coastal areas. The first thing for the walker to be aware of is Spain's excellent network of marked walking trails. These are divided into **pequeño recorrido** (PR), short trails marked with yellow and white signs, and **gran recorrido** (GR), longer-distance walks marked in red and white. These take in places often inaccessible by car; the GR trails are planned so that nights can be spent at *refugios* (walkers' hostels) or in villages with places to stay. Detailed maps and descriptions of these routes can be found in good bookshops or outdoor equipment shops; web coverage is good for some routes but still patchy overall. The magnificent Pyrenees and Picos offer trails for all abilities, from picturesque morning strolls to the challenging coast-to-coast Pyrenean traverse. Walks are detailed in the travel chapters of this guide.

Climbers, too, will have a good time of it in the Pyrenees and Picos. There are many peaks offering varying degrees of challenge; some of these are mentioned in the text.

Walkers and climbers in these areas should take every precaution, even in the height of summer. Get a weather forecast if you're heading into the mountains, and watch what's going on, as mists can roll in pretty

Walking the Camino de Santiago

To use the network of *albergues* (pilgrim hostels), you'll need to be an accredited pilgrim. This status comes in the form of a Pilgrim Passport or *credencial*, issued by various organizations outside Spain and many places on the route itself. This document should be stamped daily at *albergues*, churches or town halls to help prove you've travelled the route. At Santiago, presenting a completed pilgrim passport at the Pilgrim Office (www.archicompostela.org) entitles you to a compostela, a Latin certificate of completion of the pilgrimage. To be eligible for this, you have to have walked at least the last 100 km, or cycled the last 200 km. If you are only doing the last section of the pilgrimage, get at least two stamps a day in the *credencial*. Religion is not a requirement either to obtain the *credencial* or the *compostela*, but a suitable attitude and respect for the journey is expected.

There are many *albergues* along the *camino*; these are typically simple places that ask for a small fee or donation (€4-10) for dormitory accommodation. Most also serve cheap meals and have cooking facilities. As most pilgrims set off early to avoid the fierce afternoon sun, *albergues* generally have a curfew of 2200-2230, and a checkout of 0600-0700. The curfews are a handicap, as you'll miss much of Spanish life, so many pilgrims alternate with nights in *pensiones* or hotels. You'll need your own sleeping bag for *albergues*; a sleeping mat is also advisable as you may need to kip on the floor.

To look like an authentic medieval pilgrim, many people don the traditional garb. A long staff is a sensible option anyway, as are a gourd for water and broad-brimmed hat to keep out sun and rain. The scallop shell is a badge of Santiago. In former times, it was forbidden to sell scallops except in Santiago itself, so arriving pilgrims would quickly chow one down and take the shell as proof of the journey. Sturdy walking boots, sun protection, a weatherproof jacket, first-aid kit and a decent level of fitness are essential. Be prepared to encounter all weathers, as the route crosses mountain passes and scorching plains.

Spring and autumn avoid the worst of the heat, but it will be cold at nights on the plains and wet in the mountainous parts. In summer, Galicia and Navarra are pleasant, but the haul across the plains from Logroño to León is gruelling. May or September is best. For further information, see pages 10-11 as well as relevant sections throughout the guide.

---

fast. A compass is invaluable, as is a decent map and protective clothing (including good boots). If you're not on a well-used trail, let someone know where you're going and when you expect to be back.

In summer and during Spanish holidays trails can become conga lines at weekends, so if you're after a bit of peace and solitude, use the lesser-known trails or go at different times. **Contact** See page 51 for tour operators. Tourist offices have details of local routes and *refugios*. For climbing, see **Federación Española de Deportes de Montaña y Escalada**, T914 451 382, www.fedme.es.

Getting there

Air

With budget airlines having opened up several regional airports to international flights, it's easier than ever to get to Northern Spain. **Ryanair** fly to Santiago de Compostela, Valladolid, Santander, and Zaragoza from London, while **Easyjet** serve Bilbao and Asturias, **Vueling** link Bilbao, Santiago and A Coruña with London or Edinburgh, and **Air Berlin** go to Bilbao and Asturias (among others), with a connection, from many German and Austrian airports. These airlines also run routes to other European cities. Other international airlines serve Bilbao (which is connected with London, Paris, Frankfurt, and several other European cities), Vigo, Santiago de Compostela, Zaragoza and Asturias. If you're not on the budget carriers, however, it's often cheaper to fly to Madrid and connect via a domestic flight or by land transport. Madrid is a major world airport and prices tend to be competitive.

Domestic connections via Madrid or Barcelona are frequent. **Iberia** connects Madrid with most cities of the north, while **Spanair** and **Air Europa** also operate some flights. Flights are fairly expensive, with a typical Madrid–Bilbao return costing €200. There are often specials on various websites (see below) that can bring the price down considerably. If flying into Madrid from outside Spain, an onward domestic flight can often be added at little extra cost.

While budget carriers often offer excellent value (especially when booked well ahead), they offer very little flexibility. Be aware that if you're only booking a week or so in advance, it may be cheaper with other airlines such as **British Airways** or **Iberia**. Cheap fares will usually carry a heavy financial penalty for changing dates or cancellation; check the small print carefully before buying a ticket. Some airlines don't like one-way tickets; it's (ridiculously) often cheaper to buy a return.

Before booking, it's worth doing a bit of online research. Two of the best search engines for flight comparisons are www.kelkoo.com and www.kayak.com, which compare prices from travel agencies and websites. To keep yourself up to date with the ever-changing routes of the bewildering number of budget airlines www.whichbudget.com is recommended. **Flightchecker** (http://flightchecker.moneysavingexpert.com) is handy for checking multiple dates for budget airline deals.

Airport information

Madrid Barajas is the main international airport of Spain, and for non-European visitors, is the most convenient point of entry for the north. Situated 13 km northeast of the centre, it has two distinct sections: Terminal 4, used for most EU flights, as well as services run by **Iberia** and partner airlines, and the old Terminals 1-3 (used by the rest). A free shuttle bus runs between terminals, and the metro stops at both T1-3 and T4. There are tourist information offices in Terminals 1, 2, and 4 and many multinational car hire companies and banks with ATMs. There's also a hotel booking service. ▶ *Information on smaller airports can be found in the Transport section of the relevant city.*

The most convenient way of getting into Madrid is by taxi, which costs around €30 (including a €5.50 charge that the driver will add on: don't let them add on any other extras unless you're going to a bus or train station, in which case it's an extra €2.95), or to use the metro. There are entrances to the metro (www.metromadrid.es) from Terminals 2 and 3 and a separate station for Terminal 4. On the metro, you can be in central Madrid in as little as 20 minutes; a single ticket costs €2 from the airport. If you're moving straight on to the north, change at Nuevos Ministerios (the end of the line). Jump on Line 10 (Dirección Fuencarral) for four stops to reach Chamartín, the main northbound train station. Nine stops on Line 6 (Dirección Legazpi), on the other hand, will get you to Méndez Alvaro, which has a passage connecting to the main northerly bus station. There are also buses into town from outside Terminal 1, but these can take significantly longer in traffic.

Flying from the UK and Ireland

Competition between airlines serving Spain has benefited the traveller in recent years. Budget operators have taken a significant slice of the market and forced other airlines to compete. There are several options for flying to Northern Spain from the UK and Ireland.

The cheapest direct flights are with the budget operators, whose fares can be as low as €30 return but are more usually €85-160. It's easier to get hold of a cheaper fare if you fly off-season or midweek, and if you book well in advance. The routes offered at time of writing are: **Ryanair**: London Stansted to Santiago de Compostela, Santander, Valladolid, and Zaragoza. **Easyjet**: London Stansted to Bilbao, Asturias (Oviedo/ Gijón/Avilés). **BMI**: Birmingham to Bilbao. **Aer Lingus**: Dublin to Santiago de Compostela and Bilbao. **Vueling**: London Heathrow to Bilbao and A Coruña and from Edinburgh to Santiago. **Ryanair** also flies to Biarritz, France, which is 30 minutes on the train to the Spanish border, from where it's another 30 minutes to San Sebastián. Check **www.whichbudget.com** to keep apace of the changes.

Bilbao is also served from London by **Iberia** and **British Airways**. These flights often end up cheaper than **Easyjet** if you are flying at a weekend with less than a month's notice. APEX fares tend to be about €150-220 return and can be more economical and flexible than the budget airline if you are connecting from another British city.

Direct flights from London to Madrid are operated by **Easyjet**, **Ryanair**, **Iberia**, **British Airways**, **BMI**, **Air Europa**, **Aerolíneas Argentinas**, **Lufthansa** and others. **Iberia/British Airways** also connect to Madrid directly from Manchester, Edinburgh, Glasgow and Birmingham, while **Easyjet** fly to Madrid from Edinburgh, Bristol, and Liverpool, and **Spanair** from Edinburgh.

KLM, **Lufthansa** and **Air France** are also major carriers to Spain for those who don't mind changing at these airlines' hub airports. As well as Madrid and Barcelona these airlines all fly to Bilbao. **Iberia** and **British Airways** code share on direct flights between London and Santiago de Compostela and Oviedo/Gijón several times a week, but these flights tend to be a lot dearer; it's nearly always cheaper to connect via Madrid.

From Madrid airport (Barajas), it's very easy to hop in a taxi or the metro to the bus station (metro stop: Méndez Alvaro) or train station (Chamartín) and be in Northern Spain in a jiffy.

Iberia and **Aer Lingus** code share daily direct flights from Dublin to Madrid and Barcelona, while **Aer Lingus** runs budget flights from Dublin to Bilbao and Santiago. **Ryanair** operate budget flights between Dublin and London if you can find a cheap flight from the UK.

Flying from Europe

There are many direct flights from Europe to Northern Spain, but most are overpriced apart from those on budget airlines; you're often better flying in to Madrid. Budget routes to the north include **Air Berlin** services from numerous German, Austrian, and Swiss cities to Bilbao, Asturias, and Santiago de Compostela, usually via their Mallorca hub. **Ryanair** link Valladolid, Santander, and Zaragoza with European destinations such as Brussels Charleroi, Milan Bergamo, Roma Ciampino and Frankfurt Hahn. Other airlines, such as

German Wings, Brussels Airlines, Wizzair and Vueling, fly a few select European routes; check www.whichbudget.com for up-to-date routes in this rapidly changing market.

On full-fare airlines, Bilbao is directly connected with several other European cities, including Frankfurt, Zürich, Brussels, Paris, Milan and Lisbon. There are flights to Madrid from most European capitals with both budget and full-fare carriers.

Flying from North America and Canada
To reach Northern Spain from across the Atlantic, the best way is to fly in via Madrid. From the east coast, flights can rise well over US$1400 in summer but, in winter or with advance purchase, you can get away with as little as US$600. Prices from the west coast are usually only US$100 or so more. Iberia flies direct to Madrid from many east coast cities and British Airways often offers reasonable add-on fares via London. A domestic extension from Madrid won't necessarily add much to the fare but it might be cheaper and/or more convenient getting the train. Flying in via other European hubs such as Paris or London is often less expensive, but adds a good few hours on to the journey. Travellers from Canada will sometimes find that it's cheaper to fly via London than Madrid.

Flying from Australia and New Zealand
There are no direct flights to Spain from Australia or New Zealand; the cheapest and quickest way is to connect via Frankfurt, Paris or London. The trip takes about 30 hours in total. It might turn out cheaper to book the Europe–Spain leg separately via a budget operator. You may want to consider a round-the-world option, which can work out not much more expensive, although these are not as good value as they once were.

Flying from South Africa
There are no direct flights from South Africa, the cheapest and quickest way is to connect via Europe; Zurich, Amsterdam, Frankfurt or London normally work out best.

Airlines

Aer Lingus, www.aerlingus.com.
Air Berlin, www.airberlin.com.
Air Canada, www.aircanada.ca.
Air Europa, www.aireuropa.com.
Air France, www.airfrance.com/uk,
www.airfrance.fr.
American Airlines, www.aa.com.
BMI, www.flybmi.com.
BMI Baby, www.bmibaby.com.

British Airways, www.ba.com.
Delta, www.delta.com.
Easyjet, www.easyjet.com.
Iberia, www.iberia.com.
KLM, www.klmuk.com.
Lufthansa, www.lufthansa.co.uk.
Ryanair, www.ryanair.com.
Spanair, www.spanair.es.
US Airways, www.usairways.com.
Vueling, www.vueling.com.

Rail

Travelling from the UK to Northern Spain by train is unlikely to save either time or money; the only advantages lie in the pleasure of the journey itself, the chance to stop along the way, and the environmental impact of flying versus rail travel. Using Eurostar ① T0870 160 6600, www.eurostar.com, changing stations in Paris and boarding a TGV to Hendaye can have you in San Sebastián 10 hours after leaving Waterloo if the connections are kind.

Once across the Channel, the trains are reasonably priced, but factor in £100-200 return on **Eurostar** and things don't look so rosy, unless you can take advantage of a special offer. Using the train/Channel ferry combination will more or less halve the cost and double the time.

The main rail gateway from the rest of Europe is Paris (Austerlitz). There's a Paris–Madrid sleeper daily, which stops at Vitoria, Burgos and Valladolid. Standard tourist class is €162/189 in a reclining seat/couchette to Madrid one-way, and proportionally less depending on where you get off. Check www.elipsos.com for specials. The cheaper option is to take a **TGV** from Paris to Hendaye, from where you can catch a Spanish train to San Sebastián and beyond.

For students, the **InterRail** pass is an attractive and cheap possibility, which can be obtained from travel agents, but note that the pass is not valid on the high-speed **AVE** or **EuroMed** trains. If you are planning the train journey, **Rail Europe** ① *T0844 484 064, www. raileurope.co.uk*, is a useful company. **RENFE**, Spain's rail network, has online timetables at www.renfe.es. Also see the extremely useful www.seat61.com.

Road

Bus

Eurolines (www.eurolines.com) run several buses from major European cities to a variety of destinations in Northern Spain. From London, there's a bus that leaves London Victoria at 0800 on Monday and Saturday, and arrives in Bilbao at 0430 the next morning. The return leaves Bilbao at 0030 on Thursday and Saturday night, getting to London at 1945 the next evening. There's an extra bus in summer. A return fare costs about £100; it's marginally cheaper for pensioners and students, but overall isn't great value unless you're not a fan of flying. Book on T01582 404 511 or www.gobycoach.com.

Car

The main route into Northern Spain is the E05/E70 motorway that runs down the southwest coast of France, crossing into Spain at Irún, near San Sebastián. More scenic but slower routes cross the Pyrenees at various points. The other motorway entrance is the E7 that runs down the east coast of Spain from France. At Barcelona you can turn inland for Lleida and Zaragoza. Both these motorways are tolled but worthwhile compared to the slow, traffic-plagued *rutas nacionales*. Most other motorways are free and in good condition.

Cars must be insured for third party and practically any driving licence is acceptable (but if you're from a country that a Guardia Civil would struggle to locate on a map, take an International Driving Licence). Unleaded petrol costs €1.10-1.25 per litre in Spain.

Sea

Bear in mind that from the UK it's usually cheaper to fly and hire a car in Northern Spain than bring the motor across on the ferry. For competitive fares by sea to France and Spain, check with **Ferrysavers** ① *T0844 576 8835, www.ferrysavers.com* and **www.ferrycheap. com**, which list special offers from various operators. The website **www.seat61.com** is good for investigating train/ferry combinations.

Now that P&O no longer run a Bilbao service, the only UK-Spain ferry is the service run by **Brittany Ferries** ① *T0871 244 0744, www.brittany-ferries.co.uk*, from Plymouth and

Portsmouth to Santander. There's one weekly sailing on each route, taking around 24 hours from Portsmouth and 20 hours from Plymouth. Prices are variable but can usually be found for about £70-90 each way in a reclining seat. A car adds about £150 each way, and cabins start from about £80.

At time of writing, a trial ferry service had started up between Gijón and St Nazaire in France, potentially saving a good deal of driving. See page 402 for details.

Getting around

Public transport between the larger towns in Northern Spain is good; you can expect several buses a day between adjacent provincial capitals; these services are quick and efficient. The new network of high-speed **AVE** trains link major cities in double-quick time, but are significantly more expensive than the bus. Other train services are slow. If you want to explore much of rural Northern Spain, however, you'll probably want to hire a car, take a bike, or walk the Camino de Santiago.

Air

Most provincial capitals in Northern Spain have an airport that is serviced from Barcelona and Madrid at least once daily. The drawback is the cost; a full fare return from Madrid to Oviedo, for example, costs around €300. If you are fairly flexible about when you fly, you can pick up some good advance-purchase prices; there are some budget routes operated by **Ryanair**, **Easyjet**, **Vueling**, and other airlines. Otherwise, by far the best way is to go to a local travel agent, who can often find excellent deals on domestic flights. Flying within Northern Spain itself is less attractive, as you usually have to go via Madrid, although there are connections to Bilbao from Vigo, A Coruña and Santiago.

Most internal flights in Spain are operated by **Iberia**; **Spanair** and **Air Europa** also run some routes. If you're flying into Spain from overseas, a domestic leg can often be added at comparatively little cost.

If you're flying into Spain from outside Europe on a **OneWorld** affiliate airline, you may want to consider the *OneWorld* Visit Europe airpass, which offers set-rate flights with Iberia that cost €55 for up to 318 km, or €80 up to 638 km. The same rates apply for flights all around Europe. See www.oneworld.com for more details. **Spanair** have a *Spanair Pass*, but you have to buy 10 vouchers and it's not very good value.

Rail

The Spanish national rail network **RENFE** ① *T902 240 202 (English-speaking operators)*, *www.renfe.es*, is, thanks to its growing network of high-speed trains, becoming a very useful option for getting around Northern Spain. AVE trains run from Madrid to Valladolid, Zaragoza and Huesca, with other routes under construction to nearly all of Northern Spain's major cities. These trains cover these large distances impressively quickly and reliably. It is an expensive but excellent service that refunds part or all of the ticket price if it arrives late. Elsewhere though, you'll find the bus is often quicker and cheaper than the train.

Prices vary significantly according to the type of service you are using. The standard fast-ish intercity service is called *Talgo*, while other intercity services are labelled *Altaria, Intercity, Diurno* and *Estrella* (overnight). Slower local trains are called *regionales*.

It's always worth buying a ticket in advance for long-distance travel, as trains are often full. The best option is to buy them via the website, which sometimes offers advance- purchase discounts. You can also book by phone, but they only accept Spanish cards. In either case, you get a reservation code, then print off your ticket at the terminals at the station. If buying your ticket at the station, allow plenty of time for queuing. Ticket windows are labelled *venta anticipada* (in advance) and *venta inmediata* (six hours or less before the journey). A better option can be to use a travel agent; the ones that sell tickets will display a **RENFE** sign, but you'll have to purchase them a day in advance. Commission is minimal.

All Spanish trains are non-smoking. The faster trains will have first-class (*preferente*) and second-class sections as well as a *cafetería*. First class costs about 30% more than standard and can be a worthwhile deal on a crowded long journey. Other pricing is bewilderingly complex. Night trains are more expensive, even if you don't take a sleeping berth, and there's a system of peak/off-peak days that makes little difference in practice. Buying a return ticket is 10-20% cheaper than two singles, but you qualify for this discount even if you buy the return leg later (but not on every service). A useful tip: if the train is 'full' for your particular destination, try to buy a ticket halfway (or even one stop), get on, and then ask the ticket inspector whether it's possible to go further. You may have to shuffle seats a couple of times, but most are fairly helpful – you can pay the excess fare on board. Don't board a train without a ticket though.

An **ISIC student card** or **under-26 card** grants a discount of between 20% to 30% on train services. If you're using a European railpass, be aware that you'll still have to make a reservation on Spanish trains and pay the small reservation fee (which covers your insurance).

The other important Northern Spanish network is **FEVE** ① *www.feve.es*, whose main line runs along the north coast from Bilbao to Santander, Asturias, and as far as Ferrol in Galicia; there's another line from Bilbao to León. It's a slow line, but very picturesque. It stops at many small villages and is handy for exploring the coast. They also operate the luxury *Transcantábrico*, a week's journey along the whole network, with numerous side trips, and gourmet meals. A third handy network is **Eusko Trenbideak** ① *www.euskotren.es*, a short-haul train service in the Basque country. It's an excellent service with good coverage of the inland towns.

Both **FEVE** and **RENFE** operate short-distance *cercanías* (commuter trains) in some areas, essentially suburban train services. These are particularly helpful in Asturias and around Bilbao.

Road

Bus

Buses are the staple of Spanish public transport. Services between major cities are fast, frequent, reliable and fairly cheap; the five-hour trip from Madrid to Oviedo, for example, costs €31. When buying a ticket, always check how long the journey will take, as the odd bus will be an 'all stations to' job, calling in at villages that seem surprised to even see it. *Directo* is the term for a bus that doesn't stop; it won't usually cost any more either. Various premium services (called *Supra*, *Ejecutivo* or similar) add comfort, with onboard drinks service, lounge area in the bus station and more space, but cost around 60% more.

Most cities have a single terminal, the *estación de autobuses*, which is where all short- and long-haul services leave from. Buy your tickets at the relevant window; if there isn't one, buy it from the driver. Many companies don't allow baggage in the cabin of the bus, but security is pretty good. Most tickets will have a seat number (*asiento*) on them; ask when buying the ticket if you prefer a window (*ventana*) or aisle (*pasillo*) seat. There's a huge number of intercity bus companies, some of which allow phone and online booking; the most useful in Northern Spain is **ALSA**① *T902 422 242*, *www.alsa.es*, which is based in Asturias and runs many routes. The website www.movelia.es is also useful. The platform that the bus leaves from is called a *dársena* or *andén*. If you're travelling at busy times (particularly a fiesta or national holiday) always book the bus ticket in advance. If the bus station is out of town, there are usually travel agents in the centre who can do this for you at no extra charge.

Rural bus services are slower, less frequent and more difficult to coordinate. They typically run early in the morning and late in the evening; they're designed for villagers who visit the big city once a week or so to shop.

All bus services are reduced on Sundays and, to a lesser extent, on Saturdays; some services don't run at all on weekends. Local newspapers publish a comprehensive list of departures; expect few during siesta hours. While most large villages will have at least some bus service to their provincial capital, don't expect there to be buses running to tourist attractions like monasteries, beaches or castles; it's assumed that all tourists have cars.

Most Spanish cities have their sights closely packed into the centre, so you won't find local buses particularly necessary. There's a fairly comprehensive network in most towns, though; the Ins and outs and Transport sections in this guide indicate where they come in handy. In most cities, you just board and pay the driver.

Car

The roads in Northern Spain are good, excellent in many parts. While driving isn't as sedate as in parts of Northern Europe, it's generally of a very high standard, and you'll have few problems. To drive in Spain, you'll need a full driving licence from your home country. This applies to virtually all foreign nationals, but in practice, if you're from an 'unusual' country, consider an International Driving Licence or official translation of your licence into Spanish.

There are two types of motorway in Spain, *autovías* and *autopistas*; the quality of both is generally excellent, with a speed limit of 120 kph. They are signposted in blue and may have tolls payable, in which case there'll be a red warning circle on the blue sign when you're entering the motorway. An 'A' prefix to the road number indicates a motorway; an 'AP' prefix indicates a toll motorway. Tolls are generally reasonable, but extortionate in the Basque country. You can pay by cash or card. Most motorways in Northern Spain, however, are free.

Rutas Nacionales form the backbone of Spain's road network. Centrally administered, they vary wildly in quality. Typically, they are choked with traffic backed up behind trucks, and there are few stretches of dual carriageway. Driving at siesta time is a good idea if you're going to be on a busy stretch. *Rutas Nacionales* are marked with a red 'N' number. The speed limit is 100 kph outside built-up areas, as it is for secondary roads, which are numbered with a provincial prefix (eg BU-552 in Burgos province), although some are demarcated 'B' and 'C' instead.

In urban areas, the speed limit is 50 kph. Many towns and villages have sensors that will turn traffic lights red if you're over the limit on approach. City driving can be confusing, with signposting generally poor and traffic heavy; it's worth printing off the directions that your hotel may send you with a reservation. In some towns and cities, many of the hotels are officially signposted, making things easier. Larger cities may have their historic quarter blocked off by barriers: if your hotel lies within these, ring the buzzer and say the name of the hotel, and the barriers will open.

Police are increasingly enforcing speed limits in Spain, and foreign drivers are liable to a large on-the-spot fine. Drivers can also be punished for not carrying two red warning triangles to place on the road in case of breakdown, a bulb-replacement kit and a fluorescent green waistcoat to wear if you break down by the side of the road. Drink driving is being cracked down on more than was once the case; the limit is 0.5 g/l of blood, slightly less than the equivalent in the UK, for example.

Parking is a problem in nearly every town and city in Northern Spain. Red or yellow lines on the side of the street mean no parking. Blue lines indicate a metered zone, while white lines mean that some restriction is in place; a sign will give details. Parking meters can usually only be dosed up for a maximum of two hours, but they take a siesta at lunchtime too. Print the ticket off and display it in the car. Once the day's period has expired, you can charge it up for the next morning to avoid an early start. If you get a ticket, you can pay a minimal fine at the machine within the first half hour or hour instead of the full whack. Underground car parks are common and well signposted, but fairly pricey; €12-20 a day is normal. However, this is the safest option if you are going to leave any valuables in your car.

Liability insurance is required for every car driven in Spain and you must carry proof of it. If bringing your own car, check carefully with your insurers that you're covered, and get a certificate (green card). If your insurer doesn't cover you for breakdowns, consider joining the **RACE** ⓘ *T902 120 441, www.race.es*, Spain's automobile association, which provides good breakdown cover.

Hiring a car in Spain is easy but not especially cheap. The major multinationals have offices at all large towns and airports; the company with the broadest network is **National/ATESA** ⓘ *www.atesa.es*. Brokers, such as **Holiday Autos**, www.holidayautos.co.uk, are usually cheaper than booking direct with the rental companies. Prices start at around €150 per week for a small car with unlimited mileage. You'll need a credit card and most agencies will either not accept under 25s or demand a surcharge. Rates from the airports tend to be cheaper than from towns. Before booking, use a price-comparison website like www.kelkoo.com to find the best deals.

Cycling

Cycling presents a curious contrast; Spaniards are mad for the competitive sport, but comparatively uninterested in cycling as a means of transport. Thus there are plenty of cycling shops but very few bike lanes, though these are rapidly being constructed in most cities in the region. By far the best places to cycle are the north coast and the Pyrenees; these are where interest in cycling is high. Trying to enjoy a Castilian highway in 40°C heat with trucks zipping past your ears is another matter, although the Camino de Santiago route is a good alternative, with long off-road sections. Contact the **Real Federación de Ciclismo en España** ⓘ *www.rfec.com*, for more links and assistance.

Motorcycling

Motorcycling is a good way to enjoy Spain and there are few difficulties to trouble the biker; bike shops and mechanics are relatively common. Hiring a motorbike, however, is difficult; there are few outlets in Northern Spain. The **Real Federación Motociclista Española** ⓘ *www.rfme.net*, can help with links and advice.

Taxis

Taxis are a good option; flagfall is €2-3 in most places (it increases slightly at night and on Sundays) and it gets you a good distance. A taxi is available if its green light is lit; hail one on the street or ask for the nearest rank (*parada de taxis*). In smaller towns or at quiet times, you'll have to ring for one. All towns have their own taxi company; phone numbers are given in the text.

Maps

The Michelin road maps are reliable for general navigation, although if you're getting off the beaten track you'll often find a local map handy. Tourist offices provide these, which vary in quality. The best topographical maps are published by the **Instituto Geográfico Nacional (IGN)**. These are not necessarily more accurate than those obtainable in Britain or North America. A useful website for route planning is www.guiarepsol.com. Car hire companies have navigation systems available, though they cost a hefty supplement.

Stanfords ① *12-14 Long Acre, Covent Garden, London WC2E 9LP, T020 7836 1321, www.stanfords.co.uk*, with over 80 well-travelled staff and 40,000 titles in stock, is the world's largest map and travel bookshop. It also has a branch at 29 Corn Street, Bristol.

Sleeping

There are a reasonable number of well-equipped but characterless places on the edges or in the newer parts of towns in Spain. Similarly, chains such as NH, AC, and Hesperia have stocked Northern Spain's cities with reasonably comfortable but frequently featureless four-star business hotels. This guide has expressly minimized these in the listings, preferring to concentrate on more atmospheric options, but they are easily accessible via their websites or hotel booking brokers. If booking accommodation without this guide, always be sure to check the location if that's important to you – it's easy to find yourself a 15-minute cab ride from the town you want to be in. Having said this, the standard of accommodation in Northern Spain is very high; even the most modest of *pensiones* are usually very clean and respectable. Places to stay (*alojamientos*) are divided into three main categories; the distinctions between them follow an arcane series of regulations devised by the government.

All registered accommodations charge an 8% value-added tax (IVA); this is often included in the price at cheaper places and may be waived if you pay cash. If you have any problems, a last resort is to ask for the *libro de reclamaciones* (complaints book), an official document that, like stepping on cracks in the pavement, means uncertain but definitely horrible consequences for the hotel if anything is written in it. If you do write something in it, you have to go to the police within 24 hours and report the fact.

Hoteles, hostales and pensiones
Hoteles (marked H or HR) are graded from one to five stars and usually occupy their own building. *Hostales* (marked Hs or HsR) go from one to three stars. *Pensiones* (P) are the standard budget option, and are usually family-run flats in an apartment block. Although it's worth looking at a room before taking it, the majority are very acceptable. Spanish traditions of hospitality are alive and well; even the simplest of *pensiones* will generally provide a towel and soap, and check-out time is almost uniformly a very civilized midday. Most *pensiones* will give you keys to the exterior door; if they don't, be sure to mention the fact if you plan to stay out late.

Agroturismos and casas rurales
An excellent option if you've got transport are the networks of rural homes, called a variety of things, normally *agroturismos* or *casas rurales*. Although these are under a different classification system, the standard is often as high as any country hotel. The

Sleeping price codes

LL over €200	**L** €170-200	**AL** €140-170
A €110-140	**B** €90-110	**C** €70-90
D €55-70	**E** €35-55	**F** €25-35
G under €25		

These price codes refer to a standard double/twin room, inclusive of the 8% IVA (value-added tax). The rates are for high season (usually June-August).

best of them are traditional farmhouses or old village cottages. Some are available only to rent out whole, while others operate more or less as hotels. Rates tend to be excellent compared to hotels, and many offer kitchen facilities and home-cooked meals. While many are listed in the text, there are huge numbers, especially in the coastal and mountain areas. Each regional government publishes its own listings booklet, which is available at any tourist office in the area; some of the regional tourism websites also list them. The website www.toprural.com is another good place to find them. If you have a car, this can be a hugely relaxing form of holiday accommodation and a great way to meet Spaniards.

Albergues and refugios
There are a few youth hostels (*albergues*) around, but the accessible price of *pensiones* rarely makes it worth the trouble except for solo travellers. Spanish youth hostels are frequently populated by noisy schoolkids and have curfews and check-out times unsuitable for the late hours the locals keep. The exception is in mountain regions, where there are excellent *refugios*; simple hostels for walkers and climbers along the lines of a Scottish bothy, see box, page 203.

Campsites
Most campsites are set up as well-equipped holiday villages for families; many are open only in summer. While the facilities are good, they get extremely busy in peak season; the social scene is good, but sleep can be tough. They've often got playground facilities and a swimming pool; an increasing number now offer cabin or bungalow accommodation, normally a good-value option for groups or families. In other areas, camping, unless specifically prohibited, is a matter of common sense.

Eating and drinking

Nothing in Spain illustrates its differences from the rest of Europe more than its eating and drinking culture. Whether you're halfway through Sunday lunch at 1800, ordering a plate of octopus some time after midnight, snacking on *pintxos* in the street with the entire population of Bilbao doing the same around you, or watching a businessman down a hefty brandy with his morning coffee, it hits you at some point that the whole of Spanish society more or less revolves around food and drink. ▶▶ *See Food glossary, page 540.*

Eating hours are the first point of difference. Spaniards eat little for breakfast, usually just a coffee and maybe a croissant or pastry. The mid-morning coffee and piece of tortilla

A bed for the night

Occasionally, an area or town will have a short period when prices are hugely exaggerated; this normally corresponds to a fiesta or similar event. Low-season prices can be significantly lower; up to half in some areas such as the seaside.

Many mid- to top-range hotels in cities cater for business travellers during the week and so keep prices high. The flipside is that they have special weekend rates, which can be very good value. Typically, these involve staying on the Friday and Saturday night and pre-booking. Breakfast will often be thrown in and the whole deal can save you over 50% of the quoted price. Check the hotel website for these deals.

is a ritual, especially for office workers, and then there might be a quick bite and a drink in a bar before lunch, which is usually started between 1400 and 1530. This is the main meal of the day and the cheapest time to eat, as most restaurants offer a good-value set menu. Lunch (and dinner) is extended at weekends, particularly on Sundays, when the *sobremesa* (chatting over the remains of the meal) can go on for hours. Most folk head home for the meal during the working week and get back to work about 1700; some people have a nap (the famous siesta), some don't. It's common to have an evening drink or *tapa* in a bar after the *paseo*, if this is extended into a food crawl it's called a *txikiteo* (Basque country) or *tapeo*. Dinner (*cena*) is normally eaten from about 2200 onwards, although sitting down to dinner at midnight at weekends isn't unusual. In smaller towns, however, and midweek you might not get fed after 2200. Be aware that any restaurant open for dinner before 2030 could well be a tourist trap. After eating, *la marcha* (the nightlife) hits drinking bars (*bares de copas*) and then nightclubs (*discotecas*; a *club* is a brothel). Many of these places only open at weekends and are usually busiest from 0200 onwards.

Eating and drinking hours vary between regions. Week nights are quieter but particularly so in the Basque country and in rural areas, where many restaurants close their kitchens at 2200. Bar food changes across the area too. In the Basque country, *pintxos* (bar-top snacks) are the way forward; in León or Salamanca a free small plate of food accompanies the smallest drink; while in some other places you'll have to order *raciones* (full plates of tapas).

Food

While the regional differences in the cuisine of Northern Spain are important, the basics remain the same. Spanish cooking relies on meat, fish/seafood, beans and potatoes given character by the chef's holy trinity: garlic, peppers and, of course, olive oil. The influence of the colonization of the Americas is evident, and the result is a hearty, filling style of meal ideally washed down with some of the nation's excellent red wines.

Regional specialities are described in the main text, but the following is an overview of the most common dishes.

Even in areas far from the coast, the availability of good **fish and seafood** can be taken for granted. *Merluza* (hake) is the staple fish, but is pushed hard by *bacalao* (salt cod) on the north coast. A variety of farmed white fish are also increasingly popular. *Gambas* (prawns) are another common and excellent choice, backed up by a bewildering array of molluscs and crustaceans as well as numerous tasty fish. Calamari, squid and cuttlefish are common; if you can cope with the slightly slimy texture, *pulpo* (octopus) is particularly good, especially when simply boiled *a la gallega* (Galician style) and flavoured with paprika

Eating price codes

♈♈♈ over €20   ♈♈ €10-20   ♈ under €10

Price refers to the cost of a main course for one person, without a drink.

and olive oil. Supreme among the seafood are *rodaballo* (turbot) and *rape* (monkfish/anglerfish). Fresh trout from the mountain streams of Navarra or Asturias are hard to beat too; they are commonly cooked with bacon or ham (*trucha a la navarra*).

Wherever you go, you'll find cured ham (*jamón serrano*), which is always excellent, but particularly so if it's the pricey *ibérico*, taken from acorn-eating porkers in Salamanca, Extremadura and Huelva. Other cold **meats** to look out for are *cecina*, made from beef and, of course, *embutidos* (sausages), including the versatile *chorizo*. Pork is also popular as a cooked meat; its most common form is sliced loin (*lomo*). The Castilian plains specialize in roast suckling pig (*cochinillo* or *lechón*), usually a sizeable dish indeed. *Lechazo* is the lamb equivalent, popular around Aranda de Duero in particular. Beef is common throughout; cheaper cuts predominate, but the better steaks (*solomillo, entrecot, chuletón*) are usually superbly tender. Spaniards tend to eat them rare (*poco hecho*; ask for *al punto* for medium-rare or *bien hecho* for well done). The *chuletón* is worth a mention in its own right; a massive T-bone best taken from an ox (*de buey*) and sold by weight, which often approaches a kilogram. It's an imposing slab of meat, best shared between two or three unless you're especially peckish. *Pollo* (chicken) is common, but usually unremarkable (unless its free-range – *pollo de corral* – in which case it's superb); game birds such as *codorniz* (quail) and *perdiz* (partridge) as well as *pato* (duck) are also widely eaten. The innards of animals are popular; *callos* (tripe), *mollejas* (sweetbreads) and *morcilla* (black pudding in solid or liquid form) are all excellent, if acquired, tastes. Fans of the unusual will be keen to try *jabalí* (wild boar), *potro* (foal), *morros* (pig cheeks) and *oreja* (ear, usually from a pig or sheep).

Main dishes often come without any **accompaniments**, or chips at best. The consolation, however, is the *ensalada mixta*, whose simple name (mixed salad) often conceals a meal in itself. The ingredients vary, but it's typically a plentiful combination of lettuce, tomato, onion, olive oil, boiled eggs, asparagus, olives and tuna. The *tortilla* (a substantial potato omelette) is ever-present and often excellent. *Revueltos* (scrambled eggs), are usually tastily combined with prawns, asparagus or other goodies. Most **vegetable** dishes are based around that New World trio: the bean, the pepper and the potato. There are numerous varieties of bean in Northern Spain; they are normally served as some sort of hearty stew, often with bits of meat or seafood. *Fabada* is the Asturian classic of this variety, while *alubias con chorizo* are a standard across the region. A *cocido* is a typical mountain dish, a massive stew of chickpeas or beans with meat and vegetables; the liquid is drained off and eaten first (*sopa de cocido*). Peppers (*pimientos*), too, come in a number of forms. As well as being used to flavour dishes, they are often eaten in their own right; *pimientos rellenos* come stuffed with meat or seafood. Potatoes come as chips, *bravas* (with a garlic or spicy tomato sauce) or *a la riojana*, with chorizo and paprika. Other common vegetable dishes include *menestra* (delicious blend of cooked vegetables), which usually has some ham in it, and *ensaladilla rusa*, a tasty blend of potato, peas, peppers, carrots and mayonnaise. *Setas* (wild mushrooms) are a delight, particularly in autumn.

Desserts focus on the sweet and milky. *Flan* (a sort of crème caramel) is ubiquitous; great when *casero* (home-made), but often out of a plastic tub. *Natillas* are a similar but more liquid version, and *arroz con leche* is a cold, sweet, rice pudding typical of Northern Spain. **Cheeses** tend to be bland or salty and are normally eaten as a tapa or entrée. There are some excellent cheeses in Northern Spain, however; piquant Cabrales and Basque Idiázabal stand out.

Regional cuisine

Regional styles tend to use the same basic ingredients treated in slightly different ways, backed up by some local specialities. Most of Spain grudgingly concedes that Basque cuisine is the peninsula's best, the San Sebastián twilight shimmers with Michelin stars, and chummy all-male *txokos* gather in private to swap recipes and cook up feasts in members-only kitchens. But what strikes the visitor first are the *pintxos*, a stunning range of bartop snacks that in many cases seem too pretty to put your teeth in. The base of most Basque dishes is seafood, particularly *bacalao* (salt cod; occasionally stunning but often ordinary), and the region has taken full advantage of its French ties.

Navarran and Aragonese cuisine owes much to the mountains, with hearty stews and game dishes featuring alongside fresh trout. Rioja and Castilla y León go for filling roast meat and bean dishes more suited to the harsh winters than the baking summers. Asturias and Cantabria are seafood-minded on the coast but search for more warming fare in the high ground, and Galicia is seafood heaven, with more varieties of finny and shelly things than you knew existed; usually prepared with confidence in the natural flavours; the rest of the area tends to overuse the garlic. Inland Galicia relies more heavily on that traditional northern staple, pork.

Food-producing regions take their responsibilities seriously, and competition is fierce. Those widely acknowledged to produce the best will often add the name of the region to the foodstuff (many foods, like wines, have denomination of origin status, DO, given by a regulatory body). Thus *pimientos de Padrón* (Padrón peppers), *cogollos de Tudela* (lettuce hearts from Tudela), *alubias de Tolosa* (Tolosa beans), *puerros de Sahagún* (Sahagún leeks) and a host of others.

Eating out

One of the great pleasures of travelling in Northern Spain is eating out, but it's no fun sitting in an empty restaurant so adapt to the local hours as much as you can; it may feel strange leaving dinner until 2200, but you'll miss out on a lot of atmosphere if you don't.

The standard distinctions of bar, café and restaurant don't apply in Spain. Many places combine all three functions, and it's not always evident; the dining room (*comedor*) is often tucked away behind the bar or upstairs. *Restaurantes* are restaurants, and will usually have a dedicated dining area with set menus and à la carte options. Bars and cafés will often display food on the counter, or have a list of tapas; bars tend to be known for particular dishes they do well. Many bars, cafés and restaurants don't open on Sunday nights, and most are closed one other night a week, most commonly Monday or Tuesday.

Cafés will usually provide some kind of **breakfast** fare in the mornings; croissants and sweet pastries are the norm; freshly squeezed orange juice is also common. About 1100 they start putting out savoury fare; maybe a *tortilla*, some *ensaladilla rusa* or little ham rolls in preparation for pre-lunch snacking. It's a workers' tradition – from labourers to executives – to drop down to the local bar around 1130 for a *pincho de tortilla* (slice of potato omelette) to get them through until two.

Lunch is the biggest meal of the day for most people in Spain, and it's also the cheapest time to eat. Just about all restaurants offer a *menú del día*, which is usually a set three-course meal that includes wine or soft drink. In unglamorous workers' locals this is often as little as €8; paying anything more than €13 indicates the restaurant takes itself quite seriously. There's often a choice of several starters and mains. To make the most of the meal, a tip is to order another starter in place of a main; most places are quite happy to do it, and the starters are usually more interesting than the mains, which in the cheaper places tend to be slabs of mediocre meat. Most places open for lunch at about 1300, and stop serving at 1500 or 1530, although at weekends this can extend; it's not uncommon to see people still lunching at 1800 on a Sunday. The quality of à la carte is usually higher than the *menú*, and quantities are larger. Simpler restaurants won't offer this option except in the evenings. **Tapas** has changed in meaning over the years, and now basically refers to all bar food. This range includes free snacks given with drinks (now only standard in León and a few other places), *pinchos/pintxos*, see box, page 106, small saucer-sized plates of food (this is the true meaning of *tapa*) and more substantial dishes, usually ordered in *raciones* and designed to be shared. A *ración* in Northern Spain is no mean affair; it can often comfortably fill one person, so if you want to sample a range of things, you're better to ask for a half (*media*) or a *tapa* (smaller portion, when available). Prices of *raciones* basically depend on the ingredients; a good portion of *langostinos* (king prawns) will likely set you back €12, while more *morcilla* (black pudding) or *patatas* than you can eat might only be €4 or so.

Most restaurants open for dinner at 2030 or later. Although some places do offer a cheap set *menú*, you'll usually have to order à la carte. In quiet areas, places stop serving at 2200 on week nights, but in cities and at weekends people sit down at 2230 or later. A cheap option at all times is a *plato combinado*, most commonly offered in cafés. They're usually a greasy spoon-style mix of eggs, steak, bacon and chips or similar and are filling but rarely inspiring.

Vegetarians in Spain won't be spoiled for choice, but at least what there is tends to be good. There's a small but rapidly increasing number of dedicated vegetarian restaurants, but most other places won't have a vegetarian main course on offer, although the existence of *raciones* and salads makes this less of a burden than it might be. *Ensalada mixta* nearly always has tuna in it, but it's usually made fresh, so places will happily leave it out. *Ensaladilla rusa* is normally a good bet, but ask about the tuna too, just in case. Tortilla is simple but delicious and ubiquitous. Simple potato or pepper dishes are tasty options (although beware of peppers stuffed with meat), and many *revueltos* (scrambled eggs) are just mixed with asparagus. Annoyingly, most vegetable *menestras* are seeded with ham before cooking, and bean dishes usually contain at least some meat or animal fat. You'll have to specify *soy vegetariano/a* (I am a vegetarian), but ask what dishes contain, as ham, fish and chicken are often considered suitable vegetarian fare. Vegans will have a tougher time. What doesn't have meat nearly always contains cheese or egg. Better restaurants, particularly in cities, will be happy to prepare something to guidelines, but otherwise better stick to very simple dishes.

Drink

In good Catholic fashion, **wine** is the lifeblood of Spain. It's the standard accompaniment to most meals, but also features very prominently in bars, where a glass of cheap *tinto* or *blanco* can cost as little as €0.80, although it's more normally €1.20. A bottle of house wine in a restaurant is often no more than €5 or €6. *Tinto* is red (although if you just order *vino* it's assumed that's what you want); *blanco* is white, and rosé is either *clarete* or *rosado*. A well-regulated system of *denominaciones de origen* (DO), similar to the French *appelation controlée* has lifted the reputation of Spanish wines high above the party plonk status they

Getting to grips with the grapes

Crianza Must be at least two years old, at least six months of which have been spent in oak (12 months in the case of Rioja).

Reserva A red which has passed its third birthday, of which 12 months (often more) have been in oak.

Gran reserva The softest and most characterful of Spanish wines, although sometimes tending to be over-aged. At least five years old, with two or more in oak. Only produced in good years.

Cosechero A young red from the latest vintage.

Vino Corriente/normal/de mesa The cheap option in bars and restaurants, table wine that can vary from terrible to reasonable. Often high in acid, which balances the oily Spanish food. Served in a tumbler in bars so there's no pretending.

Fresco Most bars will keep a bottle of red *fresco*, or chilled; a refreshing option.

Tinto de verano A refreshing summer mix of cheap red wine, ice and lemonade.

Calimocho The drink of choice for students and revellers, red wine mixed 50-50 with Coca-Cola. Often served in *cachis*, paper cups holding a litre that are nursed solo or shared with straws.

Vino generoso 'Generous', ie fortified, wine, such as sherry.

DO *Denominación de origen* is a regional wine appellation controlled by a regulatory body. Rioja is a DOC (*denominación de origen calificada*), with extra strictures. DO status also exists for other products.

once enjoyed. Much of Spain's wine is produced in the north, and recent years have seen regions such as the Ribera del Duero, Rueda, Navarra, Toro, Bierzo, and Rías Baixas achieve worldwide recognition. But the daddy, of course, is still Rioja.

The overall standard of Riojas has improved markedly since the granting of the higher DOC status in 1991, with some fairly stringent testing in place. Red predominates; these are mostly medium-bodied bottles from the Tempranillo grape (with three other permitted red grapes often used to add depth or character). Whites from Viura and Malvasia are also produced: the majority of these are young, fresh and dry, unlike the traditional powerful oaky Rioja whites now on the decline. Rosés are also produced. The quality of individual Riojas varies widely according to both producer and the amount of time the wines have been aged in oak barrels and in the bottle. The words *crianza, reserva* and *gran reserva* refer to the length of the ageing process (see box, above), while the vintage date is also given. Rioja producers store their wines at the bodega until deemed ready for drinking, so it's common to see wines dating back a decade or more on shelves and wine lists.

A growing number of people feel, however, that Spain's best reds come from further west, in the Ribera del Duero region east of Valladolid. The king's favourite tipple, Vega Sicilia, has long been Spain's most prestigious wine, but other producers from the area have also gained stellar reviews.

Visiting the area in the baking summer heat, it's hard to believe that nearby Rueda can produce quality whites, but it certainly does. Most come from the Verdejo grape and have an attractive, dry, lemony taste; Sauvignon Blanc has also been planted with some success.

Galicia produces some excellent whites too; the coastal Albariño vineyards produce a sought-after dry wine with a very distinctive bouquet. Ribeiro is another good Galician white, and the reds from there are also tasty, having some similarity to those produced in nearby northern Portugal. Ribeira Sacra is another inland Galician denomination producing whites and reds from a wide range of varietals.

Among other regions, Navarra, long known only for rosé, is producing some quality red wines unfettered by the stricter rules governing production in Rioja, while Bierzo, in western León province, also produces interesting wines from the red Prieto Picudo and Mencía grapes. Other DO wines in Northern Spain include Somontano, a red and white appelation from Aragón and Toro, whose baking climate makes for full-bodied reds. Some Toro wines have achieved a very high worldwide profile.

An unusual wine worth trying is *txakolí*, with a small production on the Basque coast. The most common is a young, refreshing, acidic white which has a green tinge and slight sparkle, often accentuated by pouring from a height. The best examples, from around Getaria, go well with seafood. The wine is made from under-ripe grapes of the Ondarrubi Zuria variety; there's a less common red species and some rosé.

One of the joys of Spain, though, is the rest of the wine. Order a *menú del día* at a cheap restaurant and you'll be unceremoniously served a cheap bottle of local red (sometimes without even asking for it). Wine snobbery can leave by the back door at this point: it may be cold, but you'll find it refreshing; it may be acidic, but once the olive-oil laden food arrives, you'll be glad of it. It's not there to be judged, it's a staple like bread and, like bread, it's sometimes excellent, it's sometimes bad, but mostly it fulfils its purpose perfectly. Wine is not a luxury item in Spain, so people add water to it if they feel like it, or lemonade (*gaseosa*), or *cola* (to make the party drink called *calimocho*). Tinto de verano is a summer slurper similar to sangría, a mixture of red wine, gaseosa, ice, and optional fruit.

In most bars, you can order Rioja, Ribera, Rueda, or other regions by the glass (usually €1.20-2.50). If you ask for *crianza* or *reserva*, you'll usually get a Rioja. A *tinto* or *blanco* will usually get you a cheapish local wine, sometimes excellent, sometimes awful. As a general rule, only bars serving food serve wine; most *pubs* and *discotecas* won't have it.

Spanish **beer** is mostly lager, usually reasonably strong, fairly gassy, cold and good. On the tapas trail, many people order *cortos* (*zuritos* in the Basque lands), usually about 100 ml. A *caña* is a larger draught beer, usually about 200 ml. Order a *cerveza* and you'll get a bottled beer. Many people order their beer *con gas*, topped up with mineral water, sometimes called a *clara*, although this normally means it's topped up with lemonade. In some pubs, particularly those specializing in different beers (*cervecerías*), you can order pints (*pintas*).

Cider (*sidra*) is an institution in Asturias, and to a lesser extent in Euskadi. The cider is flat, sour and yeasty; the appley taste will be a surprise after most commercial versions of the drink. Asturias' *sidrerías* offer some of Spain's most enjoyable bar life, see box, page 415, with excellent food, a distinctive odour, sawdust on the floor, and the cider poured from above head height by uniformed waiters to give it some bounce. In Euskadi in springtime, people decamp to cider houses in the hills to eat massive meals and serve themselves bottomless glasses of the stuff direct from the vat.

Spirits are cheap in Spain. Vermouth (*vermut*) is a popular pre-lunch *aperitif*, as is *patxarán* (see glossary, page 540). Many bars make their own vermouth by adding various herbs and fruits and letting it sit in barrels; this can be excellent, particularly if its from a *solera*. This is a system where liquid is drawn from the oldest of a series of barrels, which is then topped up with the next oldest, resulting in a very mellow characterful drink. After dinner or lunch it's time for a *copa*: people relax over a whisky or a brandy, or hit the mixed drinks (*cubatas*): gin tonic is obvious, as is *vodka con cola*. Spirits are free-poured and large; don't be surprised at a 100 ml measure. A mixed drink costs €3.50-6. Whisky is popular, and most bars have a good range. Spanish brandy is good, although its oaky vanilla flavours don't appeal to everyone. There are numerous varieties of rum and flavoured liqueurs. When ordering a spirit, you'll be expected to choose which brand you want; the local varieties (eg *Larios* gin, *DYC* whisky) are marginally cheaper than their imported brethren but lower in quality. *Chupitos* are shots; restaurants will often throw in a free one at the end of a meal, or give you a bottle of *orujo* (grape spirit) to pep up your black coffee.

Juice is normally bottled and expensive; *mosto* (grape juice; really pre-fermented wine) is a cheaper and popular soft drink in bars. There's the usual range of **fizzy drinks** (*gaseosas*) available. *Horchata* is a summer drink, a sort of milkshake made from tiger nuts. **Water** (*agua*) comes *con* (with) or *sin* (without) *gas*. The tap water is totally safe to drink, but it's not always the nicest; many Spaniards drink bottled water at home.

Coffee (*café*) is usually excellent and strong. *Solo* is black, mostly served espresso style. Order *americano* if you want a long black, *cortado* if you want a dash of milk, or *con leche* for about half milk. A *carajillo* is a coffee with brandy, while *queimado* – a Galician drink of ritual significance – is a mixture of coffee and *orujo* (grape spirit), made in a huge vessel. **Tea** (*té*) is served without milk unless you ask; herbal teas (*infusiones*) are common, especially chamomile (*manzanilla*) and mint (*menta poleo*). **Chocolate** is a reasonably popular drink at breakfast time or in the afternoon (*merienda*), served with *churros*, fried doughsticks that seduce about a quarter of visitors and repel the rest.

Entertainment

Bars and clubs
Northern Spain's nightlife is excellent, but you won't find cutting-edge music in many places, nor a huge clubbing scene like in Ibiza or Madrid. Although there's always a busy bar every night of the week, it's Thursday to Saturday nights when things get going; most pubs and *discotecas* only open at weekends. Even the smallest town will usually have some place that's packed out. Late-night bars are known as *bares de copas*, and *la marcha* ('the march') doesn't usually hit them until after midnight, when people have stopped eating. These places will be at their fullest around 0100-0300, but *discotecas* (nightclubs) fill up later, and in some cities are busiest between 0400 and 0600 (the wee hours are known as the *madrugada*). *Discotecas* are often out of town.

Theatre, cinema and galleries
There are theatres in almost every medium-sized town upwards. They tend to serve multiple functions and host changing programmes of drama, dance, music and cinema. There's often only one or two performances of a given show. Tickets are cheap by European standards.

Nearly all foreign films shown at cinemas in Spain are dubbed (*doblada*) into Spanish; a general change to subtitling is resisted by the acting profession, many of whom have careers as dubbers for a Hollywood star. Entrance to cinemas is usually about €4-7; usually cheaper on weekdays. When a film is shown subtitled, the term is *versión original* (*v.o.*).

There are many museums and galleries throughout the area, including stunning modern icons like the Guggenheim. Every provincial capital will have a museum. These are often free (or charge a low admission of €1 or so), and full of interesting objects from the province. While most modern museums have multilingual information, the majority are Spanish-only, although a general leaflet or audio guide might be available in English.

Bullfighting

The bullfight, or *corrida*, is an emblem of Spanish culture, a reminder of Roman times when gladiators fought wild beasts in amphitheatres. It is emphatically not a sport (the result is a given) but a ritual; a display of courage by both animal and human (there are and have been several female *toreros*, although it remains a male-dominated field). While to outside observers it can seem uncomfortably like the bull is being humiliated, that is not the way Spaniards perceive it at all. Many Spaniards are contemptuous of the foreign anti-bullfighting lobby, whom many see as meddling hypocrites, but there is significant opposition to the activity within the country (it has recently been banned in parts of Catalunya), mainly in large cities, but *los toros* are destined to be with us for some time yet.

The myth that bullfighting is blood-thirsty needs to be dispelled. Nobody in the crowd likes to see a *torero* hurt, a less-than-clean kill, or overuse of the lance. What keeps many people going is that all-too-rare sublime fight, where the matador is breathtakingly daring, and the bull strong and courageous.

The fighting bull, or *toro de lidia*, is virtually a wild animal reared in vast ranches where human contact is minimal. It enters the ring when it is about four years old, and weighs about 500 kg.

In a standard bullfight there are six bulls and three matadors, who fight two each. The fights take 15 minutes each, so a standard *corrida* lasts about two hours, usually starting in the late afternoon. The fight is divided into three parts, or *tercios*. In the first part, the bull emerges, and is then played with the cape by the matador, who judges its abilities and tendencies. The bull is then induced to charge a mounted *picador*, who meets it with a sharp lance, which is dug into the bull's neck muscles as it tries to toss the horse. Although the horses are padded these days, it's the most difficult part of the fight to come to terms with, and *picadores* overdo it with the pic, tiring and dispiriting the animal.

The second *tercio* involves the placing of three pairs of darts, or *banderillas*, in the bull's neck muscles, to tire it so that the head is low enough to allow the matador to reach the point where the sword should go in. The placing of the *banderillas* is usually rapid and skilful, done on foot, occasionally by the matador.

The last part is the *tercio de la muerte*, or the third of death. The matador faces the bull with a small cape, called a *muleta*, and a sword. After passing it a few times he'll get it in position for the kill. After profiling (turning side on and pointing the sword at the bull), he aims for a point that should kill the bull almost instantly. Unfortunately this rarely happens; there are often a few attempts and then a *descabello* in which the spinal cord is severed below the base of the skull using a special sword. If the poor beast is still going, someone takes a knife to it.

If the crowd have been impressed by the bullfighter's performance, they stand and wave their handkerchiefs at the president of the ring, who may then award ears and, exceptionally, the tail. These are chopped off the animal and paraded around the ring by the fighter. Meanwhile, the dead bull has been dragged out by mules; if it has fought the good fight, it will be applauded. Another type of bullfight is the *corrida de rejones*, where skilled riders fight the bull from horseback atop highly trained mounts; it's an impressive combination of skill and showmanship.

Festivals and events

Fiestas

Even the smallest village in Spain has a fiesta, and some have several. Although mostly nominally religious in nature, they usually include the works; a mass and procession or two to be sure, but also live music, bullfights, competitions, fireworks and copious drinking of *calimocho/kalimotxo*, a mix of red wine and cola (not as bad as it sounds). A feature of many are the *gigantes y cabezudos*, huge-headed papier-mâché figures based on historical personages who parade the streets. Adding to the sense of fun are *peñas*, boisterous social clubs who patrol the streets making music, get rowdy at the bullfights and drink wine all night and day. Most fiestas are in summer, and if you're spending much time in Spain in that period you're bound to run into one; expect some trouble finding accommodation. Details of the major town fiestas can be found in the travel text. National holidays and long weekends (*puentes*) can be difficult times to travel; it's important to reserve tickets in advance.

Public holidays

The holidays listed here are national or across much of Northern Spain; local fiestas and holidays are detailed in the main text. These can be difficult times to travel; it's important to reserve travel in advance to avoid queues and lack of seats. If the holiday falls mid-week, it's usual form to take an extra day off, forming a long weekend known as a *puente* (bridge).

1 Jan Año Nuevo, New Year's Day.
6 Jan Reyes Magos/Epifanía, Epiphany; when Christmas presents are given.
Easter Jueves Santo, Viernes Santo, Día de Pascua (Maundy Thu, Good Fri, Easter Sun), Lunes Santo (Easter Mon; Euskadi only).
23 Apr Fiesta de la Comunidad de Castilla y León and Día de Aragón (Castilla y León and Aragón).
1 May Fiesta de Trabajo, Labour Day.
25 Jul Día del Apostol Santiago, Feast of St James (Navarra, Euskadi, Galicia; Cantabria's holiday is on **28 Jul**).
15 Aug Asunción, Feast of the Assumption.
12 Oct Día de la Hispanidad, Spanish National Day (Columbus Day, Feast of the Virgin of the Pillar).
1 Nov Todos los Santos, All Saints' Day.
6 Dec El Día de la Constitución Española, Constitution Day.
8 Dec Inmaculada Concepción, Feast of the Immaculate Conception.
25 Dec Navidad, Christmas Day.

Shopping

Although chain stores are gradually swallowing them up, one of the most endearing aspects of the country is the profusion of small shops, many little changed in recent decades and always family-run. While there are many supermarkets, people buy their bread from bakers, their newspapers from kiosks, their tobacco from tobacconists, and they get their shoes repaired at cobblers. Food markets are still the focus of many towns.

Standard shop opening hours are Monday to Friday 1000-1400, 1700-2000, and Saturday mornings. Big supermarkets stay open through the lunch hour and shut at 2100 or 2200. Bargaining is not usual except at markets but it's worth asking for a *descuento* if you're buying in bulk or paying in cash. Non-EU residents can reclaim VAT (*IVA*) on purchases over €90; the easiest way to do this is to get a tax-free cheque from participating shops (look for the sticker), which can then be cashed at customs.

What to buy

Clothing is an obvious choice; Spanish fashion is strong. While the larger chains have branched out into Britain and beyond, there are many smaller stores with good ranges of gear that you won't be able to get outside the country. The big cities of Bilbao and Zaragoza are the best places, but every medium-sized town will have plenty on offer. The average Spaniard is smaller than their British or American counterpart, so don't be offended if you have to check a few places to find something in your size.

Leather is another good buy; jackets tend to be at least 30% less than in the UK, although the range of styles available isn't as great. There are plenty of places that will make bespoke leather goods, although they usually aren't in a huge hurry about it. If Spaniards seem to be obsessed by **shoes**, it's because the shoe shops normally display their wares only in the window, so all the browsing is done outside in the street. Shoes are fairly well priced and unusual, although the long-footed will struggle to find anything. A popular souvenir of León and Asturias is the *madreña*, a wooden clog worn over normal shoes.

Ceramics are a good choice: cheap, attractive and practical in the most part. Galicia is known for its ceramics, local styles are everywhere. Zamora has a ceramics fiesta in June.

Local **fiestas** usually have handicraft markets attached to them; these can be excellent places to shop, as artisans from all around the region bring their wares to town; you'll soon distinguish the real ones from the the imported mass-produced versions.

An obvious choice is **food**. Ham keeps well and is cheap. Many ham shops arrange international deliveries. *Chorizo* is a more portable alternative. Most shops will vacuum-pack these things for you: ask for *envasado al vacío*. *Aceitunas con anchoa* (olives stuffed with anchovies) are a cheap and packable choice, as is the range of quality canned and marinated seafood.

Spanish wine is another good purchase. However, the price differential with the UK is only about 30% so try to find bottles that you can't get at home. *Vinotecas* (wine shops) are common in wine-producing areas, but elsewhere you'll find the biggest selection in department stores such as the **Corte Inglés**. **Spirits** are significantly cheaper than in most of Europe; a bottle of gin from London, for example, can in Spain cost as little as 50% of the British price. A good souvenir is a *bota*, the goatskin winebags used at fiestas and bullfights. Try and buy one from a *botería*, the traditional workshops where they are made, rather than at a tourist shop.

Cigars (*puros*) can be as little as a tenth of UK prices, and there's a large range in many tobacconists (*estancos*). **Cigarettes**, meanwhile, are seriously cheap too; about €3.50 a packet for most international brands.

Responsible travel

Spain sees a lot of tourists. While it's true that in many places the local community is reliant on tourism, it's important to understand that it can be frustrating if people don't show sensitivity to local habits and customs. People are used to speaking English in well-visited areas, but trying even a couple of words of Spanish is basic courtesy. If some aspect of Spanish society frustrates you, remember the cultural context; abusing a slow waiter or waitress in a stream of English isn't going to get you anywhere. Talking loudly about the locals in English (or any other language) is a sure way to be instantly disliked, and won't do the next passing traveller any favours either. Treat people with courtesy and patience; it's very easy to misinterpret local behaviour. You may think the waiter who throws the plates down on the table in front

How big is your footprint?

- Where possible choose a destination, tour operator or hotel with a proven ethical and environmental commitment – if in doubt, ask.
- Spend money on locally produced (rather than imported) goods and services, buy directly from the producer or a locally owned shop, and use common sense when bargaining.
- Use water and electricity carefully.
- Learn about local etiquette and culture – consider local norms and behaviour and dress appropriately for local cultures and situations.
- Protect wildlife and other natural resources – don't buy souvenirs or goods unless they are clearly sustainably produced and are not protected under CITES legislation.
- Always ask before taking photographs or videos of people.
- Consider staying in local accommodation rather than foreign-owned hotels – the economic benefits for host communities are far greater – and there are more opportunities to learn about local culture.
- Make a voluntary contribution to Climate Care, www.co2.org, to counteract the pollution caused by tax-free fuel on your flight.

of you is rude, but he/she may well throw in a free coffee and liqueur at the end of dinner. Small courtesies grease the wheels of everyday interaction here: greet the proprietor or waiter when entering a shop or bar, and say '*hasta luego*' when leaving. It is quite common to say '*que aproveche*' (enjoy your meal) when passing other diners' tables.

Environmental issues are also an individual's responsibility, and the type of holiday you choose has a direct impact on the future of the region. Opting for more sustainable tourism choices – picking a *casa rural* in a traditional village and eating in restaurants serving locally sourced food rather than staying in the four-star multinational hotel – has a small but significant knock-on effect. Don't be afraid to ask questions about environmental policy before making a hotel or *casa rural* booking.

You may consider offsetting the carbon debt of your flights or other transport (for example via Climate Care (www.co2.org), or trying to use public transport as much as possible. More obvious choices are to respect the rules and restrictions of any protected areas, stick to walking trails and carry rubbish with you. Recycling containers are now available in even small villages, so make use of them, even if locals haven't got around to doing so yet.

Responsible tourism also applies to safety issues. If you're striking off on a seldom-used trail in the mountains, let someone know where you're going and when you expect to be back – it might save your life if the weather changes or you have an accident. Don't camp where you're not allowed to; prohibitions are usually there for a good reason. Fire danger can be high in summer, so respect local regulations.

Essentials A-Z

Accident and emergency

There are various emergency numbers, but the general one across the nation is now T112. This will get you the police, ambulance, or fire brigade. T091 gets just the police.

Children

Kids are kings in Spain, and it's one of the easiest places to take them along on holiday. Children socialize with their parents from an early age here, and you'll see them eating in restaurants and out in bars well after midnight. The outdoor summer life and high pedestrianization of the cities is especially suitable and stress-free for both you and the kids to enjoy the experience.

Spaniards are friendly and accommodating towards children, and you'll undoubtedly get treated better with them than without, except perhaps in the most expensive restaurants and hotels. Few places, however, are equipped with highchairs, unbreakable plates or baby-changing facilities. Children are expected to eat the same food as their parents, although you'll sometimes see a *menú infantil* at a restaurant, which typically has simpler dishes and smaller portions.

The cut-off age for children paying half or no admission/passage on public transport and in tourist attractions varies widely.

RENFE trains let children under 4 travel for free, and its discount passage of around 50% applies up to the age of 12. Most car rental companies have child seats available, but it's wise to book these in advance.

As for attractions, beaches are an obvious highlight, but many of the newer museums are hands-on, and playgrounds and parks are common. Campsites cater to families and the larger ones often have child-minding facilities and activities.

Conduct

Northern Spaniards are fairly reserved, particularly towards foreigners. They are usually polite and courteous, but cultural differences can give first-time visitors the opposite impression. Use of 'please' and 'thank you' is minimal, but it is usual to greet and bid farewell to shopkeepers or bartenders when entering/exiting. There's a different concept of personal space in Spain than in northern Europe or the USA; the idea doesn't really exist. People speak loudly as a matter of course; it doesn't mean they are shouting.

Every evening, people take to the streets for the *paseo*, a slow stroll up and down town that might include a coffee or pre-dinner drink. It's a great time to observe Spanish society at work; the ritual is an integral part of Spanish culture. Especially in summer, the whole evening is spent outdoors.

Customs and duty-free

Non-EU citizens are allowed to import 1 litre of spirits, 2 litres of wine and 200 cigarettes or 250 g of tobacco or 50 cigars. EU citizens are theoretically limited by personal use only though individual countries may specify what they regard this as being.

Disabled travellers

Spain isn't the best equipped of countries in terms of disabled travel, but things have improved. By law, all new public buildings have to have full disabled access and facilities (as do all hotels built since 1995), but disabled toilets are rare in other edifices. Facilities are significantly better in the touristed south than in Northern Spain. Most trains and stations are wheelchair friendly to some degree, as are many urban buses, but intercity buses are often not accessible for wheelchairs. **Hertz** offices in Madrid and Barcelona have a small range of cars set up for disabled drivers, but book them well in advance. Nearly all underground and municipal car parks have lifts and disabled spaces, as do many museums and castles. An invaluable resource for finding a bed are the regional accommodation lists, available from tourist offices. Most of these include a disabled-access criterion. Many *hostales* are in buildings with ramps and lifts, but there are many that are not, and the lifts can be small. Nearly all paradores and modern chain hotels are fully wheelchair-accessible, but it's best to check. While major cities are quite straightforward, towns and villages often have uneven footpaths, steep streets (frequently cobbled) and little disabled infrastructure.

Blind visitors are comparatively well catered for in Spain as a result of the efforts of **ONCE**, www.once.es, the national organization for the blind, which runs a lucrative daily lottery. Contact them for information and contacts.

Useful organizations
Confederación Nacional de Sordos de España (CNSE), www.cnse.es. Links to local associations for the deaf.
Federación ECOM, T934 515 550, www.ecom.es. A helpful Barcelona-based organization that provides information on disabled-friendly tourist facilities in Spain.
Global Access, www.globalaccessnews.com. Reports from disabled travellers and links.
Jubilee Sailing Trust, Hazel Rd, Woolston, Southampton, SO19 7GB, T023 8044 9108, www.jst.org.uk. Tall ships running sailing journeys for disabled and able-bodied people, some around Northern Spain.

RADAR, T020 7250 3222, www.radar.org.uk. A British network for disabled people that can help members get information and contacts for disabled travel around Europe.

Dress

Away from the beach, Northern Spaniards generally cover up, but no one in cities is going to be offended by brief clothing; things are a bit more conservative in the countryside, however. Consider wearing long trousers, taking off hats and covering shoulders if you're going in to a church or monastery. Spaniards seldom wear shorts except when on holiday. Topless sunbathing is acceptable on most Spanish beaches and there are many nudist areas along the north coast. Nudism on beaches is very mainstream in Spain.

Drugs and prohibitions

The laws in Spain are broadly similar to any western European country. You are legally required to carry a passport or ID card at all times (although this is rarely an issue, you'll need photo ID to use a credit card anyway). Smoking *porros* (joints) is widespread, although far more common in public in Euskadi than anywhere else (locals say the Spanish government ships the hash In to keep the Basques placid). It is technically illegal, but police aren't too concerned about discreet personal use. Use of cocaine, speed and ecstasy is widespread but means serious trouble if caught.

Electricity

Spain uses the standard European 220V plug, with 2 round pins.

Embassies and consulates abroad

Australia, 15 Arkana St, Yarralumla, Canberra ACT 2600 T6273 3555, emb.canberra@maec.es.

Austria, Argentinierstr.34. A 1040 Wien, T505 5788, emb.viena@maec.es.

Belgium, 19 rue de la Science, 1040 Bruxelles, T230 0340, emb.bruselas@maec.es.

Canada, 74 Stanley Av, Ottawa, T747 2252, emb.ottawa@maec.es.

Denmark, Kristianiagade 21, 2100 Copenhagen, T35 424700, emb.copenhague@maec.es.

France, 22 Av Marceau, 75008 Paris, Cédex 08, T44-431 800, emb.paris@maec.es.

Germany, Lichtensteinallee 1, D-10787, Berlin, T254 0070, emb.berlin@maec.es.

Ireland, 17A Merlyn Park, Ballsbridge, Dublin 4, T269 1640, emb.dublin@maec.es.

Italy, Palacio Borghese, Largo Fontanella di Borghese 19, 00186 Rome, T684 0401, emb.roma@maec.es.

Japan, 1-3-29 Roppongi Minato-ku, Tokyo 106-0032, T3583 8531, emb.tokio@maec.es.

Netherlands, Lange Voorhout 50, 2514, The Hague, T302 4999, emb.lahaya@maec.es.

New Zealand, 50 Manners St, Wellington 6142, T04-802 5665, emb.wellington@maec.es.

Norway, Halvdan Svartes gate 13, 0268 Oslo, T22 926 690, emb.oslo@maec.es.

Portugal, Rua do Salitre 1, 1296 Lisbon, T213-472 381, lisboa@maec.es.

South Africa, 337 Brooklyn Road Menlo Park Pretoria 0181, T460 0123, emb.pretoria@maec.es.

Sweden, Djurgårdsvägen 21, 11521 Stockholm, T667 9430, emb.estocolmo@maec.es.

UK, 39 Chesham Place, London SW1X 8SB, T020-7235 5555, emb.londres@maec.es.

USA, 2375 Pennsylvania Av, Washington DC 20037, T452 0100, emb.washington@maec.es.

Gay and lesbian travellers

Homosexuality is legal, and all ages of consent have been equalized (age 13, though charges can be laid if deceit is used with someone under 16). Northern Spain has nothing to compare with the pink scene of Barcelona/Sitges, Madrid and Ibiza, but most middle-sized towns will have at least 1 venue; most have several.

Euskadi's political awareness and antipathy to Spanish conservatism means that the Basque cities are among the most tolerant in the peninsula. Gay tourism has increased dramatically in Bilbao since the opening of the Guggenheim, and it has the busiest scene. San Sebastián has plenty of life in summer, as do other places along the north coast, like Santander, Laredo and A Coruña. Overt displays of homophobia are rare and couples on the street shouldn't encounter any unpleasantness in the city; some of the smaller Castilian towns may be a different story. In rural areas amazed stares are the order of the day. It's very rare to see couples kissing in public.

Useful organizations

Cogailes, www.cogailes.org. A gay organization with a handy information service on e-ros@cogailes.org or a freephone hotline, T900 601 601 (daily T1800-2200).

COLEGA, www.colegaweb.org. A gay and lesbian association with offices in many Spanish cities.

Shanguide, www.shangay.com, is a useful magazine with reviews, events, information and listings for the whole country.

Useful websites

www.damron.com Subscription listings and travel information.

www.gayinspain.com Wide-ranging listings of bars, clubs, zones, etc.

www.guiagay.com, www.gay.com, www.gaywired.com (English), are websites with listings and information about various Spanish cities.

Health

Health for travellers in Spain is rarely a problem. Medical facilities are good, and the worst most travellers experience is an upset stomach, usually merely a result of the different diet rather than any bug.

The water is safe to drink, but isn't always that pleasant, so many travellers (and locals) stick to bottled water. The sun in Spain can be harsh, so take adequate precautions to prevent heat exhaustion/sunburn. Many medications that require a prescription in other countries are available over the counter at pharmacies in Spain. Pharmacists are highly trained but don't necessarily speak English. In all medium-sized towns and cities, at least one pharmacy is open 24 hrs; this is organized on a rota system; details are posted in the window of all pharmacies and in local newspapers.

Insurance

British and other European citizens should get hold of a **European Health Insurance Card** (**EHIC**), available via www.dh.gov.uk or from post offices in the UK, before leaving home. This guarantees free medical care throughout the EU. Other citizens should seriously consider medical insurance, but check for reciprocal Spanish cover with your private or public health scheme first.

Insurance is a good idea anyway to cover you for theft, etc. In the event of theft, you'll have to make a report at the local police station within 24 hrs and obtain a report to show your insurers. (English levels at the police station are likely to be low, so try to take a Spanish speaker with you to help).

Internet

Now that internet access in the home is so widespread, internet cafés aren't as common as they were. Nevertheless, even small towns should have at least one place where you can get online. The connection is normally pretty good and access costs €1-3 per hr. Many cybercafés are open late, although you'll have to cope with the shellbursts and automatic weaponfire from online games, which are also very popular. Other places that often offer access are *locutorios* (call shops), which are common in areas with a high immigrant population. Most hotels and modern hostales offer wireless internet facilities, and an increasing number of cafés and restaurants also have free Wi-Fi. While we have listed internet places in the text of the guide, these tend to appear and disappear rapidly, so ask the tourist information office where to get online. Mobile phone providers like Vodafone offer pay-as-you-go USB modems at a reasonable rate.

Language

For travelling purposes, everyone in Northern Spain speaks Spanish, known either as *castellano* or *español*, and it's a huge help to know some. Most young people know some English, and standards are rapidly rising, but don't assume that people aged 40 or over know any at all. Spaniards are often shy to attempt to speak English. While many visitor attractions have some sort of information available in English (and to a lesser extent French and German), many don't, or have English tours only in times of high demand. Most tourist office staff will speak at least some English, and there's a good range of translated information available in most places. See page 536 for useful words and phrases in Spanish.

While efforts to speak the language are appreciated, it's more or less expected, to the same degree as English is expected in Britain or the USA. Nobody will be rude if you don't speak any Spanish, but nobody will think to slow their rapidfire stream of the language for your benefit either, or pat you on the back for producing a few phrases in their tongue.

The other languages you'll come across in Northern Spain are *Euskara/Euskera* (the Basque language), *Galego* (Galician), *Bable* (the Asturian dialect) and perhaps *Aragonés*. (Aragonese). Euskara is wholly unrelated to Spanish; if you're interested in Basque culture, by all means learn a few words (and make instant friends), but be aware that many people in Euskadi aren't Basque, and that it's quite a political issue. Bable and Galego are more similar to Spanish, but you won't need to learn any to travel in the regions.

Media

Newspapers and magazines

The Spanish press is generally of a high journalistic standard. The national dailies *El País* (still a qualitative leap ahead), *El Mundo* and the rightist *ABC* are read throughout the country, but regional papers often eclipse these in readership. In the Basque lands, there is *El Correo*, a quality Bilbao-based syndicated chain. *El Diario Vasco* is another Basque daily, while there's also *El Norte de Castilla*, *El Diario de León*, *El Heraldo de Aragón*, *El Comercio* (Asturian) and *El Correo Gallego* (Galician). Overall circulation is low, partly because many people read the newspapers provided in cafés and bars.

The terribly Real Madrid-biased sports dailies *Marca* and *As*, dedicated mostly to football, have an extremely large readership that rivals (eclipses, in *Marca*'s case) any of the broadsheets. There's no tabloid press as such; the closest equivalent is the *prensa de corazón*, the gossip magazines such as *¡Hola!* (forerunner of Britain's *Hello!*). English-language newspapers are widely available in kiosks in the larger towns.

Radio

Radio is big in Spain, with audience figures relatively higher than most of Europe. There's a huge range of stations, mainly on FM wavelengths, many of them broadcasting to a fairly small regional area. You'll be unlikely to get much exposure to it (beyond the top-40 music stations blaring in bars) unless you're in a car or take your own set, however.

Television

TV is the dominant medium in Spain, with audience figures well above most of the EU. The main television channels are the state-run *TVE1*, with standard programming, and *TVE2*, with a more cultural/sporting bent alongside the private *Antena 3*, Berlusconi-owned *Cuatro* and *Tele 5*, *La Sexta (6)*, and *Canal Plus*. Regional stations such as *ETB1*

and *ETB2* in the Basque country also draw audiences. Overall quality is low, with reality shows and lowest-common-denominator kitsch as popular here as anywhere. Cable TV is widespread, and satellite and digital have a wide market.

Money → €1 = £0.85/US$1.33 (Jan 2011).

Currency

In 2002, Spain switched to the euro, bidding farewell to the peseta. The euro (E) is divided into 100 *céntimos*. Euro notes are standard across the whole zone, and come in denominations of 5, 10, 20, 50, 100, and the rarely seen 200 and 500. Coins have one standard face and one national face; all coins are, however, acceptable in all countries. The coins are slightly difficult to tell apart when you're not used to them. The coppers are 1, 2 and 5 cent pieces, the golds are 10, 20 and 50, and the silver/gold combinations are €1 and €2. The exchange rate at the switchover was approximately €6 to 1000 pesetas or 166 pesetas to the euro. So if someone says they paid *cien mil*, they probably mean 100,000 pesetas; €600. People still tend to think in pesetas when talking about large amounts like house prices.

ATMs and banks

The best way to get money in Spain is by plastic. ATMs are plentiful in Spain, and just about all of them accept all the major international debit and credit cards. The Spanish bank won't charge for the transaction, though they will charge a mark-up on the exchange rate, but beware of your own bank hitting you for a hefty fee: check with them before leaving home. Even if they do, it's likely to be a better deal than exchanging cash. The website www.moneysavingexpert.com has a good rundown on the most economical ways of accessing cash while travelling.

Banks are usually open 0830-1400 Mon-Fri (and Sat in winter) and many change foreign money (sometimes only the central branch in a town will do it). Commission rates vary widely; it's usually best to change large amounts, as there's often a minimum commission of €6 or so. Nevertheless, banks nearly always give better rates than change offices (casas de cambio), which are fewer by the day. If you're stuck outside banking hours, some large department stores such as the Corte Inglés change money at knavish rates. Traveller's cheques are accepted in many shops, although they are far less common than they were.

Tax

Nearly all goods and services in Spain are subject to a value-added tax (IVA). This is only 8% for most things the traveller will encounter, including food and hotels, but is as high as 18% on some things. IVA is normally included in the stated prices. You're technically entitled to claim it back if you're a non-EU citizen, for purchases over €90. If you're buying something pricey, make sure you get a stamped receipt clearly showing the IVA component, as well as your name and passport number; you can claim the amount back at major airports on departure. Some shops will have a form to smooth the process.

Cost of living and travelling

Prices have soared since the euro was introduced; some basics rose by 50-80% in 3 years, and hotel and restaurant prices can even seem dear by Western European standards these days. Spain's average monthly salary of €1300 is low by EU standards, and the minimum monthly salary of €600 is very low indeed.

Spain can still be a reasonably cheap place to travel if you're prepared to forgo a few luxuries. If you're travelling as a pair, staying in cheap pensiones, eating a set meal at lunchtime, travelling short distances by bus or train daily, and snacking on tapas in the evenings, €65 per person per day is reasonable. If you camp

and grab picnic lunches from shops, you could reduce this considerably. In a cheap hotel or good hostal and using a car, €130 each a day and you'll not be counting pennies; €250 per day and you'll be very comfy indeed unless you're staying in 4- or 5-star accommodation.

Accommodation is more expensive in summer than in winter, particularly on the coast. The Basque lands are significantly more expensive year-round than the rest of Northern Spain, particularly for sleeping, eating and drinking. The news isn't great for the solo traveller; single rooms tend not to be particularly good value, and they are in short supply. Prices range from 60% to 80% of the double/twin price; some establishments even charge the full rate. If you're going to be staying in 3- to 5-star hotels, booking them ahead on internet discount sites can save a lot of money.

Public transport is generally cheap; intercity bus services are quick and low-priced and trains are reasonable, though the fast AVE trains cost substantially more.

Petrol is relatively cheap: standard unleaded petrol is around €1.20 per litre and diesel around €1.10. In some places, particularly in tourist areas, you may be charged up to 20% more to sit outside a restaurant. It's also worth checking if the 8% IVA (sales tax) is included in menu prices, especially in the more expensive restaurants, it should say on the menu whether this is the case.

Post

The Spanish post is notoriously inefficient and slow by European standards. Post offices (correos) generally open Mon-Fri 0800-1300, 1700-2000; Sat 0800-1300, although main offices in large towns stay open all day. Stamps can be bought here or at tobacconists (estancos). A letter or postcard within Spain costs €0.39, within Europe €1.07, and elsewhere €1.38.

Safety

Northern Spain is generally a very safe place. While port cities like Bilbao, Vigo and Santander have some dodgy areas, tourist crime is very low in this region, and you're more likely to have something returned (that you left on that train) than something stolen. That said, don't invite crime by leaving luggage or cash in cars. If parking in a city or, particularly, a popular hiking zone, try to make it clear there's nothing to nick inside by opening the glovebox, etc. Muggings are very rare, but don't leave bags unattended.

There are several types of police, helpful enough in normal circumstances. The paramilitary Guardia Civil dress in green and are responsible for the roads (including speed traps and the like), borders and law enforcement away from towns. They're not a bunch to get the wrong side of but are polite to tourists and have thankfully lost the bizarre winged hats they used to sport. The Policía Nacional are responsible for most urban crimefighting. Brown-shirted folk, these are the ones to go to if you need to report anything stolen, etc. Policía Local/ Municipal are present in large towns and cities and are responsible for some urban crime, as well as traffic control and parking. The Ertzaintza are the most dashing force in Spain, with cocky red berets. They are a Basque force who deal with the day-to-day beat and some crime. There's a similar corps in Navarra.

Smoking

Smoking is widespread in Spain, but controversial new legislation banned it in all enclosed public spaces (ie bars and restaurants) from January 2011. There are still rooms for smokers in some hotels, but these are limited to 30%. Prices are standardized; you can buy smokes at tobacconists or at machines in cafés and bars (with a small surcharge).

Student travellers

An International Student Identity Card (ISIC), for full-time students, is worth having in Spain. Get one at your place of study, or at many travel agencies both in and outside Spain. The cost varies from country to country, but is generally about €6-10 – a good investment, providing discounts of up to 20% on some plane fares, train tickets, museum entries, bus tickets and some accommodation. A Euro Under 26 card gives similar discounts, and is for anyone under 26 years of age.

Telephone → *Country code +34.*

There's a public telephone in many bars, but hearing the conversation over the ambient noise can be a hard task and rates are slightly higher than on the street. Phone booths on the street are mostly operated by Telefónica, and all have international direct dialling (00 is the prefix for international calls). They accept coins from €0.05 upwards and phone cards, which can be bought from *estancos*.

For directory enquiries, dial T11818 for national or T11825 for international numbers. The local operator is on T1009 and the international one on T1008.

Domestic landlines have 9-digit numbers beginning with 9 (occasionally with 8). Although the first 3 digits indicate the province, you have to dial the full number from wherever you are calling, including abroad. Mobiles numbers start with 6.

Mobiles (*móviles*) are big in Spain and coverage is very good. Most foreign mobiles will work in Spain (although older North American ones won't); check with your service provider about what the call costs will be like. Many mobile networks require you to call up before leaving your home country to activate overseas service ('roaming'). If you're staying a while, it may be cheaper to buy a Spanish mobile or SIM card, as there are always numerous offers and discounts.

Time

Spain operates on western European time, ie GMT +1, and changes its clocks in line with the rest of the EU.

'Spanish time' isn't as elastic as it used to be, but if you're told something will happen *'enseguida'* ('straight away') it may take 10 mins, if you're told *'cinco minutos'* (5 mins), grab a seat and a book. Transport, especially buses, leaves promptly.

Tipping

Tipping in Spain is far from compulsory, but much practised. Around 10% is considered extremely generous in a restaurant; 3-5% is more usual. It's rare for a service charge to be added to a bill. Waiters do not normally expect tips for lunchtime set meals or tapas, but here and in bars and cafés people will often leave small change, especially for table service. Taxi drivers don't expect a tip, but will be pleased to receive one. In rural areas, churches will often have a local keyholder who will open it up for you; if there's no admission charge, a tip or donation is appropriate (say €1 per head; more if they've given a detailed tour).

Tour operators

Australia
Explore Holidays, www.exploreholidays.com. au. Organizes several northern Spanish trips.
Ibertours, www.ibertours.com.au. Spanish specialist and booking agent for **Parador** and **Rusticae** hotels.
Outdoor Travel, www.outdoortravel.com. au. Affiliated with several Spanish outdoor tourism operators.
Timeless Tours and Travel, www.timeless. com.au. Specializes in tailored itineraries for Spain.

North America
Abercrombie and Kent, www. abercrombiekent.com. High-class packages and tailor-made trips.

Heritage Tours, www.htprivatetravel.com. Interesting, high-class itineraries around the north of Spain, including one tour of the Jewish history of Tarazona and its region.
Magical Spain, www.magicalspain.com. American-run tour agency based in Sevilla, which runs a variety of tours in the north, including a wine-tasting one. San Francisco office also.
Sarah Tours, www.sarah tours.com. City and study trips, activity breaks, culinary courses. Spain specialists.
Saranjan Tours, www.saranjan.com. Tours to the Sanfermines in Pamplona, as well as a yacht tour around the Rías Baixas and Santiago, the Camino de Santiago, the Batalla de Vino in Haro, the Transcantábrico train route, and gourmet wine and food tours.

Spain
Olé Spain Tours, www.olespaintours.com. All types of tours.

UK and Ireland
Abercrombie and Kent, www. abercrombiekent.co.uk. Upmarket operator offering packages and tailor-made itineraries in Spain.
Alternative Travel Group, www.atg-oxford. co.uk. A variety of interesting trips to Northern Spain, many involving walking.
Blue Green Spain, www.bluegreenspain. com. Organizes self-catering accommodation in Asturias. The boss is from Gijón and knows the area well.
Casas Cantábricas, www.casas.co.uk. Self-catering holidays in Northern Spain.
Mundi Color, www.mundicolor.co.uk. An offshoot of Iberia, specializing in Spanish fly-drive packages.

Specialist operators
Adventure
Exodus, www.exodus.co.uk. Walking and adventure tours.
Spirit of Adventure, www.spirit-of-adventure. com. All kinds of activities, from caving to kayaking, mountain biking to windsurfing.

Archaeology and art history

ACE Cultural Tours, www.acestudytours. co.uk. Tours to Castilla y León, Aragón, Camino de Santiago and more.

Martin Randall Travel, www.martin randall.com. Excellent cultural itineraries accompanied by lectures.

Battlefields

Holts Tours, www.holts.co.uk. Regular tours of the Napoleonic battlefields of Northern and Southern Spain.

Birdwatching

Spain Birds, www.spainbirds.com. A variety of birdwatching excursions all over Spain.

Cycling

Bravo Bike Travel, www.bravobike. com. Biking tours, including wine-tasting itineraries in La Rioja and the Ribera del Duero.

Cycling Through The Centuries, www. cycling-centuries.com. Guided tours of the Camino de Santiago and Picos de Europa.

Irish Cycling Safaris, Belfield House, University College Dublin, Dublin 4, Ireland, www.cyclingsafaris.com. Runs tours to Northern Spain.

Saddle Skedaddle, T44 1912 651 110, www.skedaddle.co.uk. Mountain biking and cycling trips in Northern Spain.

Fishing

GourmetFly, www.gourmetfly.com. Fly-fishing excursions to Northern Spain.

Food and wine

Epiculinary Tours, www.epiculinary.com. Culinary tours and lessons that get into the heart of San Sebastián gastronomic societies.

Euroadventures, C Velásquez Moreno 9, Vigo, Spain, www.euroadventures.net. Interesting tours and lessons, including culinary tours of the Basque region.

San Sebastián Food, www. sansebastianfood.com. Gourmet breaks in Donostia, Rioja and the Basque coastline,

either all-inclusive or individually bookable activities. Recommended.

The Unique Traveller, www.theunique traveller.com. Spanish specialists offering good Rioja wine tours, and gourmet Basque country excursions, among other trips.

Vintage Spain, www.vintagespain.com. Tailor-made tours in Northern Spain, including wine tasting.

Language

Amerispan, PO Box 58129 Philadelphia, PA 19102-8129, www.amerispan.com.

Spanish Abroad, 5112 N 40th St, Suite 103, Phoenix AZ 85253, www.spanishabroad. com. 2-week immersion courses in Salamanca and San Sebastián.

Walking

Pico Verde Holidays, www.picoverde.com. Guided walking holidays in the Picos de Europa, the Pyrenees, and southwestern Asturias.

Spain Adventures, www.spainadventures. com. Hiking and biking in Northern Spain.

Walk Picos, www.walkpicos.co.uk. 1-week walking adventures.

Tourist information

The tourist information infrastructure in Northern Spain is organized by the regional governments and is generally excellent, with a wide range of information, often in English, German and French as well as Spanish. Offices within the region can provide maps of the area and towns, and lists of registered accommodation, usually with 1 booklet for hotels, *hostales*, and *pensiones*; another for campsites, and another, especially worth picking up, listing farmstay and rural accommodation, which has taken off in a big way; hundreds are added yearly. Opening hours are longer in major cities; many rural offices are only open in summer. Average opening hours are Mon-Sat 1000-1400, 1600-1900, Sun 1000-1400. Offices are often closed on Sun or Mon. Staff often speak English and other European languages and are well trained. The offices (*oficinas de turismo*) are often signposted to some degree within the town or city. Staff may ask where you are from; this is not nosiness but for statistical purposes.

The regional tourist boards of Northern Spain have useful websites, the better of which have extensive accommodation, restaurant, and sights listings. You can usually order brochures online too. They are:

Aragón, www.turismodearagon.com

Asturias, www.asturias.es

Cantabria, www.turismodecantabria.com

Castilla y León, www.turismocastillayleon.com

Galicia, www.turgalicia.es

La Rioja, www.lariojaturismo.com

País Vasco (Euskadi), www.turismoa.euskadi.net

Navarra, www.turismonavarra.es

Other useful websites

http://maps.google.es Street maps of most Spanish towns and cities.

www.alsa.es Northern Spain's major bus operator. Book online.

www.bilbao.net The city's excellent website.

www.cyberspain.com Good background on culture and fiestas.

www.dgt.es The transport department website has up-to-date information in Spanish on road conditions throughout the country. Useful for snowy winters.

www.elpais.es Online edition of Spain's biggest-selling non-sports daily paper. English edition available.

www.feve.es Website of the coastal FEVE train service.

www.guiarepsol.com Excellent online route planner for Spanish roads, also available in English.

www.idealspain.com A good source of practical information about the country designed for people relocating there.

www.inm.es Site of the national metereological institute, with the day's weather and next-day forecasts.

www.movelia.es Online timetables and ticketing for several bus companies.

www.paginasamarillas.es Yellow Pages.

www.paginasblancas.es The White Pages.

www.parador.es Parador information, including locations, prices and photos.

www.red2000.com A good introduction to Spanish geography and culture, with listings.

www.renfe.es Online timetables and tickets for RENFE train network.

www.soccer-spain.com A website in English dedicated to Spanish football.

www.spain.info The official website of the Spanish tourist board.

www.ticketmaster.es Spain's biggest ticketing agency for concerts, etc, with online purchase.

www.todoturismorural.com and **www.toprural.com** 2 excellent sites for *casas rurales*.

www.tourspain.es A useful website run by the Spanish tourist board.

www.typicallyspanish.com News and links on all things Spanish.

Visas

Entry requirements are subject to change, so always check with the Spanish tourist board or an embassy/consulate if you're not an EU citizen. EU citizens and those from countries within the Schengen agreement can enter Spain freely. UK/Irish citizens will need to carry a passport, while an identity card suffices for other EU/Schengen nationals. Citizens of Australia, the USA, Canada, New Zealand and Israel can enter without a visa for up to 90 days. Other citizens will require a visa, obtainable from Spanish consulates or embassies. These are usually issued very quickly and valid for all Schengen countries. The basic visa is valid for 90 days, and you'll need 2 passport photos, proof of funds covering your stay and possibly evidence of medical cover (ie insurance). For extensions of visas, apply to an *oficina de extranjeros* in a major city.

Women travellers

Northern Spain is a very safe destination for female travel; there's none of the harassment that you'll find in some parts of the south or elsewhere. While attitudes of the older generation are still prehistoric in some areas, this will rarely translate into anything less than perfect courtesy. Aggressive sexuality isn't part of the makeup of the Northern Spanish male; if you go out on your own, you can expect to be chatted to, but it's very rarely going to be anything more than mild flirtation.

Working in Spain

The most obvious paid work for English speakers is to teach the language. Even the smallest towns usually have an English college or two; it's a big industry here. Rates of pay aren't great except in the large cities. The best way of finding work is by trawling around the schools, but there are dozens of useful internet sites; www.eslcafe.com is still one of the best. There's also a more casual scene of private teaching; noticeboards in universities and student cafés are the best way to find work of this sort, or to advertise your own services.

Bar work is also relatively easy to find, particularly in summer. Irish theme bars in the larger cities are an obvious choice, but smaller towns along the north coast also have plenty of seasonal work, though this has decreased with economic conditions in recent times. Live-in English-speaking au pairs and childminders are also popular with wealthier city families wanting to give young children some exposure to the English language.

EU citizens are at an advantage when it comes to working in Spain; they can work without a permit. Non-EU citizens need a working visa, obtainable from Spanish embassies or consulates, but you'll need to have a firm offer of work to obtain it. Most English schools can organize this for you but make sure you arrange it before arriving in the country.

Contents

Footprint features

País Vasco

At a glance

⊖ **Getting around** Excellent transport connections throughout the region mean a hire car's not a necessity. Bilbao airport has many flights, including budget connections.

◉ **Time required** 7-10 days.

☀ **Weather** Plenty of precipitation, mostly in the form of drizzle, from autumn to spring, but good, not-too-hot summers.

✖ **When not to go** Prices on the coast are sky-high in August, but Bilbao is good year-round.

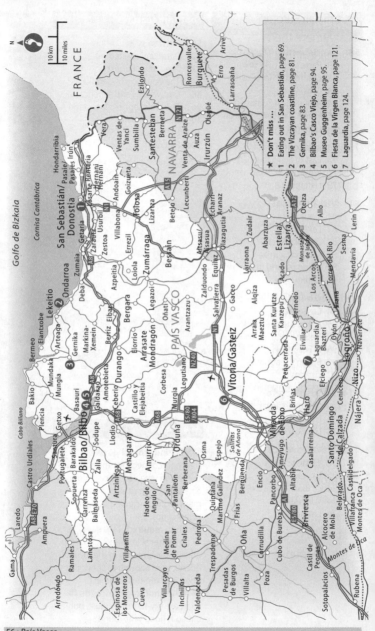

Don't miss ...

★ Eating out in San Sebastián, page 69.

1 The Vizcayan coastline, page 81.
2 Gernika, page 83.
3 Bilbao's Casco Viejo, page 94.
4 Museo Guggenheim, page 95.
5 Fiesta de la Virgen Blanca, page 121.
6 Laguardia, page 124.

It's official: Europe's oldest people have been reborn, and everywhere the visitor looks there's some celebration or affirmation that it's good to be Basque again. Euskadi is back with a bang, and the old feeling that Bilbao is the centre of the world has rapidly returned.

Whatever your views on independence movements, Euskadi (the Basque name for this part of the world) doesn't feel very Spanish. Even the most imperialistic of the Madrid establishment refer to it as 'El País Vasco', the Basque country. The name for the region in Basque (Euskara or Euskera) is either Euskadi or Euskal Herría. Things are certainly different here; there's a strange language on road signs that would break Scrabble scoring records, weird sports are played to packed houses, it rains an awful lot and there's a subtle vibrancy that infects even the most mundane of daily tasks.

The region's biggest city, Bilbao, has managed superbly to reinvent itself from declining industrial dinosaur to optimistic European metropolis. The Guggenheim museum is a powerful symbol of this, but it's the vision and spirit that put it there that are even more invigorating. San Sebastián, meanwhile, is perennially popular for its superb natural setting and wonderful gourmet scene, and Vitoria, the peaceful Basque capital, is also very appealing.

Euskadi isn't very large, which means that most of the rural areas are within easy reach of the three cities. The rugged coast has a few excellent beaches and some very personable fishing towns. Inland, medieval towns still preserve an excellent architectural heritage, while Laguardia, by happy coincidence, is both one of the most attractive walled towns in Northern Spain and an important centre of the Rioja wine region. Outside the towns, the green hills and rocky peaks of this corner of the peninsula are an invitation into the open air.

San Sebastián/Donostia

→ *Colour map 3, B3. Phone code: 943. Population: 185,357.*

The sweep of La Concha bay and the hills overlooking it draw comparisons for San Sebastián with Rio de Janeiro. One of the peninsula's most beautiful cities, it's a place with a light and leisurely feel, and draws throngs of summer holidaymakers. With a superb natural setting, lovely sandy beaches, and a regular influx of international stardom during its film festival, it's a relaxed and enjoyable place that has been invigorated by the addition of two excellent museums and a piece of world-class modern architecture in the Kursaal auditorium. It's also the gourmet capital of Spain, whether you splash out on sumptuous degustation menus in gastronomic temples or graze elaborate pintxos in the livewire bars.

The pedestrianized Old Town lies at the foot of the Monte Urgull hill, and is unabashedly devoted to tapas bars; the pintxos here are astoundingly inventive, small works of art in their own right. The bars are in constant competition to take gourmet cuisine in miniature one step further. From the old town, the main beach stretches west right around the bay to steep Monte Igueldo, the spot to head for if you want your holiday snaps to have that panoramic postcard feel. The hills behind town are green and studded with villages that seem totally oblivious to the city's presence. This is where cider is made: in spring when the stuff's ready, people descend like locusts on the cider houses to drink it straight from the vat and eat enormous meals over sawdust floors. It's amazing any cider's left to be bottled. ▸▸ *For listings, see pages 67-75.*

Ins and outs

Getting there San Sebastián's airport is at Hondarribia, 20 km east of the city (see page 75). It's connected with Madrid and Barcelona. Most inter-urban buses leave from the main bus station on Plaza Pío XII. Regular buses leave to and from Plaza Guipúzcoa to the outlying districts. San Sebastián's main **RENFE** terminus is the Estación del Norte just across the river from the new town area. ▸▸ *See Transport, page 74.*

Getting around San Sebastián is reasonably compact and most sights are within easy walking distance of each other. Buses run from one end of the city to the other.

Tourist information The efficient, English-speaking San Sebastián **tourist office** ① *Boulevard 8, T943 481 166, www.sansebastianturismo.com, Mon-Thu 0900-1330, 1530-1900 (1630-2000 in summer), Fri-Sat 0930-1900 (2000 in summer), Sun 1000-1400,* is busy but helpful. You can download city information to your mobile phone here. There's also a summer information kiosk on the beach promenade. The tourist office runs a booking agency for accommodation and events, www.sansebastianreservas.com, T902 443 442.

Background

San Sebastián is well past its days as a significant port or military bastion though it still has a small fishing fleet. Ever since royalty began summering here in the 19th century, the city has settled into its role of elegant seaside resort to the manner born. It was once, however, one of the important ports of Northern Spain, part of the *Hermandad de las Marismas* trading alliance from the 13th century on. In the 18th century, the Basques established a monopoly over the chocolate trade with Venezuela centred on this city. San Sebastián suffered during the Peninsular War: captured by the French, it was then besieged by English, Spanish and Portuguese forces. The valiant French garrison held out on the Monte Urgull hill for another week after the town had fallen, while the victorious British, Spanish and Portuguese pillaged the town. They also managed to set it on fire; Calle 31 de Agosto was the only street to survive the blaze. This was just one of several 'Great Fires' the city has endured.

Parte Vieja (Old Town)

The liveliest part of San Sebastián is its old section at the eastern end of the bay. Although most of it was destroyed by the 1813 fire, it is still full of character, with a dense concentration of *pintxo* bars, *pensiones*, restaurants and shops. Protecting the narrow streets is the solid bulk of **Monte Urgull**, which also shelters the small harbour area.

El Muelle

One of the city's nicest meanders is along Paseo Nuevo, which runs around the hill from the river mouth to the harbour. Beyond the town hall, San Sebastián's small fishing and recreational harbour, El Muelle, is a pleasant place to stroll around. There's a handful of cafés and tourist shops, and you can see the fishermen working on their boats while their wives mend the nets by the water. Halfway round the harbour is a monument to 'Aita Mari' (father Mari), the nickname of a local boatman who became a hero for his fearless acts of rescue of other sailors in fierce storms off the coast. In 1866 he perished in view of thousands attempting yet another rescue in a terrible tempest.

The **Museo Naval** ① *Paseo del Muelle 24, T943 430 051, Tue-Sat 1000-1330, 1600-1930, Sun 1100-1400, €1.20*, is a harbourside museum, which unfortunately makes a potentially intriguing subject slightly dry and lifeless. While there's plenty of information about Basque seafaring, the interesting aspects are hurried over and there's little attempt to engage the visitor. Descriptions are in Spanish and Euskara only.

At the end of the harbour, San Sebastián's **aquarium** ① *Plaza Carlos Blasco de Imaz s/n, T943 440 099, www.aquariumss.com, Tue-Thu 1000-1900 (2100 in summer), Fri-Sun 1000-2000 (2200 in summer), €12 (€6 for kids)*, is well stocked. The highlight is a tank brimming with fish, turtles, rays and a couple of portly sharks to keep the rest of them honest. There's a perspex tunnel through the tank, which can be viewed from above. Unfortunately, there's not much in the way of identification panels and viewing space can get crowded, particularly around shark-feeding time (Tuesday-Sunday at 1200), which isn't quite as dramatic as it sounds. Most fascinating are the shark egg cases, in which you can observe the tiny embryos. There is a bar/restaurant and shop on site.

Monte Urgull

The bulk of Monte Urgull is one of several Donostia spots that you can climb up to appreciate the view. An important defensive position until the city walls were taken down in 1863, it saw action from the 12th century onwards in several battles. The hill is topped by a small fort, the **Castillo de la Mota** ① *daily 1100-1330, 1700-2000, summer only*, once used as the residence of the town's *alcalde* and as a prison. It has a small collection of old weapons, including a sword that belonged to the last Moorish king Boabdil. There's also a large statue of Christ, the **Monumento al Sagrado Corazón**, adding to San Sebastián's credentials as a Rio lookalike.

Motorboats to Isla Santa Clara in the middle of the bay leave from Monte Urgull, as do boats offering cruises round the harbour.

San Sebastián/Donostia

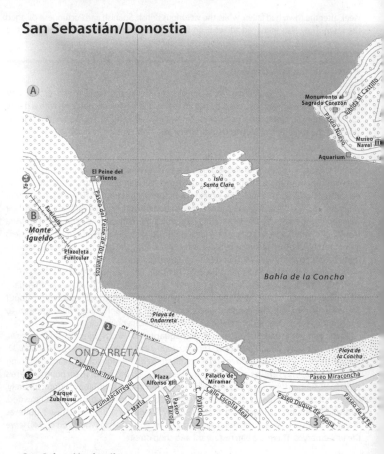

A

Monumento al
Sagrado Corazón

Subida al Castillo

Paseo Nuevo

Museo
Naval

Aquarium

El Peine del
Viento

Isla
Santa Clara

B

Monte
Igueldo

Plazoleta
Funicular

Bahía de la Concha

Playa de
Ondarreta

C

Av Satrustegui

ONDARRETA

C. Pamplona-Iruña

Plaza
Alfonso XIII

Palacio de
Miramar

Calle Escolta Real

Playa de
la Concha

Paseo Miraconcha

Parque
Zubimusu

Av Zumalacárregui

Matía

Pío Baroja

Paseo
Palacio

Paseo Duque de Baena

Paseo de la Fe

1

2

3

San Sebastián detail

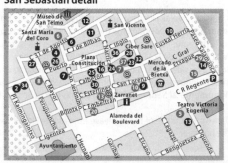

Museo de
San Telmo

San Vicente

Santa María
del Coro

C 31 de Agosto

C de Bilbao

C Inglo

Ciber Sare

Euskal Herria

Paseo Salamanca

Plaza
Constitución

C Puerto

C Mayor

C San Jerónimo

C Esterlines

C Calbetón

Mercado
de la
Bretxa

C Gral
Etxague

C San Lorenzo

C R Regente

Zarranet

C Embeltrán

Bilintx

C Iñigo

Teatro Victoria
Eugenia

Alameda del
Boulevard

Ayuntamiento

C Gentea

C Hernani

C Garibay

C Elcano

C Legazpi

C Bengoetxea

C Oquendo

Pl Kaimingainto

Peruladncha

N

200 metres
200 yards

Sleeping

De Londres y
de Inglaterra 3 *B4*
Ezeiza 2 *C1*
Hostal Alemana 1 *C4*
Izar Bat 7 *detail*
María Cristina 12 *B5*

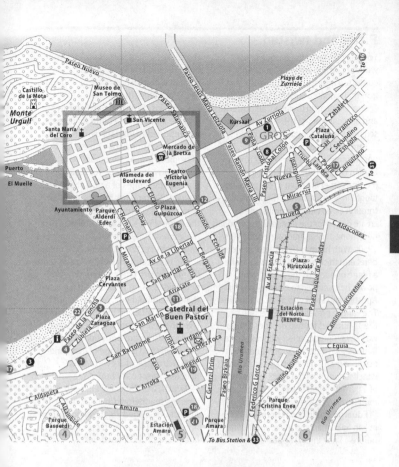

Mercure Monte Igueldo **14** *B1*	Villa Soro **16** *A6*	Casa Vergara **27** *detail*	Urepel **14** *detail*
Niza **4** *C4*		Ganbara **7** *detail*	Zeruko **28** *detail*
Pensión Aída **5** *B6*	**Eating** 🍽	Garbola **8** *A6*	
Pensión Altair **17** *A6*	A Fuego Negro **6** *detail*	Goiz Argi **32** *detail*	**Bars & clubs** 🍸
Pensión Amaiur **6** *detail*	Arzak **31** *A6*	Iturralde **33** *C5*	Altxerri Bar **15** *detail*
Pensión Bellas Artes	Astelena **10** *detail*	La Cepa **11** *detail*	Bataplán **17** *C4*
18 *C5*	Barbarin **2** *detail*	La Cuchara de	Be Bop **29** *detail*
Pensión Edorta **8** *detail*	Bar Gorriti **9** *detail*	San Telmo **12** *detail*	Bideluze **18** *B5*
Pensión Gran Bahía	Bar Ondarra **1** *A6*	La Fábrica **34** *detail*	El Nido **19** *C5*
Bernardo **13** *detail*	Bodegón Alejandro	Munto **30** *detail*	Garagar **20** *detail*
Pensión Kursaal **9** *A5*	**23** *detail*	Oquendo **13** *detail*	Komplot **21** *C5*
Pensión San Lorenzo	Borda Berri **24** *detail*	Portaletas **26** *detail*	Mendaur **37** *detail*
10 *detail*	Café de la Concha **3** *C4*	Rekondo **35** *C1*	Museo del Whisky
Pensión San Martín **11** *B5*	Casa Gandarias **4** *detail*	Tamboril **16** *detail*	**5** *detail*
	Casa Urola **25** *detail*	Txepetxa **36** *detail*	Rotonda **22** *C4*

Bitter and twisted

You can't go far in the Basque lands without coming across a hauntingly contorted figure or sweep of rusted iron that signals a creation of Jorge de Oteiza or Eduardo Chillida. The powerful and original work of these two Basque sculptors is emblematic of the region.

Jorge de Oteiza, forthright and uncompromising well into his 90s, was born in Orio in 1908. After ditching a medical career in favour of sculpture he taught in South America. His big break-through came when commissioned to create pieces for the façade of the visionary new monastery at Arantzazu in the early 1950s. With his grey beard, leather jacket, beret and thick glasses, Oteiza cut quite a figure on site, but the anguish and power he managed to channel into his Apostles and Pietá was quite extraordinary. The Vatican prevented the erection of the 14 apostles for two decades. Oteiza was always preoccupied with relevance, famously saying that "a monument will be no more than a pile of stones or a coil of wire if it does not contribute to the making of a better human being, if it is not … the moulded key to a new kind of man".

Eduardo Chillida was born in 1924 in San Sebastián and in his youth (and before a knee injury) appeared between the sticks for Real Sociedad. A sculptor of huge world renown, the spaces he created within his work are as important as the materials that comprise it. The Peine de los Vientos at San Sebastián and the Plaza de los Fueros in Vitoria are designed to interact dynamically with their setting, while his exploration of oxidized iron as a medium was particularly appropriate for Euskadi, built on the glories of a now-faded iron industry. Softer work in alabaster and wood is less confronting, but evokes the same theme of space. Chillida-Leku museum outside San Sebastián houses a large cross-section of his massive output.

The two sculptors were on bitter terms for many years: Oteiza, perhaps jealous of Chillida's rising profile, held the view that he had 'sold out', refused to use his name, and criticized him bitterly in public. Over the years there were accusations of plagiarism from both sides. Oteiza eventually had a change of heart and after many peaceful overtures were rejected, they finally buried the hatchet in 1997 with the 'Zabalaga embrace'. In fact, it seems that before Chillida's death in August 2002, aged 78, they had become firm friends. Oteiza died only months later, in April 2003, aged 94.

Iglesia de Santa María del Coro

In the heart of the old town, and with a façade about as ornate as Spanish baroque ever got, the church of Santa María del Coro squats under the rocks of Monte Urgull and faces the newer cathedral across the city. After the exuberant exterior, the interior is a contrast of low lighting, heavy oil paintings and incense. Above the altar is a large depiction of the man the city was named after, unkindly known by some as the 'pincushion saint' for the painful way he was martyred. Facing him at the other end of the nave is a stone crucifix in the unmistakable style of Eduardo Chillida, the late Basque sculptor (see box, above).

Museo de San Telmo

ⓘ *Plaza Zuloaga 1, T943 424 970, www.museosantelmo.com, Tue-Fri 1000-1400, 1500-1730, Sat-Sun 1000-1730, free. Currently closed for renovation.*

The San Telmo museum, set in a 16th-century Dominican convent, is worth a visit if only for its perfect Renaissance cloister set around a green lawn. The ground floor of the museum has a dedicated space for temporary exhibitions and a series of grave markers paired with evocative poetic quotes on death. Upstairs is mostly devoted to painting and sculpture. Fittingly, as the museum sits on a square named after him, Ignacio Zuloaga is well represented. A worthy successor to the likes of Velázquez and Goya in the art of portrait painting, one of the best examples here is his Columbus, who is deep and soulful (and suspiciously Basque-looking). There's also a small memorial to Zuloaga in the plaza outside. Upstairs, the gallery of Basque painting is a good place to get an idea of how different the local landscapes and physiques are to those of Spain; the quality is good, although there's not a sniff of the controversial, political or avant-garde.

Iglesia de San Vicente

The most interesting of San Sebastián's churches, San Vicente is a castle-like sandstone building that squats in the northeast of Parte Vieja. Started in the early 16th century, it features a massive *retablo* with various biblical scenes, and a gallery with an impressive organ. Jorge Oteiza's wonderfully fluid, modern *Pietá* stands outside the southern door.

La Bretxa

This modern complex lies at the point where the besieging English and Spanish forces entered the city during the Peninsular War – the name means 'the breach'. The main attraction is the underground food market, with fish, in particular, of spectacular quality.

Centro and New Town

Playa de la Concha

This beautiful curving strip of sand, has made San Sebastián what it is. Named *La Concha* (shell) for its shape, it gets seriously crowded in summer but is relatively quiet at other times, when the chilly water makes swimming a matter of bravado. Behind the beach, and even more emblematic, is the **Paseo**, a promenade barely changed from the golden age of seaside resorts. It's still the place to take the sea air and is backed by gardens, a lovely old merry-go-round, and a row of desirable beachfront hotels and residences that still yearn for the days when royalty strolled the shore every summer season.

Isla Santa Clara

Out in the bay this is a pretty rocky island that could have been placed there purposely as a feature. There's nothing on it but a lighthouse and a jetty, but it's prime picnic territory and the setting is unbeatable. It's only accessible by public transport during the summer, when a motorboat leaves from the harbour close to the end of the beach.

Ondarreta

Where the beach of La Concha graciously concedes defeat at a small rocky outcrop, the beach of Ondarreta begins. This is a good place to stay in summer, with less hustle and bustle. Atop the rock sits the **Palacio de Miramar**; commissioned by the regent María Cristina in the late 19th century, it would not look out of place offering bed and breakfast in an English village.

The **beach** of Ondarreta gazes serenely across at the rest of San Sebastián from beyond the Palacio de Miramar. It's a fairly exclusive and genteel part of town, appropriately watched over by a statue of a very regal Queen María Cristina. The beach itself feels somewhat more spacious than La Concha and, at the end the town, gives way to the jagged rocky coastline of Guipúzcoa. Integrating the two is *El Peine del Viento*, the comb of the wind, one of sculptor Eduardo Chillida's (see page 62) signature works. It consists of three twisted rusty iron whirls, which, at times, seem to be struggling to tame the ragged breezes that can sweep the bay. After a vain attempt to borrow helicopters to place the sculptures, the task was finally accomplished using a specially designed floating bridge.

Monte Igueldo
Above Ondarreta rises the steep Monte Igueldo, which commands excellent views of all that is San Sebastián. It's not a place to meditate serenely over the panorama – the summit of the hill is capped by a luxury hotel and a slightly tacky **amusement park** ① *€1.80 entrance by road*. The view makes it special though, and is unforgettable in the evening, when the city's lights spread out like a breaking wave below.

There's a **funicular** ① *1100-2000, €1.45/2.60 return*, running from a station behind the tennis club at the end of the beach. Otherwise it's a walk up the winding road beside it, which gives occasional views both ways along the coast. To reach Ondarreta and the funicular, walk or take bus No 16 from Plaza Guipúzcoa.

Catedral del Buen Pastor
The simple and elegant neo-Gothic Catedral del Buen Pastor is light and airy with an array of geometric stained glass, but in reality, there's little to detain the visitor – it's more impressive outside than in. Lovers of kitsch art will, however, have a field day – the Christ with sheep above the altar is upstaged by the painted choirboy with donation box in hand.

Gros

A bit more down-to-earth and relaxed than the rest of San Sebastián, Gros lies across the river and backs a good beach, which sees some decent surf. It's dominated by the Kursaal, but is also worth exploring for its off-the-beaten-track *pintxo* bars.

Kursaal
① *Av Zurriola 1, T943 003 000, www.kursaal.org, guided tours Fri-Sun 1330, €2.*
In a space that was derelict for three decades since the old Kursaal was demolished, these two stunning glass prisms opened their doors in 1999. Designed by Navarran architect Rafael Moneo to harmonize with the river mouth, the sea and 'communicate' with the hills of Uría and Urgull to either side, the concert hall has inspired much comment. The architect fondly refers to his building as 'two stranded rocks' – critics might agree – but the overall reaction has been very positive, and in 2001 the building won the European Union prize for contemporary architecture. The main building hosts concerts and conventions, while its smaller sidekick is an attractive exhibition centre. It's also the new home of the San Sebastián Film Festival and it houses a café and an upmarket modern restaurant as well. The Kursaal looks at its most impressive when reflecting the setting sun, or when lit up eerily at night.

Around San Sebastián

Museo Chillida-Leku
① *Ctra Hernani-Rekalde, T943 336 006, www.museochillidaleku.com, Sep-Jun daily 1030-1500, Jul-Aug Mon-Sat 1030-2000, Sun 1030-1500, €8.50, under-12s free.*

The Museo Chillida-Leku is a very relaxing place to spend a few hours out of the city. The late Basque sculptor Eduardo Chillida (see box, page 62) gracefully restored a 16th-century farmhouse with his own concepts of angles and open interior space. The lower floor, lit by a huge window, has a selection of large pieces; upstairs is some of his smaller, earlier work, as well as preparatory drawings. Around the house is a large park, which has about 40 of his larger sculptures (these are changeable depending on exhibition commitments). It's a very peaceful and shady place to stroll; the organized should pack a picnic. Bus No G2 from Calle Oquendo runs to the museum every 30 minutes on the half-hour.

Cider houses
① *The tourist office in San Sebastián has a map and list of the cider houses, several are in very picturesque locations with walking trails through the hills and valleys from Astigarraga and Hernani, a 15-min bus ride from Plaza Guipúzcoa in the centre.*
In the hills around Hernani and Astigarraga a short way south of town, apples are grown among stunning green hills. Although it's not hugely popular as a day-to-day drink in San Sebastián these days, cider has an important place in Guipúzcoan history. It's nothing like your mass-produced commercial ciders, being sharpish, yeasty and not very fizzy. It's best drunk fresh, poured from a height to give it some bounce after hitting the glass. The cider is mostly made in the hills in the many small *sagardotegiak*, or *sidrerías*. When it's ready, in early January, cider houses stoke up their kitchens, dust down the tables and fling the doors open to the Donostian hordes, who spend whole afternoons eating massive traditional cider house meals and serving themselves freely from taps on the side of the vats. It's an excellent experience even if you're not sold on the cider itself. Tradition has it that this lasts until late April or so, although several are now open year-round.

The typical meal served starts with *tortilla de bacalao* (salt-cod omelette), continues with a massive slab of grilled ox, and concludes with cheese, walnuts, and *membrillo* (quince jelly, delicious with the cheese). The best of the places are the simpler rustic affairs with long, shared, rowdy wooden tables and floors awash with the apple brew, but these tend to be harder to get to. Expect to pay from €15-30 for the *menú sidrería*, which includes as much cider as you feel like sinking.

Inland from San Sebastián → *For listings see pages 67-75.*

Guipúzcoa is crisscrossed by valleys that are lush from rainfall and dotted with small towns, some agricultural centres for the surrounding farmland, some seats of heavier Basque industry such as cement or paper manufacture.

In many ways this is the 'real' Basqueland and the smaller, poorer communities are still where separatism flourishes most strongly. The valleys also conceal beautiful churches (as well as the massive Loiola basilica), and plenty of walks and picnic spots. Due to Euskadi's good transport connections, many of these places are within easy day-trip range of both San Sebastián and Bilbao. However, there are good accommodation options, especially in *casas rurales* or *agroturismos*, usually Basque farmhouses with good welcoming accommodation in the heart of the countryside.

Santuario de Loiola → *Colour map 3, B3.*
Now here's a strange one. A massive **basilica** ① *Tue-Sat 1000-1230, 1500-1815, Sun 1000-1230, €2, best time to visit is during the week as at weekends it's overcrowded with pilgrims*, not quite St Peter's or St Paul's but not very far off, standing in the middle of Guipúzcoan

pasture land. All is explained by the fact that St Ignatius, founder of the Jesuits (see page 77) was born here. The house where he first saw daylight has bizarrely had the basilica complex built around it; it's now a museum.

The most arresting feature of the basilica from a distance is the massive dome, which stands 65 m high. Designed by Carlo Fontana, an Italian architect from Bernini's school, it's topped by an ornate cupola. Lavish is the word to describe the rest of the decoration of the church; minimalist gurus will probably drop dead on the spot. The building is designed to be viewed from a distance – this is the function of the formal promenade in front of it – and what first strikes the visitor are the harmonious proportions. On closer inspection, the intricacy of the decoration becomes apparent. Inside, the baroque style is grandiose (almost to the point of pomposity), with a silver-plated statue of Ignatius himself gazing serenely at some very elaborate stonework and massive slabs of marble.

Those with a keen interest in the saint might want to take themselves down to nearby **Azpeitia** to see the font where he was baptized, in the church of San Sebastián.

Oñati → Colour map 3, B2.

The town of Oñati is one of the most attractive in the region and has a proud history as a university town and, until the mid-19th century, as a semi-independent fief of the local lord. The university, **Universidad de Sancti Spiritus**, was established in 1540 and is a beautiful example of cultured Renaissance architecture with an attractive colonnaded quadrangle. The stately red-balconied **Casa Consistorial** overlooks the main square where the two principal pedestrian streets, Calle Zaharra and Calle Barria, meet. These streets are the centre of the lively weekend nightlife as well as being the town's major axes. Oñati's **tourist office** is on Plaza de los Fueros.

Santuario de Arantzazu

Some 9 km south of Oñati is the Franciscan Santuario de Arantzazu, perching on a rock in a valley of great natural beauty. The basilica, built in the 1950s, is one of the most remarkable buildings in Euskadi. Incredibly avant-garde for the time, its spiky stone exterior is a reference to the hawthorn bush: according to tradition, a statue of Mary was found by a shepherd in 1468 on the spines of a hawthorn. A tinkling cowbell had led him to the spot, and the discovery ended years of war and famine in the area. The statue now sits above the altar, surrounded by the visionary abstract altarpiece of Luzio Muñoz. Although it appears to be made of stone, it's actually treated wood, and 600 sq m of it at that. Above the iron doors, sculpted by Eduardo Chillida, are Jorge Oteiza's fluid apostles and *Pietá*. He created great controversy by sculpting 14 apostles; for years they lay idle near the basilica as the Vatican wouldn't permit them to be erected. In the crypt, the impressive paintings of Néstor Basterretxea also caused problems with the church hierarchy. He originally painted the crucifixion backwards; when this was censured, he agreed to repaint it but with an angry Jesus. He succeeded – his powerful red Christ is an imposing figure. See box, page 62, for further information on Oteiza and Chillida.

There are some excellent opportunities for walking in the area, which is one of the most beautiful parts of Euskadi.

For Sleeping and Eating price codes and other relevant information, see Essentials pages 31-39.

☉ Sleeping

San Sebastián *p58, map p60*

The Parte Vieja is the best spot for budget accommodation, with an unbelievable number of *pensiones*, some quite luxurious; there's also some near the cathedral around C San Martín. All accommodation in San Sebastián is overpriced; there is no getting away from the fact. High season is Jun-Sep; prices are at least 30% lower in most places outside this period. In the Kursaal, there's an office of Nekatur, which has a large portfolio of rural accommodation in the Basque lands. Be aware that the pedestrianized part of the old town can be extremely noisy at night, especially at weekends.

LL Hotel de Londres y de Inglaterra, C Zubieta 2, T943 440 770, www.hlondres. com. Grand old beachfront hotel that is an emblem of the city's glory days. The rooms could do with a refit, but it's all about the location here. If royalty don't drop by as often as they once did, no one's letting on. Spend the extra for a room with the stunning bay view, but consider elsewhere if you can't find a discounted rate online.

LL Hotel María Cristina, C Oquendo 1, T943 437 600, www.starwoodhotels. com. Taking up an entire block, its elegant sandstone bulk has cradled more celebrities than you could drop a fork at. It has all the services, luxury, and style you would expect, including a child-minding service and a proper concierge, as well as prices that boot other Basque hotels into the campsite class. A double costs about €450 in summer, a bit more with views.

LL Villa Soro, Av de Ategorrieta 61, T943 297 970, www.villasoro.com. To the east of Gros, this sumptuous 19th-century villa is something of an oasis, set in large grounds with manicured gardens. It really feels like a rural hotel, with discreet service, a refined, relaxing feel, and seriously comfortable rooms, some in an annexe. No restaurant (but wonderful Arzak is a short walk away). Free bikes offer a good way to zip around town. Recommended.

L Mercure Monte Igueldo, Paseo del Faro 134, T943 210 211, www.monteigueldo. com. It's all about the view here: the hotel itself needs a bit of a refit. Right at the top of Monte Igueldo, most of the hotel's rooms offer spectacular vistas towards town or west along the coast. It's not really walking distance from the old centre though, and you can feel a bit isolated. There are often good special offers on booking websites.

AL Hotel Niza, C Zubieta 56, T943 426 663, www.hotelniza.com. Right on the beach, this hotel is an odd mixture of casual seaside and starchy formality. About half the comfortable, modernized rooms have views – but you can't book these ahead – the others face the road and can be a little noisy. The singles are a little dark but offer very good value.

A Hotel Ezeiza, Av Satrustegui 13, Ondarreta, T943 214 311, www.hotelezeiza. com. Well situated at the peaceful western end of Ondarreta beach, this is a welcoming place with the added attraction of an excellent terrace bar.

A Pensión Gran Bahía Bernardo, C Embeltrán 16, T943 420 216, www. pensiongranbahiabernardo.com. This attractive and upmarket *pensión* is convenient for both the beach and Parte Vieja. Recently renovated, the beds are very comfortable, and the rooms well equipped, a/c and quietish. There are a few different room categories. **C** off-season.

B Hostal Alemana, C San Martín 53, T943 462 544, www.hostalalemana.com. An efficient modern *hostal* with warm personal service and a location just seconds away from the beach. Despite its *hostal* category it is effectively a hotel, with all the conveniences, plus some nice views and a pretty breakfast room. Minimum 5-night stay in Aug. It's **D** off season.

B-C Pensión Edorta, C Puerto 15, T943 423 773, www.pensionedorta.com. Overpriced but charming, this beautiful *pensión* is right in the old town near the fishing harbour. Recently opened, with beautiful rooms with rough stone-faced walls, polished floorboards and elegant iron-headed beds. The bathrooms are also very elegant, but some are shared (**D**).

C Pensión Aída, C Iztueta 9, Gros, T943 327 800, www.pensionesconencanto. com. A very good place to stay in Gros, and convenient for the station. The gleaming rooms are appealing, and the breakfast in bed is a great way to start the day. There's free Wi-Fi and internet, and they rent bikes.

C Pensión Altair, C Padre Larroca 3, T943 293 133, www.pension-altair.com. Gleaming, friendly, and with a decent location in Gros, this stylish and comfortable choice takes the humble *pensión* to stratospheric levels. With modern conveniences like free Wi-Fi, swipe cards and safes in the rooms, decorated with a soft contemporary scheme, this is one of the city's best. Book it ahead. Recommended.

C Pensión Bellas Artes, C Urbieta 64, T943 474 905, www.pension-bellasartes.com. A 15-min walk from the old town, this ultra-friendly *pensión* is well located for the bus and train stations, and easily found if arriving by car. The stylish rooms offer excellent comfort for this price. Recommended.

C Pensión Kursaal, C Peña y Goñi 2, T943 292 666, www.pensionesconencanto.com. A good place to stay just across the river in Gros, and very near the beach. The attractive rooms have large windows, bathrooms and TV. As in many of these old buildings, the plumbing and heating can make a racket. Internet access in the lobby and free Wi-Fi. Parking available under the Kursaal for €12 a day – a good deal. Recommended.

D Izar Bat, C Fermín Calbetón 6, T943 431 573, www.pensionizarbat.com. Kitted out in warm colours and with bathrooms so bright and clean you need sunglasses, this is a top Parte Vieja option. High beds are extremely comfortable, there are great modern facilities and a fridge in every room, and the front rooms are double glazed to avoid the worst of the noise. Recommended.

D Pensión San Martín, C San Martín 10, T943 428 714, www.pensionsanmartin.com. One of the better of the host of choices on this street. The rooms are good and comfy, and have bathrooms and TV. Very handy for the train station. Free Wi-Fi.

D-E Pensión Amaiur, C 31 de Agosto 44, T943 429 654, www.pensionamaiur. com. Situated in the oldest house in the Parte Vieja (few others survived the 1813 fire), this is one of the best budget options in town. Lovingly decorated and sympathetically run, there's a variety of smallish but homely rooms, most with satellite TV and some with balconies. Guests have free use of the pretty (stoveless) kitchen, and there's coin-operated high-speed internet access and free Wi-Fi. Highly recommended.

D-E Pensión San Lorenzo, C San Lorenzo 2, T943 425 516, www.pensionsanlorenzo. com. A friendly star of the old town near the Bretxa market. The 5 well-priced rooms are brightly decorated and come with full bathroom, TV, fridge, kettle and piped radio. Internet access and Wi-Fi. It's a quiet place and highly recommended, but fills very fast. **F** off-season.

Camping

Camping Igueldo, Paseo Padre Orkolaga 69, T943 214 502, www.campingigueldo. com. Open all year, this big San Sebastián campsite is back from Ondarreta beach behind Monte Igueldo. They've got bungalows, and it's easily accessed on bus No 16 from near the tourist office.

Santuario de Loiola p65

C-D Hotel Loiola, Av de Loiola s/n, Loiola, T943 151 616, www.hotelloiola.com. Although the building itself won't win many prizes for harmonious rural architecture, it's handy for the basilica, and reasonable value. The rooms are a touch dull but don't lack conveniences.

E Laja, Santa Cruz, Azkoitia, T943 853 075. A good choice on the edges of Azkoitia in a traditional-looking *baserri* farmhouse that offers home-cooked meals and very good-value rooms in striking distance of the basilica.

Oñati p66

The cheaper beds in Oñati fill up quickly at weekends.

D Ongi Etorri, C Zaharra 19, T943 718 285. This family-run hotel is well located on the main pedestrian street. The rooms are thoughtfully decorated, a touch small, but snug with heating and a/c.

E Arregi, Ctra Garagaltza-Auzoa 21, T943 780 824, www.nekatur.net/arregi. An excellent *agroturismo* a couple of kilometres from Oñati. A big farmhouse in a green valley with beautiful dark-wood rooms, a ping-pong table, and pleasant owners. You can use the kitchen, or they can provide dinner with advance notice. Recommended.

F Etxebarría, C Barria 15, T943 780 460. A cheap *pensión* not far from the main square. Rooms are clean and good value but it's definitely worth ringing ahead. It can get a little noisy at weekends.

Santuario de Arantzazu p66

There are a couple of hotels and restaurants in Arantzazu but, happily, nothing else.
C Hotel Santuario de Arantzazu, Arantzazu 29, T943 781 313, www.hotelsantuariodearantzazu.com. Right next to the basilica, this monk-run guesthouse has recently been converted to a modern hotel with spa and conference facilities. It's all very comfortable, but the restaurant leaves a bit to be desired. Great location.

❶ Eating

San Sebastián p58, map p60
San Sebastián is the gourmet capital of Spain, with some seriously classy restaurants dotting the city and the hills around. Several of the nation's finest eateries are here; as well as those we list, **Akelarre** (www.akelarre.net), **Martín Berasategui** (www.martinberasategui.com) and **Mugaritz** (www.mugaritz.com) are gourmet temples in and around town. It's also a great place for crawling around bars eating *pintxos*; the best zone for this is the Parte Vieja, where 'eat street' is C Fermín Calbetón, with several excellent places. **Gros** is a quieter but equally tasty option. Cold *pintxos* are arranged on the bartops here, but most places offer hot ones cooked to order. These can be a real highlight – look out for the board listing them. To order, get a waiters attention and say, for example, 'dos de foie' (2 foie *pintxos*). *Pintxos* cost €2.50-4. Eating in the city is far from cheap by Spanish standards. If you're here in spring, make sure you make a trip into the hills to one of the many cider houses (*sagardotegiak*) around the towns of Hernani and Astigarraga for no-frills good cheer, eating, and drinking. See www.sagardotegiak.com for a list of these establishments.

♦♦♦ Arzak, Alto de Miracruz 21, T943 278 465, www.arzak.info. On a hill in the eastern reaches of town, this is many foodies' choice as Spain's top restaurant and it doesn't disappoint. The Arzak family has been running it for over a century, and it maintains some of that traditional atmosphere; it's no aloof gastronomic Parnassus, though the interior is darkly contemporary. The quality and innovation doesn't come cheap though. The degustation menu (€155 plus drinks) is the way to go here. Highly recommended.
♦♦♦ Bodegón Alejandro, C Fermín Calbetón 4, T943 427 158. This popular spot has a homely, unpretentious interior; the focus is on the quality cuisine, which draws

influences both from the new Basque wave and from upmarket French bistro traditions. Eating is via a bistro menu, which costs €37, and might see you follow crab ravioli with roast trotters. Drinks are extra.

¶¶¶ Rekondo, Paseo de Igueldo 57, T943 212 907, www.rekondo.com. On the slopes of the Igueldo hill, with great views, this offers traditiónal but upmarket Basque cuisine that includes excellent grilled meats and well-treated fish. The real highlight is the wine cellar. With some 100,000 bottles, this is one of the nation's top wine collections.

¶¶¶ Zuberoa, Barrio Iturriotz 8, T943 491 228, www.zuberoa.com. Outside San Sebastián, near the town of Oiartzun/Oyarzun is the lair of top chef Hilario Arbelaitz, in an attractive stone farmhouse with a wooden porch and terrace. Arbelaitz combines an essential Basqueness with a treatment inspired by the very best of French and Mediterranean cuisine. Everything is delicious, from a typical fish soup to the untypical grapefruit, spider crab and trout roe jelly with potato and olive oil cream. The degustation menu (€115) focuses on flavour more than fanciness and is a memorable feast.

¶¶ A Fuego Negro, C 31 de Agosto, www. afuegonegro.com. Darkly modish and moody in red and black, this bar has become one of Donostia's in-vogue eating options. A bewildering mixture of Euskara and Spanish covers the blackboard – ask the waiter to recommend something or for the English translation if you're not sure what they're on about. The *pintxo* combinations are incredibly imaginative; they don't all work but you can have fun trying. Pricier than most.

¶¶ Astelena, C Euskal Herría 3, T943 426 867, www.restauranteastelena.com. In a quiet side street near the Bretxa market, this modern place buzzes with chat during the week, when its €24 *menú* (available lunch Tue-Fri and dinner Tue-Thu), using fresh market produce, pulls in the punters. It offers excellent value for its stylish cuisine at any time.

¶¶ Barbarin, C Puerto 21, T943 421 886, www.restaurantebarbarin.com. It's not gourmet, but this old-fashioned, friendly, comfortable and spacious restaurant specializes in well-priced seafood and rices. The *rollitos de txangurro* (fried crab rolls) are especially tempting; they also do a good paella (€40 for 2) and cheap steaks as well as various set menus from €20 a head.

¶¶ Casa Urola, C Fermín Calbetón 20, T943 423 424. An enticing choice whether for *pintxos* or a full meal, this small and busy bar has exquisite gourmet snacks on the counter. There are 2 dining areas; upstairs is more peaceful. The fish dishes are excellent and the *solomillo*'s tasty too. Recommended.

¶¶ Ganbara, C San Jerónimo 21, T943 422 575. This is a fairly upmarket tapas bar and *asador* with a worthwhile array of *pintxos* to accompany the cheerfully poured wine. The *raciones* are delicious, with such delicacies as *trufas* (truffles) and *percebes* (goose barnacles) making an appearance.

¶¶ La Fábrica, C Puerto 17, T943 432 110, www.restaurantelafabrica.es. If *pintxo*-hopping is all getting a bit much and you want a sit-down meal without sacrificing quality or maxing out the credit card, head here. A good-quality set menu is only €25 lunch or dinner during the week (€38 at weekends), and is accompanied by friendly service in this stylishly appointed but comfortable space.

¶¶ Munto, C Fermín Calbeton 17, T943 426 088. This thoroughly worthwhile place is one of many good choices on this street. The downstairs *comedor* is very attractively lit and decorated, the service is attentive, and the food – tasty steaks and delicately-treated seafood – is of excellent quality for the price.

¶¶ Oquendo, C Oquendo 8, T943 420 932. A good, fairly formal restaurant near the Hotel María Cristina, serving a range of fresh fish around €18 a plate. It's a fine option at any time though, for there's a range of breakfasty pastries and tortillas, fine bar-top *pintxos*, and oysters and champagne for special occasions. The photo wall from the San Sebastián Film Festival is great for testing your silver-screen knowledge.

¶¶¶ Petritegi, Astigarraga s/n, T943 457 188, www.petritegi.com. In the cidery hills near town, this is one of the few *sagardotegiak* (cider house) to open year-round. The traditional cod omelette is excellent, and you pour your own cider straight from the barrel. The set menu is €28. It's open for dinner only, and lunch at weekends.

¶¶¶ Urepel, Paseo Salamanca 3, T943 424 040. A long and brooding restaurant with a fairly Spanish feel. The food is lighter, and the highlight is an elegantly treated shellfish. A good wine list accompanies the classy nosh.

¶ Borda Berri, C Fermín Calbetón 12, T943 425 638, www.bordaberri.com. The checked tiles and *pintxo*-free wooden bar make it feel like you've stepped into another country suddenly. But once you get your lips around the melt-in-the-mouth foie, the slow-cooked duck magret, or the carrilleras, you're back in gourmet heaven. All prepared to order. Recommended.

¶ Bar Gorriti, C San Juan 3, T943 428 353. An unglamorous bar that's been going since the 1920s. Somewhat surprisingly, on entering you are confronted with a mighty impressive spread of cold *pintxos* during the day and early evening. You could spend all day in here if you weren't careful. A great spot and an antidote to the overelaboration in some of the newer places.

¶ Bar Ondarra, Av de la Zurriola 16, T943 326 033. Opposite the Kursaal exhibition centre in Gros, this is a no-frills tapas bar with a small street level and an underground den featuring regular live jazz and soul. Good cold *pintxos*.

¶ Casa Gandarias, C 31 de Agosto 25, T943 428 106. This busy tapas bar is near the Santa María church and has an adjoining restaurant. The *pintxos* are excellent and are served by efficient and cordial staff. The *solomillo* or the grilled foie are particularly recommended. Good whisky selection, too.

¶ Casa Vergara, C Mayor 21, T943 431 073. This highly recommendable tapas bar is on the corner of the ever-popular 31 de Agosto. While it's worth sitting down in the simple but comfortable *comedor* to try *raciones* of stews like *callos* (tripe), *chipirones* (squid) or *pulpo* (octopus), the *pintxos* at the bar are delightful. Try the *gulas* wrapped in smoked salmon if they're about. It's well priced too.

¶ Garbola, Paseo Colón 11, T943 285 019. Legendary for its scrumptious mushroom creations and *caipirinhas*, this Gros bar also offers more unusual snacks, such as kangaroo and shark. It's very plush and old-fashioned inside.

¶ Goiz Argi, C Fermín Calbetón 4, T943 425 204. A warmly welcoming family-run place, this specializes in skewered *pintxos*. The hot ones are very tasty: prawns with a spicy garlic and chilli sauce might have you ordering seconds.

¶ La Cepa, C 31 de Agosto 7, T943 426 394. Perennially and deservedly popular tapas bar lined with hams and featuring the head of a particularly large *toro* on the wall. You can eat better in other places, but a good atmosphere is guaranteed here..

¶ La Cuchara de San Telmo, C 31 de Agosto 28 (back), T943 420 840. An extraordinary bar up the side of the museum. The Cuchara's tiny open kitchen pioneered the idea of *pintxos* in the form of made-to-order gourmet dishes in miniature, now something found in several of Donostia's bars. There's a short, changing menu, but everything is delicious. It's an inspiring and down-to-earth place. Highly recommended.

¶ Portaletas, C Puerto 8, T943 423 888. This welcoming establishment offers unpretentious hospitality, with its stone-faced walls and wooden beams. There are appetizing *pintxos*, mostly on slices of bread. There's also a cheap *menú del día* and good value *raciones* (€5-10).

¶ Tamboril, C Pescadería 2, T943 423 507. San Sebastián's pretty plaza is largely devoid of appealing bars, but this smart little spot partly redresses that. Quality gourmet *pintxos* and decent wines served politely make it a worthwhile stop. Just watch your glass on the rickety wooden rests. There's a pleasant terrace on the square in summer.

Txepetxa, C Pescadería 5, T943 422 227. Nobody seems to like anchovies any more, but you'll like these: the fresh kind, not the salted ones. They come in myriad ways, advertised by lifelike plastic models. With foie gras and apple? Doesn't sound like it'd work, but it does.

Zeruko, C Pescadería 10. Don't mind the sawdust on the floor, this is a very smart bar that produces *pintxos* and *raciones* of the highest class. The main dishes are based around stew-type meals, with *chipirones en su tinta* (squid in ink) particularly delicious. The bar snacks are so elaborate you'll have to ask what most of them are.

Cafés
Café de la Concha, Paseo de la Concha s/n, T943 473 600. A pretty place to stop for a coffee or a glass of wine during a stroll along the beach. It's also got a decent restaurant with good views and a terrace. €13 *menú del día*, a euro more if you eat outside.

Iturralde, Av Libertad 11, T943 428 690. You might struggle to squeeze into this narrow spot, but it's worth it. There's really excellent coffee and teas and infusions bursting with flavour. The owner knows what she's doing, so if she suggests something say yes. Recommended.

Ni Neu, Av Zurriola 1, T943 003 162. The outdoor part of this Kursaal restaurant is an excellent spot for an early evening *pintxo* and drink, with superb views over the river mouth and sea.

Santuario de Loiola *p65*
Kiruri, Loiola Auzoa 24, T943 815 608, www.kiruri.com. The best option in the area, directly opposite the basilica. It does some good traditional dishes and is popular for its *rabas* (calamari strips). Service can be slow if there's a coachload of pilgrims in. There's a good terrace outside.

Oñati *p66*
The **Etxebarría** (see Sleeping, above) runs a good cheap restaurant a couple of doors down the street. The **Zelai-Zabal** (www. zelaizabal.com) in Arantzazu has a sound reputation.

Bars and clubs

San Sebastián *p58, map p60*
The Parte Vieja has many options and the crossroads of C Larramendi and C Reyes Católicos near the cathedral is full of bars. There's studenty nightlife around C San Bartolomé, just back from the beach.

Altxerri Bar, C Reina Regenta 2, www. altxerri.com. An atmospheric cellar bar by the tourist office that regularly showcases live jazz and other acts. Draws an interesting crowd and is worthwhile even if there's nothing on. Open 1700 to late.

Bataplán, Playa de la Concha s/n, T943 460 439, www.bataplandisco.com. San Sebastián's most famous *discoteca*, right on La Concha beach. Open Thu-Sat from 2400 and attracts a smart young crowd. The music is mostly club anthems and pop crowd pleasers. Rises to prominence during the film festival when it hosts various after-parties. €7-15 entry.

Be Bop, Paseo de Salamanca 3. This well-visited bar by the river mouth is quiet and relaxing and has regular live jazz music playing; entry is usually about €5.

Bideluze, Plaza Guipúzcoa 14, T943 422 880. A lively and interesting bar, with 2 floors of eccentric furniture, on the south side of Plaza Guipúzcoa. Simple food is served downstairs and *pintxos* upstairs. It's popular with young and old; you may be addressed in Euskara.

El Nido, C Larramendi 13. A sizeable pub that fills after work and doesn't empty again until late. Friendly crowd and board games.

Garagar, Alameda del Boulevard 22, T943 422 840. Slightly overpriced pub at the edge of the Parte Vieja with some comfy booths. Busy till 0200 most nights (0400 at weekends), and more relaxed than some of the other late openers. There's a DJ upstairs at weekends.

Komplot, C Pedro Egaña 5, T943 472 109, www.komplot.es. Small and fashionable club featuring probably the best house music in San Sebastián.

Mendaur, C Fermín Calbetón 8, T943 422 268. Crowded and lively, this Parte Vieja spot packs them in every night with frequent drink specials. If you're looking for the action on a quiet weeknight, it'll be here.

Museo del Whisky, Alameda Boulevard 5, T943 426 478. Elegant and refined, this 2-level bar does indeed have a sizeable whisky collection on shelves all around. The mixed drinks are pricy and delicious, and there's an atmosphere of well-heeled good cheer.

Rotonda, Playa de la Concha 6, T943 429 095, www.rotondadisco.com. Another club on La Concha beach and open very late weekend nights. The music hovers around popular dance, with some salsa and reggae thrown in as required.

Oñati *p66*
For later action, head for one of the bars on C Zaharri, such as **Bar Irritz**, which is friendly and has a popular techno scene at weekends.

Entertainment

San Sebastián *p58, map p60*
Bullfighting
Near the stadium is the bullring, **Illumbe**, which includes a massive cinema complex.

Football club
Estadio de Anoeta, Paseo de Anoeta 1, T943 462 833, www.real-sociedad-sad.es. This is the home of **Real Sociedad**, the city's football team. Given the title 'Real' (Royal) in 1910 by the king, who spent much time in the city, the club is one of comparatively few to have won the Spanish league title. Tickets €25-40 (sold at the stadium from the Thu afternoon before a game to the Sat evening, then 2 hrs before kick-off, usually 1700 on Sun).

Theatre
The beautiful **Teatro Victoria Eugenia** is a sparklingly atmospheric place to catch a show, and benefits greatly from its recent restoration. The box office, T943 481 818, www.victoriaeugenia.com, is open 1130-1330, 1700-2000; there's also a good café-restaurant.

Festivals and events

San Sebastián *p58, map p60*
19-20 Jan **Tamborrada**, the feast day of San Sebastián, is celebrated with a deafening parade of drummers through the streets from midnight on the 19th.
Week before 15 Aug Aste Nagusia or 'big week', the city's major fiesta, kicks off in San Sebastián with world-renowned fireworks exhibitions.
3rd week of Sep International Film Festival.

Shopping

San Sebastián *p58, map p60*
La Bretxa, Plaza de Bretxa, Market complex in the Old Town. The food market downstairs is the best bit.
Solbes, C Aldamar 4, T943 427 818. A delicatessen and wine shop with a high-quality, not particularly cheap line-up.
Zaporejai, C San Jerónimo 21, T943 422 882, www.zaporejai.com. In the old town, this place sells a variety of excellent hams. It's a friendly spot, and they'll be pleased to explain about piggy products and let you taste things.

☾ Activities and tours

San Sebastián *p58, map p60*
The tourist office hires out multilingual
audio guides for the city; these cover the
old town and cost €10 for a day. There's
a hop-on, hop-off bus that runs Oct-Jun
daily except Tue (mornings only in winter
months), and daily Jul-Sep. Ticket (€12)
valid for 24 hrs; another service goes to the
Chillida museum. There's also a small tourist
train (www.txu-txu.com) running around
the streets. It leaves every hour from the
corner of Miramar and Andia just behind
the beach in the centre of town.

The boat *Ciudad San Sebastián*, T670
977 877, www.ciudadsansebastian.com,
runs ½-hr trips around the bay, with
hourly departures daily in summer and at
weekends in sping and autumn, €8 (leaves
from halfway along aquarium wharf).

San Sebastián Food, T634 759 503, www.
sansebastianfood.com, is an excellent
English-speaking set-up that offers various
gourmet options from *pintxo* tours of the
old town – a good way to get the hang of
this sometimes intimidating way of eating
– *pintxo* cookery classes, wine tastings,
Rioja visits and more. You can book online.
Recommended.

⊖ Transport

San Sebastián *p58, map p60*
Bicycle hire Bici Rent Donosti, Av
de la Zurriola 22, T943 279 260, www.
bicirentdonosti.galeon.com. Open daily
0900-2100, this shop on Gros beach rents
bikes by the hour and by the day. They're
not cheap at €18 per day, but there's a
decent range, and the staff will help with
planning trips. Alai Txirrinduak, Av Madrid
24, T943 470 001, www.alaitxirrinduak.com,
and Grosgreen Bicicletas, C Peña y Goni 3,
are other places to rent bikes.

Bus The main bus station is an
inconvenient 20-min walk from the old

town; buses No 26 and No 28 run there
regularly from the Alameda del Boulevard.
For the tickets, you have to go to the
company offices, situated on Paseo Vizcaya
and Av Sancho el Sabio on either side of the
bus bays.

Bilbao (1 hr 20 mins, €10) is served at
least hourly, and **Vitoria** (1 hr 40 mins, €8)
7 or more times a day.

Other destinations include **Pamplona**
(8 daily, 1 hr 15 mins), **Madrid** (11 daily,
5 hrs 45 mins), **Burgos** (4 daily, 3-4 hrs), and
Santander (9 daily, 3-4 hrs). There are also
buses to **Bayonne** and **Biarritz** in France.

Shorter-haul buses to Guipúzcoan
destinations leave from the central Plaza
Guipúzcoa. Destinations include **Zumaia**,
Zarautz, **Azkoitia** and **Loiola** (the exception;
this leaves from the bus station), **Tolosa**,
Oiartzun, **Hernani**, **Astigarraga**, all with
very frequent departures.

Train There are mainline train departures
to **Madrid** (3 daily, 5 hrs 30 mins, from €50)
and other Spanish cities.

There are 7 trains a day for **Vitoria** (1 hr
40 mins, from €10). Euskotren connects the
city with other Basque destinations on the
coast and inland: its hub is Amara, on Plaza
Easo in the south part of the new town.
Bilbao is served hourly via the coast (2 hrs
40 mins). **El Topo** (the Mole) is a train service
running from Amara to **Hendaye** in France,
it runs every 10-15 mins and takes 35 mins.
At Hendaye you can change to mainline
SNCF train services.

Santuario de Loiola *p65*
Bus You can reach Azkoitia and Loiola
by bus from **Bilbao's** bus station (3 a day),
and from **San Sebastián** (hourly, 1 hr)
(destination may be marked 'Azpeitia').

Oñati *p66*
Bus Oñati is accessed by bus from **Bilbao's**
bus station with Pesa once daily Mon-Fri,
otherwise connect with local bus from
Bergara. There's no public transport from

Oñati to Arantzazu; a taxi costs about €10 each way. Walking from Oñati takes about 2 hrs, but the return trip downhill is significantly quicker. There's plenty of traffic, and it's easy to hitch a ride.

❶ Directory

San Sebastián *p58, map p60*
Internet and telephone Locutorio Puerto, C Puerto 14, cheap internet plus phone calls; **Navinet**, C Fermín Calbetón 11, in the heart of the old town. **Language courses** Lacunza, C Mundaiz 8, T943

326 680, www.lacunza.com; **Tandem San Sebastián**, C Pasajes 4, T943 326 705, www.tandemsansebastian.com. **Laundry** Wash'n Dry, C Iparragirre 6, San Sebastián, T943 293 150, is an Aussie laundromat across the river in Gros offering self-serve and drop-off facilities. **Medical services** Hospital Nuestra Señora de Arantzazu, Av Doctor Begiristain 115, T943 007 000. **Police** The emergency number for all necessities is T112, while T091 will take you to the local police. Policia Municipal San Sebastián, C Larramendi 10, T943 450 000, is the main police station. **Post office** C Urdaneta s/n.

Guipúzcoan Coast

Crossing the French border, the first stretches of Spain are well worth investigating, starting with the very first town. Hondarribia is a beautiful walled place completely free of the malaise that seems to afflict most border towns; if you don't mind a few day trippers, this is one of the most attractive towns in Euskadi. It's a good place to stay, but is easily reached as an excursion from San Sebastián.

The coast west of San Sebastián is characterized by some fairly muscular cliffs interspersed with a few excellent beaches, a popular summer playground. As with Vizcaya, the area's history is solidly based on the fishing of anything and everything from anchovies to whales. While Zarautz's aim in life seems to be to try and emulate on a smaller scale its big brother San Sebastián just along the coast, Getaria is a particularly attractive little port. ▸▸ *For listings, see pages 79-81.*

East of San Sebastián → For listings, see pages 79-81.

Hondarribia/Fuenterrabia → Colour map 3, B4.
This old fishing port sits at the mouth of the Río Bidasoa looking directly across at France, a good deal more amicably now than for much of its history. The well-preserved 15th-century walls weren't erected just for decoration, and the city has been besieged more times than it cares to remember.

Although there's a fishing port, very busy marina, and a decent beach, the most charming area of Hondarribia is the walled part, a hilly grid of cobbled streets entered through arched gates. The stone used for many of the venerable old buildings seems to be almost luminous in the evening sun. The hill is topped by a plaza and a 16th-century **palace of Carlos V**, now a parador; its imposing bulk is offset by a very pretty courtyard. Nearby, the **Iglesia de Santa María de Manzano** is topped by a belltower and an impressive coat-of-arms. It was here in 1660 that María Teresa, daughter of Felipe IV, married Louis XIV of France, the Sun King. **Plaza Guipúzcoa** is even nicer than the main square, with cobbles and small but ornate buildings overhanging a wooden colonnade.

Outside the walls, the marina is busy with yachts and sits at the river mouth, just behind the beach. It's worth exploring the headland beyond here. Passing the fishing harbour, you reach a lighthouse with spectacular views. Below here, the Asturiaga bay has some remains from its days as a Roman anchorage. Above it is a small fort, the Castillo de San Telmo, not open to the public.

Information is available from Hondarribia's **tourist office** ① *C Ugarte 6, T943 645 458, www.bidasoaturismo.com, Oct-Jun Mon-Fri 0930-1330, 1600-1830, Sat-Sun 1000-1400, Jul-Sep daily 1000-1500, 1600-1900.* Hondarribia makes an excellent place to stay, with several appealing hotels.

Near Hondarribia, the town of **Irún** is joined by road and rail to **Hendaye** in France but has little of interest except **Museo Oiasso** ① *Eskoleta 1, T943 639 353, www.oiasso.com, €4.50, Tue-Sun 1000-1400, 1600-1900 (2000 summer),* attractively displaying finds from the ancient Roman settlement here of the same name.

Pasaia/Pasajes

West of Hondarribia, the GI-3440 rises steeply, affording some fantastic views over a long stretch of coastline. Between Hondarribia and San Sebastián, it's worth stopping at Pasaia/Pasajes, the name given to a group of towns clustering around a superb natural harbour 6 km east of San Sebastián. **Pasajes San Juan** (Pasai Donibane), distinct from the other parts that are devoted to large-scale shipbuilding, is a very charming town that literally only has one street, which wends its way along the water, twisting around some buildings and simply going through others. While now dwarfed by the industry across the water, this was for periods in history the most important Basque port. The Romans made use of it to export mining products; whaling expeditions boldly set off for some very far-flung destinations indeed; and a good part of the Spanish Armada was built and crewed from this area. A later boost was given to the town as a result of the chocolate trade with Venezuela but by the time Victor Hugo came to live here for a spell, it was no longer the shipping centre it had been.

Pasajes gets a fair number of French tourists strolling through, which means that there are several restaurants (although, at time of writing, no accommodation). Apart from eating and strolling, there's not much going on, although you might want to investigate **Ontziola** ① *T943 494 521,* an organization that builds traditional Basque boats, such as were used in Pasajes' heyday. There's a **tourist office** ① *daily 1100-1400, 1600-1800,* in Victor Hugo's old pad. Their website www.oarsoaldea-turismo.net gives ideas for activities in the area.

West of San Sebastián → *For listings, see pages 79-81.*

Zarautz → *Colour map 3, B3.*

While similarly blessed with a beautiful stretch of sandy beach and a characterful old town, like its neighbour San Sebastián, Zarautz has suffered from quick-buck beachfront high-rise development, which seems to appeal to the moneyed set who descend here by the thousand during the summer months. Nevertheless, along with the rows of bronzed bodies and the prudish but colourful changing tents, it can be quite a fun place. There's a good long break for surfing – one of the rounds of the world championship is often held here – and there's scope for more unusual watersports such as windboarding.

The old town is separated from the beach by the main road, giving Zarautz a slightly disjointed feel. There are a few well-preserved medieval structures, such as the **Torre Luzea**, and a handful of decent bars. Zarautz is known for its classy restaurants; after all, there's more to a Basque beach holiday than fish 'n' chips. There is a **tourist office**

The army of Christ

There can be few organizations that have had such an impact on all levels of world history than the Society of Jesus, or Jesuits. Their incident-filled five centuries of existence matches the strange life of their founder, Iñigo de Loiola (see page 65), a Basque from a small town in the valleys of Guipúzcoa.

Born in 1491 to a wealthy family, Iñigo was the youngest of 13 children. Sent as a pageboy to the court of Castilla, he embarked on a life of gambling, womanizing and duelling. Fighting alongside his brother in an attempt to relieve the French siege of Pamplona, he was badly wounded in the legs by a cannonball. After being taken prisoner and operated on, he was sent home on a stretcher by the French, who admired his courage. His leg didn't mend, however, and it had to be rebroken and set. Although near to death several times, the bones eventually healed, but the vain Iñigo realized to his horror that a knob of bone still protruded from his leg, which had become shorter than the other. Desperate to strut his stuff as a dashing courtier again and despite anasthetics not being available, he ordered the doctors to saw the bone off and lengthen the leg by repeated stretching.

During the boredom and pain of his lengthy convalescence, he began to read the only books at hand, the lives of the saints and a book on Jesus. Finally recovered in 1522, he set off on a journey, hoping to reach Jerusalem. Not far from home, riding muleback, he came across a Moor, with whom he argued about the virginity of Mary in her later life. When they parted company at a fork in the road, Iñigo decided that if his mule followed the Moor, he would kill him, and if it went the other way, he would spare him. Luckily the mule went the other way.

After further enlightening experiences, and a spell in jail courtesy of the Inquisition, Iñigo ended up in Paris, meditating on what later became his Spiritual Exercises. His sceptical roommate was Francis Xavier, another Basque, whom Iñigo eventually won over. He and some companions travelled to Rome and, with the Pope's blessing, formed the Society of Jesus.

Iñigo died in 1556 and was canonized along with Francis Xavier in 1609. Since then the Jesuits, 41 saints on, have shared his passion for getting their hands dirty, being involved in education, charity and, more ominously, politics. They are a favoured target of conspiracy theorists, who see them as the real power behind the Vatican – the top Jesuit, the Superior General, is often called the 'Black Pope'.

For many centuries, however, the Jesuits were the prime educational force in western Europe and the New World: they have been called the 'schoolmasters of Europe'. The *reducciones*, communities of native Amerindians that they set up in Paraguay and Argentina were a brave and enlightened attempt to counteract slavery. These efforts, made famous by the film *The Mission*, were lauded by Voltaire (an unlikely source of praise) as "a triumph of humanity which seems to expiate the cruelties of the first conquerors". As a direct result of these works they were expelled from South America and Spain. In more recent times, the Jesuits have again courted the displeasure of western powers by advocating human rights in South America, so-called liberation theology seen as a grave danger to US muscle power in the region.

① *Nafarroa Kalea s/n, T943 830 990, www.turismozarautz.com, winter Mon-Fri 0930-1300, 1530-1930, Sat 1000-1400, summer Mon-Sat 0900-2030, Sun 1000-1400*, on a modern square on the main street through town.

Getaria/Guetaria → *Colour map 3, B3.*

Improbably perched on a hunk of angled slate, Getaria is well worth a stop en route between Bilbao and San Sebastián. Despite being a large-scale fish cannery, the town is picturesque with cobbled streets winding their way to the harbour and, bizarrely, through an arch in the side of the church.

Getaria gets its fair share of passing tourists, which is reflected in the number of *asadores* that line its harbour and old centre. For an unbeatable authentic local feed, order a bottle of sprightly local *txakoli* and wash it down with a plate of grilled sardines – you'll turn your nose up at the canned variety for ever more.

The **Iglesia de San Salvador** is intriguing, even without the road that passes under it. The wooden floor lists at an alarming angle; to the faithful in the pews the priest seems to be saying mass from on high.

You won't stay long without coming across a statue of **Juan Sebastián Elkano**, winner of Getaria's most famous citizen award for nearly 500 years running, although fashion designer Cristóbal Balenciaga has come close in more recent times. Elkano, who set sail in 1519 on an expedition captained by Magellan, took command after the skipper was murdered in the Philippines. Sailing into Sevilla with the scant remnants of the expedition's crew, he thus became the first to circumnavigate the world. Not a bad finish for someone who had mutinied against the captain only a few months after leaving port.

Beyond the harbour, the wooded hump of San Antón is better known as **El Ratón** (the mouse), for its resemblance to that rodent. There are good views from the lighthouse at its tip; if the weather is clear you can see the coast of France northwards on the horizon.

Behind Getaria, a country road winds its way into the hills through the vineyards of the local *txakoli* producers. It makes a pleasant stroll from town, rewarded with some spectacular coastal views.

Zumaia/Zumaya

Some 5 km further along, Zumaia is not as attractive, but has the worthwhile **Museo Zuloaga** ① *Ctra San Sebastián-Bilbao, T943 862 341, Apr-Sep only, Wed-Sun 1600-2000*. Ignacio Zuloaga, born in 1870, was a prominent Basque painter and a member of the so-called 'Generation of 98', a group of artists and thinkers who symbolized Spain's intellectual revival in the wake of the loss of the Spanish-American War, known as 'the disaster'. Zuloaga lived in this pretty house and garden, which now contains a good portion of his work as well as other paintings he owned, including some Goyas, El Grecos and Zurbaráns. Zuloaga himself is most admired for his expressive portraiture, with subjects frequently depicted against a typically bleak Spanish landscape. In the best of his work, the faces of the painted have a deep wisdom and a deep sadness that seems to convey both the artist's love and hatred for his country. The museum is a 15-minute walk on the Getaria/San Sebastián road from the centre of Zumaia.

For Sleeping and Eating price codes and other relevant information, see Essentials pages 31-39.

🛌 Sleeping

Hondarribia *p75*
LL Parador de Hondarribia, Plaza de Armas 14, T943 645 500, www.parador.es. This fortress was originally constructed in the 10th century, then reinforced by Carlos V to resist French attacks. Behind the beautiful façade is a hotel of considerable comfort and delicacy, although the rooms don't reach the ornate standard set by the public areas. A pretty courtyard and terrace are the highlights.
L Hotel Pampinot, C Mayor 5, T943 640 600, www.hotelpampinot.com. Behind a charming façade, this wonderfully restored *palacio* has added yet another immensely appealing place to stay in Hondarribia. The rooms, opulent and stylish, are charismatically and distinctively decorated, including whimsical ceiling frescoes to gaze at as you recline in the plush beds. The price (at the low end of this range) seems a bargain for this level of quality and service. Recommended.
AL Hotel Obispo, Plaza del Obispo s/n, T943 645 400, www.hotelobispo.com. The former archbishop's palace is also overflowing with character; it's a beautiful building and features some pleasant views across the Bidasoa. The rooms are delightful, particularly those on the top floor. Free internet access for guests and frequent special offers.
B Hotel Palacete, Plaza Guipúzcoa 5, T943 640 813, www.hotelpalacete.net. Winningly situated on Hondarribia's prettiest plaza, and with modern, compact rooms with a colourful, airy feel, this hotel offers good value and welcoming service in the heart of things. There's a pleasing garden patio for quiet moments.
C Hostal Txoko-Goxoa, C Murrua 22, T943 644 658, www.txokogoxoa.es. A pretty little place in a peaceful part of town by the town walls (enter from the street below). The

bedrooms are on the small side but homely, with flowers in the window boxes, and spotlessly clean.
D Hostal Alvarez Quintero, C Bernat Etxepare 2, T943 642 299. A tranquil little place with a distinctly old-fashioned air. The rooms are simple but not bad for this price in this town. It's a little difficult to find: the entrance is through an arch on the roundabout by the tourist office.

Camping
Faro de Higuer, Paseo del Faro 58, T943 641 008, F640 150. 1 of 2 decent campsites, slightly closer to town on the way to the lighthouse. There's a pool, lively bar, and a few bungalows.

Zarautz *p76*
See also Eating, below.
C Pensión Txikipolit, Plaza Música s/n, T943 835 357, www.txikipolit.com. One of the nicest budget options. Very well located in a square in the old part of town, with comfy and characterful rooms with plenty of facilities including a popular restaurant. Significantly cheaper off season.

Camping
Gran Camping Zarautz, T943 831 238, www.grancampingzarautz.com. A massive campsite with the lot, open all year but packed in summer's dog days.

Getaria *p78*
C Pensión Katrapona, Plaza Katrapona s/n, T943 140 409, www.katrapona.com. Set in a great restored stone building tucked away behind the **Mayflower** restaurant, this upmarket modern *pensión* has spotless and comfortable rooms with plenty of natural light and little balconies.
D Hotel Itxas Gain, C San Roque 1, T943 141 033, www.hotelitxasgain.com. Lovely place overlooking the sea (that's what the name means). This warm-hearted and open place

has some lovely rooms with impressionist pictures on the walls. On the top floor there's a suite with a spa-bath. There's also a garden, which is a top place to relax in hot weather, and a friendly dog.

D Pensión Iribar, C Nagusia 34, T943 140 451, iribarjatetxea@yahoo.com. Clean and comfy little rooms with bathroom around the back of the restaurant of the same name, right in the narrow heart of the old town.

E Gure Ametsa, Orrua s/n, T943 140 077, www.caseriogureametsa.com. Off a backroad between Zumaia and Getaria, this friendly, simple rural accommodation is in a superb location with hilly views over the sea. There are also cheaper rooms without en suite.

⊘ Eating

Hondarribia p75

The town is notable for its excellent restaurants; the location between San Sebastián and France is propitious.

₮₮₮ Alameda, C Minasoroeta 1, T943 642 789, www.restalameda.com. Pushing hard for the Hondarribia gold medal, this exquisite spot serves elaborate gourmet dishes with a confident, well-presented flair. The short menu is bolstered by appealing daily specials, and there are also 3 multi-course set menus to choose from.

₮₮₮ Sebastián, C Mayor 9, T943 640 167, www.sebastianhondarribia.com. Closed during Nov and on Mon. This excellent restaurant is attractively set in a dingy old grocery packed with interesting aromas. The food goes far beyond the humble decor, with a good-value *menú de degustación*.

₮ Bar Itxaropena, C San Pedro 67, T943 641 197. A good bar in the new town offering a variety of cheap foodstuffs and plenty of company at weekends. Turns into a pub later in the evening.

Zarautz p76

₮₮₮ Karlos Arguiñano, C Mendilauta 13, T943 130 000, www.hotelka.com. This is the lair of Spain's most famous TV chef, a

cheerful, almost ubiquitous fellow. Right on the beach, his restaurant, converted from a stone mansion, boasts high-class cuisine that's innovative without losing its local roots. There are also comfortable hotel rooms (**L** in summer) set in the tower of the building and great views over the beach from the castellated rooftop terrace.

₮₮₮ Kulixka, C Bixkonde 1, T943 134 604. This is a welcoming waterfront restaurant with an unbeatable view of the beach. There's good seafood as you'd expect, roast meats and a decent *menú del día* for €12.90, as well as a night-time version for €18.

Getaria p78

₮₮₮ Kaia-Kaipe, C Katrapona Aundia 10, T943 140 500, www.kaia-kaipe.com. The best and priciest of Getaria's restaurants with a sweeping view over the harbour and high standard of food and service. Whole fish grilled over the coals outside are a highlight, as is the exceptional and reasonable wine list. Try some of the local *txakolí*, the best around.

₮₮ Mayflower, C Katrapona 4, T943 140 658. One of a number of *asadores* in this attractive harbour town, with the bonus of an excellent *menú del día*. Grilled sardines are a tasty speciality.

₮ Politena, Kale Nagusia 9, T943 140 113. A bar oriented towards weekend visitors from Bilbao and San Sebastián. There's a very enticing selection of *pintxos*, and a €13.50 'weekend' *menú*, which isn't bad either.

₮ Txalupa, C Herrerieta 1, T943 140 592. A great place to buy or taste the local fish and *txakolí* in a hospitable bar, which offers *pintxos* as well as *cazuelitas*, small portions of bubbling stews or seafood in sauce.

⊘ Activities and tours

Getaria p78
Diving

K-Sub, C Txoritonpe 34, T943 140 185, www.ksub.net. Offers PADI scuba courses, and hires out diving equipment. Also gives advice on good locations.

Hondarribia *p75*

Bus There are buses to and from Plaza Guipúzcoa in **San Sebastián** every 20 mins. A few buses cross the border into France. There are frequent buses linking Hondarribia with **Irún**, just a few kilometres down the road, from where there's more regular cross-border transport to neighbouring **Hendaye**.

Boat Boats run across the river to the French town of **Hendaye**.

Train The most common way of crossing the border is by the *topo* train that burrows through the mountain from between **San Sebastián** or **Irún** and **Hendaye**.

Zarautz *p76*

Bus Buses run regularly to/from **San Sebastián** bus station.

Train Zarautz is serviced by Euskotren hourly from **Bilbao's** Atxuri station and **San Sebastián's** Amara station.

Getaria *p78*

Bus Getaria is serviced by bus from **San Sebastián** bus station regularly.

Train Zumaia is serviced by Euskotren trains hourly from **Bilbao's** Atxuri station and **San Sebastián's** Amara station. Regular buses connect the two towns.

Vizcayan Coast

The Vizcayan section of the Basque coastline is some of the most attractive and dramatic of Northern Spain: cliffs plunge into the water around tiny fishing villages, surfers ride impossibly long breaks, and the towns, like spirited Ondarroa, are home to a convivial and quintessentially Basque social scene. The eastern section is the most rough-edged, with stirring cliffs and startling geological folding contrasting with the green foliage. Fishing is god around here: some of the small villages are far more accessible by sea than by land. The main town of this stretch is Lekeitio, one of Euskadi's highlights. ▸▸ *For listings, see pages 87-90.*

Ondarroa → *For listings, see pages 87-90.*

The friendliest of towns, Ondarroa marks the border of Vizcaya and Guipúzcoa. Situated at the mouth of the Río Artibai, the town is straddled by two bridges, one the harmonious stone **Puente Viejo**, the other a recent work by Santiago Calatrava, which sweeps across with unmistakable panache. Although low on glamour and short on places to stay, Ondarroa could be worth a stop if you're exploring the coast, particularly on a Friday or Saturday night, when the nightlife rivals anywhere in Euskal Herría.

Music has long been a powerful vehicle of Basque expression, and here the bars pump not with salsa or *bacalao* but nationalist rock.

Markina-Xemein → *Colour map 3, B2.*

This village in the Vizcayan hills, a short distance inland from Ondarroa, is set around a long leafy plaza. Not a great deal goes on here but what does is motivated by one thing and one thing only: *pelota* (see box, page 21). Many 'sons of Markina' have achieved star status in the sport, and the *frontón* is proudly dubbed the 'university of *pelota*'. As well as the more common *pelota a mano*, played with bare hands, there are regular games of *cesta punta*, in which a long wicker scoop is worn like a glove, adding some serious velocity to the game.

Games are usually on a Sunday evening, but it's worth ringing the tourist office for details, or checking the website, www.euskalpilota.com – go to the 'Cartelera' section.

The hexagonal chapel of **San Miguel de Arretxmago** is a 10-minute stroll from the plaza on the other side of the small river. The building itself is unremarkable but inside, surprisingly, are three enormous rocks, naturally balanced, with an altar to the saint underneath that far predates the building. According to local tradition, St Michael buried the devil here; a lingering odour of brimstone would tend to confirm this. This is the place to be at midnight on 29 September, when the village gathers to perform two traditional dances, the *aurresku*, and the *mahai gaineko*. There's a summer **tourist office** in a palace across the iron footbridge over the river.

Lekeitio → *For listings, see pages 87-90. Colour map 3, B2.*

Along the Basque coastline, Lekeitio stands out as one of the best places to visit and stay. Its fully functioning fishing harbour is full of cheerfully painted boats, and the tall old houses seem to be jostling and squeezing each other for a front-row seat. Once a favourite of holidaying royalty, the town is lively at weekends and in summer, when it's a popular destination for Bilbao and San Sebastián families. There are two **beaches** – the one a bit further from town, across the bridge, is better. Both look across to the pretty rocky islet of the **Isla de San Nicolás** in the middle of the bay, covered in trees and home only to goats. The countryside around Lekeitio is beautiful, with rolling hills and jagged cliffs. The emerald green colour unfortunately doesn't come for nothing though – the town gets its fair share of rainy days.

The narrow streets backing the harbour conceal a few well-preserved medieval buildings, while the harbour itself is lined with bars. The **Iglesia de Santa María de la Asunción** is worth a visit. Lauded as one of the best examples of Basque Gothic architecture, it seems to change colour completely from dull grey to warm orange depending on the light. The *retablo* is an ornate piece of Flemish work, while the exterior has extravagant flying buttresses. The helpful **tourist information office** ① *C Independencia s/n, T946 844 017, turismo@learjai.com, Mon-Tue and Thu-Sat 1030-1330, 1600-1900, Sun 1030-1430; summer daily 1000-1400, 1600-2000*, has a good range of information.

Elantxobe → *Colour map 3, B2.*

If tiny fishing villages are your thing, Elantxobe, west of Lekeitio, might be worth adding to your itinerary. With amazingly steep and narrow streets leading down to a small harbour, it seems a forgotten place, tucked away at the bottom of a sheer escarpment. It's authentic without being overly picturesque. There's now a road that winds around the hill down to the port, but the bus still gets spun around on a turntable in the tiny square up above. There are a few places to try the catch of the day, and a *hostal*. **Bizkaibus** A3513 between Bilbao and Lekeitio stops here. It leaves Bilbao every two hours from Calle Hurtado Amezaga by Abando train station.

Beyond Elantxobe, the coast is broken by the **Urdaibai estuary**, home to many waterbirds. The good beach of **Laia** looks across at the surfing village of **Mundaka**, but the road heads a fair way inland, crossing the river at the area's main town, Gernika.

Gernika/Guernica → *For listings, see pages 87-90. Colour map 3, B2.*

A name that weighs on the tongue, heavy with blood and atrocity, is Gernika, but this thriving town and symbol of Basque pride and nationalism has moved on from its tragic past, and provides the visitor with a great opportunity to experience Basque culture.

Today, Gernika is anything but a sombre memorial to the devastation it suffered (see box, page 84). While it understandably lacks much of its original architecture, it's a happy and friendly place that merits a visit. The Monday morning market is still very much in business and entertaining to check out. The **Casa de Juntas** ① *1000-1400, 1600-1800 (1900 in summer), free,* symbolically placed next to the famous oak tree, is once again the seat of the Vizcayan parliament. The highlight of the building itself is the room with a massive stained-glass roof depicting the oak tree. The tree itself is outside by the porch, while part of the trunk of an older one is enshrined in a slightly silly little pavilion. Behind the building is the **Parque de los Pueblos de Europa** ① *1000-1900 (2100 summer),* which contains sculptures by Henry Moore and Eduardo Chillida. Both recall the devastated buildings of the town and are dedicated to peace.

● *"...The concentrated attack on Guernica was the greatest success" (from a secret memo to Hitler written by Wolfgang von Richthofen, commander of the Condor Legion and cousin of the Red Baron First World War flying ace).*

Museo de la Paz

① *Plaza Foru 1, T946 270 213, www.museodelapaz.org. Tue-Sat 1000-1400, 1600-1900 (summer 1000-2000), Sun 1000-1400, €4.*

Gernika's showpiece, the Museo de la Paz (Museum of Peace), is an excellent and moving museum. It focuses on peace as a concept and as a goal to strive for, examines the Gernika bombing, then crucially, the importance of reconciliation and an optimistic outlook. Two excellent audiovisual presentations are included; the staff cleverly put these in the right language as they monitor your progress through the museum. A visit to Gernika is highly recommended for this museum alone.

The **Euskal Herria Museoa** ① *C Allendesalazar 5, T946 255 451, Tue-Sat 1000-1400, 1600-1900, Sun 1100-1430, 1600-2000, €3,* is housed in a strikingly beautiful 18th-century *palacio* and is the repository for a sizeable collection of artefacts relating to the history and ethnography of the Basque country.

Gernika has a **tourist office** ① *Artekale 8, T946 255 892, turismo@gernika-lumo.net, Mon-Sat 1000-1400, 1600-1900, Sun 1000-1400; guided tours of the town leave here daily at 1100,* with English-speaking staff.

Around Gernika → *For listings, see pages 87-90.*

Gernika sits at the head of the estuary of the Río Oka, the **Urdaibai Reserve**, a varied area of tidal sandflats and riverbank ecology that is home to a huge amount of wildlife. UNESCO declared it a Biosphere Reserve in 1984. It's a great spot for birdwatching, but mammals such as the badger, marten and wild boar are also present. The **park headquarters** ① *T946 257 125,* are on the edge of the town centre of Gernika in the Palacio de Udetxea on the far side of the Parque de los Pueblos. Vistas of the estuary can be had from either side of the estuary, but to really appreciate the area, you might be better off taking a tour.

The bombing of Gernika

During the Spanish Civil War, in one of the most despicable planned acts of modern warfare there has ever been, 59 German and Italian planes destroyed the town in a bombardment that lasted three gruelling hours. It was 26 April, 1937, and market day in Gernika, thousands of villagers from the surrounding area were in the town, which had no air defences to call on. Three days earlier a similar bombardment had killed over 250 in the town of Durango, but the toll here was worse. Splinter and incendiary bombs were used for maximum impact, and fighters strafed fleeing people with machine guns. The attack resulted in about 1650 deaths.

Franco, the head of the Nationalist forces, simply denied the event had occurred; he claimed that any damage had been caused by Basque propagandists. In 1999 Germany formally apologized for the event, making the Spanish conspicuous by their silence. Apart from a general wish to terrorize and subdue the Basque population, who were resisting the Nationalist advance on Bilbao, Gernika's symbolic value was important. For many centuries Basque assemblies had met here under an oak tree – this was common to many Vizcayan towns but the Gernika meetings became dominant. They were attended by the monarch or a representative, who would swear to respect Basque rights and laws – the *fueros*. Thus the town became a powerful symbol of Basque liberty and nationhood. The first modern Basque government, a product of the Civil War, was sworn in under the oak only six months before the bombing.

One of the most famous results of the bombing was Picasso's painting, named after the town. He had been commissioned by the Republican government to paint a mural for the upcoming World Fair, and this was the result. It currently sits in the *Reina Sofía* gallery in Madrid although constant Basque lobbying may yet bring it to Bilbao. A ceramic copy has been made on a wall on Calle Allende Salazar in Gernika itself. Picasso commented on his painting: "By means of it, I express my abhorrence of the race that sunk Spain in an ocean of pain and death".

Cueva de Santimamiñe

ⓘ *Tours cost €5 and are limited to 20 people on a first-come, first-served basis so should be booked ahead by phone T944 651 657, or email santimamine@bizkaia.net. They run Tue-Sun at 1000, 1030, 1200, 1230, 1500, 1530, 1700, and 1730. The visit lasts about 90 mins.*

The cave of Santimamiñe was an elegant and spacious home for thousands of generations of prehistoric folk, who decorated it with an important series of paintings depicting bison, among other animals. Apart from the entrance chamber, the cave is now closed to the public to protect the paintings and allow ongoing archaeological investigation, but it's still worth booking a guided visit. Starting with a stroll through the holm-oak hillside, you then visit the cave entrance and end up in an interpretation centre where you embark on a virtual visit of the entire cave while wearing 3D specs. Apart from the paintings, you see the eerily beautiful rock formations. The bus from Gernika to Lekeitio (approximately every two hours) can drop you at the turn-off just before the town of Kortezubi. From there it's a half-hour walk.

Bosque Pintado de Oma

① *Free.*

Near the caves is an unusual artwork: the Bosque Pintado de Oma. In a peaceful pine forest on a ridge, artist Agustín Ibarrola has painted eyes, people and geometric figures on the tree trunks in bright, bold colours. Some of the trees combine to form larger pictures – these can be difficult to make out, and it doesn't help that most of the display panels have been erased. Overall, it's a tranquil place with the wind whispering through the pines, and there's a strangely primal quality about the work. It's hard not to feel that more could have been made of the original concept though. A dirt road climbs 3 km to the wood from opposite the **Lezika** restaurant next to the Santimamiñe caves. The forest is accessible by car, but it's a pleasant walk. If on foot, it's worth returning another way. Take the path down the hill at the other end of the Bosque from the entrance. After crossing a couple of fields, you'll find yourself in the tiny hamlet of **Oma**, with attractive Basque farmhouses. Turning left along the road will lead you back to the caves.

Mundaka and Bermeo → For listings, see pages 87-90. Colour map 3, B2.

From Gernika, following the west bank of the estuary takes you back to the coast. A brisk half-hour's walk is all that separates the fishing towns of Bermeo and Mundaka, but they couldn't be more different. Mundaka is petite and slightly upmarket as visitors come to admire its beautiful harbour. Bermeo puts it in the shade in fishing terms: as one of the most important ports on this coast some of its boats seem bigger than Mundaka's harbour. There's a good atmosphere though, and an attractive old town.

Mundaka

While Mundaka still has its small fishing fleet, it's better known as a surfing village. It's a Mecca of the global surf community, with a magnificent left-break (a wave that breaks from right to left, looking towards the beach). When the wind blows and the big waves roll in, a good surfer can jump in off the rocks by Mundaka harbour and ride a wave right across the estuary mouth to Laida beach, a couple of kilometres away. Even if catching waves isn't your thing, Mundaka is still well worth visiting, with a beautiful bonsai harbour and relaxed ambience. The village is a small maze of winding streets and an oversized church. There are some good places to stay or camp, and it's within striking distance of several highlights of the Basque coast. In summer, boats run across to **Laida beach**, which is the best in the area. It's almost worth the trip merely to taste the *tigres* at the small bar on the estuary. There's a small **tourist office** ① *Mon, Wed, Fri 1130-1430, longer hours in summer*, near Mundaka's harbour. The town's surf shop, www.mundakasurfshop.com, is the place to go for equipment and advice.

Bermeo

Bermeo is a bigger and more typical Basque fishing town with a more self-sufficient feel. One of the whaling towns that more or less pioneered the activity on this coast, Bermeo has a proud maritime history documented in its museum. The ships for Columbus's second voyage were built and largely crewed from here. There's much more action in the fishing harbour here than in peaceful Mundaka.

The old town is worth a visit. There's a cobbled square across which the church and the Ayuntamiento vie for power; the latter has a sundial on its face. There's a small chunk of the old town wall preserved, with a symbolic footprint of John the Baptist, who is said to have

Cod, whales and America

In former times whales were a common species off the northern coast of Spain. The Basques were among the first to hunt the giant mammals, which they were doing as far back as the seventh century. It became a major enterprise and, as the whales grew scarcer, they had to go further afield, venturing far into the North Atlantic. It's a good bet they reached America in the 14th century at the latest, signing the native Americans' visitors book under the Vikings and the shadowy, debatable scrawl of St Brendan.

The whaling expeditions provisioned themselves by fishing and preserving cod during the trip. The folk back home got a taste for this *bacalao*, and they still love it, to the bemusement of many tourists. Meanwhile, Elkano added to the Basques' seafaring CV by becoming the first man to circumnavigate the globe, after the expedition leader, Magellan, was killed in the Philippines. Basque whalers established many settlements along the coast of Labrador during the 16th century and, later, Basques left their homes in droves for the promise of the New World; Basque culture has been significant in the development of the USA, particularly in some of the western states, as well as in Argentina and Chile.

made modern triple jumpers weep by leaping from here to the sanctuary of Gaztelugatxe in three steps. The **Museo del Pescador** ① *Plaza Torrontero 1, T946 881 171, Tue-Sat 1000-1400, 1600-1900, Sun 1000-1415, €3*, is set in a 15th-century tower and is devoted to the Basque fishing industry. The tourist office is opposite the station.

If you want to get out on the water, **Hegaluze** ① *T666 791 021, www.hegaluze.com*, runs coastal trips, whale- and dolphin-watching excursions, and cruises in the Urdaibai estuary in a small covered boat.

Santuario de San Juan de Gaztelugatxe and around

West of Bermeo, some 6 km from town, is the spectacular sanctuary of San Juan de Gaztelugatxe. In the early 11th century, Sancho the Great, King of Navarra, was in Aquitaine, in France, when a surprising gift was presented to the local church hierarchy: the head of John the Baptist, which had mysteriously turned up a short while before. As a result, the cult of the Baptist received an understandable boost and many monasteries and sanctuaries were built in his name, including several in northeastern Spain, with the express encouragement of the impressed Sancho.

San Juan de Gaztelugatxe is one of these (although the church dates from much later). A rocky island frequently rendered impressively bleak by the coastal squalls, is connected by a bridge to the mainland, from where it's 231 steps to the top. Apart from the view, there's not a great deal to see, but the setting is spectacular. The island is a pilgrimage spot, particularly for the feast of St John on 24 June, and also on 31 July. To get there from Bermeo, take a bus (about every two hours) along the coast road towards Bakio; you can get off opposite the sanctuary. While you're here, have lunch at the Eneperi, overlooking the sanctuary with a superb terrace, cheap lunches and *pintxos* in the bar, an excellent, more upmarket, restaurant, and even a small museum.

For Sleeping and Eating price codes and other relevant information, see Essentials pages 31-39.

⊜ Sleeping

Ondarroa *p81*
F Patxi, Arta Bide 21, T609 986 446. On the sloping street heading down into the town when coming from the west, this is an exceedingly good-value *pensión* with comfortable rooms and a shared bathroom.

Markina Xemein *p81*
D-E Intxauspe, Barrio Atxondo 10, T652 770 889, www.intxauspe.com. Just north of the centre of Markina, this beautifully restored stone farmhouse is a *casa rural* that has a caring owner and 5 pretty, comfortable rooms, ideal for a relaxing stay in this corner of rural Vizcaya.

Lekeitio *p82*
A Hotel Palacio Oxangoiti, Gamarra Kalea 2, T944 650 555, www.oxangoiti.net. This loving new conversion of a 17th-century palace in the heart of town will win you over with its friendly welcome and elegant old-style decor. It's an intimate place with just 7 rooms (the bathrooms are gleamingly modern), so you'll need to book ahead.
B Hotel Zubieta, Portal de Atea, T946 843 030, www.hotelzubieta.com. A superbly converted coachhouse in the grounds of a *palacio*. With surprisingly low prices, this is one of the best places to stay, with friendly management, a lively bar, and cosy rooms with sloping wooden ceilings. Light sleepers, however, will enjoy it more at weekends, for the woodyard next door can be noisy on weekday mornings. Recommended. Also has reasonably priced apartments for 2-4.
C Emperatriz Zita/Aisia Lekeitio, Santa Elena Etorbidea s/n, T946 842 655, www.aisiahoteles.com. This slightly odd-looking hotel was built on the site of a palace where Empress Zita had lived in the 1920s. Married

to the last Austro-Hungarian emperor, who unluckily acceded to the throne in a losing position in World War 1; she was left with 8 children when he died of pneumonia on Madeira in 1922. The hotel is furnished in fading but appropriately elegant style and is also a thalassotherapy (sea water) health centre. It was badly in need of a refit when we last passed by, so until that happens, look elsewhere.
D Piñupe Hotela, Av Pascual Abaroa 10, T946 842 984. The cheapest place in town and a sound choice. The rooms have en suite, phone and TV and are far more comfortable than the bar downstairs indicates.

Elantxobe *p82*
D-E Elantxobe Ostatua, Aita Arriandiaga 5, T946 276 344. This spruce little place has just 4 rooms, with small modern bathrooms and great views down over the fishing harbour.

Gernika *p83*
B Hotel Katxi, Morga/Andra Mari s/n, T946 270 740, www.katxi.com. A few kilometres west of Gernika in the hamlet of Morga is this excellent rural hotel. The rooms, some much larger than others, are extremely comfortable, and there's a friendly lounge area. It's a great place to get away from things, with a warm atmosphere, and plenty of opportunity for relaxing on the terrace or in the garden. The owners run a good *asador* next door.
C Hotel Gernika, C Carlos Gangoiti 17, T946 250 350, www.hotel-gernika.com. Gernika's best hotel is nothing exceptional, situated on the main road at the edge of town. But it's had a recent facelift, and the comfortable rooms are backed up by facilities including a café, and helpful service.
D-E Pensión Akelarre, C Barrenkale 5, T946 270 197, www.hotelakelarre.com. This enjoyable place has funky little rooms with TV and varnished floorboards. There's a terrace to take some sun and it's in the heart of the

pedestrian area. There's free Wi-Fi access. There are discounts if you stay more than 1 night, and it's significantly cheaper off-season. If there's nobody there, you can access and pay via a computer terminal. Recommended.
E Hotel Boliña, C Barrenkale 3, T946 250 300, www.hotelbolina.net. In the centre of Gernika, this hotel has some good-value doubles with TV and telephone. It's well run and makes a good choice, although it can be stuffy in the height of summer.
E Pensión Madariaga, C Industria 10, T946 256 035. Very attractively furnished rooms with TV, bathroom and heating. Good value.

Mundaka *p85*
Accommodation in Mundaka isn't cheap.
A Hotel Atalaya, C Itxaropen 1, T946 177 000, www.hotelatalaya.es. The classier of the town's options, recently refurbished and with a summery feel to its rooms and café. Garden and parking adjoin the stately building. Very nice breakfasts (not included) and excellent service round out the package.
C Hotel El Puerto, Portu Kalea 1, T946 876 725, www.hotelelpuerto.com. The best value of Mundaka's 3 hotels, set right by the tiny fishing harbour. Delightful rooms, very cosy and some overlooking the harbour (worth paying the few extra euro). The bar below is one of Mundaka's best but noise can carry to the rooms above it. Free Wi-Fi. Recommended.
C Hotel Mundaka, C Florentino Larrinaga 9, T946 876 700, www.hotelmundaka.com. This well-cared for hotel offers rather pleasant rooms just back from the water, with plenty of space and comfortable beds. There's also a garden and café-bar as well as internet access and Wi-Fi.

Camping
Portuondo, 1 km out of Mundaka on the road to Gernika, T946 877 701, www.campingportuondo.com. Sardined during the summer months, this is a well-equipped campsite with a swimming pool, cafés and laundry. There are several bungalows

(a week minimum stay in high summer) that sleep up to 4, but are not significantly cheaper than the hotels in town if you're only 2. They do come with kitchen, fridge, and television though.

Bermeo *p85*
D Hostal Torre Ercilla, C Talaranzko 14, T946 187 598, barrota@piramidal.com. A lovely place to stay in Bermeo's old town, between the museum and church. Rooms are designed for relaxation, with small balconies, reading nooks and soft carpet. There's also a lounge, terrace, chessboard and BBQ among other comforts. Recommended.

❼ Eating

Ondarroa *p81*
♈ Eretegia Joxe Manuel, C Sabino Arana 23, T946 830 104. Although it does a range of other appetizing dishes, the big charcoal grill outside this restaurant caters to carnivores with large appetites. Forget quarter-pounders; here the steaks approach the kilogram mark and are very juicy and tasty. Go for the *buey* (ox) for extra flavour.
♈ Sutargi, Nasa Kalea 11, T946 832 258. A popular bar with an excellent restaurant upstairs serving traditional Basque seafood specialities. Difficult to get a table at weekends.

Lekeitio *p82*
Despite the busy summer scene, there are lots of fairly traditional places to eat and drink.
♈ Kaia, Txatxo kaia 5, T946 840 284. One of the many harbourside restaurants and bars, this serves excellent grilled fresh fish. There's a daily lunch *menú* for €12 too.
♈ Zapiraín, C Igualdegi 3, T946 840 255. This cosy family-run spot is something of a Lekeitio classic and excels itself with warm personal service and fantastic fresh fish.

Gernika *p83*
♈ Arrien, C Eriabarrena 1, T946 258 551. Overlooking the flowery Jardines de El Ferial,

this terraced restaurant/bar has a good *menú del día* for €9 and various other set meals from €10 as well as à la carte selections.

Ψ Foruria, C Industria 10, T946 251 020. A good option for a cheapish meal, with a selection of hot dishes around the €9 mark as well as a wide selection of *jamón*, *chorizo* and cheese for cold platters. There are several other options on this street.

Around Gernika *p83*

ΨΨ Lezika, Cuevas de Santimamiñe, Kortezubi, T946 252 975. The whole of Vizcaya seems to descend on the beer garden here at weekends with kids and dogs in tow; the restaurant is worthwhile as well and better value than the meagre *raciones* on offer at the bar.

Mundaka *p85*

ΨΨ Asador Bodegón, Kepa Deuna 1, T946 876 353. Mundaka's best restaurant, despite a slight air of 'we know what you want to eat'. Meat and especially fresh fish are grilled to perfection over the coals. Try the home-made *patxarán*, a liqueur made from sloe berries. Upstairs is **Casino**, a traditional members' club that's also a high-quality restaurant with a very old-fashioned feel and great views from the gallery. Fish is the thing to try here.

⓪ Bars and clubs

Ondarroa *p81*

Ondarroa's nightlife scene revolves around the main streets of the old centre. **Nasa Kalea** is well-stocked with bars, many of which are temples to Basque rock, which is heavily identified with the Independence movement. **Music school**, corner of Iñaki Deunaren and Sabino Arana (Arana'tar Sabin). Often has live Basque alternative rock on Fri or Sat nights – it's usually free.

Lekeitio *p82*

Hotel Zubieta, Portal de Atea, T946 843 030. The lively café bar in this beautifully restored coachhouse is an excellent spot for a chat and a beverage in uplifting surroundings.

Talako Bar, above the fisherman's cooperative on the harbour, is a great spot for one of Lekeitio's rainy days, with a pool table, board games and a 180° view of the harbour, town and beaches.

Txalupa, Txatxo kaia 7. While Lekeitio isn't as out-and-out Basque as Ondarroa, this bar on the harbourside keeps the Basque rock pumping, and does a range of simple snacks.

Gernika *p83*

Arrana, C Juan Calzada 6. A vibrant Basque bar with a lively young crowd spilling outside at weekends.

Metropol, corner of C Unamuno and Iparragirre. A cavernous and comradely bar, open later than anywhere else.

⊛ Festivals and events

Lekeitio *p82*

5 Sep Fiesta de San Antolín. In a land of strange festivals, this is one of the strangest. It involves a long rope, a few rowing boats, plenty of able-bodied young folk and a goose. Thankfully these days the goose is already dead. The hapless bird is tied in the middle of the rope, which is stretched across the harbour and held at both ends. Competitors take turns from rowing boats to grab the goose's head (which has been liberally greased up) under their arm. The rope is then tightened, lifting the grabber high into the air, and then slackened, dunking them in the water. This is repeated until either the goose's head comes off, or the person falls off, when it's time for the next boat's turn.

⊖ Transport

Ondarroa *p81*

Ondarroa is served by **Bizkaibus** from **Bilbao** bus station (hourly) via **Markina** and Pesa from **San Sebastián** bus station (50 mins), 4 times a day (twice at weekends).

Lekeitio *p82*

Bizkaibus hourly from the bus station in **Bilbao** (30 mins), Pesa 4 a day from the bus station in **San Sebastián** (2 at weekends, 1 hr 25 mins).

Gernika *p83*

There are hourly trains to Gernika from **Bilbao**'s Atxuri station, and buses ½ hourly (hourly at weekends) from C Hurtado de Amezaga next to Abando station (30 mins).

Mundaka and Bermeo *p85*

Hourly trains to both towns from **Bilbao**'s Atxuri station, and ½-hourly buses from C Hurtado de Amezaga next to Abando station.

● Directory

Lekeitio *p82*
Internet Ziber Jaure, C Agirre Solarte 17, €2 per hr.

Bilbao/Bilbo

→ *Colour map 3, B1. Phone code: 944. Population: 354,860 (but almost 1 million in the total urban area). In an amazingly short time, and without losing sight of its roots, Bilbao, the dirty industrial city, has successfully transformed itself into a buzzing cultural capital. The Guggenheim museum is the undoubted flagship of this triumphant progress, a sinuous fantasy of a building that will take your breath away. It inspires because of what it is, but also because the city had the vision to build it. While the museum has led the turnaround, much of what is enjoyable about modern Bilbao was already there. Bustling bar-life, harmonious old and new architecture, a superb eating culture, and a tangible sense of pride in being a working city are still things that make Bilbao special, and the exciting new developments have only added to those qualities.*

The Casco Viejo, the old town, still evokes a cramped medieval past. Along its web of attractive streets, designer clothing stores occupy the ground floors where families perhaps once huddled behind the city walls. El Ensanche, the new town, has an elegant European feel to it. The wealth of the city is more evident here, with stately banks and classy shops lining the planned avenues. The riverbank is the most obvious beneficiary of Bilbao's leap into the 21st century: Calatrava's eerily skeletal bridge, designer promenades and Gehry's exuberant Guggenheim bring art and architecture together and make the Río Nervión the city's axis once more. It doesn't stop there, as ongoing work is further softening the remaining industrial edges.

The seaside suburbs, once reached by hours of painstaking river navigation, are now a nonchalant 20 minutes away by metro. Fashionable Getxo has a relaxed beach atmosphere, while, across the estuary, Portugalete still seems to be wondering how Bilbao gets all the credit these days: for hundreds of years it was a far more important port. ►► *For listings, see pages 102-113.*

Ins and outs

Getting there Bilbao's airport is one of two international ones in Euskadi, and is a good gateway to Northern Spain with connections to several European destinations. The Portsmouth–Bilbao ferry service is no longer operational. The city is well served by buses from the rest of the nation and is exceedingly well connected with Vitoria, San Sebastián and smaller destinations in Euskadi. There are a few train services to other Spanish cities and a narrow-gauge line along the coast to Santander, Oviedo and Galicia. ►► *See Transport, page 111.*

Getting around Central Bilbao isn't too large and is reasonably walkable. The Guggenheim museum, as far afield as many people get, is about 20 minutes' walk from the old town along the river. For farther-flung parts of Bilbao, such as the beach or the bus station, the metro is excellent. Sir Norman Foster's design is simple, attractive and, above all, spacious. Although there's a reasonable network of local bus services in Bilbao, they are only generally useful for a handful of destinations; these are indicated in the text. The newly re-established tram network is handy, particularly for reaching the Guggenheim from the old town. There's just one line so far; a scenic one, running from Atxuri station along the river, skirting the Casco Viejo (stopping behind the Teatro Arriaga), then continuing on the other side of the Nervión, stopping at the Guggenheim and the bus station among other places.

Best time to visit Bilbao's summers are warm but not baking. This is the best time to visit, but be sure to book ahead during the boisterous August fiesta (see Festivals and events, page 111). At other times of year, Bilbao is a fairly wet place, but never gets especially cold. The bar life and museums provide ample distraction from the drizzle.

Tourist information Bilbao's main **tourist office** ⓘ *Plaza Arriaga s/n, T944 795 760, bit@ ayto.bilbao.net, Mon-Fri 1100-1400, 1700-1930, Sat 0930-1400, 1700-1930, Sun 0930-1400,* has temporarily moved to the Teatro Arriaga on the edge of the old town. There's another in the **new town** ⓘ *Plaza Ensanche 11, Mon-Fri 0900-1400, 1600-1930.* There is also a smaller office by the **Guggenheim museum** ⓘ *Abandoibarra Etorbidea 2, Tue-Fri 1100-1800, Sat 1100-1900, Sun 1100-1700,* and an office at the airport. There's also a **tourist information line** ⓘ *T944 710 301, operational daily 0830-2300.* The offices can provide a good free map of the city; they can also sell you the **Bilbao Card**, which allows free transport on local buses, metro, tram and the Artxanda funicular, as well as providing discounts in several shops and museums. It costs €6 for a day, €10 for two days, or €12 for three days. Make sure you also pick up a copy of the excellent bi-monthly tourist magazine *Bilbao Guía*. The city's website, www.bilbao.net, is also a good source of information. The tourist board also runs an accommodation and event-booking website, www.bilbaoreservas.com, T902 877 298.

Background
In 1300 the lord of the province of Vizcaya, Don Diego López de Haro V, saw the potential of the riverside fishing village of Bilbao and granted it permission to become a town. The people graciously accepted, and by the end of the 14th century history records that the town had three parallel streets: Somera, Artekale and Tendería. These were soon added to: Belostikale, Carnicería Vieja, Barrenkale and Barrenkale Barrena, forming the Siete Calles – the seven original streets of the city. It was a time of much strife and the fledgling town was walled, but at the end of the 15th century these original fortifications came down and the city began to grow.

◑ *The city's coat of arms features two wolves; these were the family symbol of Don Diego – his surname López derives from the Latin word* lupus, *wolf.*

Bilbao suffered during the first Carlist war in the 19th century, when the liberal city was besieged (ultimately unsuccessfully) by the reactionary Carlist forces. The one bright spot to emerge was the invention of *bacalao al pil-pil*, now the city's signature dish, but originally devised due to lack of any fresh produce to eat. Not long after the war, Bilbao's boom started. The Vizcayan hills harboured huge reserves of haematite, the ore from which the city's iron was produced. By the middle of the century, it had become evident that this was by far the best ore for the new process of steelmaking. Massive foreign investment followed, particularly from Britain, and the city expanded rapidly as workers flooded in

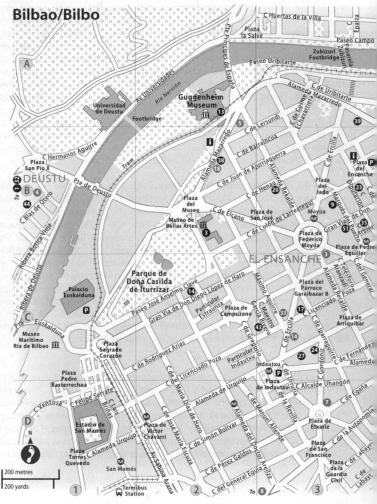

Bilbao/Bilbo

C Huertas de la Villa

Plaza la Salve

Paseo Campo

Zubizuri Footbridge

Plaza Príncipes de España

Paseo Uribitarte

Alameda Mazarredo

C de Uribitarte

A

Río Nervión

Universidad de Deustu

Footbridge

Guggenheim Museum **13**

5 C de Lersundi

C de Barraincua

i

C de Juan de Ajurriaguerra

Plaza del Ensanche

i P

C Hermanos Aguirre

Plaza San Pío X

Tram

38 **18**

C de Henao **20**

Plaza del Jado

Plaza de San José

C de Elcano

C de Colón de Larreategui

Moyúa **9**

DEUSTU

1 P

B **4**

44

C Blas de Otero

Pte de Deusto

Plaza del Museo

Museo de Bellas Artes **3**

Plaza de San José

Plaza de Federico Moyúa **51**

35

Plaza de Pedro Eguiller

Albert de Deustu

C

El ENSANCHE

Parque de Doña Casilda de Iturrizar **14**

Paseo José Anselmo Clavé

Gran Vía de Don Diego López de Haro

Particular Estraunza

Plaza de Campuzano

Plaza del Párroco Garaibazar B

17

Plaza de Arriquibar

Palacio Euskalduna P

Pre Euskalduna

Museo Marítimo Ría de Bilbao **III**

Plaza Sagrado Corazón

C de Rodríguez Arias

33

C de Gregorio

43

27 **24**

C de Fernánde

Alameda

Plaza Pedro Basterrechea

C de Licenciado Poza

Particular Indautxu

Indautxu **M**

7

C Ventosa

C de Felipe Serrate

Alameda de Urquijo

Plaza de Indautxu

C de Alcalde Uhangón

C de Egaña

Plaza de Etxariz

Estadio de San Mamés

Plaza de Victor Chávarri

C de José María Escuza

C de Simón Bolívar

Alameda del Doctor Areilza

Plaza de San Francisco

C de la Autonomía

C de Labayru

N

200 metres

200 yards

Plaza Torres Quevedo

Alameda Urquijo

AV Sabino Arana

San Mamés **M**

Termibus Station

C de Pérez Galdós

C del General Eguía

To **8**

Plaza de la Guardía Civil

C de Labayru

1 **2** **3**

Sleeping

Albergue Bilbao Aterpetxea **8** *D3*
Apartamentos Atxuri **19** *C6*
Arriaga **1** *detail*
Carlton **3** *B3*
Deusto **4** *B1*
Ercilla **14** *C3*
Gran Domine Bilbao **5** *A2*
Hostal Begoña **2** *B4*

Hostal Gurea **6** *detail*
Hostal Mardones **10** *detail*
Hostal Méndez **11** *detail*
Indautxu **7** *D3*
Iturrienea Ostatua **17** *detail*
Miróhotel Bilbao **18** *B2*
Pensión Ladero **16** *detail*
Pensión Manoli **9** *detail*
Petit Palace Arana **13** *detail*
Sirimiri **12** *B6*

Eating

Arbola Gaña **3** *B2*
Artajo **2** *B4*
Asador Ibáñez
  de Bilbao **5** *A4*
Asian Chic **21** *B4*
Bar Irintzi **15** *detail*
Berton **4** *detail*
Boulevard **8** *detail*
Café-Bar Bilbao **6** *detail*

Café Iruña **16** *B4*
Café La Granja **52** *B4*
Café Lamiak **22** *detail*
Capuccino **24** *C3*
Casa Vasca **32** *B1*
Colmado Ibérico **7** *C4*
Egiluz **25** *detail*
El Globo **35** *B3*
El Kiosko del Arenal **10** *A5*
Garibolo **11** *C4*

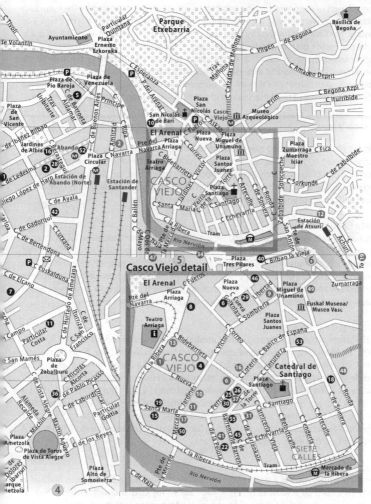

Casco Viejo detail

from all parts of the peninsula. The good times didn't last, however, and by the early 20th century things were looking grimmer. Output declined and dissatisfied workers sank into poverty. The Civil War hit the city hard too; after the Republican surrender, Franco made it clear he wasn't prepared to forgive the Basques for siding against him. Repressed and impoverished, the great industrial success story of the late 19th century fell into gloom. The dictator's death sparked a massive reflowering of Basque culture, symbolized by the bold steps taken to revitalize the city. The Guggenheim's opening in 1997 confirmed Bilbao as a cultural capital of Northern Spain, and ongoing regeneration works proceed apace.

Casco Viejo

Bilbao's old town is a good place to start exploring the city. This is where most of the budget accommodation and bar life is based. Tucked into a bend in the river, it's the most charming part of town, a lively jumble of pedestrian streets that has always been the city's social focus. There's something of the medina about it; on your first few forays you surely won't end up where you might have thought you were going.

Siete Calles
The parallel Siete Calles (seven streets) are the oldest part of town, and even locals struggle to sort out which bar is on which street. While there aren't a huge number of sights per se, there are dozens of quirky shops and some very attractive architecture; leisurely wandering is in order. The true soul of the Casco emerges from early evening on, however, when Bilbaínos descend like bees returning to the hive, strolling the streets, listening to buskers, debating the quality of the *pintxos* in the myriad bars and sipping wine in the setting sun.

Catedral de Santiago
In the centre of the old town area is the **Catedral de Santiago** ① *Tue-Sat 1000-1300, 1600-1900, Sun 1030-1330, free*, whose slender spire rises high above the tight streets. A graceful Gothic affair, it was mostly built in the late 14th century on the site of a previous church, but was devastated by fire in the 1500s and lost much of its original character. Two of its best features are later additions: an arched southern porch and a small but harmonious cloister (if it's locked, ask an attendant). The interior is small and has an inclusive, democratic air. Also worth spotting is a beautifully worked Gothic tomb in the chapel of San Antón. Promoted to cathedral in 1950, the building has benefited from recent restoration work. A few shops are charmingly nestled into its flank.

Plaza Nueva
The 'New Square', one of a series of similar cloister-like squares in Euskadi, was finished in 1849. Described by Unamuno (see box, page 96) as "my cold and uniform Plaza Nueva", it will particularly appeal to lovers of geometry and symmetry with its courtly neoclassical arches, which conceal an excellent selection of restaurants and bars, offering some of the best *pintxos* in town. In good weather, most have seating outside in the square.

Museo Vasco
Near the Plaza Nueva, the **Euskal Museoa/Museo Vasco** ① *Plaza Miguel de Unamuno 4, T944 155 423, www.euskal-museoa.org, Tue-Sat 1100-1700, Sun 1100-1400, €3 (free on Thu)*, is attractively set around an old Jesuit college and houses an interesting if higgledy-piggledy series of Basque artefacts and exhibits covering thousands of years. There's

a fascinating room-sized relief model of Vizcaya on the top floor, a piece of one of the Gernika oak trees and some good displays on Basque fishing. Across the square and up the steps, the new **Museo Arqueológico** ① *Calzadas de Mallona 2, T944 040 990, Tue-Sat 1000-1400, 1600-1930, Sun 1030-1400, €3*, has a well-presented overview of Vizcaya's prehistory and history through material finds. Most of the prehistoric artefacts were found in caves around the province.

Arenal and around

Formerly an area of marshy sand, the Arenal was drained in the 18th century. It is now a busy nexus point for strollers, lovers, demonstrators and dog walkers, and has a bandstand with frequent performances, often of folk dancing. Next to it is the 18th-century baroque façade of **San Nicolás de Bari**. Opposite, the **Teatro Arriaga** seems very sure of itself these days, but was only reopened in 1986 after decades of neglect. It's very much in plush *fin de siècle* theatre style, with chandeliers, soft carpet and sweeping staircases, but at times presents some fairly cutting-edge art, usually of a strong standard and fairly priced.

Basílica de Begoña

Atop a steep hill above the Casco Viejo, the Basílica de Begoña is Bilbao's most important church, home of the Virgin of Begoña, the patron of Vizcaya. It's built in Gothic style on the site of a chapel where the Virgin is said to have appeared in former times. The cloister is a later addition, as is the flamboyant tower, which gives a slightly unbalanced feel to the building. To get there from the Casco Viejo, take the lift from Calle Esperanza or leave the metro station by the 'Begoña/Mallona' exit. From there, walk up the hill to the basilica. Buses No 3 and No 30 come here from Plaza Circular, or bus No 41 from Gran Vía. On your way back down, rather than taking the Mallona lift, head down the flight of stairs next to it; a charming descent into the Casco Viejo warren, emerging on Plaza Unamuno.

Along the riverbank

"You are, Nervión, the history of the town, you are her past and her future, you are memory always becoming hope." Miguel de Unamuno.

The **Nervión** made Bilbao and Bilbao almost killed the Nervión; until recently pollution levels were sky-high. Although your immune system would still have words to say about taking a dip, the change is noticeable. The riverbank has been and continues to be the focus of most of Bilbao's beautification schemes; if you only take one stroll in Bilbao, an evening *paseo* from the Casco Viejo along the river to the Guggenheim should be it.

Cross the river at the **Zubizuri** footbridge, one of the most graceful of the acclaimed bridges of Santiago Calatrava. After crossing the footbridge, you are on the **Paseo Uribitarte**; this riverside walk leading to the Guggenheim museum is where plenty of Bilbaínos gather for the evening stroll.

The tram is a good way to see the river, running more or less along it from Atxuri station to the Guggenheim and Euskalduna palace.

Museo Guggenheim

① *Abandoibarra Etorbidea 2, T944 359 000, www.guggenheim-bilbao.es, Tue-Sun 1000-2000 (Jul and Aug daily 1000-2000), €13 including audio guide, students/pensioners €7.50, children under 12 free, €13.50 including Museo de Bellas Artes; guided tours free at 1130, 1230, 1630, 1830 (Spanish, English and Euskara).*

The philosopher's last stand

One of Bilbao's most famous sons was Miguel de Unamuno, poet, philosopher and academic, born in 1864 on Calle Ronda. A member of the 'Generation of '98' – a new wave of artists and thinkers emerging in the wake of the Spanish-American war of 1898 – Unamuno, who spoke 15 languages, was a humanist and a Catholic with an idealistic love of truth. This made him enemies in a Spain where political beliefs tended to come first.

To this day, many Basques have mixed feelings about 'Don Miguel', who, although proud of being Basque, wasn't pro-independence and deplored some of the myths created in the name of nationalism.

Unamuno became rector of the university at Salamanca but after criticizing the dictatorship of Primo de Rivera, he was imprisoned in the Canary Islands, from where his rescue was organized by the editor of the French newspaper *Le Quotidien*.

In Salamanca when the Civil War broke out, Unamuno, previously a deputy in the Republic, had supported the rising, but grew more and more alarmed with the nature of the Nationalist movement and the character of the war. On 12 October, 1936 he was presiding over the Columbus day ceremony at the university. The gathering degenerated into a fascist propaganda session. Catalan nationalism was denounced as a cancer that fascism would cut out, and General Millán Astray, a war veteran, continued with more empty rhetoric; the hall resounded to the popular Falangist slogan "Viva la muerte", or "long live death".

Unamuno rose to close the meeting: "At times to be silent is to lie", he said, and went on to criticize harshly what had been said. The general responded by crying "Death to intellectuals". Guns were pointed at the 72-year-old, who continued: "You will win, because you have the brute force. But you will not convince. For to convince, you would need what you lack: reason and right in the struggle". At the end of his speech, he was ushered out of the tumultuous hall by Franco's wife to safety. Under house arrest, he died a couple of months later, it was said, of a broken heart. On the day of his death, his two sons enlisted in the anti-fascist militia.

Daring in concept and brilliant in execution, the Guggenheim museum has driven a boom in the local confidence as well as, more prosaically, the economy; its success gave the green light to further ambitious transformations of the formerly industrialized parts of the city.

It all started when the Guggenheim Foundation decided to build a new museum to enable more of their collection to be exhibited. Many cities around the globe were considered, but Bilbao was keenest and the Basque government were prepared to foot the US$100 million bill for its construction.

Frank Gehry was the man who won the design competition and the rest is the reality of what confronts visitors to Bilbao today: a shining temple of a building that completely fulfils the maxim of 'architecture as art'. Gehry's masterstroke was to use titanium, an expensive soft metal normally reserved for Boeing aircraft and the like. He was intrigued by its futuristic sheen and malleable qualities; the panels are literally paper-thin. The titanium makes the building shimmer: it seems that the architect has managed to capture motion.

One of the most impressive features of the design is the way it interacts with the city. One of Bilbao's enjoyable and surprising experiences is to look up when crossing a street in the centre of town and see the Guggenheim perfectly framed, like some unearthly craft that's just landed. Gehry had to contend with the ugly bulk of the Puente de la Salve running through the middle of his site, yet managed to incorporate the bridge fluidly into his plans. The raised tower at the museum's eastern end has no architectural purpose other than to link the building more effectively with the town upriver; it works.

The building also interacts fluidly with the river itself; the pool at the museum's feet almost seems part of the Nervión, and Fuyiko Nakaya's mist sculpture, when turned on, further blurs things. It's entitled *FOG*, which also happen to be the architect's initials. The same pool also hosts Yves Klein's Fire Fountain pyrotechnics.

A couple of creatures have escaped the confines of the gallery and sit in the open air. Jeff Koons's giant floral sculpture, *Puppy*, sits eagerly greeting visitors. Formerly a touring attraction visiting the city for the opening of the museum in 1997, he couldn't escape the clutches of the kitsch-hungry Bilbaínos, who demanded that he stayed put. On the other side of the building, a sinister spider-like creature guards the waterside approach. Entitled *Maman*, we can only be thankful that late sculptor Louise Bourgeois's mother had long since passed away when it was created. It's a striking piece of work, and makes a bizarre sight if approached when the mist is on. More comforting are Koons's colourful bunch of *Tulips* by the pool under the gallery's eaves.

So much for the exterior, which has met with worldwide acclaim. What about the inside? It is, after all, an art museum. Gehry's idea was that there would be two types of gallery within the building: "galleries for dead artists, which have classical square or rectangular shapes, and galleries for living artists, which have funny shapes, because they can fight back". The embodiment of the latter is the massive Gallery 104, built with the realization that many modern artworks are too big for traditional museums. This has been dedicated to Richard Serra's magnificent *The Matter of Time*, an installation now consisting of eight monumental structures of curved oxidised steel centered around *Snake*, whose curved sheets will carry whispers from one end to another. A hundred feet long, and weighing 180 tons, it's meant to be interactive – walk through it, talk through it, touch it. Other pieces, including one that's disturbingly maze-like, play with space, angles, and perception in different ways. Off the gallery is an interpretative exhibition on the pieces. This, however, is one of only a few pieces that live in the museum; the rest are temporary visitors, some taken from the permanent collection of the Guggenheim Foundation, others appearing in a range of exhibitions. This, of course, means that the overall quality varies according to what's on show.

Architecturally, the interior is a very soothing space, with natural light flooding into the atrium. It's a relief to realize that this isn't one of those galleries that makes you feel you'll never be able to see everything unless you rush about; it's very uncluttered and manageable. In the atrium is Jenny Holzer's accurately titled *Installation for Bilbao*, an arresting nine-column LED display that unites the different levels of the building. The effect created is a torrent of primal human sentiment expressed simply in three languages. Nearby are Jim Dine's towering but headless *Three Red Spanish Venuses*.

There are three floors of galleries devoted to temporary exhibitions radiating off the central space. For a look at some smaller-scale Frank Gehry work, drop into the reading room on the ground floor, furnished with his unusual cardboard chairs and tables, which are surprisingly comfortable and solid. The cafés also feature chairs designed by him. As well as the usual gallery shop, the museum also has an excellent modern art bookshop.

The closest metro stop to the museum is Moyúa, but it's a few blocks away; better is the tram, which stops just outside.

There's a spot in the museum designed to display Picasso's Gernika, which the Basque government persistently try to prise away from the Reina Sofía gallery in Madrid.

Palacio Euskalduna

Beyond the Guggenheim, the Euskalduna Palace is a bizarre modern building that echoes both the shipbuilding industry and Vizcaya's iron trade. It's now a major venue for conferences and concerts, particularly classical. More *simpático* is the covered Euskalduna bridge nearby, which sweeps into Deustu in a confident curve.

Museo Marítimo Ría de Bilbao

ⓘ *Muelle Ramón de la Sota 1, T902 131 000, www.museomaritimobilbao.org, Tue-Fri 1000-1800 (2000 summer), Sat and Sun 1000-2000, €5 (extra applies for special exhibitions).*

This newish museum nestles under the Euskalduna bridge and examines the maritime history of this proud city. It's on the site of what was once an important shipbuilding and cargo area; a massive derrick and various ships in dry dock are part of the exterior exhibition. Inside, the focus is on the Bilbao estuary and Vizcayan shipping in general. It's dry but fascinating, with a couple of good AV presentations in English (other displays have translation sheets). One of the highlights is the aerial photograph of Bilbao and its *ría*. There are often excellent temporary exhibitions, which have included visiting 'guest ships' that moor outside.

Deustu

Across from the Guggenheim is Deusto (recently officially renamed Deustu), a bohemian university district buzzing with purpose. Sometimes dubbed 'The Republic of Deusto', it developed separately from Bilbao for much of its history and still has a different vibe. Traditionally frequented by artists, students and agitators, the cafés and bars hum with political discussion. If you want that perfect snap of Frank Gehry's masterpiece, this is the place to come, particularly in the evening light.

The Universidad de Deustu, Bilbao's main university, was founded in 1886 by the Jesuits. It now counts over 20,000 students and staff among its several buildings. While the academic standard of the university has traditionally been very high, it was an important centre of radical opposition to the Franco dictatorship, and has also played an important role in Basque nationalism.

On Deustu's waterfront, a large sculptured stone feline defies the sky. This building was originally a pavilion to house the small workshops of local tradespeople but has now been converted into luxury apartments. Bilbaínos call it **El Tigre** (the tiger), but the city is divided; many agree that it's actually a lioness.

El Ensanche

The residents of old Bilbao had long been crammed into the small Casco Viejo area when the boom came and the population began to surge. In 1876 the Plan de Ensanche (expansion) de Bilbao was approved, and the area across the river was drawn up into segments governed by the curve of the Nervión. The Ensanche quickly became Bilbao's business district, and it remains so today, its graceful avenues lined with stately buildings, prestige shops and numerous bars.

Museo de Bellas Artes

ⓘ *Plaza del Museo 2, T944 396 060, www.museobilbao.com, Metro Moyúa, Tue-Sun 1000-2000, €6, free Wed, €13.50 with Guggenheim, €2 audio guide.*

Not to be outdone by its titanium colleague, the fine arts museum has tried to keep up with the times by adding a modern building of its own on to the existing museum. The result is a harmonious credit to its architect, Luis Uriarte, who seamlessly and attractively fused new to old. Similarly, the collection is a medley of modern (mostly Basque) art and older works – there's also a new space for temporary exhibitions.

The Basque sculptors Eduardo Chillida and Jorge de Oteiza (see box, page 62) are both well represented, but the museum confidently displays more avant-garde multimedia work by young artists too. Among the portraits, the jutting jaw of the Habsburg kings is visible in two famous works. The first, of a young Felipe II, is by the Dutchman Moro, while the Felipe IV, attributed to Velásquez, and similar to his portrait of the same king in the Prado, is a master work. The decline of Spain can be seen in the sad king's haunted but intelligent eyes, which seem to follow the viewer around the room. A lighter note is perhaps unintentionally struck by the anonymous *Temptations of St Anthony*, who is pestered by a trio of colourful demons. Among other items of interest is a painting of Bilbao by Paret y Alcázar. Dating from 1793 and painted from the Arenal, it looks like a sleepy riverside village. Here too, is a very good modern restaurant upstairs offering great views.

Plaza de Toros de Vista Alegre
ⓘ *Check the website, www.plazatorosbilbao.com, for details of* corridas *and ticketing.*
Bilbao's temple of bullfighting sees most action during *Semana Grande* in August, when there are *corridas* all week. The locals are knowledgeable and demanding of their matadors, and the bulls they face are acknowledged to be among the most *bravo* in Spain. Tickets to the spectacles don't come cheap, starting at about €30. The bullring is also home to a **museum** ⓘ *C Martín Agüero 1, T944 448 698, Metro Indautxu, Mon-Fri 1030-1300, 1600-1800, €3,* dedicated to tauromachy. There are displays on the history of the practice, as well as memorabilia of famous matadors and bulls.

Estadio de San Mamés
ⓘ *C Felipe Serrate s/n, Metro San Mamés, T944 411 445, www.athletic-club.net.*
The Estadio de San Mamés is at the far end of the new town. Few in the world are the football teams with the social and political significance of Athletic Bilbao (see box, page 100); support of the team is a religion, and this, their home stadium, is known as the Cathedral of Football. Services are held fortnightly, usually on Sundays at 1700. The Basque crowd are fervent but good-natured. It's well worth going to a game; it's a far more friendly and social scene than the average match in the rest of Europe. The Monday papers frequently devote 10 pages or more to Athletic's game. Tickets usually go on sale at the ground two days before the game. On match days, the ticket office opens two hours before kick-off. Tickets range from €25-50 depending on location. The ground also holds a small **museum** ⓘ *Tue-Sat 1000-1400, 1600-1900 (1830 winter), Sun 1000-1400, €6,* displaying trophies and other memorabilia of 'Los Leones'. Entry includes a guided tour of the stadium.

Bilbao's seafront → *For listings, see pages 102-113.*

At the mouth of the estuary of the Nervión, around 20 km from Bilbao, the fashionable barrio of Getxo is linked by the improbably massive Puente Vizcaya with the grittier town of Portugalete, in its day a flourishing medieval port. It's a great day trip from Bilbao; the fresh air here is a treat for tired lungs, and not far from Getxo stretch the languid beach suburbs of Sopelana, Plentzia and Gorliz.

Athletic Bilbao

Rarely is a football team loved quite as deeply as Athletic Club are by Bilbao. A Basque symbol in the same league as the *ikurriña* or the Gernika oak, the team, as a matter of principle, only fields Basque players. Astonishingly they have remained competitive in one of the strongest leagues in the world and have never been relegated. To date, they have won the championship eight times (more than any other club bar the two Madrid giants and Barcelona) and have won 24 Spanish Cups.

Athletic Club grew out of the cultural exchange that was taking place in the late 19th century between Bilbao and the UK. British workers brought football to Bilbao, and Basques went to Britain to study engineering. In the early years, Athletic fielded many British players, and their strip was modelled on that of Sunderland, where many of the miners were from. José Antonio Aguirre, who led the Civil War Basque government so nobly, had been a popular player up front for the club.

Getxo

Very much a separate town rather than a suburb of Bilbao, Getxo is a wealthy, sprawling district encompassing the eastern side of the river mouth, a couple of beaches, a modern marina, and a petite old harbour. It's home to a good set of attractive stately mansions as well as a tiny but oh-so-pretty whitewashed old village around the now disused fishing port-ette. There's a very relaxed feel about the place, perhaps born from a combination of the seaside air and a lack of anxiety about where the next meal is coming from.

The **Playa de Ereaga** is Getxo's principal stretch of sand, and location of its **tourist office** ① *T944 910 800*, and finer hotels. Near it, the **Puerto Viejo** is a tiny harbour, now silted up, and a reminder of the days when Getxo made its living from fish. The solemn statues of a fisherman and a *sardinera* stand on the stairs that look over it, perhaps mystified at the lack of boats. Perching above, a densely packed knot of white houses and narrow lanes gives the little village a very Mediterranean feel – unless the *sirimiri*, the Bilbao drizzle, has put in an appearance. There are a couple of restaurants and bars to soak up the ambience of this area, which is Getxo's prettiest quarter.

Further around, the **Playa de Arrigunaga** is a better beach flanked by crumbly cliffs, one topped by a windmill, which some days has a better time of it than the shivering bathers. A pleasant, if longish, walk leads downhill to the estuary end of Getxo, past the marina, and an ostentatious series of 20th-century *palacios* on the waterfront, and a monument to Churruca, whose engineering made the estuary navigable, making Bilbao accessible to large vessels; a vital step in its growth.

Passing the hulking modern **Iglesia de Nuestra Señora de las Mercedes** (which contains some highly regarded frescoes) will bring you to the unmistakable form of the Puente Vizcaya and the trendy shopping area of **Las Arenas** (Areeta).

Puente Vizcaya

① *www.puente-colgante.com, 1000-2200 crossings, 1000-dusk walkway; crossings €0.30 per person, €1.10 per car; walkway €5, Metro Areeta or Portugalete.*

A bizarre cross between a bridge and a ferry, the Puente Vizcaya was opened in 1893, a time when large steel structures were à la mode in Europe. Wanting to connect the estuary towns of Getxo and Portugalete by road, but not wanting a bridge that would block the *ría*

La Pasionaria

"It is better to be the widow of a hero than the wife of a coward." Dolores Ibárruri.

One of the most prominent figures of the Spanish Civil War, Dolores Ibárruri, from the Bilbao suburb of Gallarta, near Portugalete, was known as La Pasionaria (the passion flower) for her inspirational public speaking.

Formerly a servant and a *sardinera* (sardine seller), she suffered grinding poverty and the loss of two daughters in infancy, but rose to prominence in the Communist Party in the 1930s, becoming a deputy in the parliament in 1936 (she was released from prison to take up her post). When the Civil War broke out, she became a powerful symbol of the defence of Madrid and the struggle against fascism as well as empowered womanhood. Straightforward, determined and always dressed in black, she adopted the war cry *"No pasarán"* (they shall not pass), which

was taken up all over Republican Spain. She was instrumental in the recruitment and morale of anti-fascist soldiers, including the International Brigades. When the latter were withdrawn, she famously thanked them: "You can go proudly. You are history. You are legend … We shall not forget you". Ibárruri was never much involved in the plotting and infighting that plagued the Republican cause and was able to claim at the end of the war: "I have neither blood nor gold upon my hands". When Franco was victorious in 1939, she flew to Russia, where she lived in Moscow. The dictator died in 1975 and, after 38 years, Ibárruri was re-elected to her old seat at the first elections in 1977. On her return to Spain the 82-year-old Pasionaria, still in black, proclaimed to a massive crowd: "I said they shall not pass, and they haven't". She died in 1989.

---

to shipping, the solution taken was to use a 'gondola' suspended by cables from a high steel span. It's a fascinating piece of engineering: the modern gondola fairly zooms back and forth with six cars plus foot passengers aboard. You can also ascend to the walkway 50 m above. You'll often see the bridge referred to as the **Puente Colgante** (hanging bridge).

Portugalete

On the other side of the Puente Vizcaya from Getxo is Portugalete, a solid working-class seamen's town with a significant seafaring history. In former times, before Churruca did his channelling work, the Nervión estuary was a silty minefield of shoals, meanders and sandbars – a nightmare to navigate in anything larger than a rowing boat. Thus Bilbao was still a good few hours' journey by boat, and Portugalete's situation at the mouth of the *ría* gave it great importance as a port. Nowadays, although from across the water it looks thoroughly functional, it preserves a characterful old town and attractive waterfront promenade.

Above the waterside the old Casco is dominated by the **Iglesia de Santa María**, commissioned by Doña María the Kind at the time of the town's beginnings, although the current building, in Gothic style, dates from the early 16th century. There's a small museum inside. Next to it, the **Torre de Salazar** is what remains of the formidable compound built by Juan López de Salazar, a major landowner, in about 1380. The main living area was originally on the second floor – the first was a prison – and the tower was occupied until 1934, when a fire evicted the last residents. A member of the Salazar family who lived here, Luis García, was one of the first chroniclers of Vizcaya. He had plenty of time to devote to his writings, as he spent the last few years of his life locked up by his loving sons. For **tourist information** ⓘ *T944 958 741, turismo@portugalete.org.*

For Sleeping and Eating price codes and other relevant information, see Essentials pages 31-39.

● Sleeping

Bilbao *p90, map p92*

Finding accommodation is frequently difficult; it's worth phoning ahead, although some of the *pensiones* won't take reservations. Most budget accommodation is in or near the Casco Viejo, while the classier hotels are spread through the new town.

L Gran Domine Bilbao, Alameda Mazarredo 61, T944 253 300, www.granhoteldomine bilbao.com. This modern 5-star hotel is directly opposite the Guggenheim and has been designed with the same innovation and levity in mind. The original façade of the building consists of 48 mirrors at slightly different angles, while the delightful interior is dominated by a large central atrium. The rooms with Guggenheim views cost a little more, but it's worth it when you're paying prices of this level (though online discounts are plentiful outside peak times). There's also a good bar and restaurant. Inspiringly original. Recommended.

L Hotel Carlton, Plaza Moyúa 2, T944 162 200, www.hotelcarlton.es. This grand old hotel, set on noisy Plaza Moyúa, is considerably more luxurious inside than out. Its refurbished neoclassical ambience has colonnaded Einstein, Lorca and Hemingway, among other notables. Rooms are spacious, and there are some very interesting prices online.

L Hotel Ercilla, C Ercilla 37-39, T944 705 700, www.hotelercilla.es. Well located on the city's main shopping street, this large 4-star hotel has a cheerful entrance. It's newly renovated and is much the better for it. With quality service and a busy, metropolitan feel, it makes a convenient base, and is well priced for the amenities on offer. There are excellent weekend rates, with savings of up to 40%. Check the website for current offers.

AL Hotel Indautxu, Plaza Bombero Etxariz s/n, T944 211 198, www.hotelindautxu. com. Behind a mirrored façade that bizarrely dwarfs the older building in front, are comfortable executive-style rooms, set on a comparatively quiet square. There's a terrace, and pianists make the occasional scheduled appearance in the bar. More character than many in this category and cheerful to boot.

AL Miróhotel Bilbao, Alameda Mazarredo 77, T946 611 880, www.mirohotelbilbao. com. Also close to the Guggenheim, with some great views of it, this is a sleek hotel with a Catalan touch; both architect Carmen Abad and interior designer Antonio Miró hail from Barcelona. It's impressively modern, with a pared-back feel not without touches of whimsy. The rooms are excellent: spacious and with a Nordic feel to the white fittings. Rates vary substantially according to when you reserve; you may get better deals from an online broker or travel agent than the hotel's own website. There are all services, including an enjoyable jacuzzi and a stylish bar. Staff are helpful and friendly.

A Hotel Deustu, C Francisco Maciá 9, T944 760 006, www.nhhoteles.com, Metro Deustu. This colourfully decorated hotel is an enjoyable place to stay on this side of the river. The large rooms, featuring minibar, safe, PlayStation and inviting beds are offset by an attractively arty bar and restaurant downstairs. Extras like internet are immodestly expensive though.

A Petit Palace Arana, C Bidebarrieta 2, T944 156 411, www.hthoteles.com. With an unbeatable location at the mouth of the warren that is the Casco Viejo, this beautiful building has been very sensitively converted into a smart modern hotel. There's free internet access for guests, and the best of the rooms have a computer terminal and exercise bike. There are innovative family suites with fold-down beds (good value), a pretty upstairs breakfast room, and rooms equipped for the disabled. Book on the internet in advance for the best rates. The closest parking is the Arenal.

B Apartamentos Atxuri, Av Miraflores 17, T944 667 832, www.apartamentosatxuri. com. These beautifully sleek apartments occupy a modern building a 5-min walk east of the Casco Viejo and not far from the Atxuri terminus of the tram. Spacious, spotless, and decorated with style, they have either 1 or 2 double rooms as well as a sofa-bed in the lounge. Staff are helpful and facilities excellent.

C Hotel Arriaga, C Ribera 3, T944 790 001, www.hotelarriaga.es. Very friendly hotel with a garage (rare in the Casco Viejo) and some excellent rooms with floor-to-ceiling windows and views over the theatre. Plush, formal-style decoration and fittings, a bit old-fashioned but with plenty of charm. Free Wi-Fi. Good value.

C Hotel Sirimiri, Plaza de la Encarnación 3, T944 330 759, www.hotelsirimiri.com. Named after the light misty rain that is a feature of the city, this is a small gem of a hotel in a quiet square a short stroll from the Casco Viejo. The genial owner has equipped it with a gym and sauna, and there's limited free parking – a big saving – at the back. Rooms come with heating but not a/c. The twins are much more spacious than some of the doubles. Follow signs for Miraflores/Atxuri from the motorway and it's very easily reached. Recommended.

D Hostal Begoña, C Amistad 2, T944 230 134, www.actioturis.com. Very handy for the train station and Casco Viejo, this is a welcoming modern hotel packed with flair and comfort. From the inviting library/lounge to the large chalet-style rooms and mini-suites at very reasonable prices, this is an excellent option. The hotel also offers free internet access and Wi-Fi, and can organize a range of outdoor activities. **Pensión Bilbao** in the same building is a more than acceptable fallback if the **Begoña** is full. Highly recommended.

D Hostal Gurea, C Bidebarrieta 14, T944 163 299, www.hostalgureabilbao.com.

Carefully refurbished and well-scrubbed establishment on one of the Casco Viejo's principal axes. Welcoming and cheerfully vague about bookings. Rooms are all en suite and comfortable if by no means luxurious. Free Wi-Fi.

D Hostal Mardones, C Jardines 4, T944 153 105, www.hostalmardones.com. Run by a welcoming and chatty owner and very well situated in *pintxo* heartland. Entered by the side of a newsstand, the *pensión* is fitted in attractive dark wood, and rooms are pleasant, light and airy. There's free Wi-Fi available.

D Iturrienea Ostatua, C Santa María, T944 161 500, www.iturrieneaostatua.com. This beautiful *pensión* in the heart of the Casco Viejo *pintxo* zone is carefully lined in stone, wood, art, and idiosyncratic objects. With delicious breakfasts (€4) and homely rooms, you might want to move in. Free Wi-Fi. Recommended.

E Albergue Bilbao Aterpetxea, Ctra Basurto-Kastrexana 70, T944 270 054, http://albergue.bilbao.net. Bus No 58 from Plaza Circular and the bus station. Bilbao's HI hostel is a block-of-flats-sized structure by a motorway on the outskirts of Bilbao. Despite its inconvenient location, it does have good facilities (including bike hire). There's accommodation in dorms, singles or doubles; it's cheaper for under-25s, but *pensiones* in the centre are just as cheap. The 0930 check-out is a shock to the system when the rest of the nation runs with 1200.

E Hostal Méndez, C Santa María 13, T944 160 364, www.pensionmendez.com. A dignified building with castle-sized doors and an entrance guarded by iron dogs. The 1st floor has *hostal*-grade rooms with new bathrooms, while the 4th floor is *pensión*-style accommodation, simpler, but still very adequate. Many rooms have balconies, but there's street noise until 2400 or later.

E Pensión Ladero, C Lotería 1, T944 150 932, www.pensionladero.es. Right in the thick of it, this small and welcoming option has cork tiles, good shared bathrooms and very well-priced rooms with TV, some of which are reached by a tiny spiral staircase. There's some echoing noise but you'll receive a hearty Basque welcome – just as well, as it's on the 4th floor with no lift. Excellent value and the price doesn't change by season. Recommended. No bookings taken.

F Pensión Manoli, C Libertad 2, T944 155 636, www.pensionmanoli.com. In the heart of the Casco Viejo with some good-value exterior rooms with balcony and shared bathroom. Bright and well looked after.

Bilbao's seafront p99

Staying here is a good alternative to the city; there are plenty of options.

L Hotel Embarcadero, Av Zugazarte 51, T944 803 100, www.hotelembarcadero.com; Metro Areeta. With an excellent seafront location, this grand old villa now houses an excellent boutique hotel. The spacious, attractive rooms come with modern flowery wallpaper; pay the little extra for a wide water view. Recommended.

A Gran Hotel Puente Colgante, C María Díaz de Haro 2, T944 014 800, www.granhotelpuentecolgante.com. Euskotren Portugalete; Metro Areeta. A reconstructed 19th-century building with a grand façade, this upmarket modern hotel is superbly situated next to the Puente Vizcaya on the waterfront promenade. All rooms face outwards, and the hotel has all the facilities you need. There are good discounted rates available via the website.

B Hotel Igeretxe, Playa de Ereaga s/n, T944 910 009, www.hoteligeretxe.com, Metro Neguri. Shaded by palms, this welcoming hotel is right on Ereaga beach, Getxo's main social strand. Formerly a *balneario*, the hotel still offers some spa facilities, as well as a restaurant overlooking the slightly grubby sand. Breakfast included.

D Pensión Usategi, C Landene 2, T944 913 918, Metro Bidezabal. Well placed on the headland above pretty Arrigunaga beach, the rooms are clean and cool, and some have great views.

E Pensión Areeta, C Mayor 13 (Las Arenas), T944 638 136, Metro Areeta. Near the metro and an iron bar's throw from the Puente Vizcaya, this is a good place in the heart of the trendy Las Arenas district of Getxo. The rooms are smallish but welcoming.

Camping

Camping Sopelana, Ctra Bilbao-Plentzia s/n, T946 762 120, www.campingsopelana.com; Metro Sopelana. Very handy for the metro into Bilbao, this is the most convenient campsite within range of the city. Well equipped with facilities, and close to the shops, it's right by the beach, too. There are also 7 bungalows available.

● Eating

Bilbao p90, map p92

Bilbao's Casco Viejo is undoubtedly the prime place to head for *pintxos* and evening drinking, with the best areas being the Plaza Nueva and around the Siete Calles, with a particularly earthy and vibrant Basque scene at the top of C Somera. There's another concentration of bars on Av Licenciado Poza and the smaller C García Rivero off it. The narrow C Ledesma, a street back from Gran Vía, is a popular place to head for lunch set menus or after-work snacks and drinks. There are some good restaurants in the Casco Viejo (including a couple geared solely to tourists), but also plenty of options scattered through the New Town and Deustu.

Arbola Gaña, Museo de Bellas Artes, Plaza del Museo s/n, T944 424 657. Decorated with modern minimalism, this restaurant upstairs in the fine arts museum makes a great spot for a lazy lunch while you admire the wonderful views. The food is elaborate, but with less flashiness than other upmarket spots around here. The quality of the ingredients is very high.

Asador Ibáñez de Bilbao, C Ibáñez de Bilbao 6, T944 233 034, www.asadoribanezdebilbao.com. This smart spot is a traditional meat restaurant specializing in roast lamb, which emerges from the kitchen in enormous chunks on traditional clay dishes and beautifully tender. Service is polite and there's also a good variety of fresh shellfish and crustaceans if the meat sounds a bit much.

¶¶¶ Guggenheim Restaurant, Av Abandoibarra 2, T944 239 333, www. restauranteguggenheim.com. A good all-round option in the museum. One of Spain's most highly regarded restaurants, this offers innovative gourmet cuisine in small but beautifully presented portions in its restaurant section. The degustation menu goes for €76 plus drinks – the wine list is excellent – but there's also a decent *menú del día* for €20 in the bistro section. The furniture is Gehry's work. No bookings are taken for the bistro, which is served (slowly) from 1330 on a 1st-come basis. Both the cafés do a fine line in croissants, coffee and *pintxos*; the one inside, off Gallery 104 has more seating and a nice view over the river.

¶¶¶ Guria, Gran Vía 66, T944 415 780, www. restauranteguria.com, Metro San Mamés. One of Bilbao's top restaurants with plush red walls and a quiet elegant atmosphere. Its stock-in-trade, like many of its counterparts, is *bacalao*, which you'll never have better than here. Count on €60 a head minimum, more if you forsake the fish for the meat, which is tender and tasty: the steak tartare and the foie are both exquisite. A cheaper option is to eat in the bar, where there's a bistro menu. There's a very respectable selection of brandies too.

¶¶¶ Mina, Muelle Manzana s/n, T944 795 938, www.restaurantemina.es. Rated by many Bilbao foodies as the most enjoyable place to eat in town, this restaurant faces the Casco Viejo on the riverbank. Expect creative combinations that you haven't seen before and are unlikely to again. There's no menu, but the table d'hôte is excellent at €54 and beats more pretentious places that charge twice the price. Service is top notch. Recommended.

¶¶¶ Serantes and **Serantes II**, C Licenciado Poza 16 and Alameda Urquijo 51, T944 102 066 and 944 102 699, www. marisqueriaserantes.com, Metro Indautxu. These *marisquerías* (seafood restaurants) have a deservedly high reputation for the quality of their fish. It's all very fresh, and the chefs have the confidence to let the flavours of the seafood hold their own. Go with the daily special – it's usually excellent, or tackle some *cigalas* (Dublin Bay prawns) the 4WD of the prawn world, equipped with pincers. A third branch, **Serantes III**, is at Alameda Mazarredo 75, T944 248 004, opposite the Guggenheim.

¶¶¶ Víctor, Plaza Nueva 2, T944 151 678. A quality upstairs restaurant with an elegant but relaxed atmosphere. This is a top place to try Bilbao's signature dish, *bacalao al pil-pil*, or the restaurant's variation on it, and there's an excellent wine selection. Service is polite and formal. Don't confuse with **Víctor Montes**, also worthwhile and on the same square, see below. Recommended.

¶¶¶ Víctor Montes, Plaza Nueva 8, T944 155 603. This traditional and excellent restaurant is known for its huge collection of wines and whiskies. The elegant upstairs dining room has the best of Basque cuisine at surprisingly reasonable prices. Downstairs is a very popular *pintxo* bar; if you can shoulder your way to it in the evening, you'll find that not a square inch is free of posh and delicious bites.

¶¶¶ Zortziko, Alameda Mazarredo 17, T944 239 743, www.zortziko.es. This upmarket business-district choice focuses on fairly traditional Basque ingredients brought to perfection with modern techniques. Squid with liquid foie gras or slow-cooked pigeon breast are signature dishes, but the €92 degustation menu is the best way to see the full range of this Michelin-starred restaurant's repertoire.

¶¶ Asian Chic, C Ledesma 30, T944 231 186. Right in the heart of the Bilbao business district, this elegant and extensive Japanese/ Chinese restaurant is a favourite lunch escape for its speedily served *menú del día*,

Pintxos

In the Basque country, from about 1900 in the evening until midnight or so, everyone lives in the street, walking, talking, drinking and eating *pintxos*.

Wherever you go in the region, you'll be confronted and tempted by a massive array of food across the top of bars. Many bars serve up very traditional fare: slices of *tortilla* (potato omelette) or *pulgas de jamón* (small rolls with cured ham). Other bars, enthused by 'new Basque' cuisine, take things further and dedicate large parts of their day to creating miniature food sculptures using more esoteric ingredients. The key factor is that they're all meant to be eaten. Many places will prepare hot *pintxos* straight from the kitchen – these have to be ordered but are always well worth the wait. For the cold ones atop the bar, you can ask the bartender or usually simply help yourself to what you fancy, making sure to remember what you've had for the final reckoning. If you can't tell what something is, ask: *¿de qué es?*. *Pintxos* usually cost between €1.50 and €3 depending on the bar and ingredients.

which might include tasty sushi followed by glazed duck breast and fried rice. There are also good sashimi and tempura options à la carte, and teppanayaki for group bookings.

Casa Vasca, Av Lehendakari Aguirre 13-15, T944 483 980, www.casavasca.com. A Deustu institution on the main road – the front bar has a good selection of posh *pintxos* and a couple of comfortable nooks to settle down with a slightly pricey drink. Behind is a restaurant that serves pretty authentic Basque cuisine in generous portions. Another dining room serves a cheap *menú del día*, and there's even a nightclub downstairs, catering for an older crowd.

Colmado Ibérico, Alameda Urquijo 20, T944 436 001. A feast of piggy products, this welcoming locale is both a ham shop and a bar/restaurant, where you can munch on a basic (but delicious) *pulga* of Spain's finest ham or more elaborate pork-based creations.

Egiluz, C Perro 4, T944 150 242. Among all the bright modern lights of the Casco Viejo's newer restaurants, this sturdy old family-run place is still the place to go if you fancy a steak or similar. The dining room is upstairs at the back of the bar. They serve a huge *chuletón* – it could comfortably feed 2 – and other excellent grilled and roasted fare.

Hostaria Marchese del Porto, C Marqués del Puerto 10, T944 161 680, Metro Moyúa.

This elegant Italian restaurant goes slightly over the top with its decor but is deservedly popular with local businessfolk at lunchtime. Good pasta and gelati too.

Kasko, C Santa María 16, T944 160 311, www.restaurantekasko.com. With funky, appealing decor inspired by the fish and high-class but low-priced new Basque food, this spacious bar-restaurant is always busy, and is in the heart of the action. Service is bohemian-friendly, and there's sometimes a pianist accompanying your meal. The daily *menú del día* is good value, and there are always interesting specials on the evening menu.

La Viña, C Henao 27, T944 243 602; Metro Moyúa. You could easily miss this tiny bar wedged into a block in the Ensanche. As well as being a hospitable place to have a glass of wine, they serve some very fine food at a very fair price. Their speciality is seafood, with mussels, crabs, or whatever's fresh to choose from and eat at the handful of small tables.

Su@, C Marqués del Puerto 4, T944 232 292, www.sua.es. Metro Moyúa. One of the best of the recent designer restaurants to open in Bilbao, this is ultra-modern but comfortable, with a romantic coloured lighting scheme and a menu of new-style creations that are curiously ordered by temperature that they leave the kitchen at. A gimmick, yes, but the food and atmosphere are pretty good. There's a *menú del día* for €17.50. Evening bookings essential.

Taloaska, Av Madariaga 7, T944 758 264, www.taloaska.com. A more than solid choice in the heart of Deustu, with a bar that stretches as far as the eye can see and is very well endowed with *pintxos*. At the end is the dining room, where there's a good *menú* for €11.

Capuccino, C Gordóniz 2, T944 436 980. A place for people in the know. This café, run by a friendly Egyptian, and with a map of the old Nile painted on the roof, serves filled pitta rolls, as well as *shawarma*, musaka, and other snacks. They have an excellent range of teas.

Garibolo, C Fernández del Campo 7, T944 223 255, Metro Moyúa. Opens for lunch Mon-Sat, and dinner Fri-Sat. There are now a few vegetarian restaurants in Bilbao, but this, the original, is still the best. The colourful Garibolo packs 'em in, particularly for its €12.50 lunch special. No alcohol served.

Laga, C Merced 2, T944 164 770. This bright, simply decorated bar is one of the Casco's best places for simple, no-nonsense wholesome Basque food. Particularly recommended are the croquettes, but it's all good, including the fresh fish, the garlicky steaks and the *mollejas*. Great value.

Mr Lee, C Pedro Martínez Artola 12, T944 440 862. Free of the repetitive paraphernalia that adorns other Chinese restaurants in Spain, which tend to become caricatures of themselves, this has an elegant, spacious dining area with Asian artwork of restrained good taste. The menu has a range of decent dishes from different parts of east and southeast Asia. Good value. The street slopes up from Plaza Zabálburu.

New Inn, Alameda Urquijo 9, T944 151 043. The restored art nouveau splendour of the main bar of this popular lunch-spot is reason enough to enter. Workers in Bilbao offices sadly have little time now to grab a 3-course meal, so this place caters for them with a range of excellent sandwiches and similar.

Río Oja, C Perro 4, T944 150 871. Another good option on this street, specializing in bubbling Riojan stews and Basque fish dishes, most of which are in big casseroles at the bar. The dishes will come microwave-heated (standard practice in Spain), but it's good value and has friendly service.

Rotterdam, C Perro 6, T944 162 165. Small, uncomplicated Casco Viejo restaurant with a *simpático* boss. This is what lunch restaurants have always been like here, with a solid *menú del día* for €9.

Saibigain, C Barrenkale Barrena 16, T944 150 123. Closed Sun. This is an intensely traditional and atmospheric place, and one of the best cheap restaurants in the Casco Viejo. It's full of black and white photos of Athletic Bilbao, and has a phalanx of hams hanging over the bar. There's a *menú del día* for €9, and various other set meals from about €20 per person; it's worth waiting to grab a table upstairs.

Pintxo bars

Bar Irrintzi, C Santa María 8, T944 167 616, www.irrintzi.es. With a vibe so laid-back that there's not even a till: the takings are under colour-coordinated bottles behind the bar, this Casco Viejo bar doesn't skimp on the quality. *Pintxos* are an art form, with a superb array of imaginative snacks, all carefully labelled, freshly made and delicious.

Berton, C Jardines 11, T944 167 035. The hanging *jamones* and bunches of grapes define this cheerful bar, which has top-notch ham *pintxos* and *raciones* and some quality wines by the glass. It's mushroomed in recent years, and now has another bar around the corner and one opposite. All offer better value for tapas at the bar than sit-down meals.

Café-Bar Bilbao, Plaza Nueva 6, T944 151 671. A sparky place with top service and a selection of some of the better gourmet *pintxos* (all labelled) to be had around the old town. It's always busy, but the bar staff never seem to miss a trick.

¶¶ **Gatz**, C Santa María 10, T944 154 861. A convivial bar with warm, non-designer decor and some of the Casco's better *pintxos*, which are frequent contenders in the awards for such things. Happily spills on to the street at weekends. Friendly, no-nonsense staff. Recommended.

¶¶ **El Globo**, C Diputación 8, T944 154 221. There's an extraordinary variety of cold and cooked-to-order hot *pintxos* at this place near the Moyúa square. Traditional bites take their place alongside wildly imaginative modern creations. Recommended.

¶¶ **Lekeitio**, C Diputación 1, T944 239 240. An attentive bar that's a mile long with a fantastic selection of simple after-work eats. The variety of fishy and seafoody *pintxos* are good, as is the *tortilla*. A palisade of oars and life-buoys sections off a small sit-down eating area.

¶¶ **Okela**, C García Rivero 8, T944 415 937. A modern bar popular with the office crowd and dominated by a huge signed photo of the footballer Joseba Etxebarría in full stride for Athletic Bilbao. Decent *pintxos*. There are several other good choices on this street.

¶¶ **Oriotarra**, C Blas de Otero 30, T944 470 830. A classy *pintxo* bar in Deustu that has won an award for the best bar-top snack in Bilbao. A round of applause for the pig's ear *millefeuille*.

¶¶ **Urkia**, C Somera 40, T606 990 295. One of the more popular bars at the top of Somera, which buzzes with a pro-Basque after-work crowd from all social strata, this has elaborate *pintxos* presented on slate tablets. They change regularly, but at last visit the anchovy, brie, caviar, and tempura courgette combination was mighty impressive.

¶¶ **Xukela**, C Perro 2, T944 159 772. A very social bar on a very social street. Attractive *pintxos* and some good sit-down food – cheeses and cured meats – and a clientele upending glasses of Rioja at competitive pace until comparatively late.

¶ **Artajo**, C Ledesma 7, T944 248 596, Metro Abando. Uncomplicated and candid bar, one of many on this street, with homely wooden tables and chairs and good traditional snacks of tortilla and *pulgas de jamón*. Famous for its *tigres* (mussels in spicy tomato sauce).

¶ **Jaunak**, C Somera 10, T944 159 979. One of quite a few earthy, friendly Basque bars on this street, with a huge range of large *bocadillos* at about €3.50 a shot.

¶ **Kuku Soak**, C Barrenkale Barrena 18, T944 163 807. On a busy Casco Viejo corner, this bar doesn't mind turning the music up pretty loud, but that doesn't bother the cheerful mix of after-workers and students. Its main temptation is its wide range of *pulgas* (little sandwichy *pintxos*) with various gourmet combinations of fillings: mark your choices on the tear-off sheets, and they'll be freshly made. You can also order to take away.

¶ **Taberna Taurina**, C Ledesma 5. A tiny old-time tiles 'n' sawdust bar, which is packed top to bottom with bullfighting memorabilia. It's fascinating to browse the old pictures, which convey something of the controversial activity's noble side. The *tortilla* here also commands respect.

Cafés

Boulevard, C Arenal 3, T946 791 752. This fabulous historic café was once Bilbao's literary meeting place. Now 140 years old, it still has plenty of atmosphere as theatre-goers, workers, students and tourists coincide in its cavernous interior. There's a very glamorous downstairs cocktail bar, but the art deco upstairs is what the place is all about.

Café Iruña, Jardines de Albia s/n, T944 237 021. This noble old establishment on the Jardines de Albia has begun its 2nd century in style and is more popular than ever, with people spilling out onto the street. Well refurbished, the large building is divided into a smarter café/restaurant space with wood panelling in neo-Moorish style, and a tiled bar with old sherry ads and some good *pintxos* – including lamb kebabs sizzling on the grill in the corner.

Café La Granja, Plaza Circular 3, T944 230 813. A spacious old Bilbao café, opened in 1926. Its high ceilings and long bar are designed to cope with the lively throng that gathers throughout the day. Attractive art nouveau fittings and *pintxos*, although the simple *menú del día* is a little overpriced.

Café Lamiak, C Pelota 8, T944 161 765. A peaceful and likeable 2-floor forum, the sort of place a literary genre, pressure group or world-famous band might start out. It's a mixed gay/straight crowd, with a relaxed atmosphere.

El Kiosko del Arenal, Muelle del Arenal s/n, T657 711 352. Elegant and cool café under the bandstand in the Arenal. Plenty of outdoor tables overlooking the river. Barbecue in the corner. Recommended.

Bilbao's seafront *p99*

There's plenty of good eating in these waterside suburbs.

Asador El Puerto/Zabala, C Aretxondo 20, T944 912 166, Metro Algorta. With fresh seafood right off the boats and a great location by Getxo's old port, this makes a prime fish-eating destination. There's no menu: they just tell you what's fresh that day. Prices can add up, but the quality shines through.

Cubita, Ctra Galea 30, T944 911 700, www.cubita.biz, Metro Neguri. A highly acclaimed restaurant with a new location by the windmill above Arrigunaga beach. People rave about the *cigalas* (Dublin bay prawns) turned out by young modern chef Alvaro Martínez.

Jolastoky, Av Leioa 24, T944 912 031, www.restaurantejolastoki.com, Metro Neguri. Decorated in classy but homely country-mansion style, Jolastoky is a house of good repute throughout Euskadi. Definitely traditional in character, dishes such as *caracoles en salsa vizcaína* (snails) and *liebre* (hare) are the sort of treats that give Basque cuisine its lofty reputation.

Karola Etxea, C Aretxondo 22, T944 600 868, Metro Algorta. Perfectly situated in a quiet lane above the old port. It's a good, not too expensive place to try some fish; there are usually a few available, such as *txitxarro*

(scad) or *besugo* (sea bream). The *kokotxas* (cheeks and throats of hake in sauce) are also delicious.

El Hule, C Victor Chavarri 13, T944 722 104. In the narrow, sloping streets of Portugalete's old town (just behind the town hall on the waterfront near the Puente Colgante), this is a cracking spot for lunch. The small but cute upstairs and downstairs dining rooms are cosy and comfortable. The food is traditional, uncomplicated fare (*menú del día* €12) served with a smile and plenty of quality.

Irrintzi, C Particular de Arlamendi, off C Zalama, T944 643 372. This homely bar has appealing brick and wood decor, an upmarket clientele and about the finest reputation for *pintxos* on the right bank of the ría. There's an excellent array, and they are all very tempting. From Metro Areeta, head straight ahead and up the hill past the Mandarin Chinese restaurant, and turn right. The bar is un-signed.

Bars and clubs

Bilbao *p90, map p92*

Bilbao's nightlife is very quiet during the week, but it makes up for it at weekends. Most bars have to shut at 0400 these days, but there are some *discotecas* that go later. Nearly everywhere in the Casco Viejo shuts by 0130, but you can always dash across the Puente de la Merced to the streets around C Hernani, where there is plenty going on. Be careful in this zone though, as muggings are not unknown. There are lots of bars in the Casco Viejo, including many on the legendary streets of Ronda, Somera and Barenkale, the latter legendary for its boisterous rock 'n' roll scene.

Bars

Bizitza, C Torre 1, T944 165 882. Very chilled mixed gay-straight bar with a Basque political slant. Relaxed, atmospheric and welcoming, with frequent cultural events. One of the top spots for an after-dinner *copa* in Bilbao – they mix a great drink. Recommended.

Compañía del Ron, C Máximo Aguirre 23, T944 213 069. Friends of Ronald will be happy here, with over 100 rums at the disposal of the bar staff, who know how to handle them. Despite the chain-pub feel (it's not), this is a good early-evening spot in the heart of the new town.

El Patio de mi Casa, C Cosme Echevarrieta 13, T944 248 676. A small but quality place, which serves great *copa*s to a discerning crowd in a homely, relaxed atmosphere. Open nightly 2300-0300.

Errondabide, C Ronda 20. This is a good place to come to get a feel of what a hardline pro-independence Basque bar is like. There are political posters everywhere, photos of ETA prisoners, a spirited atmosphere, and plenty of smoke and beer.

Luz Gas, C Pelota 6, T944 790 823. A beautiful mood bar with an oriental touch. Sophisticated but friendly, and you can challenge all-comers to chess or Connect-4.

Muga, C María Muñoz 8, T944 162 781. A long-time favourite, this relaxed café and bar has a rock 'n' roll vibe, with colourful tables, fanzines and CDs for sale, and a down-to-earth clientele.

Zodiako's, C Euskal Herria s/n (corner of Telletxe), T944 604 059, Metro Algorta. This squiggly bar in the heart of Getxo is one of the best, with a terrace, *pintxos* and service with a smile. There's a *discoteca* underneath.

Zulo, Barrenkale 22. A tiny nationalist bar with plenty of plastic fruit and a welcoming set. The impressively bearded owner Txema is a notable Casco Viejo character.

Clubs

Bullitt Groove Club, C Dos de Mayo 3, T944 165 291, www.myspace.com/bullittgrooveclub. Across the river from the Casco Viejo, this retro discobar has a variety of music styles. On Sat, it's Black Roots night, with excellent soul and R&B. Other nights offer ska, reggae and 1960s rock.

Conjunto Vacío, C Muelle de la Merced 3, T944 158 338, www.conjuntovacio.net. Empty by name and packed by nature, at least from about 2 on Fri and Sat nights. The music is fairly light *bakalao*, the crowd mixed and good-looking, the drinks horrendously expensive, but entry is usually free.

El Balcón de La Lola, C Bailén 10, www.balcondelalola.com. Decorated in industrial style with sheet-metal and graffiti, this is a weekend-opening club that varies in character from fairly cheesy dance to pretty heavy garage. Open latish; concerts earlier in the night.

Santana 27, C Tellería 27, Bolueta, T944 598 617, www.santana27.com. Open nightly 2300-0600. Near the metro station in Bolueta, this vast venue has opened out here to avoid the strict opening hours in central Bilbao. There are so many dance floors that you are bound to find something you like; it often has live bands and special club nights. Usually €5-10 to get in, including a drink.

☻ Entertainment

Bilbao *p90, map p92*
For bullfighting and football, see page 99.

Cinema
Cines Renoir, C Lehendakari Aguirre 23, T944 751 210, www.cinesrenoir.com, Metro Deustu. This is one of the better central cinemas.

Music venues
Bilbo Rock, Muelle de la Merced s/n, T944 151 306. Atmospheric venue in a converted church that is now a temple of live rock with bands playing most nights of the week. No licence, but canned beer from machines.

Kafe Antzokia, C San Vicente 2, T944 244 625, www.kafeantzokia.com. An ex-cinema turned Bilbao icon, this is a live venue for anything from death metal to Euskara poetry, and features 2 spacious floors with bars which go late and loud at weekends. Sociable, friendly, and a place where you might hear more Euskara than Spanish.

Palacio Euskalduna, C Abandoibarra 4, T944 310 310, www.euskalduna.net. Top-quality classical performances from the symphonic orchestras of Bilbao and Euskadi, as well as high-profile Spanish and international artists.

Theatre
Teatro Arriaga, Plaza Arriaga 1, T944 792 036, www.teatroarriaga.com. Bilbao's highest-profile theatre is picturesquely set on the river by the Casco Viejo. It's a plush treat of a place in late 19th-century style, but the work it presents can be very innovative. The better seats go for €25 and above, but there are often decent pews available for just €5.

⊛ Festivals and events

Bilbao *p90, map p92*
Sat after 15 Aug Aste Nagusia (big week), Bilbao's major fiesta, follows on from those in Vitoria and San Sebastián to make a month of riotous Basque partying. It is a boisterous mixture of everything: concerts, *corridas*, traditional Basque sports and serious drinking.

○ Shopping

Bilbao *p90, map p92*
Bilbao is the best place to shop in Northern Spain. The majority of mainstream Spanish and international clothing stores are in the Ensanche, particularly on and around C Ercilla. The Casco Viejo harbours dozens of quirkier shops. A new commercial centre, **Zubiarte**, just by the Puente de Deustu, has a full complement of fashion chains and a cinema.
Mercado de la Ribera, the art deco market by the river where stallholders used to come for the weekly market, has over 400 stalls selling fruit, veg, meat and fish, it's the major centre for fresh produce in Bilbao. Come in the morning if you want to get the true flavour; afternoons are comparatively quiet.

There are numerous great delis for buying Basque and Spanish produce; **Txorierri**, in the old town at Artekale 19, is one, **Oka**, at Marqués del Puerto 1 near Plaza Moyúa, is another.

◐ Activities and tours

Bilbao *p90, map p92*
A double-decker tour bus (www.bus turistikoa.com) runs around the city, stopping 15 times in the standard hop-on, hop-off circuit. A 24-hr ticket is €12.
Bilbao Paso a Paso, T944 730 078, www. bilbaopasoapaso.com. Knowledgeable tours of Bilbao and the whole of Euskadi that can be tailored to suit.
Bilboats, T644 442 055, www.bilboats.com. Boat trips along the Nervión. The basic €10 jaunt takes you up past the Guggenheim – have the cameras ready – but the longer €16 trip takes you right up to the sea, past the ghosts of the city's industrial past.

Bilbao's seafront *p99*
Getxo Abentura, www.getxo.net. The Getxo tourist office can organize just about any outdoor activity you can think of in the Getxo area, from caving to canoeing, provided there are enough people to make a go of it (usually 4 for group-style outings).
Náutica Getxo, Puerto Deportivo de Getxo, T609 985 977, www.nauticagetxo.com. On the jetty at the end of Ereaga beach, this company hires out yachts with or without a skipper. Sailing knowledge isn't really required as the boats come with auxiliary power, but if you want to learn to sail, these guys can teach you that too.

⊖ Transport

Bilbao *p90, map p92*
Air
Bilbao's airport near **Sondika/Loiu**, 10 km northeast of the centre, is a beautiful building designed by Santiago Calatrava, seemingly in homage to the whale. A taxi to/ from town costs about €20-25. There's an

efficient bus service that runs to/from Bilbao's bus station via Plaza Moyúa in central Bilbao. It leaves from outside the terminal, takes 20-30 mins and runs every half hour. One-way €1.30.

Bilbao is served from several European destinations. The cheapest direct flights from the **UK** are with the budget operators **EasyJet** and **Vueling**. Bilbao is also directly connected with several other European cities. Note that although **Ryanair** seem to fly to Bilbao, the flights actually land at Santander, from where a bus service runs to Bilbao (see page 352). Bilbao also has frequent domestic connections with **Madrid**, **Barcelona** and other Spanish cities, operated by **Iberia** and **Spanair**.

Airlines offices Iberia, C Ercilla 20, Bilbao, T944 245 506, www.iberia.es; Spanair, Aeropuerto de Bilbao, T944 869 498, www.spanair.com.

Bicycle hire

Alquimoto, C Anselma de Salces 9, T944 012 563, www.alquimoto.com, rent bikes, scooters and motorbikes.

Boat

The Portsmouth–Bilbao ferry is now a thing of the past. The Basque government were making noises about subsidising a replacement service, but it at time of writing it seemed unlikely to happen. The closest ferry connection from the UK is to Santander.

Bus

The majority of Bilbao's inter-urban buses leave from the Termibus station near the football stadium (Metro San Mamés, tram stops outside). All long-haul destinations are served from here, but several Basque towns are served from the stops next to Abando station on C Hurtado Amezaga.

To **San Sebastián**: buses from the Termibus station every 30 mins weekdays, every hour at weekends, operated by PESA (1 hr 20 mins, €10). To **Vitoria**: buses from the Termibus station about every 30 mins with **Autobuses La Unión** (55 mins, €6). Other destinations include **Santander** (almost hourly, 1 hr 30 mins, from €7), **Pamplona** (7-9 daily, €2 hrs), **Logroño** (5 daily, 2 hrs), and **Burgos** (4 direct daily, 2 hrs).

Car

Though the centre is fairly well signposted, the 1-way system and extensive pedestrianization can make it difficult to find your way around. Parking in the centre is metered; if your hotel doesn't have private parking, you're best off in one of the underground stations, which cost around €15-18 for 24 hrs. The handiest for the Casco Viejo is **Arenal**; cross the Puente del Ayuntamiento from the new town and turn right. When approaching Bilbao by road from the east, it's worth paying the €1.75 (max) toll through the Artxanda tunnel, which brings you in to town right alongside the Guggenheim Museum, saving much time and potential to get lost.

Car hire The usual assortment of multinationals dominate. The process is fairly painless, and national driving licences are accepted. Atesa, C Sabino Arana 9, T944 423 290; Aeropuerto de Bilbao, T944 533 340, www.atesa.es; Avis, Av Doctor Areilza 34, T944 275 760; Aeropuerto de Bilbao, T944 869 648, www.avis.com; Hertz, C Doctor Achucarro 10, T944 153 677; Aeropuerto de Bilbao, T944 530 931, www.hertz.com.

Metro

Bilbao's metro (www.metrobilbao.net) runs Sun-Thu until about 2400, Fri until about 0200, and 24 hrs on Sat. A single fare costs from €1.40, while a day pass is €4. There's 1 main line running through the city and out to the beach suburbs, while the second line heads out to the coast on the other side of the estuary.

Tram

A single costs €1.25; there are machines at the tram stops. It runs every 10-15 mins or so. You have to validate your ticket in the machine on the platform before boarding.

Train

Bilbao has 3 train stations. The main one, **Abando**, is the terminal of **RENFE**, the national Spanish railway. It's far from a busy network but it's the principal mainline service.

Abando is also the main terminus for **Euskotren**, a handy short-haul train network that connects Bilbao and San Sebastián with many of the smaller Basque towns as well as their own outlying suburbs. The other Bilbao base for these trains is **Atxuri**, situated just east of the Casco Viejo, an attractive but run-down station for lines running eastwards as far as San Sebastián. These are particularly useful for reaching the towns of Euskadi's coast. **Gernika** is serviced every hour and on to **Mundaka** and **Bermeo**. Trains to **San Sebastián** run every hour on the hour (2 hrs 40 mins) via **Zarautz**, **Zumaia**, **Eibar**, and **Durango**.

Narrow-gauge FEVE trains connect Bilbao along the coast to **Santander**, 3 times daily (2½ hrs) and beyond. They are slow but scenic and leave from the Estación de Santander just next to Bilbao's main Abando railway station. There's also a daily service from here to **León** (7 hrs 15 mins).

Getxo p100
Bus
Buses No 3411 and No 3413 run to/from Plaza Moyúa every 30 mins.

Metro
Getxo is a large area, and the metro stations Areeta, Gobela, Neguri, Aiboa, Algorta, and Bidezabal all fall within its area. The beaches further on can be accessed from Larrabasterra, Sopelana and Plentzia metros.

Portugalete p101
Bus
Bus No 3152 from the Arenal bus station in Bilbao (Mon-Sat).

Metro
Bilbao's Metro (Line 2) now runs to Portugalete; the Line 1 station of Areeta is also handy, just across the Puente Colgante.

Train
From Abando station, the **Euskotren** service runs to Portugalete (line: Santurtzi) every 12 mins weekdays, less frequently at weekends, and takes 20 mins.

❶ Directory

Bilbao p90, map p92

Consulates Eire, T944 912 575; France, T944 249 000; Germany, T944 238 585; South Africa, T944 641 124; UK, T944 157 600; USA, the nearest consular representative is at the embassy in Madrid, T915 872 200. **Internet** There are various free Wi-Fi zones around the centre of Bilbao, including Plaza Nueva. El Señor de la Red, Alameda de Rekalde 14, T944 237 425, €2/hr; Laser Internet, C Sendeja 5, T944 453 509, Mon-Fri 1030-0230, Sat and Sun 1100-0230, €0.05 per min, handy and quick, also offers photocopier and fax services; Ciber Latino, C Carnicería Vieja 6, internet at €2 per hr; La Basca Universal, C Viuda de Epalza 12, T944 792 865, cheap phone calls and internet on the Arenal. **Language schools** Instituto Hemingway, C Bailén 5, T944 167 901, www.institutohemingway.com. **Laundry** Fast & Clean, Plaza Ensanche 9, T944 239 363. Dry cleaning and service washes. **Medical services** Hospital de Basurto, Av Montevideo 18, T944 006 000, T944 755 000, Tram Basurto. **Police** The emergency number for all necessities is T112, while T092 will take you to the local police. **Main police station**, Policia Municipal Bilbao, C Luis Briñas 14, T944 205 000. **Post office** Main post office, Alameda Urquijo 19; Casco Viejo branch, C Epalza 4 (opposite Arenal).

Vitoria/Gasteiz

→ *Colour map 3, B2. Phone code: 945. Population: 239,361. Altitude: 512 m.*

Vitoria is the quiet achiever of the trio of Basque cities. A comparatively peaceful town, it comes as a surprise to many visitors to discover that it's actually the capital of the semi-autonomous Basque region. A thoughtful place, it combines an attractive old town with an Ensanche (expansion) designed to provide plenty of green spaces for its hard-working inhabitants. While it lacks the big-city vitality of Bilbao or the languid beauty of San Sebastián it's a satisfying city much-loved by most who visit it. Perhaps because it's the political centre of the region, the young are very vocally Basque, and the city feels energized as a result. An ambitious urban improvement plan has brought escalators to the old town, a tram service, and is creating a flash new train/bus station to the north of the centre.
▸▸ *For listings, see pages 118-121.*

Ins and outs

Getting there There are frequent bus connections with Bilbao and other Basque destinations. Vitoria's **RENFE** station has better connections with the rest of Spain than does Bilbao. ▸▸ *See Transport, page 121.*

Getting around Vitoria is a good two-wheel city with more cycle ways and green spots than in busier Bilbao. There's a new tram line, but Vitoria is easily walkable with Calle Dato the focus of the evening paseo.

Tourist information Vitoria's **tourist office** ① *Plaza General Loma 1, T945 161 598, turismo@vitoria-gasteiz.org, summer daily 0930-1930, winter Mon-Sat 1000-1900, Sun 1100-1400,* is in the centre of things.

Background

Vitoria's shield-shaped old town sits on the high ground that perhaps gave the city its name (*beturia* is an Euskara word for hill). After being a Basque settlement first, then a Roman one, Vitoria was abandoned until it was refounded and fortified by the kings of Navarra in the 12th and 13th centuries. An obscure Castilian town for much of its history, Vitoria featured in the Peninsular War, when, on midsummer's day in 1813, Napoleon's forces were routed by the Allied troops and fled in ragged fashion towards home, abandoning their baggage train containing millions of francs, which was gleefully looted. "The battle was to the French", commented a British officer sagely, "like salt on a leech's tail". Vitoria has thrived since being named capital of the semi-autonomous Basque region, and has a genteel, comfortable air, enlivened by an active student population.

Casco Medieval

Calle Cuchillería and Calle Chiquita

Calle Cuchillería, and its continuation, Calle Chiquita, is the liveliest part of the old town, with several impressive old mansions, a couple of museums, dozens of bars, and plenty of pro-Basque political attitude. Indeed, there's an interesting contrast in the atmosphere of the new and old towns; whereas the former feels very Spanish and quite staid, the preserve of middle-aged strollers, the old streets hum with young Basque energy. Like several in the Casco Medieval, this street is named after the craftspeople who used to have shops here; in this case knife makers. Walking along this street and those nearby you can see a number of old inscriptions and coats of arms carved on buildings.

Housed in a beautiful fortified medieval house on Cuchillería with a sleek modern extension out the back **Bibat** ① *Tue-Fri 1000-1400, 1600-1830, Sat 1000-1400, Sun 1100-1400, free*, contains two museums. The unusual Fournier collection is devoted to the playing card, of which it holds over 10,000 packs. Diamonds are forever, but you won't see many here: the cards are mostly Spanish decks, with swords, cups, coins and staves the suits. Here also is the archaeology museum. The province has been well occupied over history, and the smallish collection covers many periods, from prehistoric through Roman and medieval. Arguably the most impressive of the objects on display is the *Knight's Stele*, a tombstone carved with a horseman dating from the Roman era.

The corner of the old town at the end of Calle Chiquita is one of Vitoria's most picturesque. The **Casa del Portalón**, now a restaurant, is a lovely old timbered building from the late 15th century. It used to be an inn and a staging post for messengers. Across from it is the **Torre de los Anda**, which defended one of the entrances in the city wall. Opposite these is the 16th-century house of the Gobeo family.

Opposite here is the current entrance to the older of Vitoria's two cathedrals, the **Catedral de Santa María** ① *tours daily 1100-1400, 1700-2000, €3 per person, pre-book on T945 255 135 or www.catedral vitoria.com*. There's an ongoing restoration project, scheduled to last until 2012. It's currently 'open for renovation'; while normal visits have been suspended, you can take a fascinating guided tour of the restoration works. Depending on the progress, you may be able to walk on gangways high above the nave, admiring the vaulting from close up, or see the delicate retrieval of crumbling stonework.

Above the busy square of **Plaza de la Virgen Blanca**, the church of **San Miguel** stands like one of a series of chess pieces guarding the entrance to the Casco Medieval. Two gaping arches mark the portal, which is superbly carved. A niche here holds the city's patron saint, the Virgen Blanca, a coloured late-Gothic figure. On the saint's day, 5 August, a group of townspeople carry the figure of Celedón (a stylized farmer) from the top of the graceful belltower down to the square.

Los Arquillos

Running off the same square, this slightly strange series of dwellings and covered colonnades was designed in the early 19th century as a means of more effectively linking the high Casco Medieval with the newer town below, and to avoid the risk of the collapse of the southern part of the hill. It leads up to the attractive small **Plaza del Machete**, where incoming city chancellors used to swear an oath of allegiance over a copy of the Fueros (city statutes) and a machete, in this case a military cutlass.

Also off Plaza de la Virgen Blanca, the picture-postcard **Plaza de España** (Basques prefer to call it **Plaza Nueva**) was designed by the same man, Olaguíbel, who thought up the Arquillos. It's a beautiful colonnaded square busy with playing children and parents chatting over coffee, housing the town hall and several bars with terraces that are perfect for the morning or afternoon sun.

Vitoria/Gasteiz

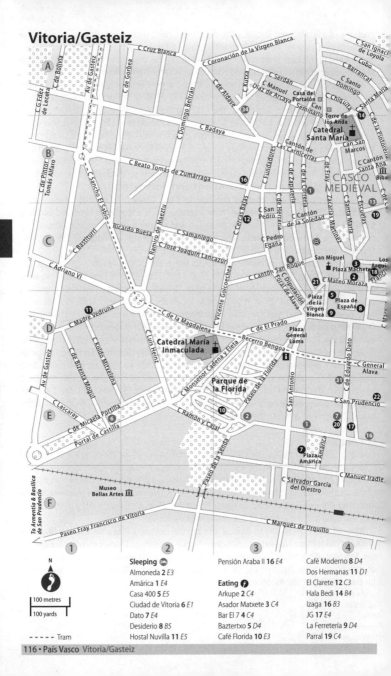

N

100 metres
100 yards

- - - - Tram

Sleeping
Almoneda **2** E3
Amárica **1** E4
Casa 400 **5** E5
Ciudad de Vitoria **6** E1
Dato **7** E4
Desiderio **8** B5
Hostal Nuvilla **11** E5
Pensión Araba II **16** E4

Eating
Arkupe **2** C4
Asador Matxete **3** C4
Bar El 7 **4** C4
Baztertxo **5** D4
Café Florida **10** E3
Café Moderno **8** D4
Dos Hermanas **11** D1
El Clarete **12** C3
Hala Bedi **14** B4
Izaga **3** B3
JG **17** E4
La Ferretería **9** D4
Parral **19** C4

New Town

Vitoria's new town isn't going to blow anyone's mind with a cavalcade of Gaudí-esque buildings or wild street parties, but it is a very satisfying place: a planned mixture of attractive streets and plenty of parkland. It's got the highest amount of greenery per citizen of any city in Spain and it's no surprise that it's been voted one of the best places to live in the coutry. With the innovative Artium adding a touch of innovation, the mantle of Basque capital seems to sit ever easier on Vitoria's shoulders.

Artium

ⓘ *C Francia 24, T945 209 020, www.artium. org, Tue-Thu 1100-1400, 1700-2000, Fri-Sun 1100-1400, 1600-2100, entry by donation.*

Artium is Vitoria's answer to Bilbao's Guggenheim and San Sebastián's Kursaal. It's an exciting project that features some excellent contemporary artwork, mostly in the form of temporary exhibitions, some of which incorporate some of the older buildings in Vitoria's Casco Medieval. Shiny and white, your attention is grabbed immediately by the building's confident angles and Javier Pérez's *Un pedazo de cielo cristalizado* (A piece of sky made glass), a large hanging-glass sculpture in the atrium. The galleries are accessed down the stairs. The website has details in English about what's on at any given time; the exhibitions are usually in place for many months. There's also a good little café.

Catedral de María Inmaculada

There's no missing the new cathedral, María Inmaculada, constructed in the 20th century in neo-Gothic style; its bulk looms attractively over this part of the town. Built in medieval style, it now houses the **Museo Diocesano de Arte Sacro** ⓘ *Tue-Fri 1000-1400, 1600-1830, Sat 1000-1400, Sun 1100-1400, free.*

Parque de la Florida

This gorgeous park is an excellent retreat right in the heart of Vitoria. Cool and shady, it has a number of exotic trees and plants and a couple of peaceful cafés. You can watch old men in berets playing *bolas* (boules), and there's an old bandstand with Sunday concerts, guarded by statues of four ancient kings. If you see anyone taking life a little too seriously, they're more than likely politicians – the Basque Parliament stands in a corner of the park.

Basílica de San Prudencio

① *Mon-Fri 1000-1400, Sat 1000-1400, 1600-2100, Sun 1000-1200, 1600-2100, guided visit €3.*
It's well worth the half-hour walk or the bus ride to see this church in the village of **Armentia**, now subsumed into Vitoria's outskirts. The village is supposedly the birthplace of San Prudencio, the patron saint of Alava Province, and the church was erected in his honour. It was rebuilt in the 18th century, but still has some excellent features from its Romanesque youth, such as a harmonious round apse and the carvings above the doors, one of Christ and the apostles, the other of the Lamb and John the Baptist. At time of writing, it was being renovated, and access to most of the building was by guided tour run by archaeologists who have exposed Romanesque foundations and an adjoining cemetery.

To reach Armentia on foot, continue past the Museo de Bellas Artes on Paseo Fray Francisco de Vitoria, then turn left down Paseo de Cervantes when you reach the modern chapel of **La Sagrada Familia**. The basilica is at the end of this road. It's a pleasant walk; you can also get bus No 9, which runs every half an hour from the new cathedral to the basilica.

◉ Vitoria/Gasteiz listings

For Sleeping and Eating price codes and other relevant information, see Essentials pages 31-39.

● Sleeping

Vitoria *p114, map p116*
AL Parador de Argómaniz, Carretera N1 Km 363, T945 293 200, www.parador.es. This parador is some 12 km east of Vitoria in a Renaissance palace. It's a tranquil place with some good views over the surrounding countryside. Napoleon slept here before the disastrous Battle of Vitoria.
A Hotel Ciudad de Vitoria, Portal de Castilla 8, T945 141 100, www.hoteles-silken.com. A massive 4-star hotel situated at the edge of Vitoria's centre, where character starts to make way for 'lifestyle'. It's airy and pleasant, with good facilities, including a gym and sauna. Chief attraction is its excellent weekend rate, when it's usually a **C**.
B Hotel Almoneda, C Florida 7, T945 154 084, www.hotelalmoneda.com. Attractively

situated a few paces from the lovely Parque de la Florida, this hotel has decent spacious rooms with a rustic touch. It's significantly cheaper at weekends. Breakfast included; you can even have it in bed if you ask nicely.
D Hotel Amárica, C Florida 11, T945 130 506. Just around the corner from C Dato and close to the train station, this friendly hotel is very well placed. The rooms are good value, with TV and good bathroom, warm, and surprisingly quiet, considering it's a busy street.
D Hotel Dato, C Eduardo Dato 28, T945 147 230, www.hoteldato.com. This *pintxo*-zone cheap hotel is a treasury of art nouveau and classic statues, mirrors and general plushness, in a comfortable rather than stuffy way. Its rooms are exceptional value too; all are pretty, with excellent facilities, and some have balconies or miradors (enclosed balconies). Free Wi-Fi. Recommended.
D Hotel Desiderio, C Colegio San Prudencio 2, T945 251 700, www.hoteldesiderio.es. This

is a welcoming hotel with unremarkable but comfy rooms with bathroom just on the edge of the Casco Medieval. It's quiet and unassuming and offers very good value. They have cheaper *hostal* rooms across the road.

E Pensión Araba II, C Florida 25, T945 232 588, www.pensionaraba.com. This elegant home makes an excellent base in central Vitoria. A variety of spotless, comfortable rooms with or without bathroom and a genuinely friendly welcome make it a budget star. Parking spaces available (€6).

E Casa 400, C Florida 46, T945 233 887, p.gandiaga@telefonica.net. This renovated *pensión* makes a sound central base. Spacious rooms have comfortable beds, decent bathrooms and electronic locks; the friendly owner will show you the ropes then leave you to your own devices. There's free Wi-Fi and it's handy for the train station.

F Hostal Nuvilla, C Fueros 29, T945 259 151. Centrally located *pensión* with small rooms with washbasin. It's friendly and cheap.

🍴 Eating

Vitoria *p114, map p116*
In the old town, C Cuchillería is a long row of simple Basque taverns; smarter places dot the new town, particularly around C Eduardo Dato.

† Arkupe, C Mateo Moraza 13, T945 230 080, www.restaurantearkupe.com. On the edge of the old town, this quality restaurant turns out imaginative dishes that are typically combinations of various quality northern Spanish products. Try the juicy *carrilleras* stewed in local Rioja, the range of gourmet salads, or, on Thu, a traditional *cocido* stew.

††† Dos Hermanas, C Madre Vedruna 10, T945 132 934, www. restaurantedoshermanas.com. One of Vitoria's oldest restaurants, this place manages to combine tradition and modernity, with an assured gourmet touch and personable service. There's a variety of set menus as well as some à la carte options.

††† El Clarete, C Cercas Bajas 18, T945 263 874, www.elclareterestaurante.com. Comfortably contemporary in style, this enthusiastically run restaurant offers confidently prepared modern Spanish cuisine with an experimental flair. Portions, while not huge, are beautifully presented and taste fabulous: try the slow-roasted lamb or anything with their home-made foie.

††† Asador Matxete, Plaza Machete 4, T945 131 821, www.matxete.com. This stylish, friendly restaurant is harmoniously inserted into this pretty plaza above Los Arquillos. The vaulted dining area is atmospheric, and dishes such as quail salad back up the excellent charcoal-grilled meat, though service is a little patchy. There's also a quality downstairs tapas bar and pleasant terrace to enjoy a drink in this peaceful square.

†† Baztertxo, Plaza de España 14, T945 157 400. A fine bar with some great wines by the glass and top-notch *jamón* and other gourmet snacks. Although service can be beneath the dignity of the staff, it's still a good choice, with a terrace on the square.

†† Izaga, Tomás de Zumárraga 2, T945 138 200, www.restauranteizaga.com. Excellent dining at this fairly formal restaurant in a smart stone building. The focus is on seafood – try the delicious Huelva prawns – but there are plenty of other specialities – such as duck's liver on stuffed pig's ear, and some sinful desserts. There's a *menú del día* on weekdays for €21.

†† Toloño, Cuesta San Francisco 3, T945 233 336. One of the city's best *pintxo* bars, this smart spot on the hill leading up to the old town is a kidney-shaped space with an upbeat and welcoming feel. The tapas are great, especially the gourmet *pintxos* chalked up on the board. For around €3, take your pick from a range of exquisite hot delights; the *foie* is great if it's on. Recommended.

†† Xixilu, Plaza Amárica 2, T945 230 068. On a small gardened square not far from the train station, this is a great place to eat. The sociable, intimate *comedor* at the back is filled with chunky wooden tables and stools; the food is quite smart, with delicate *sesos* (brains), and good house salad among a range of tempting dishes. Recommended.

¶ Bar El 7, C Cuchillería 7, T945 272 298. A Vitoria classic, this is an excellent bar at the head of the Casco Medieval's liveliest street. Its big range of *bocadillos* keeps students and all-comers happy. Order a half if you're not starving; they make 'em pretty large. They also do a very acceptable €11 *menú del día*.

¶ Hala Bedi, C Cuchillería 98, T945 260 411. A late-opening Basque bar with a cheerful atmosphere. It's very lively, and popular with the young and politically conscious. Out of a tiny kitchen come crêpes with a massive variety of sweet and savoury fillings, as well as sandwiches and other simple dishes.

¶ Parral, Cantón de San Francisco Javier 4. T945 276 833. This relaxed spot on a sloping street above C Cuchillería is a vegetarian restaurant by day and a mood bar by night, with regular live music. There's a salad buffet and a *menú del día* offering significant value.

¶ Restaurante JG, C Eduardo Dato 27, T945 231 132. Another excellent option for *pintxos* on this pedestrian street – the range of *croquetas* comes highly recommended. More substantial eating is also good value in the *comedor*.

¶ Restaurante Virgen Blanca, Plaza Virgen Blanca s/n, T945 286 199. Overlooking the picturesque Virgen Blanca square, this spacious spot features sturdy wooden tables and gnarled floorboards, as well as great outdoor tables perfect for contemplation of central Vitoria. Tasty *pintxos* are arrayed along the bar, and there's a lunch *menú* for €14.70.

¶ Saburdi, C Eduardo Dato 32, T945 147 016. There are some excellent *pintxo* bars in Vitoria, and this is one of the classics, with a great range of delicious bites. It's warmly lit and welcoming, with several decent wines by the glass. Recommended.

¶ Taberna, C San Prudencio 21. Simple dynamics: long bar, tables in the sun, big screen showing sport or films, beer, wine and *pintxos*. It spills onto the street in a happy crowd in summer.

Cafés

Café Moderno, Plaza España 4. Sunseekers should head here in the afternoon – the terrace in the picture-postcard arched square is perfectly placed for maximum rays. The trendy bar does good *pintxos*, and the terrace gets very lively in the evenings as the square packs out with socializing Vitorians.

Café Florida, Parque de la Florida. One of Vitoria's best spots, with lots of tables among the trees of this peaceful park. Regular games of *bolas* take place nearby.

La Ferretería, Plaza de la Virgen Blanca s/n, T945 133 922. In the heart of Vitoria, this trendily lit former ironmongers is not to be sneered at if you're on the prowl for a morning coffee and croissant. If you grab a spot on its terrace in the early evening you can truly say you are sitting where it's all happening.

🚺 Bars and clubs

Vitoria *p114, map p116*

The old town tends to have boisterous, no-frills bars with a Basque atmosphere, while the new town has a more chic scene.

Bar Río, C Eduardo Dato 20, T945 230 067. A decent café with outdoor tables by day, and one of the last bars to shut at night, when it caters to a good-natured gay/straight crowd. They prepare mixed drinks with an unbelievably elaborate ritual. Original live music on Thu nights.

Café Iguana, Correría 94, T945 122 837. This spot has a great ambience for an after-dinner *copa* and a friendly mix of arty people. Plenty of tables and well-mixed drinks. One of Vitoria's best.

Cairo Stereo Club, C Aldabe 9. Great club with some excellent and innovative DJs and a mixed crowd. During the week they often show cult movies or hold theme parties.

El Bodegón de Gorbea, C Herrería 26. A classic. No-frills bar with rock music, cheap beer, and a bohemian bunch of friendly Basques chatting and drinking from early until very late. On the corner of Cantón San Roque.

Gora, Cantón de San Francisco Javier s/n. A modern, spacious place just off C Cuchillería. Green, light and peaceful.

⊛ Festivals and events

Vitoria *p114, map p116*
25 Jul Santiago's day is celebrated as the Día del Blusa, when colour-coordinated kids patrol the streets.
4-9 Aug Fiesta de la Virgen Blanca, the city's major knees-up, which is recommended.
Dec Advent. Vitoria is known for its spectacular life-sized Nativity scene (*Belén*), with over 200 figures.

○ Shopping

Vitoria *p114, map p116*
Segunda Mano, C Prudencio María Verástegui 14, T945 270 007. This is an amazing shop selling second-hand goods, which seems to have everything. From books to grand pianos, skis to tractors, and carriages to confessionals. You name it, it's likely to be there.

⊖ Transport

Vitoria *p114, map p116*
Air
Vitoria's airport (VIT) is 8 km northwest of town. The airport is served by Iberia affiliates from **Madrid** and **Barcelona**. A taxi from the centre will cost about €17.

Bus
Until the new bus station is built (this will be at tram stop: Intermodal), the bus station is on the eastern side of town. Buses to **Bilbao** run about every 30 mins with **Autobuses La Unión** (55 mins, €6). There are 7-8 buses a day to **San Sebastián** (1 hr 40 mins, €8), to **Madrid** (€25, 5 hrs), **Burgos** (€8, 1½ hrs), **Pamplona** (9-14 daily, €8, 1 hr 40 mins), as well as buses to **Logroño**, **Haro**, **Laguardia**, and **Salvatierra**.

Taxi
A taxi ride from Vitoria train station to the Basilica at Armentia costs about €6.

Train
The train station has regular connections with **Madrid**, **Zaragoza**, **Logroño**, **Barcelona**, **Burgos**, and other destinations.

Tram
Vitoria's smart new tram line crosses the city centre and costs €1.05 for a ride. It's not of great use to the visitor yet, but will be once the new bus station opens north of the town in a few years.

ⓘ Directory

Vitoria *p114, map p116*
Internet and telephone Locutorio Tito, C Correría 44, and **Meknasi**, C Fueros 7, have cheap internet and phone calls.

Alava Province

The province of Alava is something of a wilderness compared to the densely settled valleys of Vizcaya and Guipúzcoa. It's the place to come for unspoiled nature; there are some spots of great natural beauty and plenty of scope for hiking and other more specialized outdoor activities. The attractive walled town of Salvatierra is worth a visit and a base for exploring the area. The southern part of the province drops away to sunny plains, part of the Rioja wine region. Laguardia, the area's main centre, is not to be missed. ▶▶ *For listings, see pages 126-128.*

Western Alava → *For listings, see pages 126-128. Colour map 3, B1.*

West of Vitoria the green pastures give way to a rugged and dry terrain, home of vultures, eagles and dramatic rock formations. The area is served by bus from Vitoria.

Salinas de Añana

This hard-bitten half-a-horse village has one of the more unusual sights in the Basque lands. The place owes its existence to the incredibly saline water that wells up from the ground here, which was diverted down a valley and siphoned into any number of *eras* or pans, flat evaporation platforms mounted on wooded stilts. It's something very different and an eerie sight, looking a little like the ruins of an ancient Greek city in miniature. As many as 5500 pans were still being used by the 1960s but nowadays only about 150 are going concerns. The first written reference to the collection of salt in these parts was in AD 822, but it seems pretty likely the Romans had a go too.

During Semana Santa, Salinas comes to life; Judas is put on trial by the villagers. However, it's something of a kangaroo court as he's always convicted and burned.

Cañón de Delika

To the west beyond Salinas, and actually reached via the province of Burgos, is this spectacular canyon that widens into the valley of Orduña. The Río Nervión has its source near here and when running, it spectacularly spills 300 m into the gorge below: the highest waterfall in Spain. There's a good 90-minute round walk from the car park. Follow the right-hand road first, which brings you to the falls, then follow the cliffs along to the left, where vultures soar above the valley below. When you reach the second mirador, looking down the valley to Orduña, there's another road that descends through beech forest back to the car park. Near the car park is a spring, the **Fuente de Santiago**. Legend has it that St James stopped here to refresh himself and his horse during his alleged time in Spain. To get to the car park, which is about 3 km from the main road, the 2625 (running from Orduña in the north to Espejo in the south and beyond) turn-off is signposted 'Monte Santiago' and is about 8 km south of Orduña. There are buses to Orduña from Vitoria bus station with **La Unión**.

Eastern Alava → *For listings, see pages 126-128. Colour map 3. B2.*

The eastern half of the Alava plain is dotted with interesting villages, churches and prehistoric remains. The town of Salvatierra is the most convenient base for exploration or walking. At the northern fringes of the plain, the mountains rise into Guipúzcoa. One of the Camino de Santiago routes passes through the natural tunnel of San Adrián here.

Salvatierra/Agurain

The major centre in eastern Alava is the not-very-major Salvatierra (Agurain), a well-preserved, walled medieval town with some interesting buildings. Around Salvatierra there's plenty of walking, canyoning and abseiling to be done, while further afield canoeing, windsurfing, paragliding and horse trekking can be arranged. The sleeping and eating possibilities are nothing to write home about, but there are a couple of *pensiones*, both attached to restaurants. The **tourist office**, on the main street half a block up from the square with the **Iglesia de San Juan**, is very helpful. They currently hold keys for the churches in Salvatierra as well as the marvellous church at Gaceo. Unfortunately, though, they don't have permission to lend the keys to visitors so currently the only option is to pay for a guided tour. A guided trip to Gaceo and Alaiza costs €2 per person: contact **Tura** ① *T945 312 535; www.agurain.biz*, for details. Tours run every Thursday and Sunday, and daily in July and August, but also by arrangement (50 per group).

Túnel de San Adrián and around

One of the most interesting walks starts from the hamlet of Zalduondo, 8 km north of Salvatierra. A section of the **Camino de Santiago**, part of it follows the old Roman/medieval highway that effectively linked most of the peninsula with the rest of Europe. It's about 5.5 km from Zalduondo to a small parking area named **Zumarraundi**. From there, the track ascends through beech forest to the Túnel de San Adrián. Shortly after meeting the old stone road, there's a right turn up a slope that's easy to miss; look for the wooden signpost at the top of the rise to your right. The tunnel is a spectacular natural cave cutting a path through the hill. It houses a small chapel, perhaps built to assuage the fears of medieval pilgrims, many of whom thought that the cave was the entrance to Hell. After the tunnel, the trail continues into Guipúzcoa, reaching the attractive town of Zegama about 90 minutes' walk further on. There are numerous adventure tourism options in the area.

Eguilaz

The area around Zalduondo and Salvatierra is also notable for its prehistoric remains; in particular a series of dolmens. Near the village of Eguilaz 45 minutes' walk from Salvatierra (just off the N1 to the east) is the dolmen of **Aitzkomendi**, which was rediscovered by a ploughing farmer in 1830. What happened to the plough is unrecorded, but the 11 impressive stones making up the structure all tip the scales at around the 10-ton mark. It's thought that the dolmen is a funerary marker dating from the early Bronze Age. On weekdays, five buses run to Zalduondo from Vitoria/Salvatierra (destination Araia); two run on Saturday and one on Sunday.

Sorginetxe and around

On the other side of Salvatierra near Arrizala is the equally impressive Sorginetxe, dated to a similar period. The name means 'house of the witch'; in the Middle Ages when the area was still heavily wooded, it could well have been the forest home of somebody of that profession. To the east of here, near the village of Ilarduia, is the **Leze Cave**, a massive crevice in the cliff face. It's 80 m high and a stream flows from its mouth, making access tricky for casual visitors. It's a good place for canyoning (see **Tura**, in Salvatierra, above).

Gorbeia

North of Vitoria, straddling Vizcaya and Alava, is the massif of Gorbeia, an enticing and inaccessible area of peaks and gorges topped by the peak of the same name, which hits

1482 m. It features in Basque consciousness as a realm of deities and purity. There are several good marked trails around **Murguia**, including an ascent of the peak itself, which shouldn't be attempted in poor weather.

La Rioja Alavesa → *For listings, see pages 126-128. Colour map 3, C2.*

Basque Rioja? The two words don't seem to go together naturally but in fact many of the finest Riojas are from Alava province. Confusion reigns because the Spanish province of La Rioja is only one of three that the wine region of the same name encompasses. Although it's not far from Vitoria, the Rioja Alavesa definitely feels Spanish rather than Basque; the descent from the green hills into the arid plains crosses a cultural and geographical border. As well as the opportunity to visit some excellent wineries, the hilltop town of Laguardia is one of the most atmospheric places in Northern Spain.

Laguardia/Biasteri

The small, walled hilltop town of Laguardia commands the plain like a sentinel – which it was; it was originally called La Guardia de Navarra (the guard of Navarra). Underneath the medieval streets, like catacombs, are over 300 small bodegas, cellars used for the making and storing of wine, as well as a place to hide in troubled times. Most are no longer used – **Bodega El Fabulista** is a fascinating exception.

Even if wine is put aside for a moment, the town itself is captivating. Founded in 1164, its narrow streets are a lovely place to wander. Traffic is almost prohibited due to the bodegas carved out 6 m below. The impressive **Iglesia de Santa María de los Reyes** ⓘ *weekend tours at 1730 and 1830, €2, at other times ask at tourist office*, begun in the 12th century, has an extraordinarily well-preserved painted Gothic façade, while the former Ayuntamiento on the arched Plaza Nueva was inaugurated in the 16th century under Carlos V.

Laguardia's **tourist office** ⓘ *C Mayor 52, T945 600 845, www.laguardia-alava.com, Mon-Fri 1000-1400, 1600-1900, Sat 1000-1400, 1700-1900, Sun 1045-1400,* is in the centre of things.

Laguardia was the birthplace of the fable writer Félix de Samaniego.

Around Laguardia

The area around Laguardia also has a few non-vinous attractions. A set of small lakes close by is one of Spain's better spots for birdwatching, particularly from September to March when migrating birds are around. There are a series of marked walking and cycling routes in this area, spectacularly backed by the mountains of the Sierra Cantábrica.

If you're coming from Vitoria by car, it's marginally quicker and much more scenic to take the smaller A2124 rather than the motorway. After ascending to a pass, the high ground dramatically drops away to the Riojan plain; there's a superb lookout on the road, justly known as 'El Balcón' (the balcony). From here, the whole of the Rioja region is visible before and below you.

Wineries

Though not strictly a winery, **Centro Temático Villa Lucía** ⓘ *Ctra Logroño s/n, T945 600 032, www.villa-lucia.com, Tue-Sun 1000-1400, 1700-2000, €5-15,* is definitely a winey experience. It offers intriguing 'virtual' tasting sessions that'll help hone your skills, and you can also pre-arrange a variety of different tasting sessions of the real stuff. There's also a botanic garden here.

Bodegas Palacio

ⓘ *Ctra de Elciego s/n, T945 621 195, www.habarcelo.es, tours Tue-Fri 1200 and 1300, Sat 1100, 1200, 1300, €5 (redeemable in shop or restaurant); booking essential.*

One of the handiest of the wineries, and worth seeing, is **Bodegas Palacio**, located just below Laguardia on the Elciego road, some 10 minutes' walk from town. The winery is modern; the older bodega alongside having been charmingly converted into a hotel and restaurant. Palacio produces a range of wines, the quality of which has increased in recent years. Their *Glorioso* and *Cosme Palacio* labels are widely sold in the UK.

The winery was originally founded in 1894 and is fairly typical of the area, producing 90% red wine from the Tempranillo grape, and a small 10% of white from Viura (as well as *crianzas, reservas* and *gran reservas*, see box, page 222). Palacio also produce a red wine for drinking young, *Milflores*, which is soft, fruity and a change from the woodier Rioja styles.

Bodega El Fabulista

ⓘ *Plaza San Juan s/n, Laguardia, T945 621 192. Tours daily at 1130, 1300, 1730, and 1900; Sun: mornings only, €6.*

A massive contrast to Palacio, which produces two million bottles a year, is **Bodega El Fabulista**, next to the tourist office in Laguardia. Eusebio, the owner, effectively runs the place alone and produces about 1/50th of that amount. The wine is made using very traditional methods in the intriguing underground cellar from grapes he grows himself. The wines, marketed as *Decidido*, are a good young-drinking red and white. He runs four tours a day, which are excellent and include lots of background information on the Rioja wine region and a generous tasting in a beautiful underground vault.

Herederos del Marqués de Riscal

ⓘ *C Torrea 1, Elciego, T945 180 888, www.marquesderiscal.com, multilingual tours Tue-Sat 1000, 1230, 1600, Sun 1100 and 1300, €10, reserve in advance.*

Founded in 1860, Marqués de Riscal is the oldest and best known of the Rioja bodegas and has built a formidable reputation for the quality of its wines. The Marqués himself was a Madrid journalist who, having cooled off in France after getting in some hot political water at home, returned to Spain and started making wine. Enlisting the help of Monsieur Pinot, a French expert, he experimented by planting Cabernet Sauvignon, which is still used in the wines today.

The innovative spirit continues, and Marqués de Riscal enlisted none other than Frank Gehry of Guggenheim museum fame to design their new visitor complex, a visual treat of a building which opened in 2006. Gehry's design incorporates ribbons of coloured titanium over a building of natural stone. The silver, gold and 'dusty rose' sheets are Gehry's response to 'the unbroken landscape of vineyards and rich tones'. The building encompasses a hotel, a restaurant, and an oenotherapy spa, which combines water treatments with applications of grape and vine extracts.

The winery is modern but remains faithful to the bodega's rigorous tradition of quality. As well as their traditionally elegant *Reserva* and *Gran Reserva*, the more recently inaugurated *Barón de Chirel* is a very classy red indeed, coming from low-yielding old vines and exhibiting a more French character than is typical of the region.

Buses from Vitoria to Logroño via Elciego pass through here and Laguardia, which is 7 km away.

Other wineries

Two kilometres north of Laguardia, with a waved design echoing the steep mountains behind it, is **Ysios Bodega** ⓘ *T945 600 640, www.domecqbodegas.com/ysios, visits are daily at 1100 and 1300, €5, they need to be pre-arranged*, designed by Santiago Calatrava, the brilliant Valencian engineer/architect who seems to have made Euskal Herría his second home.

Twenty minutes east of Laguardia is the pretty but parched town of Oyón/Oion. One of the bigger operations here is **Bodegas Faustino Martínez** ⓘ *T945 622 500, www. bodegas faustino.com, tours weekdays during working hours and Sat 1100, 1300, phone to arrange, €6*, whose range of Faustino wines are a reliable and popular choice both in Spain and the UK. They run a good tour of their operation in Spanish or English. The tour is all the better for being a bit more in-depth and a little less cursory than some of the other big wineries.

◉ Alava Province listings

For Sleeping and Eating price codes and other relevant information, see Essentials pages 31-39.

● Sleeping

Salvatierra *p123*

C-D Eikolara, Barrio Arbinatea 30, Zalduondo, T945 304 332, www.eikolara. com. An excellent *casa rural*, this great spot is a characterfully restored old stone house in the village of Zalduondo. The rooms (which vary in price and size) are colourfully and stylishly decorated, and the owners are helpful and keep it all super clean and ship shape. Breakfast included.

D Zadorra Etxea, C Zadorra 21, T945 312 427, www.zadorraetxea.com. Although often let out whole over weekends, this *casa rural* does offer accommodation on a per-room basis. Friendly owners and thoughtful decoration with exposed beams and wooden floors make this Salvatierra's best place to stay.

E Mendiaxpe, Barrio Salsamendi 22, Asparrena, T945 304 212, mendiaxpe@terra. es. Cleverly located in the wooded foothills of the Sierra de Urkilla, this is a superb base for walking in the area. There's use of a kitchen but no meals available except breakfast. The 3 en suite rooms are lovely and light.

E Merino, Plaza de San Juan 3, T945 300 052. One of 2 unremarkable *pensiones*

in Salvatierra, it offers a *menú del día* in its restaurant.

La Rioja Alavesa *p124*

There are some excellent places to stay in Laguardia.

LL Hotel Marqués de Riscal, T945 180 880, C Torrea 1, Elciego, www.starwoodhotels. com. This flamboyant structure is visible from afar and is your chance to stay in a Frank Gehry-designed building. The exuberant waves of metal conceal a modern building made from traditional stone. The rooms are, as you'd expect at this price, well designed if not enormous, and have appealingly offbeat shapes and features. You'll get better rates from the website the further in advance you book. There's also a fine gourmet restaurant.

AL Hospedería de los Parajes, C Mayor 46, Laguardia, T945 621 130, www. hospederiadelosparajes.com. Right in the heart of the old town, this recently opened hotel offers significant style and comfort and peaceful rooms with excellent facilities. There's a range of room classes at different prices and sizes, but all boast chic fabrics and modern-rustic design and great bathrooms. There's a wonderful underground bodega that makes a romantic spot for an evening glass of local wine.

A Castillo El Collado, Paseo El Collado 1, Laguardia, T945 621 200, www.hotelcollado. com. Decorated in plush but colourful style, this mansion at the north end of the old town is comfortable and welcoming. There are 10 individually decorated rooms as well as a restaurant. The owner is more than helpful, and can arrange your bodega visits for you. Recommended.

A Posada Mayor de Migueloa, C Mayor 20, Laguardia, T945 621 175, www. mayordemigueloa.com. A beautifully decorated Spanish country house, with lovely old wooden furniture and a peaceful atmosphere. Rooms are heated and a/c. The restaurant is of a similarly high standard.

C Hotel Antigua Bodega de Don Cosme Palacio, Carretera Elciego s/n, Laguardia, T945 621 195, www.hotelcosmepalacio.com. A wine lover's delight. The old **Palacio Bodega** has been converted into a charming hotel and restaurant, adjacent to the modern winery. The sunny rooms are named after grape varieties, and come with a free ½ bottle. Most rooms feature views over the vines and mountains beyond and have a/c to cope with the fierce summer heat. The rates are reasonable too.

D Hostal Biazteri, C Berberana 2, Laguardia, T941 600 026, www.biazteri.com. Run by the owners of the bar on the corner, this is a very airy and pleasant place to stay. Rooms are spacious, comfortable and reasonably priced. Breakfast is included.

E Larretxori, Portal de Páganos s/n, Laguardia, T945 600 763, larretxori@ euskaltel.net. This comfortable *agroturismo* is just outside the city walls and commands excellent views over the area. The rooms are spruce, clean and good value and the owner is very benevolent.

⊙ Eating

La Rioja Alavesa *p124*
♦♦♦ **Mesón La Cueva**, Concepción 15, Oyón (La Rioja), T945 601 022. If you're visiting wineries over this way, a hearty lunch here is in order. It's a place with a lofty and deserved reputation in the heart of the village, with a new upstairs *comedor* which is light and airy, a significant improvement. The *menú* is €22 but features some excellent Riojan staples, such as *pochas* (young broad beans) and other hearty stews. Recommended.

♦♦♦ **Castillo El Collado**, Paseo El Collado 1, Laguardia, T945 621 200. There's an excellent, well-priced restaurant with 3 attractive eating areas in this beautiful fortified hotel at the northern end of Laguardia.

♦♦ **El Bodegón**, Travesía Santa Engracia 3, Laguardia, T945 600 793. Tucked away in the middle of old Laguardia is this cosy restaurant, with a €11 *menú del día* focusing on the hearty staples of the region, such as *pochas* (beans) or *patatas con chorizo*.

♦♦ **Marixa**, C Sancho Abarca s/n, Laguardia, T945 600 165. In the **Hotel Marixa**, the dining room boasts great views over the vine-covered plains below and has a range of local specialities with formally correct Spanish service.

⊙ Bars and clubs

La Rioja Alavesa *p124*
Café Tertulia, C Mayor 70, Laguardia. With couches, padded booths and a pool table, this is the best place for a few quiet drinks in Laguardia.

⊙ Shopping

Laguardia *p124*
La Vinoteca, Plaza Mayor 2, T945 621 213. A worthwhile wine shop in the centre of town.

⊙ Transport

Salinas de Añana *p122*
Bus 5 buses daily from **Vitoria** bus station.

Salvatierra *p123*
Bus There are **Burundesa** buses hourly from **Vitoria** bus station to Salvatierra, 40 mins.

Gorbeia p123
Bus There are 4-5 daily buses to Murguia from **Vitoria** bus station.

La Rioja Alavesa p124
Bus There are 3-4 daily buses to Laguardia from **Vitoria** bus station (1 hr 45 mins). These run via **Haro** and proceed to **Elciego** and **Logroño**. There's 1 daily bus from **Bilbao** that stops here (1 hr 45 mins, €11.05), but no return service; you'd have to go to **Vitoria** or **Logroño**.

Contents

Footprint features

Navarra

At a glance

⊖ **Getting around** Pamplona is most easily reached via Bilbao. Bus services around the province are alright, but grab a car to explore the Pyrenees.
⊙ **Time required** A week.
☼ **Weather** Hot summers in the south, cool in the mountains. Pamplona gets very chilly in winter.
✕ **When not to go** Late Jul: Pamplona's still in its post-fiesta hangover and many places are shut.

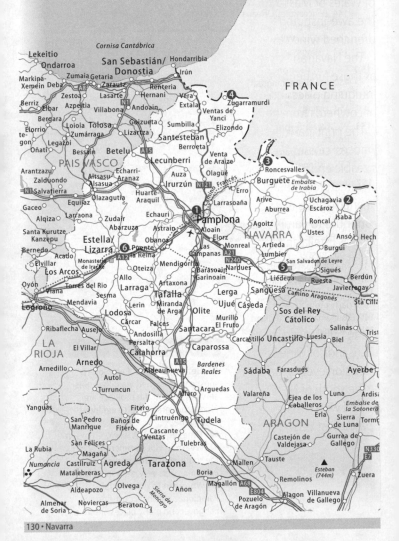

★ **Don't miss ...**

1 Running with the bulls in Pamplona, page 136.
2 Roncal Valley, page 143.
3 The long walk to Santiago from Roncesvalles, page 144.
4 Zugarramurdi, a hotbed of witches, page 146.
5 San Salvador de Leyre, page 151.
6 Estella, page 153.

Golfo de Bizkaia

Cornisa Cantábrica

Lekeitio
Ondarroa
San Sebastián/Donostia
Hondarribia
Irún
FRANCE

Markina-Xemein
Zumaia Getaria
Deba
Zarautz
Renteria
Hernani
Vera
Zugarramurdi ④
Berriz
Zestoa
Lasarte
Andoain
Elbar
Azpeitia
Villabona
Goizueta
Extalar
Ventas de Yanci
Bergara
Loiola Tolosa
Lizartza
Sumbilla
Elizondo
Elorrio-tegon
Zumárraga
Santesteban
Berroeta
Oñati
Legazpi
Bessain
Betelu
Lecunberri
Venta de Araize
PAIS VASCO
Arantzazu
Zalduondo
Altsasu
Echarri-Aranaz
Auza
Olagüe
Roncesvalles ③
Burguete
Embalse de Irabia
N1 Salvatierra
Alsasua
Huarte-Araquil
Irurzún
Erro
Arive
Aburrea
Uchagavia
Escároz
Isaba ②
Gaceo
Equilaz
Olazagutia
Larrasoaña
Agoitz
Roncal
Ustes
Alqiza
Lar.aona
Zudair
Echauri
Astrain
Aloain
Pamplona ①
Elorz
Artieda
Lumbier
Burgui
Ansó
Hech
NAVARRA
Santa Kurutze Kanzepu
Abarzuza
Obanos
Las Campanas
Monreal
San Salvador de Leyre ⑤
Bernedo
Estella/Lizarra ⑥
Puente la Reina
Mendigorría
Barásoain
Garinoain
Nardues
Sigüés
Elvillar
Monasterio de Iroche
Oteiza
Artaxona
Liédena
Ruesta
Berdún
Los Arcos
Allo
Larraga
Tafalla
Lerga
Sangüesa
Javierregay
Oyón
Torres del Rio
Sesma
Miranda de Arga
Ujué Cáseda
Camino Aragonés
Sta. Cilla
Viana
Mendavia
Lerin
Olite
Logroño
Lodosa
Cárcar
Falces
Murillo El Fruto
Sos del Rey Católico
LA RIOJA
Ribaflecha
Ausejo
Andosilla
Peralta
Santacara
Carcastillo
Uncastillo
Luesia
Biel
Salinas
Trist
El Villar
Calahorra
Caparossa
Sádaba
Farasdués
Ayerbe
Arnedo
Aldeanueva
Bardenes Reales
Arnedillo
Autol
Arguedas
Valareña
Ejea de los Caballeros
Luna
Ardisa
Embalse de la Sotonera
Turruncun
Alfaro
Erla
Sierra de Luna
Torm
Yanguas
Fitero
Cintruénigo
Tudela
Castejón de Valdejasa
Gurrea de Gallego
San Pedro Manrique
Baños de Fitero
Cascante
Ventas
Tulebras
Mallen
Tauste
N330
E7
La Rubia
San Félices
Magaña
Agreda
Tarazona
Boria
Añón
Magallón
Esteban (744m)
Remolinos
Alagon
Zuera
Numancia
Castilruiz
Matalebreras
Olvega
Sierra del Moncayo
A68
E804
Villanueva de Gallego
Almenar de Soria
Aldeapozo
Noviercas
Beraton
Pozuelo de Aragón
ARAGON

Navarra was for many centuries a small independent kingdom, and an important player in the complex diplomacy of the period. These days as a semi-autonomous province with the same boundaries, it preserves that independent feeling and has plenty of pride in its history. Although fairly small (it's about half the size of Wales or Massachusetts), it's stuffed full of things to see, from the awe-inspiring Pyrenees to dusty, castled plains and sun-drenched wine country.

The Navarran Pyrenees are beautiful, if not quite as spectacular as those further to the east. A series of remote valleys make intriguing places to explore, summer pastureland for generations of cowherds from both sides of the border.

The principal route of the pilgrims to Santiago, the Camino Francés, crosses Navarra from east to west and has left a sizeable endowment of some of the peninsula's finest religious architecture. Entering the province at Roncesvalles, where Charlemagne's rearguard was given a nasty Basque bite, it continues to Pamplona and thence through small attractive towns such as Estella and Viana. It's not all hard work though; at one lunch stop there's a drinking fountain that spouts red wine.

In the midst of it all is Pamplona, a pleasant and sober town that goes berserk for nine days in July for the Fiesta de los Sanfermines, of which the best-known event is the daily *encierro*, or running of the bulls, made famous by Hemingway and more recently by thousands of wine-swilling locals and tourists looking scared on television every year.

The south of Navarra is much more Castilian; sun-baked and dotted with castles, it produces some tasty red wines and some of Spain's best vegetables along the banks of the Río Ebro.

Pamplona/Iruña

→ Colour map 3, B4. Phone code: 948. Population: 198,491. Altitude: 444 m.

Pamplona, the capital of Navarra, conjures images of wild drunken revelry and stampeding bulls. And rightly so; for that is exactly what happens for nine days every July, Los Sanfermines. Love it or hate it, if you're around you have to check it out. At other times Pamplona is quite a subdued but picturesque city, its high-walled old town very striking when approached from below. It's a good place to stop over, with plenty of good accommodation and eating options; you can do pinchos Basque-style or sit down to a huge Castilian roast. ▸▸ For listings, see pages 138-142.

Ins and outs

Getting there Pamplona is easily reached by bus or train from major cities in Spain and from most places in the northeast of the country. There are several daily flights with **Iberia** from Madrid and Barcelona to Pamplona airport, 7 km away. There's no bus service from the airport into town; a taxi will cost about €10. ▸▸ See Transport, page 142.

Getting around Walking around Pamplona is the best option; the only time you might want to use the city buses is to reach the Hospitales district where the stadium, planetarium and several hotels and *pensiones* are located. Numerous buses plough up and down Avenida Pío XII connecting the Hospitales district with the centre. You can get on them at Avenida Carlos III, near Plaza del Castillo. The **RENFE** train station is inconveniently situated a couple of kilometres north of town, but is connected every 10 minutes by bus.

Orientation Pamplona is an easy city to get the hang of: the walled old town perches over the plain above the Río Arga. To the south and west stretch the Ensanches, the newer town, which radiates outwards along avenues beginning near the Ciudadela, a large bastion turned public park.

Best time to visit **Los Sanfermines** are the best time to visit for atmosphere; it's difficult to describe just how big a party it is. Whatever you do, don't visit immediately afterwards (ie mid- to late July); everything's shut and the city seems sunk in a post-party depression. ▸▸ See also the boxes on pages 136 and 137.

Tourist information Pamplona has an excellent **tourist office** ① Plaza de San Francisco s/n, T848 420 420, www.turismo.navarra.es, Mon-Sat 0900-1800, Sat 0900-1400, 1600-1800, Sun 1000-1400; during Los Sanfermines daily 0800-2000.

Background

The Pamplona area was probably settled by Basques, who gave it the name Iruña/Iruñea, but the city's definitive founding was by the Roman general Pompey, who set up a base here around 74 BC while campaigning against the renegade Quintus Sertorius, who had set himself up as a local warlord. No shrinking violet, Pompey named the city after himself (Pompeiopolis). The city flourished due to its important position at the peninsula's doormat, but was sacked time and again by Germanic tribes. After a period of Visigothic control, it was taken by the Moors in AD 711, although the inhabitants were allowed to remain Christian. There was more territorial exchange and debate before the final

The kingdom of Navarra

While the area has been populated for millennia, the historical entity of Navarra emerged in the ninth century after periods of Basque, Roman, Visigothic, Moorish and Frankish control as part of the Reconquista, the Christian battle to drive the Moors southwards and out of the peninsula. Under the astute rulership of King Sancho III in the early 11th century, Navarra was unified with Castilla and Aragón, which meant that Sancho ruled an area extending from the Mediterranean right across to Galicia; not for nothing is he known as 'the Great'. After his death things began to disintegrate, and provinces were lost left, right but not centre until in 1200, when it had roughly the boundaries it has today, but including Basse-Navarre, now in France. In 1512, King Fernando of Aragón (Regent of Castilla following his wife's death) invaded Navarra and took it easily.

In the 19th century, after centuries of relative peace, things kicked off, first with Napoleon's invasion, then with the rise of the liberal movement and Carlism. These events were always likely to cause schisms in the province, which already had natural divisions between mountains and plains, and families who were Basque, French, or Spanish in alignment. Navarra became the centre of Carlism and suffered the loss of most of its rights as a result of that movement's defeat. During the Civil War, the Carlists were on Franco's side; the province was favoured during his rule, in contrast to the other Basque provinces, which had taken the Republican side.

Today, as a semi-autonomous province, the divisions continue; many Basques are striving for the union of Navarra with Euskadi, but the lowland towns are firmly aligned with Spain. Navarra's social and political differences are mirrored in its geography; it is (to use a cliché) a land of contrasts. The northern and eastern parts of the province are dominated by the Pyrenees and its offshoots, and are lands of green valleys and shepherd villages, which are culturally very Basque. The baking southern and central plains seem to reflect the dusty days of the Reconquista and are more Castilian Spanish in outlook and nature.

emergence of the Kingdom of Pamplona in the ninth century. Sacked and destroyed by the feared caliph of Córdoba Abd-al-Rahman in AD 924, the city only gradually recovered, hampered by squabbling between its municipalities.

Pamplona's rise to real prominence ironically came when Navarra was conquered by Castilla; Fernando built the city walls and made it the province's capital. After a turbulent 19th century, Pamplona expanded rapidly through the 20th century, necessitating the development of successive *Ensanches* (expansions) south and west of the old centre.

Sights

Plaza del Castillo

At the southern entrance to the old town is the pedestrianized Plaza del Castillo, centre of much of the city's social life. Before the Plaza de Toros was built, the bullfights were held in this square. Behind the square to the east is the famous cobbled **Estafeta**, the main runway for the bulls during Los Sanfermines; it's lined with shops and bars. It's amazing how narrow it can look when six bulls are charging down it towards you. At the famous corner where the bulls turn into Estafeta, the new **Museo del Encierro** ① *C Mercaderes 17*,

Pamplona/Iruña

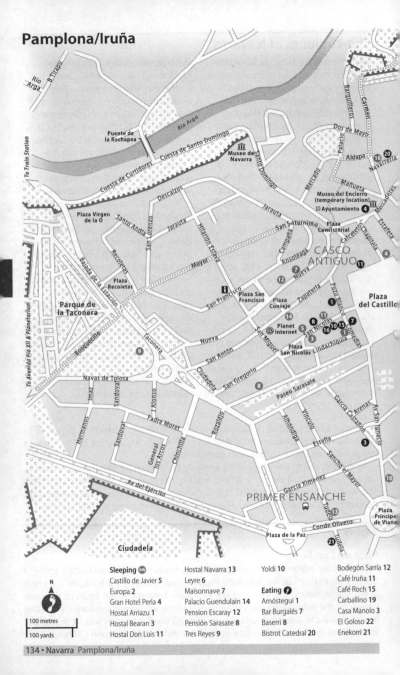

T948 225 413, Mon-Fri 1000-1400, 1600-2000, Sat-Sun 1200-2000, €10, has history and photos of the running of the bulls as well as several audiovisual exhibits including simulators that give you some of the idea of the *encierro* itself. This is just a temporary location, with the real museum due to open near the bullring some time in 2013.

Cathedral and around
ⓘ *T948 212 594, cathedral and museum, Mon-Sat 1000-1400, 1600-1900 (closed Sat pm in winter), €4.40.*

The quiet, seemingly deserted part of town east of the Plaza del Castillo is dominated by the cathedral. Don't be daunted by the rather austere 18th-century façade, as the interior is a masterpiece of delicate Gothic work. Facing the front, the entrance is up the street to your right. First stop is the gorgeous cloister, a superb space full of delicate harmony with excellent carved reliefs on some of the doorways leading off it. The cathedral itself, which is similarly impressive, houses the tombs of Carlos III ('the noble') of Navarra and his queen. The **Diocesan museum** is located in what used to be the larder, kitchen and dining room, and now holds a reasonably interesting selection of artefacts.

Behind the cathedral, past the shady **Plaza de San José**, is the tranquil corner of **El Caballo Blanco**, named after the inviting bar that looks over the ramparts. Walking down the east wall from here you'll reach the **Plaza de Santa María la Real**, another peaceful spot, overlooked by the archbishop's palace.

Plaza Consistorial and around
The centre of town is occupied by the small Plaza Consistorial, seat of the pretty baroque **Ayuntamiento**, where the crowd gathers to watch the start of Los Sanfermines. Down the hill from here, near the market, is the impressive **Museo de Navarra** ⓘ *Tue-Sat 0930-1400, 1700-1900, Sun 1100-1400, restricted opening during Los*

Fiesta de San Fermín

Better known in English as the 'running of the bulls', the nine-day Fiesta de San Fermín lays a serious claim to being the biggest party in Europe. The city goes completely *loca*, and the streets and bars burst with locals and tourists clad traditionally in white with red neckscarves, downing beer and wine with abandon while dancing to the music pumping from a dozen different sources.

It's quite possible to lose a week of your life here and never set eyes on a bull, but it's the *encierros* (bull-runnings) that add the spice. It's difficult to imagine any other country allowing over three tons of bullflesh to plough through a crowd of drunken citizens, but it happens here at 0800 every morning of the fiesta. The streets are barricaded and six bulls are released to run from their *corral* to the Plaza de Toros. If they keep in formation and don't get panicked or distracted they'll only take three minutes to cover the course, but if they find a buttock or two to gore along the way, they can be on the streets for 10 minutes or more. Rockets are let off; the first is single and signals the release of the bulls; the next, a double, means that they've all left the *corral*; and the triple is fired after they've arrived at the bullring and have been safely penned. For good measure, a few cows (with covered horns) are then released into the ring. They always toss a few people, to the amusement of the large crowd. That evening the bulls are fought in the daily *corrida*.

The festival kicks off each year on 6 July at the Ayuntamiento, with a rocket (*El Chupinazo*) fired at midday and cries of '¡Viva San Fermín!'. The saint himself was a Roman convert to Christianity who became the first bishop of Pamplona. The day proceeds with a procession of larger than life papier mâché headed figures (*cabezudos y gigantes*) who parade through town. 7 July is the biggest day with the first *encierro*, but there are plenty of things going on all week, with live bands, processions, street performers, fireworks and more. Especially noticeable are the *peñas*, large social clubs that travel Spain to find a party. Boisterous and with their own brass section, their colourful parades are a feature of the week.

When you come to Los Sanfermines, give it a little time. It can be overwhelming, and there's plenty to dislike: the stench of stale beer and urine, crowds, inflated prices ... but it's enjoyable and addictive. It's also easy to get away from the hectic atmosphere – walk a few streets into the new town, and you can mix with jovial locals enjoying an equally good-natured, but more civilized, party.

One of the best aspects of the festival is that it's still a fiesta with a strong local flavour. While things are busiest from 1900, it's great to wander around during the day, seeking out little pockets of good time in the quiet backstreets. It's a time for family and friends to get together too; you'll see long tables set up in unlikely places for massive alfresco meals.

Animal rights campaigners have correctly highlighted that the *encierro*, with its crowds and noise, is a stressful experience for the poor beasts involved. As an alternative, PETA (People for the Ethical Treatment of Animals) organize a festive protest on the 5 July. **The Running of the Nudes** (www.runningofthenudes. com) is exactly what it sounds like – a light-hearted clothing-optional fun run with an anti-bullfighting agenda.

The festival finally ends at midnight on 14 July, again at the Ayuntamiento, with a big crowd chanting the '*Pobre de mí*' (poor me), mourning the end of the fiesta. For practical information, see box, page 137.

Los Sanfermines: party protocol

Accommodation Prices literally triple during the fiesta, and rooms should be booked several months in advance. If you're too late, don't worry; there are rooms available on an impromptu basis – check noticeboards at the bus and train stations, the tourist office and the newspaper. The official campsite is packed, but more secure than the free areas set up by the council to the east of town. If all else fails, sleep out – you'll be in good company and there are plenty of green areas south of the centre or under the walls. The other option is to get a room out of town, party all night and crawl back on the bus in the morning. It's much easier to get rooms for later in the fiesta than for the first few days.

Bulls Even if you aren't going to run, come prepared to. Enthused by the revelry and a few drinks the worse for wear, it may suddenly seem like an excellent idea. Wear decent shoes; the cobbled streets are slippery, even before they hose them down. Walk the course beforehand and pick a sensible place to start your run. The tight corner at the bottom of Calle Estafeta is where most carnage occurs, with bulls and people slipping all over the shop. Get there well before the start; women should keep a lowish profile, as the police still aren't too keen for women to run. Carry something disposable – chucking a cap or a newspaper can distract a bull if you're in trouble. Don't try to attract a bull's attention; once separated from the herd they are far more dangerous. It's much better to run later in the week; on the first two days there are too many people falling over each other. Try to watch an *encierro* so you have an idea of what goes on. Above all, respect the bulls as the large, fast, lethal animals they are. People often get seriously injured, occasionally fatally. If you're not from the EU, remember that your travel insurer will probably laugh if you try to claim medical expenses for a horn wound.

Pitching a spot Watching the *encierro* can be an anti-climax. It's tough to get a good spot and even if you get one, you may not see much; it's often all over in a blur. The best spots are the private balconies along Calle Estafeta, but you'll have to pay – check for notices on the buildings. Otherwise, grab a seat on the wooden barriers. You're not allowed on the front fence, only the second one. Get there at least two hours beforehand. If you want to watch the final frolic in the ring, you'll need to queue well in advance.

Tickets You can buy bullfight tickets for that day and the next at the Plaza de Toros. These get snapped up, so you may have to buy from scalpers, who drop their prices rapidly once the *corrida* is underway. Avoid the cheap seats as they often degenerate into rowdy food fights.

Eating and drinking Prices are predictably high during Los Sanfermines and it can be tough to find space without a reservation. Most people live off *bocadillos*, which are available all over the place, with decreasing prices as you move away from Calle Estafeta. Plenty of shops stay open all night. The centre is pretty chaotic, with people drinking and relieving themselves on the street, but walk a few blocks to the new town and you'll find an equally good atmosphere, but with far more scope for tapas and restaurant meals.

Parking There are a couple of free parking areas on the approach roads to town – comparatively secure. Cars cannot enter the old town during the fiesta.

Safety San Fermín is Christmas for pickpockets. Don't carry a bag if you can help it, and watch your pockets in the crowds. Although the atmosphere can get volatile, there's remarkably little violence. See also box, page 136.

Sanfermines, €2, free on Sat afternoon and Sun, set in a stately former convent hospital. The museum contains a wide range of material, from prehistoric remains on the ground floor through to modern Navarran art at the top. There are a few Goyas, as well as much religious art that has been gathered from the many provincial churches and monasteries.

Primer Ensanche

The Primer Ensanche, the city's earliest expansion, lies immediately to the south of Plaza del Castillo. The Avenida de San Ignacio has a statue depicting the saint, founder of the Jesuit order, wounded while defending the city; the wounds more or less led to his conversion. This avenue ends at the busy **Plaza Príncipe de Viana**; a short way to the west, the bus station stands on the offbeat **Plaza de la Paz**. Beyond the old town, in the Primer Ensanche, stretches the pentagonal wall of the **Ciudadela**, a low military bastion constructed by Felipe II; it houses a chapel and a small arms exhibition. The newer parts of town south of here are blessed with plenty of green space.

Back on the edge of the old town, the **Plaza de Toros** is the first thing you see after winding up the Bajada de Labrit into town from the Puente de la Magdalena, where the pilgrims cross the river. It's no exaggeration to say that Hemingway's novel *Fiesta (The Sun Also Rises)* has had a massive impact on Pamplona's prosperity over the years, so it's fitting that there's a bust of him in front of the ring – the street outside is also named after him.

◉ Pamplona/Iruña listings

For Sleeping and Eating price codes and other relevant information, see Essentials pages 31-39.

◉ Sleeping

Pamplona *p132, map p134*
There are scores of budget options around the old town and along Av Pío XII in the Hospitales district; look for signs saying '*camas*' above bars and restaurants. The codes given here do not apply for San Fermín, when prices treble at least. At other times, finding accommodation is never a problem.
LL Gran Hotel Perla, Plaza del Castillo 1, T948 223 000, www.granhotellaperla. com. Where Hemingway lay his bearded head when he came to town, the Perla is right on the square and has recently been converted from dilapidation to a most elegant 5-star hotel, beautifully lit at night. Rooms all have balconies looking out on to Estafeta, another street, and/or the plaza, and are most spacious, with elegant period furniture. The helpful staff are particularly welcoming and there's an excellent restaurant.

L Palacio Guendulain, C Zapatería 53, T948 225 522, www.palacioguendulain.com. In the heart of old Pamplona, this noble old palace has been recently converted into a plush boutique hotel, with period furnishings and a selection of handsome carriages. Service is excellent, with little details normally absent in larger, more impersonal places. The rooms are spacious, with super-comfortable beds and luxurious bathrooms. Recommended.
AL Tres Reyes, C Taconera s/n, T948 226 600, www.hotel3reyes.com. This giant hotel towers over the edge of the old town and its rooms offer plenty of natural light and great views from their lofty position. Its mostly geared for conferences, which, for the leisure traveller translates to excellent facilities, plenty of staff on call, and weekend rates that are very good value, up to 50% cheaper with advance booking.
A Maisonnave, C Nueva 20, T948 222 600, www.hotelmaisonnave.es. A sleek but friendly modern hotel with comfortable furnishings, a decent café and a sauna among other amenities. The a/c rooms are

equipped with every comfort and are pretty good value for this type of facility, with some good out-of-season specials.

B Hotel Europa, C Espoz y Miña 11, T948 221 800, www.hreuropa.com. If there's a hint of the self-satisfied about this place, they have good reason – it is a small and superbly located hotel just off the Plaza del Castillo, with balconies overlooking C Estafeta (the main drag of the bull-running). The restaurant is also one of the better ones in town.

C Hotel Castillo de Javier, C San Nicolás 50, T948 203 040, www.hotelcastillodejavier. com. This hotel has a great central location. It's decorated with a light modern touch; the rooms are smallish but comfortable, with funky modern art on the walls. There are several nice touches throughout, and rooms have TV and telephone; for a little more cash you can have a hydromassage shower in the bathroom. Downstairs there's a café/bar and 1 room is equipped for disabled travellers.

C Hotel Leyre, C Leyre 7, T948 228 500, www.hotel-leyre.com. Although furnished in fairly unimaginative 3-star standard style, this hotel is close to the bullring and offers plenty of comfort and facilities. It's handy for both the old and new towns, and offers very good and notably friendly service.

C Hotel Yoldi, Av San Ignacio 11, T948 224 800, www.hotelyoldi.com. Hemingway stayed here after his friend Juanito Quintana lost his hotel, La Perla, during the Civil War. It happily offers modern comforts with surprisingly reasonable prices. The rooms are a/c and spacious, if a little unimaginatively furnished. They have good facilities.

D Hostal Arriazu, C Comedias 14, T948 210 202, www.hostalarriazu.com. Offering more than your average *hostal*, this is a boutique option close to the Plaza del Castillo. Prices are high, but you get rooms that have polished parquet floors and firm beds. It sometimes feels more like a homestay, and you have the run of the sitting room area.

D Hostal Bearan, C San Nicolás 25, T948 223 428. One of the better equipped of the several *hostales* on this street, this

has spacious doubles with good heating and decent bathrooms. The rooms have simple but modern furnishings, and with the location, are reasonable value, though not for single travellers. Facilities include hairdryers and free Wi-Fi though it doesn't work in all rooms. Ask in the bar next door if there's nobody around.

D Hostal Navarra, C Tudela 9, T948 225 164, www.hostalnavarra.com. Bright modern *hostal* with hotel-standard rooms just around the corner from the bus station and a short walk from the old town. There's free Wi-Fi and helpful management. No lift.

E Hostal Don Luis, C San Nicolás 24, T948 210 499. Despite a ragged exterior and dodgy staircase, this central option is very comfortable and well furnished. The double rooms have colourful pastel walls and comfy sofa. If there's nobody about, ask in the café of the same name up the street near the Plaza del Castillo.

E Pensión Escaray, C Nueva 24, T948 227 825. This simple little place is a likeable basic budget option. Run by a solicitous mother-son combination, it has clean and fairly unadorned rooms with shared bathroom. There's a fair difference in quality between the rooms on the 2 different floors.

E Pensión Sarasate, Paseo Sarasate 30, T948 223 084, pensionsarasate@wanadoo.es. A small, quiet and friendly *pensión* with well-cared-for rooms in the heart of things. This is one of Pamplona's best budget options. The rooms vary; some have balcony; all are decorated in a cheerful and homely style. Recommended.

Camping

Ezcaba, Ctra N121 Km 7, on the road to Irún, T948 330 315, www.campingezcaba.com. The closest campsite to Pamplona, with a pool and a few caravans. It's absolutely packed during Los Sanfermines. There's a bike path running from here to town.

✪ Eating

Pamplona *p132, map p134*

¶¶ Amóstegui, C Pozo Blanco 20, T948 224 327. A traditional and central upstairs restaurant that serves excellent Navarran cuisine. Try some fresh asparagus or artichokes if they're in season, but only go for the fresh foie gras if you fancy something seriously rich. Other specialities of the house include pigeon and *zarzuela* (fish stew). Politely formal service.

¶¶ Enekorri, C Tudela 14, T948 230 798, www.enekorri.com. One of Pamplona's gourmet temples, this is modishly lit and a place to be seen hereabouts. Tuna with cherry gazpacho was a taste sensation last time we passed by, but the meats are beautifully treated and presented too. It's haute cuisine without too much frippery. Recommended.

¶¶ Josetxo, Plaza Principe de Viana 1, T948 222 097, www.restaurantejosetxo.com. Closed Sun and Aug. One of Pamplona's most refined restaurants, with wines to match. The *txangurro* (spider crab) stuffed in its own shell is one of a number of outstanding dishes that focus on Navarran tradition rather than current fashions.

¶¶ Bistrot Catedral, C Navarrería 20, T948 210 152, www.bistrotcatedral.com. The artistic modern design of this small place near the cathedral, all CDs, cable curtains and cork chairs and tables, isn't let down by the food, which features exquisitely presented *pinchos* and *raciones*: try the sauteed vegetables and mushrooms with egg yolk. It's also a good place for a *copa*: the G&Ts stand out.

¶¶ Carballino, C Los Teobaldos 2, T948 224 895. A smart modern *pulpería* serving good calamari and octopus with a minimum of fuss and a Galician flair. It's a little away from the hectic centre and can be a good escape during Los Sanfermines.

¶¶ Casa Manolo, C García Castañón 12, T948 225 102. A dependable 2nd-floor restaurant proudly presenting Navarran specialities like *pichón estofado con pochas* (braised pigeon with beans). Good service.

¶¶ El Goloso, C Aoiz 12, T948 291 973. It's worth seeking out this stylish modern new town tapas bar for its relaxed but modish decor, buzzy atmosphere, and excellent array of plates, from tiny snacks to substantial portions of succulent meat and fish, all beautifully presented. Great value. If you're in the area, drop in too to the Trastienda del Colmado at C Iturralde y Suit 24, for excellent traditional food with a modern twist.

¶¶ Otano, C San Nicolás 5, T948 227 036, www.casaotano.com. Popular, attractive and central, this upbeat restaurant has tables overlooking one of Pamplona's livelier weekend streets. It specializes in its roast meats, but if there's *rodaballo* (turbot) about, definitely consider it. There's a good-value €18 *menú* that's also served in the evenings midweek and a long list of scrumptious desserts. The bar downstairs is great, with friendly service and tasty *pinchos*. The *tortilla* is superb. Recommended.

¶¶ San Nicolás, C San Nicolás 13, T948 221 319. On one of Pamplona's main eat streets, this bistro-style set-up has a small but attractive back dining area where you can chow down on tasty French-inspired Basque fare at fair prices. Good mixed salads, rich duck confit, and good-value Navarran wines make this a worthwhile experience.

¶ Bar Burgalés, C Comedias 5, T948 225 158. Recently refurbished, this spot has a fair bit of history behind it. A long curving bar now supports some rather untraditional fare, with elaborate gourmet creations alongside more typical fritos and rolls. It's all delicious.

¶ Baserri, C San Nicolás 32, T948 222 021. This popular chess-board patterned restaurant serves a good value *menú del día* (€15) daily except Sun and nightly except Fri and Sat. A more elaborate menu is served at other times. The bar does a good range of *pinchos*.

¶ Bodegón Sarría, C Estafeta 52, T948 227 713. Rows of quality ham hanging from the ceiling; you can try *pinchos* at the bar or sit at the wooden tables and snack on *raciones*, which also include tripe and stews.

¶Fitero, C Estafeta 58, T948 222 006. Award-winning bites on the main drag, which include an excellent spinach and prawn *croqueta* among other fancy delights.

¶Gaucho, C Espoz y Mina 7, T948 225 073. A buzzy little corner bar with good *pinchos* and strong coffee. It's always busy; there's a great variety of beautifully elaborate fare on the bar. Recommended.

¶Iruñazarra, C Mercaderes 15, T948 225 167. This spacious and convivial Basque tavern has been going for ages. It's a top spot to eat cheap *raciones* at tables at the back; you can accompany them with cider poured from a big barrel. A cheerful mixture of young and old.

¶Monasterio, C Espoz y Mina 11, T948 212 859. Next door to **Gaucho**, this lacks nothing by comparison; it's longer, more brightly lit and more modern in feel but has equally fine snacks, all labelled.

Cafés

Café Iruña, Plaza del Castillo 44, T948 222 064. This marvellous spot on the square is a beautifully refurbished Pamplona classic with its magnificent belle epoque interior. It's got everything; reasonably priced coffee, tasty *pinchos*, a to-be-seen-on terrace, and a good restaurant serving traditional Navarran food and wine.

Café Roch, C Comedias, T948 222 390. Well over a century old, this is a down-to-earth Navarran spot with a real mix of people dropping by throughout the day. Venerable floorboards and a buzz of chatter add to the atmosphere, and little fried morsels vanquish any hunger pangs.

● Bars and clubs

Pamplona *p132, map p134*
The streets in the western part of the old town are full of bars, while C Calderería, C Carmen and around have a vibrant Basque social scene.

Caballo Blanco, Rincón del Caballo Blanco s/n, T948 211 504. Closed Jan/Feb. Pamplona's nicest spot, a fantastic location tucked into a quiet corner of the city walls with views over the ramparts. The bar's in a beautiful stone building, but the beer garden is the place to hang out. Peaceful.

La Barbacoa, C Carmen 2, T948 224 315. This corner spot on the infamous 'Mussel Bar' square is an excellent place for a glass of wine or a *copa*, with an attractive interior, all soft greys and beiges and exposed brick. It's the sort of place where everybody knows each other by name and everybody stays a bit longer than they thought they would.

Toki Leza, C Calderería 5, T948 229 584. Long and simple, this wood and brick bar is one of the liveliest around. It's Basque, and has live music every Sun.

Tropicana, Plaza del Castillo 18, T948 225 398. The best option on the main square, with cold beer and down-to-earth attitudes.

● Entertainment

Pamplona *p132, map p134*
For bull running, see pages 136 and 137.

Cinema and theatre

Cines Carlos III, C Cortes de Navarra, T948 225 595. Handiest cinema for the old town.

Teatro Gayarre, Av Carlos III 3, T948 220 139, www.teatrogayarre.com. This noble old theatre doesn't see as much action as in its heyday, but still has regular shows.

Football

Pamplona's football team, **Osasuna**, www.osasuna.es, are a hardworking and passionately supported club; it's one of the nicer places to go and see a game in Spain, but wrap up well. They play at **Reyno de Navarra** (formerly El Sadar) stadium south of the city; you can get there by taking bus No 5 from Av Carlos III near Plaza Castilla. Tickets are €30-50 and are on sale office hours at the stadium a couple of days before the match, as well as 2 hrs before kick-off.

✴ Festivals and events

Pamplona *p132, map p134*
See San Fermín boxes, pages 136 and 137.

○ Shopping

Pamplona/Iruña *p132, map p134*
Foto Auma, Plaza del Castillo. During Los
Sanfermines, this photography shop has
excellent photos of that day's *encierro*.
Librería Abarzuza, C Santo Domingo 29,
T948 213 213. Sells decent maps of the city.

⊘ Activities and tours

Pamplona *p132, map p134*
Bideak, www.bideak.es. An association of
tour operators who will find the company
that does what you want done, from
architectural tours to canoeing and
horse trekking.
Novotur, C Dra Juana García Orcoyen 1,
T948 383 755, www.novotur.com. One of
several outfits doing guided tours of the city.
The tourist office has a full list.

⊖ Transport

Pamplona *p132, map p134*
Bus Pamplona is the hub for buses in the
area. Destinations include: **Madrid** (Conda,
7-9 daily, €27, 4 hrs 45 mins) via **Soria**
(2 hrs); **Zaragoza** (Conda, 7 daily, 2-2½ hrs);
Bilbao (ALSA/La Burundesa, 7-9 daily,
€14, 2 hrs); **Vitoria** (ALSA/La Burundesa,
9-14 daily, €8, 1½ hrs); **San Sebastián**
(Roncalesa, 8 daily, €7, 2 hrs); and **Jaca/
Huesca** (Roncalesa, 2 daily, Jaca €8, 1 hr,
Huesca €14, 2 hrs).

Train 2 fast trains daily from **Madrid** (3 hrs
10 mins, €55) and 3 to **Zaragoza** (2 hrs,
€19), some continuing to **Barcelona**.

ℹ Directory

Pamplona *p132, map p134*
Internet Kuria Net, C Curia 15, T948
223 077, 1000-2200, €3 per hr. **Medical
services** Hospital de Navarra, C
Irunlarrea s/n, T948 422 100/948 422 212
(emergencies). **Police** Main police station
at C Chinchilla. T112 (emergencies). **Post
office** Paseo de Sarasate s/n. **Telephone**
Locutorio next to the bullring at Paseo
Hemingway s/n, 1000-2230.

Western Pyrenees

Navarra's mountainous north is a series of valleys winding up into the Pyrenees towards France. It's fertile and green in summer, when Basque herders still drive their cattle up to the seasonal pasturelands. The landscapes are spectacular, particularly in the east, where the mountains are more imposing. If you're going to visit one of Navarra's valleys, make it the easternmost, the Valle de Roncal.

Continuing north from Roncal, the slopes of the western Pyrenees rise towards France. The major route of the Camino de Santiago descends to Pamplona from the pass near Roncesvalles, a place of rest for millions of pilgrims over the centuries, which still retains some medieval character. Further north, the river Bidasoa runs through some attractive Basque villages before dividing France and Spain at the coast, while one of its tributaries, the Baztan, runs down a peaceful valley that is also worthy of investigation. ▸▸ *For listings, see pages 147-149.*

Roncal Valley ▸ *For listings, see pages 147-149.*

Navarra's easternmost Pyrenean valley is also its most enchanting. Here, the mountains are really beginning to flex their muscles – it's a popular base for cross-country (and some downhill) skiing in winter. Summer, though, is when it really comes into its own, when flowers bloom from window boxes in the lovable villages, and the cobblestones aren't icy invitations to a sprained ankle.

Izaba/Isaba

While it may be the big smoke of the valley, Izaba is not more than a village. Back from the road that winds along its length are unspoiled stony lanes where sheep are still penned on the ground floors of houses and vegetable patches are tended in the heart of town. There's lots of accommodation too, as it's a popular base for walkers, skiers and cross-border weekenders. The village church, **Iglesia de San Cipriano** towers fortress-like over the settlement, and there's also a local museum. Otherwise, spend a while climbing around the streets, trying to find the perfect photo framing stone houses, geraniums and craggy peaks behind. Izaba has a **tourist office** ⓘ *Mon-Sat 1000-1400, 1630-2000, Sun 1100-1400.*

The valley above Izaba has such lush pastureland in summer that for many centuries French shepherds and cowherds couldn't help themselves and took their flocks over the border to get fat on peninsular grass. After a hard winter, the shepherds in the Roncal Valley were in no mood to be neighbourly, and much strife ensued. Finally, it was agreed that the French would give a gift of three cows to the Navarrans each summer in return for incident-free cud-chewing. The mayor of Izaba, dressed in traditional conquistador-like costume, still collects on it – you can see the two parties solemnly clasp hands on the frontier stone every 13 July at midday, before the Spanish party solemnly select three cows from a frisky herd (sadly, they don't actually keep them any more). If you're going to the ceremony, get there early or be prepared to walk a couple of kilometres, as cars are parked way back down the road on both sides.

Roncal

Down the valley from Izaba is the village of Roncal itself, famous for its sheep's milk cheese. Its another attractive Pyrenean village with crisp mountain air that must have been a boon to its favourite son, Gayarre, a tenor from opera's golden days in the late 19th century. His tomb in the village cemetery is an ornate riot of kitsch, flamboyantly out of place amid the humbler graves of cheesewrights. In December 1889 his voice gave out during a performance in Madrid. Devastated, he said *"Esto se acabó"* (it's all over), and died three weeks later, aged 45. His mausoleum was so well regarded that it went on tour to exhibitions while his poor bones stayed put.

Roncal's **tourist office** ① *Mon-Sat 1000-1400, 1630-2000, Sun 1100-1400, winter Sun-Thu 1000-1400, Fri-Sat 1000-1400, 1600-1930*, has a nature exhibition and is equipped with an internet terminal for public use.

The valley, particularly in its higher reaches, is home to a great variety of wildlife, including rare species such as bear, boar, capercaillie, ptarmigan, chamois and a variety of birds of prey. It offers numerous opportunities for exploring.

West of the Roncal area the Río Salazar, before gouging its way through the Foz de Arbayún, tracks down a low and little-visited valley of beech woods. The main town is Otsagi/Ochagavía, a small place at the point where the Salazar is formed from two tributaries. It seems to have more bridges than it needs – one is a venerable medieval span. On a hill north of town is the Marian **Santuario de Muskildu**.

Roncesvalles/Orreaga and around

→ *For listings, see pages 147-149. Colour map 3, B4. Phone code: 948. Altitude: 924 m.*

On a misty evening the stern ecclesiastical complex at Roncesvalles resembles Colditz, but offers a distinctly warmer welcome to Santiago-bound pilgrims, for whom it is the first stop for pilgrims along the camino francés from the French town of St Jean Pied-de-Port; it was also the last stop for many of Charlemagne's knights including the famous Roland (see box, opposite).

Roncesvalles/Orreaga is little more than the Colegiata church complex, pilgrim hostel, hotel and a couple of *posadas*. It sits just below the Puerto de Ibañeta pass that divides Spain from French Basqueland. Some 3 km closer to Pamplona through an avenue of trees, the village of **Burguete** offers more services, and has been made moderately famous by Hemingway, whose characters Jake and Bill put away several gallons of wine there on a fishing expedition before descending to Pamplona in his novel *Fiesta* (*The Sun Also Rises*).

Sights

A **pilgrim hostel** was originally built in Roncesvalles in 1127. Its fame grew with the growing streams of walkers who were succoured here, aided by the discovery of the Virgin of Roncesvalles, found by a shepherd who was guided to the spot by a deer with Rudolf-style illumination. The statue is said to have been buried to protect it from Moorish raiders. The **Collegiate church** ① *T948 790 480, daily 0800-2100; free, or €4.10 including visit to the Iglesia de Santiago and the Silo, which are otherwise kept closed, these guided tours run 1000-1400, 1530-1900*, that houses the silver-plated statuette is the highlight of the sanctuary, a simple and uplifting example of French Gothic architecture, with blue stained-glass windows and the Virgin taking pride of place above the altar. On her birthday, 8 September, there's a major *romería* (pilgrimage day) and fiesta here. Off the cloister is the burial chapel of the Navarran King Sancho VII ('The Strong'), whose bones were transferred here in 1912. He lies with his wife under a 2.25-m 14th-century alabaster statue of himself that's said to be life size; in the stained-glass depiction of him battling the Moors at the scene of his greatest triumph, Navas de Tolosa, he cuts an imposing figure. A **warhammer** leaning nearby is predictably said to have been Roland's. The small **museum** ① *daily 1000-1400, 1500-1800 (1900 summer, closed afternoons in Jan)*, attached to the complex is less

Charlemagne and Roland

Taking the crown of the Franks in AD 768 at the age of 26, Charlemagne embarked on a lifelong campaign to unite and bring order to western Europe, which resulted in an empire that included France, Switzerland, Belgium, Holland and much of Italy and Germany, as well as the 'Spanish March', a wedge of territory stretching down to the Ebro River. Or so he thought; the locals weren't so sure. Allowing him to pass through their territory to battle against the Moors, the local Basques were outraged at Charlemagne's conduct: he destroyed Pamplona's fortifications after taking it; and accepted a bribe from the city of Zaragoza to return to France. As the army ascended the Ibañeta Pass above Roncesvalles on their way home, their rearguard and baggage train was ambushed and slaughtered by locals. Among the dead was Hrudoland, or Roland, governor of the marches of Brittany, a shadowy historical figure immortalized in the later romantic account of the event, *Le Chanson de Roland*, which blamed the attack on the Moors.

impressive, but has a few interesting manuscripts, as well as a blue-embossed reliquary known as 'Charlemagne's chess set'.

A few paces away from the church complex are two further buildings, the tiny 14th-century **Iglesia de Santiago** and the 12th-century funerary structure known as the **Silo of Charlemagne** ⓘ *see Collegiate church, above for both*. Legend maintains that the Silo was built on the site where Charlemagne buried Roland and his stricken rearguard. Underneath it is a burial pit holding bones of various origins; some may well have been pilgrims for whom the hard climb over the Pyrenees had proved to be a step too far; the bear and wolf population likely also took a toll.

Opposite the complex, there's a **visitor centre** ⓘ *1100-1330, 1600-1900, €1*, which is half an excuse for a shop to keep the steady flow of visitors happy. There's also a small exhibition and audiovisual display on Navarra and the Roncesvalles area.

The Roncesvalles **tourist office** ⓘ *Mon-Sat 1000-1400, 1530-1900 (1500-1800 winter), Sun 1000-1400, T948 760 301*, is attentive and helpful, although queues can be long.

Puerto de Ibañeta

Not far up the road to France is the pass itself, the Puerto de Ibañeta. Here, there's a modern chapel and a **memorial to Roland**. Some say this is where the grieving Charlemagne buried Roland; at any rate the memorial is slightly incongruous, seeing as it was the Navarrans who probably did him in. A more recent and appropriate memorial in Roncesvalles commemorates his vanquishers. Continuing from Puerto de Ibañeta, the valley of **Valcarlos/Luzaide** is seen by many scholars as the most likely location of the battle itself. At the border, the town of the same name is pretty enough but is often overwhelmed with French hopefuls paying over-the-odds prices for Spanish ham and wine.

Burguete/Auritz

The austerity of Roncesvalles continues down the hill in the village of Burguete/Auritz, whose main street is flanked by drains, which give the stone cottages a fortified appearance. A severe church is the town's centrepiece but it's a solid, friendly place to stay with a handful of good-value sleeping and eating options. Hemingway fans will head for the **Hostal Burguete**, which happily seems to have changed little since his day.

Northeast of Pamplona, the road to Irún follows the course of the salmony river Bidasoa, which divides France and Spain at the Bay of Biscay. The road itself is a nightmare of speeding trucks and smelly industry, but the valley houses several likeable villages that are very Basque indeed. Lesaka and Etxalar are charming places; further into the hills Zugarramurdi was a centre of witchcraft in the 17th century, or so the Inquisition thought.

Bera/Vera de Bidasoa
Closest to the coast is Bera/Vera de Bidasoa, a place where you may hear more Euskara than Spanish, and traditionally a hotbed of support for ETA. Below the imposing grey stone church is the Ayuntamiento, with a façade painted with female figures of Fortitude, Temperance, Justice and Prudence, who sometimes seem to dominate this sober town. On the edge of town is the farmhouse where the Basque novelist **Pío Baroja** used to spend his summers; it's still a private home (used by his nephew) and rarely open to the public. The **tourist office** ⓘ *T948 631 222, Mon-Sat 1000-1400, 1600-1900,* is on Calle Errotazar.

Lesaka
Further inland from Bera, a couple of scenic kilometres off the main road, is Lesaka, prettier and more welcoming than its neighbour. Its architectural highlights are a pair of tower houses, but there are several impressive homes, many built by *indianos*, colonists returning with fortunes made in the New World. As in Bera, the stone church looms large over the town, but it seems more at ease amid gardens, brightly blooming windowboxes and tranquil pathways.

Etxalar
Some 3 km off the main road on the other side of Lesaka is peaceful Etxalar, a stone Basque village with a very attractive pinkish church surrounded by circular Basque gravemarkers, widely thought to be a continuation of pre-Christian tradition. There are several *hostales* and *casas rurales* around here.

Zugarramurdi
From Etxalar, a deserted road leads up a spectacular valley and around a couple of hills to Zugarramurdi. On entering this spotless whitewashed village you might think it a place of peaceful rural life, the only corruption to be found in shifty-eyed shopkeepers selling overpriced wine and ham to their fellow Basques from across the border. You'd be wrong.

The Inquisition weren't fooled in 1610 when they turned up. Don Juan del Valle Alvarado, sent from the tribunal at Logroño after hearing of an outbreak of witchery in the area, spent several months investigating here and found the village to be a whitened sepulchre, a seething pit of blasphemy and moral turpitude. He accused over 300 villagers (men, women and children) from the surrounding area of witchcraft, and of committing crimes, including: whipping up storms to sink ships in the Bay of Biscay; eating the dead and the living; conducting black Masses; indulging in various unspeakable acts with Satan in the form of a black goat, and more. As in most of the Inquisition's investigations, denunciations by fellow villagers were the dubious source of most of the evidence. Many people turned themselves in; the punishments were far harsher if you didn't. The most heinous of these contemptible criminals were taken to Logroño and left in prison while the evidence was debated. Many died before the verdicts were announced; their effigies were burned or pardoned accordingly. A total of 12 were sentenced to death.

Five minutes' walk from town is a large **cave complex** ① *summer daily 1000-2100, winter Tue-Sun 1100-1800; €3.50,* said to have been the site for most of the diabolical activity. It certainly would make a fine spot for a black Mass, with an impressive natural tunnel overlooked by viewing galleries. It may well be that non-Christian rituals were practised here: veneration of traditional Basque deities such as Mari, the mother goddess, was still alive well into the 20th century. It's said that in the year of the witch trials, the local priest came to the caves and daubed them with mustard, declaring that the witches would vanish for as many years as there were mustard grains.

Being so close to France, this whole area was (until the EU era) a nest of smuggling, and many marked walking trails in the area would have been used by moonlight. The unwritten contract between police and smugglers was that, if sprung, the smugglers would drop their booty and make themselves scarce. The law, for their part, would hold their fire and take the goods home with them.

◉ Western Pyrenees listings

For Sleeping and Eating price codes and other relevant information, see Essentials pages 31-39.

● Sleeping

Roncal Valley *p143*
There are dozens of places to stay in Izaba and around, many of them *casas rurales*. Check www.toprural.com or www.turismo. navarra.es for some listings of these.
B Hotel Isaba, Ctra Roncal s/n, Izaba, T948 893 000, www.isabaha.com. A modern and friendly hotel at the edge of town, this is Izaba's most upmarket lodging. Recently refurbished, it now offers mainly very slick apartments (**A**), as well as attractive and happily non-standard rooms. Handily situated right next to the municipal swimming pool.
D Onki Xin, Izaba s/n, T618 317 837, www. onkixin.com. A great choice, this warm and welcoming family-run place is in the village itself, and offers enchanting, artistically decorated rooms at a low price. There's plenty of helpful advice on what to do in the area.
E Txabalkua, C Izargentea 16, Izaba, T948 893 083. A peaceful and pretty *pensión* in the middle of the old town. One room has a bathroom; the rest share. Clean and pleasant, with wooden beams and an authentic mountain touch.
F Refugio de Belagua, Ctra Izaba–Francia Km 19, T948 394 002. On the way up to

the French border, this *refugio* looks like a big tent but is a warm base for skiers and walkers year round. Accommodation in huge dorms. Warming meals.

Camping
Camping Asolaze, Ctra Izaba–Francia Km 6, T948 893 034, www.campingasolaze. com. This year-round campsite is 6 km from Izaba but there's pine forest right up to the back door. There are various bungalows sleeping 4 or up to 8.

Roncesvalles/Orreaga and around *p144*
There are plenty of *casas rurales* around Burguete/Auritz should you fail to find a bed.
C Hotel Loizu, Av Roncesvalles 7, Burguete/ Auritz, T948 760 008, www.hotelloizu.com. Closed mid-Dec to mid-Mar. The most upmarket of the places to stay in this area, this is a decently modernized old house in Burguete with reasonable rooms with TV and heating, which can be much needed both in summer and winter. The nicest rooms are on the top floor use stripped-back stone to great decorative effect.
C Hotel Roncesvalles, Roncesvalles s/n, T948 760 105, www.hotelroncesvalles.com. Occupying an 18th-century building that's part of the Roncesvalles complex, this cosy modern hotel offers comfortable rooms,

Patxarán

One of Navarra's most emblematic products is this liqueur, usually taken as a *digestivo* after a meal. Although there are *patxaranes* made from a variety of berries and fruits, the traditional Navarran one, which now has its own DO (*denominación de origen*), is made from sloe berries macerated in an aniseed liquor. Usually served on ice,

the taste can range from the sweet and superbly delicate to medicinal. The name comes from the Euskara word for sloe, *basaran*. Some folk like to mix it: a *San Fermín* is *patxarán* and *cava* (sparkling wine), while a *vaca rosa* (pink cow) is a blend of the liqueur with milk. Adding cinnamon or coffee is another option.

---

and good-value apartments. They offer discounts for pilgrims.

E Hostal Burguete, C San Nicolás 71, Burguete/Auritz, T948 760 005, www.hotel burguete.com. Closed mid-Dec to mid-Mar. The place where Ernest used to hang out, and the base for Jake and Bill's expedition in *Fiesta* (*The Sun Also Rises*). On the main (only) street through Burguete; this is a place with plenty of character and decent double rooms.

E La Posada, Roncesvalles s/n, T948 760 225, www.laposadaderoncesvalles.com. Closed Nov. It feels like an old travellers' inn and it is one, dating from 1612. The best place to stay in Roncesvalles itself with snug, heated en suite rooms. There's also a log fire and a more than decent cheap restaurant.

Camping

Camping Urrobi, Ctra Pamplona–Valcarlos Km 42, T948 760 200, www.campingurrobi. com. Open Apr-Oct. Just below Burguete, this campsite is reasonably equipped and also has bungalows and cheap dormitory beds.

Bidasoa Valley *p146*

There are many cottages for rental, particularly in Etxalar. See www.toprural.com.

C Donamaria'ko Benta, Barrio Ventas 4, Donamaria, T948 450 708, www. donamariako. com. An excellent place to stay for those with transport, this creeper-swathed inn 3 km from the main road beyond the town of Santesteban/ Doneztebe dates from 1815. The welcoming

owners rescued it from dereliction and it's now beautiful, with rustic floorboarded rooms with comfort and style. The adjacent restaurant is excellent.

C Hotel Atxaspi, Bittiria Kalea 24, T948 637 536, Lesaka, www.atxaspi.com. A great source of relaxation and calm, this enchanting spot sits in the middle of Lesaka. There are just 6 rooms, all with original decor – one is a duplex decked out like a ship – and guests have (paid) access to a sauna and jacuzzi area as well as a sweet little terrace overlooking the village.

D-E Hostal Ekaitza, Plaza Berria 13, Lesaka, T948 637 559, www.ekaitzalesaka.com. A highly central place to stay above a bar in the heart of the village, this offers reasonable double rooms with good bathroom; the best rooms have a balcony. Upstairs is a family suite that sleeps 4. It can get noisy at weekends and during the village festival.

● Eating

Roncal Valley *p143*

▼▼ Pekoetxe, Ctra Roncal s/n, Izaba, T948 893 101. An attractive and stylish modern restaurant specializing in grilled meat and fish, featuring a range of other local options.

▼ Txiki, C Mendigatxa 17, Izaba, T948 893 118. Closed May and Nov. A lively and atmospheric local bar and restaurant serving a *menú* for €10.50 that's got few frills but plenty of authentic Navarran taste.

Roncesvalles/Orreaga and around *p144*

While the **Posada** and **Sabina** in Roncesvalles do fine fare with cheap pilgrim menus, if you fancy something a little different, head down to Burguete.

Ψ Loizu, Av Roncesvalles 7, Burguete/Auritz. T948 760 008. This hotel restaurant serves up good warming mountain food with a touch of class. There's a *menú* for €17.

Ψ Burguete, C San Nicolás 71, Burguete/Auritz, T948 790 488. If you've read *Fiesta* you'll be eating here. The piano that Bill played to keep warm is *in situ* in the dining room and, while they may have forgotten how to make rum punch, there is a *menú* for €14.25 that is good value and includes trout, as it should. Pictures of the bearded writer adorn the room but it's thankfully far from being a shrine.

Bidasoa Valley *p146*

ΨΨ Donamaria'ko Benta, Barrio Ventas 4, Donamaria, T948 450 708. Excellent modern cuisine with a homely wood-beamed rustic feel beside one of the best rural hotels in the area. There's a Basque slant to the menu, but there are even some Japanese dishes.

Ψ Ansonea, Plaza de los Fueros 1, Bera, T948 631 155. A well-priced place to try Basque specialities such as *kokotxas* (stewed hake cheeks), or *pimientos rellenos de txangurro* (red peppers stuffed with crab). There's a cheap *menú del día*, internet access, and rooms upstairs.

Ψ Kasino, Plaza Zahorra 23, Lesaka, T948 637 287. This charming building houses a dark, homely restaurant with a terrace. Don't be fooled by the humble surroundings; the *tortilla* here has been voted best in the nation by judges in San Sebastián.

⦿ Bars and clubs

Roncal Valley *p143*

Ttun Ttun, Barrikato s/n, Izaba. A great little bar with a terrace in the back streets. The *ttun-ttun* is a zither-like instrument (literally a psaltery), traditional in these parts.

⦿ Festivals and events

Roncal Valley *p143*
25-28 Jul Izaba's main festival
15 Aug Roncal festival.

Bidasoa Valley *p146*
7 Jul Lesaka is famous for its own San Fermín festival, starting at the same time as Pamplona. The major event is on the morning of 7 Jul, with a dance, the *zubi gainekoa*, performed along both sides of the river to symbolize friendship in the region.
3 Aug The start of Bera's major fiesta.
15 Aug Zugarramurdi festival.

⦿ Transport

Roncal Valley *p143*
La Tafallesa, T948 222 886, run 1 bus from **Pamplona** to Roncal and Izaba, leaving at 1700 Mon-Fri, 1300 Sat and returning Mon-Sat at 0700 (€9). 1 bus from **Pamplona** to Ochagavía (daily, leaving at 1500 Mon-Thu, 1900 Fri, and 1330 Sat. It leaves Ochagavía Mon-Sat at 0900. This changes in winter; phone T948 303 570.

Roncesvalles/Orreaga and around *p144*
Artieda, T948 300 287, run 1 bus from **Pamplona** to Roncesvalles at 1800 Mon-Fri, 1600 on Sat (€6), continuing to **Jaurrieta** Fri and Sat. The return bus leaves Roncesvalles at 0920 Mon-Sat.

Bidasoa Valley *p146*
La Baztanesa run a series of buses up and down the Bidasoa and Baztan valleys. There are effectively 3 buses to and from **Pamplona** daily the whole way, but some need a change. T948 226 712 or T948 580 129.

Camino Aragonés

→ Colour map 3, C4.

Descending from the mountains, pilgrims on the Camino Aragonés usually make Sangüesa their first stop in Navarra. It's a fine little town with more than its fair share of quirky buildings, and within reach are a few other interesting places – the Monasterio de Leyre and Castillo de Javier are steeped in religious history, while the Embalse de Yesa reservoir offers a break from the fierce heat. To the west, around the town of Lumbier, are two gorges of great natural beauty. ▶▶ For listings, see pages 152-153.

Sangüesa/Zangoza → For listings, see pages 152-153.

Originally founded by Romans on a nearby hill, Sangüesa served its apprenticeship as a bastion against the Moors before quieter times saw it moved down to the banks of the cloudy green Río Aragón. Most notable among several impressive structures is the Iglesia de Santa María by the bridge. Sweaty pilgrims trudging into town will be happy to know that in Sangüesa the stench from the nearby paper mill makes all bodily odours fade into insignificance. After an hour or so, it's actually not too bad – plenty of locals swear they miss it when they're out of town.

The **tourist office** ① *opposite the church of Santa María, T948 871 411, Apr-Oct Mon-Sat 1000-1400, 1600-1900, Sun 1000- 1400, Nov-Mar Tue-Sun 1000-1400*, is helpful.

Iglesia de Santa María
① *T620 110 581, tours of this and other churches, summer Mon-Sat 1000-1400, 1600-1800, winter Mon-Sat 1000-1400, €1.95 church only, €4 whole town.*
The church's elaborately carved portal takes Romanesque sculpture to heights of delicacy and fluidity seldom seen elsewhere, although some of the themes covered stray a fair way from lofty religion. The inside is less interesting and annoyingly only accessible by guided tour (the office is at the back of the building). This goes for most of the other buildings in town. The church can be visited independently just before Mass, which is at 1900 in winter and 2000 in summer.

Palacio de Vallesantoro
Sangüesa's town hall is based in the outrageous Palacio de Vallesantoro. The doorway is flanked by two bizarre corkscrew (Solomonic) columns, but it's the macabre overhanging eaves that draw even more attention. They make the building look like a Chinese pagoda, designed after a night of bad dreams. Leering dogs, lions and asses alternate with tortured human figures along the black overhang.

Iglesia de Santiago
① *The church is only opened at Mass times or on the town's guided tour.*
A couple of streets back is the church of Santiago, a late Romanesque building with an impressive fortified tower and several good Gothic sculptures, including one of Saint James himself. He also appears in colour on the building's façade, flanked by two pilgrims who look as though they might have made the journey from the Australian outback.

Off the main street, an elegant arched arcade points the way to the Palacio Príncipe de Viana, formerly a residence of kings of Navarra, while on Calle Alfonso el Batallador, not far from the Ayuntamiento, is a working iron forge that uses fairly traditional methods and specializes in forging individualized tokens for pilgrims. Across the river is a statue of St Christopher, patron saint of travellers, which explains the cut-out of a car that's been strangely attached to it.

Around Sangüesa → For listings, see pages 152-153.

Castillo de Javier
ⓘ *Daily 1000-1300, 1530-1830 (1700-2000 summer), €2.*
Like a lion with its mane plaited, the castle of Javier doesn't seem as formidable as it no doubt once was. Enough of a thorn in the side of Spain for Cardinal Cisneros (also known as Ximénez the Inquisitor) to have commanded its partial destruction, it is better known as the birthplace of the missionary and founding member of the Jesuits, San Francisco Javier. Unlike the birthplace of Francis' former roommate Saint Ignatius, there's not too much ostentatious piety and the castle makes for a good visit. It has been heavily restored; someone foolishly backed a basilica into it in the 19th century, and more work was done in the 1950s, but there's still some feeling of what it might have been like when young Francis roamed its corridors.

Monasterio de San Salvador de Leyre
ⓘ *T948 884 150, Mon-Fri 1015-1400, 1530-1900, Sat 1015-1400, 1600-1900; €2.10; the monks chant offices at 0730, 0900, 1900 and 2110 in the church.*
Off the N240 northeast of Sangüesa, a road winds 4 km through fragrant hills to the Monasterio de San Salvador de Leyre, a stop on the Camino de Santiago. A monastery was first founded here as early as the eighth century AD, but the beautiful, rugged spot – the name means 'eagerness to overcome' in Euskara – had been a favourite haunt of hermits before that. Nothing but foundations remain from that period – the older parts of today's structure date from the 11th and 12th centuries, when the Navarran monarchs took a liking to the spot and made it the seat of their kingdom. The centre flourished with religious and secular power and became extremely wealthy before an inevitable decline began. The abbey was abandoned in the 19th century after loss of monastic privileges and was not re-used until 1954, when it was colonized by Benedictines from the Monasterio de Santo Domingo de Silos.

The church itself is of mixed styles but preserves much simplicity and tranquillity inside, above all when it's filled with the Gregorian chanting of the monks during offices. The structure is remarkably off-kilter – lovers of symmetry and proportion will be appallingly ill-at-ease. The portal is a fascinating 12th-century work, filled with Romanesque scenes. While the main groups are of the Last Judgement, Christ and the Evangelists, the sculptors let their fancy run a bit freer elsewhere – you can spot several interesting demons and nightmarish animals, Jonah getting swallowed, and some lifelike prowling lions. Inside, the centrepiece is the Virgin of Leyre, while the adult Christ is relegated to his customary Spanish place in the wings. A large chest on one wall contains the bones of no fewer than 10 Navarran kings, seven queens and two princes – these were exhumed and boxed in 1915 – their feelings on the matter unrecorded. A small side chapel has a *retablo* in a pleasingly rustic style.

The crypt, accessed from the ticket office, is a weird space, whose stone altar and ram-horned columns suggest darker ritual purposes. The columns all vary and are tiny – it's strange to have the capitals at waist height. Next to the crypt is a tunnel leading to an image of San Virila – a former abbot. This dozy chap wandered up to a nearby stream and was so enchanted by the song of a bird that he didn't make it back for vespers for another three centuries. If you fancy some time out too, follow his lead and head up to the spring, which is signposted five minutes' walk above the complex. If you like the spot, you might consider staying in the attached *hospedería* (see Sleeping, below).

Foz/Hoz de Lumbier

① *Entry is €1.50 when the ticket booth is attended; take swimming gear on a hot day.*

A mile from the small town of Lumbier is the Foz/Hoz de Lumbier, a fashionably *petite* designer gorge. It's a top place, with gurgling stream, overhanging rock walls and a large population of vultures that circle lazily above, in the vain hope that a tourist will drop dead from the heat. Twenty minutes' walk from the car park will get you to the other end of the gorge, where you can see the ruins of the 'Devil's Bridge', destroyed in the Peninsular War but possibly none too safe before that. Return the same way or via a longer circuit around the top of the gorge.

Embalse de Yesa

The N240 continues on into Aragón, following the shore of the Embalse de Yesa reservoir. This is a pretty way to get to the Roncal Valley (see page 143) if you have a car.

The Embalse is a beautiful chalky blue colour and good to swim in (watch for submerged trees – check your spot from higher up the bank). On its north shore is the abandoned village of **Escó**, still proudly beautiful on a hilltop. The villagers had to clear out in 1959 when the reservoir was filled (some villages are completely submerged).

⊙ Camino Aragonés listings

For Sleeping and Eating price codes and other relevant information, see Essentials pages 31-39.

⊙ Sleeping

Sangüesa *p150*
D Hostal JP, Paseo Raimundo Lumbier 3, T948 871 693, www.hostalruraljp.es. A clean, fresh and good option (if slightly hospital-like) just across the river from the Iglesia de Santa María. The rooms are modern and pleasant enough, and have a good bathroom and cable TV. There are also apartments (and, in summer, pilgrim dorm beds) available.

Camping
Camping Cantolagua, Paseo Cantolagua s/n, T948 430 352, www.campingcantolagua.com. A good site by the riverside, with a swimming pool and tennis courts. There are also bungalows, caravans and rooms available at good cheapish rates.

Castillo de Javier *p151*
B Hotel Xabier, Plaza de Javier s/n, Javier, T948 884 006, www.hotelxabier.com. This is the nicer of the 2 hotels in the little touristic

zone by the castle of Javier. The old-style rooms have modern comforts, and there's a reasonable restaurant.

Monasterio de San Salvador de Leyre *p151*
C Hospedería de Leyre, Monasterio de Leyre, T948 884 100, www.hotelhospederiadeleyre.com. With great views over the plains and the reservoir below, and some very nice walks in the scented hills, this monastery hotel offers much more than monastic comfort, as well as some very good meals. The rooms are simple but welcoming; some are larger than others.

⊙ Eating

Sangüesa *p150*
⛶ Mediavilla, C Alfonso el Batallador 15, T948 870 212. A hospitable *asador* with filling *menús* for €19 and €24. There's a range of very tasty roast meat, but plenty of lighter dishes to accompany it.

⛶ Bar Ciudad de Sangüesa, C Santiago 4, T948 871 021. There are several bars on this street – this bar does good cheap meals and is popular with locals. The quality is very high for the price, and the style is traditional, with hearty country food.

¶ El Pilar, C Mayor 87, Sangüesa, T948 870 027. The posh place in town to come for a drink or a coffee, this also offers a selection of gourmet *pinchos*, such as a little pastry basket with local wild mushrooms. There's a terrace in summer.

⊖ Transport

Bus
La Veloz Sangüesina, T948 870 209, runs 3 buses daily to and from **Pamplona** (only 1 on Sun). For the Foz de Lumbier, take a **Río Irati** bus from **Pamplona** to the town of Lumbier, and walk from there (1-3 a day).

Western Pilgrim Route

The two main branches of the Camino de Santiago, the Camino Francés (which has come through Roncesvalles and Pamplona) and the Camino Aragonés (which has tracked through Aragón and Sangüesa) meet at Puente La Reina and continue westwards together. This part of the province is one of Navarra's nicest, with towns such as Estella and Viana joys for the pilgrim or casual traveller to discover. Off the main route, too, are some perfect little villages, while, to top things off, some of Navarra's best wine is made in the area. ►► *For listings, see pages 155-156.*

Puente La Reina/Gares and around → *Colour map 3, C3.*

"And from here all roads to Santiago become only one." While this, inscribed on the monument at the entrance to the village, is not completely true, the two principal pilgrim routes converge here just before reaching the medieval bridge that the town grew around, a long and beautiful Romanesque span that emerges from an arched entrance and speaks of many kilometres to come under a beating sun.

The town is small, and a good place to stop for a night if you're inclined. Arriving from the east, on the outskirts, you'll see the strange monument to pilgrims, a wild-eyed and gaunt bronze figure who might provoke more anxiety than comfort in passing peregrines. The pilgrim hostel isn't much further, and stands next to the 12th-century **Iglesia del Crucifijo**.

In the heart of town is another **church** ① *Mon-Sat 1000-1330, 1700-2000, Sun 0845-1400*, dedicated to Santiago himself. The so-called Matamoros ('Moor killer') might not be too impressed to notice that his doorway looks remarkably Muslim in style with its horseshoe notched recessed portal. Opposite is the fine façade of the **Convento de la Trinidad**. The peaceful centre of the town, the **Plaza Julián Mena**, houses the Ayuntamiento and **tourist office** ① *Tue-Sat 1000-1400, 1530-1830 (1700-2000 summer), Sun 1100-1400*.

Near Puente La Reina, the medieval village of **Obanos** is famous for its biennial staging of a mystery play based on a legend of the Camino.

Estella/Lizarra → *For listings, see pages155-156.*

The major town of western Navarra, Estella is a very likeable place to stay a while. The town likes to dust off the moniker 'the Toledo of the North'; this is a little over-the-top, but its crop of historic buildings are certainly interesting.

Estella's history as a town goes back to 1052 when King Sancho Ramírez, taking ruler and pencil to the burgeoning pilgrim trail, established it as a new stop on the official route.

On a hill, close to the Puente de la Cárcel, on the western bank, the older part of town, is the towering grey bulk of the **Iglesia de San Pedro de la Rúa**, with its crusty façade and indented Romanesque portal. The highlight inside is the semi-cloister. It was here that the Castilian kings used to swear to uphold the Navarran *fueros* after the province was annexed; it was a promise honoured in varying degrees by different monarchs. At time of last research the church was closed for restoration until at least 2012.

Opposite is the **Palacio de los Reyes** ① *Tue-Sat 1100-1300, 1700-1900, Sun 1100-1330, free*, another Romanesque edifice, which now houses a museum devoted to the early 20th-century painter Gustavo de Maeztu, who was influenced by the art nouveau movement and lived his later years in Estella.

Across the river, the **Iglesia de San Miguel** is also set above the town on a hillock. Its most endearing feature is the Romanesque portal, richly carved with a scene of Christ in Majesty surrounded by his supporting cast. It's an impressive work. Like San Pedro, the church is only open by guided tour or about an hour before 2000 Mass (1900 in winter).

The newer part of town centres around the large **Plaza de los Fueros**, overseen by the **Iglesia de San Juan**, a mishmash of every conceivable style. Nearby is the quiet **Plaza de Santiago**, in whose centre four horrible creatures spill water from their mouths into a fountain.

Estella's **tourist office** ① *T948 556 301, Easter-Oct Mon-Sat 1000-1400, 1600-1900, Sun 1000-1400, Nov-Easter Mon-Fri 1000-1700, Sat and Sun 1000-1400*, is next to the Palacio de los Reyes; guided tours of the town depart from here.

Around Estella

A couple of kilometres southwest of Estella, on the way to Ayegui on the Camino, is the **Monasterio de Irache** ① *Tue 0900-1330, Wed-Sun 0900-1330, 1700-1900 (1630-1800 winter)*, the oldest of the original Navarran pilgrim refuges. The light and airy church features an inscrutable Virgin and a bony bit of San Veremundo in a reliquary by the altar.

The monastery is famous for its palatable red table wine, and pilgrims might be tempted to linger on the way here a little: there's a tap at the back of the bodega that spouts red wine for the benefit of travellers on the road, a sight to gladden the heart!

There are numerous **wineries** in the Estella area which are happy to show visitors around. The tourist office provides a list of bodegas (phone beforehand to arrange a visit). One of the quality labels is **Palacio de la Vega** ① *T948 527 009*, in the small town of Dicastillo, south of Estella. The bodega, whose home is a striking 19th-century palace, is a modern producer that has been at the forefront of the successful establishment of French varietals like Cabernet Sauvignon and Merlot in Navarra. A more traditional producer of quality wines is **Bodegas Sarría** ① *based by Puente La Reina, T948 202 200, www.bodegadesarria.com*.

Viana

One of Navarra's loveliest towns, Viana is the last stop before the Camino descends into the oven of La Rioja. Fortified to defend the kingdom's borders against Castilla, it still preserves sections of its walls, rising above the surrounding plains. The **Iglesia de Santa María** has a monumental façade and a high Gothic interior, whose sober interior is enlivened by a great number of ornate baroque *retablos*.

In front of the church is the gravemarker of an unexpected man; Cesare Borgia, a 15th-century Italian noble who could rightly be described as Machiavellian – *The Prince* was largely based on his machinations. Son of a pope, after becoming a cardinal he most probably had his elder brother murdered as part of his scheme, one of a number of opportunistic assassinations he masterminded while conquering significant swathes of Italian territory. It all went pear-shaped for Borgia, though; after having been imprisoned in Spain, Borgia was placed under the protection of the King of Navarra, and he ended up as a minor noble in Viana. He was then elected constable of the town, but was killed in a siege by Castilian forces in 1507, aged, would you believe, only 30.

The atmospheric ruined Gothic church of **San Pedro** sheltered French troops during the Peninsular War before it collapsed in 1844. Viana has a **tourist office** ① *summer Mon-Sat 0900-1400, 1700-1900, Sun 1000-1400, winter Mon-Sat 0900-1400.*

◉ Western Pilgrim Route listings

For Sleeping and Eating price codes and other relevant information, see Essentials pages 31-39.

◉ Sleeping

Puente La Reina/Gares and around *p153*
Puente has a couple of excellent lodging choices. It's close to Pamplona, so prices soar during Los Sanfermines.
AL El Peregrino, C Irunbidea s/n, T948 340 075, www.hotelelperegrino.com. An impressively individual and classy hotel and restaurant on the approach to town. Packed with arty objects and quirky architectural kinks, but with a comfortable stone-and-wood feeling. Lovely pool and surrounding terrace. The restaurant is of a very high standard. Despite the name, one senses eyebrows might rise if a road-weary pilgrim with backpack and staff actually ventured inside.
C Bidean, C Mayor 20, T948 341 156, www.bidean.com. A charming hotel in the centre of town with welcoming staff and an old-fashioned homely feel. The beds in the colourful rustic rooms are very comfortable.
F Fonda Lorca, C Mayor 54, T948 340 127. A cheery place facing the small Plaza Mena, with a balcony, reasonable home-style food, and some cheap rooms.

Estella *p153*
AL Hotel Tximista, C Zaldu 15, T948 555 870, www.hoteltximista.com. A converted flour mill holds this, Estella's most upmarket option. The building's unusual form lends

itself to offbeat rooms, which are decorated in crisp modern fashion. The peaceful waterside location adds to the charm.
D Hotel Yerri, Av Yerri 35, T948 546 034, www.hotelyerri.es. This hotel is a reliable Estella option, situated near the bullring. The rooms are modern and have cable TV, good bathroom and telephone, but are fairly blandly decorated. Parking available.
E Cristina, C Baja Navarra 1, T948 550 772. A well-positioned *hostal* in Estella's liveliest part. Nearly all the rooms have a balcony to watch the world go by; those rooms overlooking the Plaza de los Fueros can get a bit noisy. All rooms are en suite.
E-F Pensión San Andrés, Plaza Santiago 58, T948 554 158. This is a very good, cheap option on a quiet square in the heart of town. The management is very friendly, and the rooms homely and comfortable. They come with or without bathroom. Location is excellent.

Camping
Camping Lizarra, Ctra Pamplona–Logroño Km 44, T948 551 733, www.campinglizarra.com. A range of accommodation options are available at this riverbank site. Facilities include a large swimming pool. You'll find it on the road to Pamplona a couple of kilometres from town.

Viana *p154*
B Palacio de Pujadas, C Navarro Villoslada 30, T948 646 464, www.palaciodepujadas.com. This lovely hotel is set in an historic old-town *palacio*. The interior is a lesson in

combining modern comfort while staying true to the original building; the rooms are a delight with stately tasteful furniture. There's free internet access for guests.

E Casa Armendáriz, C Navarro Villoslada 19, T948 645 078. This, a good choice for lodging, has clean and proper rooms with or without bathroom – the latter are pretty basic – as well as cheerful dining in an old wine cellar.

🍴 Eating

Puente La Reina/Gares and around *p153*
¶¶¶ El Peregrino (see Sleeping, above). The hotel's high-class restaurant offers excellent fare in small portions at high prices.
¶ Restaurante Joaquin, C Mayor 48, T948 340 931. This is a decent lunchtime option with a *menú del día* for €10. The food is typically Navarran, with fine trout and other hearty dishes.

Estella *p153*
Estella's signature dish is *gorrín*, another name for roast suckling pig, a heavy but juicy meal seeded with a potent dose of garlic.
¶¶¶ La Cepa, Plaza de los Fueros 15, T948 550 032. One of Estella's best, this restaurant makes up for its dull decor with imaginatively prepared Navarran dishes. They prepare a fine *gorrín* but also work with more subtle ingredients like local truffles.
¶¶ Astarriaga, Plaza de los Fueros 12, T948 550 802. An *asador* offering a decent *menú del día* for €15, and doing the usual good steaks, but also some traditional Navarran offerings. Good *pinchos* and a terrace on the square. It's also just about the most popular spot for afternoon coffee.
¶¶ Katxetas, Estudio de Gramática 1, T948 550 010. This cheerful spot is a Basque cider house tucked into what was once the city walls and serving challengingly large portions. The traditional *menú* is delicious but extremely filling.

☺ Festivals and events

Estella *p153*
Mid-Jul Medieval week, with troupes of *jongleurs* and crumhorn-players roaming the streets, which are enlivened by flaming torches, bales of straw and chickens and rabbits in cages.
Aug Estella's fiesta starts on the first Fri of the month, with *encierros* (bull-runnings), *corridas* and more.

Viana *p154*
Late Jul Viana goes wild for the joint fiesta of Mary Magdalene and St James; there are 2 *encierros* daily.

◉ Transport

Puente La Reina/Gares and around *p153*
Bus
La Estellesa (T948 222 223) runs frequent buses from **Pamplona** to Puente la Reina (20 mins); the buses continue to **Logroño**.

Estella *p153*
Bus
La Estellesa (T948 222 223) runs 10 buses a day to and from **Pamplona** (1 hr, €4). A similar number go to **Logroño**. There are also 6 buses daily to **San Sebastián** and 1 to **Zaragoza**.

Viana *p154*
Bus
La Vianesa (T948 446 227) run to both **Pamplona** and **Logroño** a few times daily.

Southern Navarra

→ Colour map 3, C4.

Not far south of Pamplona, the land flattens and hardens as the Spanish meseta *opens up. It's a land where the weather doesn't pull punches; the winters are cold, the summers can be merciless and massive windmills put the relentless westerlies to good use (Navarra is one of Europe's leaders in this form of energy). Corn, wheat, olives and grapes are grown where there's water, while towns and villages stand defiantly under the big sky.*

Within easy reach of Pamplona, the delightful towns of Tafalla and Olite, only 7 km apart, are well worth visiting. Although overshadowed from a tourist point of view by its neighbour, Tafalla is the larger and more complete town, whose old quarter boasts an attractively run-down web of medieval streets and little plazas centred around its impressive church. Olite stands in the middle of the baking valley like a bullfighter in the middle of the ring. In its most extravagant phase it was capital of the Navarran court, but in spite of this there's a Spanish feel to much of the area; perhaps it's just that the sun-baked sandstone seems in such contrast to the softer stone and wood buildings of the Pyrenean villages. Olite's centrepiece is its magnificent castle, which sometimes seems bigger than the town itself. The surrounding area's architecture is magnificent too: even the smallest village seems to have a church tucked away that would draw hundreds of visitors daily in other parts of the world.

Further south, Tudela is Navarra's second largest city and centre of the southern region known as La Ribera, for the Ebro, the peninsula's second longest river, meanders lazily through it, giving life to the rows and rows of grapevines that stripe the area. To the west of Tudela are winemaking villages that have given Navarra's reds a very good reputation, to the annoyance of some Rioja producers who, although literally in some cases next door, have to work under more stringent conditions and have limited scope for experimentation.
▸▸ For listings, see pages 160-162.

Tafalla

The biggest town in the area, Tafalla is a busy place, an industrial and commercial centre as well as focus for the surrounding districts. Historically an important stop on the road from Pamplona to Tudela, its architectural charm is as much in the small details – an arch here, a coat of arms there – as its selection of larger monuments.

The major structure in the narrow old town streets is the **Iglesia de Santa María**. Built in the 16th century over older foundations, it's been tweaked a fair bit over the years. The façade is curious in shape but fairly unadorned; it looks as though someone's put up a lean-to along one side. The highlight for most visitors is the *retablo*, an ornate late 16th-century work by the hand of Juan de Ancheta. After working on it for seven years, the strain (perhaps caused by the meddling patrons) killed the maestro, and the work was completed by his colleague and pupil Pedro González de San Pedro. If you find the piece over-ornate, blame the patrons: when the work was finished, they decided it wasn't striking enough, so they got a third artist to touch up some of the paintings and spray paint the rest gold. The bottom row is a brief biography of the Virgin Mary from left to right. The piece is topped by Ancheta's sensitive crucifixion.

There's no tourist office, but the **Casa de Cultura** ① *C Túbal 19, T948 701 654*, provides tourist information.

Olite

One of the oldest towns in Navarra, Olite was founded and fortified by the Romans. It wasn't until the 12th century, however that the town began to rise to prominence within Navarra. The Navarran monarchs had very itchy feet and were always decamping the court from one capital to the next. Olite became something of a favourite, and a **palace** was built, incorporating what remained of the Roman fortifications. This palace is now a parador.

It's the newer **castle** ⓘ *daily Oct-Mar 1000-1800; Apr-Sep 1000-1900; Jul and Aug until 2000; €3.10*, which turns heads though. Carlos III of Navarra, 'the Noble', felt that the ambitions of a kingdom should be reflected in its buildings. Accordingly, he went for broke, building the new palace in the early 15th century. Capitalizing on a period of peace in the Hundred Years' War between England and France (which tended to unavoidably involve Navarra), Carlos was determined that the palace would be a model of elegance, etiquette, and courtly splendour, and put in second-floor 'hanging' gardens, exotic trees, elegant galleries and towers, and a population of African animals including several lions and a giraffe. The castle was unfortunately destroyed in the Peninsular War to prevent it from falling into French hands, but it has been faithfully restored (perhaps overly) to something like its original appearance. It bristles with towers like an extravagant sandcastle, all with flags aflutter, but the highlight is certainly the restored 'queen's garden', a beautiful green space for which Carlos installed a very high-tech irrigation system for its time.

As well as several other elegant buildings from Olite's zenith, the town has an intriguing series of **medieval galleries** ⓘ *Oct-Mar Tue-Fri 1100-1300, Sat 1100-1400, 1700-1900, Sun 1100-1400, 1630-1930; Apr-Sep daily 1000-1400, 1700-2000; €1.50*, underneath it. Their origins are uncertain, but it seems likely they were created, or at least enlarged by Carlos III, who extravagantly dreamed of linking the towns of Tafalla and Olite with a secret passageway for times of trouble. You can visit the galleries under the main square – they house an exhibition on medieval life.

The **tourist office** ⓘ *Rúa Mayor, T948 741 703, Mon-Sat 1000-1400, 1500-1800 (1600-1900 summer), Sun 1000-1400*, is across the square from the parador and houses a reasonable wine museum (admission €3.50). There are several wine bodegas in and around town, most only visitable at weekends, and a great wine shop, Vinoteca Algarra, just around the corner from the tourist office at Rúa San Francisco 21.

Ujué and San Martín de Unx

Perched above concentric terraces harbouring almond trees, Ujué was founded in the early days of the Navarran monarchy in the ninth century AD. The memorably beautiful walled settlement was ennobled by Carlos I, who built much of the sanctuary complex that perches atop the hill. The **Santuario de Santa María** seems part castle and part church, which it effectively was; the town was seen as an important defensive bastion. The María in question is the 'black virgin', a dark Romanesque figure with an intense stare who refuses to shiver in the bleak stone church. Carlos II left his heart to the figure, literally; it sits in a box under the altar. How pure a heart it is, is not known: Carlos II was known as 'the Bad' for a number of dodgy political manoeuvres during his reign; he was imprisoned for a while by the French King John, whom history – the winners take it all – has named 'the Good'.

The most attractive part of the complex is the Paseo de Ronda, a covered walkway around the outside of the church with elegant galleries with beautiful vistas over the surrounding countryside. The road to Ujué starts from the attractive village of **San Martín de Unx**, worth a look in itself for its crypted church and noble old houses.

In case you were wondering, Ujué is the gorgeous hilltop village on every second Navarran tourist poster.

Monasterio de La Oliva
ⓘ *Mon-Sat 0900-1230, 1530-1800, Sun 0900-1100, 1600-1800; cloister and garden €2.*
The isolated monastery at La Oliva is actually near the village of Carcastillo (18 km east of the main N121 on the NA124) but it feels in the middle of nowhere. The monastery dates from the mid-12th century and is populated by a working community of Cistercians (white monks). Although it was only repopulated in 1927 after a century of abandonment, there's a remarkable feel of living history here. The monks farm and make wine in true Cistercian style, and the smell of the farmyard pervades the monastery air. The beautifully simple portals, long gloomy church, and supremely peaceful cloister make this a very attractive visit.

Artajona
Some 11 km northwest of Tafalla, Artajona's stunningly well-preserved walls are on a huge scale, and speak of a pride and resolve little related to the size of the village. Artajona claims to be the only place in the world whose bells are rung upside down. On fiestas, a team of *campañeros* gathers to push the four bells in a steady rhythm until they begin swinging right around. It requires a fair bit of strength and timing: the two heaviest bells each weigh over a ton.

Around Artajona are several **dolmens**, as well as the excavated Iron Age settlement of **Las Eretas** ⓘ *T948 364 247, currently accessible daily due to ongoing archaeological work but phone to check; free,* which consists of several houses and burials; some bits have been reproduced, and it's not badly done.

Tudela → *For listings, see pages 160-162. Colour map 5, A6.*

Even during its chilly winters, Tudela's got a scorched look, while in summer the heat radiating from the footpaths and brick buildings can make it feel like a kiln. There's a definite Andalucían or Middle Eastern feel to the place, so it's no surprise to find that this was a place where Christians, Moors and Jews lived in relative harmony together for centuries.

Although there had been a Roman settlement here, it was in fact the Moorish lord Amrus ibn Yusuf who founded modern Tudela in the ninth century. Tudela was a centre of learning and, at times, government during the Middle Ages but its main claim to fame these days is vegetables. Although aridity is the main feature of the area, the silty banks of the Ebro have been a grower's paradise for millennia. If you're eating *alcachofas* (artichokes) or *cogollos* (lettuce hearts) in Spain, one thing's certain: if they aren't from Tudela, they aren't the best. The town's restaurants showcase these and other famous vegetables.

Sights
Like many Spanish towns above a certain size, Tudela's outskirts look like no-man's land in a construction war and, like most Spanish towns, the centre is old and remarkably beautiful. The major sight is an example of biting the hand that feeds. When the city was taken by Christians in the early 12th century after centuries of tolerant Muslim rule, the Moors watched in dismay as their mosque was demolished and a **cathedral** ⓘ *Tue-Sat 1000-1330, 1600-1900, Sun 1000-1330, €3,* erected on top of it. Despite this un-Christian beginning, the cathedral is something of a masterpiece, although seemingly crowded by the surrounding buildings. The Puerta del Juicio is the finest of its entrances, and food for

thought for unrepentant sinners passing under it: the Last Judgement is pretty thoroughly and graphically depicted on one side, with doings from the life of Christ as comparison on the other. The high rib-vaulted Gothic interior has several elegant artistic works; the *retablo*, a work of Díaz de Oviedo recounts scenes in the life of Christ and Mary and is set around a Renaissance sculpture of the Virgin. There's also a small **museum** in the harmonious Romanesque cloister, from which you can organize a guided visit of the other monuments in the town's centre.

The **Plaza de los Fueros**, not far from the cathedral, is a good space, with a cute bandstand and several terrace bars. The square used to be used for bullfights, and the surrounding buildings are decorated with scenes of tauromachy, and with the coats of arms of the families of nobles that used to occupy the balconies. Just to the north of the centre is the hill of Santa Bárbara, topped by a statue of Christ on the spot where the old Moorish and Christian castles once stood. From here there's a nice view over the vegetable gardens and the Ebro, crossed by a stately bridge.

Tudela's **tourist office** ⓘ *T948 848 058, Mon-Fri 0930-1400, 1600-1900, Sat 1000-1400, 1600-1900, Sun 1000-1400*, is next to the cathedral. There are several free Wi-Fi zones around the historic centre of town.

Around Tudela

The town of **Fitero** is home to a beautiful **monastery** ⓘ *Mon 1730-1815, Tue-Sat 1130-1215, 1730-1815, Sun 1200 for guided tours, €3*, whose charming crumbly façade fronts a cavernously attractive church, cloisters and chapterhouse. Dating from 1140, this is the oldest of Spain's Cistercian monasteries. Less attractive, but interesting nonetheless, is the memorial to the Falangist dead of the Civil War. Next door, the **tourist office** ⓘ *T948 776 600, Mon-Fri 1100-1300, 1700-1830, Sat 1100-1300*, might be persuaded to arrange a visit at other times if you look keen.

On the outskirts of Fitero, **Baños de Fitero** and its adjoining Riojan village **Ventas del Baño** are spa towns in a craggy little valley. Thousands of people still come here to take the waters, which are considered beneficial for many ailments.

North of Tudela, the **Bardenas Reales** is technically semi-desert; a violently rugged expanse of white gypsum flats and scrawny sheep grazing on what little spiky foliage survives. It's a popular location for filmmaking: parts of the Bond film *The World is not Enough* were made here. If you've got a car, a few roads are accessible with 2WD; otherwise take a tour from Tudela. The website www.turismobardenas.com is organized by the guides' cooperative and is the best place to start.

⓸ Southern Navarra listings

For Sleeping and Eating price codes and other relevant information, see Essentials pages 31-39.

⓸ Sleeping

Tafalla *p157*
D Arotza, Plaza de Navarra 3, T948 700 716, www.hostalarotza.es. In the heart of things on this busy plaza, this *hostal*, run out of the restaurant **Túbal** next door, is clean and

comfortable. The restaurant also has simpler and cheaper rooms above it.

Olite *p158*
For budget places, head for Tafalla or San Martín.
L Parador Príncipe de Viana, Plaza de los Teobaldos 2, T948 740 000, www. parador.es. This recently restored gem of a *parador* occupies the old palace next to the

flamboyant castle of Olite. The rooms have modern bathrooms and are centred around a lovely courtyard.

A La Joyosa Guarda, Rúa de Medios 23, T948 741 303, www.lajoyosaguarda.com. Tucked away in old Olite, this stylish hotel set in a historic mansion adds yet another reason to visit this town. There are 3 grades of room with correspondingly luxurious fittings, and the abundance of natural light thanks to the interior patio and faultless modern amenities make this an excellent stay. Recommended.

C Hotel García Ramírez, R de Medios 1, T948 741 300, www.hotelgarciaramirez.com. Thankfully this place on the main square opposite the castle doesn't live up to its billing as a 'medieval hotel'; in fact it's not short on modern comforts. The best rooms have mock stained-glass windows looking over the square; all are a/c. The hearty *asador* downstairs tends to be heavily booked by tour groups.

E Albergue de Beire, Ctra Aragón 1, Beire, T948 740 041, www.beire.com. A 40-min walk from Olite, this hostel is set around the courtyard of a *palacio* and has good dorms and doubles (**D**). During summer, however, the place is often booked out as a summer camp. Prior reservation essential. Rates include breakfast and there are other meals available.

Ujué and San Martín de Unx p158

E Casa Pedro, Ctra San Martín de Unx–Ujué Km 1, T948 738 257, www.casapedro.net. A warm, welcoming place to stay just outside San Martín de Unx. Comfy and attractive doubles in a peaceful setting with home-cooked meals and a great atmosphere. There's an attached hostel section (**F**) and the place is totally 'green'. Recommended.

Tudela p159

A Ciudad de Tudela, C Misericordia s/n, T948 402 440, www.ac-hoteles.com. A stately mansion house near the Plaza de los Fueros,

converted into a modern hotel. Good facilities and crisp modern rooms, although some aren't overly blessed with natural light. The staff are enthusiastic and helpful.

D Remigio, C Gaztambide 4, T948 820 850, www.hostalremigio.com. A cool and shady *hostal* with a fine location just off Plaza de los Fueros, with basic but clean rooms with bath.

F Estrella, C Carnicerías 13, T948 821 518. A good-value set of rooms above a popular bar. Basic but acceptable; with reasonable shared bathrooms and oversoft beds.

Around Tudela p160

C Balneario Bécquer, Baños de Fitero, T948 776 100, www.fitero.com/balneario. The most historic, but less attractive of the 2 hotels.

C Virrey Palafox, Baños de Fitero, T948 776 275, www.fitero.com/balneario. Up the hill, this hotel is more peaceful.

⊕ Eating

Tafalla p157

¶¶ **Túbal**, Plaza Navarra 6, T948 700 852. A Tafalla institution and a must on any *pintxo*-hopping trip in Tafalla; it also does some tasty smart modern meals.

Olite p158

¶¶ **Erri Berri**, Rúa del Fondo 1, Olite, T948 741 116. Big chunks of chargrilled meat are very popular at this *asador*. *Chuletón de buey* is a big T-bone from a mature ox, packed with flavour and sold by weight, which usually approaches 1 kg – most people choose to share. The *sidrería* menu for €29.50 is another good way to dine heartily here.

¶¶ **Gambarte**, Rúa del Seco 15, T948 740 139. A likeable restaurant, which makes a point of doing traditional Navarran dishes well. Try the *cogollos de Tudela*, lettuce rarely reaches these heights; or the *jarrete de cordero*, a herb-flavoured lamb stew.

Tudela p159

¶¶ **Bargota**, C Virgen de la Cabeza 21, T948 824 911. A quality place, and one of the best to try the local vegetables. One way is to order a *menestra*, which is delicious here.

Iruña, C Muro (also called Abilio Calderón) 11, T948 821 000. One of Tudela's most reliably good restaurants. Smart modern dining near the plaza with an enticing menu with distinct Navarran and Riojan flavour. Good unobtrusive service and an excellent selection of the local veggies.

Bar Aragón, Plaza de los Fueros 15, T948 821 054. Bar with a shady terrace to watch things happening (or not) in the summer heat. Good beer and plenty of snacks.

Bar José Luis, C Muro 23, T948 820 091. A good, cheap place to eat with outside tables and superb *ensaladas mixtas*. There are few frills in the interior, but the tapas are reliably excellent, and quite elaborate.

Moncayo 2, C Merced 1, T948 410 946. By the food market, this bar doesn't spend any extra on decor. But come here with room for at least 2 *pinchos*: the *manita de cerdo* (de-boned pig trotter) and the home-made duck-liver foie are spectacularly good.

⊛ Festivals and events

Tudela *p159*
24-30 Jul Tudela's big party, the **Fiestas de Santa Ana**, features *encierros* and general revelry. A few days before this is the **Bajada del Ebro**, a competitive and rough-house regatta on the river.

⊖ Transport

Tafalla and Olite *p157 and p158*
Bus
La Tafallesa (T948 222 886) run regular buses from **Pamplona** to Tafalla (around 10 daily, 45 mins), most of which continue to Olite, which is also served by **Conda** 7 times daily. A handful of trains link Tafalla and Pamplona, but the bus is better.

Ujué *p158*
Bus There's one bus daily from **Tafalla** to Ujué via San Martín.

Artajona *p159*
Bus Artajona is serviced 2-3 times every Mon-Sat from **Pamplona** by Conda (1 hr).

Tudela *p159*
Bus Conda, T948 221 026, www.condasa. com, runs between **Pamplona** and Tudela 6-7 times daily (1 hr 15 mins-1 hr 30 mins, €6-7). Some of these services stop in **Olite**, while there are other buses between **Tafalla** and Tudela.

Contents

Footprint features

At a glance

⊖ **Getting around** Great transport connections to Zaragoza, including international budget flights and a fast train from Madrid. You'll want a hire car to explore the Pyrenees though.
◉ **Time required** A week.
☀ **Weather** Zaragoza bakes in summer but things are fresher in the mountains, which get heavy winter snows.
✖ **When not to go** Prices soar in Zaragoza in Oct, and around Christmas and Easter in the Pyrenees.

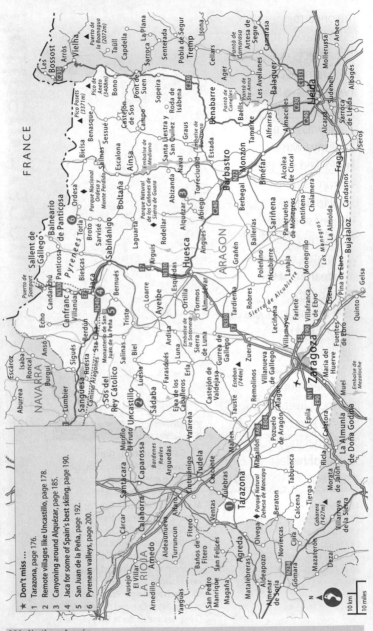

FRANCE

NAVARRA

ARAGÓN

LA RIOJA

★ **Don't miss ...**
1 Tarazona, page 176.
2 Remote villages like Uncastillo, page 178.
3 Canyoning around Alquézar, page 185.
4 Jaca for some of Spain's best skiing, page 190.
5 San Juan de la Peña, page 192.
6 Pyrenean valleys, page 200.

N

10 km
10 miles

The once-mighty region of Aragón is now one of the peninsula's lesser-known areas. It's the ruggedness of the northern extremes that attracts most visitors; walkers and climbers beckoned by the same remote beauty that once drew legions of monks to establish themselves in lonely corners.

Wandering this sparsely populated region, it's hard to imagine that it was once a major Mediterranean power. Unification with Catalunya was a major part of that and once the two separated, landlocked Aragón was never going to wield the same influence. Aragón's strong democratic tradition was a constant stumbling block for later kings desperate for war funds, and to this day the Aragonese enjoy a reputation for stubbornness in the rest of the country. The region saw some of the Civil War's bloodiest stalemates, exacerbated by the extremes of temperature that are a feature of the area.

The north of Aragón is taken up by a large chunk of Spain's most dramatic mountains, the Pyrenees. Whether you're a serious climber, trekker or skier, or you just enjoy fresh air, picturesque villages and proud granite peaks, the area is deeply satisfying and the awe-inspiring mountainscapes live long in the memory.

Further south, Zaragoza, which hosted the 2008 World Expo, is a good, lively place with enough museums, bars and Roman ruins to keep anyone happy for a couple of days. This area was the homeland of Goya, one of the world's great painters, and several of his lesser works can be seen in the city.

Zaragoza

→ *Colour map 6, B1. Phone code: 976. Population: 682,283.*
One of Spain's larger cities, Zaragoza is the nicest of places, with an easy-going modern European feel allied to some attractive architecture and good eating options. Thousands of pilgrims come from all over Spain to visit the Basílica de Nuestra Señora del Pilar, a massive construction that dominates the square of the same name. Zaragoza attracted even bigger crowds in 2008, when it hosted the World Expo, themed, appropriately for this thirsty province, on water conservation. Formerly an important Roman city, it's now a prosperous centre that stands in stark contrast to the somewhat bleak province that it commands. It sits on the Ebro and was a port in that river's livelier days. Over half of Aragón's population lives in Zaragoza.
▸▸ *For listings, see pages 172-175.*

Ins and outs

Getting there and around   There's an extensive network of local bus routes; a timetable is available from the Ayuntamiento. Zaragoza's train station, Las Delicias, is on the **AVE** fast-train network. It lies a couple of kilometres west of the centre and incorporates the bus terminal. Most of the city sits on the south bank of the Río Ebro; the old town being close to the river, and the newer sections spreading east, south and west from there. The majority of the sights are in the fairly compact old town.▸▸ *See Transport, page 175.*

Best time to visit   In high summer the pilgrim crowds in the basilica can be off-putting, but they're usually on day trips, so the rest of town is by no means cluttered, although it does get fearsomely hot in August. The week around 12 October is the **Fiesta de La Virgen del Pilar.**▸▸ *See Festivals and events, page 175.*

Tourist information   The centre of Zaragoza has various information points. The most useful are the **municipal office** ⓘ *T976 201 200, www.zaragozaturismo.es, daily 1000-2000, 0900-2100 in summer,* in a black glass cube opposite the basilica, and a **provincial office** ⓘ *T976 212 032, Mon-Fri 1000-1400, 1700-2000, Sat 1100-1400,* on the Plaza de España. You can download city information to your mobile phone at these points. They can also sell you the **Zaragoza Card**, www.zaragozacard.com, but it's worth totting up whether you'll actually save anything, as it costs €23 for three days. There are also two Aragón offices, handy if you're heading up to the mountains later. They're at Avenida César Augusto 25, T976 282 181, and Diego Dormer 21, T976 294 539. Both are open daily 1000-1400, 1600-2000.

Background

Zaragoza sits on the Río Ebro, lifeblood of central Aragón, which undoubtedly made it an attractive option for the Romans, who took over the Iberian settlement of Salduie and founded their own town in 14 BC, naming it Caesaraugusta. It became a focus of Roman culture, and then an important Visigothic city. Taken in AD 714 by the Moors, it resisted Charlemagne's attempts to conquer it and enjoyed a period of cultural and architectural pre-eminence, known throughout Moorish lands as Al Baida, or the 'White City'. It was reconquered in 1118, and enjoyed a period of religious tolerance but later became a centre of the Inquisition: one of their number was famously murdered in the cathedral.

Tension between Aragón and Castilla led to rioting in the late 16th century, and the town was annexed by the Castilian armies; effectively ending Aragonese autonomy.

The city's heroic defence against Napoleon's besieging armies in 1808 to 1809 is still a powerful symbol of Spanish independence.

Zaragoza played a full part in the tensions leading up to the Civil War too; the archbishop was murdered in 1923 by the famous anarchists Durruti and Ascaso, while a great general strike in 1933 to 1934 astounded observers, as workers went unpaid for 57 days. Despite these tendencies, the military rising in 1936 took the town by surprise and the Republican forces were never able to regain it, despite a lengthy campaign.

There are a number of noble buildings of interest in Zaragoza; many of them are described in the pamphlet *100 motivos para visitar Zaragoza*, available at the tourist office.

Sights

Basílica de Nuestra Señora del Pilar
ⓘ *Plaza del Pilar, daily 0700-2030 (2130 in summer), free.*
This enormous basilica, one of the country's foremost pilgrimage sites, is a spectacular building reminiscent of a mosque with its large coloured dome and slender towers. Saint James (who might have been surprised to learn that he was ever in Spain at all), was preaching in Zaragoza in AD 40 when the Virgin Mary descended from heaven on a jade pillar with words of encouragement for him. The pillar stayed when she disappeared and the basilica was built around it. Such is the Virgin of the Pillar's importance that Pilar has for many centuries been one of the most popular names for Spanish girls. During the Civil War, the Virgin was named Captain-General of the city, which was under attack by Republican forces. A couple of bombs landed near the basilica but failed to explode; this was of course attributed to the Virgin's presence and intervention rather than the poor quality of the ordnance. The bombs are still proudly displayed in the basilica, hopefully defused.

The church itself is a monumental edifice of a variety of architectural styles. It was built in the 17th and 18th centuries on the site of an earlier church, and not actually completed until 1961. The Santa Capilla chapel at the eastern end of the building houses the pillar itself, entombed in an ornate 18th-century *retablo*. Round the back is a small chink through which the column can be kissed. Nearby, two alcoves have ceilings painted by a young Goya.

Visitors throng the building, standing around watching the very public Masses and confessions, or lighting candles. The other item of major artistic interest is the main *retablo* by the Aragonese sculptor Damián Forment, an incredibly intricate alabaster work depicting the Assumption of the Virgin. Opposite, the impressive organ has 6250 pipes.

Behind the basilica is the **Río Ebro**, crossed by a heavily restored 15th-century stone bridge, attractively lioned at each end with modern bronze works.

Plaza del Pilar
The basilica dominates the Plaza del Pilar, a long rectangular space with a large population of pigeons and tourist shops; there's a roaring trade in religious souvenirs, some of which are in appalling taste. The plaza's western end is given character by the attractive modern **Fuente de la Hispanidad**, while in the east a bronze Goya overlooks sculpted figures derived from his paintings. Next to him is the **Lonja**, a Renaissance building that was originally the merchants' guild, but now houses exhibitions in its elegant columned hall.

Museo de Ibercaja Camón Aznar
ⓘ *C Espoz y Mina 23, T976 397 328, Tue-Sat 1000-1345, 1700-2045, Sun 1000-1345, free.*
Situated in a beautiful Renaissance palace in the heart of Zaragoza, this impressive private

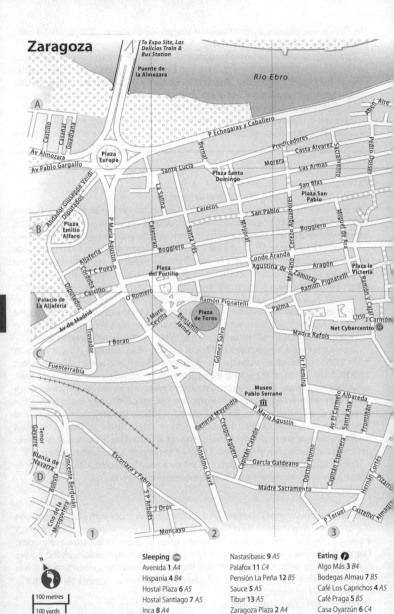

Zaragoza

To Expo Site, Las
Delicias Train &
Bus Station

Puente de
la Almozara

Río Ebro

Abad Aire

P Echegaray y Caballero

Predicadores

Casta Álvarez

Sacramento

Pedro Dosset

Av Almozara

Castillo

Casanal

Guardián

Bernal

Las Armas

Morera

Santa Lucía

Av Pablo Gargallo

Plaza
Europa

Plaza Santo
Domingo

San Blas

Plaza San
Pablo

La Salina

Cereros

San Pablo

Mayoral

Cerezo Aguadores

Andador Giuseppe Verdi

Diputados

Plaza
Emilio
Alfaro

P María Agustín

Calatorao

Santa Inés

Boggiero

Boggiero

Miguel de Ara

Aljafería

Conde Aranda

Aragón

Plaza la
Victoria

T C Pueyo

Córdoba

Plaza
del Portillo

Agustina de

Mariano

Tamoray

Ramón Pignatelli

Ramón y Cajal

Castillo

O Romero

Ramón Pignatelli

Palma

J Carmón

Palacio de
La Aljafería

Dinutados

J Muro
Sevilla

Benjamín
Jarnes

Plaza
de Toros

L'rio

Net Cybercentro

Av de Madrid

Trovador

Madre Rafols

J Borao

Gómez Salvo

Fuenterrabia

Dr Fleming

Museo
Pablo Serrano

Tenor
Gayarre

General Mayandía

P María Agustín

Av El Carmen

Santa Ana

Albareda

Fromtinan

Blanca de
Navarra

Crespo Agüero

Capitán Casado

Vincente Berdusán

Escoriaza y Fabro

Anselmo Clavé

García Galdeano

Doctor Horno

Capitán Esponera

Hernán Cortés

Pizarro

Bollría

Cno de la
Mosqueruela

S P Arbués

J Orús

Madre Sacramento

P Teruel

Castellvi

Almagro

Moncayo

N

100 metres

100 yards

Sleeping	Nastasibasic **9** A5	Eating
Avenida **1** A4	Palafox **11** C4	Algo Más **3** B4
Hispania **4** B4	Pensión La Peña **12** B5	Bodegas Almau **7** B5
Hostal Plaza **6** A5	Sauce **5** A5	Café Los Caprichos **4** A5
Hostal Santiago **7** A5	Tibur **13** A5	Café Praga **5** B5
Inca **8** A4	Zaragoza Plaza **2** A4	Casa Oyarzún **6** C4

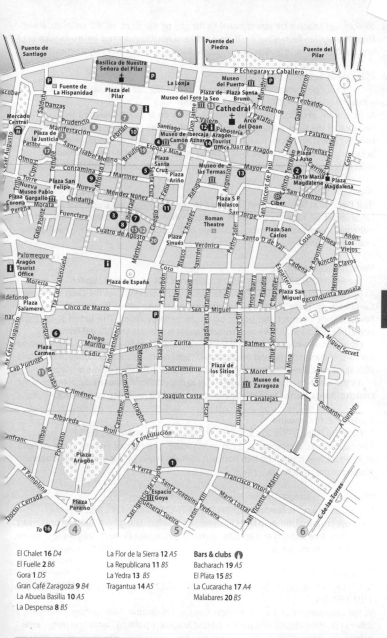

El Chalet **16** *D4*	La Flor de la Sierra **12** *A5*	**Bars & clubs** 🎵
El Fuelle **2** *B6*	La Republicana **11** *B5*	Bacharach **19** *A5*
Gora **1** *D5*	La Yedra **13** *B5*	El Plata **15** *B5*
Gran Café Zaragoza **9** *B4*	Tragantua **14** *A5*	La Cucaracha **17** *A4*
La Abuela Basilia **10** *A5*		Malabares **20** *B5*
La Despensa **8** *B5*		

collection of Spanish art was donated to the city on the death of the collector, a well-known Zaragozan literary figure. There are several notable paintings by artists such as El Greco and Zurbarán, as well as a large gallery displaying Goya's four major series of prints.

Plaza de la Seo and the cathedral

ⓘ *Cathedral open winter Tue-Fri 1000-1330, 1600-1800, Sat-Sun 1000-1200, 1600-1800; summer Tue-Sun 1000-2030, €4 including museum.*

At its eastern end Plaza del Pilar becomes Plaza de la Seo, dominated by Zaragoza's cathedral of the same name. Built on the site of the city's mosque, it's a blend of styles covering everything from Romanesque to neoclassical. Admire the *mudéjar* tiling and brickwork on its northern side before going inside, where there is an excellent tapestry collection; the amount of work involved in these masterpieces can hardly be imagined.

Arco del Dean

Near Plaza de la Seo, the street is crossed by the pretty Arco del Dean. The dean didn't fancy soiling his robes in the medieval muck when travelling between home and the cathedral, so he had an overhead passage built across the street, with ornate Gothic-*mudéjar* windows.

Roman Caesaraugusta

ⓘ *Tue-Sat 0900-2030, Sun 0900-1330, €2.50 each, €7 for all 3 and the theatre.*

As you stroll around the area of Arco del Dean, you're walking over the centre of Roman Caesaraugusta. There are **three underground museums**, where the foundations of the Roman forum, riverport and public baths can be investigated. The forum is the most interesting, although all have audiovisual displays in Spanish, English and French.

Other Roman remains to check out are the walls, of which an 80-m stretch is well conserved just west of Plaza del Pilar, and the **theatre** ⓘ *same opening hours, €3.50*, which once held 6000 spectators. There's an interpretation centre with an exhibition on water usage.

It's also worth heading down Calle Mayor to inspect the fabulous *mudéjar* tower of the church of **Santa María Magdalena**, a spectacular symphony in decorative brick.

Museo Pablo Gargallo

ⓘ *Plaza San Felipe 3, T976 724 923, Tue-Sat 0900-2030, Sun 0900-1330, €3.50.*

The Pablo Gargallo museum is set in an attractive 17th-century *palacio* in the old part of Zaragoza, and fronted by two horses. It contains works by the impressive Aragonese sculptor of the same name.

Museo de Zaragoza

ⓘ *Plaza de los Sitios 6, Tue-Sat 1000-1345, 1700-1945, Sun 1000-1345, free.*

The main provincial museum is set in an elegant building dating from 1908. It contains art and architecture sections and includes several Goyas, as well as much Aragonese religious art and more modern works.

Espacio Goya

ⓘ *C San Ignacio de Loyola 16, Tue-Fri 0830-1430, 1800-2100, Sat 1100-1400, 1800-2100, Sun 1100-1400, free.*

In the headquarters of a bank, Espacio Goya is a decorative 16th-century patio from a different building, around which are exhibited Aragonese paintings, including many Goyas.

The Master of Darkness

"Goya, a nightmare full of the Unknown" Baudelaire.

The man who reputedly threw a plaster bust at the Duke of Wellington for moving during a portrait sitting was born in the Aragonese village of Fuendetodos in 1746. Francisco José de Goya y Lucientes is widely recognized as being the first artist of the modern age. An artist of great technical skill and imagination, Goya was a master of painting and engraving who managed to combine his role at the heart of Spain's art establishment with his own uncompromising artistic vision.

Goya became known outside Spain with the publication in 1864 of his 80-etching series *The Disasters of War*, which depicts in a brutal manner the horrors of the war in Spain after the French invasion of 1808. Not published during his lifetime, this series is unusual in art history for the dark view of humanity that it portrays. Along with his other series of etchings, *Los Caprichos*, of 1799, a wicked satire on Spanish society, and the 18 etchings of *Los Proverbios*, Goya's vision can seem overwhelmingly bleak.

Goya was, however, a man of the Enlightenment and believed that art could instruct and educate. An examination of his enormous number of paintings reveals an artist who worked on many different levels. His designs for the Royal Tapestry factory are rustic and optimistic while his portraits of the family of Carlos IV show him subverting his role as courtly painter by revealing the coldness and ugliness at the heart of the Royal Court.

The darker side of Goya's work was produced during the latter part of his life. The 12 works known as the *Black Paintings*, which he painted on the walls of his house in Madrid, are undoubtedly influenced by his many illnesses which had left him deaf and unable to communicate except through hand signals. His experimentation with new forms and techniques is at its most obvious in these works, typified by the almost abstract *Dog on a Leash*.

Goya's most famous paintings of the clothed and unclothed *Maja* shows his skill in revealing our common humanity stripped of pretensions. His finest works place him in the very highest echelon of European painters and, although his paintings and etchings show at times a pessimistic view of humanity, in much of his work there there is something life-enhancing. Goya died in Bordeaux in 1828.

Palacio de la Aljafería

ⓘ *T976 289 683, Sat-Wed 1000-1330, 1600-1830 (1930 in summer), closed all Thu and Fri am except during Jan, Jul and Aug, €3, free Sun.*

A kilometre west of the old town, the Aljafería was once a sumptuous Muslim palace. After the city was reconquered, it was lived in by the Aragonese kings, before Fernando and Isabel obtained planning permission to put on a second storey. Felipe II later had the building converted into a military fort, building exterior walls and a moat – he was having problems with the locals at the time. Today the complex holds the Aragonese regional parliament. The most impressive part to visit is the Muslim courtyard, a modern reconstruction with original fragments still visible. It gives a good sense of what it must have been like, with characteristic scalloped arches and delicate carved intricacies. There's a small, ornate prayer room; the niche is the *mihrab*, which points towards Mecca. Upstairs, little remains of the Catholic Monarchs' palace other than some very elaborate ceilings of superb polychrome wood. As it's a parliament building, there's a scanner on the way in, so leave swords and penknives at your *pensión*.

Museo Pablo Serrano

ⓘ *Paseo María Agustín 20, Wed-Sat 1000-1400, 1700-2000 (1800-2100 summer), Sun 1000-1400.*
A curious bunker-like building, the Pablo Serrano museum exhibits the work of the sculptor, as well as the painter Juana Francés who married him. It was closed for construction works at time of last research.

Monasterio Cartuja de Aula Dei

ⓘ *Open last Sat of each month, but numbers are limited; there's usually a lengthy waiting list; T976 714 934, to get on it.*
On the outskirts of Zaragoza, north along the Z-123, this Carthusian monastery has some wall paintings by Goya, but is almost impossible to get into unless you plan a visit well in advance.

The Expo Site

On a bend in the Río Ebro to the northwest of the centre, the 2008 World Expo site was built to the show's theme of water and resource management. The curvilinear **Torre del Agua** tower is the most emblematic building of the area, which is being converted into a business park and regional government offices. The main reason to come to the site now that the party's over is to visit the excellent **Acuario Fluvial** ⓘ *T976 076 606, www.acuariodezaragoza.com, Mon-Thu 1000-1715, Fri-Sun 1000-1915, adult/child €14/7.* This freshwater aquarium focuses on various riverine environments from around the world and has several hundred species divided between dozens of tanks. The building itself is a striking sight with water cascading from atop it. Catch bus No 20 or 23 from the centre to get here, or walk or cycle the riverside path.

◉ Zaragoza listings

For Sleeping and Eating price codes and other relevant information, see Essentials pages 31-39.

● Sleeping

Zaragoza *p166, map p168*
There are over 100 places to stay in Zaragoza, although many of them are business hotels or functional *pensiones*. Prices rocket in mid-Oct for the Virgen del Pilar long weekend.
L Hotel Palafox, Casa Jiménez s/n, T976 237 700, www.palafoxhoteles.com. The most classic of Zaragoza's hotels has undergone a recent redesign, and has been kitted out in attractive minimalist style. The rooms are large and light, and come with all the trimmings, including video games, a free minibar and round-the-clock room service. There are some rooms available for disabled guests.
A Zaragoza Plaza, C Manifestación 16, T976 205 858, www.hoteles-catalonia.com. Set in a historic house on a perfectly located square, this offers fine business-standard

facilities and friendly service in the heart of town. There's a raft of helpful facilities and there are frequently excellent deals available via the website. No parking.
B Hotel Avenida, Av César Augusto 55, T976 439 300, www.hotelavenida-zaragoza. com. A clean, fresh spot with mock-Roman decor on the street where the old walls used to run. The a/c rooms have parquet floors and are attractive and comfortable. Out of season it's extremely good value (**D**).
B Hotel Hispania, Av César Augusto 103, T976 284 928, www.hotelhispania.com. Well located near the Plaza del Pilar, this handy, pleasant option has modern rooms with many facilities. It's very good value off season and has parking available for €15.
B Hotel Inca, C Manifestación 33, T976 390 091, www.hotelinca-avil.com. A likeable and stylish small hotel south of the basilica. The wood-floored rooms have simple elegance and the attractive restaurant is suitably classy. Rooms have a safe and internet access.

B-C Hotel Sauce, C Espoz y Mina 33, T976 205 050, www.hotelsauce.com. Handily central, with simple but spacious rooms, some rather unusually shaped, with plenty of comfort, powerful showers, and Wi-Fi that works a treat. Amiable staff. There's a decent breakfast for (usually) €7.50. Recommended.

C Hotel Nastasibasic, Plaza del Pilar 11, T976 394 250, www.nastasibasiczgzhotel.com. Directly opposite the basilica, this pleasant old hotel with friendly staff has large, comfortable modernized rooms, all recently refurbished, and most of which have views and a balcony rail. Don't ask us why they changed the name – Hotel Las Torres was perfectly acceptable. Parking available close by.

C Hotel Tibur, Plaza de la Seo 2, T976 202 000, www.hoteltibur.com. A smart place in a quiet corner of the Plaza del Pilar area. The rooms have every convenience and are spacious and tastefully furnished. There's also a good restaurant.

D Hostal Santiago, C Santiago 3, T976 394 550, www.hostal-santiago.com. A well-placed warren of a hotel near the tourist office and basilica. Management is slightly odd, but it's clean, comfortable, and with a/c. Some rooms are more expensive than others.

E Hostal Plaza, Plaza del Pilar 14, T976 294 830, www.hostalplazazgz.com. A reasonable choice with a top location opposite the basilica. Decent a/c rooms with bathroom. Confirm any bookings.

G Pensión La Peña, C Cinegio 3, T976 299 089. Simple, cheap clean rooms with washbasin, in the old part of town, right in the heart of the tapas district.

● Eating

Zaragoza p166, map p168

Zaragoza's main tapas area is known as *El Tubo*, a cluster of narrow old-town streets around C Libertad. It's common for groups to order a mixed tapas plate, or *verbena de tapas*, which might cost around €10-15.

₮₮₮ El Chalet, C Santa Teresa 25, T976 569 104, www.elchaletrestaurante.com. An excellent and not exorbitant restaurant run by chef Angel Conde, an avid historian of Aragonese cuisine. Although his beef dishes are sublime, the careful treatment of vegetables marks the restaurant out from most of its compatriots. In good weather, there's a beautiful garden terrace.

₮₮ La Despensa, C Libertad 3, T976 297 614, www.la-despensa.es. A world away from some of the Tubo's rowdier choices, this quiet spot focuses on a short menu of delicious dishes made with quality deli-style ingredients. There's a bar for tapas and an attractive downstairs dining area. Service is polite and attentive.

₮₮ Casa Oyarzún, Plaza Nuestra Señora del Carmen 1, T976 232 473, www.casaoyarzun. com. Popular with business workers for its good-quality lunchtime *menú* and sunny terrace. The cuisine is Basque in style and features carefully prepared fish dishes and delicious red meats.There's also a good array of *pinchos* and a pleasant terrace.

₮₮ La Abuela Basilia, C Santiago 14, T976 390 594. A good downstairs restaurant specializing in suckling pig and milk-fed lamb cooked in a wood-fired oven. There's a good selection of Aragonese wines, and prices are reasonable.

₮₮ La Yedra, C Mayor 28, T976 393 705. Central, but away from the Tubo's sometimes suffocating crowds, this cosy place offers plenty of tapas fare at the bar, as well as tables to eat more substantial fare. It's all very friendly and atmospheric: grilled meats, fresh fish, and more elaborate creations are all on offer. There's also a tasting menu for €33 which makes no pretensions to haute cuisine but is toothsome and fun.

₮₮ Tragantua, Plaza Santa Marta s/n, T976 299 174. This excellent little tapas bar specializes in seafood. It's always busy with people competing for elbow room to crack open their crustaceans. Good value and very cheerful; there's also a downstairs dining room. One of several tapas bars in this worthwhile little zone.

₮ Algo Más, C Estébanes 2, T976 205 595. Small, light, and incredibly popular, this tapas bar has become one of the Tubo's favourite spots for its exquisite gourmet *pinchos* – try the black rice – and generous glasses of wine. You may have to resort to violence or wheedling to actually squeeze into the place on a weekend evening.

¶ Bodegas Almau, C Estébanes 10, T976 299 834. This enchanting wine bar is well into its 2nd century. It's a temple to Spanish tradition, with old wooden shelves rising to the ceiling laden with bottles of all shapes and sizes. It's a great place to have a glass of local wine. There's an outdoor terrace opposite. Recommended.

¶ El Fuelle, C Mayor 59, T976 398 033. This tapas spot is large and homely, decorated with farming implements and the neckscarves from dozens of fiestas. Definitely drop by for a glass of wine but eat elsewhere.

¶ Gora, C Francisco de Vitoria 1, T976 227 983. This trendy modern tapas bar has a stellar reputation for its tortilla, which is succulent in the extreme. At weekends it turns into a trendy disco bar once the tapas are cleared away.

¶ La Flor de la Sierra, C San Valero 8, T976 291 198. A long-standing Zaragoza favourite, this attractive and spacious bar specializes in grilled sardines, which are delicious. They also do recommended skewers of *morro* (pig snout) that taste much better than they sound if you can cope with the rubbery texture.

¶ La Republicana, C Méndez Núñez 38, T976 396 509, www.larepublicana.net. Closed Sun. A cheap and cheerful little old town tapas bar, cosy and warm. They serve tasty *pinchos* as well as simple, hearty plates of comfort food. The decor, full of bric-a-brac, reminds one of a French bistro, but the cheap breakfasts are pure Spanish: they include the option of a glass of wine.

Cafés

Café Los Caprichos, C Espoz y Mina 25. A good little backstreet bar with a few outdoor tables in summer. The interior is elegant and comfortable, full of character with various Goya prints on the walls and coloured glass. It's a fine spot for a pre- or post-dinner *copa*. DJs play downstairs at weekends.

Café Praga, Plaza Santa Cruz 13, T976 200 251. A good summer option, with a large terrace and good service in a quiet square. Particularly atmospheric in the early evening.

Gran Café Zaragoza, C Alfonso I 25, T976 290 882. A Zaragoza classic: a beautiful, traditional old Spanish café with a range of small eats. Set on the main pedestrian street, it's a de rigueur stop for an evening coffee during the *paseo*, or a lunchtime vermouth and *pincho*.

◑ Bars and clubs

Zaragoza *p166, map p168*

Bar Bacharach, C Espoz y Mina 10, T976 390 660. A small and very popular bar, decorated in white wood. The walls are decorated with black and white photos of films that Bacharach scored. It's usually full of interesting people; it's also a place where you can eat simple meals and is open late. There are a couple of other options nearby on this street.

El Plata, C 4 de Agosto 23, T647 619 326. In the heart of El Tubo, this is a historic venue for cabaret/burlesque performances that run from comic songs to gentle striptease. It's a lot of fun, and you don't really need to understand Spanish to have a good time here. There's a pleasant outdoor bar area around the back.

La Cucaracha, C Temple 25. One of many rowdy bars on this street. This is Zaragoza's prime zone for weekend festivities and you can take your pick of dozens of places.

Malabares, C Cinegio 2, T976 292 557. This popular new bar is mainly worth visiting for its great setting, in an old *palacio* in El Tubo with a beautiful antique ceiling. The interior design is modern and stylish, with a cosy little lounge as well as plenty of tables. There's a range of innovative *pinchos*, but the place really gets going around 2400. Poor service, though.

◉ Entertainment

Zaragoza *p166, map p168*

Cinema

Filmoteca de Zaragoza, Plaza San Carlos 4, T976 721 853, shows excellent repertory cinema, mostly English-language films with Spanish subtitles. Admission €2.

Theatre
Teatro del Mercado, Plaza Santo Domingo s/n, T976 437 662.
Teatro Principal, C Coso 57, T976 296 090, www.teatroprincipalzaragoza.com.

❈ Festivals and events

Zaragoza p166, map p168
12 Oct Fiesta de La Virgen del Pilar. A week of parties, concerts and fireworks as well as serious veneration of the Virgin.

◎ Shopping

Zaragoza p166, map p168
Most shops are around the broad avenues south of the old town.

Markets
Try the modernista Mercado Central, just southwest of the Plaza del Pilar. Also worth a look is the flea market on Sun morning by the bullring, and the clothes market on Wed and Sun mornings by the football stadium.

◑ Activities and tours

Zaragoza p166, map p168
A tourist bus runs around 2 city routes. A hop-on hop-off ticket costs €7. The service runs daily from Jul to mid-Oct, and weekends only from Easter-Jun and mid-Oct to mid-Dec. The tourist office also run a variety of tours of the city and province, www.turismozaragoza.com.

⊖ Transport

Zaragoza p166, map p168
Air The city's airport (ZAZ) is served by Iberia from **Madrid**; by Ryanair from **London** Stansted, **Brussels** Charleroi, **Rome** Ciampino and **Milan** Bergamo; there are also flights to **Frankfurt**, **Paris**, Romania,

and other Spanish cities. Airport buses leave from the corner of Gran Vía and Paseo Pamplona to connect with flights (20-30 mins, €1.60). Costs about €25 in a taxi.
Airport enquiries T976 712 300.

Bus There are many bus companies serving a huge variety of destinations. All buses now leave from the new bus station, in the same complex as the Las Delicias train station. Bus No 51 runs from the centre (passing Puerta del Carmen) to this station.
The major long-distance destinations are: **Madrid** hourly (3 hrs 45 mins, €15), **Barcelona** more or less hourly (4 hrs, €15), **Valladolid** 3 daily (7 hrs), **Bilbao** 4-5 daily (4 hrs, €21), **San Sebastián** (€22), via **Tudela** and **Pamplona** (€15), **Huesca** more than hourly (55 mins, €7) and on to **Jaca** 5 daily (2 hrs 10 mins, €14). **Teruel** and **Tarazona** are also serviced regularly; for other Aragonese destinations, see the relevant section.

Taxi T976 383 838.

Train There are roughly hourly AVE fast trains from the Las Delicias station to **Madrid** (1½ hrs, €55) and to **Barcelona** (1 hr 40 mins, €63) as well as a few slower, cheaper options on the same routes. Other trains run to **Bilbao**, **Pamplona**, **Burgos**, **Huesca**, **Jaca**, **Calatayud**, **Teruel**, **Valencia** and more. Bus No 51 runs between the centre (Puerta del Carmen is 1 stop) and Las Delicias station.

⊙ Directory

Zaragoza p166, map p168
Internet Ría Internet, C Predicadores 22, cheap internet and phone calls, **Ciber**, C San Lorenzo 26, internet. **Laundry** A lavandería is on C Pedro María Ric s/n. **Medical services** C Isabel La Católica s/n. T112 in an emergency. **Police** C Doctor Palomar 8, T976 396 207. T092 or T112 in an emergency.

Northwest from Zaragoza

The most interesting corner of Zaragoza province seems to encapsulate Aragón with its deserted, epic, dry and dusty landscapes and fascinating, forgotten towns and villages redolent of past glories. Intriguing Tarazona takes you back centuries to the era when three faiths lived side by side. With its superb ensemble of mudéjar *brick buildings and its precariously perched old town, it has a distinct feel of sandswept North Africa or the Levant. North of here, the enticing Cinco Villas are backwaters today, with beautifully preserved buildings and squares and steep paved streets. Who would believe that remote Sos was the birthplace of one of history's most powerful monarchs, the Catholic King Fernando de Aragón?* ▶▶ *For listings, see pages 178-179.*

Tarazona and around → *For listings, see pages 178-179. Colour map 5, A5.*

Those who hold stone and wood to be the only noble building materials should pay Tarazona a visit. Brick can be beautiful too, as this town's many *mudéjar* edifices prove. Once home to thriving Muslim and Jewish populations, Tarazona still seems to pine for these expelled people, although a look at the *turiaso* faces suggests that the Catholic purists happily didn't come close to erasing every last drop of non-Christian blood.

The best time to see Tarazona is a summer evening, just as the sun decides it's baked the bricks enough. People emerge from hiding and the buildings glow with a cheery light. Tarazona is an easy day trip from Zaragoza or Soria, but is a nice, peaceful place to stay too.

Background

Tarazona was populated by Celtiberians from way back but flowered in the 13th and 14th centuries, when it sheltered a flourishing population of Jews, Muslims and Christians. A frequent target for Castilian expansion, it suffered several sieges. The Aragonese crown generally protected its non-Christian citizens from the pogroms that plagued the land in the late 14th century but, once it had unified with Castilla, the population was doomed to convert or leave. Later, even the converted Muslims were expelled.

There's a **tourist office** ① *on the roundabout in the middle of town, T976 640 074, turismo@ tarazona.org, Mon-Fri 0900-1330, 1630-1900, Sat-Sun 1000-1330, 1630-1800 (1900 summer).*

Sights

Most of Tarazona's *mudéjar* architecture is clustered on a knoll above the struggling Río Queiles. The tower rising imperiously over the town belongs to the **Iglesia de Santa María Magdalena**, built in a mixture of architectural styles from the Romanesque to the Renaissance. Next to it stands the episcopal palace, formerly a residence of Muslim rulers and Aragonese kings. The ornate Plateresque façade overlooking the river suggests that the local bishops weren't exactly prepared to rough it.

Descending from here, Calle San Juan was the centre of the *morería*, or Moorish quarter. Little remains of the *judería*, the Jewish quarter, which was clustered at the foot of the hill, overhung by houses perched above. The **Ayuntamiento** is an unusual and attractive building adorned with pictures of the labours of Herakles, perhaps an attempt to flatter Carlos V, the king and emperor at the time it was built. An intriguing sculpture in front depicts *El Cipotegato*, a jester-like character who appears to open the town's annual fiesta on 27 August. He attempts to run from the Ayuntamiento across the town; an easy enough task apart from the minor inconvenience of the entire citizenry trying to stop him by pelting him with tomatoes.

Across the river stands the **cathedral** with an extraordinary *mudéjar* brick tower. Currently closed for renovation, it's another fascinating hotchpotch of styles; the attractive cloister is one of its best features. Nearby, the Plaza de Toros is interesting. Annoyed by the lack of a bullring, a group of citizens in the late 18th century decided to build their balconied houses in an octagon that both gave them a place to live and the town a tauromachy venue.

Monasterio de Veruela
① *Oct-Mar, Wed-Mon 1030-1830; Apr-Sep Wed-Mon 1030-2030.*

Beautifully situated in a valley to the southeast of Tarazona is the Veruela monastery. The Cistercian order, bent on a return to traditional monastic values, found Aragón a suitably harsh terrain for their endeavours. Veruela was the first of many monasteries founded by the White Monks in the 12th century. Its small, gardened entrance conceals the size of the complex, girt by a formidable hexagonal wall. The relatively unadorned church is a blend of Romanesque and early Gothic styles. The cloister is similarly attractive and understated, its capitals crowned with simple fronds and leaves. The monks still work the fields, both inside and outside the walls. During summer there are occasional classical concerts in the grounds. Turn off the Zaragoza–Tarazona road at the second of the junctions for Vera de Moncayo; the monastery is 4 km from here. Zaragoza–Tarazona buses can drop you here.

Parque Nacional Dehesa de Moncayo
① *Visitor centre open at weekends in spring and summer 1000-1400, 1500-1900.*

The Dehesa de Moncayo National Park straddles the border of Zaragoza and Soria provinces and is an attractive spot for walks, with scented pine hills and a couple of interesting sanctuaries and villages.

Cinco Villas → *For listings, see pages 178-179.*

Northwest of Zaragoza in a land of harsh hills, cold winds and beating sun are situated these five towns, granted their charter by the Bourbon King Felipe V but important places long before that. If you've got transport you might want to check out all five, but if limited by time or bus timetables, Sos del Rey Católico and Uncastillo are the most rewarding to visit.

Sos del Rey Católico
Once just called Sos, words were added in memory of its most famous son. Not only did young Fernando become king of Aragón, he also united Spain in partnership with his wife Isabel. She was quite a catch; although she only bathed twice in her life that was twice more than most people of the time, and what's more, she was heiress to the Castilian throne.

It's a beautiful, atmospheric village; the city wall is partly intact, with houses built into it. It has become a very popular spot for summer outings and weekends but at other times of year you may have it to yourself – pace the lonely streets and plot your own Reconquista. It's the village as a whole that impresses. In the centre of town is the **Plaza de la Villa**, presided over by the decorative **Ayuntamiento**, featuring a stern warning from Ecclesiastes. The square used to be used for markets; a hole in one of the columns was for hanging a balance, and next to it is etched an official measure of length of the time, the *vara jaquesa* (Jaca bar).

Ascending from the square you'll reach the church via a haunting underpass. The high-vaulted interior is impressive. The highlight is the crypt, which preserves some excellent wall-paintings of the life of Christ and the Virgin. At the far end of the village, remains of a

Mudéjar

Mudéjar is a style of architecture that evolved in Christian Spain, and particularly Aragón, from the 12th century. As the Reconquista took towns from the Muslims, Moorish architects and those who worked with them began to meld Islamic tradition with the influences of Romanesque and Gothic. The result is distinctive, typified by the decorative use of brick and coloured tiles, with the tall, elegant belltowers a particular highlight. The style became popular nationwide; in certain areas, *mudéjar* remained a feature for over 500 years of building.

castle and walls are backed by the parador. Fernando himself was born in the **Palacio de Sada**, one of the largest of the town's buildings, which holds the **tourist office** ⓘ *summer daily 1000-1400, 1600-2000, winter Wed-Fri 1000-1300, 1600-1900, Sat-Sun 1000-1400, 1600-1900.* There are guided walks through the village twice a day from here.

Uncastillo

The most remote of the Cinco Villas, Uncastillo is also its most charming. It's much less visited than Sos and, although not as architecturally perfect, perhaps less austere. Originally fortified by Muslims to counter the Christian Reconquista, it changed hands and became an important bastion for the Navarran King Sancho the Great, before it passed to the Aragonese monarchy. The town also had a flourishing Jewish quarter.

What's left of the castle, above the town, has been transformed into a small but excellent **museum** ⓘ *T976 679 121, Jul-Aug daily 1100-1400, 1700-2000, Sep-Jun Wed-Fri 1100-1400, Sat-Sun 1100-1400, 1600-1800, €2.* The visit commences with a short audiovisual presentation (Spanish or English), which is an epic, and then sends you up the tower where some accessible displays give good information about the history of the town and the region. There's a small **tourist office** open all week during the summer.

Ejea de los Caballeros

The 'capital' and largest of the Cinco Villas (whose two other villages are Sádaba and Tauste), Ejea de los Caballeros at first glance lacks the charm of its neighbours. However, make your way to the church of **San Salvador**, which has some vestiges of colour in its portal, which depicts the *Last Supper* and the *Nativity*. The real reason to come here, however, is inside; the main *retablo* is a masterpiece. The Gothic painted panels show clear Flemish influence and have been carefully restored. They depict scenes from the life of Christ, from the *Adoration* to the *Last Judgement*, all in high colour and lively detail.

◉ Northwest from Zaragoza listings

For Sleeping and Eating price codes and other relevant information, see Essentials pages 31-39.

◉ Sleeping

Tarazona and around *p176*
C Hostal Santa Agueda, C Visconti 26, T976 640 054, www.santaagueda.com. This modern and well-manicured establishment just off the main plaza is Tarazona's most appealing lodging option. The interior is beautiful, with wooden beams and antique furniture. It's very stylish, and the management friendly.
E Palacete de los Arcedianos, Plaza Arcedianos 1/C Marrodón 16, T976 642

303, www.palacetearcedianos.com. Good, if sometimes stuffy, rooms with small modern bathrooms in a curious domed building.

Sos del Rey Católico *p177*
A Parador de Sos del Rey Católico, C Sainz de Vicuña 1, T948 888 011, www.parador. es. At the far end of town, this parador is mostly modern but characterful, with a nice veranda terrace and slightly sombre but comfortable rooms and some much nicer mini-suites.
A El Sueño de Virila, C Coliseo 8, T948 888 659, www.elsuenodevirila.com. In the heart of Sos, and 1 of several *casas rurales*, this boutique spot offers enchantment in its 6 rooms, with exposed stone and comfortable beds.
D Hostal Las Coronas, Plaza de la Villa s/n, T948 888 408, www.hostallascoronas.com. In the heart of town, these doubles are slightly overpriced but have TV and bathroom above a good restaurant. Some rooms look onto the plaza.

Uncastillo *p178*
There are several *casas rurales*; check www.turismodearagon.com for a list.
C Posada la Pastora, C Roncesvalles 1, T976 679 499, www.lapastora.net. This rural hotel is an excellent option. The decor combines light modernity with rustic colours and textures, and the rooms are a delight, particularly the top floor suite, which has great views and a cosy attic roof (**A**). Breakfast is extra but very good, and the owner is delightful.

● Eating

Tarazona and around *p176*
El Galeón, Av La Paz 1, T976 642 965. It's a fair way from the sea, but this good ship does some excellent seafood – the mussels are especially delicious. There's a *menú* for €9.15 that's pretty good value.
Amadeo I, Paseo de los Fueros de Aragón s/n, T976 642 290. A fine terraced café by the Río Queiles, a spot for early evening drinks

and ice creams as well as for an excellent variety of appetizing *pinchos*.
Bar Visconti, C Visconti 19. The locals' choice, with a range of *raciones* and tapas, many of them fried morsels of various things. Tasty steamed mussels too.

Sos del Rey Católico *p177*
Many hotels also have decent restaurants.
As Bruixas, C Mayor 25, T948 888 415. Colourful and modern behind the noble historic façade, this place brings a breeze of fresh air to rural Aragón. The bar features some fine *pinchos* and good atmosphere, while the restaurant does local specialities like roast lamb or pigeon with a confident modern touch.
Vinacua, C Pintor Goya 1, T948 888 071. Recently redecorated, this village stalwart Eschew the *menú* for à la carte; it's no more expensive. Well-prepared Aragonese classics and wines are the order of the day. They also have good rooms available down the road
Bar Landa, C Alfaro s/n, T948 888 158. Good for morning coffee, with a peaceful back terrace and cheap evening meals.
El Caserío, C Pintor Goya s/n, T948 888 009. A welcoming bar serving *raciones* of ham and sausage.

● Transport

Tarazona and around *p176*
Bus Therpasa buses leave from the corner of Av de Navarra and C Arenales. They service **Zaragoza** and **Soria** 6-7 times daily. Cada leave from Av Estación just off Cra de Zaragoza for **Tudela** 6 times a day, with no service on Sun.

Cinco Villas *p177*
Autobuses Cinco Villas run from **Zaragoza** to **Tauste**, **Ejea de los Caballeros**, and **Sádaba** 3-4 times daily, some continuing to **Uncastillo** 1-2 times daily. **Sos del Rey Católico** can be reached on the Sangüesa bus that leaves **Zaragoza** 1 daily.

Huesca and around

→ *Colour map 6, B3. Phone code: 974. Population: 52,059.*
Huesca is in a slightly strange situation – in spite of being the capital of Aragón's Pyrenean province, it has been eclipsed by Jaca as 'gateway to the mountains'. Its old town, albeit interesting, feels a little bit neglected, and although the town has plenty of character, it's hard to pin down. That said, it's far from unpleasant, and has some worthwhile restaurants in the eating zone around Plaza Navarra. ▸▸ *For listings, see pages 183-184.*

Ins and outs

Getting there and around Huesca is small and easily traversed on foot. The old town is ringed by a road, which changes name several times; south of here is the main area for bars and restaurants, as well as the combined bus and train station on Calle Zaragoza. There are frequent connections with Zaragoza and regular connections to all major cities in Spain. The new fast train and airport have made Huesca, and the snow beyond, more accessible. ▸▸ *See Transport, page 184.*

Tourist information Huesca's active **tourist office** ⓘ *Plaza López Allué s/n, T974 292 170, www.huescaturismo.com, daily 0900-1400, 1600-2000,* has a new location in the southern part of the old town. As well as being a good source of information, they run guided tours of the city (1100 and 1700 depending on numbers, two hours, €2). An excellent initiative is a vintage bus that has been beautifully restored and runs day trips into the Huescan countryside from Easter to October. It leaves Plaza de Navarra at 0900 daily, returning around 1430. There are dozens of different excursions; it's a great way to reach some hard-to-get-to places. There are details in English on the website; booking is essential. The trip costs €5. There's also a small **information kiosk** on Plaza de Navarra open summer only.

Background

Huesca's history is an interesting one. An important Roman town, it was known as Urbs Victrix Osca and was used by Sertorius as an education centre for Romanizing the sons of local chieftains. Taken by the Muslims, it was known as Al-Wasqa before Pedro I retook it. It became a significant bastion in the continuing Reconquista, a walled town with 90 sturdy towers that was capital of the young Aragonese kingdom for a few years. Its importance declined, along with Aragón's, after union with Castilla. Republicans besieged it for a long period during the Civil War but unsuccessfully; George Orwell tells how an optimistic general's catchcry "Tomorrow we'll have coffee in Huesca" became a bitter, cynical joke in the loyalist lines as the weeks went by.

Sights

Cathedral

ⓘ *Mon-Fri 1030-1400, 1600-1745, Sat 1030-1400 (cathedral but not museum also open Sat afternoon and Sun), €3.*

The cathedral is a sober Gothic edifice. It has an attractive portal with apostles, and an interesting Diocesan museum, but the highlight is a magnificent alabaster *retablo* sculpted by the Aragonese master Damián Forment. The vivid central pieces depict the crucifixion; the sculpture's beauty makes the gold-painted *retablos* in the side chapels look tawdry.

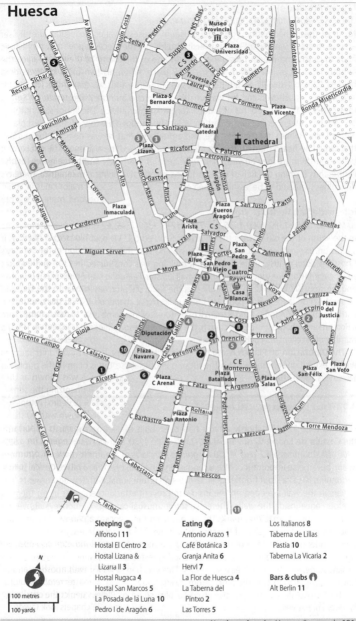

Huesca

Sleeping
Alfonso I **11**
Hostal El Centro **2**
Hostal Lizana &
  Lizana II **3**
Hostal Rugaca **4**
Hostal San Marcos **5**
La Posada de la Luna **10**
Pedro I de Aragón **6**

Eating
Antonio Arazo **1**
Café Botánica **3**
Granja Anita **6**
Hervl **7**
La Flor de Huesca **4**
La Taberna del
  Pintxo **2**
Las Torres **5**

Los Italianos **8**
Taberna de Lillas
  Pastia **10**
Taberna La Vicaria **2**

Bars & clubs
Alt Berlin **11**

100 metres
100 yards

N

Museo Provincial

① Tue-Sat 1000-1400, 1700-2000, Sun 1000-1400, free.

North of the cathedral, the Provincial Museum houses a varied collection, prettily set around the old royal palace and university buildings. The pieces range from prehistoric finds to Goyas and modern Aragonese art. In one of the rooms of the royal palace the famous incident of 'the bell of Huesca' took place. When his two older brothers died heirless, Ramiro II unwillingly left his monk's cell in France and took the throne. The nobles saw him as a pushover, and he was unable to exercise authority. Desperate, he sent a messenger to the abbot of his old monastery, asking for advice. The abbot said nothing, but led the messenger out to the garden, where he chopped the tops off the tallest plants with a knife. Ramiro got the message, and announced that he was going to forge a bell that would be heard through the kingdom. He summoned the nobles to the palace, and beheaded them as they arrived, making a circle of the heads and hanging one in the centre, thus forming the Bell of Huesca. It was an effective political manoeuvre: Ramiro's difficulties were said to be less from then on.

Iglesia de San Pedro El Viejo

① Mon-Sat 1000-1330, 1600-1930, Sun 1100-1215, 1300-1345, €2, English tour available.

In the south of the old town is the church of San Pedro El Viejo, of old stock indeed, as it stands on the location of a Visigothic church, and was the place of worship of the city's Christians during Muslim rule. The current building was constructed in 1117 and features some superb Romanesque capitals in its small cloister. Featuring scenes of the Reconquista and the story of Christ's life, it's thought that the same sculptor was involved both here and at San Juan de la Peña (see page 192). The plain burial chapel off the cloister houses the earthly remains of Alfonso I and Ramiro II (the monk), whose tomb is faced with a panel from a Roman sarcophagus. Inside the church, the soft Romanesque lines are complemented by a number of excellent wall paintings.

The **Diputación** on Plaza Navarra has an impressive ceiling fresco by Antonio Saura as well as exhibitions of other works. The room is in official use, but is open to the public on weekdays 1800-2100.

Loarre → For listings, see pages 183-184.

First recorded in 1033, shortly after it had been built by Sancho the Great of Navarra, the **Castillo de Loarre** ① Nov-Feb 1100-1330, 1500-1730, Mar-Oct daily 1000-1400, 1600-1900 (2000 summer), €2, plus €1.50 for guided tour, one of the finest castles in Northern Spain, became an important centre, a monastery, and also briefly a royal residence, before continuing life as a stout frontier post. The design is functional, with few adornments. The towers in the wall are open on the inside, to prevent attacking enemies using them as a refuge once inside the walls. There are some unusual carvings of monkeys above the entrance, while a small dog marks the ascent from the crypt up a narrow staircase that emerges in front of the altar of the church, an unusually high Romanesque structure. The grim dungeons and remains of the royal hall are other highlights, along with the imposing watchtowers. After the early construction used limestone, the masons decided to switch to sandstone, which is much easier to work. This was bad news for the Muslim prisoners, however, who had to drag the blocks from 20 km away.

The Castillo de Loarre was also used to film some of Ridley Scott's crusader film, *Kingdom of Heaven*.

For Sleeping and Eating price codes and other relevant information, see Essentials pages 31-39.

⊙ Sleeping

Huesca *p180, map p181*

A La Posada de la Luna, C Joaquín Costa 10, T974 240 857, www.posadadelaluna. com. An unusual and offbeat small hotel, set in a sensitively and handsomely renovated Aragonese mansion with mystic and astrological decor. The a/c rooms have all the facilities of a business hotel, including Wi-Fi, flatscreen TV and safe, but it still feels intimate, if overpriced. The location on the edge of town is the only other downside.

A Pedro I de Aragón, C del Parque 34, T974 220 300, www.gargallo-hotels.com. This is a typical modern Spanish hotel, with quiet and cool but vaguely dull rooms and an unremarkable exterior. There are special offers and a large outdoor swimming pool.

C-D Hostal Lizana and **Lizana II**, Plaza Lizana 6/8, T974 220 776, www.hostal-lizana.com. These 2 neighbouring places offer good value. The smallish rooms come with or without bathroom and are clean and comfortable. No 2, where reception is located, is a bit more modern.

D-E Hostal El Centro, C Sancho Ramírez 3, T974 226 823, www.hostalelcentrohuesca.es. An old-fashioned establishment with decent rooms with bathroom and TV. It's near the cafés and restaurants, but can be noisy at weekends if you face the street. Free Wi-Fi.

D Hostal Rugaca, Porches de Galicia 1, T974 226 449, www.hostalrugaca.com. Right in the heart of things above a popular café, the rooms are simple and smallish but have a/c, TV and en suite bathrooms. Parking is also available.

D Hostal San Marcos, C San Orencio 10, T974 222 931, www.hostalsanmarcos.es. A friendly spot in the café/bar zone, with clean rooms and attractive new wooden furniture. Breakfast served and parking available at €6.

E Alfonso I, C Padre Huesca 67, T974 245 454, hostalalfonso@terra.es. Small but pleasant rooms with and without bathroom. Hospitable management.

Loarre *p182*

B Hospedería de Loarre, Plaza Miguel Moya 7, T974 382 706, www.hospederiadeloarre. com. A beautiful place to stay, in a big stone building with commodious rooms. The major attraction lies 6 km above, on a rocky outcrop. There's a decent restaurant, and breakfast is included.

⊘ Eating

Huesca *p180, map p181*

Most eating options are south of the old town, around Plaza Navarra.

ŸŸŸ Las Torres, C María Auxiliadora 3, T974 228 213, www.lastorres-restaurante.com. In rather uninspiring residential surrounds, this place fights it out with the Lillas Pastia for the title of Huesca's best restaurant. Solid Aragonese produce with a gourmet touch is the key to its success.

ŸŸŸ Taberna de Lillas Pastia, Plaza Navarra 4, T974 211 691, www.lillaspastia.es. A classy, slightly snooty restaurant in the old casino with undeniably good rich fare served in exquisitely presented small portions. Expect to pay around €50-60 a head à la carte. House speciality is *revuelto de trufas*, a delicate combination of truffles and scrambled eggs.

ŸŸ Antonio Arazo, C Alcoraz 2, T974 212 736, www.antonioarazo.com. For a cheaper but still delicious binge on wild mushrooms than at **Lillas Pastia**, head around the corner to this spot, which specializes in various of these local *setas*, as well as game and pork in season. There's a number of excellent rices too, including one with pigeon, and a slow-food menu of produce garnered from within 100 km. Recommended.

ŸŸ Hervi, C Santa Paciencia 2, T974 240 333. A popular spot with an outdoor terrace and some excellent fish dishes. Its calamari tapas are particularly highly regarded hereabouts.

¶¶ La Flor de Huesca, C Porches de Galicia 4, T974 240 402. In the Diputación (provincial government) building, this excellent spot is a favoured lunching place for the not-too-hard-working *funcionarios* tucked under the colonnade on this central street. Modern lines, a high ceiling, and colourful contemporary art on the walls are complemented by good service and plenty of value for a short menu that includes great grilled meats. Lunch *menú* for €17.20. Recommended.

¶ La Taberna del Pintxo, C San Orencio 7, T974 226 063. This place specializes in *pinchos*; just help yourself from the little boxes that line the bar. It's an honesty system whereby you leave the toothpicks on your plate and get charged accordingly. The service is excellent, and you can also enjoy *raciones*, or a €10.90 *menú del día* at the small wooden tables.

¶ Taberna La Vicaria, C San Orencio 9, T974 225 195. With stained glass out front, and some pew-like seats at the tables, this has a churchy theme but is far more about earthly indulgence. A fine range of *pinchos* and tapas are complemented by a selection of meat and seafood *raciones*. The €10 *menú del día* is great, but there are very few tables.

Cafés

Café Botánica, Plaza Universidad 4, T974 240 401. A popular and attractive spot next to the museum. It's a student favourite and offers a huge range of teas, and usually has some relaxing world music on the stereo.

Granja Anita, Plaza Navarra 5, T974 215 712. A smart coffee spot opposite the Diputación, with an ornate façade and huge doors. It's popular with Huesca's parliamentarians and as a smart stop on the evening *paseo*.

Los Italianos, Cosa Baja 18, T974 224 539. An excellent ice-cream parlour with tempting pastries and coffee. Try a *pastel ruso*, a traditional confection of almonds, meringue, and hazelnut paste. The sign outside made our day on last visit.

☻ Bars and clubs

Huesca *p180, map p181*

The main bar zone is around C Sancho Ramírez and C Padre Huesca, where you can pick and choose the most inviting option.

Alt Berlin, Plaza de López Allue 8, T974 230 429. This bar is one of Huesca's best. It offers good beer on an attractive plaza that comes to life during San Lorenzo. Some German food is available in the evening.

❀ Festivals and events

Huesca *p180, map p181*

9 Aug San Lorenzo, a week-long festival, with processions of giants, bullfights, cow-dodging in the ring and partying.

❍ Transport

Huesca *p180, map p181*

Air The new Huesca-Pirineos airport, 10 km from town, works with **Pyrenair** (www.pyrenair.es), which offers winter budget flights operated by other airlines from **Madrid** among other cities. Their website has offers that include transport to the ski fields and lift passes.

Bus Buses run from Huesca to **Zaragoza** more than hourly (55 mins, €7). Other destinations include **Barcelona** (4 a day), **Pamplona** (5 a day) and **Lleida** (6 a day). Several buses go to **Jaca** (€7.50, 1 hr), **Barbastro** and **Monzón**. 1-2 buses daily to **Loarre**, leaving at 0825 (Mon-Sat) and 1330 (Mon-Fri).

Train 6-8 trains daily to **Zaragoza** (40-60 mins, from €7.30), a slow train to **Jaca** (2 hrs, €8.60) and a fast train to **Madrid** (2 hrs 20 mins, €59).

☺ Directory

Huesca *p180, map p181*
Internet Casa Blanca, C Cuatro Reyes 10, cheap internet and telephone. Also terminals in the bus/train station.

East of Huesca

The southern part of this zone is an agricultural area at the feet of the soaring Pyrenees, little touched by tourism but boasting some good sights, including the excellent Templar castle of Monzón. Aragón's best wine, Somontano, comes from here, around Barbastro, which is also the spiritual home of the Catholic organization Opus Dei. Nearby is the spectacular canyoning mecca of Alquézar while, further northeast, towards the Pyrenees, is one of Spain's more enchanting villages, Roda de Isábena. ▸▸ *For listings, see pages 188-189.*

Alquézar and the Guara Canyon

The village of Alquézar, tucked away in the Pyrenean foothills, is one of Aragón's prettiest places, a heavily restored sand coloured village nestling among crags that makes a great destination in its own right but also happens to be the launchpad for some of Europe's finest canyoning. There are over 200 canyons in the surrounding Sierra de Guara; some can be strolled without equipment, while others require full climbing, abseiling and water gear. Try and avoid going in the height of summer, as the region gets ridiculously crowded, as well as seriously hot. Alquézar is a 45-minute drive from Huesca, signposted off the Barbastro road. There's a **tourist office** ⓘ *C Arrabal, summer daily 0930-1330, 1630-2000, mid-Oct to mid-Jun weekends only.*

The village's twisting medieval streets – no cars – are dominated by a large rock, on which once sat a **Muslim fortress** ⓘ *entrance by guided tour only; Wed-Mon 1100-1330, 1600-1800 (1630-1930 summer), €1.80*, hence the town's name. The foundations and walls are still visible, but following the Christian reconquest of the town in 1067, it was converted into a fortified collegiate church. Although much of it dates from the 16th century, there are some attractive Romanesque elements still present, particularly the irregularly shaped double-columned cloister, which has some capitals carved with Old Testament scenes.

The area's most famous canyon is the **Cañón del Vero**, a popular destination for the tour companies. It's not very difficult, but you'll need to get wet in some parts at most times of year. The canyon is spectacular, wide and deep, with immense numbers of vultures; the rare lammergeier occasionally puts in an appearance too. Descending the canyon takes about six hours; during summer there's a shuttle bus to the starting point 20 km from Alquézar, otherwise it's about a 4½-hour walk. If you don't fancy doing the whole thing, you can see part of it by walking from Alquézar about an hour to the 'Roman' bridge of Villacantal. ▸▸ *See Activities and tours, page 189.*

Barbastro and around → *For listings, see pages 188-189. Colour map 6, B3.*

After enlisting in Barcelona, to fight alongside the Republican Army in the Spanish Civil War, Barbastro was George Orwell's first stop en route to the front. While things have changed since those dark days, you can see what he was getting at when he referred to Barbastro as "a bleak and chipped town"; he had few good words to say about Aragonese towns in general. The place has taken on new life recently as the centre of the **Somontano** wine region, a small core of producers who have risen to prominence with modern winemaking methods allowing high production and consistent quality.

Barbastro was an important Muslim town in its time, but it's the 16th-century **cathedral** ⓘ *1000-1300, 1800-1930; summer 1000-1330, 1630-1930*, which dominates today. Built between 1517 and 1533, it's an elegant structure with a newer, separate bell tower. Archaeological unearthings have revealed parts of a former church and a mosque alongside the building.

The church's pride is the 16th-century *retablo*, sculpted from alabaster and polychrome wood by Damián Forment (whose work is also in Huesca cathedral), an Aragonese of considerable Renaissance kudos. He died before he could complete the work, but you wouldn't know – it's a remarkable piece. Barbastro's **tourist office** ① *T974 308 350, Mon 1000-1400, Tue-Sat 1000-1400, 1630-1930*, is in the Museo del Vino complex on Avenida de la Merced on the edge of town.

Wineries
The Somontano DO (*denominación de origen*) was approved in principle in 1974 and in practice a decade later. Most of the producers are modern concerns, using up-to-date techniques to produce a range of mid-priced wines from 12 permissible red and white grape varieties, some local, some French. The region's cold winters and hot, dry summers are ideal for ripening wine grapes and production has soared in the bodegas. The **Museo de Vino** ① *above the tourist office, Mon-Sat 1000-1400, 1630-2000, free*, is an arty but not particularly informative display. There's also a shop downstairs and a good restaurant.

Most of the wineries are on the road to Naval relatively close to Barbastro. The best known both inside and outside Spain is **Viñas del Vero** ① *T974 302 216, www.vinasdelvero. es, Mon-Fri 1000-1400, 1600-1900, Sat 1000-1400, guided visits last 1 hr and include a tasting*, 3 km from the centre on this road, whose Cabernet Sauvignon- and Merlot-based wines are appealingly good value. They're open.

Monzón → *Colour map 6, B3.*
Though seldom visited, Monzón is one of those surprising Spanish towns that has a superb attraction, in this case its relatively unspoiled **castle** ① *Tue-Sat 1000-1300, 1700-2000, Sun 1000-1400, 1700-1900, winter Tue-Sat 1130-1300, 1500-1700, Sun 1000-1400; €2*, an atmospheric Templar stronghold that feels impregnable, albeit bare. The castle was fought over during the Reconquista, and often changed hands. The mercenary El Cid came here a few times to accept contracts from Muslim governors, while his renowned blade *El Tizón* was later kept here as a relic. Although some reconstruction has been effected, the buildings still preserve the Templar austerity and ambience. There are underground passageways to be explored (take a torch). The **tourist office** is in the bus station, but the admissions booth at the castle also functions as one.

Torreciudad → *Colour map 6, B3.*
The holy shrine of **Opus Dei** ① *daily 0900-1900 (later in summer)*, is worth a visit, but don't expect revelation; it's likely to reinforce anyone's pre-existing love or otherwise of the organization (see box, opposite). In a spectacular setting on a rocky promontory amid craggy hills, it overlooks the Embalse de El Grado and Franco's dam that created it. The main building, once you're past the security guard, is a curious affair. Virtually windowless, the brick design seems to recall the designs of both Oriental temples and Victorian power stations. Inside, the altarpiece is the main attraction, an ornate sculptural relief. In the centre is a Romanesque statue of the Virgin – a passage behind leads to a kissable medallion.

Many Catholic theologians see Opus Dei as an organization looking backwards towards ritual piety rather than a more enlightened spirituality; the complex certainly bears this out – visitors are encouraged to seek God in the rosary and stations of the cross in several admittedly attractive locations. The structure was conceived by Saint Josemaría himself, who was born in nearby Barbastro. He died suddenly in 1975, 11 days before the official opening.

Opus Dei

For this secretive Catholic organization, the stunning success enjoyed by the *The Da Vinci Code*, which portrays it in a distinctly unflattering light, was anathema, and spokesmen reacted angrily to what was, after all, a detective novel that made no claim of objectivity. Whatever the mysteries of Opus, we can be fairly certain that self-mutilating albino monk assassins aren't within their *modus operandi*.

It's ironic that after centuries of severe persecution of Freemasons on the grounds that they were a "secretive, power-hungry cult", Spain should have produced Opus Dei, a Catholic sect with marked similarities to the Lodgemen. It was founded in 1928 by Josemaría de Escrivá, a Barbastro lawyer turned priest appalled at the liberalism prevalent in 1920s Spain. He saw Opus (the name means "the work of God" as a way for lay people to devote their life to the Lord; one of his favourite phrases was "the sanctity of everyday life". His book *The Way* is the organization's handbook, with 999 instructions and thoughts for achieving greater spirituality in daily matters. Members are both men and women (although *The Way* has been heavily criticized for its archaic attitude to the latter) and, although some follow a semi-monastic life, the majority continue in their worldly professions.

The organization has members all around the world, but Spain has remained its heartland, where membership in boardrooms, staffrooms and parliament remains high but undisclosed. Politically and religiously conservative, Opus was a powerful peacetime ally of Franco's government. This explains part of the considerable hostility towards the sect, as do its capitalistic ventures; the group is very wealthy and owns numerous newspapers, television channels and companies worldwide. Allegations of secrecy about Opus centre around the lack of transparency in its involvement in these enterprises as much as the private nature of personal participation. More serious, perhaps, is its backward-looking approach to Catholicism, with holiness deemed to derive in a large part from the regular performance of the ritual of the sacraments, and the more recent devotions of the rosary and the stations of the cross, an approach bemoaned by forward-thinking Catholic theologians. The late Pope John Paul II, a devoted admirer of capitalism and conservatism, had a lot of time for Opus, and granted them a privileged status within the Vatican. On 6 October 2002, Escrivá was canonized in Rome as San Josemaría; a controversial event both celebrated and mourned in Spain.

Graus

This small service town doesn't seem much to most who pass through it en route to higher ground. In fact, it's a town with plenty of history, an important bastion of the Reconquista, and long-time marketplace for much of the eastern Pyrenees.

The **Plaza Mayor** is an extravagant and beautiful square. Surrounded by beautiful mansions, the **Casa de Barrón** stands out for its red colour and two large paintings on its façade. The female forms are depictions of Art and Science, supposedly created to please the owner's Andalucian wife, perhaps longing for a touch of Mediterranean decadence in dusty Aragón. It's also been suggested, though, that there are several symbols of freemasonry in the paintings, an amusing thought in Opus Dei heartland. Another former resident of the square would not have been amused – Tomás de Torquemada, one of the masterminds of the Spanish Inquisition and scourge of the Spanish Jews, who lived here for a period, see box, page 303. Not to be outdone, however, the owner of the **Casa de**

Heredía did his eaves up with a series of Renaissance female figures. Unable to compete, the **Ayuntamiento** on the square is distinctly restrained by comparison.

Abizanda → Colour map 6, A3.

Heading north from Barbastro towards Aínsa, the village of Abizanda is unmissable, with its **atalaya** (defensive tower) looming over the road. The *atalaya* dates from the 11th century but has been recently rebuilt. Typical of the area, it functioned as a watchtower, one of a chain that could relay signals up and down the valley. A series of levels (sometimes spruced up by art exhibitions) leads to a vertiginous wooden platform with views in all directions through narrow wooden slots. Adjacent is the **Museo de Creencias y Religiosidad Popular** ① *tower and museum Jul to mid-Sep daily 1100-1400, 1700-2100; Easter-Jun and mid-Sep to early Dec Sat and Sun only 1100- 1500, €1.50*, a small but interesting collection of pieces focusing on the local customs that were (and still are, in some villages) designed to keep evil spirits at bay.

Roda de Isábena → Colour map 6, A4.

One of Aragón's gems is tiny Roda, an unlikely cathedral town with a population of 36 in a valley south of the Pyrenees. Apart from the odd tourist shop, the hilltop settlement preserves a superb medieval atmosphere. The Romans established it as a commanding fortification overkooking the valley, but it owes its current appearance to the powerful counts of Ribagorza, sometime troublemakers who made this a major residence. The town invites wandering around its stone buildings and fortifications; there are several coats-of-arms for heraldists to decipher, and occasional art exhibitions and music recitals.

The **cathedral** ① *admission by guided tour only; €2*, claims to be the smallest in Spain, but it's no chapel. The intricate 12th-century façade (with a later porch) is the portal to several architectural and artistic treasures. It is impressive, with columns crowned with rearing lions around a massive studded door. The delicate crypt has superb Romanesque wall paintings of which the best is a Pantocrator. There are more in a chapel off the cloister. The earthly remains of San Ramón are housed in a carved tomb, while the 350-year-old organ still belts out. The cloister is beautiful, swathed with grass and flowers.

⊙ East of Huesca listings

For Sleeping and Eating price codes and other relevant information, see Essentials pages 31-39.

⊙ Sleeping

Alquézar and the Guara Canyon *p185*
C Hotel Santa María, C Arrabal s/n, T974 318 436, www.hotel-santamaria.com. Perhaps the nicest place to stay, with some good views over the valley, castle, and village. Attractive rooms. The hotel runs the **Avalancha** agency (see page 189).
E Casa Jabonero, C Mayor s/n, T974 318 908. One of the nicest of the *casas rurales*. Friendly with attractive rooms, some with en suite.

F Albergue Casa Tintorero, C San Gregorio 18, T974 318 354, www.vertientesaventura. com. A convivial and well-priced hostel in the town centre, with a tour agency.

Camping
Camping Alquézar, T974 318 300, www. campingalquezar.com. The closer to town (1 km) of the 2 campsites and open all year.

Barbastro and around *p185*
Monzón has more charm than Barbastro.
C Hotel Clemente, C Corona de Aragón 5, T974 310 186, www.hotelclemente.com. A touch sterile but spacious, modern and friendly, with a/c and a restaurant.

Monzón p186
D Vianetto, Av de Lérida 25, T974 401 900,
www.hotelvianetto.com. The best option in
Monzón, with dull but comfortable doubles
with a/c. Decent restaurant.

Graus p187
D Hotel Lleida, C Costa s/n, T974 540 925,
www.hotel-lleida.com. The best bet if you
want to stay. With a popular bar/restaurant.

Roda de Isábena p188
Roda can get busy in summer at the weekends.
D Hospedería Roda de Isábena, Plaza la
Catedral s/n, T974 544 554, www.hospederia-
rdi.com. Virtually touches the cathedral steps,
and garlanded with grapevines. A good,
well-priced place. Rooms are comfortable,
but more atmospheric is the restaurant in the
old refectory of the monks who founded the
cathedral, or the patio overlooking the valley.

● Eating

Alquézar and the Guara Canyon p185
※ Casa Gervasio, C Arnal Cavero 13, T974
318 282, www.hotelmaribel.es. In the heart of
the village, this offers traditional Aragonese
cuisine, including tasty home-made pâtés
and cured meats. There's convivial dining
inside, and a pretty patio terrace.

Barbastro and around p185
※ Europa, C Romero 8, T974 310 350. A fairly
upmarket place specializing in gourmet steaks,
rabbit and *longaniza* (an Aragonese sausage).
The bar serves cheaper *platos combinados*.
※ San Julián, Av de la Merced 64, T974
315 575. A restaurant on the ground
floor of the Museo del Vino behind the
tourist office. They specialize in typical
Aragonese cuisine.

Monzón p186
※ La Taberna del Muro, C Juan de Lanuza 4,
T974 403 281. A reasonable, well-frequented
restaurant, with internet access.

Graus p187
※ Itaka, C Joaquín Costa 27, T677 301 601.
A good lunch or drink option on the southern
edge of Graus, with a very pleasant garden
terrace; there's also an internet terminal.

Roda de Isábena p188
※ Hospedería Roda de Isábena, see Sleeping.
A good place for an atmospheric bite to eat.
※ Restaurant Catedral, Plaza Sorolla 2,
T974 544 545, set in the cathedral building
itself. Closed Nov. Aragonese cuisine with
game such as partridge, rabbit and quail, the
most unusual being *jabalí al chocolate* (wild
boar with chocolate). There's a reasonable
menú de la casa for €12.

● Activities and tours

Alquézar and the Guara Canyon p185
There are several companies offering guided
descents of canyons. Competition keeps
prices very similar, but be sure to check what
is offered, as well as insurance; standard
travel insurance may not cover this type of
activity. The standard day trip costs around
€60, usually including a packed lunch.
Avalancha, C Arrabal s/n, T974 318 299,
www.avalancha.org. Solid reputation.

● Transport

Barbastro and around p185
Bus Barbastro is a major transport junction
for the eastern Pyrenean towns. The bus
station is near the cathedral.
  Buses include **Barcelona** 4 daily (3½ hrs),
Huesca 11 daily (50 mins); **Benasque** 2 a
day (2 hrs), **Lleida** 10 a day, **Monzón** hourly
(15 mins), **Aínsa** 1 daily, another on Sun and
in summer, **Graus** 3 daily, and 1 to **Alquézar**.

Monzón p186
Bus Many daily buses to **Huesca** via
Barbastro; 4-6 a day to **Lleida**; 4 to **Fraga**,
and a couple to **Benabarre**.

Western Pyrenean valleys

Although on a world scale the Pyrenees are no giants, their awesome ruggedness is mightily impressive; they are a formidable natural barrier between the peninsula and the rest of Europe. They gain steadily in height from west to east and are accessed by a series of north- south valleys; just to the south of these, Jaca is the effective capital of the region, a fun-loving outdoorsy place that acts as a supply centre to holiday favourites such as Sallent de Gállego and top ski resorts such as Candanchú or Astún. Pilgrims on the Camino Aragonés have their first taste of Spain in this area, which also harbours the stunning carved capitals of San Juan de la Peña, while the quieter vales of Echo and Ansó are home to the distinctive cheso culture. ►► For listings, see pages 196-199.

Jaca → *For listings, see pages 196-199. Colour map 6, A2.*

→ *Phone code: 974. Population: 13,396. Altitude: 820 m.*

A relaxed spot in northern Aragón, Jaca is far from being a large town but it ranks as a metropolis by the standards of the Pyrenees, for which it functions as a service centre and transport hub. The town has enthusiastically bid for three Winter Olympics, most recently for the 2010 event, but with no luck so far. Most visitors to this part of the Pyrenees are in Jaca at some point, and its also the major stop on the Camino Aragonés pilgrim route, so there's always plenty of bustle about the place.

Jaca's **tourist office** ① *Plaza San Pedro 11, T974 360 098, oficinaturismo@aytojaca.es, winter Mon-Sat 0900-1330, 1630-1930, summer Mon-Sat 0900-1400, 1630-2000, Sun 1000-1300, 1700-2000*, is down the side of the cathedral in the heart of town.

Background
Jaca was the centre of the Aragonese kingdom in the early Middle Ages under Ramiro I and his son Sancho Ramírez, who established the *fueros* (see page 504). It was a crucial base in the Reconquista after having been under Moorish control in the eighth century, and a Roman base before that. The city sits on a high plateau above the rivers Aragón and Gállego.

Sights
"It does exist, love for a building, however difficult it may be to talk about. If I had to talk I would have to explain why it should be this particular church that, when I can no longer travel, I will want to have been the last building I have seen." Cees Nooteboom, *Roads to Santiago*.

Jaca's treasure is its delightful Romanesque **cathedral** ① *1100-1330, 1600-2000*, which sits moored like a primitive ship, surrounded not by boats but buildings. Neither majestic nor lofty, it was built in the late 11th and early 12th centuries, although the interior owes more to later periods. The main entrance is a long open portico, which approaches a doorway topped by lions and the Crismon symbol. The idea was perhaps that people had a few paces to meditate on their sins before entering the house of God.

The south door has a wooden porch and fine, carved capitals depicting Abraham and Isaac, and Balaam with the angel. These were beautifully carved by the 'Master of Jaca'. The interior is slightly less charming; the most ornate of the chapels is that of San Miguel, which contains a fanciful 16th-century *retablo* and a carved portal. Next to this is a 12th-century figurine of a wide-hipped virgin and child, dedicated to Zaragoza's Virgin of the Pillar. The main altar is recessed, with an elaborately painted vaulted ceiling. The cathedral is usually dark; a coinbox just inside the main door takes half-euro pieces, each of which provides light for five minutes.

Worthy of a quick peek is the **Iglesia del Carmen**, with its interesting façade columns and a Virgin seemingly flanked by a pair of mandarins.

In the cathedral cloister is the **Diocesan Museum** ① *Tue-Sun 1100-1300, 1600-1[...] €2,* which houses a superb collection of Romanesque and Gothic frescoes, taken from other churches in the area and cleverly reconstructed. The best is an awesome 11th-century set

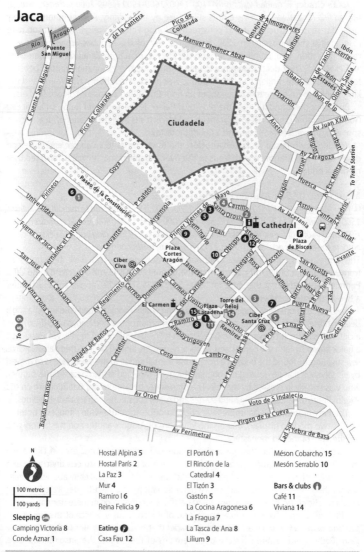

Jaca

Sleeping 🛌	Hostal Alpina **5**	El Portón **1**	Méson Cobarcho **15**
Camping Victoria **8**	Hostal París **2**	El Rincón de la	Mesón Serrablo **10**
Conde Aznar **1**	La Paz **3**	Catedral **4**	
	Mur **4**	El Tizón **3**	**Bars & clubs** 🍸
	Ramiro I **6**	Gastón **5**	Café **11**
	Reina Felicia **9**	La Cocina Aragonesa **6**	Viviana **14**
		La Fragua **7**	
Eating 🍴		La Tasca de Ana **8**	
Casa Fau **12**		Lilium **9**	

...om Bagües, depicting an abbreviated history of the old and new Testaments, comic-strip style. Another highlight is the apse paintings from Riesto, featuring some marvellously self-satisfied 12th-century apostles. Of the paintings, a prim Saint Michael is standing, as is his habit, on a chicken-footed demon who is having a very bad time of it; a wood-carved Renaissance assembly of figures around the body of Christ is also impressive.

Jaca's **citadel** ① *guided visits only 1100-1400, 1600-1900 (1600-2000 summer); wait at the red line for a guide to arrive, €10*, is still in use by the military. A low but impressively large star-shaped structure, it was constructed during Felipe II's reign. The garrison here rose against the monarchy in 1930, before the rest of the Republican movement was ready for action: two young officers who decided to march on Zaragoza were arrested and executed. Their deaths were not in vain, though, as the indignation caused boosted feeling against the monarchy – the Republic was proclaimed shortly afterwards, and the king went into exile. The tour takes about an hour (including a museum of lead soldiers).

Built over the foundations of the old Royal Palace is the **Torre del Reloj**, an attractive Gothic affair that is now HQ to a Pyrenean taskforce. It sits in Plaza Lacadena, an attractive spot at night, with several bars and a floodlit fountain.

Walking down **Paseo de la Constitución**, the town comes to an abrupt end in a slope down to the **Río Aragón**. A path leads to the river, a bathing spot, which is traversed by a medieval bridge.

Monasterio de San Juan de la Peña → *Colour map 6, A2.*
① *Nov-Mar 1030-1400, 1530-1730, Apr-May 1000-1400, 1530-1900, Jun to mid-Jul 1000-1400, 1500-2000, mid-Jul to Aug 1000-2000, Sep-Oct 1000-1400, 1530-1900, €6 old monastery only, €9 including one of the exhibitions in the new monastery, €12 including both. All tickets include entry to the monastery at Santa Cruz de la Serós, 10 km further north.*

The monastery is difficult to reach without a car, although you can walk the whole way from Jaca on the GR65.3.12 path, part of the Camino de Santiago; otherwise jump off a Pamplona-bound bus at the cruce for Santa Cruz de la Serós; the monastery is just under a two-hour walk from here.

This famous monastery allegedly came into being when a noble named Voto was chasing a deer on horseback. The despairing creature took the Roman option and leaped to its death over a cliff. Voto's horse was unable to stop itself from following. Still in the saddle, Voto launched a quick prayer to John the Baptist and, to his amazement, landed safely outside a small cave. Investigating, he found the body of a hermit and a small shrine to the saint. He was so moved by his salvation that he decided to continue the hermitage and settled here with his brother, who was equally impressed by the tale. The monastery became an important centre on the Pilgrim Route to Santiago in the Middle Ages and today constitutes two separate buildings.

The new monastery is an impressive brick baroque structure which houses a hotel as well as two modern displays, one on the kingdom of Aragón, another on the history and architecture of the old monastery.

It's the older monastery that draws visitors, spectacularly wedged into the cliff 1 km down the hill. Built around bedrock, the lower part consists of a spooky 11th-century church and dormitory, with fragmentary wall paintings and the tombs of several early abbots. Upstairs is a pantheon, where nobles could (with a hefty donation) be buried; it's decorated with the characteristic *ajedrezado jaqués* chessboard pattern that originated in these parts.

The high church features three apses, one of which holds a replica of the Holy Grail, see box, page 194, and a martial funerary chapel that holds the remains of the Aragonese kings Pedro I and Ramiro I. It's the open remains of the cloister that inspire most awe;

are decorated with superbly carved Romanesque capitals under the conglomerate cliff. Scenes from the life of Christ and the book of Genesis are superbly portrayed; Cain takes on Abel with a particularly fearsome sledgehammer.

Canfranc Valley → *For listings, see pages 196-199. Colour map 6, A2.*

The Canfranc Valley stretches north from Jaca to the French border at Somport, traversed by a long tunnel. Apart from the spectacular mountains at its northernmost extremity, the valley is attractive but not breathtaking. There's not a huge amount of interest; some fine walks to be sure, but the townships seem listless most of the year, perhaps too busy anxiously scanning the skies for the first signs of snow. Pilgrims on the Camino Aragonés branch of the route to Santiago enter Spain along this valley, but the area's main source of tourist revenue is skiing, with two important resorts close to the border.

Villanúa
The first large settlement in the Canfranc Valley is Villanúa, whose main attraction is a limestone cave, **La Cueva de las Güixas** ① *T974 378 139, the opening schedule is impossibly complex but it's basically summer daily 1000-1330, 1630-2000, rest of the year weekends only; morning visit at 1230 and evening one at 1730, €5.80.* Formerly a home for prehistoric man, there are some calcified formations and an underground river. The tour takes about one hour.

Canfranc and Canfranc-Estación
The village of Canfranc was destroyed by fire in 1944 and plays second fiddle to its neighbour up the valley, Canfranc-Estación, where most of its residents settled after the blaze. Between the two is a small but impressive moated defensive tower built by Felipe II. It now functions as an information centre for the **Somport tunnel** linking France and Spain, which was finally opened in 2003 despite much opposition from environmentalists. Canfranc-Estación's main feature is, sure enough, its railway station, inaugurated in 1928 in a spirit of Franco-Hispanic cooperation. A massive edifice with a platform of prodigious length, it will look familiar to fans of the film *Dr Zhivago*, in which it featured. It's a sad place now, derelict and awaiting rehabilitation work; France closed the rail link in the 1970s.

Candanchú and Astún
The ski resort of Candanchú sits amid pretty mountains 1 km short of the border. An ugly place, it's nevertheless equipped with excellent facilities, 40 skiable kilometres at heights from 1.5-2.5 km, a variety of accommodation, and a full range of runs, as well as a cross-country circuit. The intimidating 'Tubo de la Zapatilla' is a legendary steep and narrow descent best tackled by experts. Check the website www.candanchu.com for further information and for current snow conditions.

Nearby, at just 4 km distance, Astún is a smaller but equally professional centre, with a range of high-end accommodation. A day's skiing at either resort costs €34, or €140 for a five-day pass.

Echo and Ansó valleys → *For listings, see pages 196-199.*

Echo and Siresa
Echo (also spelt Hecho) is a small place popular with weekenders. There's a sculpture of a couple in traditional *cheso* costume – these valleys are home to a distinctive micro-culture

The Holy Grail

Relics have always been big in Spain. Fragments of the true cross, feathers from the archangel Gabriel's wings, half-pints of the Virgin's milk, the last breath of San Sebastián in a bottle ... But the daddy of them all is the Holy Grail, the cup used to knock back the bevvy at the Last Supper. Several Aragonese monasteries have held this over the years although, irritatingly for Northern Spain, it's now in Valencia. St Peter thoughtfully took the goblet with him after dinner, and brought it to Rome, where it was in the possession of pope after pope until things got dicey and it was handed to a Spanish soldier, who took it home to Huesca in the third century.

When the Moors got too close for comfort, the local bishop took to the hills, and hid the Grail in the monastery of Siresa. After a century or so it was transferred to safer Jaca, where it sat in the cathedral awhile before monks took it to nearby San Juan de la Peña, where it was guarded by Templar knights. The Aragonese King Martino V thought it would look nice on his sideboard, however, and took it to his palace in Zaragoza in 1399. The monks weren't too happy, but he managed to fob them off with a replica (a replica of the replica is still there; the original replica was destroyed in a fire). When the king died, the Grail showed up in Barcelona. When Alfonso V, King of Valencia, acceded to the Aragonese throne, he took it home with him, and it was eventually placed in the cathedral, where you can see it today.

Spoilsport art historians have revealed that it has been embellished in the ninth, 15th and 16th centuries, but its heart is an agate cup dating from Roman times, so you never can tell.

– with a very distinct dialect and customs – but it's close enough to Basque lands that there's a *frontón* for playing *pelota*. There's a small **ethnographic museum** ① *summer 1030-1330, 1800-2100 (except Mon afternoon), €1.20.* Behind the **tourist office** ① *1700-2000*, on the main road is a **sculpture garden**, a legacy of a former annual festival.

North of Echo, the village of Siresa houses a monastery that was another stop on the long journey of the Holy Grail (see box, above). The **Monasterio de Siresa** ① *1100-1300, 1700-2000, €1.50*, a blocky Romanesque construction, dominates the surrounding hillside. There are a few places to stay, including a youth hostel (T974 375 385), which rents bicycles and provides information about walking in the area. Further up, the valley becomes more spectacular; the most popular spot for starting a hike is 11 km north at Selva de Oza, where there's a campsite and a bar.

Ansó

Overlooking a river, Ansó is a characterful town. Belying its chunky exterior, the **church** houses a massive *retablo* and several large gold-framed paintings as well as a small **ethnographic museum** ① *€2*. From Ansó you can cross to the Roncal Valley in Navarra (see page 143).

Tena Valley → For listings, see pages 196-199. Colour map 6, A2.

While not as spectacular as the valleys to the east and west, the Tena Valley is pretty and accessible, with a good wide road all the way to France. It holds two ski resorts, Panticosa and Formigal, and sees most action in winter; during summer it seems a little bit ill at ease without a coating of snow.

Sabiñánigo and around

The town at the head of the valley is Sabiñánigo, a fairly dull and uninteresting place useful only for transport connections, see page 199. On the edge of town is a good ethnographic museum, worth a visit if you're stuck here for a few hours. West of here, the semi-abandoned villages of the **Serrablo** region are worth exploring with time and a car; there are numerous small Romanesque gems throughout the near-deserted land.

Biescas and around

Moving on into the valley, Biescas is a nice quiet little place divided by a pebbly river. There's a road from here leading to **Torla** (see page 200) and the Ordesa Valley, with occasional buses plying the route. There's not a lot going on in Biescas, but it's an authentic Pyrenean village and makes a quiet base. The **tourist office** ① *1000-1330, 1700-2030*, is above the main square by the river.

If you've got a car, you may want to drop in at **La Cuniacha** ① *winter 1100-1800, summer 1100-2000 (last entry 2 hrs before closing), €13.50, children 5-12 €10.50, under 5 free*, an open-plan wildlife park/zoo up a side road 5 km north of Biescas. It's a good chance to see some of the Pyrenean animals and plant species, as well as other alpine and cold-climate fauna, although some are a little reclusive.

Panticosa and around

Some 10 km beyond Biescas, a road branches right to the ski town of Panticosa. It's a pleasant little place, although the odd shop and restaurant break the symmetry of the hotels lining the streets. A cable car takes skiers up to the chairlift 800 m higher; it also runs in summer, when most visitors are using the town as a base for walks in the area. The hotels are fairly cheap – the skiing is low-key compared to Formigal. You can rent bikes to explore the countryside from **Sport Panticosa**. There's a **tourist office** ① *1000-1300*.

Further up the narrow valley of the river is an old spa resort, **Balneario de Panticosa**. It's a stately sort of place, given over to leisurely summer lunches and a little light strolling. It's a bit like Hyde Park in the mountains, with a small lake, rowing boats and a tourist train. The location is pretty, and this is the starting point for some more serious hiking up into the mountains; there's a *refugio* (T974 487 571), which can be used as a walking base.

Sallent de Gállego and around

Back on the main road through the valley, the destination of choice for most of the valley's visitors is Sallent de Gállego, a stone village on the banks of a stream, still bravely trying to be pretty through the mushrooming clusters of hotels that surround it. There are several easy walks in the area, detailed by the tourist office, but the main attraction outside skiing season is the **Pirineos Sur** world music and culture festival (see Festivals and events, page 199), with high-quality international performers and a market. One of the positives to spring from the festival has been the rebirth of the town of **Lanuza**, a couple of kilometres away on the shore of an *embalse*. The Sallent **tourist office** ① *1000-1300, 1700-2000*, is unfailingly friendly; it's set in a square with a curiously attractive sculpture. It's only open in summer; there's tourist information in winter at nearby Formigal.

Formigal

The ski resort of Formigal, 4 km above Sallent, enjoys a bleak but spectacular mountain setting, but is by no means attractive; you're better off, as most people do, staying in Sallent. The skiing is good, with dozens of runs, although the wind can bite as it sweeps over the bare hills. For current snow conditions check www.formigal.com. Apart from winter sports, there's little reason to stop, unless it's for the last drops of Spanish petrol before hitting pricier France. There's a **tourist information centre** ⓘ *daily*. For skiing, see Activities and tours, page 199.

⊚ Western Pyrenean valleys listings

For Sleeping and Eating price codes and other relevant information, see Essentials pages 31-39.

⊜ Sleeping

Jaca *p190, map p191*
It's worth booking accommodation ahead here in both high summer and high winter.
AL Hotel Reina Felicia, Paseo Camino de Santiago 16, T974 365 333, www.pronihoteles. com. This hotel in a new suburb a couple of kilometres from the centre stands out for its avant-garde modern design. Rooms are comfortable, with dark chocolate colours and swish bathrooms. Facilities include a spa and pool complex, but it's a little disappointing that they cost extra. There's a good breakfast buffet.
B Hotel Conde Aznar, Paseo de la Constitución 3, T974 361 050, www. condeaznar.com. A charming hotel whose modernization hasn't affected the original charm of the place, but has brought facilities up to an excellent level for the price. The doubles vary substantially in size; some are quite small. For a little more money, you can procure one with a hydromassage unit, or a 'special', which is part way to being a suite. At peak times, they may only take bookings on a half-board basis; no hardship, as the restaurant is the best in town. Excellent service. Recommended.
C Hotel La Paz, C Mayor 41, T974 360 700, www.alojamientosaran.com. A very decent place run by decent folk. The rooms are standard modern Spanish, with TV, tiled floors and bathrooms. Some have balconies. Run out of the same establishment are various apartments, as well as the **Hostal Alpina** (**D-E**), just down the road. The latter is simple but offers decent value on the main street. It gets noisy if there's a school group in, though.

C Hotel Mur, C Santa Orosia 1, T974 360 100, www.hotelmur.com. This is a historic Jaca hotel with a good feeling about it. Bedrooms are airy and have full facilities; the best overlook the citadel, so you can watch the top-secret manoeuvres of the Spanish army.
D Ramiro I, C del Carmen 23, T974 361 367. Closed Nov. Middle-of-the-road hotel with courteous management and fairly simple but spacious enough rooms. The restaurant is uninspiring but decent value.
E Hostal París, Plaza San Pedro 5, T974 361 020, www.jaca.com/hostalparis. A good option near the cathedral with clean doubles with excellent modern shared bathrooms. The doors are locked at night until about 0700, so be sure to make some arrangement if you've got an early start.

Camping
Camping Victoria, Ctra Jaca–Pamplona, T974 357 008, www.campingvictoria.es. A year-round site with bungalows that's less campervan traffic than many, and only 15 mins' walk from town.

San Juan de la Peña *p192*
A Hospedería San Juan de la Peña, T974 374 422, www.touractive.com. This hotel occupies the southern wing of the upper monastery and adds plenty of modern comforts to the historic building. The rooms are attractive and spacious, with polished wooden floors; some are appealing duplexes that cost some €20 more. Wi-Fi, gym, and other business-standard facilities are present, but the isolated location and short wander down the path to the ancient cloister under the overhang are the real reasons to stay here. The restaurant isn't up to much.

Canfranc and Canfranc-Estación *p193*
There are several *albergues* and hotels.
A Hotel Santa Cristina, Ctra Candanchú
Km 669, T974 373 300, www.santacristina.es.
You can't miss this massive hotel, a couple
of kilometres beyond Canfranc-Estación. The
rooms are spacious and warm and decorated
with more subtlety than the exterior would
suggest. All facilities for skiers are present, and
there's a lively bar and restaurant. The views
are great when it's clear.
E Pepito Grillo, T974 373 123, www.
pepitogrillo.com. This simple mountain
hostel has friendly management, dorm beds,
and simple doubles and rooms for groups.
It's a lively hillwalkers' bastion.

Candanchú and Astún *p193*
B Hotel Candanchú, T974 373 025,
www.hotelcandanchu.com. Closed Oct-Nov
and May-Jun. One of the more characterful
of the hotels, an old-style Spanish winter
hotel with rustic decor, views and a terrace,
with a good restaurant. The tariff rises
sharply (**AL**) over a few of the crucial ski
weekends, but this is compensated for by
attractive full-board rates. In summer it's
much cheaper. The restaurant is good.

Echo and Siresa *p193*
D Casa Blasquico, Plaza Palacio 1, Echo,
T974 375 007, www.casablasquico.com, and
its restaurant **Gaby**, with charming rooms,
good hospitality and great food. There are
also cheaper *casas rurales*.

Ansó *p194*
D Posada Magoria, C Milagros 32, T974 370
049, www.posadamagoria.com. The nicest of
several places to stay in the old town, this is
a very homely *casa rural* run by welcoming
folk. Vegetarian meals are available.

Biescas and around *p195*
A Hotel Tierra de Biescas, Paseo del
Canal s/n, Biescas, T974 485 483, www.
hoteltierradebiescas.com. This tasteful
modern hotel on the edge of the town

makes a peaceful and attractive base for
the area. The rooms feature crisp white
sheets, plenty of natural light and inspiring
mountain views. Spacious grounds, a pretty
outdoor pool, a spa complex, and a family-
friendly attitude add value.
D Casa Ruba, C Esperanza 18, T974 485 001,
www.hotelcasaruba.com. In the heart of
the village, this has offered solid mountain
hospitality since the 19th century, and offers
value for its simple, comfortable modern
rooms. A popular place for a hearty meal too.
E-F Habitaciones Las Heras, C Agustina de
Aragón 35, T974 485 027. A friendly place
with renovated rooms with or without bath.

Panticosa and around *p195*
D Navarro, Plaza de la Iglesia s/n, T974 487
181, www.hotelnavarro.com. One of several
cheap hotels, it's decked out in typical
mountain style with polished wood, cosy
rooms, laundry service and ski-rack. There's
also a restaurant and pleasant terrace.

Sallent de Gállego and around *p195*
There are plenty of places to stay in Sallent.
A Almud, C Espadilla 3, T974 488 366,
www.hotelalmud.com. This stone hotel in
the heart of the village is a welcoming and
elegant place, full of antique furniture. The
nicest room is at the top, with a mirador to
sit and admire the view over the lake.
D Hostal Familiar Maximinia, C La Iglesia
3, T974 488 436, www.valledetena.com/
maximina. A hospitable stone mountain
lodge, with good rooms, some perfect for
housing families or groups on a ski trip.
The price is very reasonable for these parts.
Rooms have bathroom, TV and phone.

Formigal *p195*
The hotels are predictably pricey. If you're
here to ski, you'll get better deals booking
a package from a travel agent.
A Hotel Villa de Sallent, Formigal s/n, T974
490 223, www.hotelvillasallent.com. Excellent
service and a warm welcome make this a
spot to look forward to returning to after a

🍴 Eating

Jaca *p190, map p191*

🍴🍴🍴 El Portón, Pl Marqués de la Cadena 1, T974 355 854. This elegant rustic restaurant sits in Jaca's most attractive square. Quality ingredients are prepared and served with some style, and the waiting staff are polite and helpful. They're at their best here with traditional Aragonese plates given modern flair.

🍴🍴🍴 La Cocina Aragonesa, Paseo de la Constitución 3, T974 361 050, www.condeaznar.com. Jaca's best, a friendly spot serving up classy Aragonese cuisine with a distinctly French touch. Part of the Hotel Conde Aznar. There's a *menú del día*, but it's not really representative of the quality on offer. There's a lovely covered and heated terrace; a contrast to the, cosier interior.

🍴🍴🍴 Mesón Cobarcho, C Ramiro I 2, T974 363 643. There are several spots in town that specialize in grilled and roast meats, but this spacious and inviting restaurant might just be the best. Truly excellent ox *entrecots* come sizzling, juicy, tasty, and sizeable, and salads or grilled vegetable platters balance out the meal. Recommended.

🍴🍴🍴 Gastón, Av Primer Viernes de Mayo 14, T974 361 719. This upstairs establishment offers a €18 set menu that features good home-style cooking. On the main menu, the *lenguado* (sole) in cava is excellent.

🍴🍴🍴 La Fragua, C Gil Berges 4, T974 360 618. A good hearty *asador*, popular with locals at weekends for its excellent *chuletón de buey* (ox steaks) and other hearty meat dishes. All portions are enormous.

🍴🍴🍴 Lilium, Av Primer Viernes de Mayo 8, T974 355 356. On the main street, this spot has a covered terrace and an artistic touch that is manifest in its beautifully presented Pyrenean cuisine. There are a number of menus showcasing local food, as well as one for kids.

🍴🍴🍴 Mesón Serrablo, C Obispo 3, T974 362 418. An attractive and delicious restaurant in an antique-style stone building. 2 levels, and a good weekend *menú* for €18. The value-for-money is high here.

🍴 Casa Fau, Plaza de la Catedral 3, T974 361 594. This is a great place by the cathedral, with a homely wooden atmosphere perfect after a day on the slopes; or a sunny terrace for warmer weather. The bar proudly displays an array of tasty *pinchos*, including a tasty terrine from across the border, and the service comes with a smile. Recommended.

🍴 El Rincón de la Catedral, Plaza de la Catedral 4, T974 355 920. The place to sit and admire the soft Romanesque lines of the cathedral. Large range of French-style meals, salads, and gourmet *montaditos* costing around €2.

🍴 El Tizón, Av Primer Viernes de Mayo 14, T974 362 780. Gregarious and hospitable, this restaurant is a family favourite after a day on the slopes or walking in the hills. There's something for everyone in the ample menu, from pizzas (€5-9) to a huge range of tasty salads, steaks and game. There's also a decent wine list and helpful service.

🍴 La Tasca de Ana, C Ramiro I 3, T974 364 726. An indispensable stop on the Jaca food trail with a very large variety of quality hot and cold tapas, great salads, good wine and more. The only problem is that it's so good, it can be tough to get in the door.

Panticosa and around *p195*

🍴 Manél, Panticosa, T974 874 470. A nice place to eat, a stone café/restaurant with a shady terrace; they do a solid *menú del día* for €12.

Sallent de Gállego and around *p195*

🍴🍴🍴 Martón , Plaza Valle de Tena s/n, T974 488 251. A quiet riverside terrace and cosy interior serving cheap dishes, including good roasts cooked in an open brick oven.

🍴 Bar Casino Ctra Francia 4, T974 488 046. There are many places to eat in Sallent, but if you've never had a beer in a town hall before, this is the place to do it.

♥ Bars and clubs

Jaca *p190, map p191*
Café, Plaza de Lacadena s/n. Unremarkable-looking spot, this is actually one of Jaca's best bars, with a great collection of vinyl and a good vibe to boot.
Viviana, Plaza de Lacadena s/n. With a mixed selection of Asian prints on the walls, a pool table, and drum 'n bass sounds, this is one of Jaca's most frequented bars. Stick to beer here though: the mixed drinks aren't great.

⊛ Festivals and events

Sallent de Gállego and around *p195*
Mid-Jul Pirineos Sur, T974 294 151, www.pirineos-sur.es. A 3-week world music and culture festival with high-quality international performers and a market.

♦ Activities and tours

Jaca *p190, map p191*
Jaca has several tour operators who offer activities throughout the Aragonese Pyrenees.
Alcorce Pirineos Aventura, Av Regimiento Galicia 1, T974 356 437, www.alcorcea ventura.com. Specialize in mountains, particularly skiing, trekking, climbing and caving.
Aragón Aventura, C Pablo Iglesias 12, T974 362 996, www.aragonaventura.es. Experts in canyoning and skiing, but also offer other activities.
Deportes Goyo, Av Juan XXIII 17, T974 360 413, www.deportesgoyo.com. Hire mountain bikes.
Ur Pirineos, Av Premier Viernes de Mayo 14, T974 356 788, www.urpirineos.es. Primarily a summer operator, running, climbing, canyoning, canoeing trips and more.

Formigal *p195*
Escuela de Esquí de Formigal, T974 490 135, www.escuelaesquiformigal.com. Has a monopoly on skiing courses in Formigal.

⊖ Transport

Jaca *p190, map p191*
Bus
Jaca's bus station is conveniently located on Plaza Biscos in the centre of town. 5-10 daily buses run between Jaca and **Huesca** (1 hr, €7). These connect in Huesca with buses to **Zaragoza**. There are 2 buses daily to Pamplona (1 hr 40 mins, €7).
Alosa run buses from Jaca via **Sabiñánigo** up the Valle de Tena as far as **Sallent de Gállego** and **Formigal**, detouring to **Panticosa** on the way.
There are 5 daily buses from Jaca up the **Canfranc Valley**.
For **France**, get a bus or train to Canfranc, and change there for a French rail bus, which runs 3-5 times daily to Oloron-Sainte-Mairie, from where you can connect by train to Pau and beyond.
For the **Echó** and **Ansó** Valley, there is 1 daily bus from Jaca, leaving Mon-Sat at 1850. The return leaves Ansó at 0630.

Train
The trains are neither as handy nor as useful as the buses and the station is to the east of town. A shuttle bus links to it from outside the bus station. 2 daily trains head down to **Huesca** and on to **Zaragoza**. There are also trains to Canfranc.

Tena Valley *p194*
From Sabiñánigo buses run to **Torla**, gateway to the Ordesa Valley, at 1100 daily, continuing to **Aínsa**. In Jul/Aug, an additional bus runs at 1830 – both go via **Biescas**. The trip to Torla takes 55 mins.

♦ Directory

Jaca *p190, map p191*
Internet Ciber Santa Cruz, C Mayor 42-44 (in arcade), charges €2 per hr, open Mon-Sat 1100-1400, 1700-2300, Sun 1200-1730.

Eastern Pyrenean valleys

The eastern section of the Aragonese Pyrenees contains some of Spain's most spectacular scenery; towering mountainscapes that loom large over delightful grey stone villages. This is walking and climbing country par excellence, with favourites being the Ordesa National Park, demesne of the mighty lammergeyer, and Maladeta, where the range's highest peaks cluster. There is activity for any ability, from leisurely flower-filled valley strolls to high-altitude traverses and assisted climbs. A network of hospitable mountain refugios (see box, page 203) and hearty alpine cuisine adds to the appeal. Most of the eastern region is deserted in winter, with most services closed until March. ▶▶ *For listings, see pages 204-208.*

Torla → *For listings, see pages 204-208. Colour map 6, A3.*

Although heavily visited in summer, there's still something magical about Torla, the base most people use to reach the Parque Nacional Ordesa. Torla's sober square grey belltower stands proud in front of the soaring background massif of **Mondarruego** (2848 m); this imposing wall of rock looks like a citadel built by titans. The village is well equipped with places to stay, eat and stock up on supplies and gear for trekking. The beautiful church houses a small ethnographic museum with a small display of traditional working and domestic life – apart from that it's the great outdoors that beckons. There are several banks in town. Torla's summer-only **tourist office** ① *1000-1400, 1700-2000,* is on the Plaza Mayor.

Further down the valley, **Broto** and **Sarvisé** are pleasant villages with a good range of facilities, handy for Torla and the national park shuttle bus if you've got transport. Broto's star attraction is its amazingly muscular and bulky church; there's plenty of accommodation here. Even better is the tiny village of **Oto**, a 10-minute walk from Broto, and featuring some excellent medieval buildings; there's also a good campsite here and a couple of *casas rurales*.

The area isn't one for winter sports; indeed, nearly everything is closed between November and March. You'll find more action in the Tena Valley to the west, around Biescas and Sallent de Gállego, or to the east around Benasque.

Parque Nacional Ordesa y Monte Perdido → *Colour map 6, A3.*

① *Access to the park is usually confined to the shuttle bus from Torla in summer, see Transport, page 207. There's also a very pleasant 2-hr walk starting from the bridge on the main road in town. Most trails start from La Pradera car park where the bus stops. There's a bar/restaurant here, as well as meteorological information (an important consideration for longer walks even in summer).*

From Torla you can spot the beginning of the Ordesa Valley, taking a sharp right in front of the bulk of Mondarruego. It's the most popular summer destination in the Aragonese Pyrenees, and understandably so, with its dramatic sheer limestone walls, pretty waterfalls, and good selection of walking trails. The valley was formed by a glacier, which chopped through the limestone like feta cheese, albeit over many thousands of years. Beyond the end of the valley looms **Monte Perdido** (Lost Mountain, 3355 m); it's not recorded who managed to lose it, but it must have been a misty day.

The valley and national park is an important haven for flora and fauna – the latter have retreated further into the hills as the stream of visitors became a torrent. You're likely to spot griffon vultures, choughs and wild irises even from the most-used trails, and you may see isard (Pyrenean chamois) and the massive lammergeyer (bearded vulture).

Hiking in the park

The most popular route is an easy four-hour return up and down the valley, passing the pretty waterfalls of **El Estrecho** and Gradas de Soaso before arriving at the aptly named **Cola de Caballo** (Horse's Tail). It climbs gently most of the way before levelling and widening out above the Gradas. Hit the ground running when you get off the bus to avoid the crowds on this popular trail.

A much better option, if more strenuous, is to head across the bridge from the car park, following signs for the **Senda de los Cazadores**. As long as the weather is clear you needn't be fazed by the danger sign – the trail has been much improved, although it's not recommended if you don't have a head for heights. After crossing the bridge, you're led straight into a steep ascent 650 m up the valley walls to the small shelter of **Calcilarruego**, where there's a viewing platform. The worst is now over; it's flat and gentle downhill from here on in. The path spectacularly follows the *faja* (limestone shelf) along the southern edge of the valley, with great views north to the **Brecha de Roldán**, a square-shaped pass on the French border. If you think it looks man-made, you may well be right – Charlemagne's knight Roland is said to have cleared the breach with one blow of his sword. The path continues through beautiful beech and pine forest until you slowly descend to the Cola de Caballo waterfall (three to 3½ hours after starting). From here it's a two-hour stroll back down the valley floor. There are several *refugios* around the area, some of which are unmanned.

For attempts on **Monte Perdido** (hard on the thighs but no technical experience required in summer), continue up another hour or two to the **Refugio de Góriz** (see Sleeping, page 204), usually quite full. From here, you can continue east towards the Pineta Valley and Bielsa, or northwest towards France.

Aínsa → *For listings, see pages 204-208. Colour map 6, A3.*

Characterized by its hilltop location and spectacular mountainous backdrop, Aínsa (L'Aínsa) is a remarkably attractive town as well as being an important service centre and transport hub for some of the high Pyrenean villages. Unfortunately, this has its downside in the heart of summer, when the medieval quarter can feel a little like a theme park with hundreds of day trippers. Come the evening, though, you'll have a freer run, and the sleeping and eating options are good; even the plentiful gift shops are fairly tasteful.

The 12th- to 13th-century **old town** stands proud high above the gravelly junction of the Cinca and Ara rivers. From the entrance portal, two narrow streets lead past beautifully preserved houses to the massive cobbled main square, lined with arcades. Every odd year on 14 September there's a play performed here, with most of the town participating – it tells of the defeat of the Moors in AD 724. Legend has it that García Jiménez, attacking the Muslim town with 300 men, was facing defeat. He called on God, and a glowing red cross appeared on a holm oak tree; heartened by this, the Christians won. The top left corner of the Aragonese coat of arms actually refers to this event.

At the other end of the square is what's left of the **castle**, basically just the still-impressive walls and a reconstructed tower, home to an exhibition of Pyrenean ecology, with a fiendishly complex opening schedule. Back in the narrow streets, there's a better **museum** ① *Plaza San Salvador 5, T974 510 075, summer 1000-1400, 1600-2100, €2.50,* devoted to traditional Pyrenean art. The Romanesque church is Aínsa's other highlight. There's a strangely shaped cobbled cloister, frequently hung with the work of local artists. The semi-crypt behind the altar has a small view out of the window, while the tower offers excellent vistas. Arrive stocked with €1 coins to switch on the lights; this also activates a jukebox-style Gregorian chant. The **tourist office** ①*Mon-Sat 1000-1400, 1600-1930 (1700-2000 summer, plus Sun 1000-1400)*, is on the main crossroads below the old town; guided tours of the town run in summer.

There are several marked walking routes radiating out from Aínsa, which are marked on maps supplied by the tourist office but also illustrated on boards near the castle at the top of town (where the tourist parking area is). They range from jaunts of a couple of hours to serious up-hill down-dale treks to other towns and villages in the area.

Bielsa and around → *For listings, see pages 204-208.*

One of the most peaceful centres in the Aragonese Pyrenees, Bielsa sees most action during the day at weekends, when French Pyreneans nip over the border to secure stashes of cheap whisky and cigarettes. Although the setting isn't as dramatic as Benasque or Torla, it's beautiful here, and the rather unspoiled village atmosphere makes this one of the nicest places to hang out in the area, which is useful as you may end up staying longer than you meant to – it's easy to miss the only bus out at 0600.

Bielsa was mostly destroyed in the Civil War; a posse of determined Republicans held the town against the Nationalist advance before finally retreating up the valley and across the border. The artillery in the car park, however, is used for a less destructive purpose, to trigger avalanches in controlled conditions. The **Plaza Mayor** houses the helpful **national park office** and a small ethnographic exhibition; nearby is the simple but attractive 15th-century church.

Valle de Pineta

Beyond Bielsa the main road makes its way into France via a long tunnel. Above the town, a side road winds over a hill and into the Valle de Pineta, a 15-km stretch of road that admits defeat when confronted with the imposing bulk of Monte Perdido. The car park at the road's end is the start or finish for a number of trails, one heading across the Ordesa National Park towards Torla. There's also a parador here, and the Ronatiza *refugio*, as well as a small chapel with a local Virgin. An information kiosk will give you a map of the trails.

Some 2.5 km short of the car park, you'll see a sign to **Collado de Añisclo**, a tiring but spectacular ascent of the mountain across the valley. Allow eight to nine hours for a return trip in summer – at other times you'll need snow gear to reach the top.

Cañón de Añisclo

South and west of Bielsa, a small, slow and spectacular route links the village of **Escalona** with **Sarvisé** near Torla (there's a quicker way through Aínsa). The road snakes along a pretty gorge before arriving at a car park, about 12 km from the main Bielsa–Aínsa road. This is the head of the Cañón de Añisclo, a small-scale but beautiful gorge with a popular path running down it. Some sections wind easily through oak and beech forest, but other sections are slightly precipitous on one side, although the path isn't steep. Most day trippers walk as far as **La Ripareta**, a level grassy plain about three hours from the car park (the return is slightly quicker), but you can continue to the Fuen Blanca waterfall, about 5½ hour's walk from the car park. From Fuen Blanca it's possible to continue to the Góriz *refugio* and thence to the Ordesa valley and Torla, or to continue to the Pineta valley over the Collado de Añisclo. It's difficult to get to the canyon without your own transport or a tour from Bielsa or Torla, but it's

Refugios

If you spend time walking in the Pyrenees, you're likely to want to use these comradely places, which are essentially mountain hostels along Scottish 'bothy' lines. The word can mean anything from a one-person lean-to upwards, but the better ones have cosily packed dormitories where wet socks are hung from every nail, and most of the staffed ones offer meals at good rates; the communal atmosphere is usually excellent. It's always worth booking in summer; people aren't usually turned away (at least in remote areas), but you might find yourself on the floor or outside. The staff are usually knowledgeable about the area; it's a good idea to inform them if you're climbing a peak so they can give advice and alert emergency services in case of trouble. Most also have a book where walkers and climbers write hints, describe routes, and give warnings and advice.

possible to walk in on the GR15 path, staying at one of the two good *refugios* in tiny **Nerín**, a hamlet with a view. If you're in a car, the return road to Bielsa takes you back a different way, over the top of the hills, while the other option is to continue on to Sarvisé.

Benasque and around → *For listings, see pages 204-208. Colour map 6, A4.*

One of the major towns of the Aragonese Pyrenees, Benasque is a relaxed resort dedicated to outdoor pursuits. Although some of the modern development is reasonably tasteful, it has buried the old centre, which was outgrown by the massive surge in Pyrenean tourism in the years since Spain's return to democracy. It's a good base – there's plenty of accommodation (though few beds come cheap) several restaurants and bars, and resources for guides, tours, information and equipment.

The intelligent and helpful **tourist office** ① *T974 551 289, 1000 1400, 1600 1900 (2100 in summer)*, in Benasque is just off the main road. It's more than adequate for most needs, but for more detailed information about the park there's a **visitor centre** ① *daily in summer from 1000-1400, 1600-2100 and weekends only the rest of the year*, about 1 km from Benasque off the road to Anciles, and also a small exhibition.

The main attraction in the area is the **Parque Nacional Posets Maladeta**, named after the two highest summits in the Pyrenees, which it encompasses. It's a terrain of valleys gouged by glaciers that extends well into Catalunya. Wild and high, the park includes seven summits over 3000 m. The Maladeta's highest peak, **Aneto**, is the Pyrenees' highest at 3404 m – it's climbable from the **Refugio de la Renclusa** (T974 552 106, 45 minutes beyond the bus stop at La Besurta, see Transport, page 208), but come fully equipped, even in summer: not for nothing is the chain known as the 'Cursed Mountains'. On the other side of the main road, to the east, the dark summit of **Posets** is a similarly difficult climb. There are several marked trails and *refugios* around it – one of the most used is the **Refugio Angel Oíns in Eriste** (T974 344 044). It's worth checking out some of the area's glaciers, the southernmost in Europe, sadly rapidly diminishing; some estimates give them less than 30 years of life. There are summer restrictions on vehicles entering the park; you're better off using the bus services provided from Benasque.

There's much scope for shorter walks in the area, around the **Hospital**, **La Besurta** and the **Vallibierna Valley** (also accessible by bus), which is traversed by the GR11 long-distance path. There are several mountain biking routes recommended by the Benasque tourist office.

Some 6 km above Benasque stands the village of **Cerler**, which purports to be the highest place in Aragón to be inhabited year round. It's dominated by a ski resort of average quality but with plenty of runs. There's no shortage of sleeping and eating options, although it lacks the atmosphere of Benasque.

Further up the valley, **Baños de Benasque** is another example of the enduring popularity of spa towns in Spain; there's a hotel here with various regimes targeted at any number of ailments – the spectacularly beautiful location contributes greatly to the healing and relaxation potential.

◉ Eastern Pyrenean valleys listings

For Sleeping and Eating price codes and other relevant information, see Essentials pages 31-39.

● Sleeping

Torla *p200*

A Hotel Villa Russell, C Ruata s/n, T974 486 770, www.hotelvillarussell.com. This modern hotel is right in the centre of Torla but has stayed true to the attractive stone look of the place. Inside, it's a gem too, with luxurious rustic decoration. The rooms are well equipped, with DVD player, internet access, fridge and microwave; and they are handsome too – some have a terrace but all are of high comfort.

D Casa Frauca, Ctra de Ordesa s/n, Sarvisé, T974 486 182, www.casafrauca.com. Closed Jan/Feb. A faded but charming old inn, with characterful and unusual bedrooms with bathroom. Decent restaurant. Great views.

D Edelweiss, Ctra Ordesa s/n, T974 486 168, www.edelweisshotelordesa.es. The best of the cluster of main road hotels, with good, simple en suite rooms, many with pretty wooden balconies and views.

D Villa de Torla, Plaza Nueva 1, T974 486 156, www.hotelvilladetorla.com. Another excellent place to stay in Torla; although the rooms are nothing to write home about, there's a terrace with great views, a swimming pool, good eating and it's in the heart of town.

E Casa Lali, C Fatas s/n, T974 486 168. A welcoming and well-priced *casa rural* in the heart of Torla. The rooms can be a bit noisy with pub-bound revellers passing under the windows, but it's still a very good option, cosy and homely.

F Refugio L'Atalaya, C Ruata 1, T974 486 022. Although the manager rubs plenty of people up the wrong way, the rest of the staff and the decoration are welcoming. The bar/restaurant is great, but the 2 dorms don't have a lot of breathing space.

F Refugio Lucien Briet, C Ruata s/n, T974 486 221, reflucienbriet@ordesa.com. The roomier of the 2 *refugios* in town, with a couple of doubles too. Good restaurant, and board rates offered.

Camping and out-of-town refugios

Camping Río Ara, T974 486 248, www.campingrioara.com. A peaceful campsite in the river valley below Torla. Access by car is 1.5 km beyond town, but there's a quicker footpath.

Refugio de Góriz, T974 341 201, www.goriz.es. A crucial *refugio* (see page 201) despite frequent shortages of beds. Book ahead if you don't want to camp out. Meals provided.

Refugio Valle de Bujaruelo, T974 486 348. Open Apr-Oct. A well-equipped and beautiful site further up the valley.

Aínsa *p201*

Many of Aínsa's hotels are unattractive options in the new town and budget accommodation is in short supply in the summer months.

AL Monasterio de Boltaña, www.monasteriodeboltana.es. A couple of miles down the road from Aínsa near the town of Boltaña, this luxurious spa hotel is partly set in a historic monastery, which the modern additions have tried to remain faithful to. It makes a fine base for exploring the Pyrenees, with a good restaurant, and comfortable, light rooms, many of which offer spectacular views. The decor is artistic in an offbeat way, with period features alongside tribal art and modern designer flourishes. Off-season there are some appealingly discounted prices (**C**) on their website.

A-B Hotel Posada Real, C de las Escalaretas s/n, T974 500 977, www.posadareal.com. An establishment run out of the Bodegón de Mallacán restaurant, this stately place has an odd mixture of the old and new, with 4-poster beds side by side with modern tiling and art. Still, it's a very comfortable place to stay just off the plaza.

D Casa El Hospital, C Santa Cruz 3, T974 500 750, www.casadelhospital.com. A good *casa rural* in a stone house next to the church, with charming doubles at a good price.

F Albergue Mora de Nuei, Portal de Abajo 2, T974 510 614, www.alberguemoradenuei. com. Just above the lower entrance to the old town, this attractively refurbished stone townhouse is a rather charming walkers' hostel with comfortable bunks and a welcoming atmosphere. There are also doubles available (**D**).

Bielsa and around *p202*
AL Parador de Bielsa, Valle de Pineta, T974 501 011, www.parador.es. At the end of the Valle de Pineta road, under looming Monte Perdido, this makes an excellent base for walks in the area. Modern but sensitive construction, recently renovated. It's basically just you and the Pyrenees out here; it feels like a last outpost.

C Valle de Pineta, C Los Ciervos s/n, T974 501 010, www.hotelvalledepineta.com. Reasonably priced rooms, some overlooking the river valley. There's also a swimming pool and a pleasant restaurant.

E Vidaller, C Calvario 4, T974 501 004, www. vidaller.com. One of the best places to stay in Bielsa, with pleasant top-value rooms with and without bathroom above a small and

friendly shop. Simple but very comfortable for this price, which includes a simple breakfast.

Refugios
G Añisclo Albergue, Nerín, T974 489 008, www.nerinrural.com. A good place to stop if you're heading for the Cañón de Añisclo on foot. A top situation, with great valley views, dorm beds (€12 per person), and simple but happy meals.

Benasque and around *p203*
A Gran Hotel Benasque, Ctra Anciles s/n, T974 551 011, www.hotelesvalero.com. This large, comfortable hotel is built in modern rustic style and is conveniently close to the centre of town. There's an excellent swimming pool and spa facilities (which cost extra). Rooms are spacious and light, and there's a relaxing mountain retreat feel to the whole place.

B Hotel San Marsial, Av Francia 77, T974 551 616, www.hotelsanmarsial.com. One of the classier options in Benasque, although often booked out by package tourists. They organize several activities. Elegant hunting lodge-style decor. There's a range of apartment-style rooms available also.

B Hospital de Benasque Hospedería, Llanos de Hospital, T974 552 012, www.llanosdelhospital.com. With a variety of rooms, this remote inn offers every comfort. There's a very welcoming bar and restaurant, but come prepared to stay a while in winter – every now and then it gets cut off by snow.

B Hotel Ciria, Av Los Tilos s/n, T974 551 612, www.hotelciria.com. Very nice balconied rooms on the main street with cheerful fittings and many facilities. There are also suites with hydromassage units to soothe those muscles ailing from hiking or skiing.

C-D Hostal Solana, Plaza Mayor 5, T974 551 019, www.hotelsolanabenas.com. Good clean rooms above an unmemorable but bustling bar/restaurant. There are 2 separate sections, a *hostal* and a hotel – both are decent value and recently refurbished, but make sure they charge according to the rate sheet.

C-D Hotel Avenida, Av Los Tilos 14, T974 551 126, www.h-avenida.com. A friendly family-run concern in the heart of Benasque, with spotless rooms overlooking the main street and a pleasant terrace restaurant.

E Casa Mariano, C Unica s/n, Eresué, T974 553 034. A top spot for people who want a base in the great outdoors in a village 10 km southeast of Benasque. This *casa rural* is very homely, with 2 large bedrooms and excellent home-cooked meals. One of the owners is a mountain guide and will happily help organize activities and give advice.

Camping and refugios

Camping Aneto, Ctra Francia, Km 100, T974 551 141, www.campinganeto.com. Several facilities as well as some simple bungalows.

Refugio La Renclusa, T974 551 490. Run by the Hotel Avenida, this is the best base for climbing Aneto.

🍴 Eating

Torla *p200*

♛ **El Rebeco**, Plaza Mayor s/n, T974 486 068. Not the friendliest of places, but there's a good restaurant upstairs, as well as 2 terraces, 1 shady, 1 sunny. It's named after the isard/Pyrenean chamois, which thankfully doesn't feature on the menu, although it is a traditional local dish.

♛ **L'Atalaya**, C Ruata 1, T974 486 022. Funky bar and restaurant doing a range of quality dishes in a colourful atmosphere. Menú del *día* for €9, and a drinkless evening *menú* for €13. The bar does tapas and *platos combinados*.

♛ **A'Borda Samper**, C Travecinal s/n, T974 486 231. One of the nicest places to eat in Torla – a great range of simple tapas in a welcoming family atmosphere, and a good upstairs restaurant.

♛ **El Taillón** C Ruata s/n, T974 486 304. A no-nonsense bar featuring a lawn terrace with superb views of Mondarruego. The good-value restaurant upstairs does cheap and filling *menús*.

Aínsa *p201*

♛♛♛ **Bodegas del Sobrarbe**, Plaza Mayor 2, T974 500 237, www.bodegasdelsobrarbe. com. A high-class restaurant with traditional Pyrenean cuisine, based around game. Last count featured 11 different land-based creatures on the menu, but vegetarians can be consoled by the excellent wild mushrooms. There's a *menú* for €22.50, but it doesn't feature the best on show.

♛♛♛ **Callizo**, Plaza Mayor, T974 500 385. Innovative, playful cuisine can be enjoyed here at comparatively moderate prices. Their tasting menu (€5) is full of unusual touches; it doesn't all work, but enough does that you'll leave satisfied.

♛♛ **El Portal**, C Portal Bajo 5, T974 500 138. Just about the first building you pass climbing up into the old town, this restaurant has some great views over the rivers below and a *menú* for €15.

Bielsa and around *p202*

♛♛ **La Terrazeta**, C Baja s/n, T974 501 158. Well set with a dining room overlooking the valley, this is one of Bielsa's better options in summer or winter. There's a *menú* for €10.50 (excluding drinks), but à la carte isn't too pricey either.

♛ **El Chinchecle** is an excellent place in a small courtyard serving home-made liqueurs to the sound of traditional music. Also serves some very nice *cecina de ciervo* (cured venison), and put on 1 or 2 nightly dishes for some excellent simple eating.

Benasque and around *p203*

♛♛♛ **Ixeia**, C Mayor 53, T974 552 970. The smartest restaurant in Benasque with some very classy food. The general tenor is Aragonese, with a variety of meats carefully prepared with local Pyrenean fare: forest fruits and mountain herbs.

¶¶ El Pesebre, C Mayor 45, T974 551 507. A dark stony traditional restaurant with a small terrace, serving traditional Aragonese food, with plenty of lamb and game.

¶¶ La Sidrería, C Los Huertos s/n, T974 551 292. An excellent restaurant run by welcoming Asturians. Cider is the obvious choice but there are several good wines to accompany the delicious food. If there's some home-made cheesecake around, grab a slice – it's a short-priced favourite for the best dessert in Aragón.

¶¶ Restaurant La Parrilla, C Francia s/n, T974 551 134. A spacious and smartish restaurant dealing in well-prepared steaks – eat 'em rare if you want to do as the Aragonese do. There's a *menú del día* for €15.

¶ Hostal Pirineos, Ctra Benasque s/n, T974 551 307. A couple of kilometres back down the valley on the main road, this terrace is a nice place to sit and enjoy simple but well-done food and wine. There are good rooms available too.

◑ Activities and tours

Torla *p200*
See also Jaca, page 190, for activities in the Aragonese Pyrenees.
Casa Blas, Sarvisé, T974 486 041, www.caballoscasablas.com. All manner of equine activities.
Center Aventura, Av Ordesa s/n, T974 486 337. Has a good supply of trekking equipment and maps.
Compañía Guías de Torla, C Ruata s/n, T974 486 422, www.guiasdetorla.com. The other major operator in Torla for excursions in the area.

Aínsa *p201*
Aguas Blancas, Av Sobrarbe 11, T974 510 008, www.aguasblancas.com. Run white-water rafting and canoeing expeditions.

Benasque and around *p203*
Barrabés, C Francia s/n, T974 551 056, www.barrabes.com. Run a series of alpine, rock climbing, rafting and canyoning activities for all levels. Their massive shop is full of equipment and maps.
Escuela Montaña de Benasque, Campalet s/n, T974 552 019, www.prames.com. Serious mountaineering, canyoning and skiing courses throughout the year; lasting from 3-5 days, book well in advance. It's part of the **Escuela Española de Alta Montaña**, which has a reputation for excellence.
Compañía de Guías de Benasque, Av de Luchón 19, T974 551 336, www.guias benasque.com. Organizes all sorts of mountainous activities in the area.
Centro Ecuestre Casa Paulo, C La Fuente 14, Cerler, T974 551 092. Horse-riding trips into the valleys.
Escuela Español de Esquí, Centro Cerler, Cerler, T974 551 553, www.escuela esquicerler.com. Run skiing and snowboarding courses.

◒ Transport

Torla *p200*
Bus
Torla is accessed by bus from **Aínsa** 1 daily on Mon, Wed, and Fri at 1430 (1 hr), the return bus leaves Torla at 1200. 2 buses a day arrive from **Sabiñánigo**, via **Biescas**; they return at 1530 and 1945.

From Jul-Oct (and Easter) a shuttle bus runs from the parking lot at Torla to **La Pradera**, in the valley of Ordesa. Leaving every 15-20 mins from 0600-1900, the last return bus leaves the park at 2200. A return trip costs €3; outgoing buses stop at the park's visitor centre El Parador. This bus is often the only way to reach the park by road, as private vehicle access tends to be cut off. Parking in the car park at the entrance to Torla costs €0.50 per hr or €5.50 per day, but there are other places to park.

Aínsa *p201*
Bus
A bus line runs between Barbastro and Aínsa, leaving **Barbastro** Mon-Sat 1945 (1 hr), and leaving Aínsa at 0700. A Sun bus runs to Zaragoza via Barbastro and Huesca. In Jul and Aug a 2nd bus runs, leaving Barbastro Mon-Sat 1100, and leaving Aínsa at 1510. A bus leaves Aínsa for **Bielsa** at 2045 Mon, Wed, Fri (Mon-Sat in Jul and Aug). The return bus leaves Bielsa at 0600. The service connects with the Barbastro bus. A daily bus runs to **Sabiñánigo** via **Torla** and **Biescas**, leaving at 1430.

Bielsa and around *p202*
Bus
Services run from Bielsa to **Aínsa** at 0600 Mon, Wed, Fri (Mon-Sat in Jul and Aug), with a connection to **Barbastro**. The bus into town leaves **Aínsa** at 2045.

Benasque and around *p203*
Bicycle hire
El Baúl, C Francia s/n, hire bikes from €13 a day, as do **Ciclos A Sánchez**, Av del Luchón.

Bus
There are buses departing Benasque for **Barbastro** at 0645 and 1500 (2 hrs), which connect directly with buses to **Huesca**, **Lleida** and Zaragoza. For **Parque Nacional Maladeta**, a bus runs from Benasque to the trailhead of **La Besurta**, leaving at 0430, 0900 and 1300, returning at 1400, 1830 and 2130. The bus also runs to **Vallibierna** and shuttles between La Besurta and the Hospital de Benasque.

Contents

La Rioja

At a glance

⊖ **Getting around** It's easy to get to Logroño or Haro, but you'll want a car (and a designated driver) to visit wineries, or the dinosaur footprint region.

◉ **Time required** 3-5 days.

☼ **Weather** Baking hot in summer, and fairly cold in winter.

✕ **When not to go** Many wineries are closed to the public during the vintage, which is mid-Sep to early Oct.

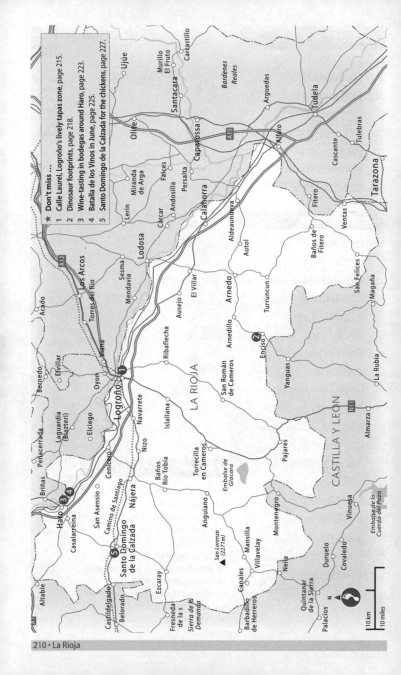

★ Don't miss ...

1 Calle Laurel, Logroño's lively tapas zone, page 215.
2 Dinosaur footprints, page 218.
3 Wine-tasting in bodegas around Haro, page 223.
4 Batalla de los Vinos in June, page 225.
5 Santo Domingo de la Calzada for the chickens, page 227.

The province of La Rioja is known above all for its red wines. The Río Ebro runs down a wide, shallow valley of enormous fertility, which also produces important cereal, fruit and vegetable crops. The region was well known by the Romans, who produced and exported much of the good stuff from here; they referred to the zone as Rioiia; the name comes from the Río Oja, a tributary of the Ebro.

La Rioja is Spain's smallest mainland region, given semi-autonomous status for the same political reasons as Cantabria: it was felt that if it was just one more province of Castilla, the people would be more easily swayed by whisperings from separatist movements in Euskadi and Navarra, of which the territory was historically a part. In truth, though, it feels very conservative and Spanish, particularly when the summer sends temperatures soaring over 40°C. Pilgrims have a hard time of it walking across this sun's anvil en route to Santiago.

The southern part of the province is hillier and has an excellent attraction in its multitude of dinosaur footprints hardened and fossilized in the Mesozoic mud.

The cuisine is wholly unsuited to the heat, being designed more for the chilly winters. Riojan dishes include hearty stews of beans, or large roasts of goat and lamb, perfect with a local red. In recent years, Spanish wineries have finally woken up to the potential of tourism. The major bodegas have competed with each other erecting ever-more ambitiously designed modern wineries, and dozens of them offer excellent guided visits and tasting sessions. Logroño is a peaceful base for exploring the area's wineries, as is Haro, while smaller villages like Briones are enchanting too. It's a compact area, and easily navigable by car: all the major wineries will be within half an hour's drive wherever you base yourself.

The wine denomination of La Rioja actually extends into other regions; a good third of it is in the neighbouring País Vasco; see Laguardia, page 124, for more wineries.

Logroño

→ Colour map 3, C2. Phone code: 941. Population: 152,107. Altitude: 379 m.

The capital of La Rioja province is a pleasant, small city with plenty of plane trees and opportunities for leisurely outdoor life. It's also an important stop on the Camino de Santiago. If you've got transport it makes an excellent base for exploring the area's bodegas, and, happily, has several excellent restaurants with Riojan cuisine that's a suitable match for the region's reds and a great old-town zone packed with tapas bars. ➤➤ For listings, see pages 214-217.

Ins and outs

Getting there and around Logroño is a good transport hub, with connections to most of Northern Spain. Bus services run from the station on Avenida España. The train station is just south of the bus station. ➤➤ See Transport, page 216.

Tourist information The good regional **tourist office** ① *T902 277 200, info@larioja turismo.com, Mon-Fri 0900-1400, 1700-2000 (1600-1900 winter), Sat 1000-1400, 1700-2000 (1600-1900 winter), Sun 1000-1400, 1600-1900,* is in the central Parque Espolón. The new **municipal office** ① *C Portales 50, T941 273 353, www.logroturismo.org, Jul-Sep daily 0900-1400, 1700-2000, Oct-Mar Mon-Sat 1000-1400, 1630-1930, Sun 1000-1400,* is on the western side of the old town.

Background

Logroño emerged in history in Visigothic times, and later, along with much of Northern Spain, became part of the Navarran kingdom until it was annexed by Castilla in 1076 under the name *illo gronio*, meaning 'the ford'. The town prospered as pilgrims flooded through on their way to Santiago, but the city's development was plagued throughout history by fighting; the rich agricultural lands of the region were a valuable prize. The city's name rose when it mounted a legendary defence against a French siege in 1521 and when it became an important tribunal of the Inquisition. In more peaceful times, with Rioja wine drunk all over the world, it has prospered significantly.

Sights

Logroño's Casco Antiguo sits on the south bank of the Ebro, while the newer town's boulevards stretch west and south to the train station, a 10-minute walk away. Centred around its elegant Renaissance cathedral, not all the old town is actually very old, but it's a pleasant space with arcades and outdoor tables at which to bask in the summer sun.

Logroño's outdoor life is centred around its cathedral, **Santa María de la Real** ① *Mon-Sat 0800-1300, 1800-2045, Sun 0900-1400, 1830-2045, free,* a handsome structure, with an ornate gilt *retablo* and elaborate vaulting. The impressive baroque façade still has a faded inscription proclaiming the glory of the Nationalist rising and the *Caudillo*, Franco.

West of the cathedral, along the arcaded Calle Portales, you'll come to **Plaza de San Agustín**, with its impressive post office and the **Museo de la Rioja**. It's a typical provincial museum, the usual mixed bag of archaeological finds and art; the highlight here is a portrait of Saint Francis by El Greco. At time of research it was closed temporarily for a facelift.

The **Iglesia de Santiago** is a bare and atmospheric Gothic edifice with a sizeable *retablo* of carved polychrome wood. There's an inscription outside to the Falangist leader José

Antonio Primo de Rivera, but the front is dominated by a statue of Santiago Matamoros trampling some Moorish heads onboard a monster stallion. The **Iglesia de San Bartolomé** is worth a visit for its intricate Gothic portal and *mudéjar*-influenced tower.

Wineries

Most bodegas have set visiting hours, but you'll nearly always have to phone in advance to arrange a tour or tasting. The tourist office has an excellent book, *Datos Enoturismo*, with a list of various bodegas in the region that welcome visitors. It's in Spanish and

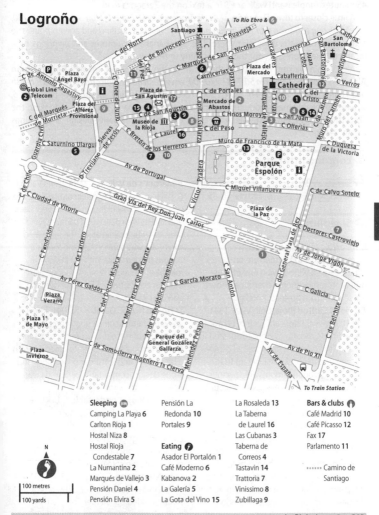

Logroño

Sleeping	Pensión La	La Rosaleda **13**	Bars & clubs
Camping La Playa **6**	Redonda **10**	La Taberna	Café Madrid **10**
Carlton Rioja **1**	Portales **9**	de Laurel **16**	Café Picasso **12**
Hostal Niza **8**		Las Cubanas **3**	Fax **17**
Hostal Rioja	Eating	Taberna de	Parlamento **11**
Condestable **7**	Asador El Portalón **1**	Correos **4**	
La Numantina **2**	Café Moderno **6**	Tastavin **14**	····· Camino de
Marqués de Vallejo **3**	Kabanova **2**	Trattoria **7**	Santiago
Pensión Daniel **4**	La Galería **5**	Vinissimo **8**	
Pensión Elvira **5**	La Gota del Vino **15**	Zubillaga **9**	

N

100 metres
100 yards

English. A smaller pamphlet carries the vital details too. ▸▸ *See the Rioja Alavesa, page 124, and the Rioja Alta, page 221, for more wineries in the area.*

One of the closest bodegas to Logroño is **Marqués de Murrieta de Ygay** ① *Ctra Zaragoza Km 5, T941 271 370, www.marquesdemurrieta.com, phone or email to arrange a visit, closed Aug, the cost of the tour depends on which wines you choose to taste; tours available in Spanish and English.* An attractive traditional winery, Murrieta has one of the best reputations for quality in the entire Rioja region. Its reds, though complex, are remarkably smooth for a wine with such lengthy ageing potential. To get there, it's about 45 minutes' (unpleasant) walk or €8 in a taxi on the Zaragoza road.

A little closer to town, **Ontañón** ① *Av de Aragón 3, T941 234 200, Mon-Sat 1230 and 1730, Sun 1230; ring to book a tour (€6 including tasting),* is just a bottling and ageing point; the actual winemaking is done elsewhere. The Bacchanalian sculptures and paintings by a local artist are impressive, but the wine is fairly unremarkable.

Also within walking distance of the centre is the spectacular, modern **Bodega Juan Alcorta** ① *Camino Lapuebla 50, T941 270 900, www.bodegasjuanalcorta.com, tours (English and French available) Mon-Fri 1100, 1300, 1600, Sat 1100, 1300, must be pre-booked, €5,* where the reliable mass-produced Campo Viejo reds are made. On a hill overlooking the Ebro, this low, modern masterpiece is a great example of innovative design, and includes a giant cellar.

◉ Logroño listings

For Sleeping and Eating price codes and other relevant information, see Essentials pages 31-39.

◉ Sleeping

Logroño *p212, map p213*
As many visitors to Logroño are on expenses-paid wine-buying junkets, the hotel accommodation is overpriced. There are several chain business hotels.
AL Hotel Carlton Rioja, Gran Vía 5, T941 242 100, www.pretur.com. One of Logroño's better hotels, though overpriced, located in the new town, 5 mins from the old centre. The ageing interior doesn't live up to the smart façade, but the rooms are spacious enough, and the service is good. Discount for internet bookings.
B Hotel Portales, C Portales 85, T941 502 794, www.hotelportales.es. Right in the centre, with parking available, this excellent modern hotel is a welcome newcomer to the Logroño scene. The clean lines of the rooms feel almost Nordic, and the fair prices, with free Wi-Fi and breakfast often included, make this the best choice in town. Recommended.

B Marqués de Vallejo, C Marqués de Vallejo 8, T941 248 333, www.hotelmarquesdevallejo. com. This friendly old town hotel is very sleek and stylish, with dark wood parquetry and grey and white minimalism. The renovated rooms are very comfortable and there's a curious modern suite with the bed in the middle of the room. Business lounge with internet access, free Wi-Fi, and underground parking close by.
D Hostal Niza, C Gallarza 13, T941 206 044, www.hostalniza.com. A good choice right in the centre of the old town, perfect for tapas time. The rooms have been touched up with a bit of style, and feature exposed brick and stone design, comfortable beds and clean spacious bathrooms.
D Hostal Rioja Condestable, C Doctores Castroviejo 5, T941 247 288, hosrioja@fer.es. This clean and modern *hostal* has a slightly cramped, lugubrious feel but offers good-value rooms on a pedestrian street. The owners are welcoming and thoughtful.
D La Numantina, C Sagasta 4, T941 251 411, www.hostalnumantina.com. This *hostal* is rather faded but still very comfortable.

The rooms are all doubles, with en suite bathroom and the location is great, in the heart of the old town.

E Pensión Daniel, C San Juan 21, T941 252 948. One of 3 *pensiones* in the same building, right in the middle of town. This is the best of them; it offers comfort at a low price.

E Pensión Elvira, C María Teresa Gil de Garate 20, T941 240 150. This *pensión*, situated in the new town, is smart and has good-value rooms.

E Pensión La Redonda, C Portales 30, T941 272 409. In the heart of town, this cute spot offers simple but correct rooms; try and get the one that looks out at the cathedral.

Camping

Camping La Playa, T941 252 253, www.campinglaplaya.com. By the River Ebro on the opposite bank from town, this is a good place to stay, and relatively handy for town. There are several cabins available.

🍴 Eating

Logroño *p212, map p213*
Logroño has a busy tapas scene; the place to head for is Calle Laurel, which proudly claims to have the highest concentration of bars per square metre in Northern Spain (although there are several pretenders to this throne). It's a place to buzz from bar to bar; you'll work out what each one specializes in by scanning the other diners' plates or the floor. Order *cosechero* if you want the young, cheap local wines, or *crianza* for older, oak-aged reds. Nearby C San Agustín has several good restaurants. The central market near here is a great place to buy fresh meat, fruit, and vegetables.

℀℀℀ Kabanova, C Benemérito Cuerpo de la Guardia Civil 9, T941 212 995, www.kabanova.com. Just outside the old town, this stylish but reasonably priced restaurant has interesting nouvelle Riojan cuisine. The menu is short but features delicacies such as pigs' feet stuffed with foie and pear. There's a set 4-and-a-bit course lunch for €26.

℀℀℀ La Galería, C Saturnino Ulargui 5, T941 207 366, www.restaurantelagaleria.com. This restaurant has gone from strength to strength in the few years it has been open, and is now one of the Rioja's best places to eat. Local Riojan vegetables, delicately-treated fish, and juicy meat are presented in innovative ways without detracting from their natural flavours. The best way to go here is to let the owners pick a tasting menu for you. Recommended.

℀℀℀ Las Cubanas, C San Agustín 17, T941 220 050, www.lascubanas.net. A historic Logroño restaurant, this looks very modern and swish. In the heart of eating territory, it's an upmarket spot serving variations on traditional dishes as well as delicious avant-garde creations. The €30 lunch *menú* is popular with local wine execs.

℀℀ Asador El Portalón, C Portales 7, T941 241 334, www.asadorelportalon.es. While this *asador* does excellent heavy roast meat, it also has a very nice line in salads to balance out a meal. It's one of several worthwhile *asadores* around the centre.

℀℀ La Gota del Vino, C San Agustín 14, T941 210 146. The tapas bar of a successful restaurant (which is upstairs), this is a long, simple, smart and minimalist spot with shell-like chairs and a high metallic bar. There are several wines to choose from at the bar which has excellent and artistic *pinchos*; there are also small rolls and *cazuelitas* (small pots of stew).

℀℀ Trattoria, C Bretón de los Herreros 19, T941 202 602. Modern and stylish, this is an excellent Italian restaurant with a split-level interior and a €12 *menú del día*.

℀℀ Vinissimo, C San Juan 23, T941 258 828. A good choice, with a €10 *menú*. There's a slightly North African flavour, with dishes like couscous and tagine featuring on the menu, but it's a place to learn about the local wine too. You can book a tutored tasting session in English (€15) as well as purchase bottles.

℀℀ Zubillaga, C San Agustín 3, T941 220 076. A wide mix of northern Spanish cuisine, with many tasty fish dishes – try the *merluza* con setas, a tasty dish of hake and wild mushrooms. There are also hearty roast meats, as well as more delicate fare, such as crêpes.

La Taberna del Laurel, C Laurel 7, T941 220 143. This narrow spot is a C Laurel classic. It's very famous around here for its *patatas bravas*: fried potatoes with lashings of tomato and garlic sauce.

Taberna de Correos, C San Agustín 8. This excellent place does regular specials on good local wines and specializes in a range of great hot *pinchos*: 'La Pluma' is a delicious mini brochette of succulent pork for just €1.80. Recommended.

Tastavin, C San Juan 25, T941 262 145. Bright and modern, this is one of a few bars on this old-town street. Delicious gourmet *pinchos* are arranged along the bar, using quality ingredients and a dash of flair. There's a good choice of well-poured wine too.

Cafés

Café Moderno, Plaza Martínez Zaporta 7, T941 220 042. A very popular local spot lavishly decorated in swish neo-baroque style with bright lights and black and white photos. It's popular for a pre- or post-cinema drink, but also does tapas and a cheap *menú del día*.

La Rosaleda, Parque Espolón s/n, T941 220 053. open summer only. An outdoor café with heaps of tables in the park. A great place to while away the hot afternoon.

Bars and clubs

Logroño *p212, map p213*
There are a number of British-type pubs popular with young Riojans; many of these cluster around C Siervas de Jesús, C Saturnino Ularguí and Av de Portugal.
Café Madrid, C Bretón de los Herreros 15. Many of Logroño's young and smartly dressed meet here for an evening coffee or large drink. On weekend nights, it becomes a disco-bar.
Café Picasso, C Portales 4, T941 247 992. A cool café-bar with imported beers

fronted by a sleek grey parrot. It's cheerful, open-minded, and there's always some local banter.
Fax Bar, Plaza San Agustín s/n. A good dark little bar with a mixed crowd. Its best feature is the summer terrace outside.
Parlamento, C Barriocepo s/n, T941 212 836. Lively café-bar with a small stone-faced interior and a terrace. it's opposite the Riojan parliament but often filled with folk much younger than your average politician.

Entertainment

Logroño *p212, map p213*
Cines Moderno, Plaza Martínez Zaporta. A conveniently central cinema.
Teatro El Bretón, C Bretón de los Herreros, T941 207 231. A theatre but also occasionally shows *versión original* (subtitled) English-language films.

Festivals and events

Logroño *p212, map p213*
11 Jun San Bernabé, which is used to commemorate the town's defence against the French. Free fish and wine are given out to the multitudes.
21 Sep Harvest Festival. The most enjoyable time to be in La Rioja is during harvest time. The festival coincides with the feast day of San Mateo.

Transport

Logroño *p212, map p213*
Bus
For bus station information: T941 235 983.
Numerous buses go daily to **Nájera**, 2 daily to **San Millán de Cogolla**, 6 daily to **Calahorra** (3 on Sun), 7 daily to **Haro** (3 on Sun, 1 hr), 4 to **Laguardia** (20 mins) in **Alava**.
To **Pamplona** (3-5 daily, 1 hr, €8), **San Sebastián** (3-5 daily, 3 hrs), **Vitoria** (6 daily, 2 hrs, €8.50), **Zaragoza** (6-7 daily), **Valencia** (2 daily), **Barcelona** (4 daily, 6 hrs), **Bilbao**

(5 daily, 2 hrs), **Burgos** (7 daily, 1 hr, €5.60), **Madrid** (6 daily, 4 hrs 20 mins).

Train
Trains run regularly east to **Zaragoza** (7 daily, 2 hrs, from €13); there are fewer services to Vitoria, Burgos, Bilbao and Haro.

⚙ Directory

Logroño p212, map p213
Internet Global Line Telecom, C Benemérito Cuerpo de Guardia Civil 13, is a *locutorio* which also has internet access. **Post office** The main post office is a pretty affair on Plaza San Agustín, next to the Museo de la Rioja.

La Rioja Baja

The Rioja Baja east of Logroño is a land where wine isn't the be-all and end-all; it's a fertile country (at least near the river), and produces large quantities of high-grade vegetables and cereals. In the southeast, the main attraction is dinosaurs: 100 million years ago prehistoric beasts roamed this land, leaving massive footprints all across the region.

Calahorra is the major town of the Rioja Baja, the province's eastern portion. Wine lovers won't find this as good a base as the Rioja Alta, although there are plenty of producers around. It's a pleasant enough place, but there's little reason to stay unless you're parador-hopping; if you want to check it out, you might be better off making it a day trip from Logroño.➤➤ *For listings, see pages 219-220.*

Calahorra

Baking hot in summer, the settlement of Calahorra is of Roman origin; its fertile riverside situation was what attracted them, and it remains a prosperous agricultural market town. The **old centre** is on a hillock above the river; some of the sloping paths still seem medieval, with chickens running among broken stones and weeds on the side of the hill. The **cathedral** ① *0900-1330, 1700-2030 (1600-1830 winter), free*, is by the river, noticeable for its ornate white sculpture on a sandy façade, a side doorway depicting the Assumption and a tiled turreted belltower. Next to it is the similarly hued **Palacio Episcopal**, but the centre of town is the **Plaza del Raso**, down by the square **Iglesia de Santiago**, a church that seems to want to be a town hall. The **tourist office** ① *T941 146 398, calahorra@lariojaturismo.com*, is just off Plaza del Raso, next to the town museum.

There are **Roman ruins**, but they are so fragmentary as to be almost invisible, although it was once an important town, with a circus for chariot-racing. It was the home of the Roman Christian poet Prudentius; the city was one of three in Spain mentioned by the geographer Strabo in the early first century AD. Some of the remains can be found in the **Museo de Romanización** ① *C Angel Oliván, near Plaza del Raso, Tue-Fri 1100-1330, 1800-2100, Sat 1100-1400, 1800-2100, Sun 1200-1400, free*.

Dinosaur country → *For listings, see pages 219-220.*

The southern part of La Rioja province feels a bit left out, with few grapevines and less arable soil. There's a major attraction, however: the area's former residents, namely stegosaurs, iguanodons and the like, who lived in considerably wetter conditions and left footprints wherever they trod. Some of these tracks have been extraordinarily well preserved. A hundred-odd million years on, it's an unforgettable and slightly eerie sight.

Footprint guide

In the early Cretaceous period, about 120 million years ago, what we now see as hot, dry, craggy hills was a flat place with dense vegetation, marshes and lagoons. Herbivorous dinosaurs were drawn here by the abundant plant life, carnivorous ones by the plump prey on offer. While most of the tracks the dinosaurs left in the mud were erased, some hardened in the sun and, over time, filled with a different sediment. This eventually turned to stone, making the footprints clearly distinguishable as the layers eroded again over tens of millions of years.

There are 20-odd marked sites (*yacimientos*) in the region. Just across the river from Enciso is the site of Virgen del Campo, a large flat bed of rock with a confusing mixture of trails and fossilized mudslides and ripple patterns. One intriguing set of tracks seems to show an iguanodon being run down and attacked by an allosaurus. The road east from here has a great variety of sites, with fossilized trees, footprints of the massive brachiosaurus, tracks of whole herbivore families, and more. Six kilometres north of Enciso, in the village of Munilla, a dirt road leads a couple more kilometres around the hills to the excellent sites of Barranco de la Canal and Peña Portillo. The former has a long trail of 33 clear iguanodon prints, while the latter has a number of well-preserved tracks, including some posited to be those of a stegosaur dragging its tail. Other beds include one, 30 minutes' walk above Arnedillo, and several over the border in Soria province (needless to say, there's no cooperation between the two authorities). The sites are enlivened by decent life-size models of the beasts, with frighteningly pitiless eyes.

Heading into the area south of Calahorra, you hit **Arnedo**, a major Riojan town nestling among rust-red hills. It's a nice enough place, and an important Spanish shoemaking centre, but there's better further on, in the heart of dinosaur country.

Arnedillo, 12 km beyond Arnedo, makes a good base. It sits in a gully carved by the Río Cidacos. Compared to many other Spanish villages, it's upside-down – the church is at the very bottom of town, and the main road at the top of the steep streets. Half a kilometre from town is a **spa**, which offers a large array of treatments and courses, and draws a good number of (mostly elderly) visitors. From here, a path follows the banks of the river as far as Calahorra; it's part of a series of former train lines turned walking paths named **Vías Verdes**.

Enciso, some 10 km further on the road to Soria, is set in the heart of things Cretaceous. Some of the best sites are within a short walk of here, and the village houses the **Centro Paleontológico** ⓘ *www.dinosaurios-larioja.org, Jun to mid-Sep daily 1100-1400, 1700-2000; mid-Sep to May Mon-Sat 1100-1400, 1500-1800, Sun 1100-1400; €3*. It's worth stopping here before you go off looking at footprints. There's a decent audiovisual display (in Spanish) and some average exhibits; the overviews of the different sites are the most valuable. They can organize guided visits of some of the footprint sites (€42 for a group): book on T941 396 093. Near one of the main footprint sites, a massive new complex called **El Barranco Perdido** ⓘ *www.elbarrancoperdido.com, daily 1100-1900, closes 1830 in winter, closes Mon in summer; adult/child €15/10*, is designed to add some dinosaur-themed activities for kids to the area. There's a 3D audiovisual, make-your-own-footprint workshop, a fossil trail, and a large pool area. If you just want to swim, it's only €5/3 for adults/kids.

Beyond Enciso, the road continues into Soria province, and to the city itself. **Yanguas** (actually just over the Sorian border) is a delightfully homogeneous town of stone buildings and cobbled streets on the road between Soria and Arnedo. It's got a very unspoilt feel, and those in need of a quiet stop could do little better. There's a fairly ruinous castle at the eastern end of town that used to house the local lairds; work is in progress to spruce it up a bit. North of the town is another reminder from days when these places were thriving; Yanguas actually had a suburb, **Villaviejo**, but it's now in ruins apart from a church, **Iglesia de Santa María**, in rapid decline but still a pretty sight with its curious cupola.

La Rioja Baja listings

For Sleeping and Eating price codes and other relevant information, see Essentials pages 31-39.

Sleeping

Calahorra *p217*
AL Parador Marco Fabio Quintiliano, Era Alta s/n, T941 130 358, www.parador. es. Calahorra's modern parador sits on the edge of town overlooking the plains below. The Roman remains around can accurately be described as ruins, but the spacious and polished rooms are most comfortable and have (of course) a/c, a prerequisite in the baking Riojan summers.
C Ciudad de Calahorra, C Maestro Falla 1, T941 147 434, www.ciudaddecalahorra. com. A good, comfortable option, but slightly old-fashioned, in the heart of town. The rooms offer excellent value and lack for nothing except perhaps a dash of levity or character.
E Hostal Teresa, C Santo Domingo 2, T941 130 332. A clean and tidy place not far from the old town. The recently renovated rooms are spotless and cheap.

Dinosaur country *p217*
B Hospedería Las Pedrolas, Plaza Félix Merino 16, Arnedillo, T941 394 401, www. laspedrolas.com. By far the best in town and one of the nicest places to stay in this part of the country. Situated opposite the church at the bottom of town it is decorated in smart yet welcoming white. The atmosphere is homely and the rooms, which vary in size, are superbly comfortable. Breakfast included, and home-cooked dinners available. Recommended.

E El Rimero de la Quintana, C La Iglesia 4, Yanguas, T975 185 432, www. elrimerodelaquintina.net. There are a couple of *casas rurales*, and this, on the plaza in the heart of the little town, is the most atmospheric. Good meals are also served.
E Hostal Parras, Av Velasco s/n, Arnedillo, T941 394 034. Right by the massive spa complex, this is a very well-priced retreat. Spacious modern rooms with or without bathroom are available and there's an attractive bar/café as well as a restaurant.
E La Tahona, C de Soria 4, Enciso, T941 396 066. A great base; this is a friendly *casa rural* on the main road, with appropriate displays of local fossils, welcoming rustic rooms, and a big terrace by the river. They also rent mountain bikes for €9 a day; the perfect way to get around the footprint sites. The owner can give you all sorts of advice on where to go, and serves a great breakfast. Recommended.
E Posada de Santa Rita, Ctra de Soria 7, Enciso, T941 396 071, www.posadasantarita. es. Beautifully restored, with gleaming wooden floors, this noble old building is a great-value *hostal* with colourful and comfortable rooms and plenty of peace and quiet.

Eating

Calahorra *p217*
Casa Mateo, Plaza del Raso 15, T941 130 009. A smart restaurant with typical Riojan cuisine, a good spot for lunch on a day trip if you can handle the jowly men flashing their bulging wallets. Its *menestra de verduras* is justly famous.

¶¶ Taberna Cuarta Esquina, C Cuatro
Esquinas 16, T941 134 355. Tucked away in
the back streets, this is another good bastion
of Riojan cuisine with a friendly atmosphere.
¶ El Mesón, C de los Monetes s/n, T941 148
056. Up an arcade off C Ipatro, this *asador*
does sizeable roasts and has a *menú del día*
for a paltry price.
¶ Porqus Porqus, C Cuatro Esquinas 9.
A hearty shop to try (and buy) *jamones*.

Dinosaur country *p217*
Eating options in Arnedillo abound, but be
aware that late nights aren't the town's forte;
many kitchens close shortly after 2200.
¶¶ Bodega La Petra, Av del Cidacos 22,
Arnedillo, T941 394 023. Near the bridge, this
atmospheric cave-restaurant is a great place to
eat. It does hearty traditional home-style food,
with tasty mushroom croquettes, and good
grilled meats in a dark and intimate grotto.
¶¶ Casa Cañas, Av Cidacos 23, Arnedillo, T941
394 022. This appealing restaurant spreads
over 2 floors and is best for meat and game,
which are prepared with Riojan pride.
¶¶ La Fábrica, C de Soria 2, Enciso, T941 396
051. There are several restaurants in Enciso,
but if you're there at a weekend, try this
likeable set-up in an old flour mill.

¶ Bars and clubs

Calahorra *p217*
Cinema Lope de Vega, on the main square,
doubles up as a *discoteca* at weekends.
Oasis, Paseo del Mercadal 25. This bar is one
of a few nightspots on this street.

◯ Shopping

Dinosaur country *p217*
Factoria, Av de la Industria s/n, Arnedo, T941
380 005. On the outskirts of Arnedo, this
factory outlet has some of Spain's bigger
shoe brands for sale at knock-down prices.

Vinoteca Elias, Av Cidacos 36, Arnedillo,
T941 394 010. A good wine shop, which has
a comprehensive range of Riojas.

◐ Activities and tours

Dinosaur country *p217*
Spa Balneario Arnedillo, Av Velasco s/n,
T941 394 000, www.balnearioarnedillo.
com. If you want to take the waters, this
hotel (**B**) offers the most comprehensive
range of services with various 1- to 6-day
programmes as well as one-off sessions.
Use of the pool is expensive for non-guests,
though some accommodations in the
region can offer you discounted entry.

⊖ Transport

Calahorra *p217*
Bus
The bus station is convenient and connects
the town 6 times daily (3 on Sun) with
Logroño. Buses also run to **Zaragoza**,
Pamplona, **Soria** and **Vitoria**.

Train
It's a weary uphill trudge from the train
station with heavy bags. Most eastbound
trains from **Logroño** (7 daily, 30 mins)
stop here.

Dinosaur country *p217*
Bus
3 buses a day (1 on Sun) run from **Calahorra**
via **Arnedo** to **Arnedillo** and **Enciso**;
1 continues to **Soria** (and vice versa).

La Rioja Alta

If you're on the trail of the good drop, you should be investigating this area northwest of Logroño, as well as the adjacent Rioja Alavesa in the País Vasco (see page 124). The Rioja Alta is home to many of the big names of Spanish wine and is increasingly well geared up for wine tourism. Haro, the main town of the region, makes an excellent base, as do the smaller, pretty villages of the region, hilltop settlements overlooking the wide expanses of vines that stretch as far as the looming mountains beyond. ▸▸ *For listings, see pages 224-225.*

Wine route

On the road to Haro from Logroño, the first stop is **Fuenmayor**, 16 km out of the capital. It's a pleasant place with a square and a couple of *pensiones*, and makes a peaceful base for visiting wineries if you've got a car. In town is **Bodegas AGE** ① *T941 293 500, Mon-Fri 0900-1400, 1500-1800 (last visit 1 hr before)*, who operate out of a lovely old 19th-century bodega. You don't have to prearrange this visit, but call ahead to arrange a tour in English or French or a weekend visit. Their Azpilicueta crianza is commonly encountered and tasty.

Cenicero is given over completely to wine, with several bodegas and the mansions lived in by those who own them. As with all these towns, the backdrop is the mountains of the **Sierra de Cantabria** to the north, rising sharply from the Riojan plain. Although it sounds mellifluous in English, *cenicero* actually means 'ashtray'; don't worry, it's really rather nice.

In town is one of the big Rioja names, **Marqués de Cáceres** ① *T941 455 064*, whose wines are a staple throughout the country. However, they don't encourage visitors. At nearby Torremontalbo, is **Bodegas Amezola de la Mora** ① *T941 454 532, www.bodegas amezola.net, daily 0930-1230, 1500-1900*, who make their very tasty wines in a small castle.

Just south of the main road, **San Asensio** is home to several bodegas, and features a smaller version of Haro's **Batalla del Vino** in July, but this free-for-all is strictly rosé only.

Further west, **Briones** is a typically handsome Riojan village, perched on a hilltop over-looking the Ebro with a panorama of vines all around. The brow of the hill houses two churches, one of which, Santa María, has a high and ornate steeple. It's a beautiful place enclosed by substantial sections of city wall; the sandstone buildings glow in the evening sun. The town's **tourist office** ① *T606 202 066, Mon-Wed 1000-1400, Thu-Sat 1000-1400, 1600-1800*, is by the Ermita, the other church, at the top of town.

At the entrance to Briones, it's hard to miss **Bodega Dinastía Vivanco** ① *Ctra Nacional s/n, T941 322 323, www.dinastiavivanco.com, Apr-Sep Tue-Sun 1000-2000, Oct-Mar Tue-Thu and Sun 1000-1800, Fri-Sat 1000-2000, museum €7.50, bodega €6.50, combined €12; phone ahead or reserve online*, whose impressive modern wine museum, **Museo de la Cultura del Vino**, is a must-see for wine lovers. You'll need a couple of hours to make the most of the large exhibition, which, despite starting with an overblown video, is down-to-earth and informative. It covers the history and processes of winemaking around the world, and includes a substantial collection of wine-related art and archaeological artefacts. Highlights include an aroma section. Price of admission includes a glass of wine at the end. Information is in Spanish, so it's worth the extra €1.50 for a multilingual audio guide if you don't read it. You can also visit the bodega and there's a restaurant with great views across the vineyards towards San Vicente de la Sonsierra.

In town, on the way up the hill to the old centre, one of the area's quality producers is **Miguel Merino** ① *Ctra Logroño 16, T941 322 263, www.miguelmerino.com, Mon-Fri 0900-1700, Sat-Sun 0900-1400, tour and tasting €7.50*, who only produce *reservas* and *gran reservas* in limited quantity from old vines.

Rioja wine

Spain's most famous wine-producing area is not solely located in the province of the same name, but extends into Basque Alava and a small part of Navarra. The Ebro Valley has been used for wine production since at least Roman times; there are numerous historical references referring to the wines of the Rioja region.

In 1902 a royal decree gave Rioja wines a defined area of origin, and in 1926 a regulatory body was created. Rioja's DO (*denominación de origen*) status was upgraded to DOC (*denominación de origen calificada*) in 1991, with more stringent testing and regulations in place. Wine was formerly produced in bodegas dug under houses; the grapes would be tipped into a *lagar* (fermentation trough) and the wine made there; a chimney was essential to let the poisonous gases escape. Techniques changed with the addition of French expertise in the 19th century, who introduced destalking and improved fermentation techniques. Now, the odd wine is still made in the old underground bodegas, but the majority of operations are in large modern buildings on the edges of towns, with ever more striking edifices designed by heavyweights of the architecture world.

Rioja's reputation worldwide is now thriving. Sales are around the 250 million litre mark, about a quarter of which is exported, mostly to the UK, USA, Germany, Scandinavia, and Switzerland.

By far the majority of Riojas are red (85-90%); white and rosé wines are also made. There are four permitted red grape varieties (with a couple of exceptions), these being Tempranillo, which is the main ingredient of most of the quality red Riojas, Garnacha (grenache), Mazuelo, and Graciano. Many reds are blends of two or more of these varietals, which all offer a wine something different. Permitted white varieties are Viura (the main one), Malvasia, and Garnacha Blanca.

The region is divided into three distinct areas, all suited to producing slightly different wines. The Rioja Alavesa is in the southern part of the Basque Country and arguably produces the region's best wines. The Rioja Alta is in the western part of Rioja province and its hotter climate produces fuller-bodied wines, full of strength and character; parts with chalkier soil produce good whites. The Rioja Baja, in the east of Rioja province, is even hotter and drier, and favours Garnacha; wines from here don't have the same long-term ageing potential. Most of the best Rioja reds are produced from a combination of grapes from the three regions.

Oak ageing has traditionally been an important part of the creation of Rioja wine; many would say that Riojas in the past have been over-oaked but younger styles are currently more in fashion. The quality of individual Riojas varies widely according to both producer and the amount of time the wines have been aged in oak barrels and in the bottle. Riojas are classified according to the amount of ageing they have undergone. The words *crianza*, *reserva* and *gran reserva* refer to the length of the ageing process, while the vintage date is also given. Rioja producers store their wines at the bodega until ready for drinking, so it's common to see wines dating back a decade or more on shelves and wine lists.

Many bodegas accept visitors, but arrange the visit in advance. The best bases for winery visiting are Briones and Haro in the Rioja Alta (pages 221 and 223), and beautiful Laguardia in the Rioja Alavesa (page 124).

The nearby town of **San Vicente de la Sonsierra** is also worth a detour. The main town of a small subsection of the wine region, it's got a most picturesque sandstone centre with a harmonious plaza and dramatic church housed within the walls of the crumbling castle compound. It sits high above the Ebro, which is crossed by a handsome medieval bridge. There are several bodegas in and around the town. **Hermanos Peciña** ① *Ctra Vitoria Km 47, T941 334 366, www.bodegashermanospecina.com, Mon-Fri 0930-1330, 1530-1830, Sat 1000-1400, 1600-1900, Sun 1000-1400*, is welcoming and offers a 30-minute tour (English-speaking guide available) with tasting.

Haro → For listings, see pages 224-225.

Haro, the major town of the Rioja Alta, is a lively little place. It definitely feels like a wine town, with a clutch of bodegas on its outskirts, several decent wine shops, a museum and a very active tapas and restaurant scene. While its outskirts apparently were designed by a child megalomaniac with a Lego set, the centre is compact and pleasant; most of the bodegas are situated on the opposite bank of the river, a 15-minute walk downhill from the centre. For information contact the **tourist office** ① *Plaza Florentino Rodríguez, T941 303 366, haro@lariojaturismo.com, summer Mon-Sat 1000-1400, 1600-2000, Sun 1000-1400, winter Mon-Fri 1000-1400, Sat 1000-1400, 1600-1900*, opposite **Los Agustinos** hotel.

The **Centro de Interpretación del Vino de la Rioja** ① *C Bretón de los Herreros 4, Mon-Fri 1000-1430; 1530-1900, Sat 1000-1900, Sun 1000-1400, €3*, is situated in the complex of the **Estación Enológica**, a grapey thinktank. The museum is to the point and excellent, with three no-frills floors explaining the winemaking process and regional characteristics in an informative fashion (in Spanish, English and French). It's more didactic than interactive, and rather than giving information about individual wineries, it provides details about the region as a whole.

At the top of town is the **Iglesia de Santo Tomás Apostol**, with an impressive portal decorated with scenes of the crucifixion flanked by the Evangelists. Inside it's gloomy and lofty; an ornate organ the most impressive feature. The balconied tower is also attractive. Have a peek at the noble house next door, with its twisted *salomónica* columns and a large coat-of-arms with a very strange base.

Wineries

One of the best wineries to visit is **Bodegas Muga** ① *T941 310 498, www.bodegasmuga.com, tour in Spanish Mon-Thu 1130 and 1630, Fri 1000, Sat 1030, 1115, 1200, tour in English Mon-Fri 1100, must be pre-booked, €5, €10 for the 'full tour'*. Founded in 1832, the firm relocated here in 1969; it's an attractive and traditional-style bodega. There's a firm commitment to time-honoured processes, so everything is fermented and aged in wood; there's no stainless steel in sight. Even the filtration uses actual egg-whites, painstakingly separated, rather than the powdered albumen favoured by most operators. Most interestingly, Muga make their own barrels on site; if the cooperage is working, it's fascinating to see. The wines are of very good quality; an appley white takes its place along a full range of aged reds. The tours are worth the money, and there's a tasting session at the end.

Near to Bodegas Muga is the **Bodegas Bilbaínas** ① *T941 310 147, www.grupocodorniu. com, Apr-Sep Tue-Sat 1000, 1100, 1200, Sun 1100, ring to book, Oct-Mar Tue-Sat 1630 only, €3*, another historic bodega set in a beautiful building.

Ask the tourist office for their booklet *Enoturismo en la Rioja* and an updated list of opening hours in the area. Most require a prior phone call in advance, but they've recently woken up big-time to the marketing value of tours and tastings, so are very accommodating.

⊙ La Rioja Alta listings

For Sleeping and Eating price codes and other relevant information, see Essentials pages 31-39.

⊙ Sleeping

Wine route *p221*

C Las Vistillas, Camino Briones s/n, San Vicente de la Sonsierra, T941 334 533, www.lasvistillas.net. The name means 'the views', and this spot just below San Vicente delivers, with amazing panoramas from this elevated position over the flat vinelands and healthy Ebro below. There are good facilities, including a garden, pool, and bikes at guests' disposal; the restaurant is also a romantic place to eat. Rooms are warmly decorated and comfortable.

D Hostal Los Calaos de Briones, C San Juan 13, Briones, T941 322 131, www. loscalaosdebriones.com. Between the 2 churches at the top of town, this appealing base offers great views from some rooms, which are all spacious, with cool nouveau-rustic decor. The restaurant downstairs offers good-value Riojan cuisine and wines and the atmosphere is very welcoming.

E El Mesón, Travesía de la Estación 3, Briones, T941 322 178, www.elmeson briones.es. Another great Briones base at the bottom of town just around the corner from the Dinastía Vivanco museum. The 7 rooms are decorated with *cariño* in rustic style and have plenty of space. The helpful owner can organize bodega visits and puts on a good breakfast (€3.50). There's a large garden to relax, but also conveniences like free Wi-Fi. Despite the name, there's no restaurant.

F Mozart, Plaza de España 8, Cenicero, T941 454 496. A small, clean and likeable *pensión* on the main square. 6 comfortable rooms and spotless shared bathrooms. Good value.

Haro *p223*

AL Hospedería Señorío de Casarreina, Plaza Santo Domingo de Guzmán 6, Casalarreina, 6 km west of Haro, T941 324 730, www.alojamientosconencantodelarioja. com. Peaceful and romantic, this grand but intimate village hotel occupies an elegant Plateresque monastery. Rooms, which are all distinct and vary substantially in price, are extremely spacious and elegant, and service is excellent.

A Los Agustinos, C San Agustín 2, T941 311 308, www.hotellosagustinos.com. A peaceful place set in a beautiful old monastery with a cloister/patio as its focus; this is Haro's best choice. The rooms offer value for the quality, with plush carpets and beds, and impeccable service. There are often excellent deals available on their website.

C Hotel Arrope, C de la Vega 31, T941 304 025, www.hotelarrope.com. Opposite the Agustinos, and with a pleasant vine-shaded outdoor terrace, this newly opened hotel has smart, spacious rooms with a minimalist feel. There are numerous stylish touches, modern facilities, and the building, lift and many of the rooms have particularly good disabled access.

E Pensión La Peña, C La Vega 1, T941 310 022. Don't be put off by the musty staircase; this central budget option is an excellent deal, with spotless, comfortable modernized rooms. Some have interconnecting doors making them good for families. Recommended.

F Pensión Aragón, C La Vega 9, T941 310 004. Slightly taciturn but oddly likeable place. Decent rooms with shared bathrooms. The mattress springs gave up the ghost years ago but there's a certain charm to the place; perhaps it's the price.

Camping

Camping de Haro, Av de Miranda s/n, T941 312 737, www.campingdeharo.com. Only a 10-min walk from town across the river, this is a good campsite with some shady spots and decent facilities that include cabins.

🍴 Eating

Haro p223

🍴🍴🍴 La Vieja Bodega, Av de la Rioja 17, Casalarreina, T941 324 254. In the scenic village of Casalarreina, 6 km west of Haro, this is one of the zone's best places to eat, an atmospheric stone and wood-beamed barn of a former winery run with attentive good cheer. The Rioja speciality *menestra* is given new life here: it bursts with fresh vegetable flavour, and the expertly cooked meats – suckling pig, delicate *solomillo* steaks and more – are a treat. Recommended.

🍴🍴🍴 Mesón Atamauri, Plaza Gato 1, T941 303 220, www.atamauri.com. This quiet, discreet place is just about the town's best restaurant, and specializes in fish, prepared with finesse. Richer offerings include delicious *tournedos* and more traditional Riojan dishes. There's a bar with elaborate and delicious *pinchos* too, with creations featuring tempura vegetables and mushrooms.

🍴🍴 Beethoven I & II, C Santo Tomás 3 y 10, T941 310 018, www.restaurantebeethoven. com. The former, a spacious place with comfy wooden furniture serving tapas and *raciones* based around ham and seafood (and an excellent 4-course lunch for €15), the latter, a smarter restaurant with a menu of all things fishy and meaty, as well as an excellent house salad (closed Tue). There's now a third one located opposite Santo Tomás church.

🍴🍴 Terete, C Lucrecia Arana 17, T941 310 023, www.terete.es. Founded in 1877, this is a mainstay of the Haro eating scene, but picturesquely unchanged, with the upstairs *comedor* set up with no-frills long wooden tables and benches. The speciality here is roast lamb, whose aroma pervades the building from the oven by the front door. It won't be the best you'll ever have, but the atmosphere makes it worthwhile.

🍴 Mesón Los Berones, C Santo Tomás 24, T941 310 707. A good and popular bar serving inexpensive portions of Riojan food in a warm, friendly atmosphere. Don't bother with the overpriced *menú del día* though.

🎉 Festivals and events

Haro p223

29 Jun Batalla de los Vinos ('Battle of the Wines'). Haro's best-known festival takes place at the Riscos de San Bilibio, 2 km from town. It has its origins in a territorial dispute between Haro and Miranda de Ebro. The mayor climbs the hill, where a medieval castle used to stand, to symbolize Haro's possession of the area. There's a Mass in the chapel, a lunch and then all hell breaks loose, with litres of red wine being sprayed over everyone. A fair bit disappears down throats too.

21 Sep The grape harvest celebration with floats and dancing.

🛍 Shopping

Haro p223

Vinícola Jarrera, C Castilla 3, T941 311 425, www.gonzalezmuga.com. Open daily 1000-2200. One of the better places to buy wine. There's a large range of Riojas, including some very old examples. While most prices here are good compared with the competition, some of the rarer wines are alarmingly overpriced, so shop around before splashing out. Tapas and tastings available. Case discounts.

🚌 Transport

Haro p223

Bus

Haro's bus station is situated in the Casa de Cune. To **Logroño** (1 hr, 7 daily, 3 on Sun), **Burgos** and **Santander** (1 daily), **Laguardia** (40 mins, 3 daily), **Vitoria** (1 hr, 4 daily), **Bilbao** (1 hr 15 mins, 4 daily), **Santo Domingo de la Calzada** (4 daily, 1 on Sun) and **Nájera** (2 daily).

Train

Services are few, and the station is a fair walk from town, but there are trains to **Logroño** (3 a day, 40 mins) and **Bilbao**.

Pilgrim Route to Santiago

For those heading to Santiago, the stretch from Logroño is often completed under baking sun, but there are a couple of characterful towns in which to stop and find some shade. Nájera and Santo Domingo de la Calzada are appealing places, and the imposing monasteries of San Millán merit a detour. The area prides itself on being the birthplace of the Spanish language; the earliest known texts in that idiom derive from here. ▸▸ *For listings, see pages 229-230.*

Nájera → *Colour map 3, C2.*

After passing through the rosé wine centre of Navarrete, the town of Nájera is the first major stop for pilgrims on the road from Logroño to Burgos. It doesn't seem as large as its population of 7000 would suggest; most are housed in the modern sprawl close to the highway, leaving the river and careworn but attractive old town in relative tranquillity. The town's name derives from an Arabic word meaning 'between rocks', referring to its situation, wedged among reddish crags that jut over the buildings of the centre. These rocky walls are riddled with caves, some of which were used extensively in medieval times and were dug through to make a series of interconnecting passageways. These can be accessed to the south of the town's imposing highlight, the Monasterio de Santa María la Real.

In former times Nájera was an important medieval city and a capital of many Navarran kings; under Sancho the Great in the early 11th century most of Northern Spain was ruled from here. In the 14th century, Nájera was the site for two important battles of the Hundred Years War, both won by Pedro the Cruel, while a famous short-term resident was Iñigo de Loyola, waiting on the Duke of Navarra during the period immediately before his wounding at Pamplona and subsequent conversion from dandy to saint (see box, page 133).

The impressive **Monasterio de Santa María la Real** ⓘ *Mon-Sat 1000-1300, 1600-1730 (1900 summer), Sun 1000-1230, 1600-1730 (1830 summer), €3*, is a testament to this period's glories. It was originally founded by Sancho's eldest son, King García, who was out for a bit of falconry. His bird pursued a dove into a cave; following them in, García found them sitting side by side in front of a figure of the Virgin Mary with a vase of fresh lilies at her feet. After his next few battles went the right way, he decided to build a church over the cave; the rest, as they say, is history. Today the figure is in the main *retablo*, still with fresh lilies at her feet, and the cave holds a different Virgin. The present monastery church is a much-altered Gothic construction, which was heavily damaged during the Peninsular War and later, when much looting followed the expulsion of the monks by government order in 1835. Heavy investment in restoration has restored many of its glories. The cloister is entered via an elaborate door crowned by the coat of arms of Carlos V, who donated generously to monastery building projects. Above is an elaborately painted dome. The cloister is pleasant, although many of the artistic details have been destroyed. The church itself is a fairly simple three-naved affair. The *retablo* features the statue of Mary; to either side kneel King García and his queen. Most impressive is the rear of the church, where elaborately carved tombs flank the entrance to the original cave. The tombs hold the mortal remains of several 10th to 12th-century dukes, Navarran kings and other worthies, but were made several centuries later. The exception is the sepulchre of Doña Blanca, a beautifully carved Romanesque original with Biblical reliefs and funerary scenes. Above in the gallery the *coro* (choir), although damaged, is a superb piece of woodwork, an incredibly ornate late Gothic fusion of religious, naturalistic, and mythological themes adorning the 67 seats.

Around the corner is the moderately interesting **Museo Arqueológico** ⓘ *Plaza Navarra, Mon-Sat 1000-1400, 1700-2000, Sun 1000-1400, €1.20*, with a range of finds from different periods mostly garnered from volunteer excavations. The area was inhabited by prehistoric man and later by a succession of inhabitants, including Romans, Visigoths and Moors.

The **Iglesia de Santa Cruz** is smaller and simpler than La Real and dates from the 17th century. It seems to be the preferred home for the town's stork population, which have built some unlikely nests in its upper extremities.

The **tourist office** ⓘ *Plaza San Miguel 10, T941 360 041, Tue-Sat 1000-1400, 1600-1800, Sun 1030-1400*, will provide a map of the town.

A half-hour walk from Nájera takes you to **Tricio**, famous for its peppers and the **Ermita de Santa María de Arcos** ⓘ *Sat 1030-1330, 1630-1930, Sun 1030-1330*, which is worth a look. Built over extensive Roman remains, some of it dates to the fifth century AD; it's a curious architectural record and a peaceful little place. Phone the keyholder (T636 820 589) ahead to check it's open, or if you hope to visit outside opening hours.

San Millán de Cogolla
ⓘ *Suso Tue-Sun 0930-1330, 1530-1800, €3; Yuso: Tue-Sun 1000-1300, 1600-1830, €4, admission by guided tour only. Visits to Suso must be booked ahead on T941 373 082.*
Some 18 km into the hills is the village of San Millán de Cogolla, which grew up around its two monasteries. The original is the **Monasterio de Suso**, tucked away in the hills a kilometre or so above town. It was started in the sixth century to house the remains of San Millán himself, a local holy man who lived to be 101 years old. It feels an ancient and spooky place, with low arches and several tombs. Mozarabic influence can be seen in the horseshoe arches and recessed chapels. The saint himself was buried in a recessed chapel off the main church but was dug up by Sancho the Great, who built a solemn carved cenotaph in its place. The bones were taken down the hill and had another monastery built around them, **Monasterio de Yuso** (the word means 'low' in a local dialect; *Suso* means 'high'). The current structure is on a massive scale and is a work of the 16th century, far more ornate and less loveable than Suso. Still an active monastery, the highlight is the galleried library, an important archive, some of whose volumes can barely be lifted by one person. San Millán finds himself in an ivory-panelled chest in the museum; this ascetic hermit would also be surprised to see himself depicted over the main entrance door astride a charger with sword in hand and enemies trampled underhoof. There's also a **tourist office** in the grounds of Yuso. A minibus makes the ascent from Yuso to Suso during visiting hours.

The monastery has styled itself the 'birthplace of Spanish', as the first known scribblings in the Castilian language were jotted as marginal notes by a 10th-century monk in a text found in Yuso's library. A couple of centuries later, the nearby village of **Berceo** produced a monk, Gonzalo, who penned the first known verse to have been written in the language.

Santo Domingo de la Calzada → *Colour map 3, C2.*
Santo Domingo is a lovely town, worth a stop for anyone passing through the area. It has a curious history, mostly connected with the man for whom it is named. Born in 1019, Domingo dedicated his young life to the pilgrims. He built a hospice, a bridge and generally improved the quality of the path; it's no wonder he's the patron saint of road workers and engineers in these parts. He made himself a simple tomb by the side of the *camino* before dying at the ripe old age of 90, but admirers later had him transferred to the cathedral, which was built in the town that grew up around his pilgrims' rest stop.

Chickens in the church

A buff 18-year-old German by the name of Hugonell was heading for Santiago with his parents in the Middle Ages when they stopped here for the night.

The barmaid at the inn liked what she saw but got a terse 'nein' from the boy. In revenge she cunningly replaced his enamel camp-mug with a silver goblet from the inn and denounced him as a thief when the family departed. Finding the goblet in his bags, the boy was taken before the judge, who had the innocent teenager hanged outside town. The parents, grief-stricken, continued to Santiago.

On their way back months later, they passed the gallows once again, only to find Hugonell still alive and chirpy; the merciful Santo Domingo had intervened to save his life.

The parents rushed to the judge and told the story, demanding that their son be cut down. The judge laughed sardonically over his dinner and said "Your boy is about as alive as these roast chickens I´m about to eat". At that, the chickens jumped off the plate and began to cluck. The boy was duly cut down.

In memory of this event, a snow-white cockerel and hen have been kept in an ornate Gothic henhouse inside the cathedral ever since. They are donated by local farmers and changed over monthly.

The **cathedral** ① daily 0930-1330, 1600-1830, €3.50, with its ornate free-standing tower, is the town's centrepiece. Time and the elements haven't quite rubbed off the fascist slogans on the façade, but inside it's pleasant and light. There's much of interest after you've made it through the officious bureaucracy at the entrance. Santo Domingo himself is in an elaborate mausoleum with a small crypt underneath it. Around it are votive plaques and offerings from various engineering and road maintenance firms. An attractive series of 16th-century paintings tell some incidents from the saint's life. One of these concerns his 'miracle of the wheel': a weary pilgrim foolishly had a nap on the road and was run over and killed by an oxcart; Santo Domingo prayed on his behalf and he rose again. In memory of this event a cartwheel is hung in the cathedral every 11 May.

Otherwise, the chooks are the main attraction in their ornate coop, punctuating the pious air with the odd cock-a-doodle-doo (see box, above). There's a 16th-century retablo with a few nasty fleshy relics of various saints in small cases and a museum around the cloister. Climb onto the roof for some fresh air and a good view over the many narrow streets below. The guided visit includes the cloister and the small museum of religious artefacts. There are several admirable buildings in the old town, which basically consists of three parallel streets and the northwest section of the old walls is still intact; pilgrims who have passed through Puente la Reina may experience a bit of déjà vu. Not far from the cathedral, on the main pedestrian street (Calle Mayor), is an exhibition on the Camino de Santiago.

The **tourist office** ① C Mayor 44, T941 341 230, www.santodomingodelacalzada.org, Mon-Sat 1000-1400, 1800-2000, Sun 1100-1430, is on the main street.

Some 12 km south of Santo Domingo, the **convent church of Cañas** ① C Real 2, Cañas, T941 379 083, Tue-Sat 1030-1330, 1600-1800, Sun 1100-1330, 1600-1800, to 1900 summer, €3.50, is worth visiting if you've got transport. Founded in the 12th century by Cistercian monks, it's now an austere but noble spot. The visit progresses around the cloister, off which is entered the fine Gothic church, with a beautiful apse with double row of alabaster-paned windows; the altar and retable have been removed to the other end to allow the majesty of the architecture full rein. The adjacent chapterhouse has carved tombs of former abbesses, with that of Beata Urraca López still preserving traces of original colour, a particularly fine example of Gothic funerary sculpture. A display of church treasures includes skulls of some of St Ursula's alleged 11,000 virgin martyrs; an atmospherically lit exhibition of religious art rounds out the visit.

◉ Pilgrim Route to Santiago listings

For Sleeping and Eating price codes and other relevant information, see Essentials pages 31-39.

◓ Sleeping

Nájera *p226*

C Hotel Duques de Nájera, C Carmen 7, T941 410 421, www.hotelduquesdenajera. com. Right in the attractive centre of town, this hotel fulfils its mission by supplying very comfortable, modern rooms backed up by lofty standards of cleanliness and service. Good value.

C Hotel San Fernando, Paseo San Julián 1, T941 363 700, www.sanmillan.com. A faded beauty, this is a good option across the river from the old town. It's quite a charming place, and the doubles offer good value, although they aren't exactly modern. There's even a replica British telephone box in the lobby.

D Hostal Ciudad de Nájera, C Calleja San Miguel 14, T941 360 660, www.ciudaddenajera. com. A modern *hostal* decorated with verve in bright colours. The delightful owners have equipped the good-value rooms superbly, with excellent bathrooms, TVs and piped music. There's also a cheery guest lounge and downstairs bodega. Recommended.

San Millán de Cogolla *p227*

A Hospedería Monasterio San Millán, T941 373 277, www.sanmillan.com. An atmospheric place to stay, this is set in a wing of Yuso monastery and offers excellent, spacious rooms, a heavy Spanish decor, and willing service. There are often exceptional special offers, so it's always worth phoning. Opposite is an *asador*, which is a decent place to eat, if a little oversized.

Santo Domingo de la Calzada *p227*

AL Parador de Santo Domingo de la Calzada, Plaza del Santo 3, T941 340 300, www.parador.es. Right next to the cathedral, this mostly modern parador is built around the saint's old pilgrim hospital and is an attractive place with facilities and charm, backed up by a decent restaurant. Another parador, **Bernardo Fresneda**, with 3-star facilities in a converted monastery, offers similar comfort. It's a hospitality training school, so service is exceptionally willing.

B Hotel El Corregidor, C Mayor (Zumalacárregui) 14 Av Calahorra 17, T941 342 128, www.hotelelcorregidor.com. Bright and breezily decorated modern hotel (although the pink curtains in the rooms are a bit sugar sweet) in the old town; it's a friendly and comforting spot to stay.

D Hostal Rey Pedro I, C San Roque 9, T941 341 160, www.hostalpedroprimero. es. Pushing the boundaries between *hostal* and hotel, this new and modern place on the main road offers plenty of comfort and conveniences, including electronic locks and appealing rooms with free Wi-Fi.

E Pensión Miguel, C Juan Carlos I 23, T941 343 252. On the main road around town, this *pensión* has rooms that are noisy but not overly so. The en suite ones are significantly nicer than the ones without bathroom, although all are reasonable.

◉ Eating

Nájera *p226*

† **El Buen Yantar**, C Mártires 19, T941 360 274. This *asador* does a very good *menú* for €10, with hearty Riojan bean dishes washed down by tasty grilled meat and decent house wine.

¶ **La Taberna de Manu**, C Mayor 21, T941 410 428. Much the best tapas bar in town, this spot is decked out with slightly bizarre original paintings, and signed shirts of notable handball players. The bar snacks include plump *tigres* (mussels topped with bechamel sauce and grilled) as well as the local speciality, fried sheep's ears, a waste-not-want-not Riojan dish.

Santo Domingo de la Calzada *p227*
There's good, cheap eating in Santo Domingo; although it might be wise to stay off the roast chicken.

¶¶ **Casa Amparo**, C San Roque 17, T941 343 016. Sporting a comfortably traditional dining room, this friendly restaurant might be just what you need after the long trudge along the Camino. Typical Riojan dishes play a big part here, and the €11 *menú del día* is one of the best in town.

¶¶ **El Rincón de Emilio**, Plaza Bonifacio Gil 7, T941 340 527. Tucked away in a tiny plaza off the main road, this is a charming chessboard of a place with good Riojan stews and meats.

⊛ Festivals and events

Santo Domingo de la Calzada *p227*
12 May The town celebrates the anniversary of the **Santo Domingo's** death in style, with a series of processions for a couple of weeks prior to the fiesta.

⊖ Transport

Nájera *p226*
Bus
Frequent services run from the bus terminal by the **Hotel San Fernando** to **Logroño** and **Santo Domingo**, and 3 or 4 daily go to **Burgos** and **Zaragoza**. There are 2 daily to **San Millán**, and 2 to **Haro** and **Ezcaray**.

Santo Domingo de la Calzada *p227*
Bus
Buses leave from Plaza Hermosilla just south of the old town. There are regular buses to **Logroño**, stopping in **Nájera**; to **Burgos**, and to **Bilbao** via **Haro** and **Vitoria**.

Contents

Castilla y León

At a glance

☺ **Getting around** Easy train and bus services between cities. International flights to Valladolid. Driving's easy, but with long distances to cover.

☺ **Time required** 3-4 weeks.

☼ **Weather** Dry and hot in summer, dry and cold in winter, which can be chilly into May.

✖ **When not to go** Aug, when temperatures exceed 40°. Jan-Feb if chill winds and snow are a turn-off.

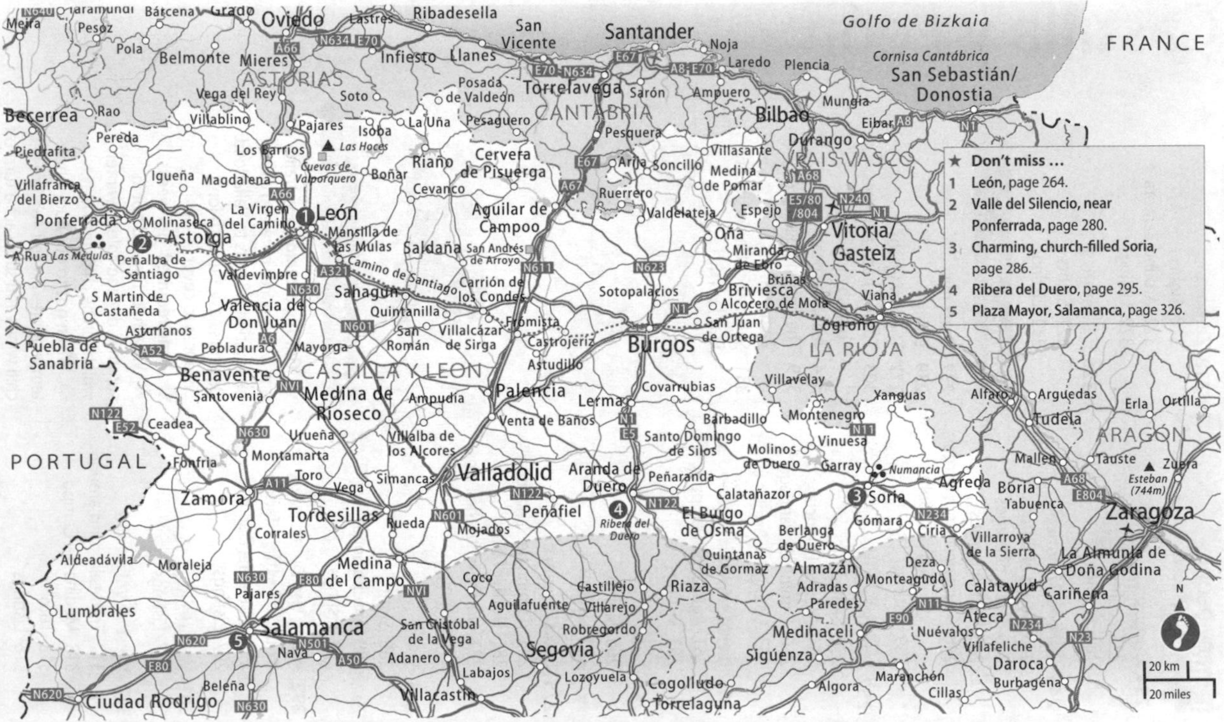

Golfo de Bizkaia
FRANCE
Cornisa Cantábrica
San Sebastián/
Donostia
Santander
Oviedo
Bilbao
Vitoria/
Gasteiz
Logroño
Burgos
León
Astorga
Ponferrada
Palencia
Valladolid
Zamora
Salamanca
Segovia
Soria
Zaragoza
PORTUGAL
ASTURIAS
CANTABRIA
PAIS VASCO
LA RIOJA
CASTILLA Y LEÓN
ARAGÓN
Camino de Santiago
Las Médulas
Las Hoces
Cuevas de Valporquero
Numancia
Ribera del Duero
Esteban (744m)
★ Don't miss …
1 León, page 264.
2 Valle del Silencio, near Ponferrada, page 280.
3 Charming, church-filled Soria, page 286.
4 Ribera del Duero, page 295.
5 Plaza Mayor, Salamanca, page 326.
N
20 km
20 miles

For many people, Castilla is the image of Spain: a dry, harsh land of pious Inquisition-ravaged cities, ham, wine and bullfighting. Visitors tend to love or hate the dusty *meseta* with its extremes of summer and winter temperatures; it's a bleak, almost desert landscape in parts.

The main route to Santiago crosses the heart of the region and is dignified by numerous churches and monasteries in noble Romanesque or Gothic. Burgos itself is much visited for its elegant cathedral and is a courteous, genteel city. Palencia doesn't attract many tourists, but it deserves more. Quiet and friendly, it's got a definite charm and boasts a province full of treasures. Despite being amicably joined with Castilla, the province of León is culturally, geographically and socially somewhat distinct. The city of León is vibrant, rich in architectural heritage and draws the crowds to its sublime Gothic cathedral. Similarly, the south of the region's major attraction is its architecture. Castilla is named for its huge number of castles, many of them found in the Duero Valley. But it has much more to offer than faded reminders of past glories. The cities of southern Castilla are all interesting: Romanesque Soria glows in the evening light, busy Valladolid preserves an imperial air, Zamora is a model for sensitive urban blending of the old and the new, and Salamanca is a stunningly beautiful ensemble of Renaissance architecture, topped off by Spain's most beautiful main square. Throughout the region, small villages harbour architectural treasures, rustic accommodation, and places to fill up on heart-warming traditional food.

This chapter roughly follows two east-west routes: firstly from Burgos west along the Camino de Santiago, then from Soria west along the Duero.

Burgos

→ *Colour map 5, A2. Phone code: 947. Population: 178,966. Altitude: 860 m.*

"They have very good houses and live very comfortably, and they are the most courteous people I have come across in Spain." Andrés Navagero, 1526.

This Venetian traveller's comment on 16th-century Burgos could equally apply today to the city where courtesy and courtliness still rule the roost. Formerly an important and prosperous trading town, Burgos achieved infamy as the seat of Franco's Civil War junta and is still a sober and reactionary town, the heartland of Castilian conservatism. But Burgos is far from being stuck in the past; the fantastic new Museum of Human Evolution sits on the Arlanzón, a committed programme of inserting cycleways along every major road that's ahead of its time in Castilla, and the S-4 urbanization project has turned heads in the architecture world.

Burgos's collection of superb Gothic buildings and sculpture, as well as its position on the Camino de Santiago, make it a popular destination, but the city copes well with the summer influx. Just don't come for gentle spring sunshine; Burgos is known throughout Spain as a chilly city, the epitome of the saying 'nueve meses de invierno, tres meses de infierno' (nine months of winter, three months of hell). The chills can be banished with the traditionally hearty local cuisine and Ribera reds from the south of the province. ▶▶ *For listings, see pages 241-245.*

Ins and outs

Getting there Burgos is roughly in the centre of Northern Spain and easily accessed from most parts of the country by bus or train. There are regular services from Madrid and the Basque country as well as Santander and all Castilian towns. ▶▶ *See Transport, page 244.*

Getting around As usual, the old centre is fairly compact, but you may want to use the local bus service to access a couple of the outlying monasteries, the new train station and the campsite.

Best time to visit Burgos has a fairly unpleasant climate with short, hot summers and long, cold winters (it often snows) punctuated by the biting wind that 'won't blow out a candle but will kill a man'. The most moderate weather is found in May, June and September.

Tourist information There is a **municipal office** ① *Plaza del Rey San Fernando 2, T947 288 874, turismo@aytoburgos.es, summer daily 1000-2000*, across from the cathedral; and also a **regional office** ① *Plaza Alonso Martínez 7, T947 203 125, oficinadeturismodeburgos@jcyl.es, mid-Sep-Jun Mon-Sat 0930-1400, 1600-1900, Sun 0930-1700, summer daily 0900-2000*. There are **city tours** and a rather tacky **tourist train** ① *daily in summer and at weekends Oct-Jun, €4*, which rolls around the sights, leaving from outside the cathedral square tourist office.

Background

Burgos is comfortably the oldest city in Europe, if you count the nearby cave-dwellers from Atapuerca, who were around over a million years ago. That aside, the city's effective foundation was in the late ninth century, when it was resettled during the Reconquista. Further honours soon followed; it was named capital of Castilla y León as early as the 11th century.

The city's position at the northern centre of the Castilian plain, near the coastal mountain passes, made it a crucial point for the export of goods. Burgos flourished, becoming a wealthy city of merchants and beasts of burden; in the 16th century its mule population often exceeded the human one, as bigger and bigger convoys of wool made their way over the mountains and by ship to Flanders.

The Consulado de Burgos, a powerful guild-like body, was created to administer trade, and succeeded in establishing a virtual monopoly; Burgos became one of three great 16th-century Spanish trading cities, along with Sevilla and Medina del Campo. The strife in Flanders hit the city hard, though, and other towns broke into the market. Burgos' population declined by 75% in the first half of the 17th century, and the city lapsed into the role of genteel provincial capital, apart from a brief and bloody interlude: during the Civil War the Nationalist junta was established here; the city had shown its credentials with a series of atrocities committed on Republicans after the rising.

Sights

Cathedral

① *Cathedral and museum are open mid-Mar to Oct daily 0930-1930, Nov to mid-Mar 1000-1900, last entry an hour before, €5, €2.50 for pilgrims. Some of the chapels are only accessible on guided tours; the guides are independent and prices vary. Before entering the cathedral, you must buy a ticket in the reception office on the square below. There's a 50% discount for pilgrims.*

Burgos's famed cathedral is a remarkable Gothic edifice whose high hollow spires rise over the city. Its beauty is an austere and solemn one, and the technical excellence of its stonework has to be admired. It also houses a collection of significant artwork.

The current structure was begun in 1221 over an earlier church by Fernando III and his Germanic wife, Beatrice of Swabia, with the bishop Maurice overseeing things. Beatrice brought him with her from Swabia, and the northern influence didn't stop there; Gil and Diego de Siloé, the top sculptors who are responsible for many masterpieces inside and throughout the province, originated from those parts, while the towers were designed by master builder Hans of Cologne.

Entering through the western door, under the spires (only completed in the 19th century), one of the strangest sights is in the chapel to the right. It's reserved for private prayer, but the figure you see through the glass is the **Christ of Burgos**. Made from buffalo hide and sporting a head of real hair, the crucified Jesus wears a green skirt and looks a little the worse for wear. The limbs are movable, no doubt to impress the 14th-century faithful with a few tricks; apparently the Christ was once so lifelike that folk thought the fingernails had to be clipped weekly. Opposite, high on the wall, the strange figure of Papamoscas strikes the hours, the closest thing to levity in this serious building.

Like those of many Spanish cathedrals, the **choir** is closed off, which spoils any long perspective views. Once inside, admire the Renaissance main *retablo* depicting scenes from the life of the Virgin. Underfoot at the crossing are the bones of El Cid and his wife Doña Jimena, underwhelmingly marked by a simple slab. The remains were only transferred here in 1927 after being reclaimed from the French, who had taken them from the monastery of San Pedro de Cardeña during the Peninsular War. They lie under the large octagonal tower, an elaborate 16th-century add-on. The choir itself is incredibly elegant and intricate – you could spend hours examining the carved wooden images; Bishop Maurice's tomb is in the centre of it.

There's a wealth of side chapels, many unfortunately shielded by *rejas* (grilles), although if an attendant is around they are happy to open them up. The chapels date from different architectural periods; some of the Renaissance ones feature stunningly fine stonework around the doorways. The **Capilla de Santa Teresa** sports a riotous

Churrigueresque ceiling, while the soaring late Gothic *retablo* in the **Capilla de Santa Ana** and the painted Romanesque tombs in the **Capilla de San Nicolás** are also striking.

The grandest, however, is at the very far end of the apse, the **Capilla de los Condestables**. The Velasco family, hereditary Constables of Castilla, were immensely influential in their time, and one of the most powerful, Don Pedro Fernández, is entombed here with his

Burgos

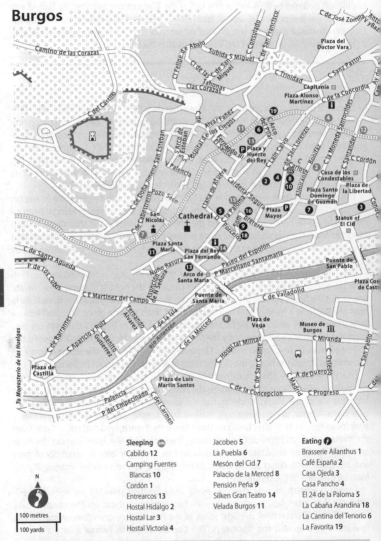

N

100 metres
100 yards

wife. Few kings have lain in a more elaborate setting, with a high vaulted roof, fabulous stonework and three *retablos*, the most ornate of which, the central one, depicts the purification of Mary. The alabaster figures on the sepulchre itself are by another German, Simon of Cologne, and his son. The room, oddly asymmetrical, is a memorable shrine to earthly power and heraldry. Just outside, around the ambulatory, a series of sensitive alabaster panels depicts Biblical scenes.

The **museum**, set around the top of the two-tiered tomb-lined cloister, is reasonably interesting. After passing through the baroque sacristy, the first stop is the chapterhouse, where, high on the wall, hangs a coffer that belonged to the Cid; possibly the one that was involved in a grubby little deed of his, where he sneakily repaid some Jews with a coffer of sand, rather than the gold that he owed them. In the adjacent chamber is a pretty red *mudéjar* ceiling. A 10th-century Visigothic Bible is the highlight of the next room, as well as the Cid's marriage contract, the so-called *Letter of Arras*. Finally, the museum has an excellent collection of well-restored 15th-century Flemish paintings. They are full of life and action – the mob mentality of the Crucifixion is well portrayed. There are several reliquaries holding various bits of saints (including Thomas Becket) and nothing less than a spine from the crown of thorns. A *retablo* depicts Santiago in Moor-slaying mode.

Iglesia de San Nicolás
ⓘ *Jun-Sep Mon-Sat 1000-1400, 1700-1900, rest of year Mon-Sat 1130-1330, 1700-1900, €1.50; free Mon.*

This small church above the cathedral has a superb *retablo*, a virtuoso sculptural work, probably by Simon and Francis of Cologne. It's a bit like looking at a portrait of a city, or a theatre audience, so many figures seem to be depicted in different sections. The main scene at the top is Mary surrounded by a 360° choir of angels. The stonework is superb throughout; have a look for the ship's rigging, a handy piece of chiselling to say the least. There's also a good painting of the Last Judgement in the church, an early 16th-century Flemish

La Posada **7**
Los Herreros **8**
Mesón Burgos **9**
Mesón La Amarilla **10**
Mesón La Cueva **11**
Mesón San Lesmes **12**
Puerta Real **13**
Taberna Pecaditos **16**

Bars & clubs 🍸
Fox Tavern **14**
La Negra
Candela **15**
Ram Jam Club **17**

work, only recently rediscovered. The demons are the most colourful aspect; one is trying to tip the scales despite being stood on by Saint Michael.

The old town is entered across one of two main bridges over the pretty Río Arlanzón, linked by a leafy *paseo*. The eastern of the two, the **Puente de San Pablo**, is guarded by an imposing mounted statue of El Cid, looming Batman-like above the traffic, heavy beard flying. The inscription risibly dubs him "a miracle from among the great miracles of the creator". The other, **Puente de Santa María**, approaches the arch of the same name, an impressively pompous gateway with a statue of a very snooty Carlos V. East of here is the **Plaza Mayor**, which is normally fairly lifeless. The **Casa Consistorial** has marks and dates from two of Burgos's biggest floods; it's hard to believe that the friendly little river could ever make it that high.

Other interesting buildings in the old centre include the **Casa de los Condestables**, with a massive corded façade. Felipe I (Philip the Fair) died here prematurely in 1506; it was also here that the Catholic Monarchs received Columbus after he returned from his second voyage. The ornate neo-Gothic **Capitanía** was the headquarters for the Nationalist *junta* in the Civil War.

Museo de la Evolución Humana and around
ⓘ *T902 024 246, www.museoevolucionhumana.com, Tue-Fri 1030-1430, 1630-2030, Sat-Sun 1000-2000, €6. You can combine your visit with a trip to the excavation site at Atapuerca by prior reservation. This includes transport from the museum and costs €10, including museum entry.*
The excavations in the caves and galleries of the Atapuerca site near Burgos in recent years have completely changed ideas about the presence of prehistoric hominids in western Europe, and this excellent new museum brings together the information gleaned from here and other sites around the globe about our ancestors and distant cousins. Set on the riverbank in a striking building with limitless space and light, the display gives an overview of finds at Atapuerca and a comprehensive picture of our current knowledge of the numerous members of the 'homo' genus, as well as background on evolutionary theory and the voyage of the Beagle.

While Neanderthal man and homo sapiens both used the Atapuerca area, it is two earlier occupations that are most of interest here. Cosmogenic nuclide dating has put the oldest (so far) remains here at 1.3 million years old; they are sufficiently different to have been named as a new species, homo antecessor. There is evidence of their presence at Atapuerca until about 800,000 years ago. Later, Homo heidelbergensis, likely ancestors of the Neanderthals, lived here from around 600,000 years ago. The Atapuerca site is responsible for some 83% of excavated hominid material from this period, the middle-Pleistocene.

All panels are translated – perfectly – into English, as are the audiovisual features. While there are a few interactive exhibits, it's mostly a fairly serious archaeological and palaentological display, so the kids might get restless.

Not far away, and attractively set around the patioed **Casa Miranda** sections of the **Museo de Burgos** ⓘ *Tue-Sat 1000-1400, 1600-1900 (1700-2000 summer), Sun 1000-1400; €1.20, free at weekends*, are prehistoric finds from Atapuerca (see page 241), Roman finds from Clunia, religious painting and sculpture, and some more modern works by Burgalese artists.

Above the town, a park covers the hilltop, which is crowned by the **Castillo de Burgos** ⓘ *T947 288 874, Oct-Mar phone for weekday visits, Sat-Sun 1100-1400, Apr-Jun phone for weekday visits, Sat-Sun 1100-1400, 1600-1900, Jul-Sep daily 1100-1400, 1700-2030, €3.70, €2.60 without tunnels*. Heavily damaged by being blown up by the French in the Napoleonic Wars, it's recently been renovated and can be visited. A new museum summarizes some of the town and fortress's history, and the visit includes the sturdy ramparts and a claustrophobic trip

El Cid

Although portrayed as something of a national hero in the 12th-century epic *El Cantar de Mío Cid* (Song of the Cid), the recorded deeds of Rodrigo Díaz de Vivar certainly give the devil's advocate a few sharp darts in the fight for places in the pantheon of Spanish heroes. Born just outside Burgos in AD 1043, El Cid (the Boss) was in fact a mercenary who fought with the Moors if the price was right.

His ability to protect his own interests was recognized even by those who sought to idolize him. The Song of the Cid recounts that, on being expelled, from Burgos the great man wrapped up his beard to protect it from being pulled by irate citizens angry at his nefarious dealings.

Operating along the border between Christian and Muslim Spain, the Cid was a man of military guile who was able to combine a zeal for the Reconquista with a desire to further his own fortune. The tawdry moment when he swindled two innocent Jewish merchants by delivering a chest filled with sand instead of gold is celebrated with gusto in Burgos cathedral where his mortal remains now lie.

Banished by Alfonso VI for double dealing, his military skills proved indispensable and he was re-hired in the fight against the Almoravids. The capture of Valencia in 1094 marked the height of his powers and was an undoubted blow to the Moors. If having his own city wasn't reward enough, the Cid was given the formidable Gormaz castle as a sort of fortified weekend retreat.

By the standards of his own time where the boundaries, both physical and cultural, between Christian and Moorish Spain were flexible, the Cid's actions make perfect sense. It is only later ages (preferring their heroes without ambiguity) that felt the need to gloss over the actual facts. By the time of his death in 1099 the Cid was well on his way to national hero status.

The Cid's horse, Babieca, has her own marked grave in the monastery of San Pedro de Cardeña. The Cid himself was buried here for 600 years until Napoleon's forces, perhaps fearing a re-appearance by the man himself, removed the body to France. He was reburied in Burgos in the1930s.

into a system of tunnels dug deep into the hillside. It's a nice place to come on a sunny day, with excellent views down over the cathedral and plenty of woods to stroll in, and there are a couple of bars up here to enjoy a coffee or a drink at night.

Monasterio de las Huelgas

ⓘ *Tue-Sat 1000-1300, 1545-1730, Sun 1030-1400, €5, free Wed; bus Nos 5, 7 and 39 run here from Av Valladolid across the river from the old town.*

A 20-minute walk through an upmarket suburb of Burgos, the Monasterio de las Huelgas still harbours some 40 cloistered nuns, heiresses to a long tradition of power. In its day, the convent wielded enormous influence. The monastery was founded by Eleanor of England, daughter of Henry II and Eleanor of Aquitaine, who came to Burgos to marry Alfonso VIII in 1170. The Hammer of the Scots, Edward I, came here to get hitched as well; he married Eleanor, Princess of Castilla, in the monastery in 1254. Las Huelgas originally meant 'the reposes', as the complex was a favourite retreat for the Castilian monarchs. Here they could regain strength, ponder matters of state – and perhaps have a bit on the side; several abbesses of Las Huelgas bore illegitimate children behind the closed doors.

To keep the nuns separate from the public, the church was partitioned in the 16th century, and the naves separated by walls. The public were just left with a small aisle, where the visit starts. In here are a couple of curios: a moving pulpit that enabled the priest to address both the congregation and the separated nuns; and a strange statue of Santiago, sword in hand. Part of the coronation ceremony of the kings of Castilla used to involve them being knighted; as they judged no-one else in the land fit to perform the task, a statue of the saint with moveable arms used to perform the deed; this is probably one of those. There's also a retablo by the tireless Diego de Siloé in here.

The real attractions are on the nuns' side of the barricade. The church contains many ornate tombs of princes and other Castilian royals. These were robbed of much of their contents by Napoleon's soldiers. All were opened in 1942 and, to great surprise, an array of superb royal garments remained well preserved 700 years on, as well as some jewellery from the one tomb the French had overlooked. In the central nave are the tombs of Eleanor and Alfonso, who died in the same year. The arms of England and Castilla adorn the exquisite tombs. They lie beneath an ornate Plateresque *retablo*, which is topped by a 13th-century crucifixion scene and contains various relics.

Around a large cloister are more treasures; a *mudéjar* door with intricate wooden carving, a Moorish standard captured from the famous battle at Navas de Tolosa in 1212, and a postcard-pretty smaller cloister with amazing carved plasterwork, no doubt Moorish-influenced. For many, the highlight is the display of the clothing found in the tombs: strange, ornate, silken garments embroidered with gold thread. The colours have faded over the centuries, but they remain in top condition, a seldom-seen link with the past that seems to bring the dusty royal names alive.

Cartuja de Miraflores

① *Mon-Fri 1015-1500, 1600-1800 (1900 summer), Sat-Sun 1100-1500, 1600-1800 (1900 summer), free. Catch bus No 26 or 27 from Plaza de España and get off at the Fuente del Prior stop; the monastery is a 5-min walk up a marked side road. Otherwise, it's a 50-min walk through pleasant parkland from the centre of town.*

This former hunting lodge is another important Burgos monastery, also still functioning and populated by silent Carthusians. Juan II de Castilla, father of Isabel (the Catholic monarch), started the conversion and his daughter finished it. Like so much in Burgos, it was the work of a German, Hans of Cologne. Inside, the late-Gothic design is elegant, with elaborate vaulting, and stained glass from Flanders depicting the life of Christ. The wooden choir stalls are carved with incredible delicacy, but attention is soon drawn by the superb alabaster work of the *retablo* and the tombs that lie before it. These are all designed by Gil de Siloé, the Gothic master and they are the triumphant expression of genius. The central tomb is star-shaped, and was commissioned by Isabel for her parents; at the side of the chamber rests her brother Alonso, heir to the Castilian throne until his death at the age of 14. The *retablo* centres on the crucifixion, with many saints in attendance. The sculptural treatment is beautiful, expressing emotion and sentiment through stone. Equally striking is the sheer level of detail in the works; a casual visitor could spend weeks trying to decode the symbols and layers of meaning.

Monasterio de San Pedro de Cardeña

① *Tue-Sat 1000-1300, 1600-1800, Sun 1215-1300, 1615-1800; wait in the church for a monk to appear; €2; accommodation available at the monastery.*

Close to the city, at a distance of 10 km, the Monasterio de San Pedro de Cardeña is worth a visit, especially for those with an interest in the Cid. The first point of interest is to one side, in front of the monastery, where a gravestone marks the supposed burial site of the Cid's legendary mare, Babieca. The monastery has a community of 24 Cistercians; a monk will show you around the church, most of which dates from the 15th century. In a side chapel is an ornate tomb raised (much later) over the spot where the man and his wife were buried until Napoleon's troops nicked the bones in the 19th century; they were reclaimed and buried in Burgos cathedral. The *mudéjar* cloister dates from the 10th century and is the most impressive feature of the building, along with a late Gothic doorway in the *sala capitular*.

Atapuerca

ⓘ *Ibeas is 13 km east of Burgos on the N120; the site is 3 km north of here. T902 024 246, www. visitasatapuerca.com, €5 for each of the excavation areas and the thematic park; tours Mar-Jun and Oct-Dec weekends at 1100 and 1300, also 1730 Apr-Jun and Oct, Jul-Sep daily 1100, 1300, 1730, ring to book at all times.*

Some 13 km east of Burgos, an unremarkable series of rocky hills have been the site of incredibly significant palaeontological and archaeological finds. Prehistoric human remains dated to over a million years were found here in 2008; the oldest known physical evidence of humans in Europe. Several fossilized remnants of Homo heidelbergensis have also been discovered here; dating has placed the bones from 500,000 to 200,000 years old. It's a crucial link in the study of hominid evolution; Neanderthals seemed to evolve directly from these Heidelbergers. A tour takes you round some of the most important excavation sites, and also to the thematic park, where there are some reconstructions and demonstrations of elements of the prehistoric hominid skillset, such as fire-making and bowmanship. You can join the tours in the main road village of Ibeas an hour before their starting time. Outside the above hours, you may be able to arrange visits by calling ahead. There are also visits from the new Museo de Evolución Humana in Burgos itself.

⊚ Burgos listings

For Sleeping and Eating price codes and other relevant information, see Essentials pages 31-39.

⊜ Sleeping

Burgos *p234, map p236*
AL Hotel Velada Burgos, C Fernán González 6, T947 257 680, www. veladahoteles.com. Set in a beautifully converted old *palacio* in the heart of town, this stylish spot features sweet rooms with small bathrooms; most are duplex, with the sleeping area accessed via a staircase. Rooms are mostly quiet despite the noisy streets around here at weekends. You can get some good prices on their website.
AL Palacio de la Merced, C La Merced 13, T947 479 900, www.nh-hoteles.com.

Attractively set in a 16th-century *palacio*, this hotel successfully blends minimalist, modern design into the old building, whose most charming feature is its cloister in Isabelline Gothic style. The rooms are comfortable and attractively decked out in wood. Extras like internet access are overpriced. Recommended.
A Hotel Cabildo, Av del Cid 2, T947 257 840, www.hotelcabildo.com. Well located, modern, and comfortable, this makes a reliable, if not spectacular, central base. Good facilities are allied with the suave contemporary decor, and helpful staff round out the experience. Closed for renovations at time of research but due to re-open in 2011.
A Hotel La Puebla, C La Puebla 20, T947 200 011, www.hotellapuebla.com. An intimate hotel in the centre of Burgos with

classy modern design, good facilities, and comfortable furnishings. Rooms are compact but comfortable, but the price seems a little elevated in high season. Parking available.

A Hotel Mesón del Cid, Plaza Santa María 8, T947 208 715, www.mesondelcid.es. Superbly located opposite the cathedral, this hotel and restaurant is an excellent place to stay, with spacious, quiet and modern rooms and helpful staff. There are larger rooms and apartments available for families.

A Silken Gran Teatro, Av Arlanzón 8, T947 253 900, www.hoteles-silken.com. Although primarily aimed at business visitors, this hotel makes a sound choice a short walk from the historic centre and right across a pedestrian bridge from the new evolution museum. Rooms are quiet and comfortable, and, as is often the case with this chain, staff are excellent. There are good rates to be found online.

B Hotel Cordón, C La Puebla 6, T947 265 000, www.hotelcordon.com. A central, reasonable option, geared up for business travellers. Nothing stunning about the rooms, but there are very reasonable weekend rates if you book ahead. Free internet; Wi-Fi in some rooms.

B Hotel Entrearcos, C Paloma 4, T947 252 911, www.hotelentrearcos.com. Under the arcades on the main pedestrian street very near the cathedral, this makes a fine modern base in the heart of town. Rooms are compact but shiny and new, with free Wi-Fi that actually works, and helpful service to back it up. Prices are more than fair, especially off-season.

C Hotel Jacobeo, C San Juan 24, T947 260 102, www.hoteljacobeo.com. This smallish central hotel is well managed and features good en suite rooms with comfortable new beds in a pretty old building. Recently renovated, it features free Wi-Fi and DVD players in the rooms. It's pretty good value, particularly outside of the summer months.

E Hostal Lar, C Cardenal Benlloch 1, T947 209 655, www.hostallar.es. This quiet and decent place has well-priced en suite rooms with TV. The management is friendly; and

despite pocket-sized bathrooms it's a good all-round budget option.

E Hostal Victoria, C San Juan 3, T947 201 542. A good choice with friendly management, this *hostal* is central and relatively quiet, and the rooms with shared bath are comfortable and fairly spacious.

F Hostal Hidalgo, C Almirante Bonifaz 14, T947 203 481. A nice quiet *pensión* on a pedestrian street. It's clean, neat and friendly; the rooms are heated and the shared bathrooms are good.

F Pensión Peña, C Puebla 18, T947 206 323. An excellent cheapie, well located and maintained on a pedestrian street. The rooms are heated and have good shared bathrooms. It's often full, however, so don't hold your breath.

Camping
Camping Fuentes Blancas, Ctra Burgos–Cartuja s/n, T947 486 016, www.campingburgos.com. A well-situated campsite in woody riverside parkland about 4 km from the centre, with a pool and bungalows on site. Take bus No 26 or 27 from Plaza de España (not terribly frequent).

⊘ Eating

Burgos *p234, map p236*

Burgos is famous for its *morcilla*, a tasty black pudding filled with rice. Roast lamb is also a speciality here.

A popular new zone for tapas and late-night bars, known as Las Bernardillas, can be found around Plaza de Roma, in the spread-out Gamonal district northeast of the centre off the road to Vitoria. Bus No 1 will get you there from near the Puente de San Pablo.

Casa Ojeda, C Vitoria 5, T947 209 052, www.restauranteojeda.com. One of Burgos' better-known restaurants, backing on to Plaza de la Libertad. Traditional cuisine a bit on the heavy side, but good. Oven-roasted meats are the pride of the house, and the homemade foie is excellent. There's cheaper food available in the bar-café.

¶¶¶ El 24 de la Paloma, C Paloma 24, T947 208 608, www.restauranteel24delapaloma.com. A smart restaurant near the cathedral with a range of succulent dishes like *cigalas* in tempura with cherry ketchup, or de-boned suckling pig. There's a degustation menu for €48, or a lunchtime one for €27 that includes roast lamb. They run regular themed Spanish wine tastings.

¶¶¶ Puerta Real, Plaza Rey San Fernando s/n, T947 265 200, www.puertareal.es. On the cathedral square, this smart *asador* specializes in succulent roast meats, with lamb foremost among them. There's a set menu for €30, which includes that, as well as the other Burgos speciality *morcilla* and a decent Ribera wine. They also show a confident touch with fish dishes. Service here is excellent.

¶¶ Brasserie Ailanthus, C San Juan 30, T947 208 990. With a small, attractive back dining room colourfully decorated with black and orange table runners, this is one of the best lunch spots about. Its €14 *menú del día* usually features soups and succulent stews like *carrillera*, accompanied by decent house wine. They also do a traditional Guipúzcoan cider house menu, and good grilled fish.

¶¶ La Favorita, C Avellanos 8, T947 205 949, www.lafavorita-taberna.com. This large barn-like spot is modern but feels traditional with its hanging hams, rows of wine bottles and wooden fittings. There's plenty of space to enjoy tasty *pinchos* – try the grilled foie gras or chopped ham with garlic mayonnaise for a rich treat – or *raciones* of traditional products. There's an attractive dining room out the back for sit-down meals. Recommended.

¶¶ La Posada, Plaza Santo Domingo de Guzmán 18, T947 204 578. This central spot is a likeable restaurant with a cheery downstairs bar that spills onto the street, and comforting and delicious home-style cooking in the upstairs *comedor*. Dishes, including soups and stews, are prepared to perfection.

¶¶ Mesón Burgos, C Sombrerería 8, T947 206 150. One of Burgos' better tapas bars downstairs is complemented by a friendly upstairs restaurant with good, if unexceptional fare. The service is good and the decor traditional and comfortable.

¶¶ Mesón La Cueva, Plaza de Santa María 7, T947 205 946. A small dark Castilian restaurant with good service and a traditional feel. The *menestra de verduras* is tasty and generous, and the roast meats are good.

¶ Casa Pancho, C San Lorenzo 13, T947 203 405. One of several good options on this street, Casa Pancho is large, warm, light and stylish, with an array of excellent *pinchos* adorning the bar, and cheerful service. Anything involving prawns or mushrooms is a good bet.

¶ La Cabaña Arandina, C Sombrerería 12, T947 261 932. This spot near the cathedral is a Burgos favourite. It's cheery and light and there's plenty of competition to sit at the wooden tables and enjoy *raciones* of cheeses, *revueltos* or *morcilla*; or stand at the bar and sample the delicious tapas. Recommended.

¶ La Cantina del Tenorio, C Arco del Pilar 10, T947 269 781. This delicatessen and bar is a buzzy and cosy retreat from the Burgos wind. A range of delicious fishy bites and small rolls is strangely complemented by baked potatoes, given a Spanish touch with lashings of paprika. Characterful and friendly.

¶ Los Herreros, C San Lorenzo 20, T947 202 448. This old favourite is an excellent tapas bar with a big range of hot and cold platelets for very little; its popularity with Burgos folk speaks volumes.

¶ Mesón La Amarilla, C San Lorenzo 26, T947 205 936. A good sunken bar serving some decent *tapas*, some seeming to use a whole jar of mayonnaise. There's a good cheap restaurant upstairs too, with a €12 *menú del día*.

¶ Mesón San Lesmes, C Puebla 37, T947 205 956. This likeable little corner place offers cheerful cheap eats in a gregarious downmarket bar. Simple *raciones* of things like *callos* (tripe), calamari and mixed salad cost €5-10 and are filling and satisfying. Or you could weigh down the checked tablecloth with a monster *chuletón* steak.

Taberna Pecaditos, C Sombrerería 3, T947 278 573. The Burgos answer to the credit crunch: this upbeat little bar uses good-quality produce from its deli opposite and offers a range of tasty snacks and drinks, all at €1. Fill in your order using the forms at the bar.

Cafés

Café España, C Laín Calvo 12, T947 205 337. There's a sepia tinge to this venerable old-style café in the heart of Burgos. Warm in winter and with a terrace in summer, it's friendly and specializes in liqueur coffees.

⦿ Bars and clubs

Burgos *p234, map p236*
During the week, nightlife is poor, but it picks up at weekends, when on C Huerta del Rey the bars spill out onto the street.
Fox Tavern, Paseo del Espolón 4, T947 273 311. Impossible to miss, this is a decent pub that doesn't push the Irish theme too far. Comfy seats including a terrace looking up at the cathedral; the food is nothing special.
La Negra Candela, C Huerta del Rey 18, T947 202 844. One of the best options in this busy weekend drinking zone, warm and dark.
Ram Jam Club, C San Juan 29, T607 7 84 339. A popular basement bar with a good vinyl collection, mostly playing British music from the 1970s and 1980s. It's always filled with interesting people. The decor changes regularly; there's live music fairly often here too.

⦿ Entertainment

Burgos *p234, map p236*
Teatro Principal, Paseo del Espolón s/n, T947 288 873, on the riverbank.

⦿ Festivals and events

Burgos *p234, map p236*
Jan 30 Fiesta de San Lesmes, Burgos' patron saint.

Mar/Apr Semana Santa (Easter week) processions are important in Burgos, with a fairly serious religious character.
End Jun Fiesta de San Pedro, Burgos' main festival of the year.

⦿ Shopping

Burgos *p234, map p236*
Burgos is a fairly upmarket place to shop, focused on the old town streets.

Books

Luz y Vida, C Laín Calvo 38, T947 265 783. A decent bookseller's spread over 2 shops.

Food

La Vieja Castilla, C Paloma 21, T947 207 367. A tiny but excellent shop to buy ham, Burgos *morcilla* (black pudding) and other Castilian produce, with friendly management.

⦿ Transport

Burgos *p234, map p236*
Burgos is a transport hub, with plenty of trains and buses for all parts of the country.

Bus

The bus station is handily close to town, on C Miranda just across the Puente de Santa María. All buses run less often on Sun.

Within the province buses run to **Aranda de Duero** 6-7 a day (1 hr 15 mins, €8), **Miranda** 3 a day, 0645, 1315, 2030, **Santo Domingo de Silos** 1 a day, 1730 Mon-Thu, 1830 Fri, 1400 Sat, none on Sun, **Roa** 1 a day Mon-Fri, 1800 (1 hr 30 mins), **Sasamón** 1 a day, 1830, none on Sun, **Castrojeriz** 2 a day, 1445, 1830, **Oña** 3 a day, 0645, 1300, 1830.

Further afield, there are services to **Madrid** hourly (2 hrs 45 mins, €17), **Bilbao** 9 a day (2 hrs, €13), **León** 4 a day (2hrs, €15), **Santander** 3-5 a day (2 hrs 45 mins, €12.50), **Logroño** 7 a day (2 hrs), **Valladolid** 5 a day (2 hrs, €8.42), and **Zaragoza** 4 a day (4 hrs, via **Logroño**).

Trains
The swish new Burgos train station is a long way from the centre in the northeast of town, and is connected by buses to the centre. There are several trains daily to **Madrid** (2½-4½ hours, €26-45) via **Aranda**, 4 west to **León** via **Palencia** (2 hrs), and services east to **Vitoria**, **Logroño**, **San Sebastián** and **Zaragoza**. You can also buy tickets at a central booking office at C de la Moneda 19.

◐ Directory

Burgos *p234, map p236*
Internet Locutorio Capitanía, C San Lorenzo 28, cheap calls and internet; Cabaret, C La Puebla s/n, a cool bar with internet access Mon-Thu 1600-0200, Fri and Sat 1600-0400, Sun 1700-0200. **Post office** Just across the river from the old town on Plaza Conde de Castro.

Burgos Province

While the barren stretches to the east and west of the city of Burgos are relatively dull and relentless, there are some very worthwhile trips to be made to the north and south, where the country is greener and hillier. To the south, the cloister of the monastery of Santo Domingo de Silos is worth a journey in its own right, but there's more to see in that region too. To the north are quiet hidden valleys and one of Northern Spain's most lovable Romanesque churches, the Iglesia de San Pedro de la Tejera. ➤➤ *For listings, see pages 249-251.*

South of Burgos → *For listings, see pages 249-251.*

Covarrubias → *Colour map 5, A2.*
This attractive village south of Burgos gets a few tour coaches but hasn't remotely been spoiled. Its attractive wooden buildings and cobbled squares make a picturesque setting by the side of a babbling brook. An impressive 10th-century **tower** stands over the big town wall on the riverbank; it's a Mozarabic work that's said to be haunted by the ghost of a noble lady who was walled up alive there. Behind it is the **Colegiata** ① *Wed-Mon 1030-1400, 1600-1900; €2 guided tour*, a Gothic affair containing a number of tombs of fat-lipped men and thin-lipped ladies, including that of Fernán González, a count of these lands who united disparate Christian communities into an efficient force to drive the Moors southwards, thereby setting the foundations of Castilla. Opposite the church is a statue of the Norwegian princess Kristina, who married the former archbishop of Sevilla here in 1257; her tomb is in the 16th-century cloister. The village has several places to stay and makes a relaxing stop.

Santo Domingo de Silos → *Colour map 5, A2.*
① *T947 390 049, www.abadiadesilos.es, Tue-Sat 1000-1300, 1630-1800, Sun 1630-1800, €3, also includes admission to a small museum of musical instruments in the village.*
The **cloister** of the monastery of Santo Domingo de Silos, the equal of any in the peninsula, should not be missed. It was started in the 11th century and the finished result is superb: two levels of double-columned harmony decorated with a fine series of sculptured capitals. It's not known who the artist was, but the expertise is unquestionable. Most of the capitals have vegetable and animal motifs, while at each corner are reliefs with Biblical scenes. Curiously, the central column of the western gallery breaks the pattern, with a flamboyant twist around itself, a humorous touch. The ceiling around the cloister

is also memorable; a colourful *mudéjar* work. A cenotaph of Santo Domingo, who was born just south of here, stands on three lions in the northern gallery.

In the 1990s the monks of Santo Domingo de Silos went platinum with a CD of Gregorian chanting.

Another interesting aspect is the old pharmacy, in a couple of rooms off the cloister. It's full of phials and bottles in which the monks used to prepare all manner of remedies; even more fascinating are some of the amazing old books of pharmacy and science that fill the shelves. Other rooms off the cloister hold temporary exhibitions. Next door, visitors are welcome to attend offices in the **monastery church** ① *Mon-Sat 0730, 0900, 1300, 1900, 2130; Sun 0800, 1200, 1900, 2130*, where the monks use Gregorian chant. The church itself is bare and uninteresting, but an office is well worth attending, especially in the evening; wrap up well.

Some 3 km away is a small natural chasm, the **Desfiladero de La Yecla**. Follow the road towards Caleruega; a snaking path leads down into the gorge just before a long tunnel. The path follows the tortuous twists of rock with vultures circling above; it's only a five- or 10-minute walk, but it's atmospheric, although the path is in need of repair.

Lerma → *Colour map 5, A2.*

Although Lerma was once a reasonably important local town, what we see today is a product of the early 17th century, when the local duke effectively ruled Spain as the favourite of Felipe III. He wasn't above a bit of pork-barrelling, and used his power to inflict a massive building programme on his hometown. Six **monasteries** were built for different orders between 1605 and 1617, but the **Palacio Ducal** tops it all; a massive structure out of all proportion to the size of the town. It bears a passing resemblance to Colditz castle; there's certainly a martial aspect to both it and the parade-ground-style square that fronts it. Inside, however, it's a more sympathetic space, and has recently been converted into a parador. Nearby, the **tourist office** ① *C Audiencia 6, T947 177 002, www.citlerma.com, Tue-Sun 1000-1400, 1600-1900 (2000 in summer)*, itself located in a former monastery, will point out the other monasteries (three of which are still functioning) on the town map for you. Their guided tour (€3, phone to book) is the only way to visit some of Lerma's notable buildings. **San Blas** is the most interesting, with a fine 17th-century *retablo* in the church.

North of Burgos → *For listings, see pages 249-251.*

The land to the north rises into the Cordillera Cantábrica, where the beautiful valleys are excellent, little-visited places to explore. Avoid coming in winter, when temperatures can drop well below zero.

El Gran Cañón del Ebro → *Colour map 2, C5.*

From Sotopalacios, the N623 continues through increasingly mountainous terrain, finally descending to the coast and Santander on the other side of the range. The Ebro, near its source here, has carved a picturesque canyon into the rock; it's a lovely cool valley full of trees and vultures. A marked trail, **El Gran Cañón del Ebro**, can be walked, starting from the spa village of **Valdelateja**; the whole trail is a six-hour round trip.

Valdivielso Valley → *Colour map 2, C5/6.*

East of here, accessible via a winding road through the village of **Pesquera de Ebro**, the Valdivielso Valley (which runs northwest to southeast) is a quiet little gem also carved by the

Ebro. Green (or white in winter), pretty and reasonably isolated, the valley is perfect for walking, climbing or even canoeing, but it also has several buildings of interest. As an important north-south conduit it was fortified with a series of towers; one of the better examples is at the valley's northern end, in the village of **Valdenoceda**. To get here direct from Burgos, take the CL-629 north from **Sotopalacios** on the main road north to Santander. It's a strange road that crosses a sort of Alpine plateau. A series of large stone waymarkers irregularly dot the route marking the road that Carlos V used on entering Spain to claim the throne.

Near here, above the pretty hamlet of Puente Arenas, is one of the finest Romanesque churches you could hope to see. The **Iglesia de San Pedro de la Tejada** ① *summer 1100-1400, 1600-1930, winter weekends only, T947 303 200 or T636 264 447 to arrange a visit at other times, €1.20*, is a beautiful little structure overlooking the valley. It's in superb condition, built in the 11th and 12th centuries. The façade is fantastic, exquisitely carved with various allegorical scenes, including a lion eating a man. Around the outside are a series of animal heads in relief. The sunken interior features more carvings of animals, musicians and acrobats as well as an impressively painted *mudéjar* gallery, installed in the 15th century. The simple apse is harmonious; it's the beautiful Romanesque proportions as much as the carvings that make this building such a delight.

Oña, a small town at the southeastern end of the Valdivielso Valley, is worth a visit for its monuments. The massive **Monasterio de San Salvador** ① *admission by guided visit only, Tue-Sun 1030, 1130, 1230, 1600, 1700, plus 1815 in summer, €2.50*, is an attractive fortified former monastery that seems bigger than the rest of the town put together. It's now a psychiatric hospital but its quite remarkable church can still be visited.

The royals of the Middle Ages always favoured burial in a monastery; they shrewdly figured that the ongoing monkish prayers for their souls (after a sizeable cash injection, of course) lessened the chance of being blackballed at the Pearly Gates. A number of notable figures are buried here in an attractive pantheon; foremost among them is the Navarran king Sancho the Great, who managed to unite almost the whole of Northern Spain under his rule in the 11th century. The main pantheon is in Gothic style, with *mudéjar* influences, and sits at the back of the church. There are lesser notables buried in the harmonious cloister, a work of Simon of Cologne.

There's a small **tourist office** ① *Easter-Oct Tue-Fri 1030-1330, 1600-1900, Sat and Sun 1030-1400, 1600-1900; Nov-Easter Tue-Sun 1000-1400, 1600-1800, Sat and Sun 1000-1400, 1530-1800*, in the square outside the church.

There's a traditional little *botería*, one of the few left of a formerly widespread craft, on the main road through town. Have a look even if you don't want to buy one; the process hasn't changed much over the years. *Botas*, goatskin winebags, once essential for every farmer and shepherd who couldn't return to their village at lunchtime, are still used to drink from at fiestas and bullfights. Drinking from them is something of an art; it's easy to spray yourself with a jet of cheap red that was meant for the mouth.

Medina de Pomar → *Colour map 2, B6.*
Northeast of Valdivielso, the town of Medina de Pomar was the stamping ground of the Velascos, a powerful Castilian family. Their legacy includes a sturdy castle and the 14th-century **Monastery of Santa Clara**, which they basically founded to be buried in; it features an attractive *retablo* by Diego de Siloé and a small museum. It's a more popular holiday base than the Valdivielso and as a result there are more facilities for tourism.

The N120 crosses wooded hills on its way to Logroño, while the N1 makes its way to Miranda de Ebro and the Basque hills. This is one of the most unpleasant roads in Spain, a conga-line of trucks enlivened by the suicidal overtaking manoeuvres of impatient drivers. It's worth paying the motorway toll to avoid it.

Some 4 km north of the N120, peaceful **San Juan de Ortega** is the last stop before Burgos for many pilgrims on the way to Santiago. In the green foothills, it's nothing more than a church and *albergue*, and has been a fixture of the Camino ever since Juan, inspired by the good works of Santo Domingo de la Calzada up the road, decided to do the same and dedicate his life to easing the pilgrims' journey. He started the church in the 12th century; the Romanesque apse survives, although the rest is in later style. It's a likeable if unremarkable place. San Juan is buried here in an ornate Gothic tomb. Pilgrims stay at the hospital that he founded.

Further along towards La Rioja, **Villafranca Montes de Oca** is an unremarkable pilgrim stop with a small *ermita* in a green valley. North again from here, just off the N1, is an unlikely picnic spot. The hamlet of **Alcocero de Mola**, 2 km from the main road on the BU703, bears the name of the general who masterminded the Nationalist rising. He was killed before the end of the Civil War in a plane crash, probably to Franco's relief. Some 3 km up a neglected side road from Alcocero is a massive concrete monument to him, on the wooded hilltop where the plane hit, with good views across the plains. All of 20 m high and completely forgotten, it's in characteristically pompous Fascist style; an intriguing reminder of a not too distant past. The concrete's in decline now, and weeds carpet the monumental staircase; take a torch if you want to climb the stairs inside.

Further east, **Briviesca** is a sizeable service town, which seems to have beaten the decline that afflicts so many towns of Castilla. The tree-lined plaza is pleasant and shady; on it stands the nicest of the three big churches, with a damaged Renaissance façade. The **tourist office** is on the square too. The town is famous for its almond biscuits but beyond its churches, there's little to see here.

Beyond here, the main road passes through a dramatic craggy pass at **Pancorbo**, which would be a nice hiking base were it not for the trucks thundering through. This is geographically where Castilla ends; the *meseta* more or less gives way here to the Basque foothills. From here, too, it's a short drive across country to Haro, heart of the Rioja Alta wine region.

Castilla officially ends at **Miranda de Ebro**, a hardbitten town which, while attractive in parts, is mostly dusty and vaguely depressing; and is full of big boulevards where nothing much happens. The main reason to come here is to change bus or train; by all means take a stroll down the pretty riverside, but don't miss your connection.

Southwest from Burgos: the Pilgrim Route → For listings, see pages 249-251.

Castrojeriz → Colour map 2, C4. For practicalities on walking the Camino de Santiago, see pages 10, 11 and 22.

West of Burgos, the principal branch of the Camino de Santiago tracks southwest to the town of Castrojeriz, a somewhat bleak place that's unlikely, despite its attractive paved main street, to cheer the heart after a long trudge across treeless Castilian terrain. It was formerly a Celtic settlement, and the *castro* hilltop structure has been preserved. There are three churches, linked by Calle Real. The **Church of San Juan** is the village's main attraction; it's a clean, if over-restored Gothic building influenced by the Burgos German tradition and features a nice double-columned cloister. As well as the bare ruin of a castle on the hill, there are a couple of other impressive buildings in the town, most notably the **Casa de Gutiérrez Barona**, a large knightly residence. This predates Castrojeriz's only moment in the spotlight. During the *comunero* revolt (see page 505) this town was deemed unlikely enough to rebel that the Council of Castilla took up residence here, and the place briefly buzzed with noblemen.

Sasamón → *Colour map 2, C4.*

A more interesting, if longer route would take the pilgrim through Sasamón, 2-3 km north of the main Burgos–León road. The **Iglesia de Santa María la Real** ① *daily 1100-1400, 1600-1900 (ask in the bar opposite if shut), €1.25 includes a helpful explanation by the knowledgeable and justly proud caretaker,* is its very lovely church in light honey-coloured stone. It was originally a massive five-naved space, but was partitioned after a fire destroyed half of it in the 19th century. The exterior highlight is an excellent 13th-century Gothic portal featuring Christ and the Apostles, while the museum has some well-displayed Roman finds as well as a couple of top-notch pieces; a couple of Flemish tapestries featuring the life of Alexander the Great, and a Diego de Siloe polychrome of San Miguel, the pretty-boy bully. It's fairly plain, a reflection of the Inquisition passing into irrelevance. In the church itself, two works of the German school stand out; the ornate pulpit, from around 1500, and a large baptismal font. A 16th-century Plateresque *retablo* of Santiago is one of many that adorn the building, so monumental for such a small town.

A statue of **Octavian** stands in a square nearby. The town of Segisama was used as a base in 26 BC for his campaigns against the Cantabrians and Asturians. The inscription reads *Ipse venit Segisamam, castro posuit* (then he came to Segisama and set up camp).

Don't leave town without checking out the **Ermita de San Isidro**, dominated by a massive 6-m carved crucifix that once would have stood at a crossroads to comfort weary travelling souls. Under Christ is the Tree of Knowledge, Adam, Eve, Cain and Abel. It dates from the 16th century and is a lovely work. Atop it is a nesting pelican; it was formerly believed that a pelican short of fish to feed the kids would wound itself in the breast to let them feed on its own blood. This became a metaphor for Christ's sacrifice, and pelicans are a common motif in Castilian religious sculpture.

⊚ Burgos Province listings

For Sleeping and Eating price codes and other relevant information, see Essentials pages 31-39.

⊜ Sleeping

Covarrubias *p245*

C Hotel Arlanza, Plaza Mayor 11, T947 400 511, www.hotelnuevoarlanza.com. This is a good option set in a stately old house. The rooms are beautiful, particularly those on the top floor with sloping attic roof. There's an atmospheric restaurant too which has riotous medieval dinners on Sat nights in spring and autumn. Prices include breakfast and are at the bottom end of this category.

D Hotel Doña Sancha, Av Barbadillo 31, T947 406 400, www.hoteldonasancha.com. On the road to Hortiguela, but close to the centre, this charming rural hotel is just about the best place to stay in town. Offering a genuine Castilian welcome and great home-style breakfasts (extra), it makes a good base for exploring the region.

D La Posada del Conde, C Fernán González 8, T609 406 698, www. laposadadelconde.es. This is a very cosy *casa rural* with original and comfortable decor backed up by welcoming owners. Breakfast is included.

E Pensión Galin, Plaza Doña Urraca 4, T947 406 552, www.casagalin.com. This *pensión* above a bar has plenty of charm. The best of the renovated en suite rooms look over the square. A bargain.

Santo Domingo de Silos *p245*

C Tres Coronas de Silos, Plaza Mayor 6, T947 390 047, www.hoteltrescoronasde silos.com. Attractive and comfortable, set in a solid stone mansion just across from the monastery. The rooms are rustic and charming. They run an annexe on the same square, with slightly cheaper rooms.

D Hotel Santo Domingo de Silos, C Santo Domingo 16, T947 390 053, www. hotelsantodomingodesilos.com. Set in 2 adjacent buildings on the main road, this offers excellent quality for the price. There's a variety of rooms available, but all have plenty of space, and comfortable furnishings. The newer ones have excellent bathrooms. The hotel restaurant does an excellent *cochinillo* (suckling pig). Recommended.

E Arco de San Juan, Pradera de San Juan 1, T947 390 074, arcosanjuan@wanadoo.es. This is a hotel and restaurant peacefully set by a stream just past the monastery. The rooms are quiet and clean, and there are some nice terraces to relax on.

Lerma *p246*

AL Parador de Lerma, Plaza Mayor 1, T947 177 110, www.parador.es. Set in the massive ducal palace, this recently inaugurated parador has a sumptuous interior and makes a fine place to stay. Built around a high-arched covered patio, it oozes class, and the cool tiled-floor rooms have excellent facilities and bathrooms; many have great views.

D El Zaguán, C Barquillo 6, T947 172 165, www.elzaguanlerma.com. This makes another very comfortable base. It's a 17th-century *casa rural* with attractive stone walls and interesting furniture. The rooms are great and equipped to hotel standard; a couple have lovely wooden sloping ceilings.

El Gran Cañón del Ebro *p246*

A Posada del Balneario, Camino del Balneario s/n, Valdelateja, T947 150 220, www.relaistermal.com. A big, attractive place by the river with a high level of comfort and service; swimming pool and jacuzzi included. Readers have recommended sleeping here but eating elsewhere. Breakfast included, and a full range of spa treatments available.

C Casa de Lolo y Vicent, C Callejón 18, T947 150 267, www.casadeloloyvicent.es. Colourful, and with a wonderful welcome, this *casa rural* is in the village of Escalada further up the road. It's set in a sensitively restored 15th-century house, and offers a good welcome and pretty views.

Valdivielso Valley *p246*

E Camino Condal, Plaza Padre Cereceda 6, Oña, T615 144 167, www.caminocondal. com. Excellent value is to be had at this great *casa rural* in the pretty heart of Oña. Rooms are compact, but most cosy, with individual colour schemes making for a soothing sleep. Recommended.

F Hostal Once Brutos, C del Pan 6, Oña, T947-300 010. A simple but clean place just off the square that also provides simple meals. Some rooms have a lot more natural light than others. It's extremely cheap.

Medina de Pomar *p247*

There are several places to stay here.

B Hotel Ciudad de Medina, Plaza Somovilla s/n, T947 190 822, www.ciudadde medina.com. Good a/c rooms with minibar and modern bathrooms set in a lovely old arcaded building on the square.

Castrojeriz *p248*

There are also 2 pilgrim *albergues*.

D Hotel Cachava, C Real 93, T947 378 547, www.lacachava.com. On the paved main street that winds through town, this is a welcoming choice for pilgrims to put their deserving feet up for a night. Rooms are simply decorated and comfortable, and meals

and bikes are available for guests. There's a patio/garden to relax in on sunny days.
D La Posada, C Landelino Tardajos 5, T947 378 610, www.laposadadecastrojeriz.es. A *casa rural* with some charm, set in a historic old mansion built around a pleasing interior patio. There's also a very good restaurant.

Sasamón *p249*

There are various *casas rurales* for complete let; check www.toprural.com for details.
E Casa Gloria, C Arco 1, T947 370 059. The village's main accommodation option, this is right opposite the church. It's cordial, clean and well presented; the simple rooms have spick and span white-sheeted beds and small bathrooms. They're heated, the owner will lend you a bike, and you can eat downstairs.

⊕ Eating

Lerma *p246*

♔ **Casa Antón**, C Luis Cervera 5, T947 170 362. Something of a local classic, this homely place specializes in the local lamb. Truth is, they serve almost nothing else – you'll get a lettuce salad and some local wine to accompany it. It's excellent. Leave room for the scrumptious home-made desserts though. Recommended.

Castrojeriz *p248*

♔ **La Taberna**, C General Mola 43, T947 377 120. One of a handful of cheap restaurants catering to locals and pilgrims. It's decent and also has internet access and simple rooms.

⊖ Transport

Covarrubias *p245*
Bus There are 3 buses a day to Covarrubias from **Burgos** (none on Sun).

Santo Domingo de Silos *p245*
Bus There is a daily bus Mon-Thu and Sat from **Burgos** in the afternoon (2 hrs), returning in the morning.

Lerma *p246*
Bus There are several daily buses and the odd train that make their way to Lerma from **Burgos** and to a lesser extent **Madrid**.

Valdivielso Valley *p246*
Bus There are daily buses from **Burgos** to Oña via Briviesca.

East of Burgos *p248*
Bus and train Briviesca is visited by 7 daily buses from **Burgos** and also several trains.

Miranda de Ebro is well connected to major cities in Northern Spain, particularly **Bilbao**, **Vitoria**, **Burgos**, **Logroño** and **Madrid**. It's a major transport hub between the Basque regions and the rest of the nation.

Castrojeriz *p248*
Bus Buses run from from **Burgos** to Castrojeriz twice a day (none on Sun).

Sasamón *p249*
Bus There are 2 buses a day to Sasamón from **Burgos** (none on Sun).

Palencia

→ *Colour map 4, A6. Phone code: 979. Population: 82,651. Altitude: 740 m.*

Though it's not that small, never a sentence seems to be written about Palencia without the word 'little'. And it's understandable; on some approaches to the provincial capital, it seems that you're in the centre of town before even noticing there was a town. It is a quiet and friendly place, bypassed by pilgrims, tourists and public awareness of its presence. This is partly an accident of geography – the town is situated in the middle of a triangle of the more important places of Valladolid, Burgos and León – but also one of history.

Palencia sits on the Carrión, so murky and green it surely merits mangroves and crocodiles. The old town stretches along its eastern bank in elongated fashion. It is studded with churches, headed up by the superb cathedral. Ernest Hemingway summed up Palencia as a "nice Castilian town with good beer".►► For listings, see pages 257-260.

Ins and outs

Getting there and around The train and bus stations are just beyond the northern end of Calle Mayor, a pedestrian street stretching the length of the old town. The main sights are all within easy walking distance of each other, concentrated in the old town. ►► *See Transport, page 260.*

Tourist information The regional **tourist office** ① *C Mayor 105, T979 740 068, oficinadeturismodepalencia@jcyl.es, mid-Sep to Jun Mon-Sat 0930-1400, 1600-1900, Sun 0930-1700, summer daily 0900-2000,* is at the southern end of Calle Mayor and has a wide range of information on the city, the province and the rest of Castilla y León. The **provincial office** ① *C Mayor 31, T979 706 523, www.palenciaturismo.es, Mon-Fri 0900-1400, 1700-2000, Sat 1030-1400, 1700-2000, Sun 1030-1430,* is more centrally located and also helpful. It opens shorter hours in winter.

Background

Palencia has a proud past. The region was inhabited in prehistoric times, then the local villages resisted the Romans for nearly a century before Pompey swept them aside in 72 BC and set up camp here. Pliny the Elder cited Palencia as one of the important Roman settlements of the 1st century AD. It wasn't until the 12th century that the city reached its zenith, however; *fueros* (legal privileges) were granted by Alfonso VIII, and Spain's first university was established. In 1378 the city became legendary for resisting a siege by the Duke of Lancaster, fighting for Pedro I. The defences were mounted by the Palentine women, as the men were off fighting at another battleground. But things turned sour in the *comunero* revolt, a Castilian revolution against the 'foreign' regime of Carlos V, which became an anti-aristocratic movement in general. The *comuneros* were heavily defeated in 1521 and Palencia suffered thereafter, as Castilian towns were stripped of some of their privileges and influence.

Sights

Palencia's scenic highlight is its superb **cathedral** ① *T979 701 347, Mon-Fri 0900-1330, 1630-1930, Sat 0900-1400, 1600-1930, Sun 1600-2000, closes half an hour earlier in winter; €1.50,* known as 'La Bella Desconocida' (the unknown beauty). Built in the 14th century on Visigothic and Romanesque foundations, it's a massive structure, although it hardly dominates the town, tucked away somewhat on a quiet square. The magnificent main portal depicts the Virgin flanked by apostles. Inside, the massive *retablo* paints the story of Christ's life; it's a work of the Flemish master Jan of Flanders, who also painted an attractive triptych on one side of the choir. The city's patron, the Virgen de la Calle, sits on a silver coffer

Palencia

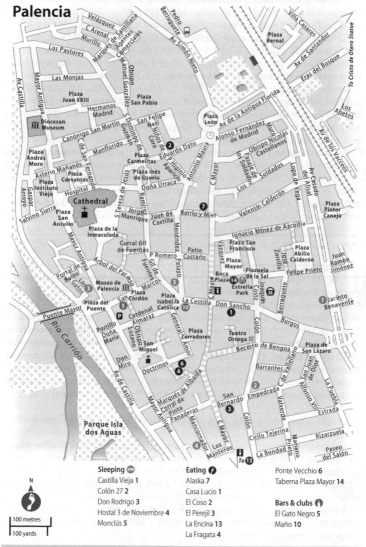

Sleeping 🛏
Castilla Vieja 1
Colón 27 2
Don Rodrigo 3
Hostal 3 de Noviembre 4
Monclús 5

Eating 🍴
Alaska 7
Casa Lucio 1
El Coso 2
El Perejil 3
La Encina 13
La Fragata 4

Ponte Vecchio 6
Taberna Plaza Mayor 14

Bars & clubs 🍸
El Gato Negro 5
Maño 10

in the ambulatory, while there's an amusing sculpture of lions eating a martyr at the back end of the *coro*. The Visigothic/Romanesque crypt is also worth a look. There's a painting by El Greco just off the cloister, but this is only accessible on a guided tour (€3, regular departures) of the whole building. Similarly annoying is the lighting system; to properly see the impressive works of art around the building will cost you a small fortune in euro coins.

A couple of blocks away is the **Diocesan museum** ① *mid-Sep to Jun open by tour only Mon-Sat 1030 and 1130, Jul to mid-Sep Mon 1030-1330, Tue-Sun 1030-1330, 1630-1930, €4*, set around a cloister, with a collection of paintings and *retablos* from around the province.

Further south, the Romanesque **Iglesia de San Miguel** ① *daily 0930-1330, 1830-1930, free*, is a knobbly affair with a hollow tower. It's fairly unadorned inside, with elegant vaulting. There's a small gilt *retablo* of the saint, and some fragmentary wall paintings. El Cid is reputed to have been married in a previous church on this site.

Nearby, the **Museo de Palencia** ① *T979 752 328, Tue-Sat 1000-1400, 1600-1900 (Jul-Sep 1700-2000), Sun 1000-1400, €1.20, free at weekends*, is housed in an attractive building on Plaza del Cordón, named for the sculpted cord that is tied around the doorway. It's a good display with plenty of artefacts from the province's Roman and pre-Roman past. The museum is situated in what was once Palencia's Jewish quarter.

Palencia's **Plaza Mayor** sits secluded just to the east of the long Calle Mayor. It's a lovely space with trees, *soportales*, and a monument to Renaissance sculptor Alonso Berruguete.

Just out of town, the looming Lego-like **Cristo de Otero** claims to be the second tallest statue of Jesus in the world (after Cochabamba, Bolivia). There are good views from the 850-m elevation. The sculptor, Victorio Macho's, last wish was to be buried at the statue's feet; his body is in the small chapel. There's a little exhibition here too.

Around Palencia → For listings, see pages 257-260.

Basílica de San Juan de Baños
① *T979 770 338, winter Tue-Sun 1030-1330, 1600-1800; summer 1000-1330, 1700-2000, €1; ring to confirm that it's open in winter.*

South of Palencia and around 2 km east of Venta de Baños, a mainline train hub with frequent connections to Palencia and Valladolid, is a church that's well worth visiting, the Basílica de San Juan de Baños. At least some of the pretty little building is awesomely old; an inscription above the altar states that it was founded by the Visigothic King Recesvinth in AD 661. To be sure, it's been altered substantially over the years, but it still preserves much of its original character, principally in the central aisle. Its architectural value is high, as clear links are evident with late Roman building traditions, but apart from all that, it's an enchanting simple structure, a relic from a time when Christianity was young.

Ampudia → Colour map 4, A5. For practicalities on walking the Camino de Santiago, see pages 10, 11 and 22.

For a good off-the-beaten track Castilian experience, head west from Palencia five leagues to the town of Ampudia, unexpectedly dominated by an imposing **castle** ① *www. castillodeampudia.com, guided visits Apr-Sep Sat 1200, 1300, 1800 and 1900, Sun 1200 and 1300 plus 1800 and 1900 Jul-Aug; rest of year Sat only 1200, 1300; €3.50; if there are a few of you, or you are especially keen, T699 484 555 to arrange a visit at other times.* It's in top nick, bristling with castellation, but visits are limited, as it's still lived in. There's an ornate collection here too, with various rooms exhibiting a traditional pharmacy, dolls and toys, guns, and religious art among other things.

The **Colegiata de San Miguel Arcángel** ① *Jul-Sep daily 1030-1330, 1700-2000, Apr-Oct Fri-Sun 1100-1330, 1700-2000, Nov-Mar Sat-Sun 1030-1330, 1700-2000, free*, is a floorboarded Gothic and Renaissance affair, light and breezy and with a spiky tower that looks ready to blast off to join the archangel himself. Its known as the *Novia de los Campos* (Bride of the Plains; this area of the province is known as *Los Campos*). The main altarpiece is a Renaissance work; more interesting perhaps is the Gothic side chapel of San Ildefonso, containing the tombs of the men who paid for the building, and also a pretty Plateresque *retablo*.

Next to the Colegiata is the **Museo del Arte Sacro** ① *May-Sep Tue-Sun 1000-1330, 1600-1900, Oct-Apr 1130-1400, 1530-1800, closed early Jan-early Mar, €2*, quite a good museum of religious art. The town itself is very pretty, with wooden soportales raising the houses over the footpaths. It has a few appealing eating and sleeping options.

Medina de Rioseco → *Colour map 4, A5.*

A little further west, and once quite an important wool and wheat merchants' town in the province of Valladolid, Medina de Rioseco still retains some historic atmosphere, and has benefitted from an excellent program of restoration and promotion of tourism. It now has plenty to offer and is well worth a look, especially on a Wednesday morning, when there's an entertaining livestock market. It lies on the main road between Valladolid and León, so makes a good stop if going between those cities too.

The most endearing aspect of the town is the pedestrian street Calle Lázaro Alonso, colonnaded in warped old wood. Following this from the main road, you'll come to one of Medina's churches, the **Iglesia de Santa Cruz**. More than a bit mausoleum-like from the outside, it houses the **Museo de Semana Santa** ① *Tue-Sun 1100-1400, 1600-1900 (1700-2000 in summer), weekends only Jan-Feb, €3*, devoted to Holy Week celebrations in different towns and villages of Castilla y León.

More beautiful is the church of **Santa María** ① *Tue-Sun 1100-1400, 1600-1900 (1700-2000 in summer), €2*, built from attractive white-ish limestone in the 15th and 16th centuries. Gothic in style, it's topped by a flamboyant baroque spire. Inside it's fairly ornate, with showy star vaulting and a big gilt *retablo*. Flashest of all is the intricately decorated funerary chapel of the Benavente family. The pretty little coloured organ provides a homelier touch. There's a small museum inside; the attendant has the keys to the **Iglesia de Santiago**, a squareish structure further down the hill. It also costs €2, but a combined ticket for all the town's attractions can be had for €7.

The recently completed **Museo de San Francisco** ① *C San Francisco 1, T983 700 020, www.museosanfrancisco.es, Tue-Sun 1100-1400, 1600-1900 (1700-2000 summer), €3*, is an innovative display of local history and religious art in a noble Franciscan monastery. Visits are by guided tour only – tours last about 45 minutes and leave on the hour.

On the edge of town, by the Canal de Castilla (see page 261), stands a huge **flour mill** ① *T983 701 923, summer daily 1100-1400, 1600-1900, winter weekends only, €2.50*, which holds an exhibition on the mill itself and also on the canal. From here, there are also one-hour boat trips (€5) running Tuesday to Sunday on the canal itself. From Thursday to Sunday, there are longer trips of 2½ and 3½ hours up to the seventh and sixth locks of this impressive waterway. Phone or check the town website (below) for times.

Tourist information is available at the town's **tourist office** ① *C San Francisco 1, T983 720 319, www.medinaderioseco.com, Tue-Fri 1000-1330, 1600-1800, Sat 1100-1300, 1600-1800, Sun 1100-1300*, in the Museo de San Francisco.

Frómista → *Colour map 2, C4. For practicalities on walking the Camino de Santiago, see pages 10, 11 and 22.*

In northern Palencia, Frómista, as well as lying on the Camino de Santiago, is a compulsory stop on the Romanesque circuit. The reason is the **Iglesia de San Martín** ① *winter 1000-1400, 1530-1830, summer 0930-1400, 1630-2000, €1, €1.50 with San Pedro*, a remarkable 11th-century Romanesque church, one of the purest and earliest, derived almost wholly from the French model that permeated the peninsula via the Pilgrim Route. From the outside it's beautiful, an elegant gem standing slightly self-satisfied in the sunlight. The church managed to survive the Gothic and baroque eras without being meddled with, but a late 19th-century restoration brought mixed benefits. While the building owes its good condition to this, it also has lost some of the weathered charm that makes the Romanesque dear. That said, the purity of its lines make it well worth a visit. Inside, it's the capitals of the pillars that attract the attention. While some were sculpted during the restoration (they are marked with an R, with creditable honesty), the others are excellent examples of Romanesque sculpture. There are no Biblical scenes – many of the motifs are vegetal, and some are curious juxtapositions of people and animals, particularly lions and birds. The church is crowned by an octagonal tower as well as two distinctive turrets.

Nearby, **San Pedro** is an attractive Gothic building with a small museum. There's a small **tourist information centre** on the main crossroads in town.

Astudillo → *Colour map 4, A6.*

Just off the Camino, southeast of Frómista, the town of Astudillo is a beautiful, out-of-the-way little place. All that remains of its medieval walls is the **Puerta de San Martín**, a striking gateway. The central square is an attractive tree-lined affair, and there are several noble *palacios* and mansions. On the small hill above town is a castle; the hill itself is honeycombed with old wine bodegas.

Villalcázar de Sirga → *Colour map 2, C4.*

The Camino continues through an awesomely empty landscape before arriving at the village of Villalcázar de Sirga, which is built around a memorable church, **Santa María la Blanca** ① *May to mid-Oct daily 1030-1400, 1700-1930, mid-Oct to Apr Sat 1200-1345, 1630-1800, Sun 1200-1345, €1, pilgrims €0.20*. It's a majestic sight, a massive Gothic affair quite out of proportion to everything else around it. The exterior highlights include a carved rose window and a portal topped by a frieze depicting the Pantocrator with evangelists and apostles, and, below, Mary in the Annunciation and the Adoration. Inside, particularly noteworthy are the painted tombs of the Infante don Felipe, prince and brother of King Alfonso X, and his wife. Both date from the late 13th century.

Carrión de los Condes → *Colour map 2, C4.*

Carrión de los Condes provides some relief after the hard slog across the Castilian plain, with a greener feel around the Carrión, the river on which the town lies. A couple of shabby churches can be found north of the main road, but the nicest part of town is around the plaza to the south of it. The **Iglesia de Santiago** is the town's showpiece, with an excellent late 12th-century façade, an unusual affair with zigzag columns and an actor doing a backflip among the figures on the archivolt. The Christ in Majesty has been described as the most impressive in Spain. There's also a small **museum** ① *Jun-Sep 1100-1400, 1700-2000, Oct-May*

Sat and Sun only, €1, inside. Another church, **Santa María**, is a clean-lined affair with a large porch and some chessboard patterning. It's relatively unadorned inside apart from a massive gilt *retablo*. A statue of St Michael is camp even by his lofty standards; the archangel looks as if he's just stepped off the set of *Starlight Express*. On Thursday mornings, a market stretches between the two churches. There's a nice park by the river too. Just west of town, the monastery of **San Zoilo** has been converted into a beautiful hotel (see Sleeping, page 258).

La Olmeda and Quintanilla → *Colour map 2, C3/4.*

Near Carrión are two of the little-known highlights of Palencia province, the Roman villas of La Olmeda and Quintanilla. **La Olmeda** ① *T979 119 997, www.villaromanalaolmeda.com, Tue-Sun 1030-1830, €5,* 18 km north of Carrión, near the town of Saldaña and just outside Pedrosa de la Vega, is the more impressive. Dating from the late first century AD, it was a sizeable building with defensive turrets, many rooms, and an attached bathhouse. Around the large central courtyard, rooms are decorated with geometrical and vegetal mosaic flooring, but in a larger room is a superb mosaic with Achilles and Ulysses as well as a hunting scene, with all manner of beasts in a flurry of complex activity. There are regular free guided tours (with English audio available), and multilingual information panels. There's also a café here.

A couple of kilometres away, **Saldaña** itself, an attractive if hard-bitten *meseta* town, has some of the finds from the two villas assembled in a **museum** set in an old church. There are some excellent pieces, particularly those found at a funerary complex by the Olmeda villa. Your entry ticket for Olmeda is valid here. Buses run to Saldaña from Palencia, Burgos and León.

Quintanilla, just off the N120 west of Carrión, has a large **villa** ① *Apr-Sep Tue-Sun 1000-1400, 1700-2000; Oct and Mar 1030-1330, 1600-1800; closed Nov-Feb; €3,* featuring some excellent mosaics as well as a hypocaust underfloor heating system for the cold Castilian winters. The entry fee is €6 if you're going to visit both villas.

① Palencia listings

For Sleeping and Eating price codes and other relevant information, see Essentials pages 31-39.

● Sleeping

Palencia *p252, map p253*
Accommodation is very reasonably priced.
B Castilla Vieja, Av Casado del Alisal 26, T979 749 044, www.hotelessuco.com. This hotel on the edge of the old town isn't interesting, but is modern, well equipped and fairly priced. The rooms are spacious, with polished wooden floorboards and decent bathrooms. The mini-suites, which have extra space and a lounge area, are only €20 more than the standard double. Parking available. There are usually **C** rates available on the hotel website.
C-D Hotel Monclús, C Menéndez Pelayo 3, T979 744 300, www.turwl.com/monclus.

This brick, slightly stuffy, hotel is in the middle of town. The rooms are comfortable but sombre brown. It's quiet and central, with parking.
D Hotel Colón 27, C Colón 27, T979 740 700, www.hotelcolon27.com. Pleasant and welcoming with spacious rooms in the heart of town. Good value for the price (which is at the bottom end of this category), although there's some morning noise from the school opposite.
D Hotel Don Rodrigo, C Los Gatos 1, T979 700 937, www.hotelessuco.com. Quiet and light, this place offers solid value in the old town near the river. Rooms are unadorned but crisp and clean, and there's parking available. Bottom of this price category.
E Hostal 3 de Noviembre, C Mancornador 18, T979 703 042. With surely the smallest

lobby of any Spanish hotel, this is a good choice. Doubles are all exterior and comfortable, although the singles are cramped (though cheap). Parking available. Reception open 1900-2330 only; phone ahead at other times.

Ampudia p254
A Casa del Abad de Ampudia, Plaza Gromaz 12, T979 768 008, www.casadelabad.com. An excellent accommodation and eating option is this beautiful and originally renovated 16th-century abbot's house in the main square. A riot of colour and subtle beauty, every room is different and comfortable, with price grades reflecting size and amenities. There's even a gym and sauna. The meals are delicious – the restaurant is of the highest class – and the wines are superb. Recommended.
E Atienza, C Duque de Alba 3, T979 768 076, www.casaruralatienza.com. Another welcoming choice, this is a *casa rural* in an old workers' cottage with a restored wine bodega. The rooms are charming, meals are served and there's a peaceful garden.

Medina de Rioseco p255
C Hotel Vittoria Colonna, C San Juan 2, T983 725 087, www.hotelvittoriacolonna. es. A welcome addition to the Medina scene, this new hotel is on the main road in the centre of town and has plenty of comfortable rooms with parquet floors and welcoming beds. Bathrooms are decked out in modish grey and facilities, which include a restaurant, are excellent.
E La Muralla, Plaza Santo Domingo 4, T983 700 577. Just at the bottom of C Lázaro Alonso, this is clean, airy and remarkably good value. Rooms without bathroom cost less.

Frómista p256
B Hotel Doña Mayor, C Francesas 8, T979 810 588, www.hoteldonamayor.com. This new Frómista hotel is in the heart of the village and features smallish, attractive, quirkily designed rooms with small

balconies. It's a relaxed place with pleasant staff; the only real downside is that the restaurant isn't up to much.
E Hostal San Telmo, C Martin Veña 8, T979 811 028, www.turismofromista.com. A great place to stay; a large, light and tranquil *casa rural* with large garden/courtyard and charming but cheap rooms.
F Pensión Marisa, Plaza Obispo Almaraz 2, T979 810 023. A good budget flop for pilgrims, this simple and welcoming choice on the main square has spotless basic rooms with shared bathroom and serves decent meals.

Villalcázar de Sirga p256
E Hostal Las Cántigas, C Condes de Toreno 1, T979 880 015, www.hostallascantigas.es. This excellent modern *hostal* is right by the church of Santa María la Blanca in this tiny and tranquil village. It makes a great rural base and is well priced. Rooms have bathroom, heating and there's a bar and restaurant.

Carrión de los Condes p256
C Real Monasterio San Zoilo, T979 880 050, www.sanzoilo.com. The best of several options. A characterful setting in an old monastery with a peaceful grassed garden. There's also a good restaurant with atmospheric beamed ceiling, offering quality local produce at fair prices.
F Hospedería Albe, C Collantes 21, T979 880 913, hostalalbe@hotmail.com. Hospitable, pleasant and cool, with charming rustic decoration. A couple of rooms have their own kitchenette and cost a few euros more.

🍴 Eating

Palencia p252, map p253
Palencia's not exactly a gourmet paradise and restaurants are a little thin on the ground here.
ᵞᵞᵞ La Encina, C Casañe 2, T979 710 936, www.asadorlaencina.com. This Castilian *asador* is considered the city's best and most reliable restaurant. It's famous for its

roast meats, but also for its *tortilla*, which has thrice been voted the best in the nation. They recite the dishes without prices, so the bill can come as a shock at the end, but the lamb is excellent.

Casa Lucio, C Don Sancho 2, T979 748 190. A bright, traditional and warmly lit bar and restaurant dealing in standard Castilian fare with a spring in its step. There's excellent service, and a reliable selection of classics like *rabo de toro* (bull's tail stew). Good value. Recommended.

El Perejil, C San Bernardo 2, T979 745 775. Just off the main pedestrian drag, this is a rewarding place to stop for lunch or a glass of wine. The tapas under the glass counter in the small bar are eye-catching and tasty; the *comedor* serves an excellent lunch menu with plenty of choice.

La Fragata, C Pedro Fernández de Pulgar 8, T979 750 129. There are 2 options on offer at this corner spot; well-prepared fish and seafood in the restaurant, or cheap, simple and effective *raciones* and *platos combinados* in the bar. Tue is hearty *cocido* day, and there's a daily lunchtime menu that's good value too.

Ponte Vecchio, C Doctrinos 1, T979 745 215. Closed Mon. Atmospheric and spacious Italian restaurant located opposite the church of San Miguel in a lovely stone building. The food is upmarket and excellent.

Taberna Plaza Mayor, Plaza Mayor 1, T979 740 410. A warm wooden tavern right on the main square, with tiled bar and walls. Hang out in the bar and enjoy *raciones* of calamari and the like, or head upstairs to the restaurant, which looks down to the bar through a hole in the floor. There's a terrace outside in summer.

El Coso, C Eduardo Dato 8, T979 746 758. A characterful and yellow-tiled café that does a range of cheap meal options. It's very convivial and fills up in the evenings.

Cafés
Alaska, C Mayor 26, T979 742 835. A compact, historic café/bar bedecked

with massive paintings, a popular terrace, and a toilet accessed by a tight spiral staircase. They also do good tapas and have free Wi-Fi.

Medina de Rioseco *p255*
Mesón la Rúa, C San Juan 25, T983 700 519. A reliable choice for traditional Castilian food. The menu bristles with local specialites such as *pichón* (squab) and hearty stews. The *menú del día* is great value at €10.

Villalcázar de Sirga *p256*
El Mesón de Villalcázar, Plaza Mayor s/n, T979 888 022. Great Castilian cooking at this hearty local.

Carrión de los Condes *p256*
Bodegón El Resbalón, C Fernán Gómez 17, T979 880 799. This dark and inviting spot is in an attractively refurbished traditional building. Stone and wood give a typical bodega feel, and the typical local cuisine matches it. The €10 *menú* is worth waiting for.

🍸 Bars and clubs

Palencia *p252, map p253*
Bar Maño, C La Cestilla 5, T979 740 210. A trendy modern bar that by day is also a restaurant, serving a bright contemporary *menú del día* and tasty tapas.
El Gato Negro, C San Marcos s/n, T979 743 343. Though it serves tasty free tapas by day, the 'black cat' comes into its own at night, when it becomes one of the city's most lively and atmospheric pubs for an after-dinner *copa*.

🎉 Festivals and events

Palencia *p252, map p253*
1st week of Sep Palencia has lots of fiestas, but the main one is **San Antolín**, with markets, stalls, bullfights, fireworks and concerts.

Ampudia *p254*
1st weekend of Sep Ampudia's fiesta includes bullfights.

Transport

Palencia *p252, map p253*
Bus For information, T979 743 222. Hourly buses to **Valladolid**, 4 a day to **Burgos** (1 hr 15 mins) and **Madrid** (5 daily, 3 hrs 15 mins, €17). 4 a day to **Aguilar de Campoo** via **Frómista** and Osorno, hourly buses to **Dueñas** via **Venta del Baños**, 2 to **Ampudia**, 2 to **Cervera**, 2 to **Astudillo** and 3 to **Saldaña**.

Train Palencia is on the main line. Lots of trains go to **Frómista** (4 daily, 25 mins), **Aguilar de Campoo** (4 daily, 1 hr, from €6.20), **Madrid** (1¾-2¼ hrs, up to 12 daily, €21-40), **Valladolid** (at least hourly, 30 mins, from €4.20), **León** (12 daily, 1 hr 10 mins, from €9.60), and other regional destinations.

Ampudia *p254*
Bus There are 2 buses daily to and from Palencia to **Ampudia**, and 1 to **Valladolid**.

Medina de Rioseco *p255*
Bus ALSA buses run here from **Valladolid** (20 a day) and **León** (8 a day). There are also services to **Madrid** and one to **Sahagún**.

Frómista *p256*
Bus and train There are regular services to **Palencia**.

Astudillo *p256*
Bus 2 daily buses to and from **Palencia**.

Carrión de los Condes *p256*
Bus Regular buses to **Palencia**.

Directory

Palencia *p252, map p253*
Internet Estrella Park, Plaza Mayor 5. There are also a couple of places on C Eduardo Dato near the station.

North towards Santander

The northern part of Palencia province is an incredible haven of Romanesque architecture; every little village seems to have a round-arched gem tucked away. Fans of the style could spend many happy days exploring the area, based at Aguilar de Campoo. The Department of Tourism has a number of useful booklets and pamphlets on the subject, which it rightly regards as the province's chief attraction. It is working towards having several dozen more churches open to the visiting public within a few years. ▸▸ *For listings, see pages 263-264.*

Canal de Castilla

North of Frómista, the road heads north towards Santander. Alongside it stretches part of the Canal de Castilla. A major work, it was started in 1749 with the aim of transporting goods from the interior to the coast more easily. In those times of war and political turmoil it took over a century to complete. One branch begins at Valladolid, one at Medina de Rioseco, and they meet and continue north to Alar del Rey, from where the mountains made a continuation impossible and goods once again were put to the road. It was a significant engineering feat for its time but sadly saw only 20-odd years of effective use before it was rendered redundant by the railway. Long stretches of it have a canalside path to walk, and there are a couple of information centres along the way.

Monasterio de San Andrés de Arroyo → *Colour map 2, C4.*
ⓘ *30-min tours Tue-Sun at 1000, 1100, 1200, 1230, 1515, 1600, 1700, and 1800, €3.*
Make every effort to get to San Andrés de Arroyo, south from Aguilar de Campoo, and 8 km west of Alar del Rey. A working monastery populated by Cistercian nuns, it boasts a superb late 12th-century cloister, which you will be shown around by a friendly inhabitant. The cloister is double-columned and features some exceptionally intricate work, especially on the corner capitals. How the masons managed to chisel out the leaves and tendrils is anybody's guess. The far side of the cloister is more recent but features equally ornate work. The Sala Capitular is a Gothic affair with an ornate tomb supported by lions, in which rest the mortal remains of Doña Mencía Lara, a powerful local countess in her day. Traces of paint remain, a useful reminder that the bare Gothic style that we admire was often probably rather garishly coloured. The centrepiece of the cloister is a Moorish fountain originally from Granada.

Closer to the main road (2 km east) is the crumbly red Romanesque monastery **Iglesia de Santa María de Mave**. The keys are in the *hospedería* that's built into the monastery.

Aguilar de Campoo → *For listings, see pages 263-264. Colour map 2, C4.*

The lovely town of Aguilar sits where the Castilian plain gives way to the northern mountains of the Cordillera Cantábrica. Chilly, even snowy, in winter, its pleasant summer temperatures make it a place of blessed relief from the *meseta* heat. It makes an excellent base for exploring the area's Romanesque heritage. Aguilar is named after its 'eagle's nest', a slightly exaggerated description of the modest hill capped by a castle that overlooks the town. In latter days, however, the town has been known for biscuit making; the rich smells wafting through the streets make a visitor permanently peckish. While iconic Fontaneda biscuits, first made by a local family in 1881, are no longer produced here, there are still three biscuit factories here, producing a wide range of crunchy delights. The

tourist office ① *Plaza de España, T979 123 641, Tue-Sat 1000-1345, 1600-1745 (1700-1845 summer), Sun 1000-1345, 1-hr guided walks leave Tue-Sun 1100, Tue-Sat 1700, €3*, is helpful.

The town sits on the Río Pisuerga and is centred on the long **Plaza de España**, which is where most things go on. At one end of the plaza is the **Colegiata de San Miguel** ① *T979 122 231, summer 1030-1330, 1700-2000, ring to visit at other times; guided tours Mon-Sat 1100, 1200, 1700, Sun 1300; €1.50*, which conceals a Gothic interior behind its Romanesque façade. Inside, there's a big *retablo*, a scary sleeping Christ with real hair and a museum.

A number of **gateways** remain from the old walls; that on Calle Barrio y Mier has a Hebrew inscription, a legacy of the once substantial Jewish population, while the one behind the church is topped by griffins.

Across the river, the **Monasterio de Santa Clara** is home to a community of nuns that follow the Assisi saint. Its **Gothic church** ① *daily 1200-0100, 1800-1900*, can be visited. Delicious pastries can be bought inside.

The **Museo Ursi** ① *C Tobalina s/n, Oct-May Fri-Sun 1200-1400, 1700-2000, Jun-Sep Thu-Sun 1200-1400, 1730-2030, €1.50*, is the workshop of the sculptor Ursicino Martínez, whose work, mostly from wood, is a blend of the sober, the abstract and the light-hearted.

Worth looking at is the Romanesque **Ermita de Santa Cecilia**, a chapel with a leaning tower below the castle. You'll have to get the key from the priest's house (the tourist office will direct you). The interior is simple; the highlight is a superb capital showing the Innocents being put to the sword by chainmailed soldiers. Above, up a path, little remains of the castle but its walls; the view is good, but the town looks better from lower angles.

Monasterio de Santa María la Real
On the road to Cervera, 1 km west is the **Monasterio de Santa María la Real** ① *Jul and Aug daily 1030-1400, 1600-2000 (guided visits 1100, 1230, 1630, 1800), Sep-Jun Tue-Fri 1600-1900; Sat and Sun 1030-1400, 1630-1930, €5, €7 guided visit*. The cloister is attractive enough, although bound to be disappointing after San Andrés de Arroyo, which is similar. The columns are doubled, but many of the capitals are missing (some are in Madrid). The Sala Capitular features clusters of multiple columns, their capitals impressively carved from a single block of stone. The **Museo Románico**, housed in the monastery, is useful for planning a Romanesque itinerary as it contains many models of churches in the province. You can stay here in a posada whose profits fund the Romanesque foundation whose HQ this is.

Cervera de Pisuerga
Some 25 km west of Aguilar is the quiet town of Cervera de Pisuerga, set in the foothills of the Cordillera Cantábrica. It's a fine base for outdoor activities; walkers will have a good time of it in the hills around here. The town's highlight is the Gothic **Iglesia de Santa María del Castillo** ① *Jul-Sep daily 1030-1330, 1700-2000, also Fri-Sun in late Jun and early Oct, €1*, imperiously enthroned above the town. It's not of huge interest inside, but worth checking out is the side chapel of Santa Ana, with polychrome reliefs adorning the walls above the *retablo*. There's also a small **Museo Etnográfico** ① *summer Tue-Sun 1100-1400, 1700-2000, spring and autumn Sat and Sun 1100-1400, 1700-2000; €2*, which is of moderate interest. The **tourist office** ① *Parque El Plantío s/n, T979 870 695, summer only Mon-Sat 1000-1400, 1700-2000, Sun 1000-1400*, on the edge of town, has lots of information on driving and walking routes.

For Sleeping and Eating price codes and other relevant information, see Essentials pages 31-39.

⊜ Sleeping

Monasterio de San Andrés de Arroyo *p261*
C Posada Hostería El Convento, T979 123 611, www.elconventodemave.com. A peaceful place to stay, apart from the odd goods train rattling by. There are various larger and more elaborate rooms costing substantially more (**A-B**).

Aguilar de Campoo *p261*
C Hotel Valentín, Av Ronda 23, T979 122 125, www.hotelvalentin.com. This slightly larger-than-life complex can't be missed as you approach. On the main road on the edge of town, it has a disco, restaurant, shops and a hotel that manages to be quite calm and pleasant, with large, light rooms. It's been recently refurbished, and offers excellent value.

C Posada Santa María la Real, Av Monasterio s/n, T979 122 000, www.alojamientosconhistoria.com. These refurbished monastery buildings 1 km west of town make a characterful place to stay, but you can tell it's not run by hospitality professionals. The split-level rooms are attractive but the upstairs sleeping area can get very stuffy in summer, and a few other details are missing too. Nevertheless, there's decent-value food on offer and this can be a good bet if you bear in mind it's not luxurious.

F Hostal Siglo XX, Plaza España 9, T979 126 040. A good choice, with cosy rooms with TV and shared bath above a restaurant. Grab one of the front rooms, which have access to enclosed balconies overlooking the square.

Camping
Monte Royal, Av Virgen del Llano s/n, T979 123 083. Near the lake to the west of town, this is a campsite with all the trappings.

Cervera de Pisuerga *p262*
A Parador Fuentes Carrionas, Ctra de Resoba s/n, T979 870 075, www.parador.es. Some 2 km above the town is this large pinkish parador, which enjoys a privileged natural setting. There are great views from all the balconied rooms (which cost a little more), particularly those in the front, overlooking a lake. It's a lovely spot.

E Casa Goyetes, C El Valle 4, T979 870 568. In the heart of town, this attractive wood-beamed *casa rural* is a relaxing and comfortable base. It's excellent value, and the homely rustic interior is a delight.

E La Galería, Plaza Mayor 16, T979 870 008. Right in the heart of this pretty village, this is a fine option with nice rooms on the charming square.

❼ Eating

Aguilar de Campoo *p261*
❖ El Barón, C El Pozo 14, T979 123 151. An excellent restaurant set in an old stone building, with atmospheric decor. There's a good tapas bar, worthwhile *menú*, plenty of cheer and hearty local cuisine. Recommended.

Cervera de Pisuerga *p262*
❖ Gasolina, La Pontaneja 2, T979 870 648. This spot near the plaza serves hearty local food, especially roast meats, in an old stone building. They also do cheap *raciones* and enormous *bocadillos* in the bar – good walker sustenance. In summer there's an appealing terrace.

⊖ Transport

Aguilar de Campoo *p261*
Bus The bus station is next to the Hotel Valentín. Regular services run to **Palencia**, **Santander**, **León**, **Burgos** and **Cervera**.

Train RENFE station is to the east of town and has frequent trains to **Palencia**, **Santander** and **Madrid**.

Cervera de Pisuerga *p262*
Bus Cervera is linked by bus to **Aguilar** and **Palencia** a couple of times daily.

❶ Directory

Aguilar de Campoo *p261*
Internet Playnet, C Comercio 8, has internet access. Open 1200-1400, 1700-2230, €2 per hr. **Laundry** Salmar, Av Ronda 16, Mon-Fri 0930-1400, 1630-2000, Sat 1030-1400.

León

→ *Colour map 2, C2. Phone code: 987. Population: 135,119. Altitude: 870 m.*
León is one of the loveliest of Northern Spain's cities, with a proud architectural legacy, an elegant new town and an excellent tapas bar scene. Once capital of Christian Spain, it preserves an outstanding reminder of its glory days in its Gothic cathedral, one of the nation's finest buildings. After crossing the dusty meseta from Burgos, pilgrims arriving here should put their feet up for a couple of days and enjoy what León has to offer. ▶▶ *For listings, see pages 270-275.*

Ins and outs

Getting there and around León's bus and RENFE train stations are close to each other just across the river from the new town, a 10-minute walk from the old town. ▶▶ *See Transport, page 274.*

Best time to visit Like Burgos, León's high altitude results in freezing winters and roasting summers; spring and autumn are good times to visit, as there's little rain.

Tourist information León's helpful **tourist office** ⓘ *T987 237 082, oficinadeturismodeleon@ jcyl.es, Sep-Jun Mon-Sat 0930-1400, 1600-1900, Sun 0930-1700, summer daily 0900-2000,* should, by the time you read this, be once again opposite the cathedral on Plaza de la Regla. There may also be a municipal office on Plaza San Marcelo.

Background

León was founded as a Roman fortress in AD 68 to protect the road that transported the gold from the mines in El Bierzo to the west. It became the base of the *Legio Septima*, the seventh legion of Imperial Rome; this is where the name originates (although León means 'lion' in Spanish). The city was Christianized in the third century and is one of the oldest bishoprics in western Europe. After being reconquered in the mid-eighth century, León became the official residence of the Asturian royal line in the early 10th century; the royals were thereafter known as kings of León. The city was recaptured and sacked several times by the Moors until it was retaken for the final time by Alfonso V in 1002. León then enjoyed a period of power and glory as the centre of Reconquista pride and prestige; the city flourished on protection paid from the fragmented *taifa* states.

In 1188 there was a meeting of nobles and ecclesiasts that set the pattern for what was later to become the system of *cortes*, regional quasi-parliaments that kept Spanish kings on a tight leash. As the Reconquista moved further south, however, León found itself increasingly put in the shade by the young whippersnapper Castilla, which had seceded from it in the 10th century.

In 1230 the crowns were united, and León is still bound to Castilla to this day, a fact bemoaned by many – spraycans are often taken to the castles on the coat of arms of the region, leaving only the Leonese lion. When the Flemish Habsburg Carlos V took the throne of Spain, León feared further isolation and became one of the prime movers in the *comunero* rebellion. One of the most extreme of the *comuneros* was a Leonese named Gonzalo de Guzmán, who declared a "war of fire, sack and blood" on the aristocracy. The rebellion was heavily put down, and León languished for centuries.

The region's coal provided some prosperity in the 19th century, but it has really only been relatively recently that the city has lifted itself from stagnating regional market town to what it is today; a relatively modern and dynamic Spanish city.

Sights

León's **old town** is to the east of the River Bernesga and surrounded by the boulevards of the newer city. Walk up the pedestrianized Calle Ancha and prepare to be stunned by the appearance of the white Gothic cathedral, a jewel in Spain's architectural crown.

Cathedral

ⓘ *Mon-Sat 0830-1330, 1600-1900; Sun 0830-1430, 1700-1900 (2000 summer); free.*

Effectively begun in the early 13th century, León's cathedral is constructed over the old Roman baths; this, combined with the poor quality of the stone used and the huge quantity of stained glass, historically made the building fairly unstable. A late 19th-century restoration replaced many of the more decayed stones, an impressive engineering feat that required removing and replacing whole sections of the building.

Approaching the cathedral up Calle Ancha, its spectacular bulk is suddenly revealed. The main western façade is flanked by two bright towers, mostly original Gothic but capped with later crowns, the northern (left hand) one by one of the Churriguera brothers. Walking around the outside, there's some superb buttressing as well as numerous quirky gargoyles and pinnacles. Back at the main door, investigate the triple-arched façade, expressively carved. The central portal features a jovial Christ above a graphic Hell, with demons cheerfully stuffing sinners into cooking pots. To the right are scenes from the life of the Virgin; a brief biography of her son is on the left side.

As you enter through the wooden doors, look up at the back corner behind you. The leathery object hanging above the door is supposed to be the carcass of the *topo maligno* (evil mole) who was blamed for tunnelling under the building works and destroying the masons' labours. In reality, the Roman baths underneath were the cause of all the tunnels; while the mole was apparently captured and killed, the hanging carcass is really that of a large tortoise.

The beautifully untouched Gothic interior of the cathedral is illuminated by a riot of stained glass, a patchwork of colour that completely changes the building's character depending on the time of day and amount of sun outside. The sheer amount of glass is impressive; some 1700 sq m. The oldest glass is to be found in the apse and in the large rose window above the main entrance; some of it dates to the 13th century, while other panels span later centuries. There's a general theme to it all; the natural world is depicted at low levels, along with the sciences and arts; normal folk, including nobles, are in the middle, while saints, prophets, kings and angels occupy the top positions. Between midnight and 0100, the floodlights are turned off and the building illuminated from the inside, a spectacular sight. From April to September, at weekends there are very worthwhile visits at 2330 to a platform that allows a close-up appreciation of the stained glass under floodlights; book ahead.

Another of the cathedral's appealing attributes is that, although there's a Renaissance *trascoro* illustrating the Adoration and Nativity, there's a transparent panel allowing a

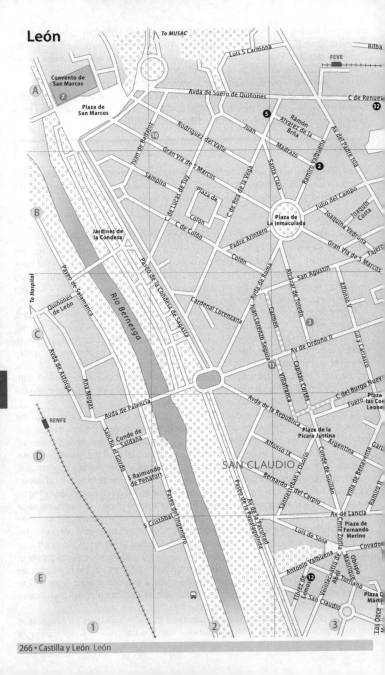

León

To MUSAC

Luis S Carmona

Bilba

FEVE

Convento de
San Marcos

7

Plaza de
San Marcos

Avda de Suero de Quiñones

C de Renuev

32

5

Rámón
Álvarez de la
Brña

Juan

Rodríguez del Valle

10

Ramiro Valbuena

Mádrazo

2

Gran Via de S Marcos

Juan de Badajoz

Sampiro

Santa Clara

Julio del Campo

Joaquín
Costa

Plaza de

Joaquina Vedruna

C de Lucas de Tuy

C de Roa de la Vega

Plaza de
La Inmaculada

Gran Via de S Marcos

Fajero

Colón

C de Colón

Padre Arintero

Jardines de
la Condesa

Paseo de la Condesa de Sagasta

Colón

Avda de Roma

Alcázar de Toledo

San Agustín

Alfonso V

To Hospital

Quiñones
de León

Paseo de Salamanca

Río Bernesga

Cardenal Lorenzana

Juan Lorenzo Segura

Carmen

Av de Ordoño II

3

Gil y Carrasco

11

Villafranca

Capitan Cortés

Avda de Astorga

Ana Mogas

C del Burgo Nuev

Plaza
Fuero las Co
Leone

RENFE

Avda de Palencia

Avda de la República

Alfonso IX

Plaza de la
Picara Justina

Argentina

Garc

Sancho el Gordo

Conde de
Saldaña

Santisteban y Osorio

Conde de Guillen

Villa de Benavente

Ramiro

S Raimundo
de Peñafort

SAN CLAUDIO

Bernardo del Carpio

Paseo de la Papalaguinda

Av de la Facultad

Av de Lancia

Plaza de
Cmte Fernando
Merino

S Cristóbal

Paseo del Ingeniero

Luis de Sosa

Cmte Zorita

Covadon

Antonio Valbuena

Veinticuatro de
Abril

Obispo
Manrique

Plaza D
Márti

Flórez de
Lemos

S San Claudio

12

León Torriano

Las Doce

1

2

3

N

100 metres
100 yards

Sleeping
Hostal Albany **2** C5
Hostal Bayón **3** C3
Hostal Casco
  Antiguo **1** C2
Hostal Guzmán el
  Bueno **5** B4
La Posada Regia **6** C4
Parador de
  San Marcos **7** A1
París **8** C5
Pensión Blanca **11** C2
Q!H **4** B5
Quindós **10** A2
Reina **9** D4

Eating
Alfonso Valderas **1** C4
Café Europa **4** B5
Casa Condeso **11** B5
El Besugo **27** C5
El Gran Café **6** B5
El Palomo **7** C5
Ezequiel **5** A2
Fornos **3** B4
La Competencia **10** C5
La Esponja **8** B4
La Poveda **2** B3
La Ribera **30** B4
La Trébede **14** B4
Las Termas **9** C5
L'Union **12** E3
Nuevo Racimo
  de Oro **15** C5
Sabor de Grecia **32** A3
Vivaldi **33** C5

Bars & clubs
Cervecería Céltica **17** B5
El Capitán **18** C5
El Universal **13** C5
Glam **28** C5
León Antiguo **21** B4
Planet Móngogo **31** A4
Taxman **16** A5

perspective of the whole church, a rarity in Spanish cathedrals. The *coro* itself is beautifully and humourously carved of walnut, although you'll have to join one of the frequent guided tours to inspect it at close quarters. The *retablo* is an excellent painted work by Nicolás Francés, although not complete. Scenes from the lives of the Virgin and the city's patron, San Froilán, are depicted.

Much venerated is the 13th-century statue of the Virgen Blanca, in one of the apsidal chapels; there's also a replica of the elegant sculpture in the portal. Inside the north door of the cathedral is another Virgin, also with child; she's known as the Virgin of the Die, after an unlucky gambler lobbed his six-sider at the statue, causing the Christ-child's nose to bleed.

Also worth a peek are two excellent 13th-century tombs in the transepts. Holding the remains of two bishops involved in the cathedral's construction, they are carved with scenes from the prelates' lives; although heavily damaged, the representations are superb.

The **cathedral museum** ⓘ *Oct-May Mon-Fri 0930-1330, 1600-1830, Sat 0930-1330, Jun-Sep Mon-Fri 0930-1330, 1600-1930, Sat 0930-1330, 1600-1900, €5, €2 cloister only, last museum visit 1 hr before closing,* is housed in the cloisters and sacristy. Most of the cloister is Renaissance in style, with several tombs of wealthy nobles and frescoes; note too the star vaulting. The museum, part of which is accessed up a beautiful Plateresque stair, has a good collection, with many notable pieces. Outstanding items include a Mozarabic bible dating from the 10th century, fragments of stained glasswork, and a superb crucifixion by Juan de Juni, portraying a twisted, anguished Christ.

Basílica de San Isidoro
ⓘ *Sep-Jun Mon-Sat 1000-1330, 1600-1830, Sun 1000-1330, Jul-Aug Mon-Sat 0900-2000, Sun 0900-1400, church free, Panteón €4, free Thu pm.*

As well as the Gothic cathedral, León also has a cracker of a Romanesque ensemble in the Basílica de San Isidoro. Consecrated in the 11th century over an earlier church, it was renamed in 1063 when Fernando I managed to get that learned saint's remains repatriated from Sevilla (see box, page 500).

The complex is built into the medieval city walls, much of which is preserved. The façade is beautiful, particularly in the morning or evening light; it's pure Romanesque in essence, although the balustrade and pedimental shield were added, harmoniously, during the Renaissance, and there are Gothic additions in other parts of the building. Facing the building, the right-hand doorway is named the **Puerta del Perdón** (door of forgiveness); pilgrims could gain absolution by passing through here if they were too infirm to continue their journey to Santiago. The door is topped by a good relief of the Descent from the Cross and Ascension.

To the left is the **Puerta del Cordero** (door of the lamb), with an even more impressive tympanum depicting Abraham's sacrifice. Atop this door is the Renaissance pediment, decorated with a large shield surmounted by San Isidoro in Reconquista mode (like Santiago, this bookish scholar made surprise horseback appearances to fight Moors several centuries after his death). The interior of the church is dark and attractive, with later Gothic elements in accord with the Romanesque; large multifoil arches add a Moorish element. The *retablo* dates from the 16th century and surrounds a monstrance in which the Host is permanently on display (the basilica is one of only two churches in Northern Spain to have been granted this right). Below is a casket containing the remains of Isidore himself – or whoever it was whose bones were found in Sevilla long after the saint's burial place had been forgotten.

The real treasure of San Isidoro lies through another exterior door which gives access to the **museum**. On entering, the first chamber you are given access to is the Panteón

Real, an astonishing crypt that is the resting place of 11 kings of León and their families. The arches, the ceiling and some of the tombs are covered with Romanesque wallpainting in a superb state of preservation (it's barely needed any restoration). There are scenes from the New Testament as well as agricultural life; if you're at all jaded with religious art and architecture, this sublime space will fix it. The short columns are crowned with well-carved capitals, mostly vegetal, but some with Biblical scenes or motifs derived from Visigothic traditions.

The next stop on the visit is the first of the two cloisters, above which rises the emblematic **Torre del Gallo** (tower of the cock), topped by a curious gold-plated weathercock that wouldn't look out of place at White Hart Lane. The original is now in the museum; recent studies have revealed that it was made in sixth-century Sasanian Persia.

The treasury and library is the other highlight of the visit to the museum. Although the complex was sacked and badly damaged by French troops in the Napoleonic Wars, most of the priceless collection of artefacts and books survived. More remains of San Isidoro reside in an 11th-century reliquary beautifully decorated in Mozarabic style; another reliquary is equally finely carved from ivory. The ornate chalice of Doña Urraca is made from two Roman cups and studded with gems. The library contains some beautiful works, of which the highlight is a 10th-century Mozarabic bible.

At the back of San Isidoro is a guesthouse, the **Casa de Espiritualidad** (C). It's a peaceful place to stay, and also has a simple restaurant; a good opportunity to see parts of the building normally not open to the public. You need to reserve by phoning T987 875 088.

Convento de San Marcos
León's other great monument is the San Marcos convent by the river, which doubles as a sumptuous parador. Not a bad place to stay, you might think; so, no doubt, did generations of pilgrims who laid their road-dusted heads down here when it was administered as a monastery and hostel by the Knights of Santiago.

The massive façade is the highlight. It postdates the pilgrim era and is 100 m long, pure Plateresque overlaid by a baroque pediment, and sensitively dignified by a well-designed modern plaza. The church itself is attractive if rather unremarkable; more inspiring is the adjoining cloister with its figure-adorned arches. You can also access it from the parador. There are daily tours of the hotel, but it's easy enough to take a stroll around the ground floor areas (ask first); the bar and lounge are attractive and open to the public.

Next to the parador on the riverbank a crowd gather at weekends and on some weekday evenings to watch the curious game of *bolos*, in which old men toss a wooden ball at skittles aiming, not to knock them over, but to roll it in an arc between them.

Beyond the parador, cheerful coloured panels greet the visitor to **MUSAC** ⓘ *T987 090 000, www.musac.org.es, Tue-Fri 1000-1500, 1700-2000, Sat-Sun 1100-1500, 1700-2100, free*, an upbeat contemporary art museum with rotating temporary exhibitions of varying quality. There's a cute gift shop and good café-restaurant here.

Old town
On the edge of León's old town, the **Museo de León** ⓘ *Plaza Santo Domingo 8, T987 236 405, Tue-Sat 1000-1400, 1600-1900 (1700-2000 summer), Sun 1000-1400, €1.20*, opened its doors in early 2007 to some acclaim. It's a very impressive modern display that comprehensively covers the city's significant Roman, royal, and Jewish past, with good information in English too. Among the pieces on display is the famous Cristo de Carraza, an exquisite 11th century ivory crucifix.

Other sights in the old town include the nearby **Casa Botines**, a *palacio* built by Gaudí in subdued (for him) fairytale style. It now functions as an exhibition centre, but the top floors are a bank. The building's façade features St George sticking it to a dragon; a bronze sculpture of Gaudí observes his creation narrowly from a park bench outside. Next door is the elegant **Palacio de los Guzmanes**, a 16th-century Renaissance palace with a fine façade and beautiful patio. Across the square, the old Ayuntamiento is from the same period; next to it is the fine tower of **San Marcelo**.

Wandering around León's old quarter will reveal many time-worn architectural treasures and hidden nooks. The area north of Calle Ancha contains several, but the area south is the most interesting. This is the **Húmedo**, the 'wet' barrio, named after its massive collection of tapas bars, the most popular of which are around Plaza de San Martín, which hums with life most evenings and explodes at weekends. Near here is the beautiful **Plaza Mayor**, an extremely elegant porticoed 18th-century design that holds a fascinating and extremely traditional Wednesday and Saturday morning fruit and veg market. Delve a little further into the area and you'll come to the **Plaza de Santa María del Camino**, popularly known as Plaza del Grano (grain square) for its one-time wheat exchange. It's a lovely time-worn space with rough cobbles, wooden arcades and a pretty Romanesque church.

Valdevimbre

An excellent lunch or dinnertime excursion is to head some 20 km south of León to **Valdevimbre**, a historic winemaking village with spacious bodegas dug into the hills. Several of these have been converted into atmospheric restaurants with fine, well-priced food (see Eating, page 273). To get to Valdevimbre, turn off the N630 or A-66 motorway 18 km south of León. A taxi either way costs €20-26.

◉ León listings

For Sleeping and Eating price codes and other relevant information, see Essentials pages 31-39.

● Sleeping

León *p264, map p266*
L Parador de San Marcos, Plaza San Marcos 7, T987 237 300, www.parador.es. One of Spain's most attractive hotels, housed in the former monastery and pilgrim hostel of San Marcos. The furnishings are elegant but not over the top, and the building itself is a treasure. The rooms are comfortable and attractive, even if they don't quite live up to the rest of the building. The restaurant is excellent.
A-B Q!H Hotel, Av de los Cubos 6, T987 875 580, www.qhehoteles.es. This brand-new boutique hotel has an excellent location on a wide pedestrian street just a few paces from the cathedral (some of the rooms

have great close-up views of it) but in a quiet zone. The rooms are decorated with comfortable modern style, and the staff are most helpful. There's a spa complex and café too.
B Hotel Quindós, Gran Vía de San Marcos 38, T987 236 200, www.hotelquindos.com. This is a very pleasant modern hotel near San Marcos, with inventively chic decor, modern art on the walls, rooms all decorated differently from each other and with plenty of colour, as well as an excellent restaurant. Good value.
B La Posada Regia, C Regidores 9, T987 218 820, www.regialeon.com. This is a superb, characterful place to stay in León's old quarter. Just off busy pedestrian C Ancha, this 14th-century building has enticing rooms with floorboards, pastel shades and many thoughtful touches; get one away from the street though, as there's

a motorcycle shop next door. There's an equally charming new annexe opposite. The restaurant is good, but overpriced. Underground parking is very close by. Recommended.

C Hotel París, C Ancha 18, T987 238 600, www.hotelparisleon.com. This is something of a León hub; a bright family-run hotel on the main pedestrian street near the cathedral. The rooms are well-equipped and very comfortable for the price – with minibar, good bathroom and pillow menu. There's also a good café, and atmospheric downstairs restaurant and tapas bar.

D Hostal Albany, C Paloma 13, T987 264 600, www.albanyleon.com. Right by the cathedral, this excellent modern hostal offers compact, comfortable rooms, friendly staff, and a worthwhile restaurant and pastry shop on site. There's no parking particularly close by though.

D Hostal Guzmán el Bueno, C López Castrillón 6, T987 236 412, hostalguzman@hotmail.com. This is a good choice in the old town, with attractive woody rooms in a spruce old building in the barrio of the Cid. They're a little dark because it's on a narrow street, but they are well equipped, and the management is friendly.

E Hostal Casco Antiguo, C Cardenal Landázuri 11, T987 074 000, www.h-cascoantiguo.com. This newish spot is attractively modern and enjoys a fabulous location in the heart of old León, very close to the cathedral but on a quiet street. The rooms aren't huge but have good bathrooms; an added plus are the ruins of a Roman camp in the basement.

E Hotel Reina, C Puerta de la Reina 2, T987 205 200. This hotel was a faded beauty until enterprising new management took it over; now it is charmingly Spanish retro and offers excellent value. Rooms are bright and cheery, and come with or without old-fashioned bathroom (only 2 rooms use each shared one). There's a lift and roof terrace, and always a genuine welcome. Recommended.

E Pensión Blanca, C Villafranca 2, T987 251 991/678 660 244. This is an exceptional budget option; the rooms are light and colourful, tastefully decorated with brand new furnishings. Rooms have private or shared bathroom; guests have use of a kitchen and there's free internet access and a friendly owner. Breakfast is included in the price, and you can have your laundry done. Highly recommended.

E-F Hostal Bayón, C Alcázar de Toledo 6, T987 231 446. This is a fine and homely choice, with comfy rooms with en suite or shared bath (**F**) in a friendly *pensión*. It's got character and it's quiet and leafy with house plants.

❶ Eating

León *p264, map p266*
Eating in León is a pleasure. Nearly all the tapas bars give a free snack with every drink; it's standard practice to order a *corto* (short beer) to take full advantage. The most concentrated tapas zone is around Plaza San Martín in the Barrio Húmedo; for a more sophisticated scene, head across C Ancha into the Barrio Romántico around Plaza Torres de Omaña.

♦♦♦ Casa Condeso, Plaza Torres de Omaña 5, T987 170 613. The gold paint and turquoise frills around the lampshades mark this place as out of the ordinary, and the great *menú del día* (€15 weekdays) is equally memorable. The solicitous chef turns out great modern cuisine in old-fashioned portions; it's worth phoning ahead for a spot in the attractive dining room. Recommended.

♦♦♦ Restaurante Vivaldi, C Platerías 4, T987 260 760, www.restaurantevivaldi.com. Widely regarded as the province's finest restaurant, this classy and welcoming spot serves up memorable gourmet food, many of the recipes using the traditional ingredients of the region. It's future was uncertain at time of research so it may have closed by the time you read this.

♥♥ Alfonso Valderas, Arco de Animas 1, T987 200 505. Famous for its *bacalao* (cod), this elegant but down-to-earth upstairs restaurant does it in myriad tasty ways. But don't be dissuaded if salt cod isn't your thing: the grilled meats are truly excellent, as are all the starters. Excellent service. Recommended.

♥♥ El Palomo, C Escalerilla 8, T987 254 225. A good little restaurant in the Húmedo area, with well-priced, high-quality fare and a friendly attitude. The cuisine is typically Leonese, with plenty of dishes to share as well as steaks and fine fish dishes. Order à la carte. Recommended.

♥♥ Ezequiel, C Roa de la Vega 4, T987 172 177, www.embutidosezequiel.es. Make a beeline for this combined chorizo shop and bar to try traditional Leonese cured meats. The tapas are incredibly generous and filling, but if you're still hungry, grab a table and try regional specialities like *botillo* or *cocido*. Good salads and warm-hearted service round out the experience. Recommended.

♥♥ La Esponja, Pl del Cid 18, T987 237 504. In the heart of the best barrio for tapas, this restaurant has warm rustic decor and attentive service. There's a simple, cheap, and good *menú del día* and excellent traditional à la carte options at very reasonable prices.

♥♥ La Poveda, C Ramiro Valbuena 9, T987 227 155. This traditional restaurant fills up fast, for the quality is very high. Dishes are mostly *raciones*, and are absolutely delicious – the *sesos* (brains) have incredible flavour and texture, and the octopus is as good as you'll get outside Galicia.

♥♥ Las Termas, C Paloma 13, T987 264 600, www.restaurantelastermas.es. An excellent lunch *menú* is the main reason to come to this spot near the cathedral. For €14, you get a wide choice of generously sized dishes. Keep your eyes peeled for rice dishes for 2, normally on Thu; they're prepared fresh to order, and are enormous and delicious. The desserts are always tasty too, as they own the pastry shop round the corner.

♥♥ Sabor de Grecia, C Renueva 11, T987 224 628. Closed Jul-Sep. A welcoming family-run restaurant not far from San Isidoro, this is much visited for its short but very delicious menu of Greek cuisine. Dishes such as meatballs or broad beans ooze with flavour, and can be accompanied by a number of Greek wines. Best to book ahead as it's always deservedly packed. Recommended.

♥ El Besugo, C Azabachería 10, T987 256 995. This is an old-style León tapas bar; a big spacious place that doesn't deal in frills but rather simple free *morcilla* and *jamón*. There are tables to devour reliable and good-value *raciones* of the same sort of fare, and an upstairs restaurant.

♥ Fornos, C El Cid 8, T680 857 544. This longstanding León favourite in new premises specializes in traditional Leonese fare, accompanied by a range of wines. Grab a table and try the delicious *ensaladilla rusa*, calamari, the *mollejas*, or any of the other tasty *raciones*. Good tapas at the bar too.

♥ La Competencia, C Conde Rebolledo 17/C Mulhacín 8, T987 212 312, www. pizzerialacompetencia.com. A León classic, this deservedly popular place serves very good cheap pizzas in 2 locations in the heart of the Barrio Húmedo. They serve until late at weekends; the 2-level bar at C Mulhacín is also much visited as a tapas bar.

♥ La Ribera, C Fernando González Regueral 8, T987 270 408. The locals crowded into this place will show you that it's one of León's best tapas options. Once you squeeze your way to the bar, you'll find out why; as well as the home-made fried potatoes, you can enjoy some of the tastiest innards around: tripe, kidneys and *asadurilla* to remember. If that's not your thing, try the delicious mussels or calamari. Recommended.

♥ La Trébede, Pl Torres de Omaña 1. Decorated with everything from old farming implements to stuffed reptiles, this cosy neighbourhood bar is consistently busy. There's always an interesting tapa to go with your wine, and the chatty buzz makes this one of the town's best.

♥ L'Unión, C Flórez de Lemos 3, T987 261 710, www.vegetarianoleon.com. Quality vegetarian places are thin on the ground in Spain, but this place certainly fits the bill. Simple decor, but excellent and innovative plates are served in generous quantity and can be washed down with organic wine. The *menú* is great value for €10.50.

¶ Nuevo Racimo de Oro, Plaza San Martín 8, T987 214 767, www.racimodeoro.com. One of the best bars on this busy square, this is a beautiful spot with old brick and timber walls and a range of *raciones* to be devoured standing up. There are also 2 atmospheric *comedores* above and below the bar, where pricier (¶¶¶-¶¶), but rich and tasty dishes are served.

Cafés
Café Europa, Plaza la Regla 9, T987 256 117. With a great location looking up at the cathedral, this café has a relaxed atmosphere, and a good range of coffees and teas.
El Gran Café, C Cervantes 9, T987 272 301, www.elgrancafeleon.com. This classic-looking café is a popular and atmospheric spot for an afternoon coffee, but it really hits its straps in the evenings, when there's regular live music. Tue jam sessions are lots of fun and pack the place out.

Valdevimbre *p270*
¶¶ La Cueva San Simón, T987 304 096. A spacious warren of a place with the main dining area in the fermentation chamber; try the *solomillo a la brasa*, morsels of tender steak that you rapidly cook on a sizzling grate that's brought to the table. This is one of several equally characterful restaurants in this small village, so just turn up and take your pick.

🌙 Bars and clubs

León *p264, map p266*
León's nightlife is busy; the **Barrio Húmedo** is the best place for concentrated action – wander around these streets and you'll find any number of bars that will suit you.

Cervecería Céltica, C Cervantes 10, T987 072 438. This large and bright bar has an excellent range of Belgian beers, and several draught options, all expertly poured. Always buzzy and cheerful.
El Capitán, C Ancha 8, T987 262 772. A reliable and atmospheric nightspot, with candlelit tables and a range of curios and furniture. The drinks aren't cheap, but it's one of the nicest places to sit with friends for a quiet chat. Open nightly until after 0200; mixed crowd than many places.
El Universal, Plaza Mayor s/n. On a corner of the Plaza Mayor, this is one of León's best bars, standing out from the crowd for its mix of all types of people, good music, well-made drinks, and busy, cheerful bar staff. In summer there's a terrace out on the square – a great place to be.
Glam, C Platerías 10. The trendiest late-night spot with León's young, this spacious and extravagantly decorated *discoteca* is absolutely mobbed at weekends around 0200. The music is far from glam rock, usually centring around the latest pop and dance hits and enlivened by live acts and go-go dancers. Live bands sometimes play here too.
León Antiguo, Plaza Ordoño IV s/n, T987 226 956. A good bar with a friendly upmarket vibe and a nice outdoor terrace in the quieter part of the old town. Always busy and cheerful.
Planet Móngogo, Plaza Puerta Castillo 5. Open Tue-Sun from 1800. People come from all over Northern Spain to visit this unique bar/restaurant, which blends trash horror, psychobilly, and high-quality, low-priced 'Hell-Mex' food among a riot of voodoo, zebra stripes and leopard spots. It's a spot you won't forget in a hurry. Highly recommended.
Taxman, C Babia 6. By the car park behind the cathedral, this bar has a loyal following thanks to its excellent service, good coffee, and beautifully poured drinks. The theme is The Beatles, whose mugshots are everywhere, but they happily play other music on request.

⊛ Festivals and events

León *p264, map p266*

Mar/Apr León's Semana Santa (Easter Week) is a very traditional, serious affair, with many mournful processions conducted by striking hooded *cofradías* (religious brotherhoods and sisterhoods). Carrying the *pasos* (floats bearing sculptures of Jesus and Mary) is thirsty work; relief comes in the form of *limonada*, a *sangría*-like punch; a throwback to Christian Spain's dark past is that going out to drink a few is traditionally known as *matar judios* ('kill Jews').

Late Jun The feasts of San Juan (24 Jun) and San Pablo (28 Jun) are León's major fiestas of the year. There's a good range of activities over 10 days, including bullfights, concerts and high alcohol consumption.

Early Oct Fiesta de San Froilán, the city's patron, is the first weekend of Oct. There's a Moorish/medieval market, processions and dances; there's also a good Celtic music festival.

✪ Shopping

León *p264, map p266*

The main shopping street is Av Ordoño II in the new town; more quirky shops can be found in the old town.

Books

Galatea, C Sierra Pambley 1, T987 272 652, near the cathedral, has a surprising and high-quality selection of English-language fiction and non-fiction.

Iguazú, C Plegarias 7, T987 208 066. A good place to go for maps and travel literature.

Food

Don Queso, C Azabachería, is a good cheese shop. Nearby is a delightful shop that sells all the necessary ingredients to make your own sausages and chorizo.

⊘ Activities and tours

León *p264, map p266*

Mundileón, T987 212 266, www.mundileon. com. This agency is a good option for people without transport. They arrange a variety of tours around this fascinating province, in English or Spanish, and will pick up from any hotel in the city.

⊖ Transport

León *p264, map p266*

Bus Within the province, **Astorga** (30-45 mins) is served hourly, **Sahagún** 2-3 times daily (1 hr), **Riaño** 3 times daily (1 hr 45 mins) **Ponferrada** hourly (1-2 hrs), and Villafranca del Bierzo 3 times daily (2 hrs 30 mins).

There are 10 to 12 daily departures for **Madrid** (3½ hrs, €23), 8 to **Valladolid** (2 hrs, stops at Valladolid airport on request, €10), a similar number north to **Oviedo** (1 hr 30 mins, €9) and **Gijón**, 5-7 to **Zamora** (2 hrs) via Benavente, 2 to **Salamanca** (3 hrs), 4 to **Burgos** (2 hrs, €5), 1 to **Palencia**, and 3 into **Galicia**.

Train From the RENFE station, trains run to **Madrid** 8 times a day (2¾-4½ hrs, from €26-45), north to **Oviedo** (2 hrs, €15.20) and **Gijón** 7 times, east to Barcelona 3 times daily (10-11 hrs) via **Palencia**, **Burgos**, **Logroño**, **Vitoria**, **Pamplona** and **Zaragoza**, and 2 daily westwards to **A Coruña** and **Santiago**.

A dozen trains run east to **Sahagún**, and several daily go west to **Astorga** and **Ponferrada**.

The FEVE station is on Av Padre Isla, northwest of the centre. The line runs to **Bilbao**; it's a scenic but slow journey via every village (1 daily, 7 hrs 15 mins, €22). The luxury train service, **Transcantábrico**, follows this route and onwards to Santiago. Leaving on Sat from Easter to Sep, it takes a week, with numerous stops for gourmet meals, or to be bussed off to various attractions. See www. feve.es for details.

Internet Locutório La Rúa, C Varillas 3, T987 230 106, provides internet access and reasonably priced phone calls.
Laundry La Paloma, C Paloma 6, near the cathedral. **Medical services** Hospital Virgen Blanca, C Altos de Nava, T987 237 400. Call 112 in an emergency.
Police Paseo del Parque s/n, T987 255 500. **Post office** The main post office is on Plaza de San Francisco and open from Mon-Fri 0800-2000 and Sat 1000-1400.

León Province

Although joined in semi-autonomous harmony with Castilla, the province of León is fairly distinct, and offers a different experience to the vast Castilian plain. In fact, it's got a bit of everything; a look at the map confirms that it's part meseta, part mountain and part fertile valley.

León was an important early kingdom of the Christian Reconquest, but soon lost ground and importance as the battlegrounds moved further south and power became focused around Valladolid and then Madrid. Mining has been a constant part of the area's history; the Romans extracted gold in major operations in the west of the province, while coal, cobalt and copper are all still extracted, although with limited future.

The west of the province is a region of hills and valleys known as El Bierzo. It's a busy, rural zone of grapevines, vegetables, mines and more; further exploration reveals superb natural enclaves and vibrant local fiestas.

The Pilgrim Route crosses León province, stopping in the towns of Sahagún, Astorga, Ponferrada and Villafranca del Bierzo as well as the capital; all good places to regain lost strength for the climb into Galicia and the last haul of the journey. The province's north includes part of the Picos de Europa (see page 374). **▶▶ For listings, see pages 282-285.**

Camino de Santiago → *For listings, see pages 282-285.*

Sahagún → *Colour map 2, C3.*
Sahagún is one of those rare towns whose population is only a quarter of that it housed in the Middle Ages. These days it's a likeable enough place; wandering its dusty streets it's hard to imagine that Sahagún was ever anything more than what it is today – an insignificant agricultural town of the thirsty *meseta*. Sahagún's main attraction is its collection of *mudéjar* buildings. These differ from Aragonese *mudéjar* and are to some extent Romanesque buildings made of brick.

The area around Sahagún was settled by Romans and the town is named for an early Christian basilica dedicated to a local saint, Facundo (the Latin name was *Sanctum Facundum*). The town began to thrive once Santiago-fever got going, and it gained real power and prestige when King Alfonso VI invited a community of Cluny monks to establish the Roman rite in the area. They built their monastery, San Benito, on the site of the old Visigothic church; once Alfonso had granted it massive privileges and lands, it became one of the most powerful religious centres of Spain's north.

Sahagún's most famous son was a 16th-century Franciscan missionary to the Americas, Friar Bernardino, a remarkable figure. His respect for Aztec culture made him a controversial figure at the time; he mastered the *náhuatl* language and wrote texts in it. He is commemorated in his hometown by a small bust near the Plaza Mayor.

The **Iglesia de San Lorenzo** is the most emblematic of Sahagún's *mudéjar* buildings; a church dating from the early 13th century and characterized by a pretty belltower punctured with three rows of arches. The interior is less impressive, remodelled in later periods. It's worth climbing the tower if restoration work permits.

The **Iglesia de San Tirso** dates from the 12th century and is similar, with a smaller but pretty tower. The interior has suffered through neglect, but it's worth popping in to see the floats from Sahagún's well-known **Semana Santa** celebrations, as well as a well-carved 13th-century tomb, later reused. A spectacular church on the hill, **Santuario de la Virgen Peregrina**, formerly a Franciscan monastery, is finally undergoing much-needed restoration; when it reopens it should be the crowning *mudéjar* glory of the town. Especially notable is the little chapel at the back of the church, where fragments of superb Mozarabic stucco work were found when the plaster that covered them began to flake off in the mid-20th century. The chapel was commissioned by a local noble in the 15th century to house his own bones.

By the church is what's left of the **Monasterio de San Benito**; a clocktower and a Gothic chapel. The portal also survived and has been placed across the road behind the building; it's an ornate baroque work from the 17th century with impressive lions. Nearby, in the still-functioning Benedictine **Monasterio de Santa Cruz** ① *guided tours Tue-Sat 1000, 1100, 1200, 1600, 1700, 1800, Sun during mornings only, €2*, is a small museum of religious art that also has architectural and sculptural fragments from the burned monastery.

Around Sahagún

If your legs aren't weary from peregrination, or if you've got a car, there's a good excursion from Sahagún. It's an hour's walk south to the **Convento de San Pedro de las Dueñas**, which preserves some excellent Romanesque capitals and attractive *mudéjar* brickwork. The keyholder is a curious old man named Pablo; if he doesn't appear, seek him out in the house below the castle by the main road.

Head east from the convent for around half an hour to **Grajal de Campos**, with an excellent castle of Moorish origin but beefed up in the 15th and 16th centuries. It's a very imposing structure indeed. There's not a great deal to see inside, but it's fun to climb the crumbling stairs and walls. While you're in town, have a look at the nearby *palacio*, which has seen better days but preserves an attractively down-at-heel patio. From here, it's about an hour back to Sahagún.

Mansilla de la Mulas → *Colour map 2, C2.*

Beyond Sahagún, the pilgrim trail continues to Mansilla de la Mulas. There are few mules around these days, and what remains of its once proud heritage are the ruins of its fortifications. Some 8 km north, however, is the lovely Mozarabic **Iglesia de San Miguel de Escalada** ① *Oct-Mar Tue-Sun 1040-1400, 1500-1750; Apr-Sep Tue-Sun 1015-1400, 1630-2000.* Dating from the 10th century, it was built by a group of Christian refugees from Córdoba. There's a pretty horseshoe-arched porch; the interior is attractively bare of ornament; the arches are set on columns reused from an earlier structure, and are beautifully subtle. A triple arch divides the altar area from the rest of the church. It's a lovely place and well worth the detour.

Valencia de Don Juan

West of Sahagún, and south of León, the chief attraction in this small town is its weird twisted ruin of a castle built in the 15th century, with strange-shaped battlements

The Maragatos

The matter of origin of the Maragatos has provoked much scholarly and unscholarly debate. They have been variously touted as descendants of Moorish prisoners, Sueves, Visigoths and Phoenicians, but no one is really sure. Until fairly recently they kept pretty much to themselves; it is still common to see them in their characteristic national dress. The men wear a red waistcoat, bowler-style hat and a black tunic, while the women have a shawl and a headscarf.

The Maragatos are famous for their *cocido*; served in reverse to the standard Spanish custom; the meal starts with the stewed meats; usually a bit of everything, chicken, lamb, sausage and chunks of pork from various parts of the pig. The chickpea and cabbage part of the stew follows on a separate plate, and is washed down by the broth after. There are many restaurants in Astorga serving it up, but some of the best are in the small villages of the *maragatería*, the surrounding district.

rising above green grass. The pretty bullring is also worth a look. The villages nearby are warrened with curious tomblike bodegas burrowed into the hills; they produce slightly effervescent red and rosé wine. South of here is Toral de los Guzmanes with a massive adobe palace. The road continues south of here into Zamora province.

West of León

The road (and the Camino de Santiago) west from León starts out through urban sprawl to the village of **Virgen del Camino**, where a modern church houses a respected Virgin. Beyond here, the village of **Hospital de Orbigo**, reached via a long medieval bridge, is a reasonably attractive little place famous for its trout soup, and the best option for pilgrims to stop over between León and Astorga; the *albergue* is a friendly spot with a pleasant patio. The bridge was the scene of a curious event in 1434. A local noble, iron chain around his neck and doubtless suffering some form of insecurity, decided to take up residence on the bridge for the fortnight leading up to the feast day of Santiago. Passing pilgrims were forced to either declare his chosen lady the most beautiful in Christendom or have a joust with the knight or one of his heavies: just what a penniless peregrine needed after another hard day's slog across the plains. The event became known as the *Paso Honroso*; how fair the fights were is not known, but the knights unhorsed over 700 pilgrims, killing one and wounding several more. Ah, for the days of chivalry. In early June, the event is commemorated in a fiesta, with everyone dressed in medieval costume, and jousts held on the vega below the bridge.

Astorga → *Colour map 2, C1.*

While Astorga has an interesting history, nothing much goes on here now. However, it's a very pleasant, relaxed place with some attractive buildings and a peaceful small-town atmosphere. Astorga and its surrounding villages are particularly famous for being the home of the Maragatos (see box, above), a distinct ethnic group that for centuries were considered the bravest and most trustworthy of muleteers and guides.

As a major Roman centre for administering the gold-mining region further to the west, Astorga was known as Asturica Augusta, having been founded by Augustus during his campaigns against the never-say-die tribes of the northwest of the peninsula. Astorga was one of the earliest of Christian communities in Spain; the archbishop of Carthage, San

Cipriano, wrote a letter to the presbyter and faithful of the town as early as AD 254. After the disintegration of the Empire, the area was settled by the Sueves who made the journey from Swabia, now in southwest Germany. They made Astorga their capital and fought constantly with the Visigothic rulers until Astorga finally fell for good in the sixth century.

Astorga's most important sight is its **cathedral** ⓘ *Mon 0900-1100, Tue-Sat 0900-1400, 1600-1800, Sun 1100-1400, cathedral free, but entry after 1100 includes the Museo Diocesano, €2.50*, on which construction began in the 15th century. The best view of the cathedral is to be had from below it, outside the city walls. Most of it is in late Gothic style, but the façade and towers are later baroque constructions and seem overlarge and ornate for the comparatively small town. The sculptural reliefs depict events from Christ's life, and are flanked by numerous cherubs and flights of Churrigueresque fancy. Inside, the marble *retablo* is impressive, while the highlight of the are the paintings of the temptations and trials of St Anthony, who is bothered during his hermitage by some memorable demons.

Next to the cathedral, the **Palacio Episcopal** ⓘ *Tue-Sat 1100-1400, 1600-1800, Sun 1100-1400; summer Tue-Sat 1000-1400, 1600-2000, Sun 1000-1400, €2.50 (€4 including Museo Diocesano)*, is something of a contrast. In 1887 a Catalan bishop was appointed to Astorga. Not prepared to settle for a modest prefab bungalow on the edge of town, he decided that his residence was to be built by his mate, a man called Gaudí. The townsfolk were horrified, but the result is a fairytale-style castle with pointy turrets. Little of the interior was designed by the man, as he was kept away by the hostility of the locals, but there are a couple of nice touches, notably in the bishop's throne room and chapel. Much of the (chilly) interior is taken up by the **Museo de los Caminos**, a collection of art and artefacts relating to the pilgrimage to Santiago. The garden is guarded by some scary angels. The **tourist office** ⓘ *Tue-Sat 1000-1400, 1600-1900, Sun 1000-1400*, is opposite the Palacio Episcopal.

Astorga's **Plaza Mayor** is attractive, and notable for the figures of a Maragato man and woman that strike the hour on the town hall clock. Some of the city's Roman heritage can be seen at the **Museo Romano** ⓘ *Tue-Sat 1000-1330, 1600-1800 (1600-2000 summer), Sun 1100-1400, €2.50 (€3 including Museo de Chocolate)*, constructed over some of the old forum by the Ayuntamiento. Finds from many of the archaeological excavations around the town are on display. There are many **Roman remains** of interest around the town; the tourist office will provide a map of the *Ruta Romana*; there are guided tours in the summer.

Another museum is the **Museo de Chocolate** ⓘ *Tue-Sat 1030-1400, 1630-1900 (2000 summer), Sun 1030-1400, €1 (€3 with Museo Romano)*, where you can learn how chocolate was, and is, made and, especially, how it can be purchased.

Around Astorga

Some 5 km from Astorga, **Castrillo de los Polvazares** is somewhat touristy, but it's the most attractive of the **Maragato villages**. Built of muddy red stone, it's been attractively restored, and you still expect the rattle of mulecarts down its cobbled streets. There are many other less-developed Maragato villages around that are worth checking out if you've got transport. There are around 40 or 50 of them in all; some of the nicest are **Murias de Rechivaldo**, **Luyego** and **Santiago Millas**. All have at least one hearty restaurant dishing up the famed **cocido**.

El Bierzo

The lands immediately west of Astorga mainly consist of low scrubby hills. There's little of interest until the Bierzo region in the west of the province. The Bierzo is crisscrossed by middling mountain ranges and pretty valleys. The Romans mined gold and other metals here, and some coal mines are still creaking on towards their inevitable closure. It's now mainly famous for red wine and vegetables; its peppers have DO (*denominación de origen*) status and are famous throughout Spain. There are many hidden corners of the region to investigate; it's one of Northern Spain's least known and most interesting corners that could merit a sizeable guidebook on its own.

Ponferrada → *Colour map 1, C6.*

Although afflicted by rampant urban sprawl, industrial Ponferrada has a small, attractive old centre above the river Sil. It's a fast-growing and vibrant young city and capital of the Bierzo region, whose fruity red wines are growing in fame outside Spain. The main feature of the centre is a superb **Templar castle** ① *Tue-Sat 1030-1400, 1600-1800, Sun 1100-1400, open until 2030 Jun-Aug, €3,* low but formidable, with a series of defensive walls and a steep underground passage descending to the river.

Some lovely buildings are preserved in the old town; check out the small lanes around the **Plaza de Ayuntamiento**, an attractive space in itself; nearby a pretty clocktower arches across the street. The **Basílica de la Virgen de Encina** sits in another square and is an attractive building. The **Museo del Bierzo** ① *Tue-Sat 1100-1400, 1600-1900 (1700-2030 May-Sep), Sun 1100-1400, €2.70,* set in an old *palacio* in the centre, is a good display, with items of interest from the region's Celtic cultures as well as the Templar period. There's a nice patio and cobbled courtyard. There's also a small **railway museum** ① *Tue-Sat 1100-1400, 1600-1900 (May-Sep 1700-2030), Sun 1100-1400, €2.70,* on the edge of the new town, with several lovable old locomotives. The **tourist office** is by the castle walls.

Molinaseca

Some 5 km southeast of Ponferrada, on the Camino de Santiago, this excellent stone village, famous for its *embutidos* – chorizo, salchichón, and the like – sits by a babbling river, scene of a frenetic water-fight during the village fiestas. It's full of bodegas that have been converted into bars, where the typical order is a cheap local wine that comes with a hunk of bread and slice of chorizo. It's particularly popular on Sundays with folk from Ponferrada. There's a pilgrim hostel here, and plenty of accommodation and eating options. For pilgrims it may make a more relaxing stay than Ponferrada itself.

Villafranca del Bierzo

West of Ponferrada, the Camino de Santiago heads west to Galicia and the road leads into dark wooded uplands. The next stop for most Santiago-bound walkers is Villafranca del Bierzo. An attractive town, it's a nice spot to gather strength and spirit before the long ascent into Galicia. In medieval times, many pilgrims were by this stage not physically capable of continuing into the harsher terrain and weather conditions. That being the case, if they reached the church here, they were granted the same absolutions and indulgences as if they had completed the whole journey to Santiago. The **Iglesia de Santiago** is where they had to go, at least from when it was built in the late 12th century. Although Romanesque, it's unusual in form, with a cavernous, barn-like interior with a calming feel. There's a crucifixion above the simple altar, with Christ looking very old and careworn; the side chapel is a more recent affair with an 18th-century *retablo*. The side door, the Puerta del Perdón, is what the pilgrims had to touch to receive all the spiritual benefits of their journey. It has some nice capitals around it, including one of the three wise men cosily bunked up in a single bed.

Nearby, the foursquare **castle** has big crumbly walls as well as a restored section. It's still lived in and therefore cannot be visited. There's a late **Gothic Colegiata** with some local architectural influences; near here make a point of walking down Calle del Agua, a superbly atmospheric street lined with old buildings. Villafranca's **tourist office** ① *daily 1000-1400, 1600-1800 (2000 summer)*, is very helpful.

Valle del Silencio

One of the most charming spots in Northern Spain is this hidden valley south of Ponferrada. The treeless plains of Castilla seem light years away as you wind through grape vines into the narrow valley carved by the River Oza. Chestnuts and oaks, as well as abundant animal and bird life accompany the cheerful stream through villages that are utterly tranquil and rural. A circular walk around the valley, waymarked PR L-E 14, is an excellent way to spend a day; it takes about six hours.

The village of **Villafrancos** is one of the prettiest in the valley, with a delightfully picturesque stone bridge, and villagers going about their business as if the passing of centuries is a curious but inconsequential matter. There's a small bar here, but no accommodation available.

Perched below the hamlet of **San Pedro de Monte**, signposted down a side road, is a monastery, mostly in ruins but of a venerable age. You can visit its baroque church, which has a Romanesque tower. The Valle del Silencio road ends at **Peñalba de Santiago**, and you feel it's done well to get this far. Peñalba, a village of slate where three mountain ranges meet, has eked out an existence on chestnuts for centuries. Although the village is in good modern repair (restored a few years ago to beautiful effect), it's a grey beauty, with wooden balconies and an ends-of-the-earth feel. Enjoy a glass of home-made wine and a tapa of *cecina* at Cantina opposite the church, a bar steeped in tradition and the focus of village life.

The centrepiece of the village is a 10th-century **Mozarabic church** ① *Oct-Mar Wed-Sat 1040-1400, 1600-1750, Sun 1040-1400, Apr-Sep Wed-Sat 1015-1400, 1630-2000, Sun 1015-1400*, which belies its solid exterior with elegant horseshoe arches inside, as well as many fragments of wall painting.

It's about a four- to five-hour stroll from Ponferrada to Peñalba, through beautiful surroundings; much of the distance is a marked trail that follows the river. ▸▸ *See Transport, page 285.*

Las Médulas and around

The Romans found gold all over Bierzo, but here at Las Médulas they had to perform engineering wonders to get at it. Mining open-cast, they diverted river waters in elaborate ways and employed thousands of labourers in what was a massive ongoing operation. Las Médulas are the eerie and surreal remains of their toil, a large stretch of terrain sculpted into strange formations and crisscrossed by paths and tunnels, some of which are amazingly extensive. To get the full idea, it's best to head first to the best viewpoint in the area, near the village of **Orellán**; from here there's an amazing vista over the tortured earth. Pliny described one of the mining techniques as *ruina montium* (the destruction of a mountain); vast quantities of water were suddenly channelled through a prepared network of wells and sluices, literally blowing the whole hillside out and down the hill to the panning areas below. A few hills survived the process; these stand forlorn, sharp little peaks red among the heathery valleys.

Near the mirador is a network of galleries to explore (entrance €1.50); ponder Pliny's account of the labour as you walk through them: "The light of day is never seen for months at a time. The galleries are prone to collapse without warning, leaving workers buried alive. Any rocks that blocked their passage were attacked with fire and vinegar, but the smoke and fumes often choked people in the caves. So they were broken into smaller pieces with blows from iron mallets and carried out on shoulders day and night, handing them along a human chain in that infernal darkness." The incomprehensible thing is that these mines were not even particularly lucrative; recent estimates put the annual production of gold at around 25 kg; extraordinarily low from such a vast operation.

Once you've got the perspective, head for the village of Las Médulas itself, where there's a small visitor centre. From here, guided walks of the area lasting about 1½ hours run four times daily and cost €3, but you can strike off along the paths yourself at any time.

The area is some 24 km southwest of Ponferrada.

North of León → *For listings, see pages 282-285.*

The mountainous northern reaches of León province are little known except by locals, but merit plenty of exploration. It's a favourite destination of cavers and rockclimbers in summer and skiers in winter. A series of spectacular mountain passes join the province with neighbouring Asturias; these are often snowbound in winter. A car is the best way to nose around the area, although the **FEVE** trains and the odd bus makes its way out from León to many outlying villages in the zone.

Las Hoces and the Cuevas de Valporquero → *Colour map 2, B2.*
A good day out from León could see you head north to the region of Las Hoces, two narrow gorges spectacularly carved from the grey stone. Take the LE-311 that follows the course of the Torío River and continue past Matallana de Torío up the first of the gorges, **Las Hoces de Vegacervera**. The villages in this area continue much as they have done for years, pasturing sheep in the summer and grimly hanging on through the cold winters. Look out for *madreñas*, a wooden clog worn over the shoes when tramping around the muddy fields, and the famous Leonese *mastín*, or mastiff, an enormous, shaggy, friendly beast.

Off the road through the gorge are the stunning limestone caves of **Valporquero** ① *Mar-Dec 1000-1700, to 1800 Jun-Sep, €6.80,* much of which remains to be discovered. Some of the chambers are amazingly large, and (in spring and autumn) there is an underground river plunging into the depths, as well as the fascinating limestone sculpture. Take warm clothing, non-slip footwear and some sort of waterproof to the caves, as it can get pretty wet if it's been raining.

Beyond the Valporquero cave turn-off, take a right turn up the LE-313 through the other gorge, the **Valdeteja**. Continuing through the gorge, take another right just after Valdeteja itself on the LE-321. About 6 km down this road, look out for a small paved area on the right. A path leads to a spectacular waterfall pounding through a hole in the rocky hill. Once you've followed the horseshoe shape through both gorges, the road ends at the village of **La Vecilla**, 4 km from the waterfall and serviced several times daily by **FEVE** trains from León. There are several accommodation options in this region.

Northeast to the Picos → *For listings, see pages 282-285.*

The northeastern section of León province is isolated and fairly poor, climbing steadily towards the Picos de Europa. Formerly a significant coal-mining region, little of that goes on here now; farming and sausage-making are the mainstays of the small towns in the area.

Boñar and around → *Colour map 2, B2.*

Vegaquemada, a small village on the way to Boñar, has nothing of interest except a strange church in an Italianate style, with an ornate layered belltower and a porch with filigreed ironwork. ▶▶ *For the Leonese Picos, see page 374.*

Boñar is served by buses from León, but also has a train connection to Santander on the private **FEVE** network. From Boñar, the quickest route to the peaks is east via Sabero, a coalmining town amid low mountains that look to be melting.

Boñar itself is liveliest in winter as there's a **ski resort** nearby. It's a somewhat bleak place like much of this region, but there are a couple of decent places to stay.

Riaño

Forgive Riaño its slightly ugly, gawky appearance overlooking an often empty lake; the construction of the controversial dam and reservoir forced the town to reluctantly relocate to the top of the hill in the 1980s.

Although it's the southern gateway to the Picos, not an awful lot goes on here except hunting and people passing through. If you're wanting to explore this side of the range, **Posada de Valdeón** makes a smaller but more inviting and convenient base (see page 374).

There's a tourist kiosk at the entrance to the town, a couple of banks, a service station and a handful of places to stay.

⊙ León Province listings

For Sleeping and Eating price codes and other relevant information, see Essentials pages 31-39.

⊜ Sleeping

Sahagún *p275*
If you're not walking the Camino, Sahagún is best seen as a day trip from León or Palencia, but there are decent places to stay.
D-E Hostal El Ruedo, Plaza Mayor 1, T987 780 075, www.restauranteelruedo.com. This is a good choice, on the main plaza with clean modern rooms, recently renovated and equipped to hotel standard, above an *asador*. There are only 4 rooms so you might want to book ahead during peak pilgrim season.
E La Codorniz, C Arco, T987 780 276. Right opposite the tourist office, these rooms are unremarkable in decoration, but large, light and comfortable and the restaurant is decent.

Valencia de Don Juan *p276*
D El Palacio, C Palacio 3, T987 750 474. One of the best places to stay in town, this is set in a beautiful old mansion and has friendly

Asturian management and a good bar (where you can try Asturian cider) and restaurant.

Astorga *p277*
C Hotel Gaudí, C Eduardo de Castro 6, T987 615 654, www.gaudihotel.es. Opposite the Palacio Episcopal, this is one of Astorga's best, a beautiful and stylish place with a good restaurant and café. There are some good-value suites available as well.
D Hotel La Peseta, Plaza San Bartolomé 3, T987 617 275, www.restaurantelapeseta. com. Good rooms above what is widely considered one of Astorga's best restaurants. The rooms are excellent for this price, and the staff incredibly welcoming.
F Pensión García, Bajada Postigo 3, T987 616 046. One of the cheaper choices in town, this is clean and decent, if fairly unremarkable.

Around Astorga *p278*
D Cuca la Vaina, C Jardín s/n, Castrillo de los Polvazares, T987 691 078, www.cucalavaina. es. If you're exploring the area, this is a top base in the village of Castrillo de los Polvazares, with a lively bar and excellent

restaurant. The rooms are rustic and beautiful, with elaborately carved headboards, and much-needed heating in winter.

D Guts Muths, Santiago Millas, El Bajo s/n, T987 691 123, www.gutsmuths.es. A superbly peaceful and welcoming place run by a Dutch expat; the rooms are decorated by art students and are out of the ordinary, to say the least.

E El Molino de Arriero, Av Villalibre 5, Luyego, T987 601 720, www.molinodelarriero.com. This is another welcoming *casa rural* with compact, simple rooms. Also serves good cheap meals. The bar gets noisy at weekends, but otherwise it's a very peaceful place.

Ponferrada *p279*

Few of Ponferrada's accommodations are in the old town; most are in the new zone across the river.

A Hotel Temple, Av Portugal 2, T987 410 058, www.templehoteles.com. The town's top hotel is set in a large stone building with pseudo-Templar furnishings; it doesn't lack comfort, although still has a of touch of 'big hotel' impersonality.

C Hotel Bierzo Plaza, Plaza del Ayuntamiento 4, T987 409 001, www.hotelbierzoplaza.com This appealing modern hotel has an excellent location in central Ponferrada, on the town hall square and warm, professional service. The rooms are decorated with a light touch, and are good value for the price. There's a popular café downstairs. Recommended.

D Hostal La Encina, C Comendador 4, T987 409 632, www.hostallaencina.com. Parked right beside the castle, this is pricier than some of the many cheaper *hostales* around Ponfe, but worth it for the warm rustic decor and the amiable owner.

Villafranca del Bierzo *p279*

There are several good places to stay in Villafranca.

A Parador Villafranca del Bierzo, Av Calvo Sotelo-Constitución s/n, T987 540 175, www.parador.es. This cheerful cottagey affair, draped in creepers, has all the comfort and style associated with the parador chain. Closed for renovation at last visit.

D Hotel San Francisco, Plaza Mayor/ Generalísimo 6, T987 540 465, www.hotelsanfrancisco.org. Closed Dec-Feb. This is a solid option on the attractive main plaza. As it's right in the centre, you pay a little for location, but it's an enjoyable place to stay.

Valle del Silencio *p280*
Peñalba de Santiago

There are 2 accommodation options, both *casas rurales* available only to rent as a whole.

Casa Elba, Arriba de la Fuente 2, T988 322 037, casaelba@telefonica.net. Very cosy, with 2 double rooms and 2 single beds, kitchen, balcony, heating and lounge with log-fire. If there are a few of you, it's a bargain for daily or weekly rental.

Turpesa, Plaza de la Iglesia s/n, T987 425 566, turpesa@eresmas.com. Not quite as cosy as **Casa Elba**, but still a good deal for €170 a weekend or €500 a week. It sleeps 3. Both need to be booked in advance.

Boñar and around *p282*

E El Negrillón, Plaza El Negrillón s/n, Boñar, T987 735 164. The nicest place to stay in Boñar, a cosy wood-lined *casa rural* on the square by the church.

Riaño *p282*

D Hotel Presa, Av de Valcayo 12, T987 740 637, www.hotelpresa.com. The best option, with views across the lake and mountains, a good restaurant, and cosy if frilly rooms.

⑦ Eating

Sahagún *p275*

♔♔ **Restaurante Luis**, Plaza Mayor 4, T987 781 085. Sahagún is famous for its *puerros* (leeks), and the best place to try them is here; it's a great restaurant with a log fire, courtyard and a large fresco depicting market day. There's a *menú* for €12 at lunchtimes but it's much more interesting to go à la carte.

Astorga *p277*

Hostal La Peseta, Plaza San Bartolomé 3, T987 617 275. See Sleeping, above. The best *cocido* in town.

Parrillada Serrano, C Portería 2, T987 617 866. This is spacious and cosily stylish; there's a big range of dishes (including an excellent fish soup) and a good-value *menú*.

Cubasol, C Ovalle 10, T987 616 489. Traditional and no-frills place for cheap *raciones* of octopus, calamari, or sweetbreads. There's a cheap *menú del día* too.

Pizzería Venezia, C Matías Rodríguez 2, T987 618 463. Popular with all types of Astorgan, this is an inexpensive option with poor service and excellent pizza.

Cafés

Café Kavafis, C Mártires de Somiedo 5, T987 615 363. This cosy little place has internet access and books, including by the Alexandrine poet after whom it is named. The peaceful atmosphere changes at weekends, when it becomes a small disco, with good DJs.

Around Astorga *p278*

Casa Juan Andrés, C Real 24, Castrillo de los Polvazares, T987 691 065, www.casajuanandres.es. Not the cheapest of the village's places, but this cosy place up the far end offers the best *cocido* in town in a beautifully decorated traditional courtyard house.

Ponferrada *p279*

There are many good tapas bars in Ponferrada, some in the old centre, and some around Plaza Fernando Miranda.

Las Cuadras, Trasero de la Cava 2, T987 419 373. A good dark Spanish restaurant down the side of the castle with gutsy fishes and meats and a good set lunch. The tables are characterfully set around a central atrium.

El Bodegón, Travesía Pelayo 2, T987 411 019. Atmospheric central tapas bar in a spacious old stone wine cellar. A hearty dish of potatoes

with sauce comes free with your drink.

Fragata, Av Montearenas s/n, Santo Tomás de las Olas, T987 401 231. It's worth tracking down this no-frills place on the edge of Ponferrada to gorge on some of Northern Spain's finest octopus, served in the traditional manner. Great value, but book ahead.

La Bodeguilla, Plaza Fernando Miranda 5, T987 411 119. One of the city's best tapas bars, this has wine-inspired decor, with wooden cases, hanging 'vines', and a soft padded bar. It's a popular meeting point for its delicious ham *pinchos*.

La Fonda, Plaza del Ayuntamiento 10, T987 425 794, with a nice covered terrace and excellent *alubias* (stewed beans) and generous meat dishes. *Menú del día* for €12.

Villafranca del Bierzo *p279*

Mesón Don Nacho, C Truqueles 2, T987 540 076, tucked off the main road just short of the square, is a cellar-type place offering an excellent *menú* for €10 full of hearty things like stews, tripe, and *caldo gallego*, a fortifying Galician soup.

Sevilla, Plaza Mayor s/n. Serves a good-value lunch *menú* with plenty of choice and lots of seating outside on the square. There's also internet access and friendly people running it.

Las Médulas and around *p280*

El Lagar, C Leirancos s/n, Orellán, T987 695 383, www.ctrellagar.com. If you're visiting Las Médulas, the best lunch stop is this rustic spot in nearby Orellán. The food is no-nonsense and abundant; it's a very typical redoubt of Bierzo hospitality.

Las Hoces and the Cuevas de Valporquero *p281*

Venta de Getino, Getino, T987 576 424. Not far north of the turn-off to the Valporquero caves, this typical rural restaurant makes a great lunch stop. The food is excellent and plentiful, and the family-run atmosphere very welcoming. There's a *menú del día* for €10

(€15 at weekends), but don't expect to be able to finish it all.

Boñar and around *p282*
La Praillona, Av Constitución 41, T987 735 810, www.lapraillona.com. Quality Leonese mountain cuisine can be had at this well-run place. Ingredients are of high quality, and the traditional dishes come with a modern twist.

Bars and clubs

Ponferrada *p279*
Ponferrada has a famously boisterous nightlife; in the streets behind the **Temple** hotel there are any number of *discobares* with all types of music. Later on, the action moves out to the large bars in the purpose-built complex known as **La Gran Manzana**.

A rather unique venue in the heart of the old town is **Sala Tararí**, C del Reloj 17, www.salatarari.com, an excellent bar with an inclusive feel, friendly folk, regular high-quality concerts, and a rocking Thu night jam session that's worth timing your visit to experience.

Festivals and events

Astorga *p277*
Aug A Roman festival, togas and all.

Transport

Sahagún *p275*
Bus A few buses stop in Sahagún but they are significantly slower than the train.

Train There are a dozen or so feasible daily trains linking **León** and Sahagún, a journey of 30 mins. Some of the trains continue to **Grajal**, 5 mins away, before heading onto **Palencia**.

Mansilla de las Mulas *p276*
Bus There are buses at least hourly from **León** to Mansilla (20 mins). 2 buses continue Mon-Fri, and 1 Sat to **San Miguel de la Escalada** (40 mins).

Valencia de Don Juan *p276*
Bus Buses run to Valencia from **León** 6-8 times a day (30 mins). A similar number head on to **Valladolid**.

Astorga *p277*
Bus There are 15 daily buses from **León** to Astorga. There are a few trains too, but the station is inconveniently situated 20 mins' walk from the centre.

Ponferrada *p279*
Bus Ponferrada's bus station is across the river from the old town; it's a bit of a trudge, but there are frequent city buses crossing the river. Many buses go to **León**, several a day go on west to **Villafranca**, and several continue into **Galicia**, mostly to **Lugo** and **Santiago**.

Train Trains run east to **León** via **Astorga** 6 times a day, and some go west to **A Coruña**, **Ourense** and **Vigo**. The train station is also across the river from the old town.

Villafranca del Bierzo *p279*
Bus Villafranca is served by ALSA buses from **León** and **Ponferrada**. Many buses continue into **Galicia**.

Valle del Silencio *p280*
Bus There are only 2 buses monthly from **Ponferrada** up the valley to Peñalba de Santiago, so grab a car or hitch.

Riaño *p282*
Bus There are 3 buses daily (only 1 on Sun) from **León** to Riaño, one continuing to the **Picos de Europa**.

Soria

→ *Colour map 5, B4. Phone code: 975. Population: 39,528.*

One of Spain's smallest provincial capitals, Soria rules a province that's incredibly empty, one of the most sparsely populated in Spain. Although much of it is dry Castilian plains, the river Duero gives it the fullest attention, carving a big horseshoe shape through the province, eventually reaching the sea at Porto in northern Portugal (where it's named the Douro). In the north of the region are some craggy hills and tranquil hilly forests, but few trees remain in the south, for centuries a battleground between Christian and Moor. Dozens of castles are testament to this, as are the gracefully simple Romanesque churches built by the eventual victors. As the Reconquista progressed, however, Christian settlers moved south in search of less thirsty lands, leaving the province a little denuded.

Soria is little known in the travel community but is worth a day or two of anyone's time, particularly for its outstanding Romanesque architecture and strong community spirit. It's one of Castilla's friendliest places, and a good spot to get a feel for this part of central Spain, its landscapes, and its cuisine. ›› *For listings, see pages 290-291.*

Sleeping
Hostal Alvi **7**
Hostal Arévacos **1**
Hostal Viena **2**

Hostería Solar de Tejada **3**
Parador Antonio
Machado **4**
Soria Plaza

Mayor **6**

Ins and outs

Getting there and around Soria is well connected by bus to other major cities in Northern Spain. The bus station is a 15-minute walk northwest from the centre of town. A yellow bus runs from Plaza Ramón y Cajal to the train station, a couple of kilometres south. The old town, where most sights of interest are to be found, is easily walkable, tucked between two attractive parks, the hilltop Parque el Castillo and the more formal Alameda de Cervantes. The pedestrianized main street changes name a couple of times but runs the length of the area. ▶▶ See Transport, page 291.

Tourist information Soria's **tourist office** ① C Medinaceli 2, T975 212 052, oficinadeturismodesoria@jcyl.es, mid-Sep to Jun Mon-Sat 0930-1400, 1600-1900, Sun 0930-1700, summer daily 0900-2000, is just around the corner from Plaza Ramón y Cajal and is very helpful.

Background

Although nearby Numancia was an important Celtiberian settlement, Soria itself didn't really get going until the Middle Ages, when it achieved prosperity as a wool town. But its relative isolation (plus the fact that the sheep ate all the grass) led to its decline, along with that of the rest of Castilla. Once the coast was under central control, there was no

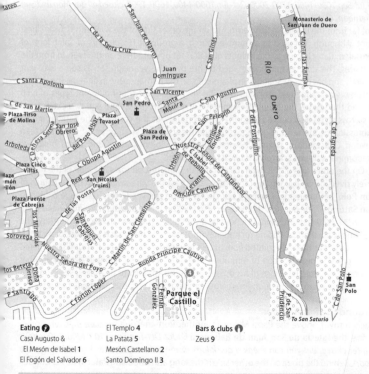

Eating ⑦
Casa Augusto &
 El Mesón de Isabel **1**
El Fogón del Salvador **6**

El Templo **4**
La Patata **5**
Mesón Castellano **2**
Santo Domingo II **3**

Bars & clubs ⑦
Zeus **9**

percentage left in towns like Soria; the conditions that led to its rise ceased to exist after the Moors had been driven out. The *cabeza* (head) *de Extremadura* – this word formerly referred to the Christian borderlands in the Reconquista – became just another decaying provincial town. Happily, this meant that there wasn't enough money to meddle with its Romanesque architectural heritage too much, a fact that the city is surely grateful for today.

Sights

Iglesia de Santo Domingo
On the northern edge of the old town, by the main road through Soria, is the Santo Domingo church, built of beautiful pale pink stone, and possessing one of the loveliest Romanesque façades in Spain. The interior is simple; barrel-vaulted and with several interesting capitals that can be a little hard to inspect in the gloom. The portal is the highlight, though, with ornately carved bands depicting a number of Biblical scenes in appealing naïve sculpture. A small plaque inside the doorway helps to identify the scenes; including the visitation of the angel to the Magi. The three seem more saucy than wise, all very cosy in bed under a single duvet.

Monasterio de San Juan de Duero and around
ⓘ *Jul-Sep 1000-1400, 1700-2000; Oct-Jun 1000-1400, 1600-1900, closed all day Mon and Sun afternoon, €0.60.*
Not far from the Iglesia de San Pedro, just on the other side of the river, this is Soria's best sight. Although it started as a humble church, a group of Hospitallers of Saint John of Jerusalem (later known as the Knights of Malta) set up base here on their return from the crusades. The simple church, damaged by fire over the years, preserves some excellent capitals and has decent Spanish display panels on the Romanesque in general. The cloister outside is a strange and striking sight. The knights blended four different types of arch around the square, the simple Romanesque, the Islamic horseshoe and two extroverted crisscross styles also derived from the east. Throughout the complex, the capitals are an expression of the returning knights' wonderment at the strange world they had seen beyond Christendom: strange beasts and plants, violent battles and weird buildings predominate; there's scarcely a Biblical scene in sight.

On the other side of the main road from San Juan, but on the same side of the river, a lovely riverside walk along the lazy Duero leads past the vine-swathed Templar church of **San Polo** (set in an apple orchard but closed to the public), to the hermitage church of **San Saturio** ⓘ *Tue-Sat 1030-1400, 1630-1830 (1930 in spring and autumn, 2030 in summer), Sun 1030-1400, free.* The saint is a popular local figure who lived in the sixth century. The building is perched on sloping rock above a grotto where he lived as a hermit for 36 years. The chapel is attractively painted floor to ceiling with wall paintings of Saturio's life; there's an impressive bearded icon of him above the altar with very haunted eyes. In another chamber are more paintings of his doings; in one he appears to be boiling sea monsters. He's still the patron of Soria, and numerous offerings and requests are made by locals.

Around the Plaza Mayor
Back in town, above the Plaza Mayor, is another Romanesque treasure in lovely Sorian stone, the **Iglesia de San Juan de Rabanera** ⓘ *Jul-Oct Tue-Sun 1100-1400, 1700-2000; winter closed, but you can sneak a quick look inside before and after Mass (times on the door).* Behind the plaza on the other side is the long and imposing **Palacio de los Condes**

de Gómara, whose Plateresque façade features a high gallery with Ionic columns; it's now used by the local government.

A mock-Roman building by the lovely Alameda de Cervantes park houses the **Museo Numantino** ① *Tue-Sat 1000-1400, 1600-1900 (1700-2000 summer), Sun 1000-1400, €1.20.* The very good display, with information in English, is mostly devoted to Roman and Celtibarian finds from Numancia and the province.

Around Soria → *For listings, see pages 290-291.*

Some 6 km north of Soria, just outside the village of **Garray**, a windswept grassy hill is the site of **Numancia** ① *Tue-Sat 1000-1400, 1600-1800 (to 2000 Apr-Sep), Sun 1000-1400, €0.60.* The inhabitants, doomed to bear the unsatisfactory name of Celtiberians until we can be surer of their origins, weren't too keen to submit to Republican Rome when it came knocking in 153 BC. Despite being outgunned, they amazingly managed to resist for 25 years. Finally, the enforcer Scipio was sent from Rome to sort them out. Not one for mucking around, he decided to encircle the walled town with a massive wall of his own, heavily fortified with camps. The despairing inhabitants lasted another 11 months before succumbing. The Romans built their own town on the site, which became one of the most important pre-Roman towns of the region, but there's not a great deal to see these days. Many years later the Numancian resistance became a powerful symbol of Spanish heroism and somewhat ironically, was used by Franco, who surely would have better identified himself with the Romans. Even Soria's have-a-go football team is named after the town.

The spread-out site is by no means thrilling today; without your own transport you might be better confining yourself to a visit to the museum in Soria. The ruins include foundations of roads, houses, public baths and a large public building; more approachable are the reconstructed Celtiberian and Roman dwellings. A couple of monuments from 1842 and 1904 commemorate the long-dead heroism of the siege. Numancia is 500 m up a road on the right after passing the centre of the village. If you don't have a car, get a cab (about €12 each way); buses to Garray run at inconvenient times.

There are several good parts of the **Sorian hills** to explore north of the capital, towards the province of La Rioja. The N-111 barrels straight north to Logroño, but ascends a picturesque mountain pass on the way, before encountering some seriously craggy hills just over the border in Rioja province. West of the road is a large expanse of forested hills, with several numbered walks. The nicest village in the region is **Molinos de Duero**, a quiet little place with lovely stone houses. Nearby, the village of **Vinuesa** is another potential base, and has a small information centre on the region.

Twenty kilometres north and west of Vinuesa is the **Laguna Negra**, reached by a potholed road. From the car park, it's a couple of kilometres up the hill to the small lake, beautifully opaque under jagged rocky peaks. There's a small information centre here, which can provide details about other walks in the vicinity.

Another good route north of Soria is on the R-115 northeast by bus or car into dinosaur country. **Yanguas**, on the Sorian side of the border, is an extremely peaceful place to stop (see La Rioja, page 217), and the numerous dinosaur footprints are well worth investigating.

East of Soria, the **Dehesa de Moncayo** is another pleasant hillforest on the Aragonese border (see page 177), while the town of **Agreda** is nice enough but has little to offer compared with Tarazona, further on. However, for a couple of decades it played an important part in Spanish history; a nun in the monastery, Sor María de Agreda, became a regular correspondent with the mighty King Felipe II, and gave him much political advice and spiritual comfort over many years.

Soria listings

For Sleeping and Eating price codes and other relevant information, see Essentials pages 31-39.

Sleeping

Soria *p286, map p286*

AL Parador Antonio Machado, Parque del Castillo s/n, T975 240 800, www.parador. es. Soria's parador is an attractive modern building peacefully set at the top of a park-covered hill above town. It's named after the famous poet, and selections of his work line the walls. The nicest rooms are suites that overlook the river and don't cost a great deal more, but it's all very comfortable, and is well staffed.

B Hotel Soria Plaza Mayor, Plaza Mayor 10, T975 240 864, www.hotelsoriaplazamayor. com. With an excellent location on the tranquil square in the heart of the old town, this hotel has plenty to offer. There are just 10 rooms, decorated in dark but elegant style, with floorboards and a/c. The ones at the top of the building are not for space freaks, but are very appealing with their sloping roof.

D Hostería Solar de Tejada, C Claustrilla 1, T975 230 054, www.hosteriasolardetejada. com. This is a great place to stay in the heart of Soria. Original decoration is backed up by warm-hearted service. The rooms, all different, are attractive and brightly coloured, and a solar and lunar theme runs throughout. Free Wi-Fi. Recommended.

E Hostal Alvi, C Alberca 2, T975 228 112, www.hostalalvi.com. Extremely central, and efficiently run, this hostal has compact rooms on the upper floors of a municipal building. The exterior rooms have much more light, although there is a little bit of traffic noise as cars echo their way up this narrow street. Interior rooms are perfect for lighter sleepers.

E Hostal Arévacos, C Clemente Sáenz 8, T975 212 832, www.hostalarevacos. com. Friendly family-run *hostal* offering comfortable modern rooms and easy parking a short distance from the town centre. Free Wi-Fi and a laundry service are among the facilities.

E Hostal Viena, C García Solier 1, T975 222 109. A short walk from the centre, this old-fashioned but hospitable *hostal* is set above a café. It's a bargain really for what you get; rooms with or without bathroom are showing their age but comfortable; all have TV and are pretty quiet. You should be able to park free somewhere nearby.

Around Soria *p289*

A-B Real Posada de la Mesta, Plaza Cañerias s/n, Molinos de Duero, T975 378 531, www.realposada.com. This is a great place to stay in this elegant village; a beautiful, large, old stone mansion with great decoration in heavy rustic style. They serve tasty gourmet meals. A highlight are the seasonal truffle-hunting outings.

Eating

Soria *p286, map p286*

Soria's eating and drinking is focused around Plaza Ramón Benito Aceña, at one end of C Mayor, and Plaza San Clemente.

♥♥♥ Mesón Castellano, Plaza Mayor 2, T975 213 045, www.mesoncastellanosoria.com. On the main square, and Castilian it certainly is, with large portions of heavy dishes such as roast goat, balanced by a decent house salad and some good Ribera del Duero reds. They'll also give you a very tasty free tapa if you drop in for a glass of wine.

♥♥♥ Santo Domingo II, Plaza del Vergel 1, T975 211 717, www.santodomingo2.es. An elegant wood-and-curtains type of Spanish restaurant, with mixed Basque and Castilian fare. There are *menús* for 2 or more, which are good value.

♥♥-♥ Casa Augusto/El Mesón de Isabel, Plaza Mayor 4, T975 213 041, www. casaaugusto.com. These 2 connected restaurants are among the city's best. In **Casa Augusto** (¶¶), you can try traditional Sorian fare such as the tasty *pecho de cordero* or a variety of stews. It's decorated in traditional Castilian style, with excellent service. Adjoining it, **El Mesón de Isabel** (¶) is a cheaper, bistro-style place with cheap set meal deals and comfort plates like meatballs and stuffed vegetables. The ambience is pleasant, with a large number of clocks and a romantic feel.

¶¶ **El Fogón del Salvador**, Pl del Salvador 1, T975 230 194, www.fogonsalvador.com. There's nothing quite like the warm lighting and enticing aromas of a Castilian *asador*. This is one of the town's best, with extremely succulent meat brought to your table on its own little charcoal grill, and plenty of lighter dishes to back it up: in season, the grilled vegetables are a treat.

¶ **El Templo**, Callejón del Pregonero 2, T975 215 162. This central bar and restaurant stands out for the warm personal service and well-priced *raciones*; things like calamari and salads come in abundant quantity and quality. There are also more substantial dishes like steaks.

¶ **La Patata**, Plaza San Carlos 1, T975 213 036. Popular for its good-value *raciones* and toasted bar-top snacks. They take a pride in their *patatas bravas*, served with a spicy home-made sauce.

◑ Bars and clubs

Soria *p286, map p286*
The main nightlife starts in C Zapatería and C Real. Later it progresses away from the centre to the **Rota de Calatañazor** zone, where there are several *discobares* and *discotecas*.

Zeus, Plaza Ramón Benito Aceña s/n, T975 231 048. A smart café/bar on 2 floors. It's a good option at any time of the day; morning coffee to late-night drinks; they cater to all.

✿ Festivals and events

Soria *p286, map p286*
Late Jun Sanjuanes, Soria's main festival. with an array of bullfights, processions, fireworks and wine drinking.
2 Oct San Saturio's feast day is a big event.

⊖ Transport

Soria *p286, map p286*
Bus
7 daily buses to **Madrid** (2½ hrs, €15), 6 to **Logroño** (1 hr 30 mins, €7), several to **Vitoria** and to **Pamplona**, some via **Tafalla** and **Olite**. 6 buses (3 on Sun) to **Zaragoza** via **Tarazona**. Heading west, 1 daily heads Mon-Fri to **Berlanga**, 3 daily to **Calatañazor** and **El Burgo de Osma**, and another 3 to **Aranda de Duero** and **Valladolid**.

2 buses daily service the dinosaur country stops of **Yanguas**, **Enciso** and **Arnedillo**.

Train
The main rail destination is **Madrid** (2 daily, 3 hrs, €16), serviced via **Guadalajara**.

❶ Directory

Soria *p286, map p286*
Internet Merlin Center, C Santa Luisa de Marillac 3, T975 225 916. An internet centre with decent connections.

Along the Duero: west from Soria to Valladolid

Travelling along the Río Duero you roughly follow the long-time frontline of the Reconquista. There are more castles than you could poke a battering ram at, although many are ruinous. The land is dry and sun-beaten except along the riverbanks, which give their name to one of Spain's best wine regions, the Ribera del Duero. Peñafiel, with its fine mudéjar *architecture and vibrant festival, makes a convenient base for exploring the Duero region, which has many bodegas to visit as well as a wine museum. Within easy reach of Berlanga is one of Castilla's more remarkable monuments, the Ermita de San Baudelio. Further west, one of the oldest dioceses in the peninsula, dating from at least AD 598, El Burgo de Osma, once an important Castilian town, makes a worthy stopover, while nearby, the castle of Gormaz stands proud and forlorn on a huge rocky hill. North of here, the spectacular Cañón del Río Lobos provides top walking and vulture-spotting opportunities.* ▶▶ *For listings, see pages 297-300.*

Calatañazor → *Colour map 5, B3.*

Some 25 km west of Soria is the village of Calatañazor. This pretty but tiny place, with its cobbled streets, toppling castle and pretty Romanesque chapel, was the unlikely venue for the fall of the great Muslim warlord Al-Manzur (see box, page 502), who was defeated here in a battle in 1002, the millennium of which was celebrated with *fiestas* and cultural events. Now home to only 30 inhabitants, Calatañazor – whose name derives from the Arabic 'Qal'at an-Nusur', which means castle of the vultures – is a picturesque place to stay. It's a touch touristy, but far enough off the beaten track that it's not really a problem; even in peak season, the day trippers disperse pretty soon after lunch. A small **tourist office** is at the bottom of the town, opposite the pretty 12th-century chapel, **Ermita de la Soledad**. In the heart of the village is the larger **Nuestra Señora del Castillo**, with a Romanesque portal and small museum. To get to Calatañazor, Burgo de Osma-bound buses from Soria will drop you at the turn-off on the main road, a 10-minute walk away.

Berlanga de Duero → *Colour map 5, B3.*

Dominated by its impressive castle, Berlanga stands on a slope above the town, which is a likeable jumble of narrow lanes and old buildings set around an attractive plaza. In the centre is the reasonably interesting late-Gothic **Iglesia de Colegiata de Santa María**.

The **castle** ⓘ *summer Tue-Sat 1100-1400, 1600-1930, Sun 1100-1400, €1, at other times ask for key in the tourist office (weekends) or Ayuntamiento (0830-1500 weekdays)*, originated as an Arab fortress, although most of it was built in the 15th and 16th centuries. The walls are preserved in a reasonable state, but little remains of the castle buildings or the elaborate gardens that once surrounded them. It is nevertheless picturesque.

Ermita de San Baudelio

ⓘ *Wed-Sat 1000-1400, 1600-1800 (2000 summer), Sun 1000-1400, €0.60.*

Some 8 km south of Berlanga is one of Castilla's more remarkable monuments. On a hillside that until the 19th century was covered in oak forest, the little chapel, Ermita de San Baudelio, was constructed at the beginning of the 11th century. It was close to the border that separated Muslim and Christian lands, and the design is a superb example of Mozarabic architecture. A horseshoe-arched doorway leads into an interior dominated by a central pillar that branches into extravagant ribs that recall a palm grove. There's even a tiny gallery, reached by an unlikely looking stair. Even more inspiring is the painted decoration, added 150 years later. Incredibly, an American art dealer was permitted to remove most of it in the 1920s (what he took is mostly now in the Metropolitan Museum in New York, although some has been repatriated to the Prado in Madrid). However, there's still enough left to excite: an Islamic hunting scene on the bottom half of the walls sits below a Biblical cycle; both preserve radiant colours and elaborate, sharp imagery.

El Burgo de Osma → *Colour map 5, B3.*

El Burgo de Osma grew in the Middle Ages, and a large stretch of the wall is still well preserved; a vigilant sentinel on this wall almost changed the course of world history when he lobbed a boulder at a passing shadow one night in 1469. He narrowly missed killing the young prince Fernando, rushing by night to his furtive wedding with Isabel in Valladolid.

The **cathedral** ① *Easter-Oct Tue-Sun 1030-1400, 1600-2000, also open Mon in Jul and Aug, Nov-Easter Tue-Fri and Sun 1100-1300, 1600-1800, Sat 1030-1330, 1600-1930, €2 (€4 for guided tour)*, was started in the 13th century but has been sorely afflicted by later architects who just couldn't leave it alone, and added chapels left, right and centre, as well as an ugly appendix that houses the sacristy. The interior is richly decorated; the *retablo* is a good piece by Juan de Juni, much of whose other work can be seen in Valladolid's sculpture museum. A guided tour will take you to the cloister and museum, the highlight of which is a superb, ornately illustrated manuscript, a copy of the *Codex of Beatus de Liébana* dating from 1086, which has been described as "one of the most beautiful books on earth". The beautiful tomb of San Pedro de Osma, who raised the Romanesque edifice, is also memorable.

The large **Plaza Mayor** has an impressive old building, a former hospital that now houses both the **tourist office** ① *T975 360 116, www.burgosma.es*, and **Antiqua Osma** ① *summer Thu-Sat 1130-1400, 1630-1930; rest of the year Sat and Sun only 1100-1400, 1600-1900*, a fun little archaeological museum with finds and reconstructed scenes from the Iberian and Roman town of Uxama, whose fragmentary ruins can still be seen to the west of town. The courtyard is also used for art exhibitions.

A more earthy note is struck by the **Museo del Cerdo** ① *C Juan Yagüe, 1200-1400, 1630-1900*, or Museum of the Pig, run by a local restaurant. The western part of Soria province is anything but New Age; stag-hunting is a popular pastime, and the eating of vegetables frowned upon. The *matanza*, when the free-range pigs are driven in from the wild and converted into ham and chorizo, is a major town event every winter.

Castillo de Gormaz

① *The castle is little visited, and is permanently open (and free); buses run from El Burgo de Osma to Quintanas de Gormaz, from where it's a 1-hr walk, including a lengthy climb.*

Some 15 km south of El Burgo de Osma, Gormaz castle, built by the Moors around AD 950 is about the oldest, and certainly one of the largest, castles in western Europe, and was one of the 'front teeth' defending Al-Andalus from the Christians. While not a lot remains inside, it's well worth a visit just to see its walls, which are nearly 1 km in length and utterly commanding, visible for miles around. The Muslim origin of the citadel can be seen in the Caliph's gate, an ornate horseshoe portal. Although it seems totally impregnable even today, it was taken barely a century after being built, by Alfonso VI. He promptly gave it to El Cid; never let it be said that old Fonsi wasn't good to his friends.

Don't confuse Gormaz castle with the castle atop the town of San Esteban de Gormaz, a town on the N122 west of Burgo de Osma.

Cañón del Río Lobos

Tucked away in the wooded hills of northwestern Soria province, this beautiful gorge is worth seeking out. The Lobos river has carved its way down through soft limestone to form a spectacular canyon that winds its way some 25 km from near the village of Hontoria del Pinar in Burgos province southeast to Ucero, situated 15 km north of Burgo de Osma. The sculptured, concave cliffs are the domain of vultures and other birds of prey, such as the golden eagle and peregrine falcon; juniper and holm oak shade the canyon floor.

A walking trail runs the length of the valley. The river's gradient is gentle, so it's not a strenuous hike, but it's a hot one in summer, so take plenty of water. There are three places you can access the canyon trail: at either end, or on the SO960 road southwest of the town of San Leonardo de Yagüe, which itself is on the N234 running northwest from Soria to Burgos.

The main access point is near Ucero. It's a small, picturesque place nestled among crags, one of which bears a ruined castle. Just beyond the village is a **park information point** ① *T973 363 564, open 1000-1400, 1600-1900, open all day at weekends and to 2000 in summer, closes 1700 in Jan and Feb*, with displays on the ecology and maps of the trail. About 1.5 km further on, there's a left turn that takes you to a large car park at the beginning of the canyon trail. From here it's 25 km to the other end. A short stroll from here takes you to the **Ermita de San Bartolomé**, a pretty Romanesque chapel a couple of kilometres up the trail (€1 entry). If you're going to walk the whole canyon, be aware that there's no bus link back. Many people walk the first half, return to their cars, and walk the second half the next day from the mid-point car park.

Aranda de Duero → Colour map 5, B2.

"That's red Aranda. I am afraid we had to put the whole town in prison and execute very many people." (Remark made by the Conde de Vallellano to Dr Junod, Red Cross representative in Spain during the Civil War.)

A cheerful and solid Castilian working town, Aranda was spared the decline of the region by its location on an important crossroads. It's a busy place also set on a junction of rivers that still functions as a market town and supply centre for the surrounding area. Aranda's pride is roast lamb, for which it is famous throughout Spain; every eatery in town seems to be an *asador*, and the smell of cooking meat pervades the air.

The main sights are two attractive churches. **Iglesia de Santa María** has a superbly ornate portal still preserving some colour from the original paint job; scenes from the Virgin's life are portrayed, including the *Nativity* and the *Adoration of the Magi*. Nearby, the **Iglesia de San Juan** has a striking, many-layered portal set around Christ and, appropriately enough, a lamb. The **tourist office** ① *Tue-Sat 1000-1400, 1600-1900, Sun 1000-1400*, is on Calle de la Sal.

Peñaranda → Colour map 5, B2.

East of Aranda is the sweet little town of Peñaranda, all cobbled streets and elegant buildings. There's a 14th-century **castle** on the hill above town, while in the heart, on the **Plaza Mayor**, the hulking **Iglesia de Santa Ana** isn't particularly loveable. Opposite is the more stylish **Palacio de Avellaneda** ① *Oct-Mar 1000-1400, 1500-1800, Apr-Sep 1000-1400, 1600-1930, tours on the hour*. Topped with a bust of Hercules, it was built by the counts of Miranda in the 16th century. The Plateresque façade is suitably grand, and attractively topped by a carved wooden roof. Inside there's an elegant galleried patio, and salons and stairways decorated in rich style. There's a **tourist office** ① *Tue-Sun 1000-1400, 1700-2000 (1600-1900 winter)*, in the centre.

Further along, near the village of **Peñalba de Castro**, are the bare hilltop ruins of **Clunia**, once a significant Roman town. It's far from a world-class attraction, but has the remains of a theatre, bathhouse and several dwellings. There are ordained opening hours when the admission fee is €1, but there are no fences to stop you going for a wander at other times.

Ribera del Duero → *For listings, see pages 297-300.*

Peñafiel → *Colour map 5, A1.*

Peñafiel is the main town of the Ribera del Duero wine region, and a good place to start your exploration of the zone. The square-jawed **castle** that sits on the hill above town was one of the Christian strongholds that flexed its muscles at the Moorish frontline, and the town grew up around it, although the settlement of Pintia nearby had been important in pre-Roman times. Peñafiel is now an attractive place by the river; there are even some trees, a rare enough site in the Castilian *meseta*.

Nicknamed 'the Ark' because it resembles a ship run aground, the citadel in Peñafiel was important because it occupied a crucial strategic ridge above the Duero. The castle is long and thin, so narrow as to almost resemble a film-set cut-out until you get close and see how thick the curtain walls are, reinforced with a series of bristling towers. Part of the castle now holds the the **Museo de Vino** ⓘ *Easter-Sep Tue-Sun 1100-1430, 1630-2030, Oct-Mar Tue-Sun 1130-1400, 1600-1900, €3 castle tour, €6 museum plus castle tour, €9 for a tutored tasting session of 4 wines*, a modern display covering all aspects of wine production. Much of it is rather unengaging – the information panels seem like sections from a textbook on agriculture – but things get more interesting with an array of aromas that you can inhale before revealing whether you sniffed correctly or not. Information is in Spanish, but there's an English/French audio guide. The cost of admission includes a guided tour around the other, unadorned, part of the castle. You can also pay extra for a tasting session.

The castle isn't Peñafiel's only point of interest. Down in the town, have a look at the excellent **Plaza del Coso**, a spacious square still used for markets and bullsports. With its beautiful wooden buildings and sand underfoot, it's an unforgettable sight. The town's major fiesta is superb (see page 300). Another highlight is the beautifully ornate brick *mudéjar* exterior of the **Iglesia de San Pablo** ⓘ *daily 1200-1330, 1730-1830, €2*. Converted from fortress to monastery in the 14th century, the interior is in contrasting Plateresque style.

Peñafiel's **tourist office** ⓘ *Plaza San Miguel de Reoyo 2, T983 881 715, www.turismo penafiel.com, Oct-Mar 1000-1400, 1630-1900, Apr-Sep 1030-1430, 1700-2030*, is a good source of information. In the same building is a radio museum.

Around Peñafiel

The area east of Peñafiel is worth exploring, even for non-vinous reasons. A good place to start is the small town of **Roa**, whose **tourist office** ⓘ *Mon-Sat 1030-1400, 1630-2030, Sun 1030-1400*, has a wealth of information on the region.

The hill on which the town sits was inhabited in pre-Roman times but lay fallow for centuries until repopulation in the 10th century. Good sections of the medieval walls are preserved, and there's an attractive walk along them, with views across the Valley of the Duero. The church of **Nuestra Señora de la Asunción** is the centrepiece of Roa, and preserves Romanesque and Gothic elements, although the majority is in early Renaissance style. The star vaulting in the interior is especially impressive. Another interesting building in the town is a well-preserved *alhóndiga*, used for storing and trading grain in the Middle Ages.

Roa's most famous inhabitant was Cardinal Cisneros (known in English as Ximenez), powerful archbishop and regent of Spain for a period. He died here in 1517, the day a letter arrived from the new king that dismissed him from his post. The smiling bust of him that looks over the city walls is a charitable interpretation of the authoritarian cleric.

North of Roa, the village of **La Horra** preserves a series of what appear to be conical cairns. Visible all over the region, they are actually air-vents and indicate the presence of an undergound wine bodega. All the region's wine was once made in these cellars and the build-up of fumes from the fermentation necessitated the chimneys, which were sometimes also used to tip grapes down.

East of here, **La Aguilera** has an unexpectedly large church complex, the **Santuario de San Pedro Regalado** ① *Mon-Sat 0900-1300, 1700-2000, Sun 1700-2000*. With an ornate interior and impressive flying buttresses, the church is dedicated to a 15th-century saint from Valladolid who spent his life as a monk here, preaching and performing the occasional miracle. He is the patron saint of bullfighters, as he once tamed a fierce bull that had escaped from the square in Valladolid; it's not uncommon for matadors to come here to give thanks for a lucky escape.

The attractive town of **Gumiel de Izán** nearby has a church with an impressive Renaissance façade and a large wooden *retablo* detailing the life of Christ, while the village of **Baños de Valderados** has the remains of a **Roman villa** ① *Jul-Aug 1030- 1400, 1600-2000, T947 534 229 to arrange a visit at other times*, with four reasonably preserved mosaïcs.

Wineries

Though the Ribera del Duero has a long history as a wine region – Vega Sicilia, the royal family's favourite tipple, was founded in 1864 – it's been since it was granted DO status in 1982 that the world has really sat up and taken notice, with its red wines winning rave reviews from experts and the public. The wines are based on the Tempranillo grape, although here it's called *Tinta del País*. Many consider the region's top wines superior to anything else produced in the country, and prices for wines such as Peter Sesseck's Pingus are stratospheric. Dealing with the cold Castilian nights gives the grapes more character, while traditionally a long period of rotation between oak barrels and larger vats has been employed. Ribera soils are also characteristic, and are probably responsible for the wines' very distinctive soft fruity nose. Most wineries can be visited, although they require a call in advance. Visits are rarely possible in August or during the vintage in late September to early October.

The excellent Pesquera is produced by **Bodegas Alejandro Fernández** ① *T983 870 037, www.grupopesquera.com*, in the village of Pesquera de Duero west of Peñafiel. Visits need to be arranged by calling a week in advance; they are are available in English, and free. In Pedrosa de Duero, near Roa, the tiny **Hermanos Pérez Pascuas** ① *T947 530 100, www. perezpascuas.com*, makes the tasty Viña Pedrosa. **Condado de Haza** ① *T947 525 254, www. condadodehaza.com*, another quality producer, is in an attractive building at the end of a long driveway between Roa and La Horra. **Vega Sicilia** is not open to the public.

In Peñafiel itself, a handy bodega to visit, clearly signposted off the main road, is **Protos** ① *C Protos 24, T983 878 011, www.bodegasprotos.com, 1000-1400, 1600-1900*, a cooperative founded in 1927 whose mellow wines are very competitively priced for their quality. Ring in advance to arrange a visit.

About 17 km west of Peñafiel, it's hard to miss the giant complex of **Bodegas Arzuaga Navarro** ① *T983 681 146, www.arzuaganavarro.com, visits bookable by phone, €5*, with a five-star hotel and enormous restaurant complementing the winery, which produces the excellent, juicy Arzuaga wines.

Just east of Sardón de Duero, on the main road some 25 km west of Peñafiel, is perhaps the most beautiful of the wineries, **Abadía Retuerta** ① *T983 680 314, www.abadia-retuerta. com, Mon and Fri 1000 and 1200, from €10 depending on wines tasted, book by phone or website; you can buy wine here Mon-Sat 1000-1400, 1600-2000*, which stands next to a gorgeous 12th-century Romanesque monastery. The winemaking facilities themselves are modern and the wines aren't actually under the Ribera del Duero denomination, but they are outstanding, some blending Tempranillo and Cabernet Sauvignon to great effect, and there are examples for every budget.

⊚ Along the Duero: west from Soria to Valladolid listings

For Sleeping and Eating price codes and other relevant information, see Essentials pages 31-39.

⊜ Sleeping

Calatañazor *p292*
Tourism is the village's only future and there are several good sleeping options.
B Casa del Cura, C Real 25, T975 183 642, www. posadarealcasadelcura.com. An upmarket *casa rural* with small but nicely decorated rooms, an attractive modern interior and a good restaurant with a large terrace. Reception is in the Hostal Calatañazor across the road.
D-E Hostal Calatañazor, C Real 10, T975 183 642, www.calatanazor.com. Good rooms and a restaurant decorated in Berber style. Value in the heart of the village.

Berlanga de Duero *p292*
E Hotel Fray Tomás, C Real 16, T975 343 033. Named after the town's most famous son, a missionary priest, the rooms are pleasant enough, though a little staid and dull. However, the restaurant is good and the prices are more than fair.

El Burgo de Osma *p293*
A Hotel Termal Burgo de Osma, C Universidad 5, T975 341 419, www. castillatermal.com. Behind a magnificent Plateresque façade, this modern hotel offers substantial elegance and comfortable rooms alongside a picturesque pool and spa area, with lots of treatment options on offer.
B Hotel Il Virrey, C Mayor 4, T975 341 311, www.virreypalafox.com. A plush but

courteous hotel in traditional Spanish style. Facilities include gym and sauna, and the rooms are comfortable enough, although some are pokier than the grand decor would suggest; you might prefer to opt for a suite (**A**), which doesn't cost too much more.
C Posada del Canónigo, C San Pedro de Osma 19, T975 360 362, www. posadadelcanonigo.es. An excellent place to stay, just inside the southern gate of the city wall. Decorated with care and style, the rooms are romantic and feature plush beds and floorboards. The *posada* also has an excellent restaurant.
D El Fielato, Av Juan Carlos I 1, T975 368 236, www.hospederiaelfielato.com. On the corner of the main road and the principal pedestrian street, this recommendable place offers spotless, comfortable rooms equipped with hotel-standard conveniences.
E Hostal San Roque, C Universidad 1, T975 341 221. A grubby exterior conceals a clean, modern and very decent option on the main road through town. The rooms have good bathrooms and you more or less have the run of the place.

Castillo de Gormaz *p293*
C Casa Grande, T975 340 982, www. casagrandegormaz.com. This excellent *casa rural* is in the village of Quintanas below the imposing fortress of Gormaz. It offers great views of the castle and is set in a spick and span yellow mansion. The rooms are delightful, with rustic touches; and there's a lounge with a fireplace. Dinners available (€20).

Cañón del Río Lobos *p294*

C Posada Los Templarios, C de la Iglesia s/n, Ucero, T975 363 528, www.posadalostemplarios.com. In a noble stone house in the village of Ucero, this is the top place to base yourself for walking the Cañón del Río Lobos. Smart modern-rustic decoration is allied with excellent facilities.

Aranda de Duero *p294*

See Peñafiel, below, for rural tourism in the villages between Aranda and Peñafiel. Nearly all Aranda's accommodation is set away from the centre on the main roads. Exceptions include:

D Hotel Julia, Plaza de la Virgencilla s/n, T947 501 250, www.hoteljulia.es. This central hotel is a comfortable place full of interesting old Spanish objects. The rooms are excellent for this price, and there's friendly management and plenty of comfort. Free Wi-Fi.

E Pensión Sole, C Puerta Nueva 16, T947 500 607. This *pensión* in the older part of town is a good budget option. It has good small clean rooms that are aging but comfortable; they all have TV and you can choose between simple en suite or shared bathroom.

Peñaranda *p294*

C Posada Ducal, Plaza Mayor s/n, T947 552 347, www.laposadaducal.com. Right on the main square, this beautiful *casa rural* was once the servants' quarters of the nearby palace. The accommodation has likely improved since those days; now it makes an excellent choice, with attractively rustic decoration and a decent restaurant too.

C Señorío de Velez, Plaza Duques de Alba 1, T947 552 201, www.hotelvelez.com. This hotel is a sound place to stay in the heart of town. Set in an attractive stone and adobe building, the rooms are clean and acceptable, if a touch overpriced. There's a nice terraced restaurant too.

Ribera del Duero and Peñafiel *p295*

If you've got a car, you might like to take advantage of the large numbers of *casas rurales* and *posadas* in the area between Peñafiel and Aranda, particularly around Roa and Gumiel de Hizán. The tourist office will provide a list; prompt them to make sure they give you it for both the provinces (Valladolid and Burgos) that this area straddles. The website www.toprural.com is also a good starting point, and the regional government website www.turismocastillayleon.com has an extensive list.

LL Bodegas Arzuaga Navarro, T983 681 146, www.arzuaganavarro.com. Despite the bulky building and unappealing main road location, this is a luxurious base in one of the Ribera's best wineries. The rooms are most commodious, and all come with jacuzzi. Opportunities for tasting can be arranged, and the restaurant specializes in game and roast lamb. You can roam the extensive vineyard and grounds.

A Convento las Claras, Pl Alonso s/n, T983 878 168, www.hotelconventolasclaras.com. In the centre of Peñafiel, just across the river from the heart of things, this excellent new convent conversion provides an historic place to stay and a comfortable base for the Ribera wine country. Rooms, set around a courtyard, are spacious and comfortable, and there's a good restaurant and spa facilities. Service is a little naïve but that will hopefully improve.

A-B Ribera del Duero, Av Escalona 17, T983 881 616, www.hotelriberadelduero.com. A large but attractive hotel cleverly converted from an old flour mill. Some of the rooms have good views of the castle and there's a well-priced restaurant.

E El Zaguán de Gumiel, C Real 54, Gumiel de Hizán, T947 544 141, www.elzaguandegumiel.com. One of the best of the rural tourism options in the Ribera del Duero area, this is an attractive stone and adobe building with plenty of character and a restaurant. The rooms are gorgeous: simple in style and wood-beamed, but with TV and a/c as well as a good bathroom. Bikes are available to explore the area.

E Hostal Campo, C Encarnación Alonso s/n, T983 873 192. This *hostal* has comfortable and clean new rooms a short stroll from the centre on the other side of the main road. The main problem is a slightly depressing location near the sugar refinery. All rooms have bathroom and modern comforts; it's run out of the down-at-heel **Bar Campo** on the road to Pesquera.

F Hostal Chicopa, Plaza de España 2, T983 880 782. This place has 2 important things going for it: price and location. Set right in the centre of the old town above a bar/restaurant, these simple rooms go for a song. Some have their own bathroom, others share; it's pretty basic, but it's not a dive.

⊙ Eating

El Burgo de Osma *p293*

♯♯♯ Virrey Palafox, C Universidad 7, T975 340 222. This restaurant is run by the same management as the **Hotel Virrey**, and is unashamedly devoted to meat, which is superbly done. On Feb and Mar weekends, the **Fiesta de la Matanza** takes place; pigs are slaughtered and devoured in their entirety.

♯♯ El Burgo, C Mayor 75, T975 341 249. Only open at weekends, this restaurant is a temple to meat. The food is great, but some of the steaks are laughably large, so be firm with the pushy owner who is sure he knows what you want.

♯ Café 2000, Plaza Mayor 7, T975 340 446. A good cheap place to eat and snack, with a terrace on the main square and a decent €10 *menú*. As everywhere, meat is the way to go here rather than fish.

Cañón del Río Lobos *p294*

♯ La Parrilla de San Bartolo, Ctra de San Leonardo s/n, Ucero, T975 363 516. On the main road through the village, this doesn't look much from the outside, but it's worth investigating for its excellent meat dishes at very reasonable prices.

Aranda de Duero *p294*

The local speciality is roast lamb, washed down with a bottle of red from the local Ribera del Duero. The lamb's not cheap or particularly subtle, but it's delicious and the portions are huge. A quarter lamb (easily enough for 2) costs around €40, and an eighth about €20; there are heaps of places to try it along the main pedestrian street Isilla, and around the Plaza Jardines de Don Diego on the road through the middle of town.

♯♯ Asador Ciprés, Plaza Jardines de Don Diego 1, T947 507 414. Many *arandinos* vouch for this *asador* as the town's best. Traditional service and delicious lamb combine well with the region's wines. If there's any room left, you can try another local speciality, *empiñonado*, a pine-nut sweet.

♯♯ El Lagar de Isilla, C Isilla 18, T947 510 683. One of several memorable *asadores* in town, this is perhaps the most atmospheric, with beams and old grape presses decorating this former wine bodega (dozens of which are dug out under the town). Lamb is cooked in the traditional wood oven and there's a great wine list and a friendly tapas bar out front. Make sure you go down to see the cellars.

Peñafiel *p295*

♯♯ Molino de Palacios, Av de la Constitución 16, T983 880 505. This is a lovely *asador* romantically set in an old watermill on the river. The speciality is predictable, namely roast lamb, but there are also plenty of game and wild mushroom dishes.

♯ Restaurante María Eugenia, Plaza España 17, T983 873 115. Friendly family-run place decorated with heavy Spanish furniture and decent landscapes. Good seafood and huge steaks.

Cafés

Café Judería, a relaxing place for a coffee or drink, nicely set in the park of the same name by the river.

⊛ Festivals and events

Aranda de Duero *p294*

Sep Aranda's annual fiesta, in the 2nd week of Sep, is a cheerfully drunken affair.

Peñafiel p295

14-18 Aug The town's major fiesta is worth attending. There are *encierros*, where bulls run through the streets, followed by *capeas* in the plaza, which is basically bull-dodging, sometimes with the aim of slipping rings over the horns. The homeowners sell off balcony seats, but interestingly some families still have hereditary rights to these seats, even if the house isn't theirs.

✪ Transport

Calatañazor p292
Bus
There are 1-3 buses a day from **Soria** to Calatañazor (25 mins). Other **Linecar Valladolid**-bound buses can drop you off just below the village.

Berlanga de Duero p292
Bus
There is 1 bus daily from **Soria** to Berlanga from Mon-Fri (70 mins).

El Burgo de Osma p293
Bus
The bus station is on the main road; there are 4-6 services to **Soria** (1 hr) and 3 to **Aranda de Duero** (45 mins) and on to **Valladolid**.

Aranda de Duero p294
Bus
Aranda has good bus connections, being at the junction of major north–south and east–west routes. The bus and train stations are across the Duero from the old part of town.

About 4 buses a day go to **Madrid** (2 hrs, €12) and 6-7 to **Burgos** (1 hr 15 mins, €8). There are 6 a day to **Valladolid** (1 hr 15 mins), 3 to **El Burgo de Osma** (45 mins) and on to **Soria** (1 hr 30 mins) and **Zaragoza** (3 hrs 45 mins) and 2 to **Roa**.

Train
Trains go to **Madrid** (1 daily, 2-3 hrs), and **Burgos** (1 daily, 1 hr).

Peñafiel p295
Bus
There are 6 buses a day from Peñafiel to **Valladolid** (45 mins) and **Aranda de Duero** (30 mins), 3 of which continue to **El Burgo de Osma**, **Soria** and **Zaragoza**.

Valladolid

→ Colour map 4, A5. Phone code: 983. Population: 317,864. Altitude: 690 m.

Valladolid, the capital of the Castilla y León region, is not outstandingly beautiful but it is a pleasant, strollable city with a very significant history. It was the principal city of Spain for most of the early 16th century and its streets are redolent with the memories of important people who walked them and events that took place in them. These days it's still an important, slightly posh administrative centre, but a fairly relaxed and friendly one; perhaps it looks down the road to sprawling Madrid and breathes a small sigh of relief, as it was odds-on favourite to be named capital at one time. ►► *For listings, see pages 307-311.*

Ins and outs

Getting there Many visitors to Northern Spain arrive in Valladolid; there's a **Ryanair** connection to the city from London Stansted as well as Brussels Charleroi, Düsseldorf Weeze and Milan Bergamo. Valladolid is a major transport hub, only two hours from Madrid by road, and less by the new fast trains. As the capital of Castilla y León, it has excellent connections within that region, as well as with the rest of Northern Spain. The bus and train stations are close together, about a 10-minute walk south of the centre. They can be reached by local buses Nos 2 and 10 from Plaza de España, or No 19 from Plaza Zorilla. ►► *See Transport, page 311.*

Getting around Situated on the east bank of the Pisuerga, Valladolid's old centre is fairly compact. At the southern end of this part, the large park of Campo Grande is flanked by two long avenues, Paseo de Zorilla, the main artery of the new town, and the mostly pedestrianized Acera de Recoletos. Nearly everything of interest is within an easy walk of the Plaza Mayor.

Tourist information The new **tourist office** ⓘ *T983 219 310, www.asomateavalladolid. com, oficinadeturismodevalladolid@jcyl.es, mid-Sep to Jun Mon-Sat 0930-1400, 1600-1900, Sun 0930-1700, summer daily 0900-2000,* is in a big glass building by the park on Paseo de Campo Grande; you pass it if you are walking from the train station into town. It has all manner of information on the city and province. There's also a **tourist kiosk** ⓘ *Tue-Sun 1000-1400, 1700-2000,* on Plaza Fuente Dorada, and an information desk at the airport.

Background

A site of pre-Roman settlements, Valladolid's profile grew with the Reconquista; it was well placed on the frontline to become an important commercial centre, driven in part by the Castilian wool trade. Although Fernando and Isabel married here in 1469 – a secret ceremony that profoundly changed the course of world history – it was in the 16th century that Valladolid became pre-eminent among Spanish cities. With a population of nearly 40,000, it was a massive place in a hitherto fragmented land, and de-facto capital of Spain; while the court was constantly on the move, the bureaucracy was based here. It was, as it is now, a city of administrators and lawyers: "courtiers died here waiting for their cases to come up" (JH Elliott, *Imperial Spain*).

Valladolid played an important part in most significant Spanish historical events, and was home for periods to people as diverse as Columbus, Cervantes and the inquisitor Torquemada. It was a major centre of the Spanish Inquisition (see box, page 303); *autos de fe* and burnings were a regular sight in the plaza.

In the year 1550-1551, a significant and famous theological debate took place here between the liberal theologian Bartolomé de las Casas and the historian and philosopher Juan Ginés de Sepúlveda. The former was arguing for an end to indigenous slavery and forced conversions in Spain's American colonies, while the latter deemed the *indígenos* inferior, being incapable of reason and therefore without rights. Las Casas' view prevailed, effectively ending the doctrine of racial purity in the colonies. Las Casas was hardly an enlightened humanist, though; he suggested the labour problem be solved by enslaving Africans instead.

Felipe II was born in Valladolid, but surprisingly chose Madrid as his capital in 1561. The city lost importance after that, but had a brief reprise. A scheming adviser of Felipe III wanted to keep him away from the powerful influence of his grandmother, and persuaded him to move the capital northwards in 1601. The glory years were back, but only for five years, after which the court moved back to Madrid. Valladolid remained fairly prosperous until the collapse of the wool and grain markets, but enjoyed renewed wealth in the early part of the 20th century. The Falange held their first national meeting here in March 1934 and when war broke out Valladolid became an important and brutal Fascist stronghold; it is estimated that over 9000 Republican civilians were shot here behind the lines.

One of Spain's most important post Civil War writers, the late Miguel Delibes, was a *vallisoletano*. His work deeply reflects the Castilian landscape but is also often bitingly anti-Francoist; much of his journalistic life was spent battling the censors while working for the liberal *El Norte de Castilla*, the regional paper. *The Hedge* is perhaps his best-known translated work; a vicious satire on totalitarian Spain.

In 1558, two members of the aristocracy turned up in Valladolid in the royal litter: the king's cat and parrot, sent back to be cared for in the city by their loving owner Carlos V, who had just died at his monastery retreat of Yuste.

Sights

Valladolid's centrepiece is its large **Plaza Mayor**, attractively surrounded by the terracotta façades of buildings. It was here that *autos de fe* and burnings were conducted during the Inquisition's long tenure in the city. Most of Valladolid's buildings of interest are to the north and east of the plaza. The **cathedral**, topped by a statue of Christ standing tall above the city, seems a little crowded-in. The façade is baroque, the interior fairly bare and disappointing, although the **museum** ① *Tue-Fri 1000-1330, 1630-1900, Sat and Sun 1000-1400; €2.50*, is worthwhile, with some excellent carved tombs among the usual assorted saints and Virgins.

Behind the cathedral stands the Gothic **Iglesia de Santa María la Antigua**, slightly down-at-heel but sporting an attractive tower. Also nearby is the **Pasaje Gutiérrez**, a belle époque shopping arcade with some pleasingly extravagant decoration. The **university law faculty**, also next to the cathedral, is worth a look for its camp baroque façade guarded by strange monkey-like lions on columns. Across the road, it's faced by a friendly looking Cervantes. Another university building is the lovely **Colegio de Santa Cruz**, a block away, with an ornate Plateresque door; it boasts an attractive central patio with the names of honorary graduates painted on the walls.

North of the cathedral, along Calle Las Angustias, is an interesting collection of buildings. The **Palacio de los Pimentel** was the building that saw the birth, in 1527, of Felipe II, likely to have been a rather serious little boy. His statue faces the palace from across the square, which also holds the **Iglesia de San Pedro**, with a very tall and ornate Gothic façade; the level of intricacy in the stonework is stunning.

Torquemada and the Spanish Inquisition

"The hammer of heretics, the light of Spain, the saviour of his country." Sebastián de Olmedo.

Founded by Fernando and Isabel in 1478, the Spanish Inquisition was unusual in that it did not report directly to the Pope but followed a more nationalistic course. Born in 1420, Tomás de Torquemada entered a Dominican monastery in his youth and was appointed as Grand Inquisitor in 1483. He pursued his tasks with considerable energy, both reforming the administration of the Inquisition and giving it its uniquely Spanish direction. Under Torquemada there was a paranoid obsession that the conversions of Muslim and Jewish *conversos* had been insincere; this was to dominate the Inquisition's activities.

Given a remit to extract confessions under torture, the Inquisition was initially content to seize the estates of those Jewish *conversos* it considered to be insincere. This enabled it to quickly build up considerable resources. Later it employed the full range of punishments available including execution by public burning following a theatrical *auto de fe* or trial of faith. It is estimated that during Torquemada's direction there were around 2000 executions, the overwhelming majority of them of Jewish *conversos*.

He was instrumental in ensuring that the Jews were expelled completely from Spain in 1492. It is reputed that when he found Fernando in negotiations with Jewish leaders over a possible payment to the Crown in order to remain, he compared Fernando's actions with those of Judas. The Jews were duly expelled, with disastrous long-term results for the country.

Torquemada's pursuit of Jewish *conversos* was largely responsible for the development of the cult of *sangre limpia* or pure blood that was to continue to obsess Spain throughout the 16th century. Based on the idea that only those of pure Christian blood could participate fully in the state, it was to cost Spain the services of most of its intellectual class, debilitating its development for centuries.

Torquemada stepped down from his role in the Inquisition in 1497. After his directorship it began to diversify into other areas including the maintenance of doctrinal purity and a concern with private morality. It was to retain a formidable grip over Spanish life until its formal abolition at the beginning of the 19th century. Torquemada retired to a monastery where he kept a unicorn's horn close at hand as an antidote to any attempt at poisoning him. He died of natural causes in 1499.

Following the pedestrian street at the side of the San Pedro church, you'll soon come to an even more amazing façade. Looking like a psychedelic fantasy in stone, it's an outrageously imaginative piece of work. A pomegranate tree perhaps represents knowledge, while the hairy men represent nature and the value of hermitry. Like much sculpture from centuries ago, it's impossible to really unlock the meaning, but it's certainly a step away from the typical. It belongs to the **Colegio de San Gregorio**, a building commissioned by Fray Alonso de Burgos to house the college he founded, and also to house him after his demise. Now re-opened after a lengthy and beautifully-realized restoration, the building contains the **Museo San Gregorio** ① *Tue-Sat 1000-1400, 1600-1800 (2100 Apr-Sep), Sun 1000-1400, €3.* The collection is what was formerly known as the National Sculpture Museum. It's a fairly specialized ensemble, excellent in its field, which is basically Spanish religious sculpture from the 16th-18th centuries. Look out

Valladolid

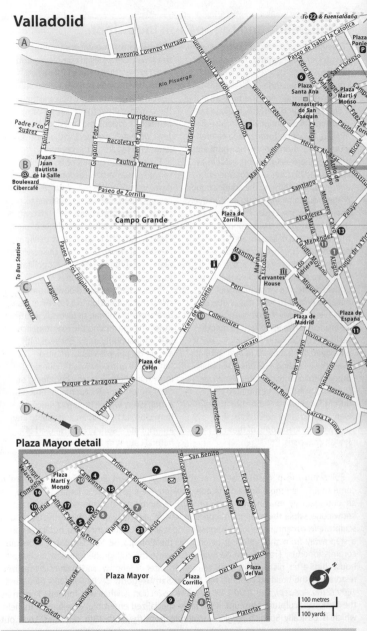

Río Pisuerga

A

To 22 & Fuensaldaña

Antonio Lorenzo Hurtado

Paseo de Isabel la Católica

Plaza Ponie

Pedro Niño Velasco

San Lorenzo

D'Angel

Plaza Marti y Monso

Veinte de Febrero

6 Plaza Santa Ana

Monasterio de San Joaquín

Fdez de Torre

Pasión

Ricote

Curtidores

Doctrinos

P

Padre F'co Suárez

Espíritu Santo

Recoletas

Gregorio Fdez

Juan Mambrilla

San Ildefonso

Héroes Alcázar

María de Molina

Zúñiga

Atrio de Santiago

Constitu

B

Plaza S Juan Bautista de la Salle

@ Boulevard Cibercafé

Paulina Harriet

Paseo de Zorrilla

Santiago

Santa María

Montero Calvo

Alcalleres

Menéndez

Palayo

13

Campo Grande

Plaza de Zorrilla

Claudio Moyano

11

Duque de la Vix

3

Mantilla

Marina Escobar

Cervantes House

Ldo. Vidriera

V. Miguel Iscar

Rastro

Santiago

To Bus Station

Paseo de los Filipinos

i

Peru

La Galera

Plaza de Madrid

Plaza de España

Aragón

C

Navarra

Acera de Recoletos

10

Colmenares

Plaza de Colón

Gamazo

Divina Pastora

Dos de Mayo

Panaderos

Vega

11

Duque de Zaragoza

Estación del Norte

Bailén

Muro

General Ruiz

Hostieros

D

1

Independencia

2

García Le smes

3

Plaza Mayor detail

D'Angel Velasco

Comedias

19

Plaza Marti y Monso

20

Cañuelos

4

15

Primo de Rivera

Rinconada Cebadería

San Benito

7

Fco Zarandona

Sandoval

14

10

Caridad

Calixto F-dez de la Torre

17

5

12

Correos

6

Peso

7

Jesús

M

Pasión

2

Ricote

Santiago

Viana

23

21

Manzana

S Fco

Del Val

Zapico

P

Plaza Mayor

Plaza Corrillo

Alarcón

Plaza del Val

3

12

Alcaz Toledo

9

Especería

8

Platerías

N

100 metres

100 yards

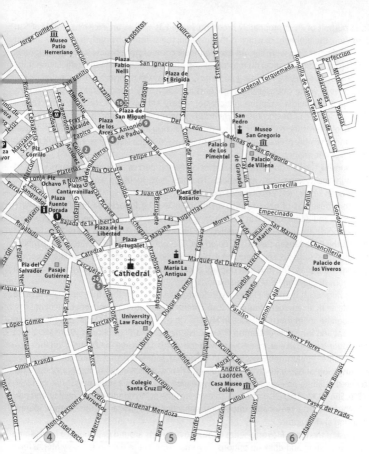

Sleeping

Amadeus **1** *C3*
El Nogal **2** *B4*
Hostal del Val **3** *detail*
Hostal Los Arces **4** *B5*
Hostal Paris **8** *detail*
Hostal Zamora **5** *C4*
Hostería La Cueva **6** *detail*
Imperial **7** *detail*
Meliá Recoletos **10** *C2*
Mozart **11** *C3*
Olid Meliá **9** *B5*
Roma **12** *detail*

Eating

Bar La Sepia **21** *detail*
Café España **1** *B4*
Degustación de Café
  Mantería **11** *C3*
El Castillo **13** *C3*
El Colmao de San
  Andrés **8** *D4*
El Figón de Recoletos **3** *C2*
Jero **7** *detail*
La Balconada **15** *detail*
La Criolla **5** *detail*
La Parrilla de San Lorenzo **6** *A3*
La Tasquita II **10** *detail*
Lion d'Or **9** *detail*
Los Zagales **2** *detail*
Méson La Sorbona **22** *A3*
Mil Vinos **14** *detail*

Otras Luces **23** *detail*
Santi I **12** *detail*
Taberna del Herrero **17** *detail*
Vinotinto **4** *detail*

Bars & clubs

Be-Bop **19** *detail*
El Soportal **16** *A5*
La Comedia **20** *detail*
La Española Cuando Besa **24** *C4*

for a portrait of an appropriately brooding Juana I as well as an excellent *retablo* of San Jerónimo, the highlight of which is the tiny lion; the painter obviously had only a limited notion of what they were like. An excellent collection of polychrome wooden sculptures by Alonso Berruguete show his mastery at depicting real emotion in that difficult medium, while a curious Zurbarán painting, *La Santa Faz*, displays that superb artist's passion for the subtleties of white cloth. Further highlights include a very creepy *Death* by Gil de Ronza, a range of Mannerist sculpture in alabaster, a gory *Martyrdom of St Bartholomew*, and a Rubens painting of *Democritus and Heraclitus*, who resembles a retired fairground boxer. A couple of interesting curios are an ensemble depicting all the events of a bullfight, and an amazing assembly of Neapolitan dolls, forming a 620-piece Nativity scene. There's a good system of information sheets in English.

Opposite, the Palacio de Villena (admission free) is part of the same museum and used for high-quality temporary exhibitions. The plan is to focus on aspects of Spanish art, bringing in key works from overseas galleries.

Other buildings of note in this part of town are the **Palacio de los Viveros**, where Fernando and Isabel married in 1469, having only set eyes on each other four days before. It now holds an archive and the university library, and isn't hugely interesting. Beyond here is the **Casa Museo Colón** ⓘ *C Colón s/n, Tue-Sun 1000-1400, 1700-2030, €2*, a replica of Columbus' son's house, where the explorer is said to have died, far from the sea and a discontented man. The museum displays a lot of pre-Hispanic American material as well as various displays on his seafaring exploits.

Moving south from the Plaza Mayor down Calle Santiago the street ends at **Plaza de Zorrilla**, with an energetic fountain. José Zorrilla was a 19th-century poet born in the city, although he spent much of his life in Mexico. On the other side of the plaza stretches the pleasant and busy park of **Campo Grande**. Numerous pro-Republican civilians were shot here during the Civil War, many dying with the words 'Long live the Republic' on their lips.

Cervantes spent three years living in Valladolid, some days of it at his Majesty's leisure on suspicion of being involved in a murder. What was probably his house, a pretty vine-covered building on Calle Miguel Iscar, is nearby; it contains a **museum** ⓘ *Tue-Sat 0930-1500, Sun 1000-1500, €3*, part of which recreates the living conditions of the day, and part of which holds a reasonably interesting collection of 19th- and 20th-century Spanish painting and sculpture.

West of the **Plaza Mayor**, a series of attractive streets around Calle Correos holds some excellent eating and drinking options. Beyond, towards the river, is the ugly **Monasterio de San Joaquín** ⓘ *Plaza Santa Ana 4, Mon-Fri 1000-1330, 1700-1900 (2000 summer), Sat 1000-1430, free*, fronted by a strangely hag-like Virgin. In the monastery museum is a collection of religious art, of which the highlight is three Goyas in the church itself.

Finally (though there are several other museums in town that we haven't space to list here) the **Museo Patio Herreriano** ⓘ *C Jorge Guillén 6; T983 362 908, www.museopatio herreriano.org, Tue-Fri 1100-2000, Sat 1000-2000, Sun 1000-1500, €3 (€1 on Wed)*, is a contemporary art museum built around a huge Renaissance patio that is elegant but rather cold and formal. The permanent collection is housed in various galleries possessed of little levity; there are some good works here (sculptures by the beachcombing Angel Ferrant and the Basque Jorge Oteiza stand out), but the worth of a visit depends largely upon the temporary exhibitions, which are frequently excellent. There are also regular concerts and other cultural events.

Near here, an artificial beach allows summer sunbathing on the banks of the Pisuerga; a small compensation for Valladolid's deep inland location.

For Sleeping and Eating price codes and other relevant information, see Essentials pages 31-39.

⊙ Sleeping

Valladolid *p301, map p304*
Valladolid is full of accommodation; the tourist office can provide a complete listing.
L Meliá Recoletos, Acera de Recoletos 13, T983 216 200, www.solmelia.com. With a peaceful location on the park between the station and the centre, very close to the tourist office, this great modern hotel is just about the city's best. Rooms are large and light, with excellent bathrooms and facilities; the hotel's staff are well informed and most helpful. Cheaper prices available via the website.
A Hotel Amadeus, C Montero Calvo 16-18, T983 219 444, www.hotelamadeus.net. A modern hotel on a central pedestrian street, smartly catering mostly for business travellers. This is good news, because they offer smart weekend rates if you book ahead. The rooms have all the facilities, including cable TV and internet point. The beds are large and comfortable. Parking available.
A Hotel Imperial, C Peso 4, T983 330 300, www.himperial.com. Located in a 16th-century *palacio* in the heart of the old town, this has considerable old-Spain charm. The bedrooms are very attractive, the furnishings plush and there's a beautiful if formal bar/lounge with a pianist. It's also right by the tapas zone.
A Hotel Mozart, C Menéndez Pelayo 4, T983 297 777, www.hotelmozart.net. The sister hotel to the **Amadeus** is set in a noble 19th-century mansion and has a classy feel. The rooms are large and light with windows looking out over the pedestrian streets below. The hotel has its own garage, plenty of charm, and excellent weekend and summer rates (**D**).
B Olid Meliá, Plaza San Miguel 10, T983 357 200, www.solmelia.com. This well-located

hotel is one of the city's most luxurious even if the decor is hardly cutting edge these days. It could do with a refit, but the rooms are spacious and light, and neither they nor the bathrooms lack comfort. You pay a little extra for a superior room or one with a balcony. The hotel has gym and parking facilities; there are occasional enticing discounts advertised via the website.
C Hostal París, C Especería 2, T983 370 625, www.hostalparis.com. Bang in the heart of town, this appealing *hostal* is really a hotel in disguise and offers neat-as-a-new-pin rooms that are compact but comfortable and, despite the busy street, pretty quiet. Bathrooms are similarly good, and the staff helpful. Free Wi-Fi. Location great. Recommended.
C Hotel El Nogal, C Conde Ansúrez 10, T983 340 333, www.hotelelnogal.com. An intimate modern hotel near the old market. It's a friendly choice and well located. The rooms are a touch cramped but have a/c and otherwise comfortable and light.
D Hotel Roma, C Héroes del Alcázar de Toledo 8, T983 354 666, www.hotelromavalladolid.com. Slightly old fashioned rooms but a helpful attitude and parking make this a good option if location is important to you. It's set in the main shopping zone just a few paces from the picturesque Plaza Mayor.
E Hostal del Val, Plaza del Val 6, T983 375 752. A sound budget option, this *hostal* is very close to the heart of town. The rooms are good for the price; some are equipped with their own bathroom.
E Hostal Zamora, C Arribas 14, T983 303 052. Right by the cathedral, this place has colourful little rooms with bathroom and TV; there are some cheaper ones with shared facilities (**F**). They're all heated, and it's pretty good value.
E Hostería La Cueva, C Correos 4, T983 330 072, daniel25sanchez@hotmail.com. This *pensión* has small, attractive rooms above a restaurant on Valladolid's nicest little street.

The better ones have compact en suite bathrooms, but there are rooms with just a washbasin available too (**F**).

F Hostal Los Arces, C San Antonio de Padua 2, T983 353 853. This is a fine budget choice, with large (if somewhat noisy) rooms, comfortable beds and a decent atmosphere. Shared bathrooms are good; rooms with en suites available.

❶ Eating

Valladolid *p301, map p304*
Valladolid is a gourmet's paradise. The zone of restaurants and tapas bars is in the small streets just west of the Plaza Mayor. Most of the options below function as both; the quality throughout this area is laudably high, with elaborate tapas creations accompanied by excellent local Rueda and Ribera wines the norm.

ŦŦŦ El Figón de Recoletos, Av Recoletos 5. This sleek traditional *asador* is confident in what it does best. While there are always daily specials, there are only 4 main dishes on the menu; the quarter roast lamb is enough for 2; the grilled kidneys are unspeakably delicious if innards are your thing. Reserve ahead if you want suckling pig; reserve somewhere else if you're vegetarian.

ŦŦŦ Los Zagales, C Pasión 13, T983 380 892, www.loszagales.com. Hanging hams by the dozen adorn this atmospheric and well-frequented spot just off the Plaza Mayor. Popular as an after-work tapas option, it's also a restaurant, whose classy and delicious fare includes pricey but quality meat, and a range of gourmet salads.

ŦŦ Jero, C Correos 11, T983 353 508. One of the most enjoyable of the bars in this tapas district, this upbeat spot specializes in *pinchos* of the most elaborate kind, taste combinations from some fantasy land. Each has about 10 different ingredients, with quails' eggs just the start: They even have elaborate dessert platters when you're done and a *comedor* for proper sit-down meals. Recommended.

ŦŦ La Criolla, C Calixto Fernández de la Torre 2, T983 373 822, www.restaurantelacriolla.es. A likeable and attractive restaurant, full of intimate nooks and adorned with quotes from *vallisoletano* writers. The fare is based around simple traditional dishes, which have been given an attractive modern boost. There's a terrace in summer and a good tapas bar, which always has an intriguing daily special; you can also order an *espejo* – a mixed tapa selection. Quality food ranges from fish to game to roast meat, all with engaging presentation.

ŦŦ La Parrilla de San Lorenzo, C Pedro Niño 1, T983 335 088. www.hotel-convento.com. Closed Jul. A romantic meaty restaurant with various atmospheric vaulted chambers in the depths of a convent building. The menu's like a medieval parchment and illustrates various traditional Castilian dishes like roast lamb, as well as fish dishes like monkfish tail, or cod salad served in a caramel basket with sweet fruity sauce. Prices are fair.

ŦŦ Mesón La Sorbona, Paraje El Barrero, Fuensaldaña, T983 583 077. Just north of the city, the village of Fuensaldaña is in the rosé wine district of Cigales. It's got a barrio of atmospheric traditional bodegas on the edge of town, many of which have been converted into restaurants, a popular lunch or dinner escape. This is about the best of them; jugs of local wine, simple salads, tortilla and good grilled meats are the way to go.

ŦŦ Mil Vinos, Plaza Martí y Monsó s/n, T983 344 336. Looking like a TV studio with its designer furniture and floor-to-ceiling trendy glass, this bar claims to offer 1000 wines (it falls short), many of which are available by the glass. There's excellent service, with staff more than happy to recommend a wine. It's also a restaurant, with a short but decent menu of grilled meat and fish as well as plenty of cheeses. The wines can also be bought at market prices. Free Wi-Fi.

ŦŦ Otras Luces, Plaza Mayor 22, T983 380 705. Offering a spacious terrace on the

Plaza Mayor, this place tries to do a bit of everything, and makes a pleasurable choice for breakfast coffee, an evening drink, or good-value set lunch. The sizeable menu is divided by points of the compass – the north (Galician, Cantabrian, and Castilian dishes) is more reliable than the hit-and-miss Moroccan and East Asian offerings. Best are the organically minded burgers and salads. Service could improve.

Santi I, C Correos 1, T983 339 355. Superbly situated in the courtyard of a historic inn, named **El Caballo de Troya** after its large painting of the same name, although the Trojan horse looks surprisingly sprightly. The restaurant serves good-quality Castilian fare; there's also a *taberna*, which is an atmospheric place for a drink; it serves tapas and *raciones*, but you're better off eating in the restaurant.

Vinotinto, C Campanas 4, T983 342 291. This high-ceilinged bar is lined with shelves of wine bottles, but the real focus is the open *parrilla*, where delicious cuts of meat, including tasty little lamb tapas skewers, sizzle over the coals. There's a *comedor* downstairs to eat, but it's more fun to eat at the wooden tables in the bar where it's all happening. There's another bar, **Vinotinto Joven**, more *pincho*-focused, opposite. Recommended.

Bar La Sepia, C Jesús 1, T983 330 769. This Valladolid classic, decorated in wood and brick, is down a side street just off the Plaza Mayor. You can smell the enticing aromas from a block away and when you sample the taste and texture of the *sepia* (cuttlefish) – it comes grilled with a garlic sauce – you'll understand why they're always busy.

El Colmao de San Andrés, Detrás de San Andrés 3, T691 111 476. This striking ensemble of eclectic furniture and objets d'art feels more like an antique dealer's or second-hand shop than a bar. A loyal local crowd keep things buzzing every night, sipping wine and munching snacks of smoked cod or salmon on toast. It's one of the city's most characterful spots. It's off Calle Mantería behind the San Andrés church.

La Balconada, C Correos 3, T983 342 114. This small mezzanine restaurant is brightly coloured and very reasonably priced. The brief menu includes *tablas* to share with friends, a good house salad enlivened by warm prawns, or a tender *solomillo* steak which is great value.

La Tasquita, C Caridad 2, T647 629 279. The main reason to come to this *cervecería*, apart from its cheerful bar staff, is for excellent *pinchos*, with winning combinations atop slices of toast. Ranging from roast beef to prawns, or octopus with paprika, they're all delicious and it's seriously difficult to not stay to try another.

Taberna del Herrero, C Calixto Fernández de la Torre 4, T983 342 310. This deservedly popular place sets out its stall to provide wholesome and traditional Castilian fare at popular prices. It succeeds superbly. *Raciones* of such delicious staples as *croquetas*, *lacón*, or a variety of stews are ridiculously cheap and filling (most plates €4-6, and a *menú del día* for €12.50). On Thu, a hearty *cocido* stew will beat the winter chills. Eat at blocky wooden tables or the solid bar. Deservedly popular.

Cafés

Café España, Plaza Fuente Dorada 8, T983 371 764, www.cafeconciertos.com. A traditional central café decorated with black and white photos. They have regular live music ranging from flamenco to jazz; check their website for upcoming performances.

Degustación de Café Mantería, C Mantería 1, T983 210 763. A most likeable café just off the Plaza de España, this narrow spot has an inclusive buzz and debatable art on the walls. The boss works his socks off, making strong, punchy coffees, and elaborately preparing little rolls with ham, olive oil, and tomato.

El Castillo, C Montero Calvo 1, T983 308 841. This is an old-fashioned spot with a row of outdoor tables on a pedestrian street. It's the place to come for hot chocolate and *churros* (fried doughsticks) – a very traditional morning or late afternoon treat.

Lion d'Or, Plaza Mayor 4, T983 342 057.
Open from 0900 until very late. A lovely
old café in the main square, complete with
fireman's poles and gilt-framed mirrors.
It's very popular in the early evenings with
people of a certain age, who have no doubt
been coming here every afternoon for
several decades; you can see why.

🍷 Bars and clubs

Valladolid *p301, map p304*
There are various zones of bars in Valladolid;
some around Plaza Martí y Monso, known as
La Coca, some smartish ones around Plaza
San Miguel, more bohemian wine bars and
nightspots around the cathedral, and a riot
of student nightlife around C Paraíso by the
university. Several *discobares* are on and
around C Padre Francisco Suárez, between
Paseo Zorilla and the river.
Be-Bop, Plaza Martí y Monsó 1. Sleek and
stylish, this upmarket jazz bar and café is a
favourite of romancing executives, perhaps
because it's so dark that when you enter
all you can see are the backlit spirit bottles
behind the bar.
El Soportal, Plaza San Miguel s/n, T983
371 940. A modern, dark and moody café/
bar with a horseshoe bar and plenty of
seats. There's hospitable service and a busy,
smart crowd at weekends, when it opens
very late.
La Comedia, Plaza Martí y Monso 4, T983 340
804. This is a reliable choice; a good lively bar
with outdoor seating when weather permits.
It fills with a fairly smart pre- and post-dinner
crowd – there's even a cigar menu – and is
lively and buzzy. There's no draught beer, but
several good wines and tasty mixed drinks.
Open until fairly late and decorated with past
stars of the silver screen.
La Española Cuando Besa, C Arribas s/n,
T983 398 379. Offbeat spot by the cathedral
that feels like you're inside the trunk of a
tree. 3 narrow levels and an upbeat, 'anyone-
welcome' atmosphere.

🎭 Entertainment

Valladolid *p301, map p304*
Cines Casablanca, C Leopoldo Cano 8, T983
374 068. An arthouse cinema that often shows
films with subtitles rather than dubbing.
Cines Roxy, C Mario de Molina 6, T983 351
672. A small but handy art deco cinema.
Teatro Calderón, C Las Angustias s/n, T983
426 444, www.tcalderon.com.The city's main
theatre, with mainstream drama and dance
in a beautifully ornate interior. Seats in the
gods can go for as little as €10, but there's
not a lot of leg room.

🎉 Festivals and events

Valladolid *p301, map p304*
Mar/Apr Semana Santa (Easter week) is
fairly serious; hooded brotherhoods parade
floats through the streets to the mournful
wailing of cornets and tubas.
Early Sep Feast of the **Virgen de San
Lorenzo**, the streets fill with stalls selling
wine and tapas, there are bullfights,
concerts and more.

🛍 Shopping

Valladolid *p301, map p304*
Valladolid's main shopping area is the
pedestrian zone between Plaza Mayor and
Plaza Zorilla, particularly along C Santiago.
Oletum, C de Teresa Gil 12, T983 213 560.
A wide range of books with a good English-
language section.

🎯 Activities and tours

Valladolid *p301, map p304*
Football Real Valladolid is the city's
football team. Their stadium, **Estadio José
Zorilla**, Av Mundial 82 s/n, T983 360 342,
www.realvalladolid.es, is to the west of town.

Valladolid *p301, map p304*
Air
Valladolid's airport (VLL), T983 415 500, is 12 km northwest of town. Linecar buses run between the bus station and the airport to connect with flights (20 mins, €3). ALSA (www.alsa.es) buses running between Valladolid and León will stop here if you have pre-booked the ticket. A taxi from Valladolid to the airport costs €20.

As well as Ryanair flights to **London** Stansted, **Milan** Orio al Serio, and **Brussels** Charleroi, there are international connections to **Paris** and **Lisbon**, as well as domestic ones to **Barcelona** and **Málaga**.

Bus
Intercity buses go from Valladolid to nearly every major city in Spain. These services include: **Madrid** hourly (2¼ hrs, €14), **León** 8-9 daily (2 hrs, €10), **Barcelona** 2 daily (10½ hrs, €45-49), **Segovia** 7-12 daily (1 hr 50 mins), **Zamora** 7-10 daily, **Palencia** hourly, **Bilbao** 3 daily (4 hrs, €20), **Santander** 2 daily (4 hrs, €13) and **Zaragoza** (5 hrs) via **Soria** (2¾ hrs) 2 daily.

Other destinations include **Aranda** (5 daily), **Roa** (2 daily), **Medina del Campo** (8 daily), **Rueda** (7 daily), **Medina de**
Rioseco hourly (30 mins), **Simancas** half-hourly and **Tordesillas** hourly.

Car hire
There are a few car hire agencies at Valladolid airport; AVIS, T983 415 530, www.avis.com; Europcar, T983 560 091, www.europcar.com; Hertz, T983 415 546, www.hertz.com.

Taxi
T983 207 755.

Train
Services run to **Madrid** 12-15 daily (slow trains 2½ hrs, €16.50, fast trains 1 hr, €35) via **Medina del Campo** very regularly, to **Palencia** more than hourly (35 mins, from €4.30), and less frequently to most mainline destinations.

● **Directory**

Valladolid *p301, map p304*
Internet Boulevard Cibercafé, Paseo de Zorilla 46, has several coin-op terminals in a stuffy café, €2.50 per hr. **Medical services** Hospital Universitario, T983 420 000, emergency T112. **Police** T092 in an emergency. **Post office** The main post office is on Plaza de la Rinconada near the Plaza Mayor.

West of Valladolid

Wandering the arid plains and dusty towns of western Castilla these days, it seems difficult to believe that this was once a region of great prestige and power. In the 15th and 16th centuries, towns like Tordesillas and Toro were major players in political and religious life, while Medina del Campo was a huge city for the time and one of Europe's principal trading towns, a sort of Wall Street of the meseta. Times have changed, and these places are backwaters, but poke about their streets with a rudimentary idea of Spanish history and you'll find them surprisingly rewarding. The excellent dry wines of Rueda or the hearty reds of Toro will banish any remaining dust from the journey across the scorched plains. ▶▶ *For listings, see pages 316-317.*

Tordesillas and around → *For listings, see pages 316-317. Colour map 4, B5.*

Heading west from Valladolid, after 8 km you come to **Simancas**, a pleasant medieval town whose spectacular castle was set up as an archive for royal documents by Carlos V and Felipe II. A couple of rooms in it are devoted to temporary exhibitions, but that's as much of the interior as you'll see unless you want to consult the archive, which you can do Monday-Friday 0815-1430 on presentation of a passport.

Beyond Simancas on the N620 you reach the town of **Tordesillas**, a place with an interesting history which boasts an imposing *mudéjar* monastery, and the attractive, arcaded 17th-century Plaza Mayor that would look even better if it were pedestrianized.

In 1494 Tordesillas was the location for the signing of a famous treaty between Spain and Portugal, two major maritime powers at the time. The treaty itself was signed in a building that now holds the **tourist office** ⓘ *Tue-Sat 1000-1330, 1600-1830 (1700-1930 summer), Sun 1000-1400*, and the Museo del Tratado, which displays relevant original and facsimile documents, most interestingly the maps showing the proposed division and how knowledge increased over time.

Background

The area around Valladolid was the centre of much of Spain's political activity in the 15th and 16th centuries, and Tordesillas was an important power. Columbus had just got back from the Americas, and there were colonial issues to be sorted out. The 1494 treaty between Spain and Portugal was basically designed to leave Africa for Portugal and the Americas for Spain, but the canny Portuguese suspected or knew of the location of the tip of what is now Brazil, so they pushed the mid-ocean dividing line far enough over to give them a foothold in South America. It had to be re-evaluated within a lifetime, but the idea of two countries meeting to divide the world gives some idea of their control over the Atlantic at the time.

Not too long afterwards, Tordesillas gained an unwilling resident in Juana La Loca (see box, page 314) who was imprisoned here, along with her daughter and the embalmed corpse of her husband. She remained an icon of Castilian sovereignty, and it was due to her presence that Tordesillas became the centre of the *comunero* revolt against the reign of her foreign son Carlos in the early 16th century. The town was viewed with suspicion thereafter and quickly became the backwater that it remains today.

Real Monasterio de Santa Clara

ⓘ *Access to convent by guided tour only; some English-speaking guides at weekends. Oct-Mar Tue-Sat 1000-1330, 1600-1745, Sun 1030-1330, 1530-1730; Apr-Sep Tue-Sat 1000-1330, 1600-1830,*

Sun 1030-1330, 1530-1730; €3.60 (free Wed to EU citizens); Arab baths Tue, Thu-Sat 1000-1200, 1600-1700 (Oct-Mar 1600-1615), Sun 1030-1200, 1530-1600; €2.25, combined ticket €4.60.

The Real Monasterio de Santa Clara, where Juana la Loca was incarcerated, is an excellent construction, built in *mudéjar* style, still home to a community of Clarist nuns. It was originally built as a palace by Alfonso XI, and he installed his mistress Doña Leonor here. After the king died of plague, Leonor was murdered on the orders of Pedro (the Cruel), the new king. Following the deaths of Pedro's longtime mistress as well as his son, he ordered his illegitimate daughter to convert the palace into a convent in their memory. The *mudéjar* aspects are the most impressive: a chapel with superb stucco work and attractive scalloped arches, and especially the small patio, an absolute gem with horseshoe and scalloped multifoil arches. Another chapel, the **Capilla Dorada**, also has a fine *mudéjar* interior. The cloister is neoclassical in appearance. The high chapel has a very elegant panelled *mudéjar* ceiling. Some fine alabaster tombs in late Gothic style can be seen in the Saldaña chapel, built by the state treasurer of John II and holding his remains, his wife's, and possibly Beatriz of Portugal, Pedro's daughter.

Urueña → *Colour map 4, A4.*

North of Tordesillas, some 4 km from the N-VI motorway, Urueña is a small gem of a town. The fantastic walls that surround the village are the main attraction; their jagged teeth and narrow gateways dominate the plains around; on a clear day you can see kilometres from the sentries' walkway along the top. Urueña has been designated as a 'book town', and several bookshops and an exhibition on the history of the book can be found in its narrow streets; regular book launches, workshops, and writing and calligraphy courses are held here. About 1 km below the town is the lovely Romanesque **Iglesia de Nuestra Señora de la Anunciada**, unusually built in the Catalan style. The distinguishing feature 'Lombard arches', a feature that resembles fingers, traced around the apses. Arrange a visit (€1) with the **tourist office** ① *town hall, Plaza Mayor 1, T983 717 445, turismouruena@wanadoo.es.*

Some 9 km south of here, the rustic sleepy village of **San Cebrián de Mazote** ① *May-Oct Fri 1700-1930, Sat-Sun 1100-1400, 1700-1930*, is named for its fine Mozarabic church. It's well worth a look; call the keyholder if it's shut (T629 000 215).

Rueda → *Colour map 4, B5.*

Between Tordesillas and Medina del Campo, the straggling town of Rueda is of little interest except for its white wine production. Rueda whites are consistently among Spain's best, and are mostly made from the Verdejo grape, a local variety (not to be confused with Verdelho) which produces wines with a distinctive lemony aroma and crisp finish. Several bodegas in the area can be visited, but the white wine process is not nearly as interesting as that of reds, so you're better off picking up a few bottles at the cellar door, and saving your visiting time for the Ribera del Duero east of Valladolid, or for Toro. One of the best wines here is made by **Marqués de Riscal**, located by the motorway just north of the town. About eight buses a day running between Medina and Valladolid stop here.

Medina del Campo → *For listings, see pages 316-317. Colour map 4, B5.*

In the early 16th century, Medina del Campo, 25 km south of Tordesillas, was one of the biggest cities in Spain, and its massive trade fairs drew merchants from around Europe in droves. Today, there are few remnants of Medina's past glories. The vast plaza is one of them, and there are some beautiful *palacios* around, but the modern town is ramshackle

Juana la Loca

There are few more tragic figures in the turbulent history of Spain than Queen Juana, who has gone down in history with the unfortunate but accurate name of 'the Mad'. The daughter of the Catholic monarchs Fernando and Isabel, she was sent off in style from Laredo in a fleet of 120 ships bound for Flanders and marriage to Felipe, heir to the throne. Felipe was known as *El Hermoso* (Philip the Fair) and poor Juana made the unthinkable mistake of falling in love with her arranged husband. He didn't feel the same way, making it clear he intended to spend his time with mistresses. This sent Juana into fits of *amorous delirium* and hunger strikes; Felipe complained that she refused to leave him alone.

When she was 27, her mother Isabel died and Juana inherited the throne of Castilla. Her husband died shortly after their arrival in Spain, and this pushed the queen over the edge. She took possession of the corpse and had it embalmed, refusing to let it be buried or approached by women. She roamed the countryside for years with Felipe, whom she occasionally put on a throne. Deemed unfit to rule, she was finally persuaded to enter a mansion in Tordesillas, where she was locked up, her husband with her. Her daughter Catalina was another unfortunate companion – Juana refused to let her be taken from her, and when she was rescued, her mother went on a hunger strike to ensure her return. The wretched Juana lived in rags for 47 years in Tordesillas; she had occasional lucid moments and was a constant focus for those dissatisfied with the new 'foreign' monarchy of the Habsburgs. Many historians (largely Protestant) have implied that her incarceration was a conspiracy, but there can be little doubt that she was mentally unfit to rule the nation. In 1555 she finally passed away at the age of 76. She is buried in Granada alongside the husband that she loved not wisely but too well.

and poor. The **tourist office** ① *T983 811 357, www.turismomedina.net, Tue-Sat 1000-1400, 1630-1900, Sun 1100-1400,* is on the square by the large church.

Background

Medina was originally an important centre for the export of wool, but diversified to become, for a while, the pre-eminent commercial city of Spain. Queen Isabel often ran Castilla from here, and she actually died in a house overlooking the square. In the *comunero* uprising of 1520 to 1521, Medina was burned to the ground by attacking royalist forces. The town's fairs recovered, but as financial activity began to surround the court once it was settled in Madrid, Medina lost influence. The commerce was greatly harmed by the royal bankruptcies of the late 16th century, and Medina drifted into obscurity.

Sights

One of the nicest of the many palaces is the Renaissance **Palacio de los Dueñas** ① *Mon-Fri 0900-1445; closed for part of Jul-Aug,* with a beautiful patio and staircase adorned with the heads of the monarchs of Castilla.

On the square, another palace, the **Palacio Real** ① *Mon-Sat 1000-1330, 1600-1900 (1700-2000 summer), Sun 1100-1400, €2,* is where Queen Isabel left this life in 1504. There's a recreation of her room and an interpretative display on the period.

The **Castillo de la Mota** ① *Mon-Sat 1000-1400, 1545-1800 (1900 summer), Sun 1000-1430, €4,* is an impressive *mudéjar* castle across the river from town. The keep has been recently renovated and opened for guided visits. Tours also run of the whole complex, though there's not a great deal to see except the magnificent walls.

The **Museo de las Ferias** ① *C San Martín 26, T983 837 527, www.museoferias.net, Tue-Sat 1000-1330, 1600-1900, Sun 1100-1400, €2*, is situated in an old church and has an interesting look at the commerce of the great trade fairs and how they influenced the art and politics of the period; there's a large collection of related documents and art.

Toro → *For listings, see pages 316-317. Colour map 4, B4.*

Toro sits high above the River Duero between Valladolid and Zamora, from either of which it can easily be visited on a day trip, if you don't fancy spending the night. Its name means 'bull', but its emblem is a stone pig dating from Celtiberian times, which sits at the eastern entrance to the city. The city was repopulated during the Reconquista and changed hands a couple of times. A significant battle occurred near here in 1476 between the Catholic Monarchs and Portuguese forces supporting the claim of Isabel's rival, Juana (not the mad one), to the throne of Castilla. The heavy defeat suffered by Alfonso V, the king of Portugal, was a boost to the joint monarchs, and he gave up interfering three years later. The prolific playwright Lope de Vega also made Toro famous by naming one of his plays, *Las Almenas de Toro*, after its battlements. These days Toro is more famous for wine: it produces reds with a worldwide reputation. The **tourist office** ① *Plaza Mayor 6, T980 694 747, turismo@toro ayto.es, Tue-Sat 1000-1400, 1600-1900 (2000 summer), Sun 1000-1400*, is on the main square.

Sights
There are several churches in town with *mudéjar* and Romanesque elements, but the highlight is the **Colegiata** ① *Mar-Sep Tue-Sun 1030-1400, 1730-1930, Oct-Feb Tue-Sun 1000-1400, 1630-1830, €1 for cloister and sacristy*, near the Plaza Mayor. The interior is graced by a high dome with alabaster windows and a baroque organ, but the real highlight is the Portada de la Majestad, a 13th-century carved doorway decorated with superbly preserved (and well-restored) painted figures in early Gothic style; the character expressed through such apparently simple paintwork is remarkable. In the sacristy is a celebrated painting, *La Virgen de la Mosca* (the Virgin of the Fly); the insect is settled on her skirt.

Overlooking the river is the **Alcázar**, a fort dating from the 12th century built on a Moorish fortification. Juana, pretender to Isabel's Castilian crown, resisted here for a while; she must have enjoyed the views, which stretch for miles across the *meseta*.

Wineries
Most wineries are happy to show visitors around, but all need to be phoned beforehand. In terms of wine quality, one of the best is **Bodegas Fariña** ① *Camino del Palo, T980 577 673, www.bodegasfarina.com*, who market their wine as Colegiata and Gran Colegiata. **Covitoro** ① *Ctra Tordesillas, T980 690 347, www.covitoro.com*, the local wine cooperative, also produce some good bottles, with *Gran Cermeño* a well-priced, oak-aged red. These are a short walk along the main road east of town. Characteristic of the new wine techniques being applied in Toro, **Viña Bajoz** ① *T980 698 023, www.vinabajoz.com*, 6 km east of Toro on the main road in Morales de Toro, is a great cooperative that produces some excellent Tempranillo reds, and even some fruity Malvasia whites. There's a wine shop here with many available for tasting, as well as some other local gourmet food items. There are plenty of other wineries within easy reach of Toro; the tourist office will supply a list. Toro wines received DO (*denominación de origen*) status in 1987.

For Sleeping and Eating price codes and other relevant information, see Essentials pages 31-39.

⊜ **Sleeping**

Tordesillas *p312*

AL Parador de Tordesillas, Ctra Salamanca 5, T983 770 051, www.parador.es. Not the most characterful, but still a good option. It is located outside the town in a mansion surrounded by pine trees. The rooms are attractive, and there's a swimming pool.
E Hostal San Antolín, C San Antolín 8, T983 796 771, www.hostalsanantolin.com. A good choice, just down from the Plaza Mayor. Rooms are excellent value for this price, and it's very professionally run. The restaurant is also one of Tordesillas' best.
F Pensión Galván, Ctra Madrid–Coruña Km 182, T983 797 600. One of the closer budget options to the interesting bits of town, this has very simple rooms with heating and TV but shared bathroom.

Camping
Camping El Astral, Camino de Pollos 8, T983 770 953, www.campingelastral.es. A decent campsite by the River Duero across the bridge from town (follow signs for the parador). On-site pool and bungalows also available.

Urueña *p313*
E Pozolico, C Santo Domingo 9, T983 717 481, www.pozolico.com. The simplicity of this *casa rural* is appealing; it also has a most friendly owner and an excellent garden, plus views of the walls from a couple of the rooms. Chilly in winter.
E Villa de Urueña, C Nueva 6, T626 847 133, www.villadeuruena.es. Run out of the restaurant of the same name on the main square, these are 2 *casas rurales* with simple doubles inside the walls. The **Casa de los Beatos** is the more and characterful building, but both are pleasant.

Medina del Campo *p313*
Medina perhaps appeals more as a day trip from Valladolid, but there are many places to stay.
L Palacio de las Salinas, Ctra de Salinas s/n, T983 804 450, www.palaciodelassalinas.es. The most opulent of the town's choices, this is a massive palace 4 km west of town. Set in huge gardens, it's also a spa hotel and has plenty of comfort for a relaxing stay. Prices normally include breakfast, and half- and full-board rates are available.
E Hostal Plaza, Plaza Mayor 34, T983 811 246, www.hostallaplaza.com. Right on the main square, this *hostal* offers excellent value. It has well-priced, spacious rooms with en suite bathroom as well as a restaurant.

Toro *p315*
B Posada Reja Dorada, C Rejadorada 13, T980 694 979, www.palaciorejadorada.com Constructed around a columned patio, this lovely stone palace has an intriguing story attached to it, from the 15th-century Civil War. Recently refurbished, it's now a lovely boutique inn, with spacious, elegant rooms that seek to recreate the period with elegant beds stately fabrics and, in some cases, canopies. The café is open to the public.
C Juan II, Paseo Espolón 1, T980 690 300, www.hoteljuanii.com. This hotel is on the edge of the old town above the cliff dropping down to the river. The rooms are comfortable; some have great views, and there's some good old-fashioned Spanish hospitality in the air.
C María de Molina, Plaza San Julián 1, T980 691 414, h.molina@helcom.es. A well-priced hotel, modern but attractive, with spacious a/c rooms that lack nothing but hairdryers and minibars. Right in the centre of town.
F Doña Elvira, C Antonio Miguelez 47, T980 690 062. Although it's rather unattractively situated by a petrol station on the main road at the edge of the old town, this is the best budget option, with clean en suite rooms at

a pittance, and rooms with shared bath for even less (**G**). There's some noise from the road, but it's not too bad.

🍴 Eating

Tordesillas p312

Hostal San Antolín, see Sleeping above, is a good eating option too.

🍴🍴🍴 **El Torreón**, C Dimas Rodríguez 11, T983 770 123. This restaurant has a lofty reputation hereabouts and is a favourite weekend lunch choice for Valladolid bureaucrats. It specializes in meat and is famous for a great steak tartare as well as home-made foie. There's a hearty, traditional Castilian atmosphere.

🍴🍴 **Palacio del Corregidor**, C San Pedro 14, T983 796 849, www.palaciodelcorregidor. com. Housed in a fine old *palacio*, this friendly restaurant specializes in good paellas and fish baked in salt. The paella should be ordered earlier in the day; if not, be prepared to wait.

Medina del Campo p313

🍴 **Mónaco**, Plaza Mayor 26, T983 801 020. The town's most characterful spot, this is a lively bar that has some great *pinchos*, and an upstairs restaurant with some excellent, rich, meaty plates and a good *menú* for €9.

Toro p315

Toro has a few cheap and cheerful places to eat around the Plaza Mayor.

🍴🍴🍴 **La Viuda Rica**, C Rejadorada 7, T980 691 581. The 'wealthy widow' has brought confident, expensive modern cuisine to this classic Castilian town, with an open kitchen, and stylishly prepared dishes that aren't afraid to break with tradition. Various set menus and plenty of Toro wines.

🍴🍴 **Juan II**, Paseo Espolón I, T980 690 300. To its great credit, this spot doesn't feel remotely like a hotel restaurant, and it's priced very fairly indeed. There's a large dining area, a terrace and a range of excellent Castilian fare.

🍴 **Restaurante Castilla**, Plaza Mayor 19, T980 690 381. This simple and friendly place has

decent hearty local cuisine and tapas. You're much better eating outside if the weather's fine, as the cramped *comedor* can get pretty stuffy. They also have cheap rooms.

🍸 Bars and clubs

Toro p315

Carpe Diem, Plaza Mayor 5, T607 601 880. This is the town's best drinking option and a stylish spot.

La Bodeguilla del Pillo, C Puerto del Mercado 34. A local-style wine bar, full of character. Nearly every Toro wine is available by the glass.

⊛ Festivals and events

Tordesillas p312

Mid-Sep The fiesta includes the **Toro de la Vega**: a bull is released in open woodlands near the town and the people start running.

⊖ Transport

Tordesillas p312

Bus Services between **Valladolid** and **Zamora** stop at the bus station just north and west of the old town. 7-10 weekdays, 3 4 at weekends, plus other services to major cities.

Medina del Campo p313

Bus There's a bus terminal next to the train station, but most buses to **Madrid** and **Valladolid** leave from a bar called **Punto Rojo** on C Artilleria near the Plaza Mayor. About 15 departures for Valladolid daily and 5 for Madrid.

Train Many trains to **Madrid**, **Valladolid**, **Palencia**, and **Salamanca**, as well as 3 a day to **León**, and 1 to **Lisbon**.

Toro p315

Bus Services between **Valladolid** and **Zamora** stop on the main road, a handier option than the train. 7-10 a day on weekdays and 3-4 at weekends.

Zamora

→ *Colour map 4, B3. Phone code: 980. Population: 66,293.*

Like so many other towns along the river Duero, Zamora was a fortress of the Reconquista frontline, although before that it was a Celtic, Carthaginian, then Roman settlement. In the Middle Ages, the city was formidably walled and famous for its resilience during sieges; the saying 'A Zamora, no se ganó en una hora' (Zamora wasn't taken in an hour) dates from these times and is still used widely.

Today the city is a relaxed and peaceful provincial capital famous for ceramics and antiques. The centre is attractive with, incredibly, a couple of dozen Romanesque churches, which are at ease with some very harmonious modern urban architecture. The city still preserves large sections of its walls around the old centre, which perches high on the rocky bank of the Duero. Zamora province is famous for its wines, with many villages riddled with traditional underground bodegas, and for its wide variety of artisanal cheeses. ▶▶ *For listings, see pages 322-325.*

Ins and outs

Getting there and around The train station (a beautiful building) and bus station are inconveniently situated a 20-minute walk to the north of town. Local buses run to them from Plaza Sagasta near the Plaza Mayor, or it's a €5 cab fare. Nearly all the sights of interest are within the walled old town, of elongated shape but still just about walkable. ▶▶ *See also Transport, page 325.*

Tourist information The city **tourist office** ① *Plaza Arias Gonzalo 6, T980 533 694, daily 1000-1400, 1600-1900 (1700-2000 Mar-Sep),* is at the cathedral end of town and is very helpful. At the other end of the old town is the similarly helpful **regional office** ① *C Príncipe de Asturias 1, T980 531 845, oficinadeturismodezamora@jcyl.es, mid-Sep to May Mon-Sat 0930-1400, 1600-1900, Sun 0930-1700, Jun to mid-Sep daily 0900-2000.* City tours (€5 per person) run at weekends from March to June and October to November, and daily from July to September. Most guides will be able to summarize in English as they go along. Ask at the tourist office about summer kayaking trips on the Duero below town (€10 per person).

Sights

Where they are preserved, the **city walls** are impressive and worth strolling around. There are a few noble entrances preserved around the perimeter. Zamora's most enchanting area is the western end of the walled town, a narrow, quiet zone of picturesque streets, noble buildings and little gardens culminating in the city's castle and cathedral.

The **castle** ① *Tue-Sun 1100-1400, 1730-2200, free,* founded in the 11th century, has a muscular keep that's largely modern inside and has been converted into a space for art exhibitions. The gardens around it house information panels; at the entrance to the area is the **Museo de Baltasar Lobo** ① *Tue-Sun 1200-1400, 1800-2100, free,* housing a number of the sensuous forms sculpted by the Zamoran artist whose name it bears.

Next to it, Zamora's **cathedral** ① *Tue-Sun 1000-1400, 1630-1830, summer daily 1000-2000, €3,* is an interesting building, especially its dome, which is an unusual feature, with scalloped tiling and miniature pagodas that wouldn't look out of place on a southeast Asian temple. In the squarish interior, you can admire the finely carved stone retrochoir as well as the 16th-century walnut choir itself. The side chapels all have elegant *rejas*, while

The fighting bishop of Zamora

In an age that saw the central state increase its power over the individual, Antonio de Acuña, Bishop of Zamora during the *comunero* revolt, stands out as a swaggering medieval throwback of an individualist whose complete lack of self awareness led to him becoming a central figure of resistance to Carlos V. Born to a wealthy Castilian family who were used to dispensing patronage, Acuña had come to the attention of Fernando and Isabel, who appointed him their ambassador to Rome in 1506.

After Isabel's death, Acuña saw an opportunity to further his own interests and deserted Fernando in preference for Felipe el Hermoso (Philip the Fair). By pledging his absolute loyalty to the Pope he was able to secure his appointment to the bishopric of Zamora despite the opposition of top local bigwig Rodrigo Ronquillo, whose objections were brushed aside when Acuña seized the bishopric by force. His Triumph-of-the-Will-style antics saw him temporarily in charge but at the expense of making a host of powerful enemies.

Although his appointment was eventually confirmed by Fernando, Zamora became a centre of intrigue with Acuña at its centre. When he was eventually expelled from the city at the start of the *comunero* revolt, he raised an army of 2000 men and found himself on the side of the rebels while his implacable enemy Ronquillo was a leading royalist commander. He conducted a series of daring but essentially meaningless campaigns in the *meseta* around Valladolid before deciding in 1521 to march on Toledo where in a great display of showmanship he persuaded the populace to declare him bishop.

It soon became apparent that his individualistic acts of empire building were no substitute for an effective political and military strategy and after the defeat of the *comuneros*, Acuña was forced to flee. But he was captured and held captive in Simancas Castle where Carlos hoped he would be quietly forgotten about.

But in 1526, while attempting to escape, Acuña killed one of his gaolers. Carlos cunningly appointed Ronquillo as custodian of Simancas Castle. Ronquillo wasted no time in settling old scores and sentenced the erstwhile bishop to be tortured and executed. His body was then displayed from the castle walls as warning to others who thought they could challenge royal power.

Although the Pope went through the motions of complaining about this breach of protocol, in reality he recognized that Acuña was a son of the Church who had signally failed to bring any credit or advantage to the Papacy. Eventually the whole matter was quietly forgotten.

---

the stone *retablo* depicts the Ascension. The highlight, however, is the **museum**, and its small collection of superb Flemish tapestries. Dating from the 15th and 17th centuries, they are amazing for their detail, colour and size (some of them are around 35 sq m). They depict scenes from antiquity: the conquests of Hannibal, the Trojan War and the coronation of Tarquin.

Zamora has an extraordinary number of Romanesque churches, a pleasing collection, particularly as several of them avoided meddlesome architects of later periods. The **Iglesia de La Magdalena** ① *Wed-Mon 1000-1300, 1700-2000, free*, is one of the nicest, with an ornate portal carved with plant motifs. Inside, it's simple and attractive, with a high single nave, and a 13th-century tomb with an unusually midget-like recumbent figure. Most of the worthwhile churches have the same opening hours.

In the **Plaza Mayor**, the **Iglesia de San Juan**, constructed in the 12th to 13th century, has a thistly façade and a big gloomy interior with unusual arches that run the length of the nave, rather than across it. The alabaster windows are an attractive feature.

The pretty **Iglesia de Santa María la Nueva** is increasingly inaccurately named as its Romanesque lines are going on 900 years old. It has some fine carved capitals outside; inside it's a simple temple with high barrel vaulting, a stone baptismal font, and the faded remains of some frescoes; you can just about make out scenes from the life of Christ and Mary. Next door is a museum detailing the traditions of Zamora's Semana Santa, while, further to the east, look out for the façade of the **Palacio de los Momos**, carved with penitents' chains seemingly at odds with the grandeur of the mansion.

The **Museo de Zamora** ① *Plaza de Santa Lucía 2, T980 516 150, Tue-Sat 1000-1400, 1600-1900 (summer 1700-2000), Sun 1000-1400, €1.20,* is housed in two connecting buildings: a 16th-century *palacio*, and a modern construction designed by Emilio Tuñón and Luis Moreno Mansilla, which has won many plaudits since its opening in 1998. The museum was conceived

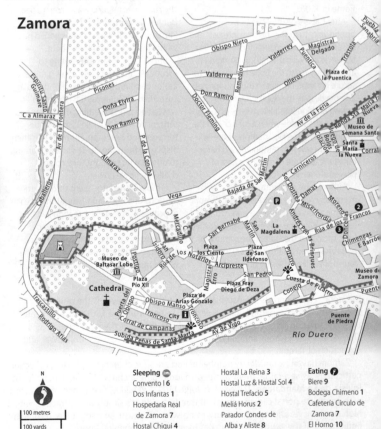

Sleeping	Hostal La Reina **3**	Eating
Convento I **6**	Hostal Luz & Hostal Sol **4**	Biere **9**
Dos Infantas **1**	Hostal Trefacio **5**	Bodega Chimeno **1**
Hospedaría Real	Meliá Horus **2**	Cafetería Círculo de
de Zamora **7**	Parador Condes de	Zamora **7**
Hostal Chiqui **4**	Alba y Aliste **8**	El Horno **10**

as a chest that would hold the city's valuables; it's imaginative without being flamboyant, and fits quietly into the city's older lines. The collection covers everything from the Celtic to the modern, and is fairly interesting: Roman funeral stelae, gilt crosses from the Visigothic period, and especially a very ornate gold Celtic brooch are all things to catch the attention.

On Plaza Viriato is the Museo Etnográfico **museum** ⓘ *Tue-Sat 1000-1400, 1700-2000, Sun 1000-1400, €3*, which holds an ethnographic display of traditional Castilian life, bolstered by regular temporary exhibitions. A little further on lies the **Museo de Semana Santa** ⓘ *Plaza de Santa María la Nueva s/n, Tue-Sat 1000-1400, 1700-2000, Sun 1000-1400, €3*, which has an interesting display illustrating the history of Zamora's famous Holy Week processions.

From parts of the old town, there are magnificent views over the ramparts and down to the Duero River and its picturesque old bridge. From **Plaza Troncoso**, just near the city tourist office, is one of the best, while **Calle Pizarro**, off Rúa de los Francos, is also worthwhile, especially at night. Another interesting street is the steep **Calle Balborraz**, which plunges down from the Plaza Mayor, and is an alluring assembly of character-laden buildings and intriguing shops.

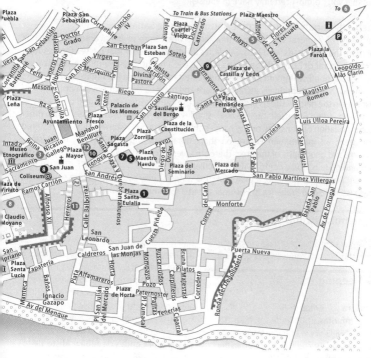

El Rincón de Antonio **2**
La Rúa **3**
Los Caprichos
de Meneses **8**
Serafín **5**

Bars & clubs 🎵
Bodega Quinti **11**
La Cueva del Jazz **13**
Ocellum **12**

Around Zamora

West of Zamora, the N122 heads towards the Portuguese castle town of **Bragança**, 100 km away. The road passes the massive and attractive reservoir of the Esla River. Some 10 km off the road (from a point 12 km west of Zamora), the church of **San Pedro de la Nave** was moved in the 1930s to protect it from submersion by the rising waters. It's a 17th-century Visigothic structure with lofty doors and some excellent capitals inside, as well as a frieze with various Christian motifs. The keyholder, María Angeles Refoyo, lives in the corner house where the road bends through the middle of the village.

North of Zamora, on the N630 just before the village of Granja de Moreruela, lie the impressive ruins of the **Monasterio de Moreruela** ① *Wed-Sun 1000-1400, 1700-2000 (winter 1530-1830), free*. Built by the Cistercians in the 12th century on a beautiful wooded site, the church and cloisters survive only in outline. Fortunately, the apse and chevet survive intact and convey an impression of the monastery's former glory. It's a romantic spot that you'll almost certainly have to yourself.

Puebla de Sanabria and Parque Natural Lago de Sanabria

Northwest of Zamora, via the unenthralling service centre of Benavente (which has a parador), the A52 heads west into Galicia. It's an attractive route that passes the beautiful **Parque Natural del Lago de Sanabria**. The lake is a hauntingly beautiful glacial feature with several good swimming beaches. The nearest town, **Puebla de Sanabria**, just off the motorway, is an exceptionally attractive place and makes a good stopover, with plenty of character in the narrow streets around its attractive 12th-century church and blocky castle.

Around the lake itself are several small villages with *casas rurales* and other accommodation options. The pretty hamlet of **San Martín de Castañeda** has in a restored monastery, an information centre on the natural park with exhibits on the history, geology, and geography of the area. There are several excellent walks around the lake and surrounding hills; horse riding is also a popular activity.

From Puebla de Sanabria, a beautiful road winds its way south through a spectacular hilly pass and on to Bragança in Portugal, about a 45-minute drive away.

◉ Zamora listings

For Sleeping and Eating price codes and other relevant information, see Essentials pages 31-39.

◉ Sleeping

Zamora *p318, map p320*
L Dos Infantas, Cortinas de San Miguel 3, T980 509 898, www.hoteldosinfantas.com. This is a modern and stylish option in the centre of town. It usually offers surprisingly reasonable online rates (**C**) for large rooms, which are equipped to business hotel standards. There's parking available as well.
L Hotel Meliá Horus, Plaza del Mercado 20, T980 508 282, www.solmelia.com. In a

stately brick building behind the market, this features attractive art nouveau fittings, helpful staff, and comfortable, classically decorated rooms; the superiors are on the top floor, with sloping attic ceilings. Facilities are excellent, and you're close to the main pedestrian drag but in a quiet zone. Excellent online rates if you book in advance.
AL Parador Condes de Alba y Aliste, Plaza de Viriato 5, T980 514 497, www.parador.es. This is a great place to stay in the heart of the old town, in a noble palace built around a beautiful courtyard. The rooms are large and attractively furnished in wood (the new wing is equally comfortable although not

quite as atmospheric), while the pool out the back helps with the summer heat.

B Hotel Convento I, Ctra la Estación s/n, Coreses, T980 500 422, www.hotel-convento.com. The stern façade of this former seminary 9 km from Zamora in the village of Coreses gives way to an opulent interior; this spa hotel bristles with columns, cherubs, frescoes, stained glass, pharaohs, and other baroque excesses. You'll either find it over-the-top or delightful, and the swimming pool area has to be seen to be believed. There's a full range of spa treatments available, and various weekend deals that include meals.

C Hospedería Real de Zamora, Cuesta Pizarro 7, T980 534 545, www.hosteriasreales.com. Between the main pedestrian thoroughfare and the river, this hotel wins several points for being in an atmospheric old building that was once the Inquisition's Zamora headquarters. It's full of religious art and antiques and has a pretty courtyard space. Rooms are OK, and the atmosphere can be a little sombre, but it's got character in spades.

D Hotel Trefacio, C Alfonso de Castro 7, T980 509 104, www.hoteltrefacio.com. Good mid-range option, with modern rooms that have excellent bathrooms in the heart of the town. The management are warm and friendly and facilities are good. The superior rooms are a few euros more but are substantially larger and face the street, which is a quiet one.

E Hostal Chiqui, C Benavente 2, T980 531 480. In the same building as the **Luz** and **Sol**, this is also a very acceptable option, with modern rooms with TV, phone and heating.

E Hostal Luz and **Hostal Sol**, C Benavente 2, T980 533 152, www.hostal-sol.com. These 2 *hostales* are in the same building and run by the same management. Both are clean and modern, with quiet rooms with bathrooms.

F Hostal La Reina, C Reina 1, T980 533 939. Superbly situated behind the church of San Juan on the Plaza Mayor, this cheery option has rooms with bathroom that are simple enough, but very good at this price.

Around Zamora *p322*

A Parador Puebla de Sanabria, Ctra Lago 18, Puebla de Sanabria, T980 620 001, www.parador.es. A good modern option, but on the other side of the river from the attractive town centre. Helpful, friendly staff and a decent restaurant.

E Hostal San Francisco, Alto de San Francisco 6, Puebla de Sanabria, T980 620 896, h_san_francisco@terra.es. With a great location in the old town, this *hostal* is comfortable, heated and has good views. Offers plenty of value.

Camping

There are 3 campsites around the Lago de Sanabria. **El Folgoso**, Ctra Puebla-San Martín Km 13, T980 626 774, www.campingelfolgoso.com, is a pretty wooded site near the village of El Vigo and a short walk away from a lakeside beach.

🍴 Eating

Zamora *p318, map p320*

🍴 **El Mirador**, Corral de Campanas 5, T980 535 440, www.rmirador.com. In a quiet street not far from the cathedral, this atmospheric little restaurant is set in an old stone bodega that looks out over the Duero. There's quite a contrast between the enclosed stone space and the sweeping views outside; the food is rich and tasty, with such delicacies as *jamón de pato* (duck ham) alongside Castilian favourites, as well as a range of salads and good fish dishes. It's a little overpriced these days, but the ambience is good.

🍴 **El Rincón de Antonio**, Rúa de los Francos 6, T980 535 370, www.elrincondeantonio.com. Zamora's culinary star is an attractive restaurant with a stone interior and a big glassed-in terrace. The cuisine is innovative and excellent; the *mollejas* (sweetbreads) are heaven, as is the *rodaballo* (turbot). There's a huge range of delicious Zamoran cheeses on the trolley, and scrumptious sweets. If you're not that hungry, they do excellent miniature gourmet plates in the bar for €2 a shot; a great way to sample some wonderful textures and flavours without busting the bank. Highly recommended.

ᵚᵚᵚ Los Caprichos de Meneses, Plaza San Miguel 3, T980 530 143, www. loscaprichosdemeneses.com. On the main square, this is a gourmet option that doesn't disappoint. Meneses is the extravagantly moustached boss, and he suggests that you choose a main course, and let them decide on the starters and desserts for you. This works well, but the grilled octopus is a treat you mightn't want to miss. Mains include succulent lamb, and several enticing *bacalao* choices, and desserts are rich and beautifully presented. Recommended.

ᵚᵚ Biere, C Benavente 7, T980 517 178. Cheerfully thronged at lunchtime, this airy café-restaurant attracts crowds for its excellent set lunches. For €12 (or €21 at dinner time) you get a wide choice of dishes featuring both heavy Zamoran classics and lighter options for those hot summer days.

ᵚᵚ El Horno, C Renova 11, T980 517 987. Just off the main square, this is a favourite for its *tablas* (shared platters) that feed 2-4 for around €25-30. They come with meats, seafood, vegetables, or other choices and are solid value.

ᵚᵚ La Rúa, Rúa de los Francos 19, T980 534 024. This likeable and comfortably decorated restaurant is solid for a range of choices, with simple *platos combinados*, a good *menú del día* and some great *zamorano* cuisine. However, it's the rices that give it its good name; the speciality, a paella-like rice with lobster, *arroz con bogavante* (€20 per person; best to order it beforehand), comes in a huge deep dish, sizzling with intent to satisfy.

ᵚᵚ Serafín, Plaza Maestro Haedo 10, T980 531 422. Good hearty Zamoran and Castilian fare at reasonable prices, with a pleasant terrace outside. As well as the café, it also has a more upmarket restaurant, serving dishes such as *arroz a la zamorana*, a hearty rice with various porcine morsels.

ᵚ Bodega Chimeno, Plaza Santa Eulalia 4, T980 530 925. Tucked away in the old town, this place looks like an apartment entrance from outside, but inside it's gloriously

traditional, with wooden tables and barrels, a range of Toro wines by the glass, and surprisingly elaborate tapas like duck ham alongside more earthy offerings like canned tuna or chunkily-cut jamón.

ᵚ Cafetería Círculo de Zamora, C Santa Clara 2, T980 530 534. On the 1st floor of a restored art deco building, this venerable Zamoran institution serves up good-value snacks and meals all day. There's also disabled access.

Around Zamora *p322*

ᵚᵚᵚ El Empalme, N-525 Km 352, Ríonegro del Puente, T980 652 016. On the *ruta nacional* about halfway between Benavente and Puebla de Sanabria, this place seems like a standard roadside diner but is in fact famous throughout Spanish gourmet circles for the quality of its dishes prepared using locally sourced wild mushrooms of various varieties. There's also plenty of game in season.

ᵚᵚ La Casona de Sanabria, Ctra Nacional N525, Puebla de Sanabria, T980 620 000, www. lacasonadesanabria.com. Puebla de Sanabria's best eating option is actually just outside the town, on the main road across the river near the big roundabout. It's an enormous hotel-café complex, but the restaurant is worth seeking out for huge and delicious dishes such as *codillo* (pork knuckle), roast lamb, and excellent octopus. Local wild mushrooms and cut-price wagyu beef are other options. The *menú del día* is perfectly adequate, but it's worth ordering off the *carta* here.

ᵚ Café Bar Remate, C Arrabal 3, Puebla de Sanabria, T980 620 920. Though it doesn't look much from the outside compared to the other choices in town, this is a top spot for simple eating, with lovingly prepared traditional dishes such as *callos* (tripe) or octopus served in a pleasant *comedor*.

❶ Bars and clubs

Zamora *p318, map p320*
The bulk of Zamoran nightlife is centred on the boisterous **C de los Herreros**, a narrow curving street off the Plaza Mayor, whose

steep length is made of one bar after another; basically you just have to stroll down and see which one you fancy. There are some quieter bars around the Plaza Mayor too, and a few secluded options throughout the old town.
Bodega Quinti, C de los Herreros 23. One of the more atmospheric of bars on this street, this underground bar is in a claustrophobic but smart brick vault. It's better earlier in the night as it gets too packed later on.
La Cueva del Jazz, Plaza Seminario 3, T980 533 436, www.lacuevadeljazz.es. Legendary Zamora jazz den in an atmospheric cellar. They have regular live music; most concerts are now in a new venue at C Puerta Nueva 30.
Ocellum, Plaza Mayor 8, T980 514 848. This high-ceilinged café/bar is popular at several points of the day. Its terrace is a great spot for an afternoon coffee after walking the pedestrian zone of the city; later, it gets busy for after-dinner drinks, then becomes a *discoteca*, with a huge selection in the DJ booth and a downstairs dance floor.

⊛ Festivals and events

Zamora p318, map p320
Mar/Apr Zamora's Semana Santa (Holy Week) is one of the most famous and traditional in Spain. Book a room well in advance if you fancy a visit. Although there's plenty of revelry in the bars and streets, the main element is the serious religious processions of hooded *cofradías* (brotherhoods) who carry or accompany giant floats; it's effectively a week-long series of funeral processions; they are very atmospheric and traditional, accompanied by mournful music that communicates both the sadness and the bitter glory. One of the most beautiful is the procession on Sat evening, when the much-loved Virgen de la Soledad is carried through the streets, preceded by a sisterhood carrying flickering candles.
End Jun Zamora's main fiesta is San Pedro, with streetlife, fireworks and bullfights. At the same time, the Plaza de Viriato holds an important ceramics fair; a picturesque sight

indeed with thousands of vessels of all shapes and sizes arranged under the trees; they range from traditional plain earthenware to imaginatively painted decorative pieces.

⊙ Shopping

Zamora p318, map p320
Zamora is full of shops dealing in antiques and ceramics; there are also characterful shops along the main pedestrian streets selling wine, delicious local cheeses and hams.

⊖ Transport

Zamora p318, map p320
Despite Zamora's proximity to the Portuguese border, there are currently no public transport connections with it; you have to go via Salamanca or Madrid.

Bus
Some 7 buses a day run north to **León** (2 hrs) via **Benavente** (4 at weekends); 7-10 run to **Valladolid**, some stopping in **Toro** and **Tordesillas** (3 at weekends); 6 service **Madrid**; a massive 13 cruise south to **Salamanca** (40 mins-1 hr, 6 on Sun), and 5 go to **Oviedo** (3 hrs 30 mins), among other northern Spanish destinations.

Train
Trains are few: 2 a day run to **Madrid** (3-4 hrs, €29); more go to **Medina del Campo** (55 mins), but you're better off using the buses.

⊙ Directory

Zamora p318, map p320
Internet Recreativos Coliseum, C Ramos Carrión, is a central gaming arcade with internet terminals. **Laundry** A friendly no-name laundry on the corner of C de Balborraz and C San Andrés just off the Plaza Mayor (look for the *Tintorería* sign) will do a service wash and dry for about €8. **Police** The police station is in the Plaza Mayor in the old town hall.

Salamanca

→ *Colour map 4, B3. Phone Code: 923. Population:155,619. Altitude: 780 m.*

Salamanca has a strong claim to being Spain's most attractive city. A university town since the early 13th century, it reached its apogee in the 15th and 16th centuries, the Golden Age of Imperial Spain. The old town is a remarkable assembly of superb buildings; a day's solid sightseeing can teach you more about Spanish architecture than you thought you ever wanted to know – Plateresque and Churrigueresque were more or less born here. By night, too, it's a good spot; today's university students just don't seem to tuck up in bed with a candle, hot milk and a theological tract like they used to, and bar life is busy seven days a week, bolstered by the large numbers of tourists and foreign students learning Spanish. If you can handle the heat and the crowds, there are few better places in Spain to spend a summer evening than the superb Plaza Mayor; sit at an outdoor table and watch storks circle architectural perfection in the setting sun.➤➤ *For listings, see pages 332-336.*

Ins and outs

Getting there Salamanca is about 200 km west of Madrid. The bus station is west of town along Avenida Filiberto Villalobos. There are plenty of buses from Madrid, Valladolid and other Castilian cities. New motorways and the straight *meseta* roads make for easy driving access; it's about an hour from Valladolid, for example, and forty minutes from Zamora. There are also several train connections. ➤➤ *See also Transport, page 335.*

Getting around You won't have much cause to stray from the old town, which is very walkable indeed. The bus and train stations are a 15-minute walk from the centre.

Best time to visit If you visit in summer you are guaranteed heat, tourists and outdoor tables. In many ways this is the nicest time to come, but the students aren't about (although there are always plenty of foreign-language students) and the nightlife is correspondingly quieter. Like the rest of Castilla, Salamanca gets cold in winter, but never shuts down and accommodation is cheap.

Tourist information There are two handy tourist offices, one in the **Plaza Mayor** ① *T923 218 342, Mon-Fri 1000-1400, 1600-1830, Sat 1000-1830, Sun 1000-1400, summer Mon-Sat 0900-2000, Sun 0900-1400,* and one at **Rúa Antigua 70** ① *Casa de las Conchas, T923 268 571, oficinadeturismodesalamanca@jcyl.es, mid-Sep to Jun Mon-Sat 0930-1400, 1600-1900, Sun 0930-1700, summer daily 0900-2000.* The former has more information on the city, the second is better for information on the rest of Castilla y León. A few summer-only kiosks are scattered about, notably at the transport terminals. Regular **walking tours** of the city run from the tourist office on the Plaza Mayor; they leave daily throughout the year at 1100 (€6, Spanish only). In summer there are usually English-language tours available. Otherwise, the tourist office can provide a list of English-speaking official guides. At either of the tourist offices you can buy the Salamanca Card (www.salamancacard.com) which, for €22, gives you two days of access to the city's monuments and museums, an audio guide, and various discounts.

Background

Salamanca's history is tied to that of its university (see box, page 331), but the town itself was founded in pre-Roman times. An Iberian settlement, it was taken by Hannibal (pre-elephants) in 218 BC. The Romans later took it over but, as with most cities in these parts, it was abandoned and only resettled during the Reconquista. The university was founded in AD 1218 and rapidly grew to become one of Europe's principal centres of learning. Flourishing particularly under the Catholic Monarchs, the city became an emblem of Imperial Spain; the think-tank behind the monarchy that ruled half the world.

Salamanca's decline in the 18th and 19th centuries mirrored that of its university and indeed the rest of Castilla. The city suffered grievously in the Napoleonic wars; the French general Marmont destroyed most of the university's buildings before his defeat by Wellington just south of the city in 1812. In the 20th century, during the Civil War, Major Doval, a well-known butcher, cracked down fiercely on Republican sympathizers after the coup. The city was the conspirators' command centre for a while, and Franco was declared *caudillo* in a cork grove just outside the town. In 2002 Salamanca revelled in its status as joint European Cultural Capital, and the city benefited from the success and structural improvements.

Sights

Plaza Mayor

Among strong competition, Salamanca's main square stands out as the most harmonious plaza in Spain. Built in the 18th century by Alberto Churriguera, it has nothing of the occasional gaudiness of the style to which he and his brother unwittingly lent their names. Paying over the odds for a coffee or a vermouth at one of its outdoor tables is still a superb option; there can be fewer nicer places to sit, especially on a warm summer's evening with storks circling above. Around the perimeter are medallions bearing the heads of various illustrious Spaniards; the more recent additions include Franco (often defaced by paint) and King Juan Carlos, and there are plenty of blank ones for new notables.

University and around

Rúa Mayor links the plaza with the cathedral and the old buildings of the university. It's lined with restaurants that take over the street with tables for pleasant overeating and drinking in the summer sun. On the right about halfway down is the distinctive **Casa de las Conchas** (House of Shells), named for the 400-odd carved scallop shells of its façades. Now a library (with occasional exhibitions), its nicest feature is the courtyard, graced by an elegantly intricate balcony and decorated with well-carved lions and shields. Opposite the Casa de las Conchas is the **Clerecía**, a Jesuit college founded in the early 17th century by Felipe III – a plaque commemorates the event. An imposing baroque cloister can be visited to the right of the church entrance.

Leave the Clerecía on your right and take the second left to reach the **Patio de las Escuelas**, a small square surrounded by beautiful university buildings. In the centre stands Fray Luis de León (see box, page 331). He faces the edifice where he once lectured, the main **university** building. Its incredible façade is an amazing example of what master masons could achieve with soft Salamanca sandstone. The key for generations of students and visitors has been to spot the frog; if you manage to do it unguided, you are eligible for a range of benefits: good exam results, luck in love and more. If you don't need any of these and want some help, see the note, page 329. It's rather underwhelming if you've just spent a couple of hours searching it out.

The **interior** ⓘ *Mon-Fri 0930-1300, 1600-1900, Sat 0930-1300, 1600-1830, Sun 1000-1300, €4, free Mon mornings; entrance includes the university museum, which is dominated by a mighty cypress*, is interesting, but not nearly as impressive, and feels positively stark after the exuberant exterior. There are several impressively worked ceilings inside. The

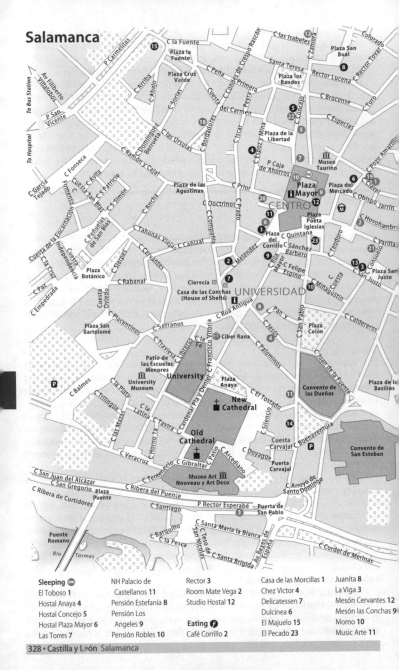

Salamanca

Sleeping
El Toboso **1**
Hostal Anaya **4**
Hostal Concejo **5**
Hostal Plaza Mayor **6**
Las Torres **7**

NH Palacio de
Castellanos **11**
Pensión Estefanía **8**
Pensión Los
Angeles **9**
Pensión Robles **10**

Rector **3**
Room Mate Vega **2**
Studio Hostal **12**

Eating
Café Corrillo **2**

Casa de las Morcillas **1**
Chez Victor **4**
Delicatessen **7**
Dulcinea **6**
El Majuelo **15**
El Pecado **23**

Juanita **8**
La Viga **3**
Mesón Cervantes **12**
Mesón las Conchas **9**
Momo **10**
Music Arte **11**

old halls radiate around the courtyard; the largest, the Paraninfo, is hung with Flemish tapestries. One of the halls is preserved as it was in the days when Fray Luis lectured here, with narrow wooden benches, while upstairs, the impressive library is a beautiful space, with ornate wooden shelves lined with thousands of ancient texts; these days you can only peer from the entrance, however. Fray Luis's remains are in the chapel.

The **university museum** is housed around a patio on the other side of the square, the Escuelas Menores. The patio is attractively grassed behind its Plateresque portal. The arches, looking a little like devils' horns, are typical of Salamanca, an exuberant innovation of the 15th century. There's a reasonable collection of paintings and sculptures, the best by foreign artists resident in Salamanca in its glory years, but the highlight is the remaining part of the fresco ceiling painted by Fernando Gallego. It illustrates the signs of the Zodiac and various constellations; a *mudéjar* ceiling in one of the rooms for temporary exhibits is also well worth a peek.

> The frog is on the right pilaster; at the top of the second tier you'll see three skulls; the frog perches on the left-hand one.

Cathedrals

Unusually for Spain, Salamanca's **Catedral Nueva** ① *Mon-Sat 0900-1300, 1600-1800 (2000 summer), Sun 0900-1300, free; cathedral tower Ieronimus exhibition daily 1000-1715, €3.50*, is built alongside, rather than on top of, its Romanesque predecessor. It's a massive affair that dominates the city's skyline from most angles. While the later tower is unimpressively ostentatious, the western façade is superb; a masterpiece of late Gothic stonework, with the transition into Plateresque very visible. It is the sheer number of statues and motifs that amazes, more than the power of any particular scene. The central figure is of the Crucifixion, flanked by Saints Peter and Paul. Around the corner to the left, the façade facing the Plaza de Anaya is also excellent. The door is named Puerta de las Palmas for the relief carving of Jesus entering Jerusalem on Palm Sunday, but take a look at the archivolts on the left-hand side; an astronaut and an imp with a large ice cream are entertaining recent additions.

Inside, the new cathedral impresses more by its lofty lines than its subtlety. It's a mixture of styles, mostly in transitional Gothic with star vaulting and colourful, high Renaissance lantern. The *coro* is almost completely enclosed; the stalls were carved in walnut by the Churriguera brothers. At the back, in a *capilla* of the squared apse, the bronze figure of the *Cristo de las Batallas* is said to have been carried into war by the Cid. In another chapel is the grisly dried hand of Julián Rodríguez Sánchez, a Salamancan priest murdered in the Civil War, and beatified in 2001. The cathedral towers have been recently restored and offer an exhibition of medieval documents, 'Ieronimus', and a terrace with a fine city view.

The **Cathedral Vieja** ① *Mon-Sat 1000-1230, 1600-1730 (1930 summer), Sun 1000-1230, €4.50*, is accessed from inside the new one. It's a much smaller, more intimate space. It dates mostly from the 12th century; while the design is Romanesque, the pointed arches anticipate the later Gothic styles. On the wall by the entrance are wall paintings from the early 17th century; they depict miracles attributed to the *Cristo de las Batallas* figurine. The *retablo* is superb, a colourful ensemble of 53 panels mostly depicting the life of Christ. Above, a good *Last Judgement* sees the damned getting herded into the maw of a hake-like monster. In the transepts are some excellent coloured tombs, one with its own vaulted ribs.

Around the cloister are several interesting chambers. The Capilla de Santa Bárbara is where, until 1843, the rector of the university was sworn in. It was also where the students used to take their final exams; if they failed, it was straight across the cloister and out via the opposite door, and thence no doubt to the nearest boozer.

Convents

The **Convento de San Esteban** ① *daily 1000-1400, 1600-1900 (2000 summer), €3*, not far from the cathedrals, is slightly cheerless but worth visiting. Its ornate Plateresque façade depicts the stoning of Esteban himself (St Stephen); the door itself is also attractive. Entry to the church is via the high cloister, which has quadruple arches. The top deck, floored with boards, is the nicest bit; it would cry out for a café-bar if it weren't in a monastery. There's a small museum with various Filipino saints, a silver reliquary in the shape of a *sombrero*, and a couple of amazing early Bibles. One of them, dating from the late 13th century or so, is so perfect it's almost impossible to believe that it was handwritten.

The church is dominated by its *retablo*, a work of José Churriguera. A massive 30 m by 14 m, it's exuberantly excessive, but more elegant than some of the style's later examples.

Opposite, the **Convento de las Dueñas** ① *Mon-Sat 1100-1245 (1030-1300 summer), 1630-1730, €2*, also houses Dominicans, this time in the shape of nuns who do a popular line in almond cakes. The irregular-shaped cloister is open for visits and is beautiful, with views of the cathedral in the background. Dating from the first half of the 16th century, its lower floor is fairly simple compared with the top level, decorated with busts and shields, as well as ornate capitals of doomed souls and beasts.

Museo Art Nouveau y Art Deco

① *C Gibraltar 14, T923 121 425, www.museocasalis.org, Apr to mid-Oct Tue-Fri 1100-1400, 1700-2100, Sat and Sun 1100-2100, mid-Oct to Mar Tue-Fri 1100-1400, 1600-1900, Sat and Sun 1100-2000, €3.*

Salamanca University and Fray Luis de León

Founded in 1218, Salamanca was Spain's second university (after Palencia) to be established. The patronage of kings allowed it to grow rapidly; in 1255 it was named by the Pope as pre-eminent in Europe, alongside Paris, Oxford and Bologna. It was the brains behind the Golden Age of Imperial Spain; its Colegios Mayores, or four Great Colleges, supplied a constant stream of Spain's most distinguished thinkers, and exerted plenty of undue political influence to get their own graduates appointed to high positions. The university had in excess of 10,000 students in its pomp and was forward thinking, with a strong scientific tradition and a female professor as early as the late 15th century.

Spain's closed-door policy to Protestant thinkers was always going to have a bad effect, and Salamanca declined in the 18th century; Newton and Descartes were considered unimportant, the chair of mathematics was vacant for decades, and theologians debated what language was spoken by the angels. The Peninsular War had a terrible effect too; French troops demolished most of the university's colleges. But the university is thriving again: although not among Spain's elite, the student atmosphere is bolstered by large numbers of foreigners who come to the beautiful city to learn Spanish.

Among many notable teachers that have taught at Salamanca, two stand out; Miguel de Unamuno (see box, page 96), and Fray Luis de León. Born to Jewish *conversos* (converts), at 14 the latter came to Salamanca to study law; he soon moved into theology, becoming a monk of the Augustinian order. In 1560 he was appointed to the chair of theology. Well versed in Hebrew, Fray Luis continued to use Hebrew texts as the basis of his Biblical teaching; he was responsible for many translations of the testaments and scriptures from that language into Spanish. Enemies and anti-Semites saw these actions as being in defiance of the Council of Trent, and on 27 March 1572, Fray Luis was arrested mid-lecture by the Inquisition and imprisoned in Valladolid, where he was charged with disrespect and imprudence. After a five-year trial he was sentenced to torture by the rack; the punishment was, however, revoked. Returning to Salamanca, he famously began his first lecture to a crowded room with "*Dicebamus hesterna die*" (As we were saying yesterday ...). He maintained his firm stance, and got into fresh trouble with the Inquisition five years later. He was made provincial of the Augustinians and died in 1591.

Apart from his theological writings, he was an excellent poet, one of the finest in Spain's history. His verses bring out the deep feelings of a man better known as having been severe and sardonic, understandably, given the religious hypocrisy that he struggled against.

If you fancy a break from sandstone and Plateresque, head for the Museo Art Nouveau y Art Deco. It's superbly housed in the **Casa Lis**, an art nouveau *palacio* built for a wealthy Salamancan industrialist; there's a particularly good view of the building from the riverbank. The collection of pieces is very good; you're sure to find something you love and something you can't stand. Representative of the traditions of many countries, there are porcelains, sculpture, glassware, ceramics, Fabergé jewelling and dolls. The stained-glass ceiling is particularly impressive too.

Nearby, check out the pretty **Puente Romano**, a bridge over the Tormes with Roman origins. There are numerous other religious buildings and museums to visit in Salamanca; the tourist office has a fuller list than can be provided here.

For Sleeping and Eating price codes and other relevant information, see Essentials pages 31-39.

⊙ **Sleeping**

Salamanca *p326, map p328*

Salamanca is replete with places to stay; there are well over 100 spots to lay your head.

L NH Palacio de Castellanos, C San Pablo 58, T923 261 818, www.nh-hotels.com. This imposing hotel occupies what was once a late 15th-century palace, although much of what remains dates from the 19th century. The rooms have all the conveniences of a business hotel but considerably more charm than most, with wrought-iron balconies, a pillow menu, video games and more. Extras, such as internet, are overpriced.

AL Hotel Rector, Paseo Rector Esperabé 10, T923 218 482, www.hotelrector.com. An excellent option near the river, this small and exclusive hotel is in a beautiful sandstone *palacio*. Its very plush inside, with leather sofas, art nouveau glass and elegant wooden furniture; the rooms are decorated with a lighter touch, with olive-wood bedheads and large windows admitting plenty of natural light. Service is excellent. Book ahead. Parking available. Recommended.

A Hotel Las Torres, C Concejo 4, T923 212 100, www.hthoteles.com. Some rooms in this sensitively refurbished 18th-century building have balconies overlooking the Plaza Mayor. It offers smart modern facilities such as internet access, hydromassage showers and, in the best rooms, PC with flatscreen monitor and exercise bike. There's free internet and business facilities for guests and specially adapted rooms for families and for the disabled. The rates are on a sliding scale and vary considerably; it's best to book over the internet to see what's on offer.

A Room Mate Vega, Plaza del Mercado 16, T923 272 250, www.room-matehotels.com. Very close to the Plaza Mayor, this stylish and upbeat chain choice offers easy-on-the-eye designer chic and very spacious rooms with plenty of facilities, including courtesy apples and free Wi-Fi.

C Hostal Concejo, Plaza de la Libertad 1, T923 214 737, www.hconcejo.com. Another well-placed option, this friendly *hostal* has faultless modern rooms around the corner from the Plaza Mayor. It's in the pedestrian zone and has been recently renovated.

C Studio Hostal, C Zamora 54, T923 280 557, www.studiohostal.com. More of a boutique hotel than a *hostal*, this super choice, like many smaller places, owes its excellence to an enthusiastic and helpful owner. Rooms are all different, with good modern extras; you can get a breakfast tray brought to your room. Much pricier at weekends. Book ahead.

D Hostal Plaza Mayor, Plaza Corrillo 19, T923 262 020, www.hostalplazamayor.es. Though not quite on the square that it's named after, it's only a few paces away. You pay a little for the location, but the rooms are compact, modern and comfortable.

D Hotel El Toboso, C Clavel 7, T923 271 462, www.hoteltoboso.com. Value-packed choice in the heart of things, with very pleasing decor in an attractive stone building. The prices are very good; the double rooms are spacious and light and the apartments (sleeping 3 or 5) are especially attractive for a family stay and priced very reasonably.

D Pensión Los Angeles, Plaza Mayor 10, T923 218 166, www.pensionlosangeles.com. The best rooms in this decent spot overlook the Plaza Mayor, and they are much nicer than the no-frills interior rooms (**F**), which are a bit grim by comparison. Get a room with a view or look elsewhere.

E Hostal Anaya, C Jesús 18, T923 271 773. A very central option, with attractive and spacious modern rooms with sparklingly clean en suite and friendly management. They can provide breakfast too, and have good-value rooms for 3 or 4.

F Pensión Estefanía, C Jesús 3, T923 217 372, www.pensionestefania.es. A very cheap and handy option in the centre of Salamanca. Though the welcome is hardly effusive, the rooms are good value, at least in summer. In winter, you might like to consider elsewhere, as there's no heating. Bathrooms are shared but clean, but there are showers in the rooms.

F Pensión Robles, Plaza Mayor 20, T923 213 197. The best reason to stay at this basic but clean place is its location on the beautiful plaza, though not all of the rooms overlook it. Rooms are simple, with an OK bathroom, and the price is super-low. It's regularly booked up.

⑩ Eating

Salamanca *p326, map p328*
Salamanca abounds in cheap places to eat. Some of the places around the Plaza Mayor and Rúa Mayor are a bit tourist-trappy, but it's hard to beat their terraces for alfresco dining. Drinks cost a little bit more in Salamanca than the Castilian norm, but you get to choose a free *pincho* to go with your tipple, and they are often excellent.

⑪⑪⑪ Chez Victor, C Espoz y Mina 26, T923 213 123. Closed Aug. Surprisingly reasonably priced for its lofty reputation, this spot deals in rich creations from traditional Spanish ingredients with a definite Gallic influence. It features warm decor, solicitous service, and a fine wine list. The owner was pondering retirement at time of last research, but hopefully it'll carry on for a year or 2.

⑪⑪⑪ El Majuelo, Plaza de la Fuente 8, T923 214 711. For great food at a fair price, head to this restaurant on the edge of the old town. Delicious foie, succulent meats roasted over the wood fire, delicate smoked fish, and a cheerful *comedor*. There's a *menú* for €25, rising to €35 at weekends, but this represents excellent value. Recommended.

⑪⑪⑪ El Pecado, Plaza Poeta Iglesias 12, T923 266 558. One of the city's more vanguardist eateries, this upstairs restaurant brings back a touch of colour and fun into modern design. Zebra stripes, bookshelves and rich red walls live up to the name (Sin), but there's substance here in abundance. The menu is startlingly original and innovative; try the turbot with onion ice cream. The *menú del día* is the price-conscious way to appreciate its charms at €17; it's also available at night in quieter times.

⑪⑪⑪ Víctor Gutiérrez, C San Pablo 80, T923 262 973, www.restaurantevictorgutierrez. com. A smart urban modern restaurant with nouvelle Spanish cuisine as well as heartier, traditional fare. Experimenting with different forms of cooking, and ingredients drawn from different cultures, the chef creates some memorable combinations; there's always something intriguing on offer. There's a €55 *menú*, or a 'surprise' degustation for €80. Recommended.

⑪⑪ Delicatessen, C Meléndez 25, T923 280 309. The beautiful patio – a wooden deck covered with a skylight dome – and worthwhile *menú del día* for €11 are reason enough to wander into this upbeat central café. It's also a popular spot for an evening drink; at night the lights come down, and DJs play moody electronic music.

⑪⑪ Mesón las Conchas, Rúa Mayor 16, T923 212 167. A top choice for a main-street bite, with excellent *raciones* and tasty *pinchos* to accompany a drink, as well as fuller choices. You can eat in the cheery upstairs dining room or out on the street. There's a wide choice, from salads and roasts to a delicately flavoured duck with honey glaze. It's all good value, especially considering its location.

⑪⑪ Momo, C San Pablo, T923 280 798, www. momosalamanca.com. A stylish modern restaurant and bar with excellent classy *pinchos* and a range of innovative modern Castilian cuisine downstairs. The *menú del día* is good for €12; mains are €10-20. There's plenty of vegetarian choice. It's also a good spot for breakfast, opening at 0800.

⑪ Sakana, C San Justo 9, T923 218 619. Rare for Northern Spain, this is a Japanese restaurant, pretty good and authentic too, although often booked out by tourist groups. The carpaccio-like beef *tataki* is very tasty, while the *menú de degustación* for 2 is a snip at €35. The decor is modern but typically thoughtful, with bamboo screens and hessian-clad walls. Another dining area offers more traditional Japanese seating.

¶¶ **Valencia**, C Concejo 15, T923 217 868. Fronting onto a small courtyard, this 50-year-old spot is devoted to bulls, with *corridas* on the telly and numerous photos of eminent Salamanca *toreros*; the current crop often drop by when in town. The tapas are delicious – try the chickpea stew if it's on, or the marinated raw sardine fillets – and the outside tables are the place to be. The interior *comedor* serves more substantial restaurant fare.

¶ **Casa de las Morcillas**, Plaza del Corrillo 18, T923 210 940. This spot, newly moved to better premises near the Plaza Mayor, has made *morcilla* its raison d'être, and has some 30 blood puddings from all over Spain, ranging from soft Cigales smeared on toast to spicy Zamoran or oniony Leonese varieties. Original and delicious.

¶ **Dulcinea**, C Pozo Amarillo 5, T923 217 843. Although it doesn't look up to much from the outside, this is a very reliable and likeable little place far from the tourist trail but only a short step from the Plaza Mayor. The fare is traditional for the region; a simple range of stews and meat dishes. Best value is at lunchtime, when there's a €9 *menú del día*; the *pollo al ajillo* (chicken pieces sizzled in garlic) is excellent if it's on.

¶ **La Viga**, C Consuelo 16, T923 210 904. When in Salamanca, do what the Salmantines do. Unfortunately, one thing they do is eat a lot of roasted pig face. Called *jeta*, it's actually very tasty, and this is the best place to try it.

¶ **Mesón Cervantes**, Plaza Mayor 15, T923 217 213. Reached up a steep staircase off the Plaza Mayor (try not to fall down it on your way out), this ultra-characterful joint is a Salamanca classic, a no-frills spot decorated in bodega style, offering tasty *pinchos* ranging from *jeta* – pig cheek – to battered prawns. The window in the sit-down area has unforgettable plaza views.

Cafés

Café Corrillo, C Meléndez 18, T923 271 917, www.cafecorrillo.com. Right in the centre, this long-running café opens at 0800 for breakfast, and also does *pinchos* and dinners. The downstairs dining area gets given over for regular concerts though; an atmospheric venue.

Juanita, Plaza de San Bual 21, T923 269 979. Situated on an engagingly dog-legged plaza, this café features warm, decadently ornate baroque decor in an intimate basement setting. These contrive to make it one of Salamanca's most loveable and atmospheric spots. Later in the evening it becomes a popular bar for *copas*.

Music Arte, Plaza Corrillo 20. An excellent place for breakfast, a friendly and stylish café near Plaza Mayor.

⊙ Bars and clubs

Salamanca *p326, map p328*
When the students are in town, Salamanca's nightlife can kick off any night of the week. The main night-owl area is on Gran Vía and around; Plaza de Bretón and C Varillas have a high concentration of spots.

Camelot, C Bordadores 3, T923 212 182. This no-frills *discoteca* occupies part of one of Salamanca's glorious stone buildings, in this case a still-working convent. It's quite a sight inside and takes the mickey with a DJ on an iron pulpit, grilles screening the upper floor, and cheapish drinks until late. No cover charge.

Capitán Haddock, C Concejo 15, T923 247 546. With plush, intriguing fittings and a small terrace in a quiet little courtyard in the heart of town, this romantic, stylish bar is much suaver than the blustering mariner after whom it's named. An atmospheric spot for a coffee or *copa*.

Cum Laude, C Prior 5, www.cvmlavde.com. It's worth popping in for a drink to admire its club's sandstone-clad pillars that recall traditional Salamanca architecture, and its dancefloor that's a mini replica of the Plaza Mayor. Long queues form later in the evening.

De Laval Genovés, C San Justo 27. One of Salamanca's best gay choices, with a spacious interior and cool shipboard decor that has earned it the nickname 'El Submarino'. It's in the heart of the main Salamanca bar zone.

El Savor, C San Justo 28, T923 268 576. This large and stylish bar packs out with people keen on dancing to salsa and other Latin American rhythms. It's a fun, uninhibited sort of place; if you want to get your feet moving right, there are free dancing classes at 2300 on Thu and Fri.

Potemkin, C Consuelo 2, T923 219 620. Another late opener in the Salamanca zone with heavyish rock music played loud. It's big, spacious and has a great atmosphere, particularly when there's a live band playing. Popular with people from all walks of life.

Tío Vivo, C Clavel 3. This intriguing bar is packed with curios; there's everything from machine guns and army uniforms to carousel horses, giving it a slightly macabre and dreamlike quality. It's a great place with a good atmosphere; there are live shows and live music several days a week, hefty coffees, and excellent G&Ts.

⊕ Entertainment

Salamanca *p326, map p328*
Teatro Liceo, Plaza de Liceo s/n, T923 272 290. A modernized theatre near the Plaza Mayor, with occasional flamenco and other performances.

⊛ Festivals and events

Salamanca *p326, map p328*
There always seems to be some type of fiesta at other times; student faculties combine to make sure there's never a dull moment.
7 Sep Salamanca's major fiesta is a 2-week binge of drinks, bullfights and fireworks.

○ Shopping

Salamanca *p326, map p328*
Bookshops
Librería Cervantes, C Azafranal 11, T923 218 602, www.cervantessalamanca.com, is one of many bookshops in this university city.

Food
A good thing to buy in Salamanca is ham; Guijuelo, one of the province's towns, is famous for it. The main shopping streets are north of the Plaza Mayor, along C Toro and C Zamora.

A convenient, if slightly overpriced, ham shop is **La Despensa**, Rúa Mayor 23, which has a good selection of all things piggy.

The market just below the Plaza Mayor is a good spot for food shopping.

⊖ Transport

Salamanca *p326, map p328*
Air
Salamanca's airport is 15 km east of town on the Avila road. Its only flights at the time of writing were a domestic connection to **Barcelona** and 2 weekly flights to **Paris**. Airport buses (€3) link to the centre; a taxi to or from the airport to the centre costs €15.

Bus
The bus station is west of town along Av Filiberto Villalobos, T923 236 717. Within the province, there are buses roughly hourly to **Alba de Tormes**, **Béjar** and **Ciudad Rodrigo**, among other destinations.

Further-flung destinations include **Avila** 4-6 weekdays, 2 at weekends, **Madrid** hourly, **Oviedo/Gijón** 4-5 daily (4½-5 hrs), **León** 4 daily, **Santiago** 2 daily (6 hrs), **Bilbao** 3 daily (6 hrs), **Zaragoza/Barcelona** 2 daily, **Zamora** more than hourly, **Valladolid** 6 daily, and **Cáceres** 10 daily (3½ hrs). There's also a daily bus to **Porto** in Portugal (5½ hrs) with a connection to **Lisboa** (9 hrs).

Taxi
For local taxis, call T923 250 000.

Train
The train station is northeast of town along Av de la Estación. There are 2 daily trains to **Burgos** (2½ hrs, €23), 7 to **Avila** (1 hr, €9.50), and 9 to **Valladolid** (1½ hrs, from €8.30). There are 7 daily trains to **Madrid** (2 hrs 45 mins, €19).

⊕ Directory

Salamanca *p326, map p328*
Internet There seems to be an internet café on every corner in Salamanca. They come and go like summer breezes. **Ciber** Rana, C Francisco Vitoria 5, is not the fastest, but is handily close to the cathedral. **Language schools** Apart from the university itself, which has a highly regarded Spanish-language programme, there are several smaller schools: **Letra Hispánica**, C Librerías 28, www.letrahispanica.com, has a reasonable reputation. **Laundry** Coin Laundry, Pasaje Azafranal 18, is a self-service laundromat in an arcade. **Medical services** Hospital Clínico, Paseo de San Vicente 58, T923 291 100. **Police** Call T092 or T923 194 433. The handiest police station is on the Plaza Mayor. **Post office** Gran Vía 25 near Plaza de la Constitución.

Contents

At a glance

⊖ **Getting around** Santander's linked by boat and plane to Britain. The coast is easily visited on the train, but grab a car to seek out the Picos de Europa's more spectacular spots.
◉ **Time required** 4-6 days.
☼ **Weather** Warm summers and cool wet winters.
✖ **When not to go** Winter, if walking in the Picos is your aim. Aug, if you like a beach to have a bit of space.

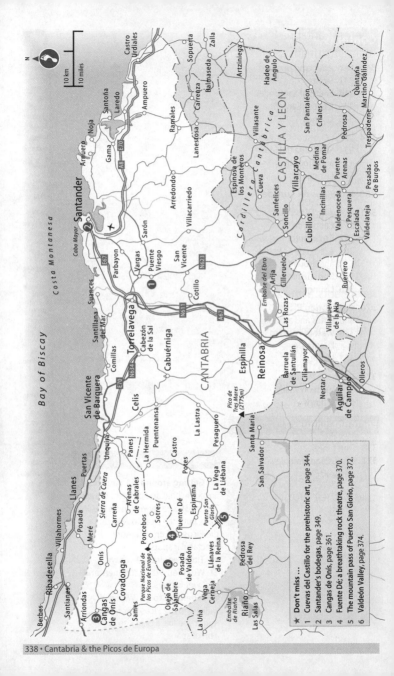

N

10km
10 miles

Castro
Urdiales

Zalla

Sopuerta

Artziniega

Hadeo de
Angulo

Quintaña
Martino Galíndez

Santoña

Gama

Laredo

Noja

Ampuero

Rañales

Balmaseda

Carrenza

San Pantaleón

Trespaderne

Pedrosa

Criales

Santander

Arnuero

E70

A8 E70

Lanestosa

Espinosa de
los Monteros

Villasante

Cueva

Cordillera Cantábrica

CASTILLA Y LEÓN

Medina
de Pomar

Puente
Arenas

Pesadas
de Burgos

Cabo Mayor

Arredondo

Villacarriedo

Villarcayo

Sarón

Parbayón

Vargas

Puente
Viesgo

San
Vicente

N623

Cotillo

Sanfelices

Soncillo

Cubillos

Incinillas

Valdenoceda

Pesquera

Escalada

Valdelateja

1

Cordillera Cantábrica

Embalse del Ebro

Arija

Cillerúelo

Las Rozas

Villanueva
de la Nía

Buerrero

Suances

Torrelavega

Santillana
del Mar

Cabezón
de la Sal

N611

A67

Espinilla

Reinosa

Olleros

Comillas

Cabuérniga

San Vicente
de la Barquera

N634

Celis

La Lastra

CANTABRIA

Barruelo
de Santullán

Cillamayor

Aguilar
de Campoo

Bay of Biscay

Puertas

Umquera

Panes

Puentenansa

La Hermida

Pesaguero

Castro

Pico de
Tres Mares
(2175m)

Néstar

Santa María

Llanes

Villahormes

Posada

Meré

Sierra de Cuera

Carreña

Arenas
de Cabrales

Sotres

Puente Dé

Potes

La Vega
de Liébana

San Salvador

Costa Montañesa

Ribadesella

Berbes

Santianes

Arriondas

Onís

Covadonga

Cangas
de Onís

Sames

Poncebos

4

Parque Nacional de
los Picos de Europa

Espinama

Puerto San
Glorio

5

Pedrosa
del Rey

Oleja
de Salambre

6

Posada
de Valdeón

Llánaves
de la Reina

La Uña

Vega
Cerneja

Embalse de
Riaño

Las Salas

Don't miss ...

★   1   Cuevas del Castillo for the prehistoric art, page 344.
    2   Santander's bodegas, page 349.
    3   Cangas de Onís, page 361.
    4   Fuente Dé; a breathtaking rock theatre, page 370.
    5   The mountain pass of Puerto San Glorio, page 372.
    6   Valdeón Valley, page 374.

Genteel Cantabria is an island of reaction between the more radical Asturians and Basques. Historically part of Castilla, it prospered for many years as that kingdom's main sea access, and is still known as a well-heeled sort of place: "people are prone to go to puerile lengths in their vanity about heraldry", claimed writer Gregorio Marañón in the early 20th century.

Way back beyond then, from 18,000 BC onwards, a thriving Stone Age population lived in the area. They've left many remains of their culture, most notably the superb cave paintings at Altamira. These are now closed to the public, but you can see a replica of their very sophisticated art; for a more authentic atmosphere, head to one of the smaller caves in the region.

Apart from the Picos de Europa, Cantabria's principal attraction is its coast. Santander itself has some superb beaches and excellent restaurants. Santillana del Mar is misnamed (it's not on the sea ...) but is within easy reach of the sand; it's a touristed but captivating and memorable town of stone mansions and cobbled streets, while Comillas has some startling modernista architecture, including a flamboyant Gaudí building.

For such a small area, the Picos de Europa has a deservedly high reputation among visitors, who eulogize this part of the vast Cordillera Cantábrica, which is blessed with spectacular scenery, superb walking, abundant wildlife and comparatively easy access. The Picos cover the corners of three provinces: Asturias, Cantabria and León, and have a fairly mild climate due to their proximity to the sea.

Santander and around

→ *Colour map 2, B5. Phone code: 942. Population:182,700.*

Still an important Spanish port, Santander has for years encouraged visitors to turn their attentions away from its industrial side and towards its series of superb beaches. These gird the barrio of Sardinero, which became a genteel and exclusive resort for the summering upper classes from the mid-19th century on. An earthier lifestyle can be found around the old centre, which has an excellent collection of restaurants and bars, where old wine bodegas have been converted into some of Northern Spain's best tapas venues. Santander's ferry link to Britain makes it many visitors' first point of entry into Spain; it's a relaxing and pleasant introduction to the country, which pleases more for its ambience and seaside than any cultural highlights.

Inland Cantabria is still very rural; mulecarts and cow traffic jams are still a common sight once off the main roads. The main road routes forge south to Palencia and Burgos respectively through attractive countryside. The principal towns in the area, Torrelavega and Reinosa, are both depressing and dull industrial centres, but there are enough small attractions to make a trip in the area interesting.

The eastern Cantabrian coast is a fairly uncomplicated place, with decent beaches and a sprinkling of resorts and fishing towns that attract many summer visitors from Madrid and the Basque lands. The nicest place by far is Castro Urdiales, while the large beach town of Laredo offers a great stretch of sand, a pretty centre, watersports and good sunny season nightlife. Smaller villages, such as Escalante, offer an inviting slice of rural Cantabria, but other sections of the coast between Santander and Laredo are blighted by ugly development. ▸▸ *For listings, see pages 346-353.*

Ins and outs

Getting there Santander is connected by bus and train with the rest of Northern Spain, and by plane domestically with Madrid and Barcelona, and internationally by **Ryanair** with London Stansted and Dublin among other European airports. It's linked by ferry from the centre of town to Plymouth and Portsmouth, operated by **Brittany Ferries**. ▸▸ *See Transport, page 352.*

Getting around Santander is long and thin, with its beaches a good couple of kilometres from its old centre. Fortunately, buses are very frequent, with nearly all lines plying the waterside. Taxis are fairly prevalent too; a fare from Sardinero to the centre won't cost much more than €4-5.

Best time to visit August is the best time to visit Santander, with the International Festival in full swing and superb weather guaranteed. The downside is the number of sunseekers, and the difficulty of finding accommodation, which increases in price. The sea is pretty chilly, so if you're not here to swim, April and May should offer decent warm weather and not too much rain; apart from Easter week, the accommodation is a bargain outside the summer months.

Tourist information and tours The main **Cantabrian tourist office** ① *T942 310 708, ofitur@cantabria.org, daily 0930-1330, 1600-1900,* is in the Mercado del Este building in the centre of town. They also run information kiosks at the ferry terminal and airport that are open to coincide with arrivals. There is a **municipal office** ① *T942 203 000, turismo@ ayto-santander.es, mid-Jun to mid-Sep daily 0900-2100, mid-Sep to Mar Mon-Fri 0900-1900,*

Sat 1000-1400, Apr to mid-Jun Mon-Fri 0830-1900, Sat and Sun 1000-1900, near the ferry terminal in the Jardines de Pereda park, as well as a **summer-only office** at the beach in Sardinero. A **tourist bus** ① *www.santandertour.com*, plies a circular route around the town and its beaches, with information and a 'hop-on hop-off' system. Tickets and schedules are available at the tourist office in the Jardines de Pereda.

From the Calderón jetty on the Paseo de Pereda, **passenger ferries** ① *T942 211 753, www.losreginas.com, single/return €2.30/4.30*, run across the bay to **Pedreña** (famous as the hometown of golfer Severiano Ballesteros) and **Somo**, from where you can walk along the extensive El Puntal beach. These are great boat trips on a pleasant day; in summer there are also circular boat trips of an hour (€9) or 2½ hours (€11.50).

Background

As the Reconquista progressed and the Moors were driven southwards, the north coast became increasingly important as an export point for Castilian produce from the expanding interior. The northern ports joined together in 1296 to form the **Hermandad de las Marismas**, a trading union that included Santander and nearby Laredo along with La Coruña and San Sebastián. Although Laredo was a more important port for much of Spain's Imperial period, Britain's Charles I picked Santander to sail home from after his incredible jaunt through France to Madrid in 1623 (see box, page 506).

Santander's major growth period as a port came in the 19th century; this was also the time that it achieved fashionable status as a resort, which it has retained. Despite the aristocratic feel of parts of the town, Santander was firmly in the Republican camp during the Civil War but finally fell in August 1937. Much of the town centre was destroyed in a fire in 1941, which originated in the Archbishop's palace. The Franco years didn't treat Santander too badly, though. So much so that a statue of the *caudillo* himself on horseback sat outside the town hall right until the last days of 2008, when he finally rode off into the sunset, considered to be a potential embarrassment to Santander's bid to be a 2016 Capital of Culture. The fascist street names remain in place, though.

Sights

Santander doesn't possess a wealth of historical buildings; the principal attraction is its picturesque shoreline, including excellent town beaches east of the centre. In the centre, the **cathedral** ① *Mon-Fri 1000-1300, 1600-2000, Sat 1000-1300, 1630-2000, Sun 1000-1330, 1700-2100*, is reasonably interesting. Largely destroyed by the 1941 fire, its church is dull, although the cloister offers a chance to relax from the street for a moment. The **crypt** ① *0800-1300, 1700-2000 (1600-2000 summer)*, around the back, is used for Masses, and is an intriguing little space, with curious stubby columns and ill-lit Roman ruins. A reliquary holds the silver-plated heads of San Emeterio and San Celedonio, the city patrons.

Nearby, the Ayuntamiento is backed by the excellent **Mercado de la Esperanza** with lashings of fruit, fish, meat and deli products; the place to buy your hams and olive oils if you're heading back home on the ferry.

Not far from here is the **Museo de Bellas Artes** ① *C Rubio 5, T942 239 485, Mon-Fri 1015-1300, 1730-2000, Sat 1000-1300; opens 30 mins later in summer; free*, a fairly mediocre collection. The highlight is many of Goya's *Horrors of War* prints, a dark and haunted series; there's also a portrait of Fernando VII, which isn't one of his better works. A small Miró is also notable, as are several sculptures by the late Basque, Jorge Oteiza, among them an expressive *Adam and Eve*.

The **Museo Marítimo** ① *C San Martín de Bajamar s/n, T942 274 962, Oct-Apr Tue-Sun 1000-1800, May-Sep Tue-Sun 1000-1930, €6*, on the waterfront, celebrates the city's fishing heritage, with good displays on navigation and boat building as well as a whale skeleton and some live fish and molluscs in tanks. There's a restaurant here with a good *menú del día*, which you can eat with great views of the bay.

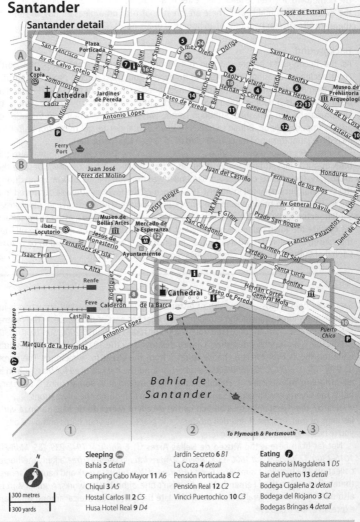

Santander

Santander detail

Sleeping 🛏
Bahía **5** *detail*
Camping Cabo Mayor **11** *A6*
Chiqui **3** *A5*
Hostal Carlos III **2** *C5*
Husa Hotel Real **9** *D4*
Jardín Secreto **6** *B1*
La Corza **4** *detail*
Pensión Porticada **8** *C2*
Pensión Real **12** *C2*
Vincci Puertochico **10** *C3*

Eating 🍴
Balneario la Magdalena **1** *D5*
Bar del Puerto **13** *detail*
Bodega Cigaleña **2** *detail*
Bodega del Riojano **3** *C2*
Bodegas Bringas **4** *detail*

300 metres
300 yards

The **Museo de Prehistoria y Arqueología** houses a collection of well-presented pieces from the province's past, many of which are creations of Neanderthal and modern man, and were found in several caves around the region. It was closed pending a move to a new location at time of research; check with the tourist office.

The **waterfront** is the nicest part of this area; it fills with people during the *paseo* and there's also a bike lane. Behind it the narrow streets are filled with tapas bars, small art

Bodegas Manzón **22** *detail*
Café Suizo **11** *detail*
Casa Albo **6** *detail*
Casa Lita **12** *detail*
La Casa del Indiano **7** *detail*
La Conveniente **5** *detail*

La Gaviota **17** *D1*
La Posada del
  Mar **10** *detail*
Las Hijas de
  Florencio **14** *detail*

Bars & clubs 🍸
Blues **24** *detail*
Floridita **16** *detail*
Rocambole **18** *detail*
Ventilador **20** *detail*

galleries, and antique shops. The **Puerto Chico** is the leisure marina; after passing this you come to the huge festival centre; quite attractive when floodlit, less winning by day.

The beaches

Past the festival centre, Avenida de la Reina Victoria heads for the sands past a millionaire's row of very upmarket houses (some of Northern Spain's most expensive residences).

The **Península de la Magdalena** protects the bay of Santander from the Atlantic and is topped by a flashy *palacio*. This was a gift from the city to the king but it now houses the renowned summer university that draws people from around the globe. Jan Morris described the building as 'like a child's idea of a palace, surrounded on three sides by the sea and on the fourth by loyal subjects'. A small **zoo** nearby holds marine animals.

On the bay side of the peninsula are a couple of pretty beaches, **Playa de la Magdalena** and **Playa de los Bikinis**; just around on the sea side is the artificial **Playa del Camello**, named for the humped rock that sticks out of the water opposite it.

Sardinero is the centre of the sand suburbs; an attractively unmodern collection of belle époque buildings that back two superb beaches named **La Primera** and **La Segunda**. The Primera is the beach to be seen at; it's backed by the elegantly restored casino and several pricey hotels. The Segunda is less crowded and usually gets better waves, either at the far end or around the spur that divides the two. Both are kept creditably clean and have enough sand that you're never hurdling bodies to reach the water. Sardinero can be reached by bus Nos 1, 2, 3, 4, 7, or 15 from the waterfront in the centre of town.

From the end of the Segunda beach, a coastal path begins that skirts a golf course around the Cabo Menor headland before reaching the **Mataleñas** beach (also accessible by car) and eventually the Cabo Mayor lighthouse.

Moving further west, the great beaches continue. Some of the best are around **Liencres**, some 12 km from the centre of Santander. The main strand here is the double beach of Valdearenas: the kiosk on the smaller of the two does great rabas for a seaside snack. There are some surfable waves here, and the beach is backed by a pretty *parque natural* of dunes. Nearby, **Arnia** and **Covachas** are other pretty beachy bays; Arnia has a bar-restaurant with great views.

South of Santander → *For listings, see pages 346-353.*

Puente Viesgo, 30 km south of Santander, is a peaceful spa village long used as a weekend retreat from Santander but of great interest because of the caves up on the hill above, 1.5 km from town and one of the highlights of the province.

Cuevas del Castillo

① *T942 598 425, May-Sep daily 1000-1300, 1600-1930; Oct-Apr Wed-Sun 0930-1555; entry is by guided tour in Spanish, but the guides speak very clearly and slowly and make every effort to be understood. €3; tours run roughly every hour and last 45 mins; daily visitors have a maximum limit; it's worth booking in summer and also in winter to avoid the lengthy wait for a group to form.*

The Cuevas del Castillo were home to thousands of generations of Neanderthal man and Cro-Magnon man (Homo sapiens); with the earliest occupation being dated at some 130,000 years ago. Both left extensive remains of tools and weapons (Teilhard de Chardin and Albert of Monaco both got their hands dirty in the excavations here), but Cro-Magnon man did some decorating in a series of paintings that extend deep into the cave complex;

these were discovered in 1903. The earliest efforts date from around 30,000 years ago and some are of several outlines of hands, created with red ochre. Interestingly, most of the prints found are of the left hand, suggesting that most folk were right-handed even back then. More sophisticated works are from later but still predate the more advanced work at Altamira. There are outlines of bison here too, as well as deer, and a long series of discs that has mystified theorists.

Although the quality of the art is nothing to touch Altamira, it's a much more satisfying experience to see the originals here than the replicas. It's atmospheric too, for the caves are fantastic; the one open for visits is a sort of Gothic cathedral in lime.

The tourist board of Cantabria produce an excellent booklet, *Patrimonio Paleolítico*, in Spanish but with clear details and well illustrated, detailing a number of other caves in the area with Palaeolithic art.

Liérganes

Picturesquely set alongside a lively burbling river, this sweet village makes a fine day trip from Santander or a peaceful overnight stop for a couple of days. Its centre is a blend of noble baroque stone mansions and turn-of-the-20th-century *indiano* dwellings, all sensitively restored. It's a popular summer retreat for wealthy Cantabrians, and has several intriguing *posadas* to stay in.

There's a small **tourist kiosk** ① *T942 528 021, aytolierganes@aytolierganes.es, summer Mon-Fri 1000-2000, winter Mon, Wed-Fri 1000-1500*, by the river that will give you a map of the town and can also advise about various marked walks in the verdant valley and surrounding hills.

Liérganes can be reached on regular **FEVE** *cercanía* trains from Santander. In a car, head along the A-8 motorway towards Bilbao from Santander, and take the Torrelavega turn off just after the Solares exit.

Eastern Cantabria → For listings, see pages 346-353.

Santoña and Escalante

Around the headland from Laredo, Santoña is a fishing town famous throughout Spain for its anchovies, which have DO (*denominación de origin*) status. Just 6 km short of it, the village of Escalante is redolent of past glories with its noble stone buildings kitted out with gnarled wooden balconies and *soportales* (ground floor wooden colonnades). It's a great spot to hole up for a couple of days and a really appealing slice of rural Cantabria, set on the edge of a wetland reserve with good birdwatching opportunities. On the western side of town, the solid parish church is set on the edge of green fields; a sizeable nearby monastery is another of several notable edifices.

Laredo

Part of the *Hermandad de las Marismas* (brotherhood of sea towns), Laredo was once an important port and the place from where Juana La Loca set sail in a fleet of 120 ships to her arranged marriage in Flanders; an ill-starred alliance that led to her complete mental breakdown. Her son Carlos V used the port too, to return to Spain weary and old, on his way to retirement and a peaceful death at the monastery of Yuste. In earlier times, Laredo was a big Roman seaport, named Portus Luliobrigensium, scene of a major naval engagement.

Laredo still nurses a handful of small fishing smacks in its harbour, but the town's sole focus these days is tourism, powered by its sunny climate and superb beach, **La Salvé**,

5 km of golden sand arcing round the bay. It's a big town, and there are kilometres of ugly resort housing along the beach; if you're prepared for that, it's a likeable place, particularly if you spend some time in its compact old town. It's worth visiting the 13th-century **Iglesia de San Francisco**, as well as sniffing out a tunnel carved in the 1860s that makes its way through the headland to a small harbour. Otherwise, relax on the sand and prepare for the lively summer nightlife. There's a cheerfully efficient **tourist office** ① *T942 611 096, daily 0930-1330, 1600-1900*, in the Alameda Miramar park.

Castro Urdiales and around

Eastern Cantabria's nicest town, Castro Urdiales is a good-humoured seaside place with just the right mixture of resort and original character to make it attractive. The coastline here has the Basque rockiness and Castro is still an important fishing port (famous for anchovies) with a big harbour and staunch nautical feel. The **tourist office** ① *Av de la Constitución, daily 0930-1330, 1600-1900*, is on the waterfront.

The **waterfront** is attractive and long; at its end is a decent beach, **Playa Brazomar**. At the other end of the harbour a couple of imposing buildings stand high over the town. The **castle**, now a lighthouse and space used for temporary exhibitions, preserves its Templar walls; nearby, the massive **church** is a surprising building of great architectural and artistic merit. The reliefs on the outside present strange but damaged allegorical scenes of animals kissing and other exotica, while the interior is beautifully Gothic, all arches and blue stained glass; the holy water is kept in a giant clam shell. A picturesque medieval bridge stands nearby. Further around the headland is a beautiful sheltered **rockpool**, occasionally used as a venue for concerts. Also worth checking is the extravagant and eclectic architecture of the early 20th-century **Toki-Eder** mansion on the main road leading east out of the centre.

Castro Urdiales is big on *traineras*, large rowing boats that are raced in regattas on the sea in fierce competition with other towns. These are testosterone-fuelled events that draw big crowds.

West of Castro, the village of **Islares** has a decent beach, but even better is **Oriñón**, an excellent stretch of sand dramatically set between rocky mountains, not too spoiled by the somewhat tasteless development behind it.

◉ Santander and around listings

For Sleeping and Eating price codes and other relevant information, see Essentials pages 31-39.

● Sleeping

Santander *p340, map p342*
As befits its resort status, Santander has dozens of places to stay. Many of these are in lofty price brackets, especially in the beachside barrio of Sardinero. There are several cheap *pensiones* around the bus and train stations, most fairly respectable if a bit noisy. Prices in Jul-Aug are outrageously high. Rates drop significantly once the summer rush is over.

LL Hotel Bahía, C Alfonso XIII 6, T942 205 000, www.gruposardinero.com. Standing proud overlooking the port and the bay, this modern hotel delivers not just on location but also on service, facilities and food. Rooms are spacious, with big beds to stretch out on, and great views over the water. You can get good deals via the website or packages with **Brittany Ferries**. Recommended.
LL Husa Hotel Real, Paseo de Pérez Galdós 28, T942 272 550, www.hotelreal.es. Santander's top hotel was commissioned by the king when the royal family started summering here in the early 20th century.

It's a luxurious and magnificent palace with a French feel to the decor; it has superb views over the bay and prices to match (a double in summer can cost up to €380). It's a byword for style and sophistication in these parts and has seen its fair share of celebrity guests.

L Hotel Vincci Puertochico, C Castelar 25, T942 225 200, www.vinccihoteles.com. With a great location right on the marina, this is a 4-star hotel with compact but comfortable rooms, the best of which look over the water. These cost about €25 more but are worth the extra. Overall, summer prices are too high for this standard of accommodation but you might feel the situation is worth it or get a better deal via a website. Can drop to **D** off season.

AL Hotel Chiqui, Av García Lago 9, T902 282 700, www.hotelchiqui.com. This large hotel is well placed at the quiet end of the Sardinero beaches. While service and staff aren't as professional as the **Real**, the front rooms have all the conveniences and superb views out to sea. Excellent off-season and weekend specials are on offer on the website.

C Hostal Carlos III, Av Reina Victoria 135, T942 271 616, www.hostalcarlos3.com. Quality beachfront accommodation doesn't always cost the earth. This century-old building offers light, comfortable rooms that offer pretty good value for Santander. Best, however, are the delightful owners.

C Jardín Secreto, C Cisneros 37, T942 070 714, www.jardinsecretosantander.com. This unusual, romantic place offers the substantial comfort and attentive welcome of a boutique hotel at the prices of a much inferior establishment. The rooms are individually decorated and delightful and there is indeed, a pretty little garden to relax in. Recommended.

D La Corza, C Hernán Cortés 25, T942 212 950. The only accommodation option in the heart of tapas and restaurant territory, this family-run spot sits right on the central Plaza del Pombo, a 1-min walk from the water. There's an old-fashioned austerity

about the place, but the rooms are spotlessly clean and spacious, and come with or without bathroom.

D Pensión Porticada, C Méndez Núñez 6, T942 227 817, www.hlaporticada.com. Convenient for the ferry and bus station, this is a good, friendly budget option. Most of the rooms have a mirador, and come with or without bathroom. The price difference is small, but there's nothing wrong with the spotless shared washrooms.

E Pensión Real, Plaza de la Esperanza 1, T942 225 787, pensionreal@hotmail.com. Good-value rooms in a warm and well-maintained family home. A very good deal at this price and located a block behind the town hall.

Camping

Camping Cabo Mayor, Ctra del Faro s/n, T942 391 542, www.cabomayor.com, is a year-round campsite on the Cabo Mayor headland, near the lighthouse and Matalenas beach north of Sardinero. The appealing location is complemented by great facilities including a pool and bungalows sleeping 2 or 4. It gets packed in summer so book ahead. Bus No 15 will take you there from the centre of town.

South of Santander *p344*

AL Gran Hotel Balneario, C Manuel Pérez Mazo s/n, Puente Viesgo, T942 598 061, www.balneariodepuenteviesgo.com. The waters of the town are reportedly effective for skin disorders and rheumatism; this massive spa hotel complex is the place to take them. These types of places are popular in Spain, and there are all manner of treatments available, as well as fine food, well-appointed rooms and pleasant grounds.

Liérganes *p345*

B Casona El Arral, C El Convento, T942 528 475, www.casonaelarral.com. The imposing bulk of this mansion sits on the edge of the old town, complete with its own baroque chapel. Rooms though, have a lighter touch, with plenty of space, and a warm, country-house feel. There are spacious grassy grounds and enough modern comforts like Wi-Fi to make for a very pleasant stay. Breakfast but no other meals available.

Santoña and Escalante p345

L San Román de Escalante, Ctra Escalante–Castillo s/n, T942 677 728, www. sanromandeescalante.com. This luxurious complex offers quality accommodation and excellent dining in a complex of modern and historic buildings near Escalante village. From the main road, turn into the village, then head through it and out the other side towards Castillo. 2 km further, you'll find the place, across the road from a gorgeous little Romanesque chapel.

C Posada Rivera de Escalante, C La Rivera 1, Escalante, T942 677 719, www. posadalarivera.com. On the main road through Escalante, this is a delightful *casa rural* decorated with a personal touch and much elan and colour. The rooms are invitingly rustic, with exposed beams and varnished floorboards, and there's warm personal service, Wi-Fi, advice on what to see in the surrounding area, and a truly great breakfast (€5-6 extra). Recommended.

Laredo p345

Most places to stay are unattractive but functional beach hotels, though surprisingly few are right on the beachfront road. There are also numerous apartments for rental.
B Miramar, Alto de Laredo s/n, T942 610 367, www.hmiramarlaredo.com. It would be staggering if there hadn't been a hotel of this name in Laredo; this isn't close to the sand but it has the best views in town, magnificent perspectives over the beach and bay from the steep road leading up to the Bilbao motorway. Apart from that it's simple but comfortable, and lonely but well-priced off-season.
D Pensión Esmeralda, Fuente Fresnedo 6, T942 605 219. Set in the old, hilly part of town this has attractive, clean doubles with

bath. It's a good budget option and has a café downstairs that'll sort you out with breakfast for €2 extra.
E Pensión Salomón, C Menéndez Pelayo 11, T942 605 081, is an excellent option despite an unremarkable exterior.
F Albergue Casa de la Trinidad, C San Francisco 24, T942 606 141. One of 2 hostels in the old town run by nuns, this sparklingly clean place is to be found up the side of the church of the same name; head through a metal gate. Facilities are excellent, with a good kitchen and comfy dorms, and the nuns (who are cloistered; if you need anything you speak to them through a hatch). When speaking to nuns, the convention is to address them *Ave María Purísima*, to which the stock reply is *Sin pecado concebida* (Hail Mary most pure/ Conceived without sin).

Castro Urdiales and around p346

A Hotel Las Rocas, C Flaviobriga 1, T942 860 400, www.lasrocashotel.com. Dominating the town beach, this large hotel has spacious rooms, most with sea view, and attentive service. It's pretty good value for this location and standard.
D Pensión La Mar, C La Mar 1, Castro Urdiales, T942 870 524. A simpler choice than **La Sota**, this central *pensión* is a good bet with decent en suite rooms with TV and heating. Some rooms have a streetside balcony; there's free Wi-Fi on offer too.
D Pensión La Sota, C Correría 1, Castro Urdiales, T942 871 188. This good-looking and sparklingly clean place is wonderfully located a street back from the water. The rooms come with TV and bathroom and are slightly overpriced in summer but good value at other times.

Camping

There's a campsite at **Oriñón** and a summer-only *fonda*; **Islares** is only a 20-min walk and has more to offer.

🍴 Eating

Santander *p340, map p342*

Santander's status as elegant holiday resort and active fishing port means there are a good selection of excellent places to eat. Top seafood restaurants and smart wine and *pincho* bars compete for attention with characterful ex-wine cellars and no-frills joints serving the best of fresh fish. Sardinero has excellent eating options, but for concentration and character, head for the old town: the streets backing the Paseo de Pereda, and especially around **Plaza Cañadío**, which is packed on summer nights. If you're travelling on a budget, ask the price before selecting a gourmet bar-top snack.

♛♛♛ Bar del Puerto, C Peña Herbosa 22, T942 212 939, www.bardelpuerto.com. One of the more upmarket choices on this foody stretch, this sleek spot serves up excellent tapas downstairs and seafood upstairs. After hours the lights dim and it becomes a cool and stylish bar.

♛♛♛ La Posada del Mar, C Castelar 19, T942 213 023, www.laposadadelmar.es. Closed Sun and all Sep. A well-established restaurant with a formidable wine list that's moved to newer premises just around the corner from its old haunts. They trot down to the local *lonja* daily for fish – try a whole salt-baked one, they're memorably juicy – but also demonstrate their know-how with meat and game bird dishes.

♛♛ Balneario la Magdalena, C La Horadada s/n, T942 032 107, www. balneariolamagdalena.com. Excellently located café and restaurant on the peaceful and calm Magdalena beach. The dining room inevitably has fantastic views and the seafood is of the highest order without breaking the bank. There's a huge range of fish and other dishes; the red mullet (*salmonete*) with a sea-urchin sauce is particularly good.

♛♛ Bodega Cigaleña, C Daoíz y Velarde 19. This warm, snug narrow bar is lined with wooden cabinets. It looks like the workshop of a mad alchemist convinced that the philosopher's stone was to be found at the bottom of a bottle of Rioja or *anis*. An excellent place for tapas, but you can also sit down for a meal; the menu focuses on game and other hearty fare. Recommended.

♛♛ Bodega del Riojano, C Río de la Pila 5, T942 216 750. This loveable bodega has what is, for Spain, an almost reverentially hushed atmosphere as people seem awed by the ageing wine bottles that line the place from floor to ceiling. This old wine merchants' is famous for its decoratively painted barrels. The *tortilla con bonito* (tuna omelette) is the best around, while there's a range of cheeses, cured meats and stews. *Raciones* cost €6-12. Closed for extensive renovations at last visit.

♛♛ Bodegas Bringas, C Hernán Cortés 47, T942 362 070. Closed Tue. An excellent tapas bar, one of several set in old wine merchants' warehouses. The atmosphere is great and the food good and well priced. It's a convivial spot with a tasty array of *pinchos* adorning its long bar.

♛♛ Casa Albo, C Peña Herbosa 15, T942 213 057, www.casaalbo.iespana.es. This unassuming place is long standing, family-run and produces some of Northern Spain's best paella, made with locally caught seafood. It really is sensational. Recommended.

♛♛ Casa Lita, Paseo Pereda 37, T942 364 830, www.casalita.es. Sporting a range of well-presented bar-top *pinchos* that won't break the bank, this features snug seating along the stone-clad wall and helpful service. Just browse the selection and pick something that takes your fancy – from basics such as delicious tortilla, to posher fare like duck ham canapés.

♛ Bodegas Manzón, C Hernán Cortés 57, T942 215 752. Open daily. This cavernous bar is big enough to park several buses in and is a Santander institution, having been in business more than a century. The huge vats of wine have the menu of cheap and cheerful *raciones* chalked up on the side; the smaller barrels still bear the names of the sherries and other wines that were once shipped from the port here. Chunky wooden tables and down-to-earth staff and customers add to the atmosphere. *Raciones* €3-10.

La Conveniente, C Gómez Oreña 9, T942 212 887. Open Mon-Sat from 1900. Another atmospheric bodega by Plaza Cañadio with a spacious, beamed interior, several shiploads of wine and a good variety of cheap food. It's a memorable place with its art nouveau panels about the only adornment to the chipped marble and aged wood, all with a patina of decades of chatter accompanied by a pianist on a honky-tonk keyboard.

La Gaviota, C Marqués de la Ensenada 35, T942 221 106. One of a series of downmarket but deservedly popular seafood restaurants in a block of the Barrio Pesquero, an earthy zone by the fishing harbour. All of them offer cheap, cheerful, and generously proportioned *raciones* of fish and seafood, as well as paella. Sardines or anything else off the grill are recommendable.

Other spots in the Barrio Pesquero include the small but excellent **La Chulilla**, and the popular **Los Peñucos**, run by the father of football star Iván de la Peña. Take bus No 4 or 14 from anywhere on the Santander waterfront to get here.

Las Hijas de Florencio, Paseo de Pereda 23, T686 160 260. Old-time in feel, with its ancient floor of coloured tiles and high ceiling, this amicable double-entrance bar draws an animated local crowd from morning coffee time onwards. Tasty and fairly priced bartop snacks, an optimistic buzz, a takeaway cheese counter, and plenty of wine make this a favourite.

Cafés

Café Suizo, Paseo de Pereda 28, T942 215 864. This large and light 2-level café's white wooden balustrades give it the feeling of a film set. It's well known as one of the best breakfast spots in town, with a range of sandwiches, pastries and little rolls, as well as a large terrace out on the waterfront road.

La Casa del Indiano, Mercado del Este s/n, T942 074 660. The recently renovated 19th-century market now houses a variety of specialist shops (including a good little wine shop), as well as this cheerful café/bar that takes up half the building and makes a great stop at any time of day.

Santoña and Escalante *p345*

San Román de Escalante, Escalante s/n, T942 677 728, www.sanromandeescalante. com. Some 2 km from the village of Escalante, this restaurant is set superbly in an old mansion house furnished with beautiful art and antiques. The cuisine is of the highest order; the memorable seafood, such as monkfish on crab paste, has won it many plaudits. Rooms also available (see Sleeping).

Laredo *p345*

For tapas, restaurants and bars, head up the steps next to the town hall to the cobbled old-town street C Rúamayor, a long, narrow affair with plentiful choice.

La Abadía, C Rúamayor 18, T942 611 489, www.mesonlaabadia.com. Attractively set in a house partly dating from the 15th century, this restaurant has a fairly traditional sort of Spanish menu drawing from different parts of the country. The paella is excellent, as is the roast lamb, but don't decide until you've found out what the stew of the day is (*guiso del día*).

Castro Urdiales and around *p346*

Castro has a good eating scene, with plenty of fish restaurants and, along C Rúa, running parallel to the waterside, a series of simple but convivial tapas bars: try **La Bodeguita** at No 4. C Ardigales also has some good eating options.

El Puerto, C Santa María s/n, T942 870 976, www.asadorelpuerto.com. Perched on top of the *lonja* by the fishing harbour, just below the church, this spot has a fabulous covered terrace offering great views over the bobbing boats and charming waterside. The menu looks seaward, with juicy mussels, tuna *ventresca* (tender meat from the belly region), and anchovies all tasty.

¶¶ El Segoviano, Plaza del Ayuntamiento s/n, T942 861 859. On the main plaza a few steps from the waterfront, this low-beamed restaurant serves up heavier fare than the seafood-based places that characterize Castro. Roast meats are the order of the day, with suckling pig a particularly tender speciality.

¶¶ Mesón Marinero, Plaza del Ayuntamiento s/n, T942 860 005, www.mesonmarinero. com. An excellent restaurant with a wooden terrace, under the arcade in the main plaza. The seafood, of which there is a huge variety, is superb and is allowed to stand on its own merits rather than being smothered in other flavours. The *marmitakos* (spicy Basque fish stews) are especially tasty, and the grilled sardines reliably good.

⊙ Bars and clubs

Santander *p340, map p342*
Blues, C Gómez Oreña 15, T942 314 305. A packed and popular bar with a good mix of people. The music, as you may have guessed, rests on a base of blues and soul.
Floridita, C Bailén s/n. A cheerful and very lively bar, with a youngish crowd and un-pretentious scene. It's got a Cuban theme, a little terrace, free Wi-Fi, and a fine attitude. They specialize in daiquiris and mojitos.
Rocambole, C Hernán Cortés 24. A late-running bar with frequent live jazz and blues and a fun dancefloor. There are often 'open jam' nights where anyone with an instrument can join in.
Ventilador, Plaza Cañadio s/n. A popular bar with outdoor tables on this lively night-time square. The atmosphere is a bit more relaxing in the quieter early evening; later on in summer it's more or less a take-away for people congregating in the square.

Laredo *p345*
Cafe IV, C Rúa Mayor 12. More a bar than a café, this cheerful nightspot is decorated with pseudo-Egyptian murals and has a few tables out on the street that are eagerly sought after. As well as a selection of wines, they have a couple of Belgian beers on tap.

⊙ Entertainment

Santander *p340, map p342*
Bahía Cinema, Av Marqués de la Hermida s/n, www.cinesa.es. A big-release cinema.
Filmoteca de Cantabria, C Bonifaz 6, T942 319 310. Arthouse films and movie festivals.
Gran Casino, Plaza Italia s/n. Open 2000-0400 (0500 in summer). Dress code and proof of age regulations apply. There's a €5 cover charge.
Palacio de Festivales, C Castelar s/n. A spacious venue for concerts and exhibitions.

⊙ Festivals and events

Santander *p340, map p342*
28 Jul The province's main rowing regatta takes place during Semana Grande, Santander's major fiesta.
Aug International Festival, www.festival santander.com. Santander's major event of the year, with some top musical and theatrical performances. The liveliest street action comes at its end, which coincides with the fiesta of the city's patron saints.

⊙ Shopping

Santander *p340, map p342*
Santander's main shopping streets are near the town hall, cathedral and to the west.
Librería Estudio, Paseo Calvo Sotelo 19. A good bookshop with a largish selection.

⊙ Activities and tours

Santander *p340, map p342*
Racing Santander, www.realracingclub.es, yo-yo between the *Primera* and *Segunda*

divisions in Spanish football. At time of writing, they had been in the top flight for a little while, and entertain the likes of **Real Madrid** in their stadium in Sardinero. Tickets can be bought at the stadium on Fri and Sat for a Sun fixture, as well as from 2 hrs before the game.

⊖ Transport

Santander *p340, map p342*
Air
Air services arrive at the Parayas airport, 5 km southwest of the centre. ALSA runs buses to the airport every 30 mins or so (€1.50, 15 mins), and also connect the airport directly with other cities, such as **Laredo** and **Bilbao**, check their website www.alsa.es for timetables. A taxi costs about €15 from the centre. Ryanair currently serve this airport from **London** Stansted, **Rome** Ciampino, **Dublin**, **Frankfurt** Hahn, Weeze, and **Milan** Orio al Serio, as well as from **Madrid**, **Alicante** and **Reus**. Iberia run domestic flights from here to **Barcelona** and **Madrid** as well as other Spanish cities. The airport phone number is T942 251 004.

    Airlines Iberia, Plaza Pombo s/n, www.iberia.es.

Bus
There's a handy online timetable at www.santandereabus.com, or you can phone the bus station on T942 211 995. Many buses ply routes from Santander to other Spanish cities. 5 a day go to **Burgos** (3 hrs) and on to **Madrid** (6 hrs, €29), while buses east to **Bilbao** (90 mins, €7) are almost hourly. Several a day follow the coast westwards as far as **Gijón** and **Oviedo** (10 daily, 2½-3 hrs) , while there are also buses serving **Zaragoza**, **Valladolid**, **A Coruña** and others.

    Within Cantabria, there are 5 daily buses (2 on Sun) running to **Santillana del Mar** (40 mins) and **Comillas** (55 mins) and 10-15 daily buses to **San Vicente de la Barquera** (1 hr if direct). **Laredo** is served roughly hourly, as is **Castro Urdiales** (1¼ hrs), while

for the **Picos de Europa**, there are 1-3 buses daily to **Potes**, some of which have a connection to **Fuente Dé**.

Car
Car hire Atesa, C Marcelino Sanz de Santuola, T942 222 926, www.atesa.es; Hertz, Puerto Ferrys, T942 362 821, www.hertz.es.

Ferry
Brittany Ferries, T0871 244 0744, www.brittany-ferries.co.uk, run a service from **Plymouth** and **Portsmouth**, UK, to Santander. There's 1 weekly sailing on each route, taking around 24 hrs from Portsmouth and 20 hrs from Plymouth. Prices are variable but can usually be found for about €80-100 each way in a reclining seat. A car adds about €170 each way, and cabins start from about €90. The service runs from mid-Mar to mid-Nov.

Taxi
If none on the street call, T942 333 333.

Train
Santander is both on the national RENFE network and the private coastal FEVE service. The stations are next to each other (as is the bus station). Call the RENFE station on T942 280 202; the FEVE station on T942 364 718.

    RENFE runs 3 trains daily to **Madrid** (4½-5 hrs, €48) and 7 or so to **Valladolid** and **Palencia** on the same line. There are *cercanía* trains to **Torrelavega** and **Reinosa** every 30 mins.

    FEVE trains run east to **Bilbao** 3 times daily (2½ hrs, €9) and west along the coast as far as **Oviedo**, **Gijón** and **Ferrol** in Galicia twice daily (to Oviedo/Gijón, it's 4 hrs and costs €16). It's a fairly slow but scenic service, and invaluable for accessing smaller coastal towns.

South of Santander *p344*
Bus
Puente Viesgo is accessible by bus from **Santander** (operated by various companies;

40 mins) up to 6 times daily. **Liérganes** is served 4 times daily (40 mins). Liérganes is also served by regular **FEVE** *cercanía* train from Santander.

Laredo *p345*
Bus
Frequent buses connected Laredo and **Santander** (every 30 mins, 40 mins).

Castro Urdiales and around *p346*
Bus
Castro Urdiales is connected very regularly by bus with both **Santander** (more than hourly, 80 mins) and **Bilbao**, which is only 30 mins away.

🜚 Directory

Santander *p340, map p342*
Internet and telephone Iber Locutorio, C Burgos 24, offers cheap internet and phone calls; **La Copia**, C Lealtad 13, T942 227 680 (by cathedral). **Post office** The main post office is on C Alfonso XIII, at the corner with Av de Calvo Sotelo.

West Coast of Cantabria

Cantabria's western coast has plenty to detain the visitor. As well as some good beaches, there are some very attractive towns; these are headed up by Santillana del Mar, a superb ensemble of stonework that also boasts the flash museum at nearby Altamira, the site of some of the finest prehistoric art ever discovered. Comillas will appeal to fans of modernista architecture and, beyond, the coast continues towards Asturias, backed spectacularly by the bulky Picos de Europa mountains. There are some fine beaches right along this stretch. ▸▸ *For listings, see pages 357-359.*

Santillana del Mar and around → *For listings, see pages 357-359. Colour map 2, B5.*

Although it may sound like a seaside town, it isn't; it's 4 km inland. A cynical old saying claims that it's the town of three lies: '*Santillana no es santa, no es llana, y no hay mar*' (Santillana's neither holy nor flat, and there's no sea). Nevertheless, Santillana is delightful, despite the high number of strolling visitors captivated by the architecture of the place that Sartre immortalized (albeit in *Nausea*) as "the most beautiful village in Spain". While it's still a dairy region – cows are still brought back into the village in the evening – every building within the old town is now devoted to tourism in some form. It's definitely worth staying overnight, as the bulk of the visitors are on day trips, and the emptier the town, the more atmospheric it is. Try and come out of season, and avoid weekends if possible. The nearby Altamira museum is also a big draw for visitors.

Background
Founded by monks, the town became important in the Middle Ages due to the power of its monastery, which had a finger in every pie cooking. What the town is today is a result of the nobility wresting control of the feudal rent system from the abbot in the 15th century. Once the peasants were filling secular coffers, the landowners grew wealthy, donated money in exchange for titles and started trying to outdo each other in ostentatious *palacio* construction. Though undoubtedly antidemocratic and tasteless at the time, these buildings are exceedingly beautiful.

Sights
The **tourist office** ① *C Jesús Otero 20, T942 818 251, santillana@cantabria.org, daily 0900-1330, 1600-1900*, at the edge of the old town near the main road, is busy and brusque. They supply a decent map/guide to the town in a variety of languages.

The **Colegiata** ① *daily 1000-1330, 1600-1830 (closes 1930 in summer), €3 (includes entrance to the Diocesan Museum at the other end of town)*, sits at the end of the town and has a jumbled, homely façade in orangey stone. The current Romanesque building replaced a former Benedictine monastery in the 12th century. An arcaded gallery runs high above the portal, and a round belltower to the right outrages symmetry fans. Wander around the side to gain access to the church and cloister, whose shady Romanesque arches also feature many different motifs on the capitals, ranging from mythological creatures to geometric figures and Biblical scenes.

The church is spacious with impressive stone vaulting; there is some of the *ajedrezado jaqués* chessboard patterning originally used in the town of Jaca and disseminated through Northern Spain by wandering masons and pilgrims. The building is dedicated to Santa Juliana, a third-century saint for whom the town is named. She was put to death by her husband for not consummating their marriage on their wedding night (or any other night); her bones were originally brought here by the community of monks that founded the monastery and town. One of her achievements in life was the taming of a demon, whom she used to drag around on a rope (to the despair of their marriage counsellor); scenes from her life can be seen on her tomb in the centre of the church, and the *retablo*, a 16th-century work. There's a figure of Juliana in the centre, standing above a chest that holds various parts of her earthly remains.

The other major sight in town is the collection of grandiose *palacios* emblazoned with coats-of-arms (in some cases hugely oversized). They are concentrated down the main street, **Calle Cantón**, and around the main square. The square has two Gothic towers, one of which is an exhibition hall. In front of the church, the former **abbot's house** was later occupied by the Archduchess of Austria; further down this street note the former marquis' house (now a hotel). The **Casa de los Villa** near the main road has a façade emblazoned with a pierced eagle and the motto *un buen morir es honra de la vida* (a good death honours the life); a precursor to the Falangist Civil War cry *¡Viva la muerte!*

As Santillana is a popular place to spend holidays, there's always plenty on for young and old, with frequent temporary exhibitions, craft displays and festivals. Permanent attractions include a decent **zoo** ① *www.zoosantillanadelmar.com, daily 0930-dusk, €16, kids €10*, on the edge of town, which has a snow leopard among its constricted but cared-for captives. There is a **Torture Museum** ① *daily 1000-2000, 2200 in summer, €4*, near the church with all sorts of horrible fantasies in iron used during the Inquisition and other dark periods in human history. Near the church, the **Fundación Jesús Otero** ① *Plaza Francisco Navarro s/n, T942 840 198, daily 1000-1330, 1600-1930 (1700-2100 summer), free*, displays works by the 20th-century sculptor of the same name, a Santillana local. The **Diocesan Museum** ① *Tue-Sun 1000-1330, 1600-1830 (closes 1930 summer, also open Mon); joint ticket with the Colegiata, €3*, on the main road, which is a good example of its kind, has a large collection that includes some Latin American pieces brought back to Santillana by *indianos*.

Altamira Caves
① *T942 818 005, http://museodealtamira.mcu.es, Jun-Sep Tue-Sat 0930-1930, Sun 0930-1500, Oct-May Tue-Sat 0930-1700, Sun 0930-1500, last admission to the Neocueva 1 hr before closing; €3, free Sat after 1430 and Sun all day. To apply to visit the original cave, write to the museum at Museo de Altamira, 39330 Santillana del Mar, or at informacion.maltamira@mcu.es, but you have to have a serious scientific reason to gain admission.*

In 1879, in the countryside 2 km from Santillana, a man and his daughter were exploring some caves only discovered a few years before when they looked up and saw a cavalcade of animals superbly painted in ochre and charcoal. The man, Marcelino Sanz de Sautuola, was interested in prehistoric art, but the quality of these works far exceeded any known at the time. Excitedly publishing his findings, he wasn't believed until several years after his death, when the discovery of similar paintings in southern France made the sceptics reverse their position. The paintings are amazing; fluid bison, deer and horses, some 14,000 years old. They became a major tourist attraction, but the moist breath of the visitors began to damage the art and admission had to be restricted; the waiting list is about three years at present and may be entirely terminated in the future. Enter the Neocueva. It's a replica of part of the original cave and paintings and is part of a museum that puts the art in context. The exhibition begins with an excellent overview of prehistoric hominids so you can get your Neanderthals sorted from your Cro-Magnons before moving on to more specific displays about the Altamira epoch and ways of life at the time.

The Neocueva itself is accessed in groups with a guide; there can be quite a wait if the museum is busy. It's an impressive reconstruction, and the explanations are good. You can admire the replica paintings, particularly as they were probably painted from a prone position but, although impressive, they lack some of the emotion that comes from actually feeling the incomprehensible gulf of 14,000 years. All told, it's a very good museum and an impressive substitute for the original cave, which the government were absolutely right to protect from destruction.

Suances
This low-key summer resort northeast of Santillana has a series of fine sandy beaches popular with swimmers and surfers alike. Playa de los Locos, with a picturesque setting backed by cliffs, is one of the best for riding the waves, but it gets busy. La Tablia, the next one along, has consistent surf too. Don't leave valuables in your car in the clifftop parking at these places.

Comillas → Colour map 2, B5.
Comillas is a fashionable Cantabrian beach resort and has been popular with the well-to-do for over a century. As well as its beach and pleasant old centre, the town is worth a visit for its architecture, out of the ordinary for a seaside summer town. Rather than drab lines of holiday cottages, it boasts some striking modernista buildings ostentatiously perched on the hilltops around the town. They are a legacy of Catalan architects who were commissioned by competitive local aristocrats to create suitably extravagant residences for them. The **tourist office** ① T942 722 591, oficinadeturismo@comillas.es, daily 0930-1330, 1600-1900 (1700-2000 summer), in the town hall building on the main road through Comillas, is efficient and helpful.

The town's most unusual architectural flourishes are found in Gaudí's El Capricho. Rightly named (the caprice), it's an astonishingly imaginative flight of fancy embossed with bright green and yellow tiles and adorned with Mediterranean sunflowers. The best feature is a whimsical tower, an ornate Muslim fantasy with a balcony. The restaurant that occupied the interior is now closed, so the only access is via the Palacio de Sobrellano.

Next door to El Capricho is the **Palacio de Sobrellano** ① Apr-Jun and Sep-Oct Tue-Sun 0930-1400, Jul and Aug daily 1000-2100, €3 palace, €3 chapel (guided tour), commissioned by the Marqués de Comillas, a heavy pseudo-Gothic structure full of quirky furniture. A small plot in the parish graveyard wasn't the marquis's vision of resting in peace, so he had an ornate chapel put up next to the family summer home to hold flashy tombs that would have done justice to a Renaissance monarch.

On the eminence opposite, the **Universidad Pontificia** was built as a theological college in similarly avant-garde style. It's a majestic and grandiose structure in reddish stone that dominates the town. Whether the priests-in-training were imbued with Christian humility in such a building is open to question, but in any event the college moved to Madrid in 1964. The building is now subject to various plans for its future and is not open for visits.

The town itself has several attractive squares and mansions that seem positively modest by comparison. Keep your eyes up as you wander around to appreciate some of the fine carved balustrades. The cobbled Plaza de la Constitución is at the heart of the area and is winningly beautiful, with fabulous balconies and rustic rubble masonry. There are two good beaches 10 minutes' walk from the centre. West of Comillas is another strand, **Playa Oyambre**, with a campsite and cheap but tasty restaurant.

San Vicente de la Barquera → *Colour map 2, B4.*

Although blessed with a stunning mountain backdrop (when you can see it for the mist), San Vicente is a fairly low-key although pleasant resort. While the town's seafood restaurants and natural setting at the mouth of two rivers appeal, the attractive old-town streets have been surrounded by some fairly thoughtless modern development. The architectural highlight is the transitional Gothic **Iglesia de Nuestra Señora de los Angeles**, which has a wooden floor like a ship's deck and attractive Gothic vaulting. The church was built in the 13th century, when Romanesque was going pointy, and it's an interesting example of this phase. There are good views from here over the river estuary and the long bridge crossing it.

On the same ridge, the **castle** ① *Tue-Sun 1030-1330, 1600-1800 (1700-2000 summer)*, €1.20, is in reasonable shape but isn't overly compelling. There's an exhibition of the town's history inside. The big **tourist office** ① *Av Generalísimo 20, T942 710 797, daily 0930-1330, 1600-1900, turismosanvicente@cantabria.org*, is on the main street; the Fascist street names live on for some reason.

◉ West Coast of Cantabria listings

For Sleeping and Eating price codes and other relevant information, see Essentials pages 31-39.

◉ Sleeping

Santillana del Mar *p354*
Santillana has a great selection of characterful old-town hotels, but it also has several that are less appealingly situated on the main road, or worse, in an ugly expansion on the other side of it that tried to retain that old-town look but failed. However, there are enough in the old centre itself to make sure you end up there, though you should definitely book ahead in summer. Many private homes put signs out advertising *camas* or *habitaciones* at peak time; some of these are very good options.
LL La Casa del Marqués, C Cantón 26, T942 818 888, www.turismosantillanadelmar. com. Santillana's priciest hotel is excellently set in a large *palacio* that belonged to the local marquis, who had to display his superior status with 3 coats of arms. The interior decoration is simpler, with attractive wooden furniture but numerous facilities. Service lets down the overall effect, but it's still a memorable place to stay.
L Parador Gil Blas, Plaza Ramón Pelayo 11, T942 028 028, www.parador.es. In a modernized *palacio* on the beautifully bare

Plaza Mayor, this parador is named after a famous fictional character from Santillana created by the French novelist Lesage in the 18th century. There's a good restaurant, and the rooms have every comfort. Another parador, **Parador Santillana**, sits on the same square, and is slightly cheaper, but not much more so, and it's not quite as appealing.
A Altamira, C Cantón 1, T942 818 025, www. hotelaltamira.com. This is cheaper than the preceding options but also characterfully set in another sumptuous *palacio*, with appropriate decor. The patio restaurant is a picturesque spot for a drink, but the food is overpriced for what it is.
B Hotel Joseín, C Manuel Noriega 27, T942 720 225, www.hoteljosein.com. On the eastern side of town, this rather ugly budget hotel doesn't look up to much from outside, but its position more than makes up for it. Perched right over the beach, it boasts stunning sea views from the big windows of all the rooms. An extra €20 gets you a balcony hanging over the sand. There's an on-site restaurant with overpriced seafood but a €12 *menú del día*.
B Posada La Casa del Organista,
C Los Hornos 4, T942 840 352, www.casadelorganista.com. Set in a smaller but still impressive 18th-century home; this is a welcoming place with lovely wooden

furnishings and rustic bedrooms. The quality of the welcome, the stone walls, old-time atmosphere, and sharp off-season prices (**D**) make this a great place. Recommended.

C Esmeralda, C Antonio López 7, T942 720 097, www.hostalesmeralda.com. This good, friendly choice is right in the centre, set in a great old stone building. The rooms are large (with good duplex family units) and sensitively modernized, good off-season prices on offer (**D-E**). Restaurant downstairs.

D Pensión Vega de Pas, Paseo del Muelle 9, T942 722 102. An upmarket *pensión* with good facilities, this is comfy if not stylish and overlooks the beach 5-10 mins' walk from the centre of town.

D Posada Ansorena Y Echevarria, C Cantón 10, T942 818 228, ansorena@hotmail. com. This delightful stone mansion is right on the main cobbled street and makes a great place to stay. Inside it's all rustic dark wooden furniture and creaking floorboards; rooms are large and varied, many with a balcony overlooking the garden. There's also a guest lounge with board games. Breakfast included; very good value.

D Posada las Ijanas, Barrio la Puentuca 10, Vivedo, T942 888 964, www.posadalasijanas. com. 3 km east of Santillana on the CA-131, this is an appealing rural hotel decorated in rustic style. There are few rooms, all new and thoughtfully appointed. The owners are very friendly and can advise on walking in the area. Breakfast features home-baking and fresh juices and can be taken on the patio.

E Casa Octavio, Plaza de las Arenas s/n, T942 818 199, www.hospedajeoctavio.com. A peaceful and very attractive spot to find a bed in an alley off the Plaza de las Arenas by the side of the church. There's a variety of rooms on offer.

San Vicente de la Barquera *p357*
You'll have no problems finding a room on spec; there are many places.

C Hotel Luzón, Av Miramar 1, T942 710 050, www.hotelluzon.net. This imposing centenarian mansion dominates the heart

of town, and its attractive recent conversion to a hotel makes it San Vicente's most recommendable accommodation choice. It's not as luxurious as you might imagine from the outside but it's comfortable; spacious rooms, some with water views, eager-to-please staff, fair prices, and modern conveniences make it a sound choice.

E Pensión Liébana, C Ronda 2, T942 710 211. This *pensión* is right in the centre of things and has decent rooms with bathroom and TV, which become exceedingly cheap (**F**) once summer is over.

🍴 Eating

Santillana del Mar *p354*
The hotel restaurants are rather unremarkable, and disappointingly there's no eating option that reaches the same standard as some of the sleeping choices. There are several tourist-trap places too.

♥♥ El Castillo, Plaza Mayor 6, T942 818 377, www.elcastillosantillana.com. Although in the heart of the town, this bar/restaurant next to the parador is refreshingly unpretentious and does some good dishes at reasonable prices. The *menú de cocido* is particularly hearty; broth followed by a big serve of chickpeas and stewed pork cuts. There's a *menú del día* for €14.

♥♥ Gran Duque, C Escultor Jesús Otero Orena, www.granduque.com. Closed Jan-Feb. The most appealing of the town's restaurants, this has views over the surrounding meadows and a warmly welcoming interior with brick, wooden beams, and clay tiles. There's much attractive seafood on the list, including a delicious seafood salad, and everything's well presented but unpretentious.

Comillas *p356*
Comillas has a reputation for being a pricey place to dine, but the quality is generally good.

♥♥ Filipinas, C de los Arzobispos s/n, T942 720 375. This is a lively bar on the intersection in the middle of town, where the locals eat. There are simple *raciones* of seafood and meat, as well as hearty stews in tin pots. The abundant €14 *menú del día* is popular, so you'll often wait for a table, especially at weekends.

Gurea, C Ignacio Fernández de Castro 11, T942 722 446. Closed Sun afternoon and Mon. A Basque restaurant that lives up to all the good things that implies. Mains such as *bacalao a la vizcaína* (a cod dish) or *kokotxas* (hake cheeks in spicy sauce; excellent) cost €12-20 and are served in a cosy atmosphere.

Siglo, Plaza Constitución 11, T942 722 257. The cosy interior of this family-run bar sports hams, hanging peppers, and just a few tables where you can enjoy solid home-style cooking at decent prices. Ask for whatever's good that day; the *solomillo ibérico*, juicy and tender chunks of prime pork cooked with garlic, is a safely tasty bet.

San Vicente de la Barquera *p357*

There are numerous seafood restaurants along the main street through town, with everything from downmarket bars selling cheap and delicious grilled sardines to upmarket *marisquerías* peddling crustaceans.

Annua, Paseo de la Barquera s/n, T942 715 050, www.annuagastro.com. With an unforgettable waterside position right on the estuary, this modern restaurant lives up to its location with excellent, creative cuisine. The staple here is seafood: they have their own oyster farm. There's a degustation menu (€66 including drinks) brimming with innovation and light-heartedness. It's a romantic place for a sunset drink too. Recommended.

Boga-Boga, Av Generalísimo, T942 710 135. The food at Boga-Boga lives up to its excellent name, which is a traditional Basque sea shanty. There's a great variety of seafood – their speciality is a lobster stew for 2 – and some good wines to knock back with it. There are also decent rooms upstairs.

Augusto, C Mercado 1, T942 712 040. This excellent seafood restaurant sees plenty of visitors at its terraced tables and in its ship-

like interior. There are plenty of good-value mixed platters to choose from; you can have a good meal here at a number of different price levels depending on what crustaceans take your fancy. They also do a good line in tasty paellas and rices.

Bars and clubs

Comillas *p356*

Don Porfirio, C Victoriano Pérez de la Riva 2, T942 722 516. In the old town, this is a friendly and boisterous bar with internet access, a Mexican feel, cold beer and pizzas. In summer, the garden gets going, with picnic-style wooden seats on the grass.

Pamara, C Comillas s/n, is a good summer *discoteca* with an upmarket set. There's sometimes live music or other events on winter weekends too.

Transport

Santillana del Mar *p354*
Bus
There are 5 daily buses (2 on Sun) running to and from **Santander** (30 mins).

Comillas *p356*
Bus
There are 5 daily buses, 2 on Sun, running to and from **Santander** via **Santillana del Mar**. They continue westwards to **San Vicente de Barquera**.

San Vicente de la Barquera *p357*
Bus
10-15 daily buses run to **Santander** (1 hr if direct), some going via **Comillas** and **Santillana**. There are also 10 westbound buses to **Oviedo** and **Gijón**.

Directory

Comillas *p356*
Internet Kiosco Ataf, C Cervantes 2, is shop with an internet terminal.

Los Picos de Europa

The Picos de Europa are a small, compact, mountainous area of the vast Cordillera Cantábrica blessed with spectacular scenery, superb walking, abundant wildlife and, most crucially, comparatively easy access (but take your hat off to the engineers who built the roads). They encompass the corners of three provinces: Asturias, Cantabria and León, and have a relatively mild climate due to their proximity to the sea. It is this proximity to the coast that probably gives them their curious name (the Peaks of Europe); they often would have been the first sight of land that weary Spanish sailors got on their return from the Americas.

The Picos are comprised of three main massifs of limestone cut and tortured over the millennia by glaciation, resulting in the distinctive rock formations typical of the karstic type. The central part of the range is a national park, expanded from the original Parque Nacional de la Montaña de Covadonga, the first such beast in Spain, denominated in 1918.

Ins and outs

Getting there The Picos de Europa are easily accessed from Gijón and Oviedo, or Santander, and are within a couple of hours' drive from León. The two principal towns for Picos tourism are Cangas de Onís (Asturias) and Potes (Cantabria); both make excellent bases, especially if you lack private transport. The main centre of the Leonese Picos is Posada de Valdeón. Potes is serviced regularly by bus from Santander and the Cantabrian coast, while there are frequent buses from Oviedo and Gijón to Cangas. ▶▶ *See Transport, page 369.*

Getting around Travelling around the Picos de Europa is simple with your own transport and time-consuming without. The Picos is basically a rectangular area with a main road running around its perimeter and several smaller roads dead-ending into the heart of the mountains from it. Buses run on the main roads and to popular destinations like Covadonga and Fuente Dé. Fewer buses run on Sundays; taxis are in any event a reasonable alternative, if there are two or more of you. There are also jeep services that act as shared taxis. Hitching is easy in the Picos too. The ideal way to explore the area is on foot; it's only three hours through the Cares gorge, and you've crossed the Picos from north to south; the journey wouldn't take less by car.

Tourist information The Picos de Europa National Park offices run free guided tours around the Picos region during summer, an excellent service. The schedule changes each year and is organized from the three regional information centres. All the major towns have year-round tourist offices, and in addition many villages have summer-only kiosks. The best tourist information offices for the Picos are Cangas de Onís and at the Sotamo visitor centre north of Potes. ▶▶ *See Cangas de Onís, page 361, and Potes, page 370.*

Best time to visit The best time to visit the Picos is either side of high summer; September/October and May/June are ideal, in July and August prices are well up and the crowds can hamper enjoyment of the natural beauties of the area. The Picos have a fairly damp and temperate maritime climate so you're never assured of clear days, but neither does it get extremely cold, at least on the north side of the range. Mists descend regularly; so take a compass and check the forecast. In winter it can snow heavily, particularly in the southern (ie Leonese) part of the range.

Flora and fauna The Picos are home to a wide variety of fauna and flora, due partly to the hugely varying climactic zones within its terrasculpted interior. Among the birds, vultures are common; rarer are eagles and capercaillies. Less glamorous species include choughs and wallcreepers. Chamois are a reasonably common sight, as are wild boar; there are also mountain cats, wolves and bears about, but they are much scarcer. A frequent and pretty sight on roads are herds of soft-eyed cows of an attractive local species. Insect and reptile life is also abundant; clouds of butterflies are about in spring and summer. The flora varies widely from the temperate to the Alpine; in spring the mountain fields are full of wildflowers.

Asturian Picos

Asturias claims the largest slab of the Picos massif and has the most advanced environmental and tourism infrastructure of the region. The area's main town, Cangas de Onís, is an excellent place to begin a trip to the Picos, while nearby Covadonga is revered as the birthplace of Christian Spain. The area is also famous for the strong blue cheese known as Cabrales after the villages in which it is produced. Similar in style to Roquefort, it lends its flavour to many a gourmet dish, but is also enjoyed by the locals as a smotherer of chips. Some of the most dramatic rocky scenery of the region is accessed south of here; there are some fantastic hikes in the area around Puente Poncebos, including the three-hour gorge walk to Caín, a route that crosses the Picos from north to south. ▸▸ *For listings, see pages 366-369.*

Cangas de Onís → *For listings, see pages 366-369. Colour map 2, B3.*

This service town is a typically cheerful Asturian centre, with plenty of places to stay, and some top *sidrerías* in which to drink and eat. Its highlight is a superb medieval bridge across the Río Sella with an alarmingly steep cobbled arch. It's at its best when eerily floodlit at night; locals inaccurately name it the **Puente Romano** (Roman bridge). Also of interest is the **Ermita de Santa Cruz**, just across the other river (the Güeña), a tiny 15th-century chapel, which has fifth-century origins and was built over a dolmen; the key can be collected from the tourist office.

After his victory at Covadonga (see below), Pelayo set up base here and Cangas proudly claims to be the first capital of Christian Spain as a result. A statue of a very rugged Pelayo stands defiantly outside the church, a 20th-century construction with *indiano* and Italian influences visible in its three-storey belltower. There are many *indiano* buildings in town; a good number of eastern Asturians left to seek their fortunes in the New World.

Cangas' **tourist office** ① *T985 848 005, www.cangasdeonis.com, daily 1000-1400, 1600-1900, Jun-Sep daily 1000-2200,* is the best equipped in the Picos region, with plenty of information about the whole Picos area. Grab all the information you can here, as the smaller offices in other towns have less regular opening and sometimes run out of maps, etc.

Around Cangas

South of Cangas the road to Riaño soon plunges into the Desfiladero de los Beyos. It's a popular spot for walking and salmon fishing and vultures are a common sight.

North of Cangas, the town of **Arriondas** is a popular base for canoeing the Río Sella, but lacks the appeal of Cangas, which also operates canoeing trips. The descent to the coast at Ribadesella is brisk but not too challenging; a fun introduction to the sport. A typical half-day involves transport to the launch point, descent, lunch and return to the town, be it Cangas or Arriondas.

Some 4 km east of Cangas, a side road leads a further 7 km up a wooded valley to Covadonga, a name written large in Spanish history, more for what it represented after the fact than for what it was. Thronged with Spanish pilgrims and visitors, its main touristic interest lies in its pretty setting and in the observation of just how deep the Reconquista is embedded as the country's primary source of national pride.

Picos de Europa

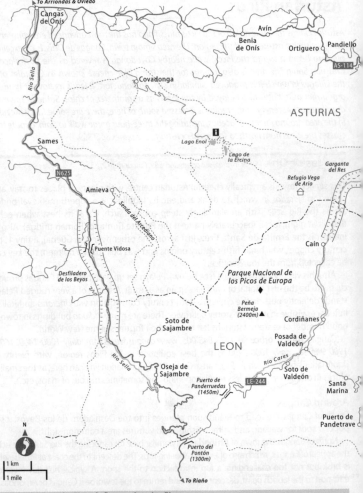

Background

The facts are few and lost in time and propaganda. What is conjectured is that Pelayo, an Asturian leader, defeated a Moorish expedition here some time around AD 718. Some accounts from the Middle Ages claim that 124,000 Moors were killed here by 30 men. This is an obvious exaggeration, it would seem more likely that the force was of a small expeditionary nature and the defeat a minor one. For the Moors, the defeat was certainly of little military significance; it was another 14 years before their first serious reverse

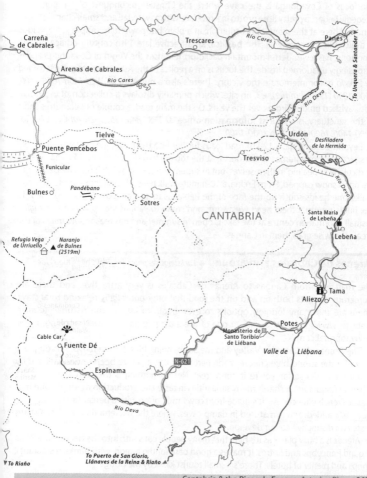

occurred at Poitiers, a good distance into France. But Spanish history has cast Covadonga as the beginning of the Reconquista, the reconquest of the peninsula by Christian soldiers, a process that wasn't complete until 1492, nearly 800 years later. In truth, the battle may have had some effect, at least in establishing Pelayo as pre-eminent among Asturian warlords and sowing the seeds for the foundation of a Christian kingdom in the mountains, a kingdom that eventually did play a significant role in unravelling Muslim dominance in Iberia. But it's hard to sit at Covadonga, watching the coaches roll in, and not ponder on how what in theory is a battleground has become a Christian shrine respected with great devotion.

Sights

The focus of Covadonga is the **cave** where the Christian reconquest of the peninsula allegedly began, a pretty little grotto in a rockface with a waterfall and small chapel. Pelayo is buried here at the scene of his triumph, in a plain but powerfully simple sarcophagus in a niche in the cave wall. The **basilica**, an attractive late 19th-century edifice in pink limestone, has a wonderful mountain backdrop; it houses the Virgin of Covadonga and is surprisingly unadorned inside; the focus is on a replica of the Asturian victory cross forged by Pelayo to commemorate the victory. There's also a **museum** ① *Wed-Mon 1030-1400, 1600-1830 (1930 summer); €3,* on site, which primarily displays a collection of expensive gifts lavished on the Virgin over the years. On the main road, a couple of kilometres short of the sanctuary, is a **tourist information office** ① *T985 846 135, open Jul-Oct Mon-Sat 1000-1400, 1600-1900, Sun 1000-1400.*

Beyond Covadonga, a 12-km road leads further into the mountains, offering a couple of spectacular panoramas to the north. At the top are two lakes, **Enol** and **Ercina**, neither particularly appealing in themselves, but in superb surroundings bristling with peaks that are often snow capped. From Ercina, a 10-minute walk beyond Enol, there are some good walks: one heads south up the face of the Reblagas to an isolated *refugio*, Vega de Ario (six hours return); others head westwards and south to various viewpoints and *refugios*. A small information centre at the lake is open in summer and has reasonable maps of the area; otherwise grab them in Cangas.

Arenas de Cabrales and around → *For listings, see pages 366-369. Colour map 2, B4.*

The road east from Cangas to Arenas de Cabrales is very attractive, and there are numerous hamlets both on and off the road that offer potentially relaxing rural stays. There are too many lodging options to even begin to list; try the Asturian tourism website, www.infoasturias.com, or one of the most popular *casa rural* booking pages, www.toprural.com.

The **Arenas de Cabrales Valley** and the surrounding hillsides are famous throughout Spain for the strong blue cheese made here; *cabrales*. If you've been underwhelmed by Spanish cheeses so far, you're in for a treat. Not for nothing is the stuff known as the 'Spanish Roquefort'; it shares many similarities in taste and production methods with that classic French blue cheese. It's made from cows' milk, often with a percentage of sheep or goat milk added, and is matured in damp caves, where the bacteria that give it its sharp taste and distinctive colour develop.

Arenas is a busy place, as it's here that many people cut south into the heart of the Picos around Poncebos and Sotres. It makes a good base for the region, with banks, restaurants, shops and plenty of hotels. There's a small tourist kiosk by the bridge.

In **Cares**, a five-minute walk across the bridge south of Arenas, the **Cueva del Cares** ⓘ *Apr-Oct daily 1000-1400, 1600-2000, Nov-Mar weekends only; €3*, is a small factory and cave where Cabrales cheese is made in the traditional manner. A guided tour takes visitors through the process and finishes up with a tasting of the blue-blooded stuff.

Into the mountains → *For listings, see pages 366-369.*

Hiking the Cares Gorge trail

An hour's walk south of Arenas, the road reaches **Puente Poncebos**, a small collection of buildings set among high, bleak mountains. There's a shared-jeep service running to here and Sotres from Arenas. Apart from the magnificent view of Naranjo de Bulnes from the hamlet of Camarmeña, 1.5 km above Poncebos, the main reason people come here is to ascend the funicular to Bulnes or to walk the Cares Gorge, one of the Picos's most popular trails. It's about three hours from here to **Caín**, at the other end of the gorge; there's accommodation there, or you can continue another two hours to **Posada de Valdeón** (see page 374), if you don't meet up with a jeep that connects those two towns. This is the best direction to walk in, it gets more spectacular as you go, and Posada de Valdeón is a welcoming place to finish up.

The trail is there thanks to a hydroelectric scheme, and it follows the course of a small, fast-flowing canal that would itch for a fairground-style dinghy ride if it didn't plunge underground every few metres. It's not the best walk if you don't like heights or enclosed spaces; there are several claustrophobic tunnels (a torch helps) and the path runs alongside steep drops to the river much of the time. It's incredibly popular, so don't do it at weekends or in high summer unless you fancy a conga-line experience. From Poncebos, the trail climbs moderately for the first hour or so, leaving the river far below. If you hear jangling far above, it comes from belled goats, who seem to reach completely impossible locations high on the precipitous rocks.

The walk gets prettier and more dramatic as you approach the tail of the **Valdeón Valley**; the massive slabs of rock get bigger and more imposing, but provide shelter for a large range of tree and plant life. You'll probably see vultures circling lazily overhead and you may spot wallcreepers thumbing their beaks at gravity as they hop up perpendicular stone faces. After two hours or so, you'll reach a large green bridge; the path gently descends from here to Caín, crossing the river a couple more times. There are swimming holes here to refresh you, although the water is never less than icy. ⋙ *See the Leonese Picos section, page 374, for Caín and beyond.*

Bulnes

Another walk from Poncebos is the steep hour-and-a-bit climb to Bulnes, a remote village in the midst of lofty mountains. Until 2001, this was the only way to get to the place, and villagers lugged their provisions up this trail as part of everyday life. There's now a **funicular railway** ⓘ *runs every 30 mins 1000-1230, 1400-1800, €15.80/19.90 single/return, free for the villagers of Bulnes*, which climbs a steep 2.2 km through a tunnel from Poncebos to Bulnes, a controversial scheme that outraged environmentalists but pleased the villagers no end (although it certainly wasn't built for their benefit). The walk leaves from near the car park for the Cares Gorge walk, and crosses the river before zigzagging steeply up the hill. The first half is the hardest, but the trail continues to climb before reaching Bulnes.

Bulnes is magnificent, set in a breathtaking valley between towering grey peaks but with enough pasture land to sustain a grazing economy. The picturesque stone buildings, tolling of cowbells, and absence of cars makes it a supremely relaxing place. There are some seven permanent (and chatty) residents, though this is augmented at weekends and in summer. There are two separate hamlets. The lower one (La Villa) is some 300 m above the funicular station, and the higher ('El Castillo') another 10 minutes' climb. With the funicular's advent, there are now several places to stay and a few simple places to eat, most of which only open summer and weekends. From La Villa, a short uphill walk will take you to a viewpoint with magnificent vistas of the Naranjo de Bulnes mountain.

Hiking from Poncebos to Sotres

From Poncebos, a spectacular road winds through the brooding mountains to the remote village of Sotres (this route is also serviced by shared jeeps in season), another walking base. Sotres is slightly on the grim side, especially in bleak weather, but there are a couple of good lodging and eating options.

Hiking from Sotres to Vego de Urriello

One of the best walks from Sotres is the 4½ hours to the *refugio* of **Vega de Urriello** ① *T985 925 200; year-round*, in a grassy meadow near the signature peak of **Naranjo de Bulnes**, which is basically a massive rock jutting out from the massif; it's not a climb for the inexperienced. The walk to the *refugio* crosses the pass at **Pandébano**, from where there are excellent views. The *refugio* offers dorm accommodation (€10) and meals (€14).

East to Panes

Panes itself isn't worth a stop; it is characterized by a modern bridge in rusted iron and a 19th-century church topped by a tacky pastel-blue Jesus. From here, the N621 heads into Cantabria, heading north to the coast at Unquera, or winding south towards Potes along the spectacular **Desfiladero de la Hermida**.

◉ Asturian Picos listings

For Sleeping and Eating price codes and other relevant information, see Essentials pages 31-39.

◉ Sleeping

Cangas de Onís *p361*

There are numerous places to stay – even in summer there should be space. The tourist office has a full list. Most are great value off-season. Among them are numerous *casas rurales*; check www.toprural.com.

AL Parador de Cangas de Onís, Villanueva s/n, T985 849 402, www.parador.es. Set in an old Benedictine monastery 3 km north of Cangas, this new parador offers excellent comfort and good views. Most of the rooms are in a modern annexe; those in the original building are less comfortable but more atmospheric.

A-B Hotel Nochendi, C Constantino González 4, T985 849 513, www.hotelnochendi.com. Stylish and comfortable, this small hotel has staff who appreciate your presence, and a good location on the river. It gets the gold medal for centre-of-town choices.

C Hotel Imperión/Puente Romano, C Puente Romano s/n, T985 849 339, www. hotelimperion.com. An authentically heavily decorated 19th-century mansion across the Sella, with courteous management and comfortable, if worn, heated rooms.

C Hotel Los Lagos, Jardines de Ayuntamiento 3, T985 849 277, www.arceahoteles. com. Right on the main square, offering fair prices, upbeat and professional staff, and reasonable rooms that could do with a facelift. Comfortable beds and decent facilities including a sunny café downstairs, and a free internet terminal. Wi-Fi is extra.

D Hotel La Plaza, C La Plaza 7, T985 848 308. Simple and cheery rooms with bathroom. The best have a balcony and look out towards the mountains.

E Pensión Reconquista, Av Covadonga 6, T985 848 275. Modern, 6th-floor rooms with balconies overlooking the town, and that rarest of beasts, a good shower. Run out of the bar on the corner. An excellent option.

Around Cangas *p361*
C El Rexacu, Bobia de Arriba s/n, T985 844 303, www.elrexacu.com. Closes Mon-Wed from Oct-May. A reader alerted us to this excellent rural hotel in a village 18 km east of Cangas. It's a welcoming, nothing-too-much-trouble sort of place, and has fabulous views. There's a sociable lounge with books, games, and films, and the restaurant serves up excellent food, including home-grown veggies and even ostrich meat from the farm. Recommended.

Covadonga *p362*
A Gran Hotel Pelayo, Covadonga s/n, T985 846 061, www.arceahoteles.com. Right in the middle of the complex at Covadonga, the Pelayo is devoid of warmth but is reasonably well equipped, with a good restaurant. The price halves off-season.
D Casa Priena, T985 846 070. Very close to the Covadonga sanctuary, this little *casa rural* offers 4 cute rooms decked out in fresh and cheerful colours. There's good walking from the doorstep (upwards) and the friendly owners rent out quad bikes.
D Los Texos, La Riera, T985 846 138, www.lostexos.com. A cosy stonebuilt rural hotel in the roadside village of La Riera, on the road to Covadonga and by the busy stream of the same name. Good value, attractive rooms in a great village location (once the traffic has died down in the evening).

Camping
Covadonga, T985 940 097, www.camping-covadonga.com. A bland campsite 4 km east of Cangas, at Soto by the main road.

Arenas de Cabrales and around *p364*
C Hotel Torrecerredo, Barrio Los Llambriosos s/n, T985 846 640, www.

hoteltorrecerredo.com. About 500 m west of the centre of Arenas, this hotel is a breath of fresh air. Plenty of space, welcoming, humorous owners, and numerous activities; it makes a great base. Add to that great breakfasts and evening meals, and you have an excellent package.
C Picos de Europa, Ctra General s/n, T985 846 491, www.hotelpicosdeeuropa.com. A little faded but still Arenas's grandest hotel, with a swimming pool, rooms with great views and an *hórreo* (granary) by the bar in the garden.
C Villa de Cabrales, Ctra General s/n, T985 846 719, www.hotelcabrales.com. In a big stone building, this is a more modern affair, with smart rooms with balconies (although there's some traffic noise). The off-season rates here are appealing.
D El Torrejón, Arenas de Cabrales s/n, T985 846 428, www.eltorrejon.com. A cordial welcome and bargain prices await at this attractive rural hotel tucked away just off the main road in Arenas. There are fine views from some of the stylish rooms and a quaint garden to relax in.

Camping
Camping Naranjo de Bulnes, Ctra Cangas–Panes Km 32.6, T985 846 578, open Mar-Oct. A 10-min walk east along the main road. They have bungalows available year-round.

Hiking the Cares Gorge trail *p365*
A El Mirador de Cabrales, Poncebos, T985 846 673, www.arceahoteles.com. Open Mar-Sep. The top accommodation option in Poncebos, this attractive place offers a great location and decent restaurant. It's a little overpriced in the height of summer, when there's a 3-night minimum stay.
D Hostal Poncebos, Poncebos, T985 846 447, hostalponcebos@wanadoo.es. Dwarfed by mountains, this bright orange building sits right on the crystal-clear rushing Cares, and has reasonable rooms and a restaurant. They'll do a packed lunch for walkers for €5.

E Garganta del Cares, Poncebos, T985 846 463. A comfortable *hostal* above a bar with en suite rooms that are heated and good value except in the height of summer (**D**).

Bulnes *p365*

D La Casa del Chiflón, T985 845 943. In the lower village of Bulnes, this is a cosy mountain retreat with wooden beams and solid stone walls. Apart from a walkers' hostel, it's currently the only place to stay in Bulnes. It's a great base for hiking and should be booked ahead in summer.

Sotres *p366*

D Casa Cipriano, T985 945 024, www.casacipriano.com. A convivial mountain *hostal*, which runs many guided excursions in the area. The rooms are good, and there's a bar and restaurant.
E La Perdiz, T985 945 011, www.laperdizsotres.com. Opposite Casa Cipriano, has good rooms with bath.
F Peña Castil, T985 945 070. Closed early Nov-Mar. A convivial stone walkers' hostel, this is a good base for hiking and has simple but clean bunks and a restaurant with a sunny terrace.

❶ Eating

Cangas de Onís *p361*

There are several cracking *sidrerías* (cider bars) that are excellent eating and drinking options.
℡℡℡ Casa Marcial, La Salgar s/n, T985 840 991, www.casamarcial.com. This is perhaps the finest restaurant in rural Asturias. Nacho Manzano, the chef, has carved a great reputation for himself by blending rustic Asturian cooking traditions with modern technique and modish innovations. The results are spectacularly tasty. You'll find this cosy rustic stone house in the hills up a spectacular road some 6 km north of the town of Arriondas.
℡℡ El Abuelo, Av Covadonga 29, T985 848 733, www.elabuelocangasdeonis.com. A cheerful, warming restaurant specializing in hearty stews and *fabadas*. There's a

pleasant covered terrace in summer, and a top-value €10 lunch menu that'll leave you wholly satisfied. Recommended.
℡℡ El Molín de la Pedrera, C Bernabé Pendas 1, T985 849 109. A smart cider bar with some great fishy stews, as well as roast chestnuts in season. One of Cangas's best. The typically Asturian stew, *fabada*, is another top thing to try here.
℡℡ La Cueva, C Turismo 3, T985 947 775. Though the grotto is made of plastic, this *sidrería* behind the tourist office is an attractive place, and has plenty of tables to sit at and enjoy the outrageously proportioned *raciones*. Calamari, salads, and octopus are all recommendable.
℡℡ Mesón El Puente Romano, Av Covadonga s/n, T985 848 110. Come for the terrace looking at the medieval bridge. Simple but reasonable Asturian fare, including *fabada*.
℡℡ Sidrería Los Arcos, Av Covadonga 17, T985 849 277. Though the bar isn't as atmospheric as others, the tables host some of the town's better food. Great quality *raciones* of some fairly classy fare are the reason to come.
℡ El Corchu, C Angel Tárano 5, T985 849 477. Near the church, this is an unpretentious traditional *sidrería*. The nearby **Potesu** is another more than sound option.

Arenas de Cabrales and around *p364*

℡℡ La Panera, C General s/n, T985 846 810. It's a good spot for a quiet drink, but the food is attractive too. There are plenty of dishes making full use of *cabrales* cheese; try it with wild mushrooms. Heavier dishes include Asturian Picos favourites like *fabada* or *cabrito asado* (roast goat).
℡ La Cabraliega, C El Parque s/n, T985 846 681. Just off the main road on the way to Poncebos, this cosy spot is part shop, selling plenty of local cheeses, and part bar, with a little sunny terrace and various tapas making good use of local products.
℡ San Telmo, Ctra General s/n, T985 846 505, gets plenty of tourists on its roadside terrace, but the food is great; try the ultimate expression of *cabrales*, chips 'n' cheese.

Bulnes *p365*

¶¶ **Bar Bulnes**, Bulnes, T985 845 934. Open weekends and summer. In the heart of the lower village, with a cosy bar serving up simple tapas and huge *bocadillos*, and a popular upstairs *comedor* doing elaborate plates, including *cabrito* and meat dishes.

❶ Bars and clubs

Cangas de Onís *p361*

Mantra, C Turismo 3. The blend of Buddhas and Moroccan art is curious, but it's a peaceful place to sip on a variety of tasty herbal teas or have a post-dinner *copa*.

❀ Festivals and events

Cangas de Onís *p361*

25 Jul The Fiesta de Santiago is celebrated with gusto at Cangas de Onís. On the same day, the **Fiesta del Pastor** is a big party with shepherds and visitors mixing on the shores of Lake Enol near Covadonga.

Aug Regattas down the Río Sella from Arriondas. This **Descenso de la Sella** features everyone from canoeists to professional partiers. The fiesta starts in Arriondas and ends in Ribadesella amid boisterous scenes. One of the region's most memorable events. **8 Sep** The Picos' biggest day is **Asturias Day**, the feast of the Virgen de Covadonga, celebrated with processions and partying.

❍ Shopping

Cangas de Onís *p361*

La Barata, Av Covadonga 13, T985 848 027. An attractive shop dealing in Asturian handicrafts, deli produce and souvenirs.

❁ Activities and tours

Cangas de Onís *p361*

Aquassport, C Juan Carlos I 26, T985 840 364, www.aquassport.com. A popular

canoeing and quad-biking operator based in Arriondas itself, with good facilities and decent prices for combined activities.

Cangas Aventura, Bernabé Pendas 2, T985 849 261, www.cangasaventura. com. Canoeing trips on the river and quad excursions into the mountains.

Escuela Asturiana de Piragüismo, C Turista 6, T985 841 282, www.piraguismo.com. Near the tourist office in Cangas, they organize canoeing trips on the Río Sella as well as horse riding and canyoning.

K2 Aventura, Las Rozas s/n, T985 849 358, www.k2aventura.com. A canoeing outfit based on the river between Arriondas and Cangas. There's a bar on hand for *après-kayak* ciders.

❒ Transport

Cangas de Onís *p361*

Bus Cangas de Onís is serviced very regularly by ALSA buses from **Oviedo** and **Gijón** (almost hourly; 1 hr 20 mins).

Covadonga *p362*

Bus From **Oviedo** and **Cangas**, 4 buses a day ascend to Covadonga. In summer a couple a day continue to the lakes; about 4 a day continue along the AS114 to **Arenas de Cabrales** and **Panes**.

Arenas de Cabrales and around *p364*

Bus There are 4 ALSA buses a day from **Cangas de Onís** and **Oviedo** to **Panes** via Arenas de Cabrales. From Arenas, ALSA run buses to the Bulnes funicular at **Poncebos**. Shared-jeep taxis also do this trip in summer, and continue to **Sotres**.

❶ Directory

Cangas de Onís *p361*

Laundry Higiensec, Av de Castilla 24, T985 947 471, just off the road to Riaño, service wash €15.

Cantabrian Picos

This is the most heavily visited section of the Picos due to its easy road access and good tourist facilities. The region's main centre is the town of Potes, a very attractive place, gouged in half by its river. The heart of the area is the Liébana Valley, a green swathe watered by mountain streams and the Río Deva. It's noted for its cheeses, its chestnuts and its orujo, a fiery grape spirit that comes in original form as well as more mellow, flavoured varieties. A hefty shot in a cup of black coffee is another popular way of taking it. West of Potes, the road winds up to the spectacular natural theatre of Fuente Dé, starting point for plenty of memorable walks. ▶▶For listings, see pages 372-373.

Potes and around → For listings, see pages 372-373. Colour map 2, B4.

Potes is a gorgeous little town on the side of a hill by the Río Deva, with cobbled streets and a few noble stone buildings (those that survived the Civil War damage). The most striking of these is a large tower, looking like a medieval fort, but in fact built as a mansion by the Marqués de Santillana in the 16th century; it's now the town hall. Another tower nearby holds changing exhibitions. Potes makes the best base in this part of the Picos, although in summer it struggles to accommodate the numbers passing through; there's an unbroken line of cars winding through its centre.

There are several banks and supermarkets in town, as well as a petrol station. In the bus station (worth a visit for its painstakingly detailed relief model of the Picos region) is the town's **tourist office** ① *summer daily 1000-1400, 1600-2000, winter Mon, Thu-Sat 1000-1400, 1600-1800, Sun 1000-1400.* More information is available 4 km north of town in Tama at the **Sotama visitor centre** ① *T942 738 109, Oct-Jun daily 0900-1800, Jul-Sep 0900-2000,* a striking, eco-friendly, wood-clad building with an environmental exhibition and national park information office. If you're going to do some walking in the area, make sure you pick up a proper map from one of these places. Even on the brightest of days, mists can descend rapidly, and in any event some trails are ambiguously marked.

A 45-minute walk from Potes, off the Fuente Dé road, is a monastery of great importance, **Monasterio de Santo Toribio de Liébana** ① *daily 1000-1300, 1600-1900.* Although in a magnificent setting, the building itself isn't of massive interest, but makes up for it with two claims to fame. The first is that it was here that the Abbot Beatus de Liébana wrote his apocalyptic commentaries on the book of Saint John; one of the superb illustrated copies of this work is kept here, far from the public gaze (see box, page 371). Prints of some of the pages of this beautiful work are displayed around the cloister (you may recognize some from the film *The Name of the Rose*), and there are some good laminates on sale for €2 in the shop. The other item of interest here is kept in a side chapel off the main church. It is nothing less than the largest fragment of the True Cross in existence, a hefty chunk of cypress wood that measures 63 cm x 40 cm and has one of the nail-holes. It's embedded in an ornate silver Gothic crucifix.

West of Potes to Fuente Dé → For listings, see pages 372-373. Colour map 2, B3.

The N621 follows the Río Deva upstream to the west of Potes, passing through several pretty hamlets. It's a well-travelled route, but just off the main road there are some pretty tranquil *casas rurales* where you can stay.

Beatus and a medieval bestseller

In the middle of the eighth century when the future of Christianity in Europe was in the balance, a monk writing in the remote mountains of Cantabria produced a work that was to be the equivalent of a European bestseller for the next 400 years. Writing from the monastery of Liébana, Beatus wrote a commentary on Saint John's Apocalypse that struck a note with readers who, as well as fearing further invasions from the Moors, also believed that the approaching millennium would bring the coming of the Antichrist. Monasteries across Northern Spain began to produce beautifully illustrated copies of the monk's work. The quality of the illustrations make these manuscripts, known as *beatos*, masterpieces of medieval art. The one in Burgo de Osma, for example, has been described as "the most beautiful book in the world". Only 22 of these manuscripts still survive, nearly all of them in academic libraries. Umberto Eco used the Beatus manuscripts as the basis for his novel *The Name of the Rose*. However, if you fancy reading the original for yourself be warned: Eco describes the Beatus text as "tortuous, even to those well acquainted with medieval Latin".

The road stops at Fuente Dé, and it's not hard to see why; there's a massive semicircle of rock ahead; a spectacular natural wall that rises 800 m and is almost sheer. It is named Fuente Dé because this is where the Deva springs from the ground, but there's little here apart from two hotels, a campsite and a cable-car station. The **cable car** ① *T942 736 610, www.cantur.com, daily 1000-1800, 0900-2000 in summer, €9.10 one way/€15.15 return*, takes 3½ minutes to trundle to the top of the rocky theatre; it's a bad one for claustrophobes, as you're jammed with 25 or so others into the tiny capsule. Expect a long wait in summer. It usually closes for a couple of weeks in February.

Hiking around Fuente Dé → *See map, page 362.*
There are some superb walks in this area, some leaving from the top cable-car station; don't worry if you don't fancy the trip up, as there's a steep path that'll get you there eventually. At the top station, there's an unremarkable tourist complex and the start of a jagged, rocky plateau, an Alpine landscape in contrast to the lush meadows below. In clear weather the views from here are magnificent, with the parador hardly more than a dot below. Following the track from here, you'll soon leave the crowds behind and start a gentle ascent to the top of a rise. Descending to the right from here, you'll come to the **Refugio de Aliva** (see page 373), a year-round hotel and *albergue*. From here, a spectacular 1½-hour descent winds around the valley and down to its floor at Espinama, from where you can follow the river back up to Fuente Dé. The whole circuit takes about four hours and is one of the most beautiful walks in the Picos. Other walks start from the campsite and provide equally spectacular valley and mountain views.

North towards Panes
North of Potes, the N621 heads into Asturias towards Panes through the very narrow gorge of La Hermida. At **Lebeña**, 500 m off the road through the gorge, and 8 km from Potes, is a worthwhile church, **Iglesia de Santa María de Lebeña** ① *Tue-Sat 1000-1330, 1600-1900, Sun 1100-1400, €2*, set against a superb backdrop of massive rock. Founded in the 10th century, its interior is Mozarabic, with horseshoe arches on a rectangular ground

plan. It's a beautifully simple space; most interesting is the altarstone, carved with a series of circles deemed to represent nature, the heavens and the redemptive power of Christ; symbols that go back to the Visigoths and beyond.

South to León
South from Potes, the road winds through the green **Liébana Valley** for a while, then begins to ascend to the **Puerto San Glorio** and **León** province. This stretch of road offers perhaps the best views in the entire Picos; the contrast between the lush green valley and the harsh grey mountains is superb.

⊚ Cantabrian Picos listings

For Sleeping and Eating price codes and other relevant information, see Essentials pages 31-39.

⊜ Sleeping

Potes and around *p370*
C La Casa de las Chimeneas, Plaza Mayor s/n, Tudes, T942 736 300, www. lacasadelaschimeneas.es. Some 9 km south of Potes off the Riaño road, this excellent complex of independent rustic apartments is a great base for exploring the Liébana valleys. The 7 apartments are all different, and charmingly decorated, with designs taken from the Beatus manuscript at the Toribio monastery. There's often a 3-day minimum stay, rising to 1 week in Jul-Aug. The owners speak English.
D Casa Cayo, C Cántabra 6, T942 730 150, www.casacayo.com. Closed Feb. A very good option above Potes' best bar and restaurant. The rooms are large, comfortable and tastefully furnished; some overlook the river. Recommended.
D Posada La Antigua, C Cántabra 9, T942 730 037, posadalaantigua@mixmail.com. Set above and behind a shop in the old part of town, this has rooms with plenty of character at a fairly decent price. Some aren't very spacious, but they are comfortable, and have efficient heating and a/c. The best rooms are on the top floor, with balustraded balconies.
F Hostal Coriscao, C La Serna s/n, T942 730 458. A simple but friendly and cheap option by the car park on the west side of the river. Rooms are basic, with shared bathroom, and can be chilly in winter.

Camping
Camping La Viorna, T942 732 021, www. campinglaviorna.com. On the road to the Santo Toribio monastery just a 15-min walk from the centre of Potes, this is a good campsite in a pleasant setting with swimming pools.

West of Potes to Fuente Dé *p370*
A Parador de Fuente Dé, Fuente Dé, T942 736 651, www.parador.es. Open Mar-Oct. The top place to stay. A modern but fairly sensitive building, this is one of the cheaper paradors but loses nothing on location, particularly when the day trippers have gone home. The rooms are spacious and attractive, most with views of some sort, and the restaurant focuses on Picos cuisine.
C Hotel del Oso, Cosgaya s/n, T942 733 018, www.hoteldeloso.com. One of numerous accommodation choices along the road between Potes and Fuente Dé, this stylish rural hotel appeals for its fine restaurant and smart, colourful rooms, many of which have balconies from which to appreciate the views and enjoy the mountain air.
C Rebeco, Fuente Dé, T942 736 601, www. hotelrebeco.com. Cheaper than the parador, with plenty of comfort despite smallish rooms, as well as a bar/restaurant. It's not de luxe, but the location makes up for it.

Camping
Camping El Redondo, T942 736 699, www.elredondopicosdeeuropa.com. 5 mins' walk past the cable car in Fuente

Dé, this campsite also has bunkbed accommodation (but only 20 places) and is at the start of walking trails.

Hiking around Fuente Dé *p371*
C Refugio de Aliva, T942 730 999, www.cantur.com. Open Mid-Jun to Oct. Atop the plateau, this hotel and hostel (**F**) is a memorable place to stay, and a wonderful base for walks. It has a popular restaurant (popular because there's a jeep running from the top of the cable-car station) that does a *menú del día* for €15.

❶ Eating

Potes and around *p370*
🍴🍴 **Asador Llorente**, C San Roque 1, T942 738 165. This restaurant has fast become a local favourite, so you'll want to book ahead. The warm rustic *comedor* sits right on the top floor, under the old building's beamed roof, and serves good-value meats and other traditional dishes.
🍴🍴 **Casa Cayo**, C Cántabra 6, T942 730 150. Closed Feb. Potes's best option, very lively and cheerful with huge portions. The *cocidos* (chickpea and pork stews) are good, as are the the *revueltos* (scrambled eggs mixed with everything). Some tables overlook the river.
🍴🍴 **El Bodegón**, C San Roque 14, T942 730 247. Atmospheric and with most friendly service, this attractive restaurant is set in a stone building off an old-timers' bar. It's a good place to tuck into a hearty *cocido lebaniego* (the local chickpea stew garnished with sausage and pork). *Revuelto de erizos* (scrambled egg with sea-urchins) is also delicious, but an acquired taste.
🍴 **Los Camachos**, C El Llano, T942 732 148. Cheap, decent food in a lively Cantabrian bar that has won prizes for its home-made *orujo*.
🍴 **Tasca Cántabra**, C Cántabra s/n, T942 730 714. A pleasing no-frills option with an upstairs *comedor*. In winter, try the *alubias con jabalí* (beans with wild boar), a real belly warmer for a pittance.

❂ Festivals and events

Potes and around *p370*
2 Jul Romería (pilgrimage procession) and festival in the Liébana Valley.
1st week in Nov Orujo festival in Potes; can be messy.

⦿ Activities and tours

Potes and around *p370*
Europicos, C San Roque 6, Potes, T942 730 724, www.europicos.com. Organizes everything from quad tours or 4WD trips to paragliding. Mountain bikes from €20 for a ½-day.
La Rodrigona, Cillorigo de Liébana s/n, Tama, T615 970 442, www.larodrigona.com. Horse-trekking operator based in a village north of Potes near the Sotama information centre.
Picos Awentura, C Cervantes 3, Potes, T942 732 161, www.lacasadelascosas.com. By the bridge in Potes, this friendly bunch offer climbing and walking activities in the area, as well as paragliding, horse riding and canoeing.
Potes Tur, C San Roque 19, Potes, T942 732 164, www.potestur.es. Specialize in quad trips into the mountains, also other options.

⊖ Transport

Potes and around *p370*
Bus 3 buses a day from **Santander** to Potes , stopping along the western Cantabrian coast, turning inland at **Unquera**, and stopping at **Panes**. This connects with 2 of 3 daily buses from Potes to the cablecar at **Fuente Dé**.

❶ Directory

Potes and around *p370*
Internet Cyber-Liébana, in the same building as Asador Llorente, offers internet access as well as DVD hire and a pool table. Open 1000-2230.

Leonese Picos

Although this part of the Picos range isn't as endowed with tourist facilities as the Asturian or Cantabrian sections, it contains much of the area's most dramatic scenery, with breathtaking mountain vistas suddenly revealed as you round a bend in the path or road. It's also colder and, in winter snowier, than the more northern sections. While Riaño (see León, page 282), is the area's biggest town, it's a bit far from the action and not especially charming; a better bet is little Posada de Valdeón, spectacularly set in a lush valley surrounded by rocky peaks.
➤➤ *For listings, see page 375-376.*

South to the Naranco Valley
The N621 running south from Potes winds its way upwards through lush alpine meadows before meeting León province at the spectacular **Puerto de San Glorio Pass**, where plans for a controversial ski station have been put on hold pending a lengthy environmental review. Descending rapidly through dark rocks and grassy pasture, the first settlement is **Llánaves de la Reina**.

Valdeón Valley → *For listings, see pages 375-376.*

Santa Marina → *Colour map 2, B3.*
Some 6 km further south is the turn-off for the Valdeón Valley (you can also access it west of Riaño via a wider, faster road), the main part of the Leonese Picos and a remote rural area famous for its strong blue soft cheese. The road climbs to the **Puerto de Pandetrave** at 1562 m, which suddenly reveals a superb view of the valley, dwarfed by the imposing stone masses of the Picos. The first village in the valley itself is Santa Marina, a very rural settlement of simple stone houses. It's a friendly village with a good campsite and a hostel.

Posada de Valdeón
Four kilometres further up the lovely grassy valley is the area's main settlement, Posada de Valdeón. This is the southern terminus for the popular walk along the Cares Gorge (see page 365), and is well equipped for such a small place, with hotels, a supermarket and bank, but no cash machine. The setting is spectacular, with the intimidating mass of **Peña Bermeja** behind it contrasting with the lush pasturelands around.

The Picos de Europa National Park has an **information office** ① *T987 740 504, Mon-Fri 0900-1700, Wed 1400-1700 only*, in Posada from where it runs free guided trips during the summer months (phone for details). There are several places to stay.

Caín
North from Posada de Valdeón, a steep and narrow road makes its way to the village of Caín, a walk of just over 1½ hours. Jeeps run a shared-taxi service between the two towns. Not far from Posada, a fantastic view opens up as the valley seems to be swallowed up by lofty mountains; it's an awe-inspiring sight in good weather. The **Mirador de Pombo** is one vantage point to appreciate the vista; it's marked by a slender chamois and a confusing diagram of the peaks around. Before you reach here, the hamlet of **Cordiñanes** has a good rustic *pensión*.

Caín itself would be about as isolated as a rural village gets were it not for the number of walkers passing through the **Garganta de Cares**. As it is, there are a couple of restaurants, shops and a few lodging options.

West to Asturias

From Posada de Valdeón, the LE244 runs west over the Panderruedas Pass to meet the main N625 near the windy Puerto de Pontón Pass a few kilometres west of Riaño. Continuing northwards, the road enters the maw of the **Desfiladero de los Beyos**, a narrow gorge framed by massive rockfaces; a haunt of vultures and anglers that winds its way into Asturias.

⊙ Leonese Picos listings

For Sleeping and Eating price codes and other relevant information, see Essentials pages 31-39.

⊜ Sleeping

Santa Marina *p374*

D Casa Friero, C Amapolas 1, T987 742 658. A very good, if slightly pricey, *casa rural* in the village; kitchen facilities are available for guests' use. Sleeps 6 and is only available as an entire rental; €90 per day or €420 for a week.

G La Ardilla Real, Plaza de la Esquina, T987 742 677, www.alberguelaardillareal.com. A friendly place in the heart of the village that offers simple but comfortable dormitory accommodation (€12 per person) and warming home-style meals.

Camping

Camping El Cares, 1 km out of town, T987 742 676. A campsite where you can rent horses to explore the valley.

Posada de Valdeón *p374*

D Posada El Asturiano, Ctra Cordiñanes s/n, T987 740 514. A favourite with many Picos regulars, this has warm and comfortable rooms just off the square and a reasonable restaurant. It's not quite so inviting in winter, when it feels a bit abandoned and musty.

E Ezkurra, Plaza Cortina Concejo s/n, T987 740 547. A stay at this warm and welcoming *casa rural* feels like sleeping at a friend's place rather than staying at a hotel. There's plenty of comfort at very low prices, and good information from the hospitable

owner. Breakfast is delicious and features home-made *bizcocho*.

E Hostal Campo, Ctra Cordiñanes s/n, T987 740 502. In the centre of the town, this friendly choice has big, warm and comfy rooms with modern bathrooms and views at a reasonable price. Fuel up for the hike with their delicious €4 breakfast.

F Pensión Begoña, Plaza Cortina Concejo s/n, T987 740 516. Run by the same management as the **Hostal Campo**, this is a friendly option, cheap, fairly basic and likeable; rooms have clean shared bathroom and a down-to-earth walkers' vibe.

Camping

El Valdeón, T987 742 605. Open summer only. The closest campsite is a couple of kilometres out on the road to Soto.

Caín *p374*

D Posada del Montañero, Caín, T987 742 711. The nicest option, open Apr-Sep, a comfortable but overpriced inn with a good simple restaurant.

E Casa Cuevas, Caín, T987 740 500, www.casacuevas.es. Recently refurbished, this walkers' spot offers comfortable, if a touch spartan, rooms, and is the village's best spot for a no-frills feed. There's a *menú* for €10; otherwise ask for *cabrito asado*, roast goat that is the region's speciality.

E Rojo, C Santiago 8, Cordiñanes, T987 740 523. A rustic *pensión*, clean and comfortable with an unbeatable location if you're not scared of big, powerful mountains.

🍴 Eating

Posada de Valdeón *p374*

🍴 **Pensión Begoña**, see Sleeping, above. Just about the best place to eat in the Leonese Picos, this simple mountain inn has fed prime minister Zapatero and offers hospitable service and hearty no-frills traditional cooking. It's a set menu (€14) with limited choice – you might get trout, which abound in the streams around here, or stew made from freshly hunted boar or venison – but it's bound to be hearty and good.

🎉 Festivals and events

Posada de Valdeón *p374*

Sep 8 The Leonese Picos's biggest day is the fiesta of the Virgen de Corona in the Valdeón Valley.

🚍 Transport

Posada de Valdeón *p374*

Bus The southern part of the Picos is a bit problematic when it comes to transport. There's 1 bus Mon-Fri from **León** to Posada de Valdeón, and on to **Caín**, currently leaving León at 1830. There are 5 buses to **Riaño** from León Mon-Fri, 2 on Sat, and 1 on Sun.

Taxi There's a shared taxi service from Posada de Valdeón to **Caín**, at the head of the Cares Gorge walk.

Contents

At a glance

⊖ **Getting around** Budget flights to Asturias, and excellent transport connections by bus and train around most of the province.
◉ **Time required** A week.
☽ **Weather** Warm but not too warm summers give way to rainy but mild winters.
✖ **When not to go** The beaches are packed in Aug, so try Sep, when the water's still warm(ish).

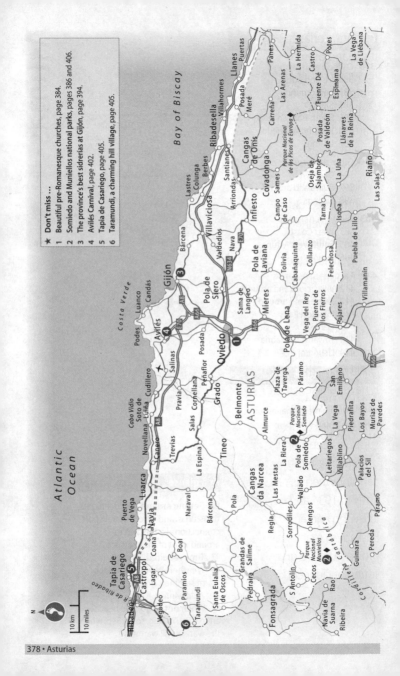

★ Don't miss...

Beautiful pre-Romanesque churches, page 384.

1 Somiedo and Muniellos national parks, pages 386 and 406.

2 The province's best sidrerías at Gijón, page 394.

3 Avilés Carnival, page 402.

4 Tapia de Casariego, page 405.

5 Taramundi, a charming hill village, page 405.

Earthy Asturias has a different feel to much of Northern Spain. It's a land of mining, fishing and good cheer, exemplified by its superb cider culture – a legacy of the Celts. There are few more interesting places to have a drink than an Asturian *sidrería*, with sawdust-covered floor and streams of booze poured from alarming heights. Round off the experience with some of the province's great seafood and you'll be in gastro heaven.

Asturias has had the foresight to look after its natural heritage. While the province is heavily industrialized, there are vast swathes of untouched old-growth forest inland that still harbour bears and wolves. A well-documented network of trails gives access to these places, maintained by an enthusiastic army of ecologists.

The cities of the region are no less appealing. Oviedo, an elegant and beautiful capital, claims some of the best of the ancient pre-Romanesque architecture left by the Asturian monarchs; Gijón is a lively place with an excellent beach; while Avilés shields a beautifully preserved old town inside an unsightly ring of industry. The nearby airport offers direct budget flights to London.

Although the sea temperatures aren't exactly Caribbean and rain is never unlikely, it's not hard to see why the Asturian coast is so popular in summer: the mix of sandy beaches and pretty fishing ports is hard to beat. Hit the east coast for a more developed summer scene, or the west for some more low-key places.

Asturias is a tough, proud land that suffered greatly in the 20th century, when its radical miners were put down brutally by the army in 1934 and again in the Civil War. It is is still one of the more left-wing and egalitarian regions in Northern Spain and, along with Euskadi, in many ways its friendliest. Wherever you head in the province you're guaranteed a gruff, genuine welcome and the sound of cider corks popping.

Oviedo and around

→ *Colour map 2, B2. Phone code: 985. B2. Population: 224,005.*

Oviedo, the capital of Asturias, seems to have come a long way since Clarín, in his biting attack on 19th-century Spanish provincialism and hypocrisy, La Regenta, wrote in 1884, "he looked down on ... the old squashed and blackened dwellings; the vain citizens thought them palaces but they were burrows, caves, piles of earth, the work of moles". Nowadays, after an extensive programme of pedestrianization and restoration, the new town is a prosperous hive of shops and cafés, while old Oviedo is an extremely attractive web of plazas and old palaces built of honey-coloured stone. Three of the best and most accessible examples of the distinctive and beautiful Asturian pre-Romanesque style are to be found in and around Oviedo; other highlights include the cathedral, the Museo de Bellas Artes, and the numerous intriguing public sculptures around town. In the local dialect, Bable, Oviedo is written and pronounced 'Uvieu'.

There's plenty to explore outside the city too. Many of the valleys south of Oviedo are pockmarked with coal mines, which are gradually being closed down. Towns to the west, such as Pravia, ancient Asturian capital, and Salas, hometown of an arch-inquisitor, can be easily visited as day trips from Oviedo or Gijón, although they also make good bases in themselves; there are several rewarding walks in the area. This is salmon country – in season, the rivers teem with them, and also with phalanxes of local and international fly-fishers.

One of the typical sights in this area are the hórreos, huts raised on legs for the storage of grain. Most of these are at least a century old, and many are much older. You'll often see strings of peppers or corn cobs hung out to dry from the eaves. ›› *For listings, see pages 387-393.*

Ins and outs

Getting there
Asturias's international airport (OVD) is 10 km west of Avilés, but is also connected by regular bus to Oviedo and Gijón. **easyJet** fly here directly from London Stansted and Geneva, and **Air Berlin** connect to Oviedo from many German and Austrian cities via their Mallorca hub. There are regular internal connections with Madrid and Barcelona with **Iberia** and **Spanair**.

Getting around
Buses are useful for reaching outlying areas – there are 12 or so routes, clearly labelled at bus stops. Taxis are easy to find, but bear in mind that, due to Oviedo's commitment to pedestrianization, many locations aren't easily accessible by car. There are several central parking stations. Hemmed in by hills, Oviedo is a fairly compact city, and easy to walk around. From the bus and train stations it's a 15-minute walk to the heart of the old town down Calle Uría; most of the accommodation is closer to the centre.

Best time to visit
Oviedo has a comparatively mild climate; usually neither winter nor summer hits uncomfortable extremes, although it is notoriously rainy in autumn and winter. Oviedo's major fiesta is in September (see page 392), but the *sidrerías* (cider bars) and other haunts are busy year-round.

 There is a life-size statue of Woody Allen in Oviedo – but people keep stealing the glasses.

Tourist information

The Asturias regional **tourist office** ① *C Cimadevilla 4, T985 213 385, ofiturio@princast.es, Oct-Jun Mon-Sat 1000-1800, Jul-Sep Mon-Fri 1000-2000, Sat-Sun 1000-1900*, is conveniently central. The helpful **main municipal office** ① *Plaza de la Constitución 4, T984 086 060, turismo-oviedo@ayto-oviedo.es, daily Oct-May 1000-1400, 1630-1900, Jun 1000-1900, Jul-Sep 0930-1930*, is just down the road from here. There's a **smaller municipal office** ① *Campo de San Francisco park, T985 227 586, 0930-1400, 1630-1930*. There's also a tourist information desk in the bus station (same hours). The website www.infoasturias.com is a valuable resource run by the tourist board.

Background

Oviedo was born in the early years of the stubborn Asturian monarchy, when a monastery was founded on the hill of 'Ovetao' in the mid-eighth century. Successive kings added other buildings until Alfonso II saw the city's potential, rebuilt and expanded it, and moved his court here in AD 808. He saw it as a new Toledo (the former Christian capital having long since fallen to the Moors). It was this period that saw the consolidation of the pre-Romanesque style, as Alfonso commissioned an impressive series of buildings. A glorious century in the spotlight followed, but Oviedo soon returned to relative obscurity when the court was moved south to León. Oviedo continued to grow through the Middle Ages, however, partly as a result of pilgrim traffic to Santiago. The university was founded in about 1600, which helped to raise the city's profile. Real prosperity arrived with the Industrial Revolution and, crucially, the discovery of coal in the green valleys near the Asturian capital. Asturias became a stronghold of miner-driven unionism and socialism, and Oviedo suffered massive damage in the 1934 miners' revolt, and again in the Civil War. Franco had a long memory, and it's only fairly recently that Oviedo has emerged from his shadow. A progressive town council has transformed the city, embarking on a massive program of pedestrianization (there are over 80 pedestrian-only streets), restoration, and commissioning of public sculpture. Now, painted and scrubbed, Oviedo is taking new pride in living up to its coat of arms as the "very noble, very loyal, meritorious, unconquered, heroic, and good city of Oviedo".

Sights

Cathedral

① *Nov-Feb Mon-Sat 1000-1300, 1600-1800, Mar-May and Oct Mon-Fri 1000-1300, 1600-1900, Sat 1000-1300, 1600-1800, Jun Mon-Fri 1000-1300, 1600-2000, Sat 1000-1300, 1600-1800, Jul-Sep Mon-Fri 1015-1915, Sat 1015-1715, admission to Cámara Santa, museum, and cloister €3.50, Cámara Santa only €2 (guided visit).*

The cathedral, a warmly-coloured and harmonious construction, dominates the **Plaza de Alfonso el Casto** with its delicate and exuberant spire. While most of the building is of 14th- and 15th-century design, it contains a series of important relics of the Asturian kings in its Cámara Santa. This chamber, originally part of Alfonso II's palace, contains the Cruz de los Angeles and the Cruz de la Victoria; the two emblematic, bejewelled crucifixes were gifts to the church by Kings Alfonso II and III respectively. The former is now the symbol of Oviedo, while the latter features on the Asturian coat of arms. Also behind glass in the Cámara Santa is a silver ark containing relics perhaps brought from the Holy Land to Spain in the seventh century. One of the relics, supposedly the shroud of Christ, is behind a

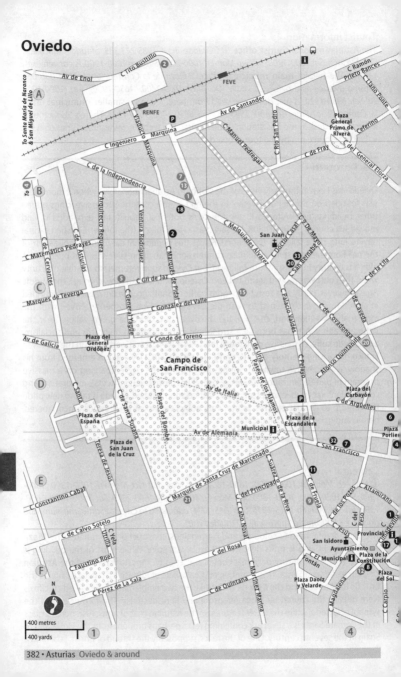

Oviedo

panel in the back wall; it is brought out and venerated three times a year. The ark itself contains a bumper crop including a piece of the true cross, some bread from the Last Supper, part of Christ's clothing, some of his nappies, and milk of the Virgin Mary. The cathedral also has an attractive cloister and a museum with a good collection of objects, although these are left to the visitor's interpretation. Across the square from the cathedral is a statue of Clarín's *La Regenta*.

Museo Arqueológico
ⓘ *C San Vicente, Tue-Sat 1000-1330, 1600-1800, Sun 1100-1300, free. Currently under renovation; should be open for summer 2011.*
Behind the cathedral is the museum of archaeology, which is built around a beautiful monastery cloister. The sparsely labelled finds lack context, but it's a pleasant stroll around the old building.

Museo de las Bellas Artes de Asturias
ⓘ *Sep-Jun Tue-Fri 1030-1400, 1630-2030, Sat 1130-1400, 1700-2000, Sun 1130-1430; Jul and Aug Tue-Sat 1030-1400, 1630-2030, Sun 1030-1430; free.*
The fine arts museum is housed in a 17th-century palace and a grand 18th-century townhouse that are joined back-to-back. There are two entrances, one on Calle Santa Ana, and one on Calle Rúa. The museum has an excellent collection of 20th-century Asturian art and a good selection of Spanish masters. In the vestibule at the Santa Ana entrance hangs José Uría y Uría's tragic *Después de una huelga* (*After a Strike*). Painted in 1895, it evocatively demonstrates that the events of 1934 and 1936 were a long time in the making.

Old town
The old town is made for wandering. The walk-through **Ayuntamiento** is on **Plaza de la Constitución**, as is the honey-coloured **Iglesia de San Isidoro**, still daubed with ancient graffiti, as graduating students traditionally painted their names there.

Other pretty plazas include **Trascorrales**, and **Porlier**; the latter is home to the mysterious sculpture *El regreso de William B Arrensberg* (The Return of William B Arrensberg), one of many street sculptures that invigorate Oviedo. From here, walk down Calle San Francisco (the Assisi saint passed through Oviedo on his way to Santiago) to the large park of the same name. *Maternidad*, a sculpture by the Colombian artist Fernando Botero, is an unmissable landmark here on the **Plaza de la Escandalera**; it's irreverently nicknamed *La Muyerona* (The Big Woman) by locals.

North of the old town

Heading north, **Calle Gascona**'s sharpish slope serves to drain away all the cider spilled in its numerous and gregarious *sidrerías*. The pre-Romanesque **Iglesia de San Julián de los Prados** ① T607 353 999, Oct-Apr Tue-Sat 0930-1130, May-Sep Tue-Fri 1000-1230, 1600-1730, Sat 0930-1200, 1530-1700; all year Mon 1000-1230 unguided; guided visits take 30 mins, last entry 30 mins before closing time €1.20, Mon free, was built by Alfonso II in the first half of the ninth century. Northeast of the old centre, beyond the fountained **Plaza de la Cruz Roja**, it now struggles for serenity beside the Gijón motorway. Designed with the characteristic triple nave, the highlight of the church is its superbly preserved frescoes.

Los Monumentos

① Apr-Sep Tue-Sat 0930-1330, 1530-1930, Sun and Mon 0930-1330; Oct-Mar Tue-Sat 1000-1300, 1500-1700, Sun and Mon 1000-1300. Admission by tour only; €3, free Mon; last tour 30 mins before closing. Tour covers both buildings, so if no one seems to be around, wait; or check the other building. The guardian's phone number is T638 260 163.

The pre-Romanesque structures of Santa María de Naranco and San Miguel de Lillo, collectively known as Los Monumentos, overlook the city on Naranco hill to the northwest. There's a good view over Oviedo, which, it has to be said, isn't super-attractive from up here, but is backed by beautiful mountains.

Santa María de Naranco, built as a palace by Ramiro I (1842-1850), is arguably the finest example of this architecture. The columns in the upper hall could almost be carved from bone or ivory, such is the skill of the stonework. Balconies at either end add to the lightness of the design; one contains an altar with an inscription of the king. A range of sculptural motifs, many of them depicting alarming animals, decorate the hall, and have been attributed to Visigothic and Byzantine influences. Underneath the hall is another chamber variously identified as a crypt, bathhouse, and servants' quarters.

The **Iglesia de San Miguel de Lillo**, a stone's throw further up the road, is a church also constructed during the reign of Ramiro I. What remains is a conglomeration of the original building – much of which collapsed in the 13th century – and later additions. The original building was undoubtedly an amazing structure for the time in which it was built. What remains is impressive, with a series of intricately carved lattices, and some remaining fresco decoration. Carved panels appear to show gladiatorial or circus scenes. To get to Los Monumentos it's about a 30-minute brisk walk up Avenida de los Monumentos from above and behind the railway station. Bus No 3 plies the route hourly from Calle Uría, or it's a €5-7 cab ride from central Oviedo. From the bus, get off at the car park – Santa María is a five-minute walk up the hill; San Miguel a short way beyond. There's an Pre-Romanesque interpretation centre (free entry) on the road before you get to the monuments.

South from Oviedo → For listings, see pages 387-393.

Due south of Oviedo, just off the motorway to León, the town of **Mieres** can be accessed very easily on the **FEVE** *cercanías* from Oviedo (line F8). It's a likeably honest place, a working town which gives a taste of Asturian mining heritage. It has excellent nightlife, even more so during **Carnaval**, see page 392. Not far to the east, in the village of El Entrego, the **Museo de la Minería y de la Industria** ① *www.mumi.es, Oct-Jun Tue-Sat 1000-1400, 1600-1900, Sun 1000-1400; Jul-Sep Tue-Sat 1000-2000, Sun 1000-1400, €5*, is a proud display of the region's coalmining history. There is a good collection of working replicas of old mining devices, but the highlight is a guided descent into an excellent replica mine, bringing to life the conditions underground. El Entrego is accessed from Oviedo on a different *cercanía* line (hourly to El Entrego station on **RENFE** C2, and **FEVE** F6-F5 five times daily; get off at San Vicente if the train stops there).

Iglesia de Santa Cristina de Lena
① *Apr-Oct Tue-Sun 1100-1300, 1630-1830, Nov-Mar Tue-Sun 1100-1300, 1600-1800; €1.20. Contact the keyholder on T985 490 525 if there's no one about.*
South of El Entrego, overlooking the motorway near the border with León province, it's worth making the effort to visit another excellent pre-Romanesque church, Iglesia de Santa Cristina de Lena. Dating from the mid-ninth century, it's a pretty thing on the outside, but its hauntingly beautiful interior is better. A delicately carved raised triple arch is topped by symbols of early Christianity, not without some Islamic influence. The altar stone inscriptions have clear Visigothic/Germanic parallels, and there are several stones reused from a Visigothic edifice. To get there, take the *cercanía* line C1 to La Cobertoria, from where it's a short walk; thus avoiding the depressing town of Pola de Lena.

Parque Natural de Somiedo → *Colour map 2, B2.*

Southwest of Oviedo, the national park (and UNESCO biosphere reserve) of Somiedo is a superbly high, wild area of Asturian forest, home to bears and wolves, as well as some exceedingly traditional Asturian villages. There are many superb walks in the park, one of the best starting from the hamlet of **Valle de Lago**, from where there's a walk to (you guessed it), Lago del Valle, a 12-km round trip up a high grassy valley with abundant birdlife. If you're see a dog the size of a pony, don't worry; these massive mastiffs are really big softies: unless you're a wolf. The trail is waymarked as PR 15.1. You can stay in Lago del Valle, or in the bigger village of **Pola de Somiedo**, a 1½-hour walk back on the main road.

West from Oviedo → *For listings, see pages 387-393.*

Salas → *Colour map 2, A1.*

West of the fishing centre of Cornellana, along a valley of eucalyptus and wild deer, is the town of Salas, a small, picturesque, and tranquil place. Salas' most famous son was Hernando de Valdés, whose formidable presence still looms large in the town over 500 years after his birth. An extremely able theologian and orator, he rapidly ascended the church hierarchy until, in 1547, he became Inquisitor-General for the whole of Spain. His rule was, like the man himself, strict, austere and inflexible. Quick to crack down on any books, tracts or people with so much as a sniff of liberalism or reformation about them, he can be seen as a symbol of the Spain that turned its back on Europe.

Valdés came from a notable local family whose small castle and tower still dominate the town. Inside is the **tourist office** and a small **museum** ⓘ *tourist office and museum, T985 830 988, turismo@ayto-salas.es; mid-Mar to mid-Jun and mid-Sep to Oct Tue, Thu-Sat 1000-1400, 1600-1830, Wed and Sun 1000-1400; Nov to mid-Mar Thu and Sat 1100-1400, 1600-1800, Sun 1100-1400, mid-Jun to mid-Sep Tue-Sun 1000-1400, 1700-2000; admission €1.20.* The museum, which is in the tower, has a display of pre-Romanesque inscriptions and ornamentation. The rest of the castle is mostly a hotel set around the pleasing courtyard.

Down the hill a little stands the **Colegiata de Santa María la Mayor**, where the body of the inquisitor now rests in an alabaster mausoleum.

Pravia and Santianes → *Colour map 2, A1.*

Little-known **Pravia** is another small gem in the crown of Asturias. Founded in Roman times, it was briefly the home of the Asturian court in the eighth century before being forsaken for Oviedo in AD 808. Now a small agricultural town, its small centre is a relaxing collage of perfect façades, which are at their best in the soft evening light. The town feels oddly South American, perhaps as a result of the large numbers of *indianos* who returned home having made their fortunes in the new colonies. Many *indiano* houses dot Pravia and the surrounding area (as well as much of Asturias) – they are typically tall and grandiose, and often have gardens planted with palms and cactus. In the heart of town there's a **tourist office** ⓘ *Parque Sabino Moutas s/n, T985 821 204, Tue-Sat 1000-1300, 1600-1900 (1700-2000 summer), Sun 1030-1300.*

The centre of Pravia is presided over by the bulky **Colegiata de Pravia** and the connected **Palacio de los Moutas**, good examples of Spanish baroque architecture. The oldest building in the town proper is the **Casa del Busto**, a large and dignified *casona* now tastefully converted into a hotel. Built in the 16th century, it was a favourite refuge of Jovellanos, the 18th-century Spanish Enlightenment figure par excellence, whose sister-in-law lived here.

The nearby village of Santianes de Pravia, 3 km from town, has a church which is the oldest of the series of existing pre-Romanesque buildings of this size. It preserves little of its original character, having been substantially altered over the years, but is an attractive building nonetheless. It stands on the site of an earlier Visigothic church. Nearby, a **museum** ① *Tue-Sat 1030-1330, 1700-1900, Sun 1130-1330, €2*, displays finds from the recent restoration of the church, including a curious stone whose acrostic inscription makes it look like a word puzzle. The entry fee includes admission to the church, which is otherwise under lock and key.

Santianes is one stop from Pravia on the **FEVE** line and is also accessible by bus. To get there by car or on foot, go down Calle de la Industria from the centre of Pravia, cross the river and two roundabouts, and continue up the hill. Santianes is signposted to the right about 1.5 km up this road.

 Spain's biggest-selling soap brand, Heno de Pravia, is named after the aromas of hay in the district.

◉ Oviedo and around listings

For Sleeping and Eating price codes and other relevant information, see Essentials pages 31-39.

◉ Sleeping

Oviedo *p380, map p382*
There's a cluster of cheap accommodation near the train station on and around the main new town street C Uría.
LL Hotel de la Reconquista, C Gil de Jaz 16, T985 241 100, www.hoteldelareconquista. com. Oviedo's top hotel is fantastically built around, and faithful to, the 18th-century Hospital of the Principality. Set around galleries, courtyards and chapels brimming with period objets d'art, the hotel makes up for in artistic charm what it lacks in top-of-the-range facilities. Visitors are welcome on the ground floor – it's well worth a look. Check the website for special offers.
AL M Hotel, C Comandante Vallespín s/n, T985 274 060, www.mhotel.es. In a building created by Santiago Calatrava, this swish designer hotel certainly looks the part, and the interior decor lives up to it, with an eclectic mix of the modern and antique lending plenty of style and high degrees of comfort. Excellent facilities include a diner-style sushi bar; the only drawback is the less-than-central location.

A Gran Hotel España, C Jovellanos 2, T985 220 596, www.granhotelespana.com. This noble giant is typical of a certain type of smart Spanish hotel slightly yearning for the glory days of the 1920s. Untypically, this has been sensitively renovated, and the courteous staff complement the plush interiors. The rooms are equipped to business-hotel standard, and the location right on the edge of the old town is also a plus. Parking and Wi-Fi available.
A Hotel Libretto, C Marqués de Santa Cruz 12, T985 202 004, www.librettohotel.com. Bright and vibrant, this strikingly innovative hotel faces the San Francisco park. Facilities are impressive, with DVD/CD players, posh TV, rentable laptops, Wi-Fi access, and even an umbrella for the regular drizzle, but it's the sleek, opera-themed design that lives long in the memory. A minimalist mix of the classic and the avant-garde, it somehow works. There are often excellent weekend or promotional deals.
B Hotel Ciudad de Oviedo, C Gascona 21, T985 222 224, www.hotelciudaddeoviedo.es. Right on cider street, this has unremarkable, but modern, spacious, spotless, and comfortable rooms. The free Wi-Fi works well and the staff are welcoming and helpful. It's much cheaper (**C**) outside Jul-Aug.

B Hotel El Magistral, C Jovellanos 3, T985 215 116, www.elmagistral.com. The steel and bottle-glass decor gives an intriguingly space-age feel to this original establishment. The rooms are softer, well-lit and with lacquered floorboards and pastel colours accompanied by the expected facilities. It's well located, competently staffed and has parking available.

B Hotel Fruela, C Fruela 3, T985 208 120, www.hotelfruela.com. An excellent location and helpful staff make this a wise choice. Smooth modern lines and shiny surfaces make it feel spotless, and everything seems to work the way it should. Prices vary wildly from **AL** to **D** depending on availability – check online.

B Hotel Vetusta, C Covadonga 2, T985 222 229, www.hotelvetusta.com. This small and welcoming central hotel has modern design that exudes warmth and personality. All rooms are exterior – there's a little traffic noise but the light and life make up for it – and half come complete with a mini sauna/massage unit. There's a sunny café-bar downstairs. There's a parking station alongside and off-season rates are great (**D**). Recommended.

C Hotel Carreño, C Monte Gamonal 4A, T985 118 622, www.hotelcarreno. com. Handily located just behind the bus station, and in striking distance of the pre-Romanesque monuments, this hotel is run by nice people and features decent-sized rooms and modern bathrooms, all spotless. The price is more than fair, and a simple breakfast is included. Parking available. Recommended.

D Hostal Arcos, C Magdalena 3, T985 214 773, www.hostal-arcos.com. A very friendly place in the heart of the old town, just off the Plaza de la Constitución. All rooms have small modern en suites; there's 24-hr access; basically it's a top central-city budget option. Recommended.

D Hostal Romero, C Uría 36, T985 227 591, www.hostalromero.net. Well located in the new town in shopping centre, this

well-renovated *pensión* has big and inviting rooms, all with bathroom and TV. The owners are welcoming and enthusiastic. Recommended.

D Hotel Alteza, C Uría 25, T985 240 404. This is a decent, cheap hotel in a flamboyant building on Oviedo's main shopping street not too far from the station. The rooms are compact but snug, and there's a comfy guest lounge. All rooms have TV and bathroom; they are warm in winter and a little hot in summer. Breakfast included.

D Hotel Favila, C Uría 37, T985 253 877. Very handily placed for trains and buses and situated on Oviedo's main shopping street, this has comfy rooms with cable TV and smart bathroom, as well as cheery staff. The restaurant downstairs does a cheap, tasty and filling lunchtime *menú*.

D Hotel Ovetense, C San Juan 6, T985 220 840, www.hotelovetense.com. In a prime central location just near Plaza Porlier, this hotel has cosy rooms, which, although small, are top value. It can be a little stuffy in summer, but it's quiet and friendly nonetheless. There's a restaurant and pay parking available nearby.

E Hostal Belmonte, C Uría 31, T985 241 020, www.hostalbelmonte.com. An inviting and hospitable option in a lovely green and cream building, this is one of a range of budget accommodation on this street. It's been attractively renovated, with a wooden floor and a variety of rooms, all with TV and bathroom.

E Pensión Fidalgo, C Jovellanos 5, T985 213 287. This homely, welcoming, and colourful set-up is well placed between the old and new towns and just a hop, skip and jump away from the cider houses of C Gascona. The rooms facing the street are a little noisy but the friendly old couple running it make up for it. Recommended.

Parque Natural de Somiedo *p386*

The best options to stay in the Somiedo area are the numerous excellent *casas rurales*. There are too many to deal with here; check www.toprural.com for a few enticing starting options.

D Meirel, T985 763 993. This appealing hotel in the centre of Pola de Somiedo is a good comfy spot to sleep and refuel on hearty Asturian food. Rooms are appealingly decorated in confident colours and rustic furnishings, and there are also apartments available (**C**).

Salas p386

C Castillo de Valdés-Salas, Plaza de la Campa s/n, T985 830 173, www. castillovaldesalas.com. This is an excellent rural hotel situated within the small castle, a beautiful setting indeed with its charming rustic central patio. The rooms are very true to the building but have much more than castle comfort. They feature bright homely fabrics on comfortable beds, pastel-shaded walls and polished floorboards. Recommended.

E Hotel Soto, C Arzobispo Valdés 9, T985 830 037. This cheap hotel is set in a pleasant old building right next to the Colegiata, which the best rooms overlook. While far from luxurious, the rooms are heated and have bathroom and television, and the price is very reasonable.

Self-catering

The hills to the northeast of Salas have a number of good options for self-catering. **Ca Pilarona**, Mallecina, T629 127 561, www. capilarona.com. One of the best options, Ca Pilarona is in the tiny village of Mallecina, 11 km from Salas. It is a series of 5 restored houses, modernized with excellent facilities. They sleep from 2 to 6, and cost from €65-90 per night, depending on length of stay.

Pravia and Santianes p386

B Casona del Busto, Plaza Rey Don Silo 1, Pravia, T985 822 771, www.casonadelbusto. es. One of the best places to stay in the area, this elegant hotel is set in a 16th-century *casona*. From the hallway to the rooms it's charming; the use of period-style furniture

perfectly sets off an already striking building. The rooms all have individual character, with plenty of wooden furniture and hessian giving a taste of the colonial era. There's also a good restaurant, with tables in the open atrium. Recommended.

E Pensión 14, C Jovellanos 8, Pravia, T985 821 148. This is a small and welcoming *pensión* with 2 home-from-home rooms, lavishly appointed with stove, sink, utensils, TV, pine wood and skylights. It's on a small street in the centre of town; don't confuse it with the hotel of the same name at the bottom of Pravia. Recommended.

🍴 Eating

Oviedo *p380, map p382*
Head to the 'Boulevard of Cider', C Gascona, for a wide choice of places to try the life-blood of Asturias; most also do tasty seafood.
¶¶¶ Casa Conrado, C Argüelles 1, T985 223 919, www.casaconrado.com. Closed Sun and Aug. A fairly traditional Spanish *mesón*, all dark wood and cigar smoke, this is a local byword for quality and elegance. The cuisine has Asturian favourites accompanied by fine meat and fish dishes; main courses are €20-30 and there's a top wine list.
¶¶¶ Casa Fermín, C San Francisco 8, T985 216 452, www.casafermin.com. Closed Sun. With a lovely atrium dining space adorned with ornate glassware, this central spot features really excellent service, a very fat wine list, and really tasty dishes ranging from local specialities to more elaborate creations. Their *merluza a la sidra* (hake cooked in cider) an Asturian speciality. Recommended.
¶¶¶ El Raitán, Plaza de Trascorrales 6, T985 214 218, www.elraitan.com. A long-term favourite for Asturian cuisine, this attractive establishment offers a smart, traditional restaurant alongside a typical Asturian cider bar. The restaurant mains are pricey but very tasty: this is an excellent place to try hearty dishes like *fabada* (bean and meat stew). There are various set menus at lunchtime (€20-40) including one for kids.

¶¶ La Corrada del Obispo, C Canóniga 18, T985 220 048. This stylish restaurant on a lovely square near the cathedral is beautifully decorated, with plenty of natural light as well as chandeliers, polished wood floors and all the trimmings. The thoughtfully prepared food matches the surroundings and feels slightly underpriced. Delicious mains include such temptations as monkfish and sea bass in asparagus sauce. There's a €50 *menú de degustación* showcasing the best on offer. They also run the place next door, **Catu**, which focuses on tapas and seafood dishes.

¶¶ Bocamar, C Marqués de Pidal 20, T985 271 611, www.bocamar.es. In the heart of the shopping district, this is a warmly lit, reasonably upmarket fish and seafood restaurant that offers a good €18 *menú* at lunchtime.

¶¶ El Cachopito, C Gascona 4, T985 218 234. At the top of Gascona, this sets the tone with well-poured cider and a range of *cachopos*, a typical Asturian plate consisting of 2 thin fried breaded steaks sandwiching various combinations of fillings, costing from €14.

¶¶ El Cogollu, Plaza de Trascorrales 19, T985 223 983. This is a little gem of a restaurant in the southeastern corner of Plaza de Trascorrales. Its peaceful stone and ochre interior is decorated with traditional ceramics; there's imaginative freshly-prepared Asturian cuisine, including delicious stews, great grilled vegetables, and tasty, fairly-priced meat. Recommended.

¶¶ Faro Vidio, C Cimadevilla 19, T985 228 624. This extremely popular restaurant specializes in well-priced Asturian home cooking. The hearty stews and casseroles are simple and filling, while the extensive seafood dishes are prepared and presented in an uncomplicated and authentic manner.

¶¶ La Bellota Asturiana, C Fruela 16, T985 200 658. Popular for an after-work wine at 1400, the 'acorn' has a bar where they do a nice line in gourmet tapas and *montaditos* (little toasted sandwiches), while the pretty

upstairs-downstairs dining areas offer elaborate and tasty plates as well as a *menú* that's a steal for around €10.

¶¶ La MásBARata, C Cimadevilla 2, T985 213 606, www.lamasbarata.com. A sparky modern but casual tapas bar specializing in rice dishes. It's popular with smart young Asturians who choose from a huge range of *raciones* for €6-13, delicious accompaniments to a *caña* at the bar; other mains are €9-19.

¶¶ Tierra Astur, C Gascona 1, T985 203 411, www.tierra-astur.com. Spacious and very popular, this cider house is one of the best-value places to eat in Oviedo. The solid wooden tables groan under the weight of some of the *raciones* that come out of the kitchen; many would feed 2, such as a selection of Asturian cheeses, all labelled with a cute little flag. The bar itself is convivial and has the smooth and lenient Trabanco cider. There's a lunchtime *menú* for €10.

¶ Casa Montoto, C San Bernabé 9. This is a simple, no-frills establishment of a sort sadly dying out in Spain. The only adornment is photos of roller-hockey teams, but the crowds flock in for a cheap wine and a *bollo preñao*, a favourite Asturian snack consisting of chorizo sausage baked in a bread roll. They don't come better than they do here.

¶ La Paloma, C Independencia 3, T985 235 397. An Oviedo classic, this double-sided bar swells with people for morning coffee or a pre-lunch vermouth and tapa, and it makes a good evening rendezvous-point. They have their own vermouth *solera*, which has been going over a century, there are daily specials such as paella, and smart seafood snacks; try some *bígaros* (winkles). They also do offer sit-down meals including a decent *fabada*.

¶ La Pumarada, C Gascona 8, T985 200 279. A busy *sidrería* with impressively fast and efficient service. The excellent value *menú del día* offers a variety of Asturian and other specialities with wine for €10. The enormous portions may intimidate those on diets, but more robust diners will be able to savour cooking of a very high standard.

Las Campanas de San Bernabé, C San Bernabé 7, T985 224 931. An attractive faded façade in the shopping district conceals a popular restaurant with beautifully painted beams and a good line in bistro-style Asturian fare, seafood dishes and rices. It's deservedly busy, and has daily blackboard specials; the warming stews are particularly good, washed down with a jar of wine.

Más Que Vinos, Plaza Constitución 6, T607 823 404. In the heart of things, this modern bar has won a loyal local following for its upbeat and cordial atmosphere, delicious range of wines from around Spain, and free tapa with your drink. Folk congregate around the barrels outside on the square if the weather permits; if you can grab a table on the terrace, don't give it up lightly.

Cafés and bars

A traditional Oviedo pastry is the *carbayón*, an eclair-like almond creation. It's named after the oak tree, the traditional centre and meeting place of Asturian villages. A large *carbayón* was controversially chopped down in Oviedo in 1879 to make more room on C Uría; a plaque marks the spot where it stood.

Café Dólar, Plaza de Porlier 2, T985 215 876. An historic central café with a relaxed ambience and prime location. It's decorated with a modern but classical touch that seems somehow very characteristic of contemporary Oviedo.

Rialto, C San Francisco 12, T985 212 164. With over 80 years in business, the Rialto must be doing something right. Its pastries are widely considered the best in Asturias and are absolutely delicious; browse them at the counter at the front, then eat them at your leisure at the cosy tables in the rear.

South from Oviedo *p385*

Plaza San Juan in Mieres is an elegant little square easily recognizable by the statue of a cider-pourer in full flow. Its placement here is no accident, as several of the town's many excellent *sidrerías* are nearby.

El Rinconín, Plaza San Juan 5, Mieres, T985 462 601. One of the best of the *sidrerías*, and notably welcoming.

Salas *p386*

Salas isn't bursting with places to eat.

Castillo, Plaza de la Campa s/n, T985 830 175. Closed Tue nights. Undoubtedly the best option in town, this is the **Castillo de Valdés-Salas** hotel restaurant. It offers a cheap and tasty lunch *menú* and cooks up game, warming traditional plates, and some of the local trout catch in season. If you're not a guest and want dinner, phone ahead to reserve a spot.

Bar La Campa, Plaza de la Campa s/n, T985 832 220. A pleasing option for simple tapas and *raciones*, with a range of wines to accompany them. Its best feature is a breezy terrace over looking the castle.

Pravia and Santianes *p386*

Balbona, C Pico de Merás 2, Pravia, T985 821 162. Don't be fooled by the somewhat garish neon sign; this is actually a restaurant with a weighty reputation for quality Asturian fare. There's always a wide selection of fresh fish caught just down the road, while the beef is also recommendable. Despite the traditional atmosphere, there's plenty of modern flair in the preparation, as well as a bar where you can relax with tapas or a bottle of cider.

La Hilandera, C San Antonio 8, Pravia, T985 822 051. This good-looking *sidrería* is immediately recognizable by its green façade. There are various cheeses and meats to enjoy with the cider, as well as heartier *raciones* like tripe. Upstairs is a very cute stone-walled dining room, with a wider selection. *Raciones* are €5-8.

Bars and clubs

Oviedo *p380, map p382*

Many of the bars only open at the weekend. Much of Oviedo's nightlife is centred in the rectangle bounded by Calles Mon, Postigo Alto, San José and Canóniga. Other areas are C Rosal, for a grungier scene and, of course, the cidery area around C Gascona and C Jovellanos.

Ca Beleño, C Martínez Vigil 4. This is a legendary Oviedo bar focusing on the Asturian folk scene with its Celtic roots fully intact. They pour a great Guinness and the front garden is a fine place on a mild evening. Frequent live music. Check their Facebook page for concerts.

La Perrera, C Postigo Alto 5. This small, attractive bar is named 'the doghouse' and it's dedicated to rock 'n' roll from the 1960s on. Beware of the pooch signs in various languages that provide the decor.

Swing Jazz Club, C Cañóniga 14. Around the side of the cathedral, this new café bar is deservedly popular for its inclusive atmosphere and live music at weekends. Check its myspace page, www.myspace.com/swingjazzclub, for upcoming concerts.

⊕ Entertainment

Oviedo *p380, map p382*
Cinema
The **Cajastur** bank on Plaza de la Escandalera has a programme of art house films.

Theatre
Teatro Campoamor, Plaza del Carbayón, T985 207 590, www.teatrocampoamor.es. A well-regarded mainstream theatre programme, opera performances, and weekly Sun morning concerts of Asturian folk music.

⊛ Festivals and events

Oviedo *p380, map p382*
Feb/Mar Carnaval in Oviedo is a big affair; the main day here is the Sat after Shrove Tue, ie 43 days before Easter Sun,when you can see the traditional end of Carnaval ceremony: the burial of the Sardine.
Sep Oviedo's major festival is the fiesta of San Mateo, the city's patron. The 3rd week of Sep is given over to street parades, dances, bullfights, an opera season and other celebration.

○ Shopping

Oviedo *p380, map p382*
Oviedo is a good place to shop, with a wide range of chain and boutique outlets. C Uría is the place to find smart fashion, as are the pedestrianized streets east of it.

Books
La Palma Libros, C Rúa 6, T985 214 782. Good bookshop for information on Asturias; also has a good English-language section.
Librería Cervantes, C Doctor Casal and C Campoamor. Bookshop with an excellent range of English-language books, as well as Asturian and Spanish literature.

Department stores
El Corte Inglés, C Uría 9. A Corte Inglés superstore with anything you could want.

Food
Mercado El Fontán, behind the Plaza Mayor. This covered central market is a good place to stock up on Asturian produce. The curious might be interested in the horse butcher.

○ Transport

Oviedo *p380, map p382*
Air
Flights arrive into and depart from Asturias international airport, see page 380. Buses run hourly (on the hour) from Oviedo's bus station to the airport, taking 45 mins and costing €6.35. A taxi costs about €50.

Bicycle hire
Salvador Bermúdez, C Postigo Alto 1, T985 212 326, rents and repairs bicycles.

Bus
Local city buses are blue and run on 13 clearly marked routes around the city (see www.tua.es for a map). The basic fare is €0.90. Bus No 3 runs hourly from C Uría up to Santa María de Naranco and San Miguel de Lillo. The intercity bus terminal is near

the train station (T902 499 949, www.
estaciondeutobusesdeoviedo.com). There
are many buses to **Gijón**, 30 mins, and many
companies run services across Asturias. The
major intercity operator is **ALSA** (www.alsa.
es), T902 422 242, who connect **Oviedo** with
A Coruña (3 daily, 4-6 hrs, €22), **Santiago**
(3 daily, 5-7 hrs, €27), **León** (9 daily, 1½ hrs,
€9), **Valladolid** (5 daily, 4 hrs, €19), **Madrid**
(14 daily, 5½ hrs, €32), **Santander** (10 daily,
2½-3½ hrs, €14), and **Bilbao** (9 daily, 5 hrs,
€21). Some of these services are premium
class, meaning they're slightly quicker and
more expensive.

Taxi
Call T985 220 919 if you can't flag one on
the street.

Train
There is a bewildering number of short-
distance *cercanía* train routes around the
central valleys of Asturias. These are run
by both FEVE and RENFE out of the train
station. Details of individual lines can be
found in the relevant destination section.
For long-distance services, RENFE links
Oviedo with **Madrid** (4 daily, €50, 4¾ hrs)
via **León** (6 daily, 1¾ hrs, €20) and
Valladolid and with **Barcelona** (2 per day,
11 hrs, €52), and points in between. FEVE's
coastal network links Oviedo (slowly) with
Santander (2 through trains per day, 4 hrs,
€15), **Bilbao** (1 per day, 6½ hrs, €23), and
westwards as far as **Ferrol** in Galicia (2 per
day, 6½ hrs, €22).

South from Oviedo *p385*
Mieres
Train FEVE trains run to Mieres from
Oviedo (Line F8, frequent, 20 mins),
and most southbound RENFE trains
also stop here.

Bus There are regular buses from **Oviedo**
and **Gijón** (at least hourly, 35 mins).

Parque Natural de Somiedo *p386*
Bus ALSA runs 4 buses on weekdays and
1 on weekends (leaves at 1000) to **Pola de
Somiedo** (2 hrs 15 mins).

Salas *p386*
Bus ALSA runs hourly buses to/from
Oviedo, 1 hr 15 mins, via **Cornellana**.

Pravia and Santianes *p386*
Train Pravia is served hourly by FEVE trains
from **Oviedo** (Line F7) and **Gijón** (F4), 1 hr.

Bus ALSA also runs buses here to/from
Gijón every couple of hours and takes 1 hr.

ⓘ Directory

Oviedo *p380, map p382*
Internet Café Oriental, C Jovellanos
8, T985 202 897. Cybercafé at €1.50 hr;
Cyber Express, upstairs in the train station,
Mon-Fri 1000-1400, 1600-1900, Sat
1000-2100, €0.04 per min. **Language
schools** Alea, C Fray Ceferino 10, T985
216 349, www.mundoalea.com. A highly
professional company that organizes
Spanish courses in Oviedo. Good reputation.
Laundry Riosol, C Capitán Almeida 31,
T985 222 090. **Libraries** The provincial
library is on C Quintana near Plaza del
Fontán, T985 211 397. **Medical services**
There's a large medical centre that deals
with emergencies at C Naranjo de Bulnes
behind the train station, T985 286 000. **Post
office** The main post office is on C Alonso
Quintanilla. **Telephone** There is a *locutorio*
(telephone centre) at C Caveda and C Alonso
Quintanilla, and another at C Foncalada 6.

Gijón and Avilés

→ Colour map 2, A2. Phone code: 985. Population: 277,554 (Gijón), 84,242 (Avilés).

Following what seems to be the established law for such things, there is no love lost between Gijón and Oviedo. People in Gijón, the larger of the two, feel that it should be capital of Asturias instead of Oviedo, which some consider posh, soft and effete. Those in Oviedo aren't too bothered, but occasionally enjoy riling Gijón by referring to it, tongue in cheek, as 'our port'.

Gijón is a fun city picturesquely set around two sandy beaches and a harbour. The larger and nicer of the beaches, Playa de San Lorenzo, is an Asturian Copacabana, fronting 2 km of city blocks with a stretch of very clean sand, which almost wholly disappears at high tide – and in summer, under rows of bronzing bodies. There are a few decent waves to surf and a good-time feel in the warm months. The small old quarter, at the base of the Cimadevilla promontory, is heady with the yeasty cider smell from dozens of small bars. The council has also done a good job of highlighting the city's heritage with small museums and information plaques. In the local dialect, Bable, Gijón is written and pronounced 'Xixón'.

A little further west is Avilés, whose reputation is slowly changing from grim to vivid. For a long time, the only travellers to pass through this large industrial centre were business visitors under company orders. Now, having tackled its pollution problems, the city is capitalizing on its major asset, a remarkably beautiful historic centre. On the back of its carnival, widely regarded as the best in Northern Spain, Avilés makes a concerted effort to welcome tourists. While there aren't many bona fide sights to visit, the beauty of the centre, the quality of the cafés and restaurants, and the openness of the people make it an excellent destination. Moreover, the beach is within walking distance, and it's a handy 10 minutes from the Asturias airport. ►► For listings, see pages 398-402.

Gijón → For listings, see pages 398-402.

Ins and outs

Getting there Gijón is under 30 minutes' drive from Oviedo by motorway. The bus station is on Calle Magnus Blikstad, with regular long-distance connections to other cities in Northern Spain and local regional services. Just about all buses inbound from and outbound to other provinces stop in both Oviedo and Gijón. Train services depart from the nearby **FEVE** station on Plaza del Humedal. Most **RENFE** trains stop here too, although the main RENFE station (Gijón Jovellanos) is on Avenida de Juan Carlos I, about 20 minutes' walk from the old centre.►► See Transport, page 402.

Tourist information The helpful **municipal tourist office** ⓘ Dársena Fomento pier, T985 341 771, www.gijon.info, daily 0900-2000 (2200 in summer), is just around the harbour from the old town. The staff are multilingual and well informed. There's also a network of summer information kiosks, including one at each end of San Lorenzo beach.

Sights

The Ayuntamiento of Gijón has been busily populating the city with small museums of varying degrees of interest. See www.gijon.info for a full list of them. There are also numerous small art exhibitions leading brief lives in unlikely places. At the tip of the Cimadevilla headland is a small hill, the **Cerro Santa Catalina**, which is topped by the remains of a castle and crowned by Eduardo Chillida's *Elogio del Horizonte*, a giant concrete

Gijón

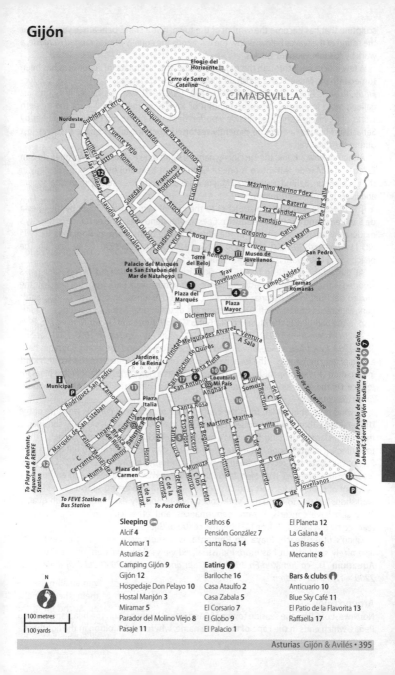

Sleeping 🛏
Alcif **4**
Alcomar **1**
Asturias **2**
Camping Gijón **9**
Gijón **12**
Hospedaje Don Pelayo **10**
Hostal Manjón **3**
Miramar **5**
Parador del Molino Viejo **8**
Pasaje **11**
Pathos **6**
Pensión González **7**
Santa Rosa **14**

Eating 🍴
Bariloche **16**
Casa Ataulfo **2**
Casa Zabala **5**
El Corsario **7**
El Globo **9**
El Palacio **1**
El Planeta **12**
La Galana **4**
Las Brasas **6**
Mercante **8**

Bars & clubs 🍸
Anticuario **10**
Blue Sky Café **11**
El Patio de la Flavorita **13**
Raffaella **17**

N
100 metres
100 yards

sculpture that has become the symbol of the town. If you stand beneath it, you can hear the sound of the waves below. Below the hill stands the equally photographed *Nordeste*, a work by Joaquín Vaquero Turcios.

A few blocks back through the old town's web, the birthplace of Jovellanos has been turned into the **Museo Casa Natal de Jovellanos** ① *Plaza Jovellanos, T985 185 152, Tue-Fri 0930-1400, 1700-1930, Sat-Sun 1000-1400, 1700-1930, free*. It's basically Gijón's art gallery; more interesting than the handful of Jovellanos memorabilia are the modern works of Navascués and the massive wooden depiction of the old Gijón fish market by Sebastián Miranda, a work he patiently restarted from scratch after the first was lost during the Civil War.

Although now a bank, the succinctly named, sandstone **Palacio del Marqués de San Esteban del Mar de Natahoyo** is one of Gijón's most beautiful buildings, particularly in the evening sun. Behind it, the **Plaza Mayor** leads a double life as stately municipal square and lively hub of cider drinking.

The **Playa de San Lorenzo** stretches to the east of here, watched over by the **Iglesia de San Pedro** and a statue of Augustus Caesar, who stands near the entrance to the city's moderately interesting remains of the Roman public baths, **Termas Romanas** ① *T985 185 151, Tue-Fri 0930-1400, 1700-1930, Sat-Sun 1000-1400, 1700-1930, €2.40, free Sun*. The beach's long boulevard is the natural choice for an evening *paseo*.

At the other end of the beach, the sluggish **Río Piles** is flanked by pleasant parks studded with palms. On the east side, about a 10-minute walk back from the beach, is the **Museo del Pueblo de Asturias** (Muséu del Pueblu d'Asturies) an open-air ethnographic park with reconstructions of various examples of traditional Asturian buildings and life. Also in the complex is the **Museo de la Gaita** ① *both Paseo del Doctor Fleming s/n, T985 182 963, Oct-Mar Tue-Fri 0930-1830, Sat-Sun 1000-1830. Apr-Sep Tue-Fri 1000-1900, Sat-Sun 1030-1900; €2.40, free on Sun*, devoted to bagpipes from around the world. Bagpipes have a long history in Asturias – the local type has a more austere tone than the Scottish kind. Information (audio) is Spanish only. The museum has a *sidrería*/restaurant with a pleasant terrace. On the other side of the river, by the **Sporting Gijón** stadium, is the busy Sunday *rastro* (flea market).

Beyond here, about 3 km from the centre, is the massive and curious structure of the **Universidad Laboral**, whose pitiless bulk evokes the Franco years; it's usually considered the nation's largest building. Begun as a project to help children who had lost their fathers to mining accidents, it soon became a larger affair dedicated to teaching traditional trades. Part of the space has recently been given over to form **Laboral** ① *T985 185 577, www.laboralcentrodearte.org, Wed-Mon 1200-2000, €5, free Wed*, an excellent and enthusiastic museum of contemporary art and design. The vast and interesting spaces of the former workshops are put to good use, with concurrent temporary exhibitions of high quality. They also have concerts, theatre performances, and other cultural events. It's easily reached by bus (Nos 1, 2, 4, or 18) from the centre of Gijón.

Gijón's other beach, **Playa de Poniente**, is a short walk west of the centre. It's also nicely sanded, but has more industrialized views. At its western end is the **Gijón Aquarium** ① *Sep-Jun Mon-Fri 1000-1900, Sat and Sun 1000-2000, Jul-Aug daily 1000-2200, €12, €6 for children*.

Around Gijón

Northwest of Gijón, the seaside towns of Candás and Luanco sit on the headland of Cabo Peñas, which ends in the cape of the same name, where an exhibition in the lighthouse explains something about the sealife of the area and the history of the building itself. Candás and Luanco make relaxed, family-friendly places to stay, close to the sights of Gijón but quieter.

Avilés and around → *For listings, see pages 398-402.*

The heart of Avilés is **Plaza de España**, from which a number of scenic pedestrian streets radiate. One side of it is occupied by the **Ayuntamiento**, an attractive arched building that is a symbol of the post-medieval expansion of the town. Opposite is the elegant bulk of the **Palacio del Marqués de Ferrera**, now converted to a luxury hotel. Avilés' **tourist office** ⓘ *C Ruiz Gómez 21, T985 544 325, turismo@ayto-aviles.es, Mon-Fri 0900-1400, 1630-1830, Sat and Sun 1000-1400, daily 1000-2000 in summer, very helpful, English spoken*, is a block down from Plaza de España. From the Plaza de España (many locals refer to it as the Plaza Mayor), Calle San Francisco runs up to the **Plaza Domingo A Acebal**, where it becomes the colonnaded Calle Galiana. This area is lined with bars and cafés, several of which have tables outdoors. It's a popular and recommended evening meeting spot. Calle San Francisco is dominated by the 13th-century **Iglesia de San Nicolás de Bari** with a pretty Romanesque cloister, now partly occupied by a school. In front is the **Fuente de los Caños** (fountain of the spouts), which pours water into a basin from six lugubrious faces. Further up Calle Galiana, the **Parque de Ferrera** was part of the impressive back garden of the counts of Ferrera before being given over to public use. It's now a rambling network of paths.

On the other side of Plaza de España, Calle Ferrería leads into the oldest part of town; this part of the city was originally walled. At the bottom of the street are the early Gothic **Capilla de los Alas**, and the earlier **Iglesia de los Padres Franciscanos**, started in the late 12th century. The latter's sandy Romanesque façade is appealing; inside is the tomb of a notable *avilesino*, Pedro Menéndez, who founded the city of San Agustín in Florida (which claims to be the oldest city in the USA). West of here, in the **Plaza Camposagrado**, is a statue of another famous local, the shaggy Juan Carreño de Miranda, a notable 17th-century Spanish painter. A few blocks further west again, past the waterfront park of **El Muelle**, is Avilés' prettiest square, the **Plaza del Carbayo**. This is in the barrio of **Sabugo**, where the majority of Avilés fisherfolk used to live. It was almost a separate town, and the plaza was its centre, where whaling and fishing expeditions were planned. Walking back towards town along Calle Bances Candamo gives further flavour of this tiny district. Between Sabugo and the centre, Plaza Hermanos Orbón, which holds the market, is memorable for its high arcade and windowed balconies glinting with dozens of panes of glass.

The nearby town of **Salinas** (4 km northwest of Avilés) is a somewhat bland place whose raison d'être is its long, sandy beach, thronged in summer but quiet at other times. At its western end is one of Asturias' best restaurants, **Real Balneario**, see page 400, and a the view from the headland is good; there's also a vaguely surreal collection of anchors. Salinas can be reached by city buses Nos 1 and 11 from Avilés bus station.

Gijón and Aviles listings

For Sleeping and Eating price codes and other relevant information, see Essentials pages 31-39.

Sleeping

Gijón *p394, map p395*

Gijón bristles with hotels, but many are dull cells for business travellers. Happily, there are several options with more charm.

AL Parador del Molino Viejo, Av Torcuato Fernández Miranda s/n, T985 370 511, www.parador.es. This parador, in a suburban setting in a duck-filled park at the eastern end of Gijón, is mostly modern but its restaurant is set within the walls of an old mill. Rooms are spacious, stylish and well lit. It's a little hard to find; look next door to the riverside **Sporting Gijón** football stadium.

A Hotel Alcif, Camino de los Quiñones 513, T984 117 700, www.hotelalcif.com. Perfect for those who like a quiet urban base, this new hotel is situated in a residential complex not far from the campsite in the eastern end of town. It's extremely peaceful, beautifully decorated, has a great garden and is run in a most welcoming manner. It's **C** off-season. Recommended.

A Hotel Alcomar, C Cabrales 24, T985 357 011, www.hotelalcomar.com. Although slightly starchy, this hotel has an excellent location at the old-town end of the San Lorenzo beach. The rooms with a view (some €20 more) are predictably lovely and light, and come with minibar, safe and the standard conveniences of a hotel of this level. There can be some noise from late-night revellers though. Breakfast included.

A Hotel Pasaje, Marqués de San Esteban 3, T985 342 400, www.hotelpasaje.net. With views of the marina from some of the rooms, this hotel makes the most of its central, but tucked-away location. The rooms are comfortable, with decent Wi-Fi access and modern bathrooms. It's overpriced in Jul and Aug, but a great deal (**D**) the rest of the year.

A Hotel Pathos, C Santa Elena 6, T985 176 400, www.celuisma.com. This is a refreshingly offbeat modern crash pad close to the Plaza Mayor and beach. Pop art decorates the walls and each of the small but stylish rooms is dedicated to a 20th-century icon: Jagger? Thatcher? Gandhi? Your choice. Bathrooms are modern and swish, while there's Wi-Fi, minibar, and a safe in the rooms. Great value off-season.

A Hotel Santa Rosa, C Santa Rosa 4, T985 091 919, www.bluehoteles.es. Decked out in minimalist white with the odd blue object as a feature, this chic recently opened hotel offers plenty of comfort and modern facilities on a central pedestrian street. Appealing and stylish without being in the least pretentious.

B Hotel Gijón, C Pedro Duro 6, T985 356 036, www.hotelgijon.com. Readers put us on to this good-value hotel a short walk from the train and bus stations and not too far from the Plaza Mayor. Spacious rooms are a steal off-season and the staff are helpful and keen to please. They also have apartment-style rooms available.

C Hotel Asturias, Plaza Mayor 11, T985 350 600, www.hotelasturiasgijon.com. There's little luxury or boutique enchantment at this spot, but it's got the best location of any Gijón hotel, right on the Plaza Mayor, steps away from restaurants, harbour, cider bars, and the beach. It's a simple establishment, with fair prices, rooms with enough light and space, and an OK included breakfast. Staff are friendly.

C Hotel Miramar, C Santa Lucia 9, T985 351 008, www.hotelmiramargijon.com. Although right in the heart of Gijón's shopping and bar-hopping area, this small hotel is remarkably quiet. The friendly management keep the rooms just-so. Can get stuffy in summer.

D Hospedaje Don Pelayo, C San Bernardo 22, T985 344 450, www.hostaldonpelayo. com. This upmarket *hostal* is in a noble old townhouse very close to the beach. The rooms are comfortable and bright, with gleaming modern bathrooms, heating, hairdryers and cable TV. Much cheaper off season.

E Hostal Manjón, Plaza del Marqués 1, T985 352 378. Very well-located *hostal* just a few paces from the restaurant and cider action of the Plaza Mayor. Rooms with a view are much nicer but noisier. The furniture and fittings are old, and don't expect extras like TV or Wi-Fi, but it's a reliable budget spot.

E Pensión González, C San Bernardo 30, T985 355 863. Basic but wholesome option with high ceilings, wooden floorboards, and a significant population of porcelain dogs. Bathrooms are shared but ok. Particularly cheap off-season.

Camping

Camping Deva, 4 km east of town just off the highway, T985 133 848, www. campingdeva-gijon.com. Well-equipped campsite with a swimming pool, and lines of simple cabins and better-equipped bungalows. Gets busy in summer.

Camping Gijón, T985 365 755, www. camping-gijon.com. Well situated at the tip of the headland to the east of the Playa de Lorenzo.

Around Gijón *p396*

B Hotel Plaza, Plaza de la Baragaña 6, Luanco, T985 880 879, www.laplazahotel. net. In the centre of Luanco near the beach, this chic but welcoming hotel has attractive modern rooms, some of which are larger than others. There's a decent variety of breakfast options too. **D** off season.

Avilés and around *p397*

AL Palacio de Ferrera, Plaza de España 9, T985 129 080, www.nh-hotels.com. This hotel has been sensitively converted from a 17th-century palace right on the main square in the heart of Avilés. The rooms aren't cheap, but they have all the facilities of a business hotel, room service, gym, sauna, and underground parking. Rates vary

extensively depending on availability and the time of year. Extras like internet access are overpriced.

B-C Hotel Don Pedro, C La Fruta 22, T985 512 288, www.hdonpedro.com. Just down the hill from Plaza de España, this small hotel is run out of a busy café. The staff are welcoming, the stone-faced rooms are charmingly grotto-like and have an Arabian feel. Recommended.

C Hotel de la Villa, Plaza Domingo A Acebal 4, T985 129 704, sebucansl@telecable.es. This likeable hotel is well situated in the historic centre, looking over a pleasant plaza and the church of San Nicolás de Bari. Rooms are appealing, with dark wood floors and prints of Kandinsky and Klee, and the staff are friendly.

E Pensión La Fruta, C La Fruta 21, T985 512 288. This well-equipped *pensión* is run out of the friendly **Hotel Don Pedro**, and is directly opposite it. Every room comes with its own bathroom (either en suite or next to the room), and TV. Recommended.

⦿ Eating

Gijón *p394, map p395*
Gijón offers some excellent eating around the Plaza Mayor and the marina. The black spiny *ericios* (sea-urchins) are a local favourite, as are *zamburiñas* (a tasty small scallop). Near the Plaza Mayor, **C Salustio Regueral** is a destination for smart tapas bars specializing in wine rather than cider. At the far end of the San Lorenzo beach (turn left to hug the headland) are several good options with magnificent views of the sea and sand. The pricey **Bellavista** is the classiest, and the cheap and cheerful **Las Terrazas del Pery** the most popular.

⦿⦿⦿ Casa Ataulfo, C Cabrales 29, T985 340 787. This *sidrería* is one of Gijón's most reliable for excellent fresh seafood. Ask what's good that day: they take the finest fish from the market, and things like calamari or *berberechos* (cockles) are always brilliant. Recommended.

₸₸₸ Casa Zabala, C Vizconde de Campo Grande 2, T985 341 731, www.casazabala. com. Near the Jovellanos museum, this Cimadevilla restaurant is run by a family, now in its 4th generation, who show a sure touch in dealing with fruits of the Bay of Biscay as well as dishes more rooted in the traditions of the Asturian farmland. The dining room is *acogedor* – a Spanish word that is somewhere between comfortable and welcoming.

₸₸ El Corsario, C Marqués de Urquijo 16, T985 338 620. It's worth tracking down this small local just back from the southeastern end of the San Lorenzo beach for its warm service and excellent-value meals. Try the *brocheta de secreto ibérico* – 2 skewers of succulent acorn-eating pork that melts in the mouth.

₸₸ La Galana, Plaza Mayor 10, T985 172 429. This distinguished looking *sidrería* on the main square is a prime spot to eat and drink, and a good introduction to Asturian cider culture, with understanding bar staff who pour well and look after you. The huge barrels, painted ceiling and heavy wooden beams give plenty of atmosphere. You can snack on tapas (€3-5 for a decent plate), or head up the back for some more serious seafood and stews. The lunchtime *menú* is great value at €11 for 4 courses.

₸₸ El Globo, C San Bernardo 13, T985 172 247, www.sidreriaelglobo.es. There's more elbow-room in the downstairs dining area than the stuffy upstairs one at this excellent traditional cider house. Great *bígaros* (winkles) and whole baked calamari (*de potera*) can be accompanied by an excellent cheeseboard featuring Asturian products. Recommended.

₸₸ El Palacio, Plaza de Marqués 3, T985 341 368. Closed Mon. In an elegant restored building between the port and the Plaza Mayor, with a popular cider joint and terrace downstairs. Above is quite an elegant restaurant. Some tables have fine views over the harbour. The *magret de pato* (duck magret) is delicious, as is the seafood and salads.

₸₸ El Planeta, Tránsito de las Ballenas 4, T985 350 056, www.el-planeta.net. It doesn't look like much when you walk in, but this no-frills place by the leisure harbour is an excellent choice for cider and seafood. A typical Gijón place and one of the most popular, so be prepared to wait for a table: they don't take bookings. Specialities are calamari and, in summer, *ventresca de bonito* – tender meat from around the belly area of the bonito fish.

₸₸ Mercante, Cuesta del Cholo 2, T985 350 244. A very good harbourside option with an excellent €10 lunch *menú* in the upstairs restaurant. In fine weather, a popular choice is to grab a cold drink from the bar and sit on the stone wall outside. Recommended.

₸ Las Brasas, C Instituto 10, T985 356 331. No-frills *parrilla* restaurant with a range of *platos combinados* and *menús*. Things such as *chorizo criollo* (an Argentinian sausage) are particularly tempting. The half *parrilla* €16; €20 with salad) can comfortably feed 2 people and features a range of meats. Eat upstairs for a quieter meal.

Cafés
Bariloche, Plaza del Instituto 1, T985 350 169. One of the city's classic cafés, with a characteristic duplex style in vogue in the 1970s in Spain. There are tasty rolls and good coffee; a good breakfast. Free Wi-Fi.

Around Gijón *p396*
₸₸ Sidrería El Muelle, Paseo del Muelle s/n, T985 880 035. In the most appealing part of Luanco by the harbour, this is an old local favourite with a great outdoor terrace. The seafood *raciones* are well prepared and fairly priced. Go for mussels, grilled bonito, sardines (*parrochas*) or fresh grilled calamari. Recommended.

Avilés and around *p397*
Avilés is an excellent place for eating out; especially C Galiana and the old streets north of Plaza de España.

₸₸₸ Real Balneario, Av Juan Sitges 3, Salinas, T985 518 613, www.

restaurantebalneario. com. One of Asturias's top restaurants, beautifully set on the beach at Salinas. Specializing in seafood, the €24 lunch *menú* is definitely the most economical way to enjoy the haute cuisine, but you might be tempted by the multi-course degustation or 'gourmet' set meals. Presentation is exquisite, and the wine list most extensive.

♥♥ Casa Lin, Av de los Telares 3, T985 564 827. This is a historic *sidrería* near the station serving up excellent seafood and well-poured cider. *Fabada* and kidneys stewed in sherry (*riñones al jerez*) also are reliably good.

♥♥ Casa Moisés, C La Muralla 4, T985 526 000, www.casamoises.com. For casual cidery dining, head to this spacious and popular offering, with a boisterous atmosphere and simple plates of high-quality food, especially fish and seafood. Prawns, *cigalas*, sea urchins: it's all good here. The *menú* for €9 is also great value.

♥♥ Casa Tataguyo, Plaza del Carbayedo 6, T985 564 815, www.tataguyo.com. Tough to find with its small sign, this wonderful split-personality restaurant has been an legend for years. The traditional bar dishes out cheap workers' lunches at shared tables in a satisfyingly no-frills atmosphere, while up the back you can dine on very classy Asturian fare in a comfortably cordial setting.

♥♥ La Posada, C Ruiz Gómez 12, T985 510 117. This restaurant is across the road from the tourist office and is warmly decorated in a modern but traditional style on 2 levels. There are plenty of warming Asturian stew-type dishes, and they prepare fine *bacalao* (cod). There's a lunch *menú* for €13 midweek, and other set meal options at various prices.

♥♥ Llamber, C Galiana 30, T984 832 348. Tucked away under the stone colonnade of this attractive street, this top-quality new restaurant offers modern Spanish cuisine drawing on influences and ingredients from around the nation. Tuck into dishes like peach and quail salad on the burner-warmed barrel terrace.

Cafés

Café Don Pedro (see Sleeping). Set in the hotel of the same name, this café is decorated in similar stony style. The coffee is very good.

Cafetería El Piano, C Alfonso VII 3, T985 512 333. Cosy and friendly, this is a place to seek out a morning coffee, which will come accompanied by a tasty small cake or slice of tortilla.

♠ Bars and clubs

Gijón *p394, map p395*
There are many cheerful drinking bars along C Rivero off the Plaza de España. The small streets around C Santa Lucía are a mass of bars, many operating only at weekends.

Anticuario, C San Antonio 9, T985 344 441. A fairly upmarket café during the day, this place changes once the sun goes down, as a white-collar (and mixed) crowd move from the *café con leche* to the gin and tonics. Particularly lively at weekends; closes late.

Blue Sky Café, C San Antonio 6, T985 356 141, next door to **Anticuario**. This compact place is a reliable option; dark, sleek, styled. A DJ and lively crowd turns it into a disco at weekends.

Raffaella, C Santa Elena 21, T699 139 085. This cheery Italian-run cocktail bar with cute lighting, cosy white vinyl seating, and outrageously colourful drinks is a winner.

El Patio de la Favorita, C Ezcuria 5. A fine spot for an evening drink, this moodily-lit place is on the beachfront, very spacious, and features regular live music. In summer there's a gimmicky camera so you can keep an eye on the beachfront action.

Avilés and around *p397*
The main area for weekend nights is the barrio of Sabugo, where pubs around C Estación are always busy. The no-frills bodegas along C Rivero also fill up fast.

⊕ Entertainment

Gijón p394, map p395
Cinemas
Cines Centro, behind Playa San Lorenzo in a shopping centre off C San Agustín, T985 353 757.

⊕ Festivals and events

Avilés and around p397
Feb/Mar Carnival, known as *Antroxu*, in Avilés is big. The town happily submits to a week of parties and events centred around the Plaza de España. On the Sat, C Galiana sees a riotous procession of boats on a river of foam, while the Tue hosts a more traditional, but equally boisterous, procession. The whole town is in fancy dress, including the bars, which also undergo a change of identity. Ash Wednesday sees the traditional Burial of the Sardine. Accommodation is tight, but FEVE run trains all night from Gijón and Oviedo on the main nights.

⊖ Transport

Gijón p394, map p395
Air Flights from Asturias international airport, see page 380, reached by bus from Gijón hourly on the hour, 40 mins, €6.35. A taxi is €45.

Bus Local services run regularly to **Oviedo** (30 mins) and **Avilés** (30-40 mins). The major intercity operator is ALSA, www.alsa. es, T902 422 242, who connect Gijón with **A Coruña** (4 daily, 5-6 hrs, €25), **Santiago** (4 daily, 6 hrs, €29), **León** (9 daily, 2 hrs, €12), **Valladolid** (5 daily, 4½ hrs, €21), **Madrid** (14 daily, 6 hrs, €35), **Santander** (10 daily, 3-4 hrs, €16), and **Bilbao** (9 daily, 4 hrs, €23). Some of these services are premium, being quicker and more expensive.

Ferry A new ferry service between Gijón and **St Nazaire** has started to operate as a trial at time of research. Run by GLD Atlantique, www.gldatlantique.co.uk, the overnight crossing takes 14 hrs. Foot passengers are not accepted; you must have a vehicle and take a cabin.

Train FEVE coastal connections to **Santander** (2 daily, 4 hrs, €15), **Bilbao** (1 daily, 6½ hrs, €23), and westwards as far as **Ferrol** in Galicia (2 daily, 6½ hrs, €22). More regular services run to **Llanes**, **Cudillero** and **Avilés**.
  RENFE links Gijón with **León** (7 daily, 2½ hrs, €22), **Madrid** (4 daily, 5¼ hrs, €51), **Barcelona** (2 daily, 11-13 hrs, €52-71) and points in between.

Avilés and around p397
Air Flights from Asturias international airport, see page 380, reached by regular bus, 25 mins, €1.35. A cab to the airport costs about €22.

Bus and train The RENFE, FEVE, and bus stations are on Av de los Telares on the waterfront to the west of the old town. Both RENFE and FEVE connect the town frequently with **Oviedo** and **Gijón** (35-40 mins), as does the bus company ALSA. Frequent buses for western Asturias.

⊕ Directory

Gijón p394, map p395
Internet and telephone Locutorio Mí País, C Instituto 9, central and cheap internet and phone calls. **Post office** Plaza 6 de Agosto, south of the centre, not far from the bus station.

Avilés and around p397
Internet Locutorio Ciber, C Alfonso VII 8, has internet access. **Post office** Plaza Alfonso VI, just north of Plaza de España.

Western Asturias

The west coast of Asturias is a rugged green landscape, speckled with fishing villages and gouged by deep ravines. George Borrow describes the arduousness of crossing these in the 1830s in The Bible in Spain, *but nowadays they are spanned by massive road and rail viaducts. It makes a great place for an enjoyably low-key Asturian stay. The fishing towns of Cudillero, Luarca and Tapia de Casariego bristle with character, and there are many excellent beaches, some with good surf.*

Southwestern Asturias is something of a wilderness, whose steep green valleys still contain villages that are not accessible by road. It's a hillwalker's paradise: there are several good bases with a range of marked trails, such as Santa Eulalia de Oscos, or Taramundi, famous for its knives and centre of a fascinating ethnographic project. The village of Grandas de Salime is another rewarding place to stay and is home to an excellent ethnographic museum. It's also worth applying to visit the Parque Nacional Muniellos, in the far southwest corner of Asturias – the old-growth European forest is home to several endangered species, including a small community of bears. ▶▶ *For listings, see pages 406-411.*

West coast ▶ For listings, see pages 406-411.

Ins and outs
The A8 motorway runs west just back from the coast, and is being completed in stages, while the **FEVE** line from Gijón and Oviedo to Galicia also follows this coast faithfully, although the stations tend to be at a short distance from the town centres, and there are only three trains a day in either direction. **ALSA** buses are much more frequent.
▶▶ *See Transport, page 411.*

Cudillero and around → *Colour map 2, A1.*
The colourful houses of this small fishing town are steeply arrayed around the harbour like the audience in a small theatre. Its picturesque setting and small fishing harbour make this prime outing territory during summer holidays. Entirely dormant during winter, in season Cudillero makes a good destination, having enough restaurants and bars to keep things interesting, but still not suffering from resort-style over-development. It's a lovely place.

The town, called *Cuideiru* in Bable, effectively has just one street, which winds its way from the village of El Pito, replete with *indiano* mansions, down the hill into Cudillero and down to the harbour, which is the easiest place to park. Here, the new **tourist office** ① *Puerto del Oeste s/n, T985 591 377, turismo@cudillero.org; Jul-Sep daily 1000-2100, Oct and Apr-Jun Mon-Fri 1000-1400, 1700-2000, Sat 1100-1400, 1700-2000, Sun 1100-1400; Nov-Mar Mon-Fri 1000-1400, 1600-1900, Sat 1100-1400, 1600-1900, Sun 1100-1400,* can furnish you with information on the town; apart from a small exhibition (€1) in the former *lonja*, there's not a lot to see; the setting and atmosphere is the main attraction. Most of the action takes place around the waterfront, where the smell of grilling fish is all-pervading at lunchtime.

There are some wildly shaped cliffs in this area, and while the summer sea might seem almost Mediterranean, in winter the waves give the sea wall a pounding. **El Pito**, just off the main road east of town, has its own **FEVE** station and a few places to stay. It's an attractive walk down into the town but an uphill return trip.

El Cambaral

El Cambaral was the most famous of the Moorish pirates who terrorized the Cantabrian and Asturian coasts. The scourge of local shipping, he was finally tricked by a local knight, who put to sea in an apparently harmless ship that was actually bristling with hidden soldiers. El Cambaral was wounded and captured. The knight took him home, for the trial had to wait until the accused had healed, but foolishly his captor let his young daughter tend to the pirate's wounds.

The two predictably fell in love and decided to elope. Reaching the port, where a boat was waiting, and thinking themselves safe, they stopped for a kiss, but the enraged knight had been warned. He arrived at the quay and chopped off both the kissers' heads with one blow.

Luarca remembers the ill-fated couple in the name of its bridge, *El Beso* (The Kiss), and the fishermen's quarter, known as *El Pirata Cambaral*.

Luarca → *Colour map 2, A1.*

The charm of Luarca, one of this coast's best destinations, is that although summer visitors are drawn by its attractive harbour and plentiful facilities, it gives the refreshing impression that fishing remains its primary concern. While it has grown a little since Borrow exclaimed that it "stands in a deep hollow ... it is impossible to descry the town until you stand just above it", it's still a compact place, centred around the Río Negro, a stream in summer that swells substantially in colder months. Luarca was formerly a major whaling port; the whale still has a proud place on the coat of arms.

Once again, the **harbour** is the biggest attraction, filled with colourful boats of all sizes. A variety of restaurants line it; beyond them you can walk around to the sea wall and watch it take a fearful pounding if the sea is in the mood. At the other end of the harbour is the **beach**, a rather apologetic affair with dirty grey sand and lined with changing huts. A much better beach is **Playa de Taurán**, a few kilometres further west.

Just by the water opposite the church is the *lonja*, where the freshly caught fish is sold throughout the day. It's decorated with tiled murals depicting the town's fishing history, one of which shows the curious custom of deciding whether to put to sea or not in bad weather: a model of a house and of a boat were put at opposite ends of a table and the fishermen lined up according to their preference. If the majority chose to stay home, nobody would go to sea that day. The **tourist office** ① *C Los Caleros 11, T985 640 083, turismo@ayto-valdes.net, Tue-Sat 1000-1400, 1630-1830, to 2000 in summer and Sun 1100-1400, 1700-1900*, is by the river at the western end of town.

Navia and around

At the mouth of the river of the same name, Navia is a more commercial port than the others on this coast, with a significant boat building and plastics industry. Unlike most of the others, Navia's charm is to be found away from its harbour, in the narrow paved streets of the old town above. The **tourist office** ① *top of C Las Armas, T985 473 795, turismo@ayto-navia.es; Oct-Jun Thu-Fri 1030-1330, 1600-1800, Sat 1030-1400, 1600-1830, Sun 1030-1330; Jul-Sep Tue-Fri 0930-2100, Sat and Sun 1000-1400, 1600-1930*, is in this part of Navia.

There's plenty to do around Navia. From town you can walk 10 km east along a marked coastal trail, rewarded by magnificent views and a good dollop of sea air and pine resin in your lungs.

The valley of the Río Navia, winding inland to **Grandas de Salime** and beyond, is one of Asturias' natural highlights, dotted with Celtic *castros*, small hillforts, most of which are between 2000 to 2500 years old. While some of the remoter ones are well worth exploring with transport, the most accessible is just 6 km from Navia, at **Coaña** ① *T985 978 401; Oct-Mar Tue-Sun 1030-1500; Apr-Sep Tue-Sun 1030-1400, 1600-1900, closed Mon; free.* A series of circular house foundations are compactly arrayed within a walled precinct on the hillside, commanding a spur in the valley and guarded by a tower that would have been the only entry point to the community. There are free hourly guided visits in the summer months. There's a café and a small visitor centre. Infrequent buses run there from Navia; if you want to walk, cross the bridge over the river and take the first road on the left. The fort is a short way past the village of Coaña.

Tapia de Casariego and around

Tapia, one of the most relaxed places on this coast, deserves a look. While there is a small harbour, the town's beautiful beach west of the centre is deservedly the main attraction. There's a small surf community here, established by the semi-mythical Gooley brothers – two Aussies who fetched up in a campervan one day in the 1970s – and it certainly feels more like a beach town than a fishing port. The town itself is charming, with a quiet elegance radiating from its whitewashed stone buildings and peaceful plazas watched over by the dominant Christ on the church tower. Opposite the church, there's a small tourist information kiosk open in summer. Apart from Tapia, the best surf beaches are **Peñarronda** to the west, where there are two campsites, and **Frejulfe**, further east. Waves also get ridden under the bridge that crosses into Galicia between Castropol and Ribadeo to the west.

Castropol and the Galician border

Asturias ends at the Ría de Ribadeo, a broad estuary at the mouth of the Río Eo, notable for the cultivation of shellfish. The N634 highway blazes straight on over a massive bridge into Galicia. While the main town in this area, Ribadeo, is across the water, Asturias still has a little more to offer in the village of Castropol.

With a great setting on the estuary, the village is a peaceful and seldom-visited gem. Formerly an important ferry crossing, it has been completely bypassed by the massive bridge, and now does little but cater to passing traffic on the Lugo road. If you've got a spare hour or two, it won't be wasted exploring the narrow streets of this lovely place. The central plaza contains a memorial to the Spanish-American war of 1898. The naval defeats of this war, and subsequent decline in shipping due to the loss of all Spain's remaining colonies, were big factors in the decline of towns on this coastline. To reach Castropol, take the Lugo turn-off from the coast road a few kilometres before Galicia.

Southwest Asturias → *For listings, see pages 406-411.*

Ins and outs

Travelling is time-consuming on these remote roads, even with your own car. ▸▸ *See Transport, page 411, for details of buses.*

Taramundi and around

More easily accessed from the coast, the road to Taramundi beetles up green valleys where mules and donkeys still draw carts, and herds of cows take priority over vehicles. The village itself is an earthy place, which draws its fair share of summer tourists, many of whom are attracted by its numerous knife workshops. The Taramundi blades are renowned throughout Spain; the range available runs from professional-standard kitchen knives to carved tourist souvenirs. Most of the workshops welcome visitors – there are plenty to choose from. Taramundi is only a couple of kilometres from Galicia, and the locals speak a bewildering mixture of Bable and Galego that they cheerfully admit is incomprehensible to outsiders. There's a **tourist office** ⓘ *Av Solleiro 18, T985 646 877, Tue-Sun 1000-1400, 1630-1930*, on the main road at the bottom of town.

In the valley around Taramundi are a number of ethnographic projects, where traditional Asturian crafts and industries have been re-established. The best of these is possibly **Os Teixois** ⓘ *T985 979 684, www.osteixois.com, daily 1100-1800, €1.50, free Wed*, in an idyllic wooded valley with a working mill and forge powered by the stream. If there aren't many people about, it feels uncannily as if you've just stepped back in time. There's a small restaurant, which cheerfully serves up simple but abundant food, much of it produced by the local projects. Teixois is about one hour's walk from Taramundi – head straight down the hill and follow the signs. The road passes near several of the other projects en route.

Grandas de Salime → *Colour map 1, B5.*
This sleepy little municipal centre is notable for an excellent museum, the **Museo Etnográfico** ⓘ *Sep-Jun Tue-Sat 1130-1400, 1600-1830, Sun 1130-1430, Jul-Aug Tue-Sun 1130-1400, 1600-1930, €1.50*, an ambitious and enthusiastic project that seeks to recreate in one place a range of traditional Asturian crafts, industries and daily life. Working mills, grape presses, and pedal-operated lathes are fascinatingly and lovingly put to work by the informative staff. Here you can see the making of the characteristic *madreñas*, wooden clogs worn over shoes when working outdoors, still very much in use. It's an important project and indicative of the deep pride Asturians hold for their heritage.

Reserva Natural Integral de Muniellos → *Colour map 1, B6.*
ⓘ *Access is strictly limited to 20 visitors a day; reservations are taken on T985 105 545.*
This large protected area of mountain oak forest is situated west of the AS-15 some 30 km south of Cangas. Much of it is unspoiled old-growth forest and it is home to many protected species including badgers, capercaillie, deer, bears, short-toed eagles, otters and serpents. The enthusiastic visitor centre is 7 km from the main road and is the starting point for a seven-hour walking trail through the forest. One inhabited village remains in the far north of the park. These days you can count the inhabitants on the fingers of one hand, a sad example of the depopulation of the Asturian mountains.

◉ Western Asturias listings

For Sleeping and Eating price codes and other relevant information, see Essentials pages 31-39.

● Sleeping

Cudillero and around *p403*
B La Casona de la Paca, El Pito, T985 591 303, www.casonadelapaca.com. Closed Jan. This red 3-storey house is a typical *casa de indiano* with a walled garden. Fairly formal in

style, it's a relaxing and secluded hideaway. As well as the comfortable rooms, there are also good-value apartments for daily or weekly hire. Take the 1st (ie easternmost) turn-off for Cudillero, and you'll see it on your right. It's just 5 mins' walk from the El Pito train station (turn left out of it).
B La Casona del Pío, C Riofrío 3, Cudillero, T985 591 512, www.lacasonadepio.com. Closed Jan. This beautiful stone hotel and

restaurant is just off the harbour. It's run by warm and friendly people, and has welcoming compact rooms with hydromassage mini-tubs. The food is great. Recommended.

D-E Pensión El Camarote, C García de la Concha 4, Cudillero, T985 591 202, www. elcamarote.es. In the top half of the main street, this upmarket *pensión* has well-equipped rooms but is often full in summer, so book ahead. They give a substantial discount to pilgrims walking to Santiago. Light breakfast included.

E Pensión Alver, C García de la Concha 8, Cudillero, T985 591 528, www.pensionalver. com. Open Easter-Sep. On the main street through the village, this friendly *pensión* in a bright blue building has good-standard rooms that are as clean as a whistle. There's free internet and Wi-Fi, and use of a kitchen.

Camping

Camping Cudillero, T985 590 663, www.campingcudillero.com. Open May-Sep. Some distance east of the town, but appealing and friendly, offering good facilities including cabins. Handy for the El Aguilar beach.

Luarca *p404*

B Hotel Villa de Luarca, C Alvaro de Albornoz 6, T985 470 703, www.hotelvilladeluarca.com. Occupying a characterful centenarian mansion in the heart of town, this worthwhile spot features individually decorated rooms with furniture befitting the building and plenty of pleasing small features. The boss can tell you about the best beaches and hidden spots in the area. This price only applies in late Jul and Aug; the rest of the year it's **D**.

B Torre de Villademoros, T985 645 264, www.torrevillademoros.com. Between Cudillero and Luarca, this is a beautiful old Asturian farmhouse with an extremely stylish modern interior situated on a cliff above the sea with a large medieval tower in its backyard. The rooms are most commodious, and the friendly owners have just created

a romantic and luxurious suite in the tower itself – perfect for an upmarket family break, or a romantic getaway. Delicious home-made food is a highlight. From Villademoros on the main road (buses stop here), cross the railway bridge and turn left when you reach a small *parrillada*. The hotel is signposted from there. Recommended.

C Hotel Báltico, Paseo del Muelle 1, T985 640 991, www.hotelbaltico.com. Right on the harbourside, this solid family-run hotel offers a great position and quiet rooms with plenty of light. There's a new annexe with more upscale modern rooms, some of which have great views over the port.

D Hotel Rico, Plaza Alfonso X, 6, T985 470 585, www.hotelrico.com. An excellent budget option, this has value-packed and spacious rooms above a café. There's cable television, heating and good en suite bathrooms. Heated debates from downstairs can echo through the building, but it's a winner at this price and a steal off-season. Recommended.

D La Colmena, C Uría 2, T985 640 278, www.lacolmena.com. This attractively modern option has smallish but newly refurbished rooms with attractive wooden floors and furnishings and plenty of light.

E Pensión Moderna, C Crucero 2, T985 640 057. A simple, old-style *pensión* with 3 spotless doubles and polished floors.

Camping

Playa del Tauran, T985 641 272, www.campingtauran.com. Open Easter-Sep. The best campsite in this part of Asturias, on a clifftop west of Luarca with access to a small beach. Excellent atmosphere and facilities. Bar, shop and cabins are among the eucalypts. It is 3 km from the main road, near the hamlet of San Martín. Quicker access by foot from the far end of Luarca beach. Recommended.

Navia and around *p404*

A Hacienda Llamabúa, La Mabona, T985 474 981, www.haciendallamabua. es. Between Luarca and Navia, this modern rural hotel is good for a families, with plenty of grounds to wander, a pool and child-friendly facilities. The rooms are comfortable, decorated contemporary-rustic with up-to-date conveniences like plasma screen TVs and iPod docks. They also have self-catering apartments available.

B Hotel Palacio Arias, Av Emigrantes 11, Navia, T985 473 671, www.palacioarias.es. One of the most lavish and eccentric *indiano* constructions in western Asturias, surrounded by a walled garden and furnished in period style. Go for the superior rooms in the *palacio* itself; the hotel's modern annexe is cheaper but less characterful.

C Hotel Casona Naviega, Av Emigrantes 37, T985 474 880, www.casonanaviega.com. This winningly blue *indiano* house sits on the main entrance road to Navia and offers a pleasing combination of original features and modern conveniences like Wi-Fi and a DVD library. It's run by enthusiastic young owners and surrounded by a pleasant garden featuring the palm trees so characteristic of these buildings. The rooms are compact but attractively furnished.

D Hotel Arco Navia, C San Francisco 2, Navia, T985 473 495, informacion@ hotelelarco.com. Attractive slate building by an arch on a historic medieval street. Apparently St Francis stayed in what is now the rental apartments.

E Pensión San Franciso, C San Francisco s/n, Navia, T985 631 351. On a tiny plaza, this whitewashed *pensión* is clean and simple.

Tapia de Casariego and around *p405*
Accommodation in Tapia is unremarkable but adequate.

C La Xungueira, T985 628 213. Closed Oct-Mar. By the beach, on the main road just west of the centre, this is the best option in Tapia. The pastel-shaded rooms are comfortable if not particularly inspiring; some of the bigger ones have fold-out couches. There's also a cider bar and a big garden with playground to keep the kids onside. Significant off season discounts.

D Hotel Puente de los Santos, Av Primo de Rivera 31, T985 628 155, www.hotelpuentedelossantos.com. On the main road, where the buses stop. The rooms are a little bit old fashioned, but comfortable enough for a beach break for a couple of days.

Camping
Camping Playa de Tapia, T985 472 721. On the other side of the beach from town, this summer-only campsite has reasonable facilities. Road access a couple of kilometres west of town but on foot it's much quicker across the beach.

Castropol and the Galician border
p405

A Palacete de Peñalba, C El Cotarelo s/n, Figueras, T985 636 125, www. hotelpalacetepenalba.com. On the hill above Figueras, this flamboyant apricot-coloured edifice dominates the fishing village. Set in a huge garden, it was built in the early 20th century by a modernista disciple of Gaudí. It's now a lavish place with an expensive French-influenced restaurant.

D Peña Mar, Ctra General s/n, T985 635 482, www.complejopenamar.com. The nicer of the 2 uninspiring hotel-motel set-ups on the main road.

Taramundi and around *p405*
A La Rectoral, Cuesta de la Rectoral s/n, Taramundi, T985 646 760, www.larectoral. com. This historic hotel is housed in the 18th-century building that used to be the home of the parish priest, with superb views over a fairytale valley. The rooms are extremely comfortable – the best have balconies overlooking the valley, as does the dining room.

D Casa Petronila, C Mayor s/n, Taramundi, T985 646 874, www.casapetronila.com. Attractive rooms in an old stone building on the main street.

D Hotel Taramundi, C Mayor s/n, Taramundi, T985 646 727, www.

hoteltaramundi.com. This friendly hotel has bedrooms plumb-full of Asturian comfort. It's a small and intimate place and real care has been paid to the decoration. Recommended.

E Pensión La Esquina, C Mayor s/n, T985 646 736. The cheapest beds in town in a simple *pensión* above a café. Small and comfy (unless you're tall, as the beds have footboards).

Casas de aldea

The area around Taramundi is brimming with *casas de aldea*. 2 recommendable ones are **D-E** Freixe, T985 621 215, near the village of Barcia, and **E** Aniceto, T985 646 853, www.casavillar.com, a small nucleus of houses in Bres. Pricier, but with character and setting is **C-D As Veigas**, T987 540 593, www.asveigas.com, where, as part of the ethnographic project, a deserted village has been restored to life; the 2 buildings of the priest's house can be rented.

Reserva Natural Integral de Muniellos *p406*

The nearest accommodation to the park is on the main road.

E Hotel La Pista, T985 911 004, www.hotellapista.net. A short distance south of the turn-off, in the village of Vega de Rengos, dominated by a massive coal plant. It is welcoming, however, with colourful rooms, a restaurant and a cosy sitting room.

E Pensión La Pescal, T985 918 903, www.lapescal.com. In the tiny village of the same name north of the turn-off, this is more a hotel than a *pensión*, with a garden, elegantly quirky bedrooms with the original furniture of the old house and comforting home-cooked meals. Great value.

● Eating

Cudillero and around *p403*

There are plenty of seafood 'n' cider places of varying quality, many featuring meet-your-meal-style aquarium tanks.

¶¶ El Faro, Río Frío 4, T985 900 092. Perhaps the pick of the litter, tucked away just off the square at the bottom of town, this warmly lit and decorated seafood spot serves enormous portions in a cordial manner. Try the Asturian classic *merluza a la sidra* (hake cooked in cider), preceded by a shared plate of steamed *berberechos* (cockles) or anything else that takes your fancy. Recommended.

¶¶ La Casona del Pío, see Sleeping, above. An excellent seafood restaurant in the slate dining room with layered wooden ceiling. The philosophy is to produce *'cocina de siempre'* with high-quality ingredients; they succeed. Lunch *menú* for €20.

¶¶ Restaurante Isabel, C La Ribera 1, T985 590 211. Bang on the harbour with lifebuoy-and-anchor style nautical decor and appropriately high-class seafood.

¶ Bar Julio, Plaza La Marina s/n, T985 590 124. A good café. Sitting on the outside terrace between the *soportales* you can watch on the whole town stretching up above you. They do decent bar-top munchies like *empanada* and little sandwiches.

¶ El Ancla, C Riofrío 2, T985 590 023. Seafood restaurant specializing in paella and a mixed seafood *parillada*, but also does a range of *raciones* and tapas. The calamari are particularly tasty, generous portions.

Luarca *p404*

¶¶¶ Restaurante Sport, C Rivero 8, T985 641 078. This smart harbourside joint specializes in seafood and especially shellfish, including river oysters from the nearby Río Eo. It is characterized by excellent service and a great wine list, whose various delights are served in lovely large glasses. There's also a bar, where they'll try and tempt you to dine by serving a delicious free *tapa*.

¶¶¶ Villa Blanca, Av de Galicia 25, T985 641 035. Another gourmet option in town, with a choice of dining rooms. The seafood is of excellent quality, as you would expect from this proud fishing town, paintings of which decorate the walls.

El Barómetro, Paseo de la Muelle 4, T985 470 662. The old wooden object in question stands on the wall outside this excellent seafood restaurant. The decor is warmly maritime, and the host is solicitous. Try a whole oven-baked *sargo* (white sea bream) or the *oricios* (sea urchins), which have an unusual but acquirable taste. High-quality dining at a very reasonable price. Recommended.

Mesón de la Mar, Paseo de la Muelle 35, T985 640 994. Massive old stone building on the harbour with plenty of character and a big range of *menús*. There are also tasty *raciones* to be eaten at homely wooden tables in the bar, which features a circular table and trough for pouring your own cider. They also do excellent seafood rices for 2 (€30-40).

Miramar, Paseo de Muelle 33, T985 640 584. On the top of the old *lonja* at one end of the harbour, this tempts with outdoor dining and drinks on a deck offering stunning views over the town and the port. The seafood has such offerings as *zamburiñas* (little scallops) or octopus straight off the grill at pretty reasonable prices.

Café Riesgo, C Uría 6, T985 640 818. Overlooking what passes for the town's traffic hub, this is a pleasant 1st-floor café with lots of windows for contemplation.

Cambaral, C Rivero 14, T985 640 983. Named after the swashbuckling pirate, see page 404, this is a great tapas and drinks option. There's a conservatory space with directors' chairs for a quiet coffee, while the bar is always lively with locals. The tapas are simple but delicious, like mussels or *lacón*.

Navia and around *p404*

La Barcarola, C Las Armas 15, T985 474 528. Fairly upmarket restaurant in a heavy 3-storey stone building in the old part of town. Attractive interior with dark wood and soft, coloured lights. Good reputation in these parts, particularly for seafood rice.

El Sotanillo, C Mariano Luiña 24, T985 630 263. Restaurant with a range of seafood with a good *menú del día*. Café upstairs does a range of snacks for smaller appetites.

Tapia de Casariego and around *p405*

The majority of restaurants and bars are huddled around the harbour. Fresh fish is understandably their stock-in-trade.

El Bote, C Marqués de Casariego 30, T985 628 282. This thoughtful seafood restaurant has a very homely feel and excellent fresh fish. Try the *percebes* (goose barnacles) if they are on offer.

La Cubierta, C Travesía del Dr Enrique Iglesias Alvarez, T985 471 016. A good *sidrería* with a simple and effective layout. A long bar crowded with locals is faced by wooden tables on 1 side, which need to be sturdy in order to support the massive *raciones* on offer at knock-down prices.

Castropol and the Galician border *p405*

El Risón, El Puerto s/n, T985 635 065. Closed Feb. The best option in town for a meal or a drink, this is a friendly and peaceful place on the water with outdoor tables looking over the oyster and clam beds of the *ría*, and over to Ribadeo in Galicia.

Taramundi and around *p405*

All 3 Taramundi hotels have good restaurants.

Hotel Taramundi, C Mayor s/n, Taramundi, T985 646 727. In the centre of town, and attractively stone-faced. The meat dishes stand out; the *churrasco* (ribs) and *solomillo* steak are particularly juicy.

Pantaramundi, C Mayor s/n, T985 646 821. Their bread is prized throughout Asturias. A friendly café, good for snacks.

Sidrería Solleiro, T985 646 706, further down the hill. A cheerily decent cider bar serving uncomplicated and delicious traditional fare.

🎵 Bars and clubs

Luarca *p404*
Saint Michel, C Párroco Camino 28, T985 640 289. The liveliest of Luarca's bars, this long dark nightspot on the pedestrian main street gets lively at weekends, when it's open very late.

Navia and around *p404*
El Bar de Siñe, C Las Armas 17, Navia. A good bar on one of Navia's nicest streets.
Te Beo, Av del Muelle. One of Navia's best bars, with a good range of beers.

Tapia de Casariego and around *p405*
El Faro, El Puerto 10. By the harbour, this is a friendly bar decorated with photos and paintings of lighthouses. A good place to discuss the surfing options hereabouts.

⚙ Activities and tours

Luarca *p404*
Jatay, based 3 km west of Luarca, T985 640 433/600 665 763, www.jatayaventura.com. Organizes tours on horses and quad buggies in the area; on more of a holiday-fun than serious-trekking footing.
Valdés Aventura, T689 148 295. Offers more serious adventures on mountain bikes or on horseback.

Castropol and the Galician border *p405*
Ondabrava, based near Castropol, T985 627 341, www.ondabrava.com. Organizes an excellent range of activities throughout the region.

⊖ Transport

West coast *p403*
Bus ALSA buses run westwards more or less hourly along the coast from **Gijón** and **Oviedo** (changing at Avilés).

Cudillero and around *p403*
Bus Most ALSA services only stop on the main road about 30 mins' walk away. A few go into town; these mostly go to/from **Avilés**.

Train The railway station is at the top of the town.

Luarca *p404*
Bus The bus station is next to **El Arbol** supermarket on Paseo de Gómez on the river. There are regular bus services to/from **Oviedo**, **Gijón** and **Avilés**.

Train The FEVE station is a little further upstream, on the accurately named Av de la Estación, 10 mins' walk from the centre of town.

Navia and around *p404*
Bus The ALSA station is on the main road, Av de los Emigrantes. **Autos Piñeiro** service the Navia valley to **Grandas de Salime**.

Train The FEVE station is on Av Manuel Suárez, Navia. There are 3 services a day to and from **Oviedo** (2 of which continue to **Galicia**).

Tapia de Casariego and around *p405*
Bus ALSA buses stop on Av Primo de Rivera in the centre of town.

Train The FEVE station is an inconvenient 20-min walk.

Taramundi and around *p405*
Bus The closest bus stop to Taramundi is Vegadeo, 18 km away on the N640 that links Lugo with the Asturian coast.

Grandas de Salime *p406*
Bus A daily bus runs to/from **Oviedo** to Grandas de Salime, stopping at every house on the way. It takes 4 hrs and costs €13.

East coast Asturias

The coast east of Gijón is popular with Spanish summer tourists but it's always possible to get away from the crowds; the sheer number of small villages and accommodation options sees to that. The scenery is majestic, with rolling green farmland, little fishing communities tumbling down to the sea and, muscling right up to the coast, the spectacular Picos de Europa mountain range. There are also dinosaur footprints scattered around; pick up the tourist office brochure or hit the museum at Lastres if you're interested in tracking them down. You'll find some good examples, although not to the standard of those in the Rioja. ►► *For listings, see pages 414-418.*

Villaviciosa and around → *For listings, see pages 414-418. Colour map 2, A2.*

Set back from the sea on a marshy inlet, Villaviciosa is a busy market town with an attractive historic centre. It's famous for *avellanas* (hazelnuts), but more importantly, it's the foremost producer of cider in Asturias, and is worth a visit even if you don't fancy trying the local juice. **Tourist office** ① *Plaza Obdulio Fernández 51, T985 891 759, www. lacomarcadelasidra.com, Oct-Mar 1200-1400, 1530-1730, Apr-Sep 1000-1400, 1600-1900.*

The centre boasts several elegant *indiano* buildings, as well as a church, the **Iglesia de Santa María de la Oliva** ① *Tue-Sun 1100-1400, 1700-1900*, a Romanesque building with very attractive zigzagged portals.

In a square nearby is a statue of Carlos V (Carlos I of Spain). In 1517, intending to make his first entry to Spain a grand one, Carlos' fleet was ravaged by storms and finally managed to limp into harbour at Tazones just north of here, thus making Villaviciosa his first sizeable stop. He stayed at a nearby *palacio*, **Casa de Hevia** ① *C José Caveda y Nava*, which is marked with a plaque.

A good chunk of the town's population work in the **cider factories**, some of which are open for tours, such as **El Gaitero**, a 10-minute walk from the centre. The tourist office will give details of visiting hours for this and others.

North of Villaviciosa, at the western mouth of its *ría* (estuary), the village of Tazones, where Carlos V washed up, is a picturesque place brimful of seafood restaurants. It gets busy with day trippers at weekends, gorging themselves on enormous rice-with-lobster dishes and suchlike. If it's the beach you want though, head up the eastern side of the estuary to Rodiles.

Southwest of Villaviciosa at a distance of about 10 km is the ninth-century pre-Romanesque **Iglesia de San Salvador de Valdedios** ① *T985 892 324, Nov-Apr Tue-Sun 1100-1300, May-Oct Tue-Sun 1100-1300, 1630-1800, €1*, one of the province's finest. Believed to have been the spiritual centre of the Asturian kingdom and part of a palace complex for Alfonso III, it is attractively proportioned with its typical three naves and carved windows. Plenty of paintwork remains, as well as charming leafy capitals and dedicatory inscriptions. Bat-phobes should avoid the place; several of the little creatures call the dark church home.

Lastres and around → *For listings, see pages 414-418. Colour map 2, A3.*

Lastres is a quiet and appealing fishing port with attractive views over the sea and rocky coast. Its steep streets see plenty of summer action, but little at other times, when the town gets on with harvesting *almejas* (clams) and fishing. The town makes a good, relaxing waterside stay, even when the nights are chillier and the sea mist rolls over the green hills.

MUJA ① *Rasa de San Telmo s/n, T902 306 600, late Sep-late Jun Wed-Sun 1030-1430, 1600-1900, late Jun-late Sep daily 1030-1430, 1600-2000, adult/child €6.60/4.40*, is the Jurassic Museum of Asturias and sits 1.5 km east of Lastres off the Colunga road. Built in the form of a dino's footprint, it serves as an interpretation centre for the area, which is rich in fossilized pawprints. Reconstructed skeletons as well as fibreglass models bring the giant creatures to life. Some 3 km away by road, **Playa La Griega**, is an excellent beach shaped strangely by a small river. There are sets of dinosaur prints on the southeast side, and a decent campsite, **Costa Verde**, see page 414.

Ribadesella → *For listings, see pages 414-418. Colour map 2, B3.*

Ribadesella is a town of two halves, separated by a long bridge. On the western side is the beach, a long, narrow strip of sand with plenty of accommodation and holiday homes behind it. Across the bridge is the fishing port, a more characterful area with plenty of good eating and drinking options, particularly in the summer season. The **tourist office** ① *Paseo Princesa Letizia s/n, T985 860 038, oficinaturismo@ayto-ribadesella.es, Oct-Jun Mon-Sat 1000-1400, 1700-2000, Sun 1100-1400, Jul-Sep daily 1000-2200*, is near the bridge on the harbourside. They have a leaflet of suggested themed circular walks from town, ranging from two to five hours in duration.

Just outside the town is a good place for a break from the beach, the **Cuevas Tito Bustillo** ① *Apr-Aug Wed-Sun 1000-1630, visits (1 hr) every 25 mins, €2.40, not recommended for children under 11*, a limestone cave complex with some prehistoric art from the Magdalenian culture that created Altamira, only discovered in 1968. Groups of up to 25 people are admitted every 25 minutes, but there's a daily limit, so get there earlier rather than later in summer. There's a small information hall and another cave alongside, open all year, which offers geological formations but no rock art.

The Sella river that flows into the sea here is a popular venue for canoeing, see page 417 for details of tour operators. The riotous descent of the Sella from Arriondas in August culminates here in one of Northern Spain's biggest parties.

Llanes → *For listings, see pages 414-418. Colour map 2, B4.*

Llanes is the most important town on this stretch of coast and a delightful place to stay. Although it sees plenty of tourists, it has retained a very pleasant character around its fishing port and walled, pedestrianized medieval centre. There are plenty of good beaches within reasonably easy reach. It was an important whaling town, and still hauls in a good quantity of smaller sea creatures every day; the best spot to see them is in the *lonja* where they are sold off daily at around midday. The **tourist office** ① *C Alfonso IX s/n, T985 400 164, www.llanes.com, turismo@ayuntamientodellanes.com, Mon-Sat 1000-1400, 1600-1830 (1700-2100 summer), Sun 1000-1400*, is located in an old tower within the walled town.

There's a tiny beach close to the town walls, **Playa del Sablón**, which soon fills up in summer. For more breathing room, head 20 minutes' walk east to **Playa de Toró**.

At the end of the harbour wall, Basque artist Agustín Ibarrola had the idea of cheering things up by painting the concrete blocks in exuberant colours. The *Cubes of Memory* are striking and best viewed from near the lighthouse on the eastern side of the harbour.

The last stretch of Asturias has many beaches and pretty pastures, with looming mountains in the background. Just across in Cantabria, **Devatur** (see Activities and tours, page 417) run all kinds of canoeing, rafting and horse-riding activities.

⊙ East coast Asturias listings

For Sleeping and Eating price codes and other relevant information, see Essentials pages 31-39.

⊜ Sleeping

Villaviciosa and around *p412*
C **Casa España**, Plaza Carlos I 3, Villaviciosa, T985 892 030, www.hcasaespana.com. This friendly and attractively renovated *indiano*-style house offers a cordial welcome in the café downstairs, and spacious bedrooms with comfort if little luxury, antique features like gnarled wooden headboards but plenty of modernity in their gleaming bathrooms. It's a steal off season but not the warmest. (**E**).

Lastres and around *p412*
LL **Palacio de Luces**, Ctra AS-257 s/n, T985 850 080, www.palaciodeluces.com. 2 km inland from Lastres, this 5-star place is a recent conversion of an historic *palacio*. Rural in feel but luxurious in every particular, it makes a relaxing stop. The spacious rooms feature excellent bathrooms, and huge windows throughout the building offer great views of the Picos. Staff are solicitous and attentive. Prices are high but there's a restaurant, Wi-Fi, and numerous other thoughtful details.
C **Hotel Eutimio**, C San Antonio s/n, Lastres, T985 850 012, www.casaeutimio.com. At the switchback where the road to the port meets the main road winding down through the town, is this well-maintained and modernized old *casona* with friendly staff and good seafood restaurant.

Camping
Costa Verde, T985 856 373. This grassy beachside campsite is open Jun-Sep.

Ribadesella *p413*
There are many places to stay; both in the centre, and along the beach, where there's a series of desirable hotels in converted *indiano* mansions.
L **Villa Rosario**, C Dionisio Ruiz Sánchez 6, T985 860 090, www.hotelvillarosario.com. As striking as any of the *indiano* buildings along this coast, this ornate blue mansion has a prime beachside position and good rooms with top views and a restaurant. It's difficult to say it offers value in high summer, but it's a better **A-C** outside of Jul-Aug.
A **Hotel Ribadesella Playa**, C Ricardo Cangas 3, T985 860 715, www. hotelribadesellaplaya.com. Right on the beach, this comfortable place has helpful staff and offers particularly good value off season, when it's a **D**. There's a small supplement for beach views, but it's worth it.
E **Hotel Covadonga**, C Manuel Caso de la Villa 9, T985 860 110. A good-value and cheerful central place with rooms with or without bath above a convivial bar.
F **Albergue Roberto Frassinelli**, C Ricardo Cangas 1, T985 861 105, www.albergueribadesella.com. Closed Nov. An official YHA hostel in an old beachfront mansion, this characterful place should be booked ahead in summer. They organize all sorts of activities. Reception is only open 1700-2100.

Camping
As well as that listed, there are a couple of campsites with bungalows near the beach.
Ribadesella, T985 858 293, www.camping-ribadesella.com, in the small village of

Cider House Rules

In contrast to the rest of the nation, where wine and, these days, beer, rules the roost, in Asturias it is cider that Bacchus calls for when refreshment seems needed. Drunk all over the province in thousands of *sidrerías*, *sidra* has developed a complex ritual of its own that at times seems as mysterious as the Japanese tea ceremony. Ordered by the bottle and not by the glass, Asturian cider is a mouth-cleansingly sour tipple containing around 6% alcohol.

The most obvious aspect to the ritual is the method of pouring (the verb is *escanciar*, or decant). It is a case of once seen, never forgotten as the waiter holds aloft the green bottle of cider and pours it from arm's length into a glass without looking. This is done not just for show but to create bubbles in the cider, which are an essential part of the drinking process. The smaller the bubbles the higher the quality of the cider.

The drinker then has a small period of grace known as the *espalmar* during which the bubbles remain in the glass and the small quantity of poured cider must be drunk. This is normally a maximum of 10 seconds. So a leisurely sip is not the norm for Asturian drinkers who usually down the glass or *culín* in one. Normal practice is then to wait until you're ready for another draught, and then give the nod to the eagle-eyed master of ceremonies to refill the glass. However, those feeling a little impatient or emboldened after a bottle or two are welcome to try themselves (at least, that is, in places with a bit of sawdust on the floor, or a trough for spillages). Just be ready to smell of fermented apples for the rest of the evening.

The different types of cider are a result of the various blends of apples used. There are around 20 varieties used in Asturias, each one falling into a different category of sweetness. Usually the cider will be made of 80% dry and semi-dry varieties. The apples are harvested between mid-September and mid-October and important local festivals are based around the harvest. The best known is in Villaviciosa. Another notable cider festival is held in Nava, another cider capital, on 11-12 July.

Not surprisingly, given its importance in Asturian culture, cider is widely used in the local cooking. Most *sidrerías* will produce their own dishes with cider added as a flavouring.

Sebreño, 1 km inland. Open Apr-Sep. This campsite has more facilities than Los Sauces (the other campsite), including a pool and bungalows.

Llanes *p413*

The town makes a sound base, with plenty of accommodation and eating choices.
B Hotel Mira-Olas, Paseo de San Antón 14, T985 400 828, www.hotelmiraolas.com. This quiet hotel is on the eastern side of the harbour and overlooks the colourful cubes. It's been recently refurbished and makes a very pleasant base. The front-facing rooms are large and light.

B La Posada del Rey, C Mayor 11, T985 401 332, www.laposadadelrey.es. This 6-roomer is a very attractive tiny hotel near the port, decorated with *cariño* and style by an enterprising and energetic old lady. The tiny cute bar is another highlight; off-season rooms are significantly cheaper. Recommended.

B Hotel Sablón, El Sablón s/n, T985 400 787, www.hotelsablon.com. A well-located hotel/restaurant, with views out to sea – perfect for dashing down after breakfast and staking a claim on the tiny beach. The old town is just a few steps away too. Great views from the restaurant terrace.

D Pensión La Guía, C Parres Sobrino 1, T985 402 577, www.pensionlaguia.com. A very pleasant central *pensión* in an old stone building in the heart of town. The rooms are decorated with a sure touch and have modern bathrooms and reading lamps; some have a glassed gallery. There's some noise from the road, but it's worth putting up with. Recommended.

Camping
Camping Entreplayas, Av Toró s/n, T985 400 888. Open Easter-Sep. There are many campsites in the Llanes area. This has a great location on a headland between, as the name gives away, 2 beaches. There are bungalows as well as tent and van sites.

❶ Eating

Villaviciosa and around *p412*
Good eating options can be found all along C Generalísimo, rising off the main road behind the town hall. In Tazones, just about anywhere down by the harbour offers good seafood and rice dishes, but beware of the prices, especially in places without a printed menu.

❦ El Catalín, La Atalaya 9, Tazones, T985 897 113. On a hill about a kilometre before you reach Tazones from Villaviciosa, this child-friendly place has brilliant views over the village and the wide sea. The seafood rice here is superb and the prices are fair. Recommended.

❦ El Congreso de Benjamín, C Generalísimo 25, T985 892 580. A characteristic Villaviciosa smell of cider permeates this convivial place, which matches considerate service with some excellent seafood eating. Their *navajas* (razor shells) or daily specials are always worth considering; for a blowout, try their *calderetas*; a giant pan for 2 or more that is plonked down awash with fish, prawns, lobster, and garlic aromas.

❦ El Centollu, C San Roque 18, Tazones, T985 897 014. There's no menu at this little

place, so don't be afraid to ask for prices. The reason there's no menu is a good one though: what's there is whatever was fresh and good that day. Try and bag one of the few outdoor tables. The home-made desserts are really excellent.

❦ El Tonel, C Alvarez Miranda 13, T985 892 359. On a sidestreet by the park, just up the hill from the big cider house called El Roxu, this is a locals' favourite that offers excellent value for extremely generous and tasty *raciones* of seafood. The *chipirones* (small cuttlefish) are especially good here, as are the stuffed asparagus.

Lastres and around *p412*
The **Hotel Eutimio** (see Sleeping, page 414) also has a good seafood restaurant.

❦ El Varadero, C Bajada al Puerto s/n, T985 334 032. On the way down to the harbour, this down-to-earth place offers a huge variety of excellent seafood rices, as well as top *chipirones* and other feasts.

Ribadesella *p413*
Head to the old town for characterful eating. Strung around the waterside opposite the *lonja* is a string of places offering seafood and cider at various budget levels.

❦ Arbidel, C Oscura 1, T985 861 440, www. arbidel.com. Tucked away off the main street through town, this lovely little place has the nicest terrace in town and serves a range of rices, fish and meats that offer significant value for this sometimes overpriced summering spot.

❦ El Campanu, C Marqueses de Argüelles 9, T670 603 694. With a cheery terrace, walls painted pastel colours in the *comedor*, and no-nonsense service, this is a reliable choice for seafood in the heart of town. The *campanu* is the first salmon caught in the rivers of Asturias each season.

❦ Sidrería Carroceu, C del Marqués de Argüelles 25, T985 861 419. A good harbourside venue for classy seafood and cider; that typical Asturian combination.

Aramburu, Gran Vía s/n, T985 857 626. This great Asturian produce shop is worth a visit for the sights and smells of its tasty range. It's good for a classy picnic, but they also do a range of daily specials in the upstairs dining room.

Llanes *p413*

Most of the action is on C Mayor, where there are many *sidrerías* and restaurants; wander along and take your pick.

El Campanu, La Calzada s/n, T985 401 021. Set on the riverside a block back from the port, this is a good seafood destination. There's an earthy downstairs cider bar, but above is a warmly lit restaurant serving excellent fresh fish. They do a good seafood paella too.

Mesón El Galeón, C Mayor 20. A very good seafood restaurant in the old town near the port. What's on offer depends on the catch. Try the *oricios* (sea urchins) or the grilled meats. There's a gregarious bar downstairs.

Siete Puertas, C Manuel Cue 7, T985 402 751. It's hard to believe that this compact place lives up to its name (7 doors) but it does. But that's not the point; It offers truly delicious meals, with warm seafood salad, for example, making an ideal starter before rice (paella is €44 for 2), fish, seafood, and meat dishes served with solicitous goodwill.

Bar Casa del Mar, C del Muelle s/n. Underneath the functional concrete fishermen's club, this place is where locals eat their seafood fresh, simple, and cheap. There's no price gouging; a *ración* of *langostinos* (king prawns) goes for a bargain €11, *chipirones* are just €5.50, and a memorable *mariscada* for 2, including a bottle of *albariño* wine, costs €75.

⚙ Activities and tours

There are many tour operators on this stretch of coast, typically offering canoeing on the Río Sella, watersports along the beaches, and quad biking or horse riding in the foothills of the Picos de Europa. See also the Picos de Europa section, page 369, for operators offering the canoe descent of the Sella river from Arriondas to Ribadesella.

Ribadesella *p413*

Cuadra El Alisal, T608 104 768. These guys near Ribadesella can organize horse riding from €20 for 1 hr.

Turaventura, Manuel Caso de la Villa 60, T985 560 267, www.turaventura.com. Canoeing the Río Sella, and canyoning and caving.

Llanes *p413*
Golf

There's a well-placed seaside links-style golf course east of town, T985 417 230.

Tour operators

Aventura Viesca, T985 357 369, www.aven turaviesca.com. These guys can sort out canyoning, mountaineering, quad biking, and canoeing excursions in the Llanes area.

Escuela Asturiana de Surf, T670 686 801, www.escuelaasturianadesurf.com. Can arrange surfing lessons at a variety of locations on the Asturian coast.

Jaire Aquasport, C El Puerto s/n, T985 841 464,. Canoe descents on the Río Sella, as well as mountain biking, caving and guided hiking.

Towards Cantabria *p414*

Devatur, Edificio Estación s/n, Unquera, T942 717 033, www.devatur.com. All kinds of canoeing, rafting and horse-riding activities.

⊖ Transport

Villaviciosa and around *p412*

Bus Several buses a day head to **Oviedo** and **Gijón**, and some heading east to Lastres.

Lastres and around *p412*

Bus ALSA buses from **Oviedo** and **Gijón** come several times a day and stop outside the summer-only tourist office.

Ribadesella *p413*
Bus Ribadesella and Llanes are linked by bus to **Gijón** and **Oviedo**, and east to **Santander**.

Llanes *p413*
For buses, see Ribadesella, above. The FEVE station is to the east of town and is another means of reaching **Oviedo**, **Gijón** and other coastal destinations.

Contents

Galicia

At a glance

☺ **Getting around** You can fly into Vigo, Santiago or A Coruña. Transport between the cities is good, but you'll want a hire car to explore the coast or interior.
☺ **Time required** 2 weeks.
☼ **Weather** Prone to rain, even in summer. In winter it's guaranteed.
✖ **When not to go** Nov-Feb; lots of places shut down, and the drizzle can get to you after a few days.

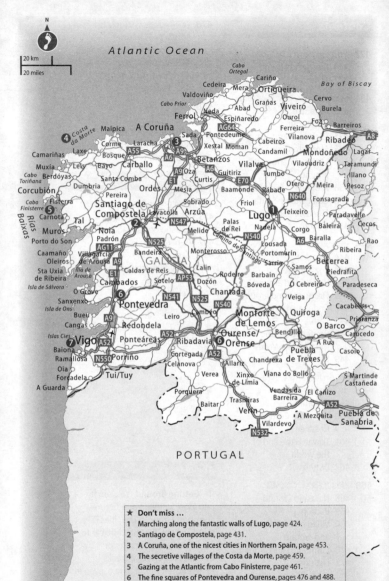

★ Don't miss ...

1 Marching along the fantastic walls of Lugo, page 424.

2 Santiago de Compostela, page 431.

3 A Coruña, one of the nicest cities in Northern Spain, page 453.

4 The secretive villages of the Costa da Morte, page 459.

5 Gazing at the Atlantic from Cabo Finisterre, page 461.

6 The fine squares of Pontevedra and Ourense, pages 476 and 488.

7 The beautifully unspoiled Islas Cíes near Vigo, page 480.

Thrust out into the Atlantic like Spain's storm shield, remote Galicia reverberates with Celtic history. Dotted with hill villages and dolmens, the *gaita*, or bagpipe, is a strong element of Galicia's musical heritage. Another point it shares with other Celtic nations is its rainfall, which is high; in the northwest, it rains 150 days of the year.

The course of Galicia's history was changed forever when the tomb of the apostle St James was allegedly discovered here. Pilgrims flocked to Galicia, progressing from across Europe, as they have begun to do again. The twin towers of the marvellous baroque cathedral of the noble granite city Santiago de Compostela which grew up around the tomb, is a fitting welcome for them.

Apart from religion, fishing is Galicia's main business; the ports of Vigo and around provide much of Spain with its fish, and shellfish are intensively farmed in the sheltered *rías* (inlets). The long, tortuous coastline is spectacular in many places. Inland, the verdant agricultural countryside still houses pockets of 'deep Spain', where, due to the small size of farm plots, modernization and Europeanization have brought comparatively little change to the traditional lifestyle.

The variety of Galicia's rural and urban landscapes make it a fascinating part of the country; the unifying factor is the seafood, which is uniformly superb, particularly the 'national' dish, *pulpo* (octopus), which is deliciously served both in no-frills *pulperías* and gourmet restaurants.

Galicians have a reputation for being superstitious and introspective, not hard to understand when you've seen the Atlantic storms in full force. A Celtic melancholy known as *morriña* is also a feature, expressed in the poems of Galicia's favourite writer, Rosalía de Castro. To visitors, though, Gallegos are generous and friendly; the region's cities are as open and convivial as anywhere in Northern Spain. You'll also notice that Galicia's a little lighter on your finances than other parts of the country: both accommodation and restaurants offer significant value here.

Pilgrim Route to Santiago

The climb from western León province into Galicia is one of the most gruelling parts of the Camino de Santiago, particularly if the local weather is on form. The first stop, O Cebreiro, is a pretty village that offers a well-deserved welcome; from here, the route to Santiago takes you through rolling green hills and a number of interesting Galician towns. Off the route, to the north, is the enjoyable city of Lugo, surrounded by a seriously impressive wall, originally built by the Romans in typically no-holds-barred fashion. ▶▶ *For listings, see pages 427-430.*

Piedrafita and O Cebreiro

The most spectacular approach into Galicia is via the pass of Piedrafita, a wind- and rain-swept mountain location that can be hostile in the extreme. Sir John Moore and his ragtag British forces were pursued up here by the French army, and many died of cold. Not much further on, they found themselves without explosive to blow up a bridge behind them, and were forced to ditch all their gold over the edge so that they could travel faster and avoid being set upon from behind.

On the main road, Piedrafita has banks, other services and lodging options, but it's best to move on down a side road to the pilgrims' rest stop of O Cebreiro. In many ways, this tiny village of attractive stone buildings is where the modern Camino de Santiago was reborn. The church and former pilgrim hostel were rebuilt in the 1960s and the energetic parish priest, Elías Valiña, found suitable people to run hostels in other waystations and began to popularize the notion of the pilgrim way once again.

Although O Cebreiro can be indescribably bleak as the winds, rains and snows roll in and the power fails, it's atmospheric and friendly and has all the services a weary pilgrim could desire. Here you'll see reconstructed *pallozas*, a circular dwelling of stone walls and straw roofs originating in Celtic pre-Roman Galicia. The church has a reliquary donated by Fernando and Isabel to accompany the chalice, which is known as the 'Grail of Galicia', after the host and communion wine became real flesh and blood one day as a skeptical priest went through the motions at Mass. In high summer, pilgrims can outnumber locals (of which there are 31) by 30 or 40 times.

Samos

Pilgrims, for a short time, have a choice of routes (they soon meet up again). The more interesting, but slightly longer, goes via the village of Samos. Significantly wetter than the Greek island where Pythagoras was born, this Samos is wholly dominated by the large monastery of **San Julián** ① *Mon-Sat 1000-1230, 1630-1830; Sun 1245-1330, 1630-1830, €2; admission by interesting tour only, leaving on the ½ hr.* The Benedictines first came here in the sixth century, and a tiny slate chapel by the river dates back to the ninth and 10th; it's shaded by a large cypress tree. The main monastery is a huge structure entered via its elegant western façade. If you think it looks a bit too square, you're right; towers were planned but the coffers ran dry before they could be erected. Ask at the monastery for a guide to visit the little chapel by the river it it's not already open.

Much of the interior of the monastery has been rebuilt: in 1951 a monk took a candle too close to a fermenting barrel in the distillery and burned most of the complex down. Although a Romanesque doorway is still in place where it used to give access to the old church, most of the architecture is baroque, but a far more elegant and restrained baroque than is usual in these parts. There are two cloisters; a pretty fountain depicting water nymphs from Greek mythology is the highlight of the smaller one, its pagan overtones appear not to trouble the monks, whose cells and eating quarters are here. Sixteen Benedictines still live here and run a small farm on the edge of the village.

The larger cloister abuts the raised church and is centred around a statue of Feijóo, the notable and enlightened writer who was a monk here early in his career. He donated much money derived from his writings to enable the dome of the church to be completed. The upper level sleeps guests (males can apply in writing or by phone, T982 546 046, to join the community for a contemplative break) and was decorated in the 1960s with a series of murals to replace those paintings lost in the fire. They're pretty bad – the artist painted cinema posters for a living – but give the monks credit for courage; it would have been all too easy to whack in a series of insipid replicas.

The church itself is large, elegant, and fairly bare. An Asturian cross above the altar is a reference to the kings that generously donated money to the early monastery; statues of them flank the nave. The dome, as with the one in the sacristy, has a touch of the Italian about it.

Sarria
Pilgrims continue on to Sarria, the major town on this stretch of the Camino. Sarria is a bit dull; a busy service and transport centre for the region, without a great deal to see. In the old town, on the side of the hill, there's a simple Romanesque church with a charming cloister and above it, a privately owned castle that needs a couple of ravens as a finishing touch to its creeper-swathed tower. The attractive pedestrianized main street that these are on is full of pilgrim hostels and peregrine-friendly eateries; it also houses a tourist information office. Sarria is famous for antiques, and there are many such shops in the town, and also several places peddling convincing replicas. The riverbank makes a relaxing spot to sit outside on a summer terrace.

Portomarín
At first glance you wouldn't know it, but this village is only about 40 years old. The original lies underwater, submerged when the river Miño was dammed. Hearteningly, the villagers were helped to move the historic buildings to the new site, and Portomarín escaped becoming the sad and soulless concrete shambles that many such relocated villages in Spain are. The main street is attractive, with an arcade and whitewashed buildings, and the Romanesque parish church is well worth a look for its rose window and beautifully carved tall portals.

Further along the Camino, it's worth taking a short detour to see the church at **Vilar de Donas**, see page 426.

Melide, Sobrado and Lavacolla
Once the Camino hits the main road, it's a rather characterless final stretch to Santiago, with fairly lifeless towns and villages straggling along the highway. The best of them is **Melide**, the geographical centre of Galicia, which has a very attractive plaza and a moderately interesting church with Romanesque origins.

If you've got transport (there are also buses here from Coruña or Santiago), it's worth heading north to the small town of **Sobrado**, where one of Galicia's largest monasteries has been saved from dereliction by the small community of monks that live there. The **church** ① *guided tour 1000-1300, 1630-1930, €2*, is impressive, with a strange sober façade of squares and geometrical patterning. The interior is softer, with ornate cupolas; there are also three down-at-heel cloisters and the massive kitchen. Sobrado is on the Camino del Norte alternative route to Santiago, and the monks run a pilgrim hostel and also offer comfortable, simple accommodation in their *hospedería*.

The last fraction of the pilgrim trail follows the busy main road due west to Santiago and has little of interest. At **Lavacolla** pilgrims used to bathe in the river so as to be clean when arriving at the apostle's tomb (the name may derive from the Latin for 'wash arse'). Ascending the hill of Monte del Gozo, now cluttered with tasteless *hostales* and roadside brothels, the first pilgrim to spot the cathedral would be dubbed the 'king' of the group. A large metal pilgrim figure marks the beginnings of the long outskirts of Santiago itself. If you're a pilgrim arriving in a very busy period, it may be an idea to overnight just before Santiago, thus arriving first the next morning to grab a cheap bed before everyone else.

Lugo and around → *For listings, see pages 427-430. Colour map 1, B4. Phone code: 982. Population: 96,678. Altitude: 470 m.*

The Romans weren't ones for half measures, so when they decided their main Galician town needed a wall, they built one with a capital W. Thanks to restoration, it's still in top condition today; it impressively circles the old town and is the most obvious feature of what is a small and remarkably pleasant inland provincial capital. Attractive architecture within the perimeter adds to the appeal, and there are several good bars and restaurants. The Miño river running far below adds to Lugo's quiet charm: it makes a great overnight stop and is small enough that things like parking and finding your way around seem to work better than in many places.

Lugo was founded in 15 BC as Lucus Augusti, named after Augustus, the emperor of the time. It rapidly became a substantial outpost; the Roman province that contained Galicia had its capital in distant Tarragona (near Barcelona), so the city had an important local administrative role. The main streets in the town still follow the Roman axes. Today, Lugo is a busy little place, a centre for the surrounding farming districts and capital of Galicia's largest province.

The main **tourist office** ① *Praza do Campo 11, T982 251 658, www.lugoturismo.com, daily 1030-1400, 1630-2000,* is near the cathedral in the heart of the tapas district. It's got a small display on the city walls. A few steps away is the **Galician regional office** ① *T982 231 361, oficina.turismo.lugo@xunta.es, Mon-Sat 1000-1400, 1600-1900, summer daily 1000-1400, 1700-2000,* which has an exhibition on the Camino Primitivo, a branch of the pilgrim route to Santiago that starts near Lugo.

Sights

Lugo's **walls** were erected in the third century AD and built to last. Made of slabs of schist, they are still almost complete and run over 2 km right around the centre of town at a height of some 10 m. Their width is impressive too; you could race chariots along the top, where the walkway is some 4-5 m wide.

The wall has been shored up over the years, and most of the 82 towers that punctuate its length are of medieval construction. If you feel a bit exposed on the top, that's because the upper portions of the towers were removed during the Napoleonic wars because it was thought they wouldn't withstand cannon fire and would topple into the town centre.

Walking around the base of the walls is the best way to appreciate their construction, and walking along the top of them is the best way to see the town. There are six points of access and 10 gates, of which the most authentically Roman is **Porta do Carme** (also called Porta Minha). In some parts the walls can feel over-restored, but they are undeniably magnificent and lend the centre inside their perimeter much character.

The 19th-century traveller George Borrow must have been having a bad day when he described Lugo's **cathedral** ① *open 1100-1300, 1600-1800*, as "a small, mean building"; although it's not the finest cathedral in Northern Spain, it's a large and interesting place. It was first built over earlier remains in the 12th century, but its big twin-towered baroque façade, somewhat reminiscent of Santiago, is what dominates today. Inside, some Romanesque features remain, such as the distinctive *ajedrezado jaqués* (chessboard) patterning associated with the Camino de Santiago.

The town was granted the right to have the consecrated host permanently on view; an honour seldom granted by the Catholic church, and still a source of some pride; Galicia's

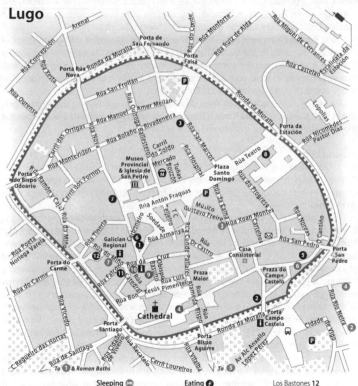

Lugo

Sleeping 🛏
Balneario de Lugo **1**
Gran Hotel Lugo **5**
Méndez Núñez **3**
Pazo de Orbán e Sangro **7**
Pensión Alba **6**
Pensión San Roque **4**
Puerta de San Pedro **2**

Eating 🍴
A Nosa Terra **6**
Bodegas de San Vicente **6**
Bodegón El Museo **7**
Campos **1**
El Castillo **2**
España **8**
La Barra **3**

Los Bastones **12**
O Figón **5**
O Pote **11**

Bars & clubs 🍸
Anagrama **4**
Jazz & Beer **9**
Medievo **10**

N

100 metres
100 yards

coat-of-arms depicts the host and the chalice for this reason. The host is displayed above the altar in an ornate silver and gold monstrance, surrounded by marble cherubs and flanked by angels. Above is a shower of silver around the eye-in-triangle symbol of the all-seeing God. In the apse is the famous and much-venerated statue of *La Virgen de los Ojos Grandes* (Virgin with the Big Eyes), a beautiful and sober Romanesque woodcarving set in a baroque chapel. The **cathedral museum** and treasury is set around the small cloisters.

Nearby, the **Praza Maior** is large, attractive, and guarded by fierce stone lions. At its top end is the town hall, an 18th-century building in Galician baroque, a style that (whisper it) owes something to Portuguese architectural traditions.

The **Museo Provincial** ① *Mon-Sat 1030-1400, 1630-2030 (2000 Sat), Sun 1100-1400, Jul and Aug Mon-Fri 1100-1400, 1700-2000, Sat 1000-1400, free*, includes the **Iglesia de San Pedro**, with a curious 15th-century door, beautiful Gothic tracery on the windows, and a strange tower. There's an eclectic display, ranging from Roman pottery and coins to sundials, Celtic jewellery, Galician painting and ethnographic displays.

Lugo's **Roman baths** were built shortly after the city was founded, taking advantage of the natural hot spring by the river. What's left of them is within the spa hotel complex by the **Miño**. A walkway over the warm waters lets you see the ancient changing rooms, with alcoves in the wall to stash your toga; another room nearby is of uncertain function. The bridge across the river nearby is also of Roman origin.

One of Lugo's pleasures, apart from strolling the walls, is exploring the small streets within their sturdy circle. **Rúa Nova** is the centre for tapas bars and restaurants, while the shopping streets are in the eastern end of the old town.

Around Lugo
The area southwest of Lugo is out of the ordinary; a sort of microcosm of Galician rural life that seems to have changed little over the decades. A web of tiny roads connects a series of hamlets where tractors are still outnumbered by mule carts and villagers still bear loads on their heads.

Within this area are two excellent buildings, both well worth visiting. The first, in the tiny settlement of **Santa Eulalia de Bóveda** ① *Mon-Fri 0800-1500 year-round, also Jan- Mar Mon-Fri 1600-1800, Sat and Sun 1100-1500, 1600-1800, Apr-Jun Mon-Fri 1600-1900, Sat and Sun 1100-1500, 1600-2000, free*, is an authentic enigma. Probably constructed in the third or fourth century AD, its main chamber, entered via a horseshoe arch, centres around a rectangular pool. Wonderful Roman frescoes of birds and trees decorate the ceiling; other ornate geometrical wall paintings have been lost through poor preservation. Though later converted to a church, it seems probable that it was a temple of sorts, perhaps a nymphaeum or place of worship of Cybele. Take the Ourense road (N540), turn right (towards Friol on the LU232) 2.5 km after crossing the bridge, left about 1 km further on, then right about 7 km down that road. It's all signposted. The church is closed, but the guardian is in a small reception building just down the road; he'll open the church up for you. Once you've seen the temple, you might want to stretch your legs a little, and a marked circular walk of 5 km from Santa Eulalia lets you do just that, while taking in this unspoiled rural zone. The villages with their low stone buildings and *hórreo* granaries are typically Galician, but the landscape, with its tilled fields, mossy stone walls, and copses, is curiously reminiscent of parts of Britain.

More easily accessible by public transport is the church at **Vilar de Donas** ① *1100-1300, 1600-1800; admission by donation (the knowledgeable and kindly warden lives nearby and may come and open it outside these hours if you hang around)*, it's also only a shortish detour off the Camino de Santiago. It's worth the trouble; it's one of Galicia's most interesting buildings. Built in the 12th century, it was modified at the behest of the Knights of Santiago to serve as a place of burial for the prestigious members of that order. The tombs line the walls after you've passed through the excellent Romanesque doorway with zigzag patterning. One of the finest tombs dates from 1378 and is mounted on two lions who are squashing a boar, representing wrath, and a wolf, symbolizing evil. In the apse are some excellent frescoes commissioned by Juan II, king of Castilla and father of Isabel, the Catholic Monarch. Dating from 1434, the paintings depict the Annunciation and Pantocrator as well as shields with the devices of Castilla y León and the order of Santiago. In the transept is a *baldacchino*, or baldachin, an ornate carved canopy commonly used over altars in Galicia; this one is made of stone. The church is easily reached by public transport; take any Santiago-bound bus from Lugo and get off at the turn-off on the main road; it's 500 m up a side road from here.

Few tourists explore the peaceful green countryside east of Lugo; the road winds its way through rolling hills to western Asturias. In a hamlet just outside the small town of **Castroverde**, 20 km or so east of Lugo, is some excellent accomodation.

◉ Pilgrim Route to Santiago listings

For Sleeping and Eating price codes and other relevant information, see Essentials pages 31-39.

◉ Sleeping

Piedrafita and O Cebreiro *p422*
There are several options in O Cebreiro, all offering similar comforts: cosy rooms in refurbished stone buildings, a convivial pilgrim bar, and warming home-cooked food.
D Hotel O Cebreiro, O Cebreiro, T982 367 125, www.hotelcebreiro.com. Just down from the church, this offers small but comfortable rooms, a range of traditional Galician cuisine, and outdoor tables in the heart of the village.

Sarria *p423*
B Alfonso IX, Rúa do Peregrino 29, T982 530 005, www.nh-hoteles.com. The town's most luxurious option, this chain hotel is modern and pleasant; the rooms have all the facilities (some are equipped for disabled visitors), and it also boasts a gym, sauna, and swimming pool as well as a restaurant. Better value than most of this chain's hotels. Extras like internet are overpriced though.

Portomarín *p423*
B Pousada de Portomarín, Av Sarria s/n, T982 545 200, www.pousadadeportomarin. com. Not the most attractive of the buildings along the Camino de Santiago, this nevertheless makes a good choice by the river a short stroll from the centre of Portomarín. Rooms are large and comfortable, if curiously furnished, and there's a pool among other facilities.
E Pensión Arenas, T982 545 386. Opposite the church on the main street, this spotless modern place makes a fine spot to put your pilgrim's head down on a pillow if you're tired of the *albergues*. There's a café and restaurant (pizza and meats) downstairs.

Lugo *p424, map p425*
B Gran Hotel Lugo, Av Ramón Ferreiro 21, T982 224 152, www.gh-hoteles.com. Lugo's top option, this massive hulk of a hotel is modern with a considerably better interior than exterior. The rooms are blessed with many facilities, including Wi-Fi, internet, and a swimming pool and spa complex.
B Hotel Puerta de San Pedro, C Neira 29, T982 222 381, www. hotelhusapuertadesanpedro.com. Around the corner from the bus station, this modern

hotel offers good amenities for a fairly low price. Though the walls are on the thin side, service is helpful, and the beds are new and comfortable. There's Wi-Fi and internet access, and, while there's no off-street parking, it's easy to get metered spaces near the hotel.

B Pazo de Orbán e Sangro, Travesía do Miño s/n, T982 240 217, www.pazodeorban. es. In a rather neglected part of the old town, tucked inside the walls, it's quite a surprise to find this wonderfully restored old baroque palace that's been caringly converted into a lovely hotel. Rooms vary in size and price – the suites are very luxurious, but all are exceptionally comfortable, and replete with numerous artistic touches. It's by far Lugo's most charismatic place to stay. Recommended.

C-D Balneario de Lugo, Barrio del Puente s/n, T982 221 228, www.balneariodelugo. com. Closed Jan. Although the atmosphere is staid, and it's a wee walk downhill from the walled town, this spa hotel is very well priced, right by the Miño river, and on the site of the old Roman baths. The rooms are well equipped, with a garden to stroll in.

D Hotel Méndez Núñez, C Reina 1, T982 230 711, www.hotelmendeznunez.com. This grand old hotel is right in the centre of town, surrounded by the pedestrianized shopping streets. It has plenty of period charm and large modernized rooms. It offers pretty good value for this location and atmosphere.

D Pensión Alba, Praza Campo Castelo 31, T982 226 056. This sparkling modern *pensión* is tucked up against (and within) the city walls near the town hall. The rooms are excellent, with firm new mattresses and wooden floorboards, and it's run with a gruff motherly air, making it a very good central spot to stay.

E Pensión San Roque, Plaza Comandante Manso 11, T982 222 700. Just outside the city walls, this modern *pensión* makes a commodious base. The rooms are compact but clean and comfy, with tight bathrooms and new parquet floors, and there's free

internet and easy metered parking in the streets hereabouts. Breakfast (in the café opposite) is included.

Around Lugo *p426*

B Pazo de Vilabade, near Castroverde, T982 313 000, www.elpazo.com. Closed Nov-Mar. One of Galicia's nicest places to stay; an old mansion with a classy but homely atmosphere and a spirited *dueña* who makes a mean afternoon tea.

🍽 Eating

Piedrafita and O Cebreiro *p422*

O Cebreiro has several places to eat, all serving inexpensive mountain food to hungry pilgrims.

¶ Casa García, Camiño Feira 2, T982 367 021. In Piedrafita, when the temperatures are low and the wind whistles through the pass, there's nothing like a hearty lunch at this friendly and traditional spot. The *menú* is €12: expensive for Galicia, but worth it, with a wide selection of homemade dishes served by a staunch local couple.

Sarria *p423*

¶ Anduriñas, Rúa Maior 29, T982 532 598. On the main pedestrian street, this place does filling plates of meat, eggs, and salad for hungry pilgrims, as well as traditional Galician favourites.

Portomarín *p423*

¶ O Mesón do Rodríguez, T982 545 054. This bastion of peregrine comforts on the main street, is a good place for a meal; the food is generously proportioned and compassionately priced.

Lugo *p424, map p425*

Lugo's excellent eating scene focuses around the 2 intersecting streets; Rúa Nova and Rúa da Cruz. Most of these bars give a small free tapa with each drink.

¶¶¶ Campos, Rúa Nova 4, T982 229 743. Right in the heart of eat street, this Lugo classic in expanded premises offers a top range of excellent seafood, as well as meat dishes and, in season, game. Prices are higher than they once were, but it's as hospitable and popular as ever.

¶¶¶ La Barra, C San Marcos 27, T982 252 920. A sleek, stylish seafood restaurant that's popular with a well-heeled traditional Lugo clientele. It's decorated in executive style; dishes such as *rodaballo* (turbot) or *kokotxas* (hake cheeks in sauce) are among the stars of the reliably excellent fish choices.

¶¶¶ Restaurante España, Rúa Teatro 10, T982 242 717, www.restespana.com. This modern restaurant serves gourmet Galician food. The menu is short and full of quality, with dishes like beef carpaccio or monkfish medallions on ratatouille well presented and delicious. Out the front is a popular bar for coffee or *pinchos*, with parchment lamps, and tables stretching as far as the eye can see.

¶¶ A Nosa Terra, Rúa Nova 8, T982 229 235. A great place to eat, this is a spot to devour tasty *raciones*, salads, and meats in an atmospheric old wine cellar, beautifully spruce in stone and wood. Out the front is a busy and excellent tapas bar; the *pinchos* are very tasty, there's a quaffable house Rioja, and the walls are decorated with wood carvings of Galician poets and quotations from them. Recommended.

¶¶ Bodegas do San Vicente, Rúa Nova 6, T982 253 318. This low, small and atmospheric deli-bar has bags of character, although the Franco and Fraga wine bottles are a little less entertaining. The boss is always chopping away at something at the front counter, be it hams, cheeses, or chorizos, which are served in the traditional manner on greaseproof paper. At the front are some barrels where people socialize with a glass of wine.

¶¶ O Figón, Rúa do Campo Castelo 47, T982 227 662. A little away from the main tapas area, in an attractive location facing the inside of the walls, this modern and handsome place offers a quiet, elegant spot to drop in for a glass of wine and a (delicious) free tapa. They also have a short menu of quality plates, ranging from grilled vegetables to stewed *jarrete*. Free Wi-Fi.

¶ Los Bastones, Travesía do Miño 13, T982 246 629. Tucked in behind the walls, this cosy Italian restaurant is perfect for a romantic dinner without busting the bank. The pastas, pizzas, and salads have a Galician flavour. Octopus pizza is one of the highlights.

¶ Bodegón El Museo, Rúa Nova 21, T982 253 351. Opposite the museum, this traditional bar is run by a hospitable Galician couple and is gloriously untrendy, with wooden beams and local folk enjoying the cheap wine. Out the back are tables where there are incredibly cheap *raciones* served; the house speciality is *pulpo* (octopus), which is absolutely delicious and only €8.

¶ El Castillo, Praza do Campo Castelo 14, T982 255 587. This attractive café and bar is an appealing spot for a coffee near the walls. It also does cheap and tasty food, ranging from good *bocadillos* to a set lunch for €9.

¶ O Pote, Rúa Miño 11, T982 228 857. Older than it looks but recently done up, this reliable standby pays attention to the important details – the food, drink and customers. They pour a generous glass of wine and you might get a free tapa to munch on while you're waiting for your free tapa to emerge from the kitchen. Now that's service.

Bars and clubs

Lugo *p424, map p425*
Lugo's lively and late bar scene is centred in the small streets around the cathedral and around Rúa de Cruz.

Anagrama, Praza Alférez Provisional 7, T982 252 827. Open nightly until late. A lively bar by the side of the cathedral with some very cool interior pseudo-classical design.

Jazz and Beer, Rúa Obispo Basulto 2, T982 250 951. This intimate and comfortable bar is a Lugo favourite for an after-dinner *copa*. With mellow music, friendly service, and well-mixed drinks, it's a very likeable place.

Medievo, Rúa Catedral 14, T982 242 021.
One of Lugo's most-frequented late-night
bars, this is a place of 2 halves. Downstairs,
the medieval decoration of armour, shields,
and the like belies a friendly bar dishing out
popcorn and jelly beans with drinks and
coffee. Upstairs is where the music is;
it tends to fill up after 0200 at weekends.

⊕ Entertainment

Lugo *p424, map p425*
Cineplex Yelmo, Praza Viana do Castelo 3,
T982 217 986.

○ Shopping

Lugo *p424, map p425*
Books There are 2 good bookshops on
Rúa Bispo Aguirre: **Aguirre**, at No 8, T982 220
336, with a good selection of maps; and **La
Voz de la Verdad**, at No 17, T982 231 104,
www.lavozdelaverdad.es.

Ceramics The famed Galician ceramic
factory Sargadelos, whose deep blue, ochre,
and white creations are very distinctive,
was founded near Lugo. There's an outlet
at Praza Santo Domingo 4 in the centre
of town.

⊖ Transport

Lugo *p424, map p425*
Bus
Lugo's bus station is conveniently located
just outside the walls near the Praza Maior;
there are services to the other Galician
cities and all over Northern Spain.

Within Galicia, regular services include to
A Coruña (roughly hourly, 1-1½ hrs), 4 to
Ferrol, 8 to **Ourense** (2 hrs), 10 to **Santiago**
(2 hrs 15 mins), 5-6 to **Viveiro** and the north
coast, 6 to **Ribadeo**.

There are 8-10 services eastwards to
Ponferrada (1½ hrs), some going via **Sarria**.
Madrid, **Barcelona**, and **Oviedo** via the
Asturian coast are also served.

Train
The train station isn't too far away from the
eastern side of the old town.

There's an overnight train to **Madrid**
(9 hrs, €51.50), and 2 to **Barcelona** (13 hrs,
from €72), which go via the rail junction
of Monforte, as well as **Sarria**, **León**, and
Burgos. You can buy tickets at a handy
RENFE office in a little arcade off the
Praza Maior.

⊕ Directory

Lugo *p424, map p425*
Post office Lugo's main post office is in
the old town on Rúa San Pedro near the
Praza Maior.

Santiago de Compostela

→ Colour map 1, B2. Phone code: 981. Population: 95,092.

"The true capital of Spain." Roads to Santiago, Cees Nooteboom.

Archaeologists in the ninth century weren't known for their academic rigour, so when a tomb was discovered here at that time it was rather staggeringly concluded to be that of the apostle Santiago, or Saint James. Christianity was in bullish mode, and the spot grew into the major pilgrimage destination in Europe as people walked thousands of miles to pay their respects, reduce their time in purgatory, or atone for their crimes.

The pilgrimage had an enormous cultural, social, and architectural effect across Northern Spain, and Santiago soon transcended its dubious beginnings to become one of the most magical cities in Spain, its cathedral the undisputed highlight of a superb ensemble of mossy granite buildings and narrow pedestrian lanes.

The late 20th century saw a massive revival of the pilgrimage tradition which has continued to grow in the new millennium. More than a 100,000 pilgrims arrive annually and Santiago is today a flourishing, happy place, seat of the Galician parliament and lively with students. Don't come for a suntan, though; HV Morton accurately if unkindly described the city as a "medieval aquarium", but the regular rain can add to the character of the place, at least for the first three days or so. Simply walking the streets here is a pleasure (even in the rain), particularly Rúa Vilar and Rúa Nova and the streets around the old university buildings. ▸▸ For listings, see pages 439-443.

Ins and outs

Getting there

The traditional way to get to Santiago is a five-week walk from the French Pyrenees, or from some closer point, but there are ways to cheat. Ryanair runs a daily service from London Stansted to Santiago's airport (**SCQ**), situated 11 km east of town in Lavacolla. Ryanair also serve the city from Liverpool, Rome, and Frankfurt Hahn. Vueling fly direct to Edinburgh, and there are daily flights from London run by **BA/Iberia**, as well as frequent internal connections (including a Ryanair flight to Madrid), and flights to other European destinations including Brussels and Amsterdam. Buses run from the airport to the the bus station via the centre. Another bus runs from Praza de Galicia to coincide with Ryanair flights. Santiago is well served by interurban buses. The bus station is a 20-minute walk northeast of the centre. Bus Nos 5 and C5 run there from Praza de Galicia via Rúa da Virxe da Cerca. If arriving by bus, head up the hill directly opposite the bus station café and turn left at the big intersection. The train station is south of the centre, about a 15-minute walk down Rúa de Hórreo (off Praza Galicia). There are trains to the rest of Galicia and Spain. ▸▸ See Transport, page 443.

Getting around

The interesting bits of town are mostly very close together. The main places you'll need public transport to access are the airport and the bus station.

Best time to visit

During summer Santiago is thronged with tourists and pilgrims; if you don't mind that, this can be the best time to be there. It rains slightly less, the old town is buzzing, and

Saint James and the Camino de Santiago

The patron saint of Spain is one of the most revered of figures in the country. St James, or Santiago, was the son of Zebedee, brother of the apostle John, and a fisherman who gave up his nets to follow Christ. In AD 44 he was martyred at swordpoint by King Herod Agrippa. Several centuries later, a small west European kingdom flexing its Christian muscles was in need of a holy warrior.

We move to Galicia, and a spot near the end of the world, Finisterre. In the early ninth century, 800 years after James was martyred and thousands of miles away, a shepherd was guided by an angel and stars to a tomb in the woods at a place now called Compostela. The local bishop, evidently not a man to reserve judgement, deemed it to be St James himself. The news spread fast, and gave the Christians new faith for their fight against the Moors. Even handier than faith on a muddy battlefield is a back-from-the-dead apostle on a white charger, and Santiago obliged. He brutally slew hundreds of hapless Muslims in battle, winning himself the nickname Matamoros, or slayer of Moors.

All very well, but how and why was his body in Spain in the first place? He had, after all, been killed in Caesarea. But tradition, however historically debatable, has it that he preached in Spain at some point, and the Virgin Mary is said to have appeared to him in Zaragoza (at the time called Caesarea too; a possible source of the confusion). James went back to the Holy Land with a few keen Spanish converts. After his death the followers rescued his body and set forth for home with it. Not experts in boat buying, they selected a stone yacht, but with the saint on board, they managed to navigate it to the Pillars of Hercules and around to Galicia. Along the way, the saint performed a miracle, saving a gentleman whose panicked horse had dashed headlong into the sea with him in the saddle. Man and horse rose from the seabed safe and sound; some traditions hold that they were covered in scallop shells; this became the apostle's symbol. His followers landed near Padrón and requested oxen from the local pagan queen so that they could transport the body inland. In mockery, she gave them a pair of ferocious bulls, but the apostle intervened and transformed them into docile beasts, thus converting the amazed queen. After the long

there's the fiesta of Santiago on 25 July. If you're prepared to get wet, spring and autumn are good times to visit; there are fewer people, accommodation prices are down, and the university is in session, guaranteeing rampant nightlife.

Tourist information

Santiago has several tourist information offices. The three most useful are the **municipal office** ① *Rúa do Vilar 63, T981 555 129, www.santiagoturismo.com, daily 0900-1400, 1600-1900*; the nearby **Galician regional office** ① *Rúa do Vilar 30, T981 584 081, otsantiago@ xunta.es, Mon-Fri 1000-2000, Sat 1100-1400, 1700-1900, Sun 1100-1400*, and a **kiosk** ① *Praza de Galicia, T981 584 400, Mon-Sat 1000-1400, 1600-1900*. There's also an information office at the airport. Galicia's tourist board, **Turgalicia**, publishes useful booklets and brochures. The website, www.turgalicia.es, is also worth a browse.

The **pilgrim office** ① *Rúa do Vilar 1, T981 568 846, www.archicompostela.org, Easter- Oct 0900-2100, Nov-Easter 1000-1900*, is around the corner from the cathedral. This is where journey, Santiago's loyal companions buried him and he was conveniently forgotten until the shepherd's discovery centuries later.

The pilgrims News that an apostle's tomb was in Christian Galicia travelled fast. A church was built and granted a perpetual *voto*, a tax payable by every inhabitant of Spain; this was levied until the 19th century. Pilgrims began to make the journey to Galicia to venerate the saint's remains. Most of the early pilgrims were from France, and the main route across Northern Spain came to be known as the Camino Francés. Waystations for pilgrims were set up, and French settlers and monks became a significant presence in the towns and villages along the route, and continued to be so; many of the churches and cathedrals are based on models from France. In the 12th century a French monk, Aimery Picaud, wrote the *Codex Calixtinus*, part of which was an entertaining guidebook for pilgrims making the journey to Santiago; the dangers mentioned include robbers, con-artists and wolves.

The pilgrimage became phenomenally popular, helped along by the Pope's declaration that all pilgrims to Santiago would have their time in Purgatory halved; if they went on a Holy Year (when the feast of St James, 25 July, falls on a Sunday) they would get a full remission (plenary indulgence). They came from all over Europe; some by boat (Chaucer's Wife of Bath made the journey), some walking for more than a year. At its peak, some half a million pilgrims arrived annually in Santiago, which rapidly became a flourishing city.

The pilgrimage declined in the 19th century, although there was a brief revival when the bones of Santiago, missing for a couple of centuries, were rediscovered (it was proved because a fragment of St James's skull from Pistoia in Italy fit exactly into a handy notch in the Compostela skull) and by the mid-20th century only a handful of people were following the route, whose pilgrim hostels had long since disappeared.

However, in the late 20th century there was a surprising revival in the pilgrimage, whose popularity has continued to grow. Well over 100,000 pilgrims arrive in Santiago on foot and bicycle every year, many more in Holy Years (the next is 2021).

you can get your pilgrim passports examined and pick up the Compostela certificate. The process has been streamlined somewhat, but there are still long queues in summer. A pile of gleefully abandoned wooden sticks sits inside the door.

Background

Relics have been a big deal in Christendom since the early Middle Ages, and especially in Spain. Christ physically ascended into heaven, and the Virgin was bodily assumed there too. With the big two out of the question, the apostles were just about the best physical remains an ambitious church could hope for. But whether you believe that the bones of Saint James are, or were ever, under the altar of the cathedral (see box, above) is beside the point; the city has transcended its origins completely, as the number of atheist pilgrims trudging towards it attests.

Santiago de Compostela

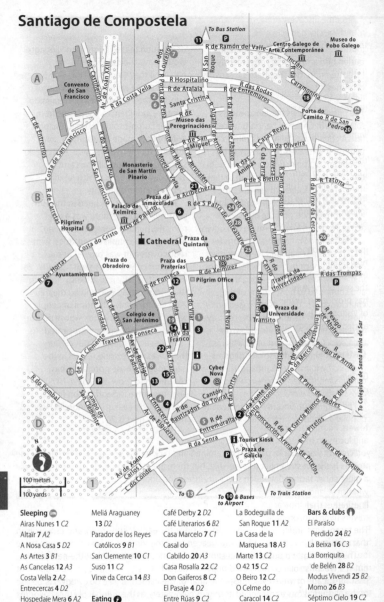

After the discovery of the tomb in the early ninth century, pilgrims soon began flooding in, and the city had achieved such prosperity by AD 968 that it was sacked by none other than the Vikings, who were never averse to a long voyage for a bit of plunder. Some 29 years later Santiago had another bad day, when Al-Manzur (see box, page 502) came from the south and sacked it again. Legend says that an old monk was praying by the tomb of Saint James while chaos reigned around. The Moorish warlord himself burst in and was so impressed by the old man's courage that he swore on his honour to safeguard the tomb and the monk from all harm.

Although the city was razed to the ground, Santiago continued to flourish as Saint James became a sort of patron-cum-field marshal of the Reconquista. Pilgrims came from across Europe and the cathedral was constructed to receive them in appropriate style; they used to bed down for the night in its interior. Constant architectural modifications followed from Santiago's swelling coffers, which also paid for the 40-something churches in the small city. This restructuring reached its peak in the 17th and early 18th centuries, from which period most of the granite-built centre that exists today dates. A rapid decline followed as pilgrimage waned and A Coruña thrived at Santiago's expense. The French occupied Santiago during the Napoleonic Wars, and carried off a large amount of plunder.

The late 20th century brought a rapid revival as the age of tourism descended on Spain in force. Santiago is high on many visitors' lists and, unexpectedly, the Camino itself is now phenomenally popular again, with pilgrims of all creeds making the journey in whole or part on foot or bicycle. Although A Coruña remains the provincial capital, Santiago is the seat of the Xunta (semi-autonomous Galician government established in 1982), which has provided a further boost to the town's economy. The Holy Year in 2004 saw a flood of visitors to the city; with more than a million in town on the feast day of Santiago, this ancient pilgrimage city is definitely back in the big time.

Cathedral and around

① *Cathedral 0730-2100, except during Mass; entry at these times is via the Praza das Praterías only. There's a Mass for pilgrims daily at 1200, and evening Mass at 1930; both last for about 45 mins. Admission is free, apart from the museum (see below).*

Santiago's past, present and future is wrapped up in its cathedral and its emblematic grey towers. Pilgrims trudge for weeks to reach it, many tourists visit Galicia specifically to see it, and locals go to Mass and confession in it as part of their day-to-day lives.

While the original Romanesque interior is superbly preserved, what first greets most visitors is the western façade and its twin towers. Granite is the perfect stone to express a more sober face of Spanish baroque; its stern colour renders the style epic rather than whimsical, and it's hard enough to chisel that masons concentrated on broader, nobler lines rather than intricacy. The façade rises high above the square, the moss-stained stone towers (which incorporate the original Romanesque ones) seem to say 'Heaven this way'. The façade was added in the 18th century and is reached by a complex double staircase that predates it.

The plaza that it dominates, named **Obradoiro**, is the main gateway to the cathedral, but it's worth strolling around the building before you enter. Walking clockwise, you pass the façade of the Romanesque **Palacio de Xelmírez**, which adjoins it and forms part of the cathedral museum. Turning the corner, you emerge in the **Praza da Inmaculada**, where the north façade is a slightly underwhelming 18th-century baroque construction that replaced the earlier Romanesque portal, which, from fragments of stone and textual descriptions, was superb. It faces the **Monasterio de San Martín Pinario**, with a huge façade that's wasted next to this magnificent cathedral; this part of it is now a student residence. The plaza used to be known as the *Azabachería*; this is where craftsmen made and sold rosaries made of jet (*azabache*) to the arriving pilgrims.

Continuing around, the **Praza da Quintana** is a curious space, with an upper and lower half; these are known as the halves of the living (the top) and the dead (below); the area used to be a cemetery. A plaque here is dedicated to the Literary Batallion, a corps of student volunteers who fought the French in the Napoleonic wars. The portal on this side is known as the Puerta Santa, or holy door. It is only opened during Holy Years, when the feast day of Santiago (25 July) falls on a Sunday. The façade is 17th century, but contains figures salvaged from the Romanesque stone choir. The 18th-century clocktower soars over the square.

The last square on the circuit is **Praza das Praterías**, with an entrance to the cathedral through an original portal, the oldest that remains, with scenes from the life of Christ.

Come back to the western façade and ascend the complex staircase. Once through the baroque doorway, you're confronted with the original Romanesque façade, the **Pórtico de la Gloria**. Built 1168-1188 by a man named Master Mateo, it is one of the finest pieces of sculpture in Spain, and a fitting welcome for weary pilgrims. Three doorless arches are intricately carved with Biblical scenes; a superb Last Judgement on the right, and variously interpreted Old Testament scenes on the left. In the centre Santiago himself sits under Christ and the Evangelists, who are surrounded by elders of the Apocalypse playing medieval musical instruments.

Upon entering the church, pilgrims queue to touch the pillar by the feet of Santiago; over the centuries five clear finger marks have been worn in the stone. On the other side of the pillar, carved with the Tree of Jesse, many then bump heads with the figure of Master Mateo, hoping that some of his genius will rub off. Many mistakenly butt the head under Santiago's feet; this is in fact Samson; Master Mateo faces into the church.

The interior itself is still attractively Romanesque in the main. High barrel vaulting and the lack of a *coro* in the centre of the nave give an excellent perspective down the church, although it's a pity the original stone *coro* by Master Mateo was destroyed in the early 17th century to make way for a wooden one that is no longer there either (the stone one has been re-assembled in the cathedral museum, the wooden one in the Monasterio de San Martín Pinario).

The massive altar is over-ornate and features some rather out-of-place cherubs on the *baldacchino* (baldachin), which is topped by an image of Santiago in Moor-killing mode; the whole thing belongs on a circus caravan. Above in the cupola is the eye-in-triangle symbol of the all-seeing God. Behind the altar is the image of Santiago himself. Pilgrims ascend behind the statue and give it an *abrazo* (embrace); this, a kiss to the back of his head, and a confession below, was the symbolic end to the pilgrimage.

On occasions, a large silver *botafumeiro* (censer) is hung from the ceiling at the crossing and slowly swung by eight men until it covers the whole length of the transept and reaches frightening velocities, diffusing incense and sparks all the while. It's a fantastic and unnerving thing to see, and it's only flown off twice (once in a Mass celebrated for Catherine of Aragón to wish her luck on her journey to wed Henry VIII in England; it was considered a bad omen, as it proved to be). The *botafumeiro* is an expensive thing to light, and is swung only on religious holidays or when a group of pilgrims get €240 together to pay for it. It needs to be reserved at least two days in advance. Contact peregrinos@ archicompostela.org.

Cathedral museum

ⓘ *Oct-May Mon-Sat 1000-1330, 1600-1830, Jun-Sep 1000-1400, 1600-2000, Sun 1000-1400, €5.*
Back in the Praza do Obradoiro, investigate the Romanesque **crypt** at the base of the main staircase. One of the three sections of the cathedral museum, it was built by Master Mateo to support the weight of his Romanesque façade above; it's an interesting space dominated by a sturdy load-bearing pillar. There are reproductions of some of the musical instruments that appear on the façade above, as well as some processional crosses and, interestingly, the 14th-century battle-horn of Alfonso XI, made from an elephant's tusk.

The main section of the museum is accessed from the cathedral or the Praza do Obradoiro. Entering from the square, the first rooms contain fragments of Romanesque sculpture, including one of the *Punishment of the Damned*, with two naked sinners having their sensitive bits eaten by beasts. The highlight of this section is the reconstruction of the stone **coro** by Master Mateo, which must have looked superb in the cathedral until it was destroyed in 1603 to make way for a wooden one. Some granite slabs elegantly painted in *mudéjar* style are also noteworthy. Upstairs, there's a range of religious sculpture in both polychrome wood and granite, including a sensitive San Sebastián in gold shorts and a fine *Last Judgement*, with an hirsute San Miguel presiding over the psychostasis (weighing of souls). There's also a wooden relief of the bells of the original church being carried back from Córdoba, whither they had been taken after Al-Manzur sacked the city. They were triumphantly reclaimed during the Reconquista, although, underwhelmingly, they were allegedly found in a pantry, being used to hold olive oil.

The **cloister** is absolutely massive in scale, and has a slightly neglected feel. The star vaulting is ornate Gothic and the arches heavily elegant. There are several tombs and fragments around, as well as some large, 18th-century bells. A small **library** contains one of the *botafumeiros* (see above), and there are some mediocre tapestries; but don't despair, there are some better ones upstairs, especially three depicting the life of Achilles by Rubens. Others are factory-made ones depicting rural life, some based on Goya cartoons.

Between the cloister and the cathedral is the **treasury**, a rather vulgar display of wealth donated by various bigwigs; the collection includes a goblet that belonged to Marshal Pétain. Next to this is the **Panteón**, which contains tombs of various kings of León and other nobles. There's also an immense *retablo* holding the cathedral's impressive collection of relics; these include the head of the other apostle James, the Lesser (Alpheus), encased in a gilt bust, and a spine from the crown of thorns.

The other section of the museum, on the other side of the cathedral façade, is the **Palacio de Xelmírez**, interesting for being a Romanesque civil building (it was built as an archbishop's residence), although it was heavily modified in the 16th century. Features include an attractive patio and large kitchen and two beautiful halls.

Praza de Obradoiro

The other buildings on the Praza do Obradoiro are also interesting. To the left as you face the cathedral is the massive **Pilgrims' Hospital**, built by Fernando and Isabel, the Catholic Monarchs. Now a parador, pilgrims still have the right a free meal here if they are one of the first 10 to queue for 0900, 1200 or 1900 sittings. The meals are served in a canteen around the back, but the food's still pretty good. The hotel has four pretty courtyards named after the evangelists and several elegant halls. Access is limited if you aren't a guest, but the bits you are allowed to wander around are worthwhile.

Opposite the cathedral, the **Ayuntamiento** is housed in an attractive neoclassical building, while the fourth side, opposite the parador, is partly taken up by the **Colegio de**

San Jerónimo, a 15th-century structure now part of the university, with a nice little patio and a portal that looks distinctly Romanesque; perhaps the architects didn't want to clash with the Pórtico de la Gloria of the cathedral. Next to it, the **Colegio de Santiago Alfeo** is a Renaissance construction used by the local government.

Monasterio de San Martín Pinario and around

North of the cathedral, the **San Martín Pinario monastery** ⓘ *Tue-Sun 1100-1330, 1600-1830, €2*, is half restricted to students, but you can enter the church and museum from the back. The door is high and rather overbearing; it's reached via an attractive downward staircase. The interior is lofty and bare, with a massive dome. In contrast to the sober architectural lines is the huge altarpiece, described by the 19th-century traveller Richard Ford: "In the *retablo*, of vilest Churrigueresque, Santiago and San Martín ride together in a fricasee of gilt gingerbread."

Similarly decorative *retablos* adorn the side chapels. Of more interest is the *coro* behind the altar; see if you can find the hidden door that the monks used to enter through. The museum has some old printing presses, an interesting old pharmacy and the wooden choir from the cathedral. There's also a multimedia exhibition on Galicia.

Near to the monastery is the **Convento de San Francisco**, founded by Saint Francis when he made the pilgrimage here in the early 13th century, and the newish **Museo das Peregrinacións** ⓘ *Tue-Fri 1000-2000, Sat 1030-1330, 1700-2000, Sun 1030-1330, €2.40, free on Sat afternoon*, a three-floor display about the pilgrimage to Santiago, images and iconography of the saint, the Pórtico de la Gloria, and the medieval life of the town. It's reasonably interesting, more so if you're a pilgrim, but ducks a few crucial Saint James issues.

Around Porta do Camino

At the eastern end of town, opposite the Porta do Camino where pilgrims enter the city, are two more museums. The **Museo do Pobo Galego** ⓘ *T981 583 620, www.museodopobo. es, Tue-Sat 1000-1400, 1600-2000, Sun 1100-1400, free*, was originally founded by Saint Dominic as a monastery. Inside is a monumental cloister and many ethnographic exhibits relating to Galician life. It's worth a look just for the architecture, including a stunning spiral staircase. There's also a chapel where the poet Rosalía de Castro is buried. Next to the museum, the **Centro Galego de Arte Contemporánea** ⓘ *www.cgac.org, Tue-Sun 1100-2000, free*, is a modern building whose attractive white spaces provide a break from the timeworn granite. Exhibitions are of a high international standard; check their website for what's on. There's also a bookshop and café.

Colegiata de Santa María de Sar

The Colegiata de Santa María de Sar is a Romanesque church a 15-minute walk south of the centre. Built in the 12th century, on insecure ground, it is remarkable chiefly for the alarming lean of its interior columns; after the Lisbon earthquake of 1755, massive buttresses had to be added. There's a small **museum** ⓘ *Mon-Sat 1000-1300, 1600-1900, €0.60*, with a tiny bit of Saint Peter in a reliquary, and a cloister, of which one side survives with carvings attributed to Master Mateo. To get there from the Rúa Fonte de San Antonio off Praza de Galicia, take the second right down Rúa Patio de Madres and follow it down the hill; the church is on your right after the railway bridge.

⊚ Santiago de Compostela listings

For Sleeping and Eating price codes and other relevant information, see Essentials pages 31-39.

⊜ Sleeping

Santiago de Compostela *p431, map p434*
There are well over 100 places to stay in Santiago, with plenty in the budget range to cater for the pilgrim traffic. Many restaurants in the centre have a few cheap rooms too. Rooms can be hard to find in summer, but it's just a matter of persistence.

LL Parador de los Reyes Católicos, Praza do Obradoiro 1, T981 582 200, www.parador. es. Although these days it's beyond the budgets of many 21st-century peregrines, the pilgrims' hostel built by the Catholic monarchs is a luxurious place to lie up and is by far the city's most atmospheric place to stay. Built around 4 beautiful courtyards, it's worth splashing out at €280 a double for the history and location alone. It's on the cathedral square, and the rooms lack nothing of the class of the building.

L Hotel Meliá Araguaney, C Alfredo Brañas 5, T981 559 600, www.araguaney.com. Not in the old town, but not far from Praza Galicia, this hotel has rather bland decor but makes up for it with good service, and plenty of space, comfort and facilities in the rooms. There's also a high-quality restaurant. You can often get much lower rates through travel agents or online discounters.

A Hotel Altaïr, Rúa dos Loureiros 12, T981 554 712, www.altairhotel.net. Modern, effortlessly attractive and stylish, this boutique hotel blends warm minimalism in the superbly comfortable rooms with exposed stone reflecting the centre of historic Santiago. Attentive staff and tasty breakfasts set you up perfectly for getting to know Compostela. Recommended.

A Virxe da Cerca, Rúa Virxe da Cerca 27, T981 569 350, www.pousadasdecompostela. com. This lovely old stone building on the road circling Santiago's old town has been

converted into this stylish and characterful hotel. While the rooms are as well equipped as in any big hotel, there's a more enchanting feel here, particularly around the delightful central patio. Rooms in the historic section are slightly dearer (**AL**). Recommended.

A-B Hotel As Artes, Travesía de dos Puertas 2, T981 555 254, www.asartes.com. A very short stroll away from the cathedral, this is a winning boutique choice with rooms named after artists of various media. If room size is a priority, look elsewhere, but if you don't mind a compact, cosy retreat in a fabulous location, you'll be charmed.

B Hotel Airas Nunes, Rúa do Vilar 17, T981 569 350, www.pousadasdecompostela.com. Right in the thick of things, this modern and stylish hotel has excellent facilities and plenty of attractive charm in a 17th-century building. Rooms are on the small side but comfortable and the location is hard to better. Bottom end of this price category.

C Costa Vella, Porta da Peña 17, T981 569 530, www.costavella.com. This smart, comfortable hotel is one of the best in this price range. It's got a romantic feel, not least for its fantastic garden studded with apple and lemon trees and offering fantastic views. Some of the rooms overlook it (they are slightly more expensive); the interior decor is stylish and beautiful, and the welcome from the owners is genuine. Highly recommended.

C Hostal 25 de Julio, Av Rodrigo de Padrón 4, T981 582 295, www.25dejulio. com. This intimate little luxury *pensión* is a charming choice. It's run by *simpático* management with an aesthetic eye. The rooms abound in good taste and are soft on mind and body. There's disabled access and an alluring little café too. It's cheaper if you stay more than 1 night. Recommended.

C Hotel Entrecercas, Rúa Entrecercas 11, T981 571 151, www.entrecercas.es. A charming little hotel that's central but tucked away from the busier parts. It has charm as well as courteous and helpful management.

Breakfast included. Underground parking close by. Recommended.

C Hotel San Clemente, Rúa San Clemente 28, T981 569 260, www.pousadasdecompostela.com. An excellent option located in the old town below and close to the cathedral. The charm of the old house still shines through, but the rooms are equipped to modern standards with good if small bathrooms and free Wi-Fi.

E A Nosa Casa, Rúa Entremurallas 9, T981 585 926, www.anosacasa.com. This friendly family-run spot is close to Praza Galicia, on an atmospheric old town street that can be loud at weekends. Handy for the Ryanair bus, but you won't get the hire car very close.

E Hospedaje Mera, Porta da Pena 15, T981 583 867. This quiet and cheap option is on a pedestrian street in the centre of town. Facilities are basic – there are rooms with and without bathroom available – but some rooms have balconies and views, and it's in a great location.

E Mapoula, Rúa Entremurallas 10, T981 580 124, www.mapoula.com. Good value for money, this is set on a narrow little street in the old town not far from Praza de Galicia. Comfortable beds, modern en suite bathrooms, and Wi-Fi make it solid budget accommodation. Noisy at weekends.

E Suso, Rúa Vilar 65, T981 586 611. This central pilgrims' favourite is handy for everything in town. Its spacious (not the singles), en suite rooms are very good value year-round (it's worth getting here early to avoid disappointment) and there's a friendly vibe from management and the happy walkers at journey's end (unlike the pilgrims of yesteryear, they don't have to turn around and walk back home again). Highly recommended.

Camping

As Cancelas, T981 580 266, www.campingascancelas.com. Open year-round. A good campsite within 30 mins' walk of the heart of town, and frequently served by city bus No 9. There are various family-sized bungalows as well as a shop and a pool.

Ciudad de Vacaciones Monte do Gozo, Ctra Aeropuerto s/n, T981 558 942, www.cvacaciones-montedogozo.com. A massive summer-only campsite and holiday village on the hill 2 km east of town with regular public transport and all facilities, including a pool.

🍽 Eating

Santiago de Compostela *p431, map p434*

Seafood is the thing to eat in Santiago, as indeed in much of Galicia. One of the main streets, Rúa Franco, is something of a tourist trap (although locals eat here too); prices are high and quality variable. *Vieiras* (scallops) are an obvious choice, served in a bacon and onion sauce, but they're expensive at about €6 per scallop. *Percebes* are also popular, as are *cigalas* (a word to the wise: *cigalas* are expensive and menus often somewhat misleadingly list the price per 100 g; 6 chubby *cigalas* can weigh well over 500 g). *Tarta de Santiago* is an almond cake often engraved with a sword; patisseries along Rúa Franco give out free morsels to taste.

₩₩₩ Casa Marcelo, Rúa das Hortas 3, T981 558 850, www.casamarcelo.net. Open Tue-Sat. This little gourmet's paradise is on one of Santiago's most picturesque streets just below the Praza do Obradoiro. You won't spend hours browsing the menu, for it's *table d'hôte* only. The feast on offer changes daily, but consists of 5-6 courses full of delicate flavours for €65. Recommended.

₩₩₩ Don Gaiferos, Rúa Nova 23, T981 583 894. A dark and moody but modernized place that offers plenty of choice of the finest Galician produce in a good location close to the cathedral. Excellent daily seafood specials, but you might also be tempted by the meat on offer; the *tournedos* are delicious, and the steak tartare just as it should be. Mains are €17-25, and there's a degustation menu.

₩₩₩ El Pasaje, Rúa Franco 54, T981 557 081. A class above the other fish restaurants on this street, this is at the open end near the

Alameda and has room for 3 or 4 outdoor tables. The seafood is sublime, though expensive. The fish cooked *a la parrilla* is memorable, and there's a fine range of wine to accompany it. The *zamburiñas* (mini-scallops) make a fine appetizer. Be aware of the price/weight equation. Recommended.

Asesino, Praza Universidad 16, T981 581 568. Discreetly signposted, this restaurant opposite the university is a long-standing Santiago classic that opens when it chooses, and offers excellent home-style food accompanied by appropriately familiar bric-a-brac decor. Almost everything is worthwhile, but the *navajas* (razor shells) are particularly succulent.

Casal do Cabildo, Rúa de San Pedro 18, T981 583 057. Off the beaten track, but still in an attractive part of Santiago close to the heart of things, this is one of several good mid-range restaurants on this street. There's great meat at good prices and huge platters of seafood on a bed of chips.

La Casa de la Marquesa, Costa de San Domingos 2. T981 573 958, www.lacasadelamarquesa.es. Nicely positioned near the modern art gallery, and with an appealing terrace with outdoor tables, this place is frequented by smart young Santiago folk and offers upmarket meals and tapas, as well as creditable sushi twice a week.

Marte, Av Rodrigo de Padrón 11, T981 584 905. Cops usually know where to eat well at sensible prices, so it's a good sign that this no-nonsense family-run place is much patronized by the police station opposite. The *menú del día* is superb value for €15 (there's an even cheaper one for €9) and doesn't hold back on the seafood; there's turbot, monkfish and plenty more. There's a terrace outside too. Top value. Recommended.

O 42, Rúa Franco 42, T981 581 009. This place on the main eat street certainly doesn't try to curry favour with pilgrims or tourists except through being authentic. The seafood is slightly pricier than at neighbouring places, but it's top quality, especially the octopus and *navajas* (razor clams). Sit at the rustic wooden tables to enjoy the traditional

Santiago *raciones*, or, if the weather's fine, head to their sister establishment at No 50, and try and grab a seat in the enclosed garden terrace out the back.

O Beiro, Rúa da Raíña 3, T981 581 370. Stocked with hundreds of wines from all over Spain, this is the place for an impromptu tasting session. The shop has an atmospheric back bar, with flagstones and a low wood-beamed ceiling, where you can try several of their wines by the glass or any of them (and there's over a 1000) by the bottle. There's a free tapa with every glass, and other local produce for sale. Recommended.

O Celme do Caracol, C Raíña 22, T981 571 746. Abuzz with upbeat Galician chat, this happy place a few paces from the cathedral turns out truly delicious bistro-style Galician fare in its intimate 2-level space. Downstairs, the bar pours good wines by the glass, and complements them with generous free tapas from the semi-open kitchen. Find a table, and enjoy a marvellous seafood soup, top salads, and, as the name suggests, snails in a spicy sauce. Prices are more than fair.

Casa Rosalía, Rúa Franco 10, T981 568 441. A tempting array of tapas is on view at the counter in this busy bar in Santiago central. There's prompt service, and it's a fine spot for a quiet bite with a glass of wine... try something like the octopus pâté.

Entre Rúas, Ruela de Entreruas 2, T981 586 108. An enchanting terrace in a minute hidden square, this is the place to conduct an illicit affair, at least when the sun's shining. It's a great spot for a drink; there's also a cheap and acceptable *menú del día*.

Jamonería Ferro, Rúa República de El Salvador 20, T981 592 399. A deli in the new part of town that's also a popular bar, with free nibbles and some good *raciones*, especially of the hammy kind.

La Bodeguilla de San Roque, Rúa San Roque 13, T981 564 379. A good bar, popular with students for its cheap and filling *raciones*. These are best eaten in the pretty upstairs *comedor* which also serves up a value-packed *menú del día*.

O Filandón, C Azabachería 6, T981 572 378. This cosy wine bar is popular with arriving pilgrims, whose messages on paper serviettes adorn the walls. There's an excellent atmosphere and very good service from the personable boss.

Cafés

There's nowhere better in town for a relaxing outdoor drink than the garden of the Costa Vella hotel (see Sleeping, above).
Café Casino, Rúa do Vilar 35, T981 577 503. This historic café is awash with 19th-century plushness. It's a massive space, beautiful, elegant and popular with young and old for evening coffee.
Café Derby, C Huérfanas 29, T981 586 417, www.cafederby.com. Just turned 80 years old, this noble old café seems to have changed little, and it's much the better for it. Polite service, cosy worn seating, cut-glass chandeliers, and plenty of space make it a Santiago classic.
Café Literarios, Praza Quintana 1, T981 565 630. A great spot on this attractive and unusual square, named after the redoubtable student batallion of this granite city. It's still got an arty feel inside, while the terrace gazes over the architectural glories of the old centre.

Bars and clubs

Santiago de Compostela p431, map p434

The student nightlife kicks off around Rúa Nova de Abaixos near Praza Roxa. Get the free newspaper *Compostelán* or *7 Días Santiago* for bar, club events and other venue listings.
El Paraíso Perdido, Rúa San Paio de Antealtares 3. This basement bar has an intriguing 'hell gate' entrance. Inside it's decorated with mosaics, and there's a chilled-out, buzzy, hippy-trippy atmosphere.
La Beixa, Rúa de Tras Salomé 3. A popular student haunt playing 1970s music in a cosy and friendly environment.

La Borriquita de Belén, Rúa San Paio de Antealtares 22. A sociable and lively bar tucked away behind the cathedral and playing host to regular live jazz and traditionally influenced Galician bands.
Modus Vivendi, Praza Feijóo 1, T981 576 109. Once a stable, you can still use the old horse trough as a table. The stone arches lend a medieval ambience to what is one of Santiago's friendliest and most characterful drinking options. Recommended.
Momo, Rúa da Virxe da Cerca. This massive bar on the edge of the old town comes equipped with its own street and zebra crossing. In summer the terrace opens – it's a fantastic spot to be, with great views.
Séptimo Cielo, Rúa da Raíña 20. This late-opening bar near the cathedral plays Spanish chart hits to a cheery crowd. There's a good atmosphere and cheapish drinks.

Entertainment

Santiago de Compostela p431, map p434

Check the website www.compostelacultura. org for upcoming concerts and events.
Auditorio de Galicia, T981 552 290, www.auditoriodegalicia.org. North of town. Classical concerts and opera.
Teatro Principal, Rúa Nova 21, T981 586 521. A council-run venue for theatre and occasional cinema festivals.

Cinemas include: **Cinesa Area Central**, Rúa Fontiñas, T902 333 231, www.cinesa.es; and **Cine Compostela**, Rúa Ramón Piñeiro 3, T981 560 342.

Festivals and events

Santiago de Compostela p431, map p434

25 Jul Santiago's main fiesta is the day of the **St James** himself. When this day falls on a Sun, it's known as a **Holy Year** (the next one is 2021). Apart from partying, there's a solemn Mass and a spectacular pyrotechnic display the night before.

O Shopping

Santiago de Compostela *p431, map p434*

Bookshops
Librería Universitas, Rúa Fernando III el Santo 3, T981 592 438; Librería San Pablo, Rúa do Vilar 37, T981 552 180.

Food and drink
The Mercado de Abastos is a lively food market in the old town on Praza de Abastos. O Beiro, Rúa da Raíña 3, www.obeiro.com, is a good place to buy (as well as drink) Galician and other Spanish wines.

Gems
Santiago is a good place to purchase *azabache* (jet), but beware of vendors near the cathedral who make a living preying on tourists.

O Transport

Santiago de Compostela *p431, map p434*
Buy a copy of the newspaper *El Correo Gallego* for a complete list of transport times.

Air
There's a daily Ryanair flight to **London** Stansted, as well as services to **Liverpool**, **Frankfurt** Hahn, and **Roma** Ciampino. Aer Lingus fly to **Dublin**, and Vueling to Edinburgh, **Paris** CDG, and **Barcelona**, while Air Berlin link Santiago with many Austrian and German cities via Mallorca. Ryanair also service **Madrid** and several other Spanish cities. There are regular flights on full-service airlines to **London**, **Brussels**, and **Amsterdam**, as well as internal ones to **Madrid** and **Barcelona** and, less frequently, **Bilbao** and **Sevilla**.

Buses connect the airport with the city centre and bus station, stopping at the corner of Av Xeneral Pardiñas and Rúa da República de El Salvador; they run approximately hourly. A Ryanair bus runs from Praza Galicia to coincide with their flights.

Bus
Local Within Galicia, buses run hourly to **A Coruña** (via motorway 45 mins, via road 1 hr 20 mins), 3 a day to **Fisterra** and **Camariñas**. 8 buses to **Lugo**, hourly ones to **Pontevedra** (45 mins) and **Vigo**, and 7 to **Ourense**. Buses run hourly to **Ribeira**, and 6 times a day to **Vilagarcía**, **Cambados** and **O Grove**.

Services connect with **Bilbao** (3 daily, 12 hrs), **Ponferrada** (5 daily, 3½-4 hrs), **Madrid** (5-6 daily, 8-9 hrs), **Oviedo** (5 a day, 5 hrs 30 mins) and **Gijón**, and **Salamanca** (2 daily, 6 hrs 15 mins) via **Zamora**, among other destinations.

Car hire
Autos Brea, C Gómez Ulla 10, T981 562 670, www.autosbrea.com is reasonably central. There are also several multinationals at the airport.

Train
Trains run regularly to **A Coruña** (45 mins, €6.10), **Vigo** (1 hr 20 mins, from €9.20), and **Ourense** (4 a day, 1 hr 30 mins, €16.80); there's also a sleeper and a day train to **Madrid** (7-9 hrs, €49.50).

O Directory

Santiago de Compostela *p431, map p434*
Internet There are many cybercafés in town, including Cyber Nova 50, Rúa Nova 50, €1.50 per hr; and Mundonet, Rúa do Xelmírez 19, from €1 per hr. **Laundry** Lavandeira, Av Rosalía de Castro 116, T981 942 110. A self-service laundromat with plenty of machines. **Medical services** The Hospital Xeral is fairly central on Rúa das Galeras, T981 950 000. **Police and emergency** T112 for an emergency; T092 contacts the municipal police. The handiest police station is on Av Rodrigo de Padrón around the corner from the post office. **Post office** The main post office is on Travesa de Fonseca a block from the cathedral. **Telephone** There are several cheap *locutorios* around Praza Roxa.

Rías Altas

→ Colour map 1, A2/3.
The north coast of Galicia, not as overdeveloped as the west coast, has some interesting fishing towns and a few cracking beaches. The inlets of the Rías Altas are deep, making perfect natural harbours and sheltered (if chilly) swimming spots. Of the two major ports on the north coast, Ferrol is an earthy industrial centre, while A Coruña is a jewel set on a promontory with a harbour on one side, a great beach on the other and a lively seafood tapas scene. For cliffscapes, Garita de Herbeira is hard to beat. ➤➤ For listings, see pages 449-452.

Ribadeo → For listings, see pages 449-452. Colour map 1, A5.

Ribadeo faces its Asturian counterpart Castropol across the broad expanse of the inlet at the mouth of the river Eo; thus the town's name. It's a functional but pleasant enough place, with a waterside promenade by the harbour at the bottom of the steep streets leading down from the old centre, which is centred on the Praza de Espanha with its ornate turn-of-the-20th century buildings. The views across to Asturias a mile away across the water are picturesque, and the modern bridge over the *ría* are impressive, despite the thundering traffic. Past the bridge there's the small **Forte de San Damián**, built to protect the town from seaward invasion. The old centre is pleasant too, with a good square with plenty of palm trees. There are many *indiano* houses, attractive structures built by Galicians returned from the Americas. There's also a **tourist office** ① *T982 128 689, turismo@ribadeo.org, Mon-Fri 1030-1400, 1600-1900, Sat 1030-1400, 1600-2000, Sun 1030-1400*, on the square.

West of Ribadeo

Along this first stretch of Galician coast are some of the region's best **beaches**, all within a 20-minute walk of the main road. **As Catedrais** (the cathedrals) is a pretty little stretch named for its spectacularly eroded cliffs and rocks lying in the water. It all but disappears at high tide. Nearby **Reinante** is a superb length of whitish sand, as is **Arealonga**, while a little further, **Praia de Lóngara** and adjacent Fontela are the best options for surfing.

Foz and around → For listings, see pages 449-452. Colour map 1, A5.

The best feature of Foz is its attractive working fishing port, where the fishermen's families come down to wave at the boats heading out to sea. The rest of the town is friendly but not particularly interesting. A good excursion is the walk or drive to **San Martín de Mondoñedo**, a hamlet whose **church** ① *Tue-Sun 1100-1400, 1600-1800 (the keyholder lives nearby)*, was once a cathedral; the bishop must have been the least stressed of primates. It's about 8 km from town along a pleasant road heavy with the scent of eucalypts. Although the church's origins are ninth century, most of what is visible is later Romanesque. It's on soft ground and is heavily buttressed; the apse has Lombard arching, a feature of the Romanesque of Catalunya. There's an attractive *cruceiro* outside, and the portal features the Lamb. Inside are some excellent Romanesque wallpaintings, good carved capitals and the tomb of Gonzalo, yet another Galician saint.

West of Foz

Moving westwards, the coast becomes a little more rugged, but there are still some decent beaches tucked into coves. As well, a multitude of rivers flow down to the sea from the Galician high country and are good spots for trout fishing. The straggling village of **Xove** is less impressive than its name, which derives from the Latin *Iovii*, meaning 'of Jupiter'.

Few places appeal as a stopover until you reach the **Ría de Viveiro**. Near the town of Celeiro is the excellent patrolled beach of **Area**, a duney stretch that looks across to an islet.

Viveiro and around → For listings, see pages 449-452. Colour map 1, A4.

Viveiro is a friendly and interesting little place that makes the best stop on this stretch of coast. Right at the tail of the *ría*, its small boats get marooned on mudflats at low tide. Viveiro is reasonably lively in summer, when there's a small but steady flow of holidaymakers, but it's very quiet for the rest of the year. The town is within easy range of many fine beaches, including Area (see above). Viveiro is particularly known for its Easter festival, a serious event with a candlelit procession enacting the stations of the cross, and the town also pushes the boat out at Christmas with a marvellous life-size Nativity scene surrounding the church.

The old town is interesting, and preserves fragments of its walls as well as a few gates, one a very tight squeeze at the top of the town. Built in the 12th century, the Romanesque **Iglesia de Santa María del Campo** is in the centre of the old town. Inside is a pretty processional cross dating from the 16th century, as well as a sculptural assembly that used to adorn one of the gates of the town wall. Nearby is a replica of the grotto at Lourdes; locals seem to trust it; there's many an offering of plastic body parts, soliciting intervention for physical ailments.

Viveiro's **municipal tourist office** ① *Av Ramón Canosa s/n, T982 560 879, www.viveiro.es, Sep-Jun Mon-Fri 1100-1400, 1630-1930, Sat 1100-1400, 1700-1900, Jul-Aug Mon-Fri 1000-1400, 1630-2000, Sat 1100-1400, 1700-1900, Sun 1130-1330*, is on the roundabout near the centre of town. The large **Centro Comarcal** ① *Mon-Fri 1000-1430, 1700-2000*, nearby, also has tourist info.

The coastline continues in rugged vein after Viveiro; as the road ascends the western headland there are some excellent views over the *ría* and out to sea. The small fishing village of **O Barqueiro** is a peaceful spot to stay, although the roadside sprawl above isn't so attractive. There's a bank in town, and a choice of places to stay on the small harbour. Just east of here, the lovely sandy crescent of Arealonga beach is one of the best in the vicinity.

From here, it's an hour's walk through eucalypt forest to **Punto da Bares**, the northernmost point in Spain. A winding road leads up to a viewpoint (signposted *Semáforo*; the signal station has now been converted into a stunning rural hotel, see Sleeping, page 449), while at the cape itself is a lighthouse and whipping winds. There are some shops in the village, a good restaurant and a superb sandy beach a mile long and sheltered by a reef that was probably built by the Phoenicians.

Ortigueira and around → For listings, see pages 449-452. Colour map 1, A4.

The town of Ortigueira is a fairly workaday fishing port, transformed in mid-July for a massive festival of Celtic music and culture (www.festivaldeortigueira.com). Otherwise, there's no real reason to stop here; a quick look at its gardened port will suffice. A short distance west of Ortigueira, the main road cuts inland, but it's worth exploring the headland, a wild and rugged landscape battered by some of Galicia's worst weather. Apart from the dull sprawl of **Carriño**, it's a bleak and lonely place populated mainly by wild horses. North of Carriño, the pretty **Cabo Ortegal** has a lighthouse and good views; it's a nice walk along the green clifftops. Further west, the **Garita de Herbeira** is an atmospheric and desolate arch of high granite cliffs 600 m high, and pounded by waves and weather.

Further west, the **Santuario de San Andrés de Teixido** is in a sturdy stone hamlet. It's a simple chapel that was established by the Knights of Malta, who brought a relic of Saint Andrew here back from the Holy Land. The saint is much venerated along this understandably superstitious coast, and there's always a good pile of *ex voto* offerings that range from representations of what intervention is being sought for, such as models of fishing boats or plastic body parts to simple gifts of pens and cigarettes. There's a well-attended *romería* (pilgrimage procession) to the sanctuary on 8 September; some of the pilgrims make the journey in coffins to give thanks for narrow escapes, mostly at sea.

Cedeira and around → *For listings, see pages 449-452. Colour map 1, A3.*

South of the sanctuary of San Andrés de Teixido, and back on the main road is Cedeira, a pleasant town on yet another picturesque *ría*. There are some excellent **beaches** around, although the town beach isn't the best of them; try **A Magdalena**, a shallow-watered strip of sand a couple of kilometres further along the coast. The two halves of Cedeira are linked by a bridge; the old town is across it from the main road, and is a warren of steep and narrow streets.

Cedeira coastline
West of Cedeira is some of the nicest coastline in these parts, heavily wooded and studded with excellent beaches, particularly **Villarube** and **Do Rodo**, one of Galicia's best surf beaches. **Da Frouxeira** is another excellent strip of sand, 2.5 km long, and backed by a lagoon that is an important haven for waterfowl. There's a good (if slightly pricey) campsite at **Valdoviño**, on the main road near Da Frouxeira beach. There's a smaller campsite near the Praia do Río, which also has good surf (see Sleeping, page 450). Buses are the only way to access the coast on public transport, as the **FEVE** line has cut inland by this point.

Ferrol → *For listings, see pages 449-452. Colour map 1, A3.Population: 74,696, but nearly 200,000 in the greater suburban area.*

While Ferrol's glory days as a naval harbour ended abruptly (along with most of Spain's fleet) during the Peninsular War, it's still an important port, and the navy is very much in evidence. Although poor and with high unemployment, Ferrol has not been shorn of its dignity; the streets around the harbour are lined with noble terraced houses, and locals are proud of their city and its hardworking heritage. Perhaps Ferrol's greatest claim to fame, however, is seldom mentioned these days: in the winter of 1892 an uptight little boy was born to a naval family in a house near the harbour. Francisco Franco y Bahamonde went on to rule Spain with a concrete fist for the best part of four decades (see box, page 447).

Hurry through Ferrol's outskirts and modern expansions, some of the more depressing urban landscapes in modern Spain. In some of the poorer, high-density areas, the council inexcusably hasn't even bothered to give the streets proper names; just letters. Nevertheless, the city centre conserves a certain maritime charm, and the council is making big efforts to spruce the place up to encourage a bit of tourism to this unfashionable place.

Although the **waterfront** is mostly taken up by naval buildings and dockyards, it's well worth strolling along: from the **Paseo de la Marina** at the western tip of the old town, you can get a good idea of just how large Ferrol's excellent natural harbour (the Ría do Ferrol) is. Near here is one of the twin forts defending the port. Another, **Castillo de San Felipe** ① *daily*

Generalísimo Franco

"A less straightforward man I never met" John Whitaker, American journalist. Francisco Franco y Bahamonde looms over 20th-century Spanish history like the concrete monoliths he was so fond of building and, like them, his shadow is long. Born in 1892 in the Galician naval port of Ferrol, this son of a naval administrator wanted to join the navy but was forced to choose the army due to lack of places at the academy. Sent to the war in Morocco at the age of 20, he excelled, showing remarkable military ability and bravery. As commander of the new Foreign Legion, he was largely responsible for the victory achieved there in 1925; this success saw him made Spain's youngest ever general at the age of 33.

The authoritarian Franco was just the man the government needed to put down the rebellion of the Asturian miners in 1934; this he achieved brutally. Having been sent to a command in the Canaries, out of harm's way as the government thought, he agreed to join the conspiracy against the Republic fairly late. Once the rising was underway, he took command of the army in Morocco, which was transported across to the Spanish mainland with German assistance, a crucial intervention in the context of the war.

Franco's advance was successful and rapid – he soon manoeuvred his way into the Nationalist leadership, reluctantly being given supreme power by his fellow generals. He assumed the title of *Caudillo*, or 'head' and installed himself in Burgos.

Throughout the war, he was known for his ruthlessness, never more so than when the German Condor Legion razed Gernika from the air on market day, killing 1650 civilians (see box, page 84). After the Nationalist victory, the Generalísimo showed no signs of giving up power,

although in 1949 he declared himself as a regent pending the choice of a king. He ensured that there was to be no leniency for those who had supported the former Republic and a cruel purge followed. Franco wasn't exactly relaxed and charismatic; after meeting him in 1940 to discuss possible Spanish involvement in the Second World War, Adolf Hitler said he "would rather have three or four teeth out" than meet him again.

After the war Franco's dictatorship was shunned by the western democracies until Cold War realpolitik made the USA adopt him as an ally, betraying the governments-in-exile they had continued to recognize. A massive aid package in exchange for military bases gave Franco the cash required to begin modernizing a country that had been crippled by the Civil War, but for much of his rule parts of Spain remained undeveloped. Franco was recognized by other countries, and Spain was accepted into the UN, but remained politically and culturally stagnant. Separatism was not countenanced; Franco banned Euskara and even Galego, the tongue of his native Galicia. He never forgot an enemy; the regions that had struggled to uphold democracy were left to rot while he conferred favours on the Nationalist heartlands of Castilla and Navarra. The ageing dictator appointed Juan Carlos, grandson of the former king, as his designated successor in 1969.

Franco died in 1975: "*Españoles*" – the Spanish people were solemnly informed – "*Franco ha muerto*". The man described as "a sphinx without a secret" was no more: those who mourned the passing of this plump, shy, suspicious, authoritarian general were comparatively few, but Francoism is still alive within the Spanish political right, and memorial services on the anniversaries of his death are still held.

1100-1830, free, is worth visiting further around the bay if you have your own transport. Most of Ferrol's character is in the five or six parallel streets back from here. The elegant balconied buildings tell of days of prosperity, as do the several *indiano* buildings. The whitewashed neoclassical church and post office show some of these influences; nearby is the busy modern market. Franco was born on Rúa María, four streets back from the shore at No 136 (although the street was called Frutos Saavedra when he was a nipper).

From the waterfront, hour-long cruises run hourly from July to September, costing €7, T620 926 958 for details. You could also take a boat across the bay to **Mugardos** (€3 each way) for a seafoody lunch.

There are several tourist offices around town. They have a number of themed leaflets in Spanish on various aspects of the city that are also downloadable from www.ferrol.es website. There is a **main tourist office** ① *C Magdalena 56, T981 944 272, ferrolturismo@ ferrol.es, daily 1030-1400, 1700-2000*; another handy **tourist office** ① *Paseo da Marina s/n, Mon-Sat 1000-1400, 1700-2000, Sun 1000-1400*, by the marina; and another less conveniently located east of the train and bus stations on Estrada de Castela, on a concrete island at a freeway junction. There's a **regional tourist office** ① *T981 311 179, Mon-Sat 1000-1400, 1600-1900 (1700-2000 summer), Sun 1000-1400*, on Praza Camilo José Cela.

Pontedeume and the Caaveiro Valley → *For listings, see pages 449-452. Colour map 1, A3.*

South of Ferrol, the river mouth town of Pontedeume is a prettier and more relaxed place to hang out despite the almost constant line of traffic through town. Its main features are its long bridge across the Eume and an impressive 14th-century tower. Both were originally built by the Andrade family, local lairds, *bon viveurs* and boar hunters (see page 450). A weathered stone boar faces across the bridge. The tower holds the **tourist office**, which can advise on things to see in the area, of which there are several.

"The valley of Caaveiro", wrote Richard Ford in the mid-19th century, "is one of the most secluded in Spain". Not much has changed. The valley, part of the Fragas do Eume natural park, is an important zone of Atlantic forest and refuge of much wildlife; there are many otters (mostly further up, above the hydroelectric station), boar, ermine and birds. Fishing has been suspended on the river to allow the salmon and trout levels to restabilize. A short way into the valley (coming from the north, cross the bridge in Pontedeume, bear left, then take the first left turn; follow this road for a while, then bear left again; it's signposted Caaveiro) is an **information centre** ① *T981 432 528, daily 1000-1400, 1600-1900*, where there are maps of walks.

At the end of the valley road, some 13 km from Pontedeume, is an atmospheric ruined monastery, **Monasterio de San Xoán de Caaveiro** ① *visits at 1100, 1200, 1300, 1530, 1630 weekends only in winter, daily in summer, free*. It was founded by the boy-bishop San Rosendo in the 10th century. The remaining Romanesque walls look over the river; it's a lovely setting. Nearby, a rapid watercourse feeds the Eume with yet more water. From the monastery, you may want to strike off for a walk: the **GR50 long-distance path** crosses the bridge at the monastery. The whole walk is recommended; it stretches from Betanzos to Cabo Ortegal at the top of Galicia, and can be done comfortably in four days, or strenuously in two. A shorter walk takes you past the monastery on the yellow-marked PR path back downstream for 3 km; you can then cross via a bridge and return up the road to your car.

The road's not designed to handle much traffic, so at busy periods, like summer weekends, you may have to leave your car at the visitors centre and travel to the monastery in a minibus.

There are other access roads to the natural park; one crosses it north to south running between the towns of Λ Capela and Monfero.

For Sleeping and Eating price codes and other relevant information, see Essentials pages 31-39.

⊜ Sleeping

Ribadeo *p444*

AL Parador de Ribadeo, Rúa Amador Fernández 7, T982 128 825, www.parador. es. The town's best place to stay, this parador is modern and not the most characterful of its kind but has views across the *ría* and a reasonable seafood restaurant.

D Hotel Mediante, Praza de Espanha 8, T982 130 453, www.hotelmediante.com. Nicely placed in the middle of the old town, where the main pedestrian street meets the square, this welcoming family-run hotel has spacious, simple, en suite rooms with chessboard tiling. It's an absolute bargain (**E**) off-season. There's also a café-restaurant. Recommended.

Camping

There are several campsites to the west of town, including **Ribadeo**, T982 131 167, www.campingribadeo.com, 2 km from Ribadeo, which boasts a swimming pool and has bungalows. Open Jun-Sep and Easter.

West of Ribadeo *p444*

C Hotel Balcón de San Bartolo, Av Acantilado s/n, Barreiros, T982 124 456, www.hotelbalcondesanbartolo.com. With direct access to the pretty San Bartolo blue-flag beach, this modern stone-clad hotel is a small, friendly, and intimate place to stay and reasonably priced for its decent facilities. It's worth paying the €10 extra to get a memorable sea view. Breakfast included.

D Casa Guillermo, Vista Alegre 3, Santiago de Reinante, Barreiros. T982 134 150, www. casaguillermo.net. A good place to stay if you've got kids; it's near to the beach and has a large garden and spotless, attractive, and comfortable rooms. The hosts are welcoming and it's open year-round.

Camping

A Nosa Casa, by Reinante beach, T982 134 065, www.campinganosacasa.com. One of several campsites in this stretch, Nosa Casa is open year-round and also has hotel accommodation (**D**) and 1- or 2-room bungalows.

Foz and around *p444*

C Hotel Leytón, Av da Mariña 6, Foz, T982 140 800, www.hotelleyton.es. This is a good option despite the slightly garish decor. The rooms are well equipped, with internet point and heating; it's particularly good value outside the height of summer. There are rooms with water views and a bit more space for and extra €25.

Viveiro and around *p445*

As well as the options below, there are a couple of intriguing *casas rurales* in noble historic buildings within a short distance of Viveiro: the **B** Casa da Torre, Toxeiras 47, Landrove, T982 598 026, www.casadatorreviveiro.com, and upmarket **A** Pazo da Trave, Trave, T982 598 163, www.pazodatrave.com.

AL Hotel Ego, Playa de Area s/n, T982 560 987, www.hotelego.com. East of Viveiro, this hotel has an excellent situation above Area beach. It's a relaxed and well-equipped hotel for stress-free summer holidays. The terrace and most rooms boast excellent views over the strand and *ría*, and there's a pool and good restaurant.

B Hotel Semáforo de Bares, O Barqueiro s/n, T981 417 147, www. hotelsemaforodebares.com. The signal station at the Bares cape has been intriguingly converted into a place to stay. Though it's Spain's most northerly hotel, it doesn't need to rely on geographical quirks: the location is stunning, and the rooms, of which there are a variety, are great. Cosy little doubles under the sloping roof are just **D**. Best though, is the suite (**AL**), formerly the control room for monitoring marine traffic; a marvellous hexagonal space with windows all around. There's a restaurant and a good welcome. Recommended.

C Hotel Orfeo, Av García Navia Castrillón 2, Viveiro, T982 562 101, www.hotel-orfeo. com. Showing its age a little these days, this is well located on the water in Viveiro itself. Many of the comfortable rooms come with a balcony and a view at no extra cost. It drops down to **E** off season. Free Wi-Fi.

D-E Hostal O Forno, O Barqueiro, T981 414 124, www.ofornobarquero.com. This is a great little place to stay, lovingly renovated and cared for; it looks over the water and also has a good seafood restaurant.

F Fonda Nuevo Mundo, Rúa Teodoro de Quirós 14, Viveiro, T982 560 025. At the upper end of town, this is a good, friendly budget option if you don't mind the sound of church bells.

Camping

Camping Viveiro, Playa de Covas s/n, T982 560 004. Open late Jun-Sep. Across the estuary from the heart of town and on a popular patrolled beach with greyish sand.

Ortigueira and around p445

D Río da Cruz, in the middle of the headland, some 9 km inland from Garita de Herbeira, T981 428 057, www.riodacruz. com. A lovely old stone farmhouse with cosy pinewood rooms, one of which is an appealing duplex that costs a little more (**C**). They serve pleasant meals, which can be eaten on an outdoor terrace.

Cedeira and around p446

E Chelsea, Praza Sagrado Corazón 10, T981 482 340, www.hostalchelsea.com. Open May-Oct only. The most appealing option in town, this is an acceptable place on a nice square very near the beach, across the bridge from the main part of town.

Cedeira coastline p446
Camping

Fontesín, T981 485 028, near the Praia do Río. Open Jun-mid Sep only. Simpler than the one at Valdoviño, but also has good surf.

Valdoviño, on the main road near Da Frouxeira beach, T981 487 076. Open Easter-Sep. A good (if slightly pricey) campsite, it has bungalows and many facilities.

Ferrol p446

Ferrol has several modern business hotels and lots of low-budget options, not all of them good.

AL Parador de Ferrol, Rúa Almirante Fernández Martín s/n, T981 356 720, www. parador.es. Situated in a good spot, at the end of the old town near the water, this parador has comfortable rooms, many with views, although these cost a little more.

C Hotel Galiano-Plaza, C Galiano 35, T981 300 000, www.hotelgalianoplaza.es. The glorious façade of this building, with its square-paned *galerías* (closed balconies) is striking, and the modern interior sensibly doesn't try to match it. There's a slight Asian minimalism to the comfortable rooms, as well as gleaming new bathrooms and friendly Ferrol service.

F Hostal da Madalena, Rúa Magdalena 98, T981 355 615, madalenahostal@wanadoo.es Clean and cheap and far better than some of the seedier options around Ferrol. Some rooms have been renovated, some not, so ask to see. Free Wi-Fi.

Pontedeume and the Caaveiro Valley p448

There are several lodging options in Pontedeume and several *casas rurales* in the area.

B Casa do Castelo de Andrade, Castelo de Andrade s/n, T981 433 839, www.castelo andrade.com. About 8 km southeast of Pontedeume, this standout rural hotel comprises 3 old farm buildings in an isolated spot surrounded by meadows and woodland. They've been beautifully converted and the blend of the historic stone with modern design features makes it a wonderfully romantic place to stay for a couple of days. Recommended.

C Casa Graña da Acea, Acea, near Monfero, T981 788 282, www.casaturismorural coruna. com. Just 2 km from the town of Monfero (labelled Rebordelo on some maps), near the natural park, this wonderful converted old stone house makes a great rural retreat. Rooms are all different but decorated with rustic style; the courteous sisters who run it put on good home-cooked dinners.

D Hotel Eumesa, Av de A Coruña s/n, T981 430 925, www.hoteleumesa.es. In the centre of Pontedeume, this simple and friendly hotel has decent rooms, many overlooking the river mouth. There's some traffic noise. Breakfast included.

E Allegue, Rúa Chafaris 1, T981 430 035, hostalallegue@hotmail.com. A little place with clean and comfortable rooms with simple bathrooms and an attractive patio.

Eating

Ribadeo p444

Ψ Solana, C Antonio Otero 41, T982 128 835. This is a reliably good seafood restaurant by the marina. Anything from the water is delicious, but the paella or *zarzuela de mariscos* (seafood stew) are excellent house specialities.

Ψ Casa Villaronta, Rúa San Francisco 9, T982 128 609. Down the pedestrian street from the central square, this is a downmarket and delightfully traditional Galician *pulpería*, where *ribeiro* wine and a plate of octopus is the way to go. It's always packed, and the low prices are only part of the reason why. Recommended.

Foz and around p444

Ψ Restaurante O Lar, Praza Conde Fontao 3, Foz, T982 140 829. This place is a good, traditional and solid harbourside eatery with reliable and cheap seafood.

Viveiro and around p445

The restaurant at the **Hotel Ego** (see Sleeping, above) has a lofty reputation for seafood.

ΨΨ O Asador, Rúa Meliton Cortiñas 15, T982 560 688. This is the most inviting restaurant in Viveiro itself, a friendly upstairs spot looking over the narrow lane below. The fish, octopus and service are superb. Recommended.

ΨΨ Vinoteca Los Leones, Pastor Díaz 12, T982 570 604. In a shopping arcade between the waterfront and the main pedestrian street, this smart little bar serves quality wines in pretty glasses and also does a few smart food options like *pirulís de perdiz*, a little partridge-flavoured flourish.

Ψ Mesón Imperial, Pastor Díaz 66, T982 562 316. Reliably buzzing at afternoon tapas time, this is a traditional tasca with a struggle to get to the bar, and delicious *raciones* like mussels, monkfish brochettes, and, of course, octopus.

Ψ O Muro, C Margarita Pardo de Cela 28, T982 560 823. This is a popular local *pulpería* with cheap bar snacks and an upstairs restaurant.

Cedeira p446

ΨΨ Badulaque, C Area Longa 1, T981 492 265. This local sits near the port in the Casa do Mar building. It's an old-fashioned sort of a place that does seafood and fish with few frills but of a very high standard.

Ferrol p446

Across the bay, Mugardos has some good and traditionally Galician seafood places.

ΨΨ Casa Rivera, Rúa Galiano 57, T981 350 759. This well-priced restaurant has excellent seafood and land-based dishes, with cheering stews and tasty octopus.

Bars and clubs

Ferrol p446

Ferrol has a lively bar scene, mostly centred in the old town.

Vétula, Rúa Cantón de Molíns 6, T981 354 712. A friendly place for a drink or a coffee, this bar, facing the park, is one of the more pleasant spots.

☉ Activities and tours

Ribadeo *p444*
At Ribadeo's waterfront you can practise or learn various aquatic activities.
¡Hola!Ola, Av Calvo Sotelo 30, T982 120 064, www.holaola.com. Offer hire of surf equipment and lessons, and also deal in waterskiing, wakeboarding and windsurfing.
Portanorte, Av Asturias 21, T982 120 429, www.portanorte.es. Boat-oriented and hire kayaks, yachts and hobby catamarans.

Viveiro and around *p445*
If you fancy a bit of boating, you can rent canoes on the Praia de Covas beach just across the *ría* from town.
Roq Sport, T646 514 602, www.roqsport.com. Land-based activities including guided hikes, mountain biking, kayaking, and abseiling.

☐ Transport

Ribadeo *p444*
Bus
8 buses daily to **Lugo**, 7 along the coast to **Oviedo**, 4 to **Santiago**, and several running to **A Coruña** along the coast. 2 buses head inland to **Vilalba** and **Mondoñedo**.

Train
The coastal FEVE train line stops here on its way between **Ferrol** and **Oviedo**. It's a good way to access some smaller coastal towns.

Viveiro and around *p445*
Bus
Buses run from here both ways along the coast and inland to **Lugo** and **Santiago**. The bus station is by the water 200 m north of the old town.

Train
The FEVE line stops at Viveiro, and also at O Barqueiro near the main road, as do buses on the coastal road.

Ferrol *p446*
The FEVE station, RENFE station and bus station are close together near Praza de España a short way north of the old centre.

Bus
There are very frequent services to **A Coruña**. **Santiago**, **Pontevedra**, **Vigo**, **Betanzos** and the north coast are also regularly serviced by bus.

Ferry
A launch service zips across the *ría* to **Mugardos** from Paseo de la Marina. Mugardos is a pretty little fishing town; you might want to stay for lunch and try the famed local recipe for octopus.

Train
4 FEVE trains a day head eastwards towards **Oviedo**; 2 of them only make it to **Ribadeo**. There's 1 RENFE train daily between Ferrol and **A Coruña** (1 hr, €6.20).

Pontedeume and the Caaveiro Valley *p448*
Bus and train
The train service between **Ferrol** and **A Coruña** calls at Pontedeume, as do buses on the same route.

A Coruña and Costa da Morte

→ *Colour map 1, A3. Phone code: 981. Population: 246,056.*

One of Spain's most enjoyable cities to visit, A Coruña is spectacularly situated and has a superb atmosphere. It's a place where, at least when it's not raining, everyone seems to stay outdoors enjoying the privileged natural setting. Coruña has a bit of everything; a harbour, a good beach, top seafood, great nightlife, Romanesque architecture, entertaining museums, quiet corners and a have-a-go football team. It's an excellent town for the tourist but also still an important working port and commercial centre.

The rugged coast west of A Coruña is named the 'coast of death', and has an interesting and dark history of marine disasters, wreckers and 'five and twenty ponies trotting through the dark' smuggling. There are some excellent beaches and some fairly authentic towns, which get on with their fishing and farming as the majority of tourists zip straight down to Finisterre.

▸▸ *For listings, see pages 462-467.*

A Coruña → *For listings, see pages 462-467.*

Ins and outs

Getting there A Coruña is connected with Madrid, Barcelona, Bilbao, and other Spanish cities by air. **Vueling** has budget flights to London Heathrow and Amsterdam, and **Iberia** also serve London, Paris, and Lisbon. It's a major railhead and bus terminus, well connected with the rest of Northern Spain. ▸▸ *See Transport, page 466.*

Getting around Most of A Coruña is easily explorable on foot. The coastal *paseo* around the headland is a long one, but a tourist tram covers the route half-hourly; a beautiful ride. The bus and train stations are a 20- to 30-minute walk south from the centre of town. City bus No 1 runs from the main road between the bus and train stations into town.

Tourist information A Coruña has several tourist offices; the handiest is the **municipal office** ① *Plaza María Pita 6, T981 184 430, Mon-Fri 0900-2030, Sat 1000-1400, 1600-2000, Sun 1000-1500*, on the main square. Nearby is the **regional office** ① *T981 221 822, oficina. turismo. coruna@xunta.es, Mon-Fri 1000-1400, 1600-1900, Sat 1100-1400, 1700-1900, Sun 1100-1400*, on the marina.

Background

Such a fine natural harbour as Coruña's was pounced upon early; it was used by the Celts and Phoenicians before becoming an important Roman port, Ardobicum Coronium. It was said that the foundations were laid by Hercules himself. The city remained (and remains) a significant port; it was the westernmost member of the **Hermandad de las Marismas**, a trading league formed in 1296 along Hanseatic lines.

Coruña's northward orientation is historically linked with Britain, whose sailors referred to it as 'the Groyne'. British pilgrims used to disembark here en route to the tomb of Saint James. This *Camino Inglés* was the easiest of the Pilgrim Routes to Santiago, at least when the Bay of Biscay was in clement mood.

In 1386 John of Gaunt, son of Edward III, decided to avenge the murder of his father-in-law, Pedro I, and landed here with an army. After a farcical progress through Galicia, a peace was finally brokered whereby John's daughter would marry the heir to the Castilian throne. The Castilian king compensated him for the expenses occurred in the invasion and he went home, honour satisfied.

A Coruña

Sleeping 🛏
Carbonara **1**
Centro Gallego **2**
Hesperia Finisterre **4**
Hospedaje Os
  Potes **3**

Hostal Mara **6**
Hostal Palas **5**
La Provinciana **7**
Meliá María Pita **8**
Riazor **9**
Santa Catalina **11**

Venecia **10**

Eating 🍴
Albeiro **2**
Alcume **3**
A Taberna de Cunqueiro **8**

When John's great-granddaughter, the Catholic Monarch Isabel, died, Philip the Fair of Flanders landed here in 1506 to meet with Fernando and claim the Castilian throne. His grandson Philip II had plenty to do with Coruña too; while still a prince, he embarked from

here to England, where he married Mary at Winchester. Some 34 years later he assembled his Armada, whose 130 ships put out from the harbour here with 30,000 men. In 1507 Francis Drake had also sailed here and set fire to the town but was thwarted by the town's heroine María Pita, who saved Coruña by seizing the British standard and rallying the townsfolk to repel the buccaneers.

In 1809 a dispirited and undisciplined British army were relentlessly pursued by the Napoleonic forces of Marshal Soult. Having abandoned all their baggage and gold, the army made for Coruña where a fleet was stationed, but Soult was hard on their heels. To save as many men as possible, the Scottish general, Sir John Moore, faced the French with a small force while 15,000 troops embarked on to the ships. Moore was killed and the force defeated, but the majority of the army got away thanks to the sacrifice.

Compared with other Spanish cities, Coruña thrived in the 19th and 20th centuries; it seems its close ties to northern Europe and its flourishing port saved it from stagnation.

Sights

One of the best ways to take in A Coruña's sights is a walk starting in the old town by the port and continuing anticlockwise around the headland. It's a long stroll, but you can hop on the tram that circles the route about every half-hour (weekends only in winter).

Avenida de la Marina and around The Avenida de la Marina is a good place to start. It's a very elegant boulevard lined with attractive old houses with trademark *galerías* or miradors, windowed balconies that look out over the water. Off here is the **Praza María Pita**, named after the city's heroine. The arcaded square is centred on a statue of María herself, defiantly brandishing a spear with a couple of Drake's mercenaries dead at her feet. She is commemorated with an eternal flame and faces the **Ayuntamiento**, a Galician *modernista* building.

A few block north of Avenida de la Marina is the modern **Museo de Bellas Artes** ① *Av Zalaeta s/n, Tue-Fri 1000-2000, Sat 1000-1400, 1630-2000, Sun 1000-1400, €2.40*, an excellent space that incorporates part of a former monastery and has a reasonable collection of European art, including some Goya sketches and some works by Rubens, as well as lesser-known but worthwhile Galician artists. Another place with good temporary art exhibitions is the striking **Fundación Caixa Galicia** ① *Cantón Grande 21, T981 185 060, www.fundacioncaixagalicia.org*.

Shipwrecks and smugglers

The indentations and rocks that abound on Galicia's coastline provide some spectacular scenery but also have a darker side. It is a sobering fact that in the last century some 140 ships have gone down with the loss of over 500 lives. The scandalously mismanaged *Prestige* oil disaster in 2002 is just one of a long series of shipping incidents on this coast.

Local legend attributes many of these wrecks to the activities of *raqueiros* (wreckers), who lured ships onto the rocks by attaching lights to the horns of cattle. More likely though, it is the combination of sea-surges and savage rocks that make this coast so hazardous.

The natural features of the coast that make it so dangerous for shipping have made it a haven for smugglers

down the years. In recent years, Galicia's smugglers have moved away from more traditional products towards drugs. A large proportion of Europe's cocaine arrives through Galicia, usually being left well offshore by a smugglers' ship, then picked up by one of the coast's fishing fleet. This has had the predictable effect of increasing problems of corruption and violence. The town of O Grove saw its former mayor facing drugs-related charges and in Vilagarcía, which experienced a sudden and highly suspicious boost in wealth in the 1990s, the local Chamber of Commerce Director was the victim of a professional hit. Recently heavy police activity has seen some of this trade move to other locations.

Ciudad Vieja East from the Praza María Pita is a very attractive network of old streets, Ciudad Vieja, a quiet place with some fine houses, squares and churches. The church of **Santa María del Campo** is a charming Romanesque building dating from the late 13th century. Its wide nave and narrow aisles make for an intriguing interior space, with a crooked, off centre alignment and solid barrel vaulting. The 13th-century portal is a good work, as is the later rose window. In the eaves, a curious carved pattern looks like dripping wax. The side portal also features elegant Romanesque stonework. Alongside, there's a small **museum** ① *Tue-Fri 1000-1300, 1700-1900, Sat 1000-1300, free*, of religious art.

Jardín de San Carlos *"Not a drum was heard, nor a funeral note, as his corse to the ramparts we hurried"*, Charles Wolfe. The small and evocative Jardín de San Carlos is the final resting place of General Sir John Moore, the Scot who turned "like a lion at bay" to engage the superior French forces of Marshal Soult to give his dispirited army time to embark on the waiting ships. He was killed by a cannonball and hurriedly buried "by the struggling moonbeam's misty light". The soldier's grave was later marked with a granite monument; in Spain, the Peninsular War is named the War of Independence, and British involvement fondly remembered, although the redcoats' behaviour and discipline was frequently atrocious. Poems by Charles Wolfe and Rosalía de Castro commemorate Moore, and fresh flowers often appear on the grave.

The marina and around Descending from here to the marina, the fort that juts into the bay was built by Felipe II and now houses the **Museo Histórico Arqueológico** ① *Sep-Jun Tue-Sat 1000-1930, Sun 1000-1430, Jul and Aug Tue-Sat 1000-2100, Sun 1000-1500, €2*, the highlight of which is a number of pieces of Celtic jewellery including distinctive torcs and the famous 'helmet of Leiro'.

Nunca Maís

In late 2002, the future of Galicia's coastline and fishing industry was put in serious jeopardy by the rupturing and subsequent sinking of the single-hulled oil tanker *Prestige*. The Spanish and Galician governments acted with culpable indecision – in an apparent effort to wash their hands of the matter, they insisted on towing the stricken vessel out to international waters, thus ensuring the oil slick spread over a larger area. The *Prestige* was carrying 70,000 tonnes of oil, over 70% of which was spilled, washing up along the Galician and Asturian coasts, reaching France and Portgual. Massive volunteer cleaning operations ensued, and the Gallego slogan *Nunca Maís* (Never Again) became a catchcry across the nation. A billion euro later and thanks to the expertise of environmental organizations and the energies of the volunteers, the long-term damage to the Galician fisheries and environment has not been as devastating as first feared. However, until sterner worldwide controls of unseaworthy vessels are applied, *Nunca Maís* remains a hope rather than a reality.

East of here, the massive glass **cuboids** of the port authority's control tower cut an impressive figure. From here, you might want to get the tram around to the Torre de Hércules, as it's a 20-minute walk with little of interest (apart from the great waterfront views).

The **Torre de Hércules** ⓘ *Oct-Mar 1000-1745, Apr-Jun, Sep 1000-1845, Jul and Aug 1000-2045 (2345 Fri and Sat), €2.50*, stands very proud at the northern tip of Coruña's peninsula. It was originally built in the second century AD by the Romans, and claims to be the oldest lighthouse still operational. Its current exterior dates from an 18th-century reformation and, in truth, there's not much Roman left of it, apart from a central core and some foundations, visible in a low-ceilinged space before you ascend. It's worth climbing the 234 steps to the top, where there's a good view of A Coruña and the coast.

Not far beyond the lighthouse is the **aquarium** ⓘ *Mon-Fri 1000-1900, Sat/Sun 1000-2000 (daily 1000-2100 in Jul and Aug), €10 (€12 for combined ticket to here, Casa de Ciencias and Domus)*. There are good displays (no English) on lots of aspects of sea life, an outdoor seal pool, an intriguing tank with growing fish embryos, and a curious underground observation area decked out to look like Nemo's office in the Nautilus. .

The ark-like **Domus** ⓘ *daily 1000-1900 (1100-2100 in Jul and Aug), €2 (€4 including IMAX projection; combined ticket with aquarium and Casa de las Ciencias €12)*, looks like the hull of a boat and has become something of a city emblem since famed Japanese architect Arata Isozaki created it. It's an entertaining modern museum of humankind, dealing in all aspects of how we function physically and mentally. There are loads of interactive exhibits, giving plenty of fun for young and old. There's also a café.

 "She belongs more to the sea than to the stony mass of mainland behind her," is how Dutch writer Cees Nooteboom has accurately described A Coruña.

Beyond the old town The curve of the city's excellent beach sweeps around the bay. It's a top stretch of sand, slightly marred by poor waterfront architecture. Although there's plenty of space, in summer it can be packed out. At its far end is the **Estadio de Riazor**. The city's football team, Deportivo La Coruña, small by European big-club standards, have achieved many notable successes.

In the Santa Margarita park, the **Casa de las Ciencias** ⓘ *daily 1000-1900 (1100-2100 Jul and Aug), €2, planetarium €2 (combined ticket with aquarium and Domus €12)*, has good displays on biology and mechanics as well as a planetarium, which can be dogged by lengthy queues.

Around A Coruña → *For listings, see pages 462-467.*

Betanzos

The town of Betanzos makes a good day trip from A Coruña. The site of a Celtic settlement, and a significant Roman port, it's an attractive, if slightly faded place that was dealt a bitter blow in the 17th and 18th centuries when the port silted up and Betanzos gradually became an inland town, although it's still a junction of the two pretty rivers that are to blame for the fiasco. In summer you can take a boat trip on them.

Betanzos's main attraction is its steep streets lined with trademark Galician housing. There are a couple of nice plazas and four churches, of which the absolute highlight is the **Iglesia de San Francisco**, a monastery church built in the 14th century. It was paid for by the count Fernán de Andrade, lord over most of this region, and dubbed '*O Bóo*', or the good; it's not clear by whom, probably himself. He had the church built with his own soul in mind: he intended to rest in peace in it, but wasn't prepared to compromise. His earthly love was boarhunting, and the number of carved boars both outside and in the church is noteworthy. The top attraction, however, is his tomb (although he's not actually in it). It's carved with excellent hunting scenes, all dogs, horns, and tally-hos, and is mounted on the back of a large stone boar and a rather brainless-looking bear. There are many other tombs of lords and ladies, as well as some representations of saints. The apse is big and light and holds a simple sculpture of Saint Francis and the Crucifixion behind the altar. The vaulting is elaborate, but the pigs still pull focus.

The **Iglesia de Santa María del Azogue** dates from the 14th century and has a pleasant, spacious interior with some slightly skewed columns with good carved capitals. The *retablo* is dark and is centred on an icon of the Virgin. The façade features the elders of the Apocalypse around a scene of the Adoration on the tympanum. Strange animals adorn the capitals.

The **Iglesia de Santiago** ⓘ *1000-1400, 1700-2100, €1*, dates from the 15th century and has a very fine carved portal of Santiago Matamoros and the Pantocrator. The capitals on either side of the door are carved with frightening beasts. The interior is simple, with a triple nave. In the **Praza Constitución** there's a small museum devoted to modern prints. There are six buses a day between Betanzos and Coruña, and a couple to Santiago.

The buses stop on the road across the river from the old town. The **tourist office** is behind the church on the plaza on the main road thorugh town.

Costa da Morte → *For listings, see pages 462-467.*

Malpica → *Colour map 1, A2.*

The first stop of interest along from A Coruña is Malpica, a lively, unadulterated fishing town ruled by a pack of large and brazen Atlantic seagulls. There's an offshore nesting sanctuary for less forceful seabirds on the **Islas Sisargas** opposite. You can get out to the islands by chartering a boat, T981 720 655, www.islasisargas.com, which costs €20 per person (minimum €100). Malpica also has a good beach, which can get pretty good surf.

Corme

There are some good wild beaches west of here. The town of Corme is reached via a side road, and sits on a nice bay used to cultivate shellfish. The port is backed by narrow streets tightly packed with the houses of fishing families. Bypass the town beach and head for **Praia Ermida**, 1 km or so further around the bay. The town doesn't give too much away; it was known as a nest of anti-Franco guerrilla activity during the Civil War, and anybody prying into the coming and going of boats in the middle of the night these days might end up sleeping with the shellfish. Suffice it to say that much of Europe's cocaine arrives through Galicia. Over 2000 kilos of the stuff were captured in one of the higher-profile police raids in 2006. A more traditional maritime harvest is the *percebe*, or goose-necked barnacle; the *perceberos* who collect them have a perilous job, but it's a much-appreciated Galician speciality.

Ponteceso and around

Ponteceso has a bridge of medieval origins that crosses the marshy river. If it's beaches you want, stop at **Laxe**, which has a top strand of white sand, and an even better one to the west; peaceful **Praia Traba**. The town itself isn't great.

Camariñas

The coast continues to be impressive; Camariñas, the next worthwhile place from Ponteceso, makes a good place to stop. It's famous throughout Spain for its lace; if that's not your thing, it also enjoys a privileged location, on a pretty inlet stocked with pines and eucalypts. It looks across the *ría* to Muxía on the other side. The port is small but serious, with some biggish boats heading far out to sea. There's a summer-only **tourist office** on the *ría*-side *paseo*.

The **Museo do Encaixe** ① *T981 736 340, Fri and Sat 1100-1400, 1700-2000, Sun 1100-1400, 1600-1930, otherwise call first, €1.50*, details the history and practice of lacemaking; they make it bobbin-style here. It is famous throughout Spain, and can be bought at several outlets in the village; on a nice day you may even see some elderly lacemakers at work in the sun outside their houses.

The best thing to do in Camariñas is explore the **headland** to the north. There's a series of dirt roads that are just about driveable, but it's nicer on foot with the smell of pine in your nose. **Cabo Vilán** is about an hour's walk, a dramatic spot with a big lighthouse building and high, modern windmills, which work pretty hard here. Further east, there are a small **beaches** and an English cemetery, with the graves of some of the dead of a British navy vessel wrecked on the coast in 1890, at a cost of 170 lives.

Muxía

The counterpart of Camariñas on the other side of the *ría*, Muxía is a tightly packed fishing town that makes up for in authenticity what it lacks in postcardy charm. It's worth visiting, though, to see the **Santuario de Nuestra Señora de la Barca** on a headland just past the town. With the waves beating the rocks to a pulp around the chapel, it's a hugely atmospheric place; it's not hard to see why fisherfolk who brave the stormy seas have a healthy religious and superstitious streak around here. The spot was originally venerated to commemorate an impressive navigational feat in the early first century AD; the Virgin Mary sailed from Palestine to this very spot in a stone boat. If you don't believe it, take a look inside the church: various fragments of the vessel are set around the sloping interior. Now, fishermen pray for the safety of their own boats, often leaving small models as ex-voto offerings.

On the first Sunday after 8 September, there's an important *romería* to the sanctuary in Muxía; part of the ritual is a claustrophobic crawl under a huge rock. It's one of the most atmospheric and meaningful of Galicia's fiestas.

Corcubión and Cée

At the foot of the Finisterre peninsula, the fishing ports of Corcubión and Cée have grown into each other, stretching around the bay. It's a fairly serious fishing spot, and Corcubión is the epitome of a picturesque Galician fishing town, with plenty of hotels and restaurants. Cée has a small ship-wrecking industry, a fairly tough business, but nothing compared to what confronts you a little further around the bay; a giant alloys plant that manages to effectively recreate Hell on the Galician coast. Pity the workers.

Towards the end of the world → *For listings, see pages 462-467.*

Fisterra and Cabo Finisterre

Further west from Cée, the town of Fisterra makes a fine place to drop anchor for the night. It's an attractive if slightly wind-bitten fishing port, and there are plenty of facilities catering to the passing tourists and pilgrims heading for Cabo Finisterre a couple of kilometres beyond. There are the remains of a small fort and good views across the bay. Fish restaurants crowd the lively waterfront, where you can visit the important *lonja* (fish market) where the day's catch is traded. Entry costs €1.

The most westerly point in mainland Europe is not Cabo Finisterre. It's in Portugal, and the most westerly point in Spain is a little further up the coast, but Finisterre has won the audience vote. Part of its appeal comes from its name, derived from the Latin for 'end of the earth', part from its dramatic location: a small finger of land jutting into the mighty Atlantic. Gazing westwards from the rocks around its scruffy lighthouse (which houses a small pilgrimage exhibition) is a magical experience, particularly at sunset; imagine what it would have been like if you believed the world ended somewhere out there, dropping off into a void. The cape is 2 km uphill from Fisterra, accessible by road. There's a small bar at the top, and you can stay at the *pousada* here. In recent years, the journey from Santiago to Finisterre has become a popular extension to the pilgrimage, and you'll likely see weary souls perched atop the cliffs, contemplating the sea at the end of their journey. Many leave an item of clothing here: those worn-out shoes, maybe, as a token.

Carnota

Moving south again towards the Rías Baixas, the village of Carnota is set 1 km back from a magnificent and wild beach 7 km long and rolling with enormous dunes. This is one of Galicia's most spectacular coastal spots. Carnota itself has a **tourist office** at the top of town and a hotel. It also boasts the longest *hórreo* (raised granary, very typical of the region) in Galicia. The vaguely ridiculous 18th-century structure is 35 m long. You'll find it tucked away in a back street on the western side of the main road.

☻ A Coruña and Costa da Morte listings

For Sleeping and Eating price codes and other relevant information, see Essentials pages 31-39.

☻ Sleeping

A Coruña *p453, map p454*

A Coruña has a large number of good-quality budget accommodation options, concentrated in the tapas zone a couple of streets back from Av de la Marina. All choices are notably cheaper outside Jul and Aug.

L Hotel Hesperia Finisterre, Paseo del Parrote 2, T981 205 400, www.hesperia-hoteles.com. Superbly located on the headland, this is the nicest place to stay in A Coruña. Recently renovated, the rooms are smallish but bright, furnished with style, and many have superb views over the harbour and sea. There are all the facilities you could ask for, and an excellent restaurant.

L Meliá María Pita, Av Pedro Barrié de la Maza 1, T981 205 000, www.solmelia.com. Cavernously large, this imposing business hotel has an excellent location overlooking the city beach. Rooms that actually have water views cost a little more, but are worth it, as other views are rather uninspiring. Service is courteous, but extras like Wi-Fi are expensive. Good off-season rates (**C**).

A Hotel Riazor, Av de Pedro Barrié de la Maza 29, T981 253 400, www.riazorhotel.com. This is a big but pleasant beachfront hotel near the stadium. Recently renovated, it has rooms with excellent bathrooms and great views – make sure you specify that you want one when reserving. It's a lot cheaper outside high summer.

C-D Hotel Santa Catalina, C Fernando Arenas Quintela 1, T981 226 704, www.hotelstacatalina.es. Right in the heart of Coruña with top tapas a couple of steps from the door, this recently remodelled choice has upgraded from *hostal* to hotel status but still offers a very reasonable rate for comfortable accommodation.

D Centro Gallego, C Estrella 2, T981 222 236. This is a very good option above a friendly café, with no-frills but excellent-value rooms with decent bathrooms. It's a remarkably good deal considering its proximity to water, tourist office, bars and octopus taverns. Off season, it's one of the cheapest places in town.

D La Provinciana, Rúa Nueva 7, T981 220 400, www.laprovinciana.net. An excellent spot to stay off season, as the rooms are good and drop to a very low price. The rooms are heated and there's parking available; it's a good deal. Although not exactly charismatic, it's run with old-fashioned courtesy.

D Carbonara, Rúa Nueva 16, T981 225 251, www.hostalcarbonara.com. One of the better choices, this is a very good central spot with friendly management and decent rooms with bathrooms in a typically attractive Coruña house. It's in the heart of the tapas zone.

E Hospedaje Os Potes, C Zapatería 15, T981 205 219. This simple but comfortable budget option is beautifully located in a narrow street in the heart of the old part of Coruña, near the delightfully wobbly Plaza Azcárraga.

E Hostal Mara, C Galera 49, T981 221 802, www.hostalmara.com. In tapas bar heartland, this is a reliable option with good, clean en suite doubles at the quiet end of the street. They're sound people running it, and there's a decent cheap restaurant. Good value off-season. Parking available.

E Hostal Palas, C Marqués de Amboage 21, T981 247 400, www.pensionpalas.com. This is a good option if you arrive late or are leaving early; it's right next to the bus station and just across the overpass from the train station. It's run by cheerful old folk and is modern and clean as a whistle; the rooms are quiet and spacious with cable TV and heating (make sure it's on!). They're used to people coming and going at odd hours.

E Venecia, Praza Lugo 22, T981 222 420. A very cheap option on a square a couple of blocks from the main bar zones. Rooms with or without bath (**F**) available in this old but character-packed building. Great value.

Betanzos *p459*
B Hotel Garelos, C Alfonso IX 8, T981 775 922, hotel@garelos.e.telefonica.net. This hotel is about the best non-budget option in Betanzos, which doesn't really inspire with its selection of accommodation. It's a little overpriced but has reasonable facilities and is central. Rooms are spacious with polished parquet floors and decent bathrooms.

Camping
El Raso, T981 460 676. A campsite near Betanzos by the beach of the same name. It's open year-round and there's an on-site café.

Malpica *p459*
B Hotel Fonte do Fraile, Playa de Canido s/n, T981 720 732, www.hotelfontedofraile. com. Right on the beach, this 3-star hotel is the most luxurious option hereabouts. Its rooms are airy and spacious, there's a pleasant little area to enjoy the sunshine or hop in the jacuzzi, and it's at the low end of this price category.
D Hostal JB, C Playa 3, T981 721 906. This is a good bet, with appealing rooms overlooking the beach.
D Panchito, Praza Villar Amigo 6, T981 720 307. With snug rooms and nice folk on the convivial square in the centre of town.

Ponteceso and around *p460*
E Hostal Bahía, Av Generalísimo 24, Laxe, T981 728 207, www.bahialaxe.com. A clean and decent year-round option if you're staying – the beach is the main reason to hang out in this town. For €20 extra, you get a room with a balcony and views.

Camariñas *p460*
There are several accommodation options in Camariñas, which gets a fair few tourists

in summer. Most of them are simple, family-run *pensiones* and *hostales*; there's nothing in the luxury class.
C Hotel Lugar do Cotariño, T659 923 693, www.docotarino.com. By far the best option hereabouts, this rural hotel is set in spacious grounds a couple of kilometres from Camariñas near the hamlet of Mourín. The rooms are classically modern rustic Spanish, with the exposed stone and wooden beams of the 3 old buildings artfully blended with new furniture and objets d'art.
E Hostal Scala, Tras Playa 6, T981 737 109, www.hostal-scala.com. This the sort of building that planning permission was invented to stop, but the structure craning to get a glimpse of the water has clean, light, and airy rooms; there's a choice of en suite or simpler pads with shared bathroom. Some rooms have a balcony.

Muxía *p460*
C-D Casa de Lema, T650 797 357, Morpeguite s/n, www.casadelema.com. A short way from Muxía in the hamlet of Morpeguite, this excellent *casa rural* gets plenty of repeat custom from folk that can't get enough of the pretty stone building or excellent hospitality. The rooms are exquisite for this price, with exposed stone, colourful walls, and iron-headed beds. Home-cooked meals are available for €18.
D Hostal La Cruz, Av López Abente 44, T981 742 084, www.hostallacruz.es. A big building with more than adequate modern comfort and little character. The best option in Muxía itself.

Fisterra and Cabo Finisterre *p461*
There are several pilgrim *albergues* and other budget accommodations in Fisterra.
A-B Pousada O Semáforo, Estrada do Faro s/n, Cabo Finisterre, T981 725 869, www. osemaforo.com. Closed Nov. Right on the headland, this is an unbeatable spot to stay. Situated in a former observatory and telegraph station, it offers considerable comfort and excellent meals (although not

to the public unless previously arranged) above the wild and endless sea.

C-D Dugium, San Salvador 26, T981 740 780, www.dugium.com. Closed Oct-Easter. In the middle of the Finisterre headland, the village of San Salvador harbours this small and peaceful rural hotel with excellent rooms, a tranquil garden and a good restaurant. Pricesinclude breakfast.

E Cabo Finisterre, Rúa Santa Catalina 1, Fisterra, T981 740 000. Closed Nov-Easter. This is one of several decent *hostales* in Fisterra, with just 6 rooms and a café.

Carnota *p461*

E Hostal Miramar, Plaza de Galicia 2, T981 857 016, www.hostalmiramar.es. Just off the main road in the centre of town, this is a convenient and comfortable place to stay. The rooms are well equipped and warm, with a slightly run-down beach-*hostal* feel, and there's a decent restaurant.

❷ Eating

A Coruña *p453, map p454*
A Coruña has a superb tapas scene, with *pulpo* (octopus) the excellent local speciality. It's usually served boiled, simply garnished with paprika, olive oil and salt, and accompanied by *cachelos* (boiled spuds). If you don't mind the slimy texture, it's superb.

From the Plaza de María Pita, C Franja and its continuation Galera form the heart of the eating zone. They are wall-to-wall *tascas*, simple spots with small tables and few frills dealing out delicious *raciones*; most locals eat in this way, hence, there are comparatively few traditional restaurants. There's little purpose to a lengthy list of recommendations; just wend your way along that route and pick a place you like. They're nearly all good: the more locals inside, the better.

¶¶¶ El Manjar, C Alfredo Vicenti 29, T981 142 552. A cosy restaurant with excellent old-time decor near the Riazor Stadium. They do a great *zarzuela de pescado* (fish stew)

and succulent *chipirones*. Ask for whatever's good that day; it's that sort of place.

¶¶¶ Pablo Gallego, Plaza María Pita 11, T981 208 888. On the picturesque central square, this intimate, romantic restaurant deals out good-quality seafood with a confident modern slant. Service is formal but friendly and there's a long wine list.

¶¶¶ Pardo, C Novoa Santos 15, T981 280 021. Coruña's finest restaurant treats its fish just right and is far from overpriced. It also does delicious partridge in season and good salads too. The seafood croquettes are justly famed. The decor is modern and stylish. Recommended.

¶¶ A Taberna de Cunqueiro, C Estrella 22, T981 212 629. With warm, enticing decor and helpful service, this popular tapas bar attracts a loyal following. They'll serve you a free snack with your glass of decent wine. Locals get rid of their pesky copper coins by sticking them in cracks in the stone wall.

¶¶ Albeiro, C de la Franja, T981 224 592. Simply decorated, this old-fashioned restaurant is a reliable choice for fruits of the sea just off the plaza. They do a good mixed grill of fish, as well as tasty *cigalas* and other seafood.

¶¶ Casa Varela, Plaza María Pita 12, T981 222 764. Just off the corner of the square, this is a homely, traditional Galician restaurant with few frills but plenty of quality. Big portions means it's easy to overorder: the meat dishes, including giant *chuletón* steaks and *codillo* (pork knuckle) are enormous.

¶¶ O Bo, C Menéndez Pelayo 18, T981 927 237. A traditional type of place, this sticks to what the Galicians know best; all the recipes have been handed down for generations. The *cocido gallego* is a guaranteed winter warmer, while the *pulpo* is delicious and the *tortilla* famous throughout the city. Recommended.

¶¶ Taberna da Penela, Plaza María Pita 9, T981 209 200, www.lapenela.com. Buzzing with chatter and conviviality, this lively spot on the main square is an excellent place to eat. The octopus is superb and backed up by tasty fish and meat dishes as well as swift service. There's a quieter, more formal restaurant, **La Penela**, with similar prices and dishes, just around the square at no 12.

¶ Alcume, C Galera 44, T981 210 174. A wooden-clad BBQ restaurant on the main tapas strip, this Argentine-style eatery has a cosy front terrace and tempting smells of grilled meats. No-frills options like chorizo *criollo* or *costilla* (ribs) are exceedingly tasty and priced low.

¶ El Serrano, C Galera 21, T981 220 353. If all that seafood is starting to make you feel a bit jaded, stop off here for excellent hams and cheeses, including the great Basque Idiazábal. They do several *tablas* (mixed boards) that are great for sharing.

¶ Mesón do Pulpo, C de la Franja 9, T981 202 444. The name says it all; on the street of octopus, this place does some of the best; just follow the locals. There are several choices of our 8-legged friend, and also a good selection of other seafood.

Cafés

Café Tortoni, Cantón Grande 21, T981 185 060. This posh, modern open-plan space occupies part of the ground floor of the Fundación Caixa Galicia building. It's a popular spot for tasty, good-value breakfasts and also has several Internet terminals.

La Bodeguilla, C Riego de Agua 33, T981 923 332. New ownership has transformed this traditional Coruña café into a modish spot for morning coffee or lunchtime tapas. Excellent service, great coffee, and small, individual tables are complemented by handsome decor, with intriguing lighting and exposed stone. There's a selection of interesting wines.

Playa Club, Andén Riazor s/n, T981 250 063. An airy café with a superb location and views down the beach. Serves a good range of *platos combinados* and tapas. There's also an upmarket restaurant, also with unbeatable views.

Betanzos *p459*

The bars with outdoor seats on the big Plaza Mayor do decent tapas.

¶¶ Os Arcos, C Argentina 6, T981 772 259. A friendly local restaurant; try the swordfish or *buey* (king crab). They also do decent budget accommodation.

Ponteceso and around *p460*

¶¶ Casa do Arco, Praza Ramón Juega 1, Laxe, T981 706 904, www.casadoarco.es. Has a good seafood restaurant.

Camariñas *p460*

There are several cafés and seafood restaurants in Camariñas.

¶¶ Gaviota, C Río 20, T981 737 032. Worthwhile seafood restaurant where you just have to eat whatever's fresh and finny that day.

Muxía *p460*

¶¶ A Pedra do Abalar, Rúa Marina 35, T981 742 063. A typically dependable seafood place with warm-hearted old-style service.

Fisterra and Cabo Finisterre *p461*

There are some excellent seafood restaurants in Fisterra.

¶¶¶ O Centolo, Paseo del Puerto s/n, T981 740 452, www.centolo.com. The classiest of Fisterra's restaurants, O Centolo serves an excellent range of fish and seafood in a spacious, light dining room, and also organizes dinner cruises on the bay in summer. You can eat here fairly cheaply or break the bank on the finest crustaceans.

¶¶ Casa Velay, Paseo da Ribeira s/n, T981 740 127. This place offers cordial, helpful service, and a terrace by the beach. The seafood is tops, with a generous *arroz con bogavante* (rice dish with lobster) for 2 costing €42, but it could feed a family.

🜚 Bars and clubs

A Coruña *p453, map p454*

After tapas time is over, folk tend to move on to 1 of 2 areas. A smarter scene goes on in the streets around Praza España and the Museo de Bellas Artes. A more alternative crowd hangs out in the bars and clubs around C del Sol, C Barrera and C Juan Canalejo de Corralón between the tapas zone and the beach. It's dead on weekdays, but at weekends it's as lively as anywhere in Northern Spain. Wander around and take your pick.

Entertainment

A Coruña *p453, map p454*
Centro Rosales, Rosales, T981 128 092, www.yelmocineplex.es. A very big cinema complex in a shopping centre.
Palacio de la Opera, T981 140 404, www.palaciodelaopera.com. As well as being an opera venue, this is the home ground of the Galician symphony orchestra.

Festivals and events

A Coruña *p453, map p454*
Aug Coruña's main festival is in honour of María Pita and lasts the whole month, with all sorts of cultural events and a mock naval battle. The main week, **Semana Grande**, is in the middle of Aug.

Shopping

A Coruña *p453, map p454*
C del Real, one street back from Av de la Marina, is the handiest shopping street.

Activities and tours

A Coruña *p453, map p454*
Diving
Centro de Buceo Nauga, Manuel Azaña 41, T981 129 811, www.nauga.es. Offer diving courses and equipment rental.

Camariñas *p460*
Horse riding
If you fancy a gallop, there's a small horse-riding operation outside town, T981 737 279.

Sport
The city's football team, **Deportivo La Coruña**, T902 434 443, www.canaldeportivo.com, play their home games at the Riazor stadium, right by the sea. It's one of the best places in Spain to watch a game, and the team are notoriously difficult to beat on their home patch. Games are normally on a Sun evening; tickets are available from the *taquilla* a couple of hours before the match; you can also book by phone or internet if you speak Spanish. Tickets booked this way must be picked up from a branch of Caixa Galicia bank.

Transport

A Coruña *p453, map p454*
Air
A Coruña's airport (**LCG**) lies to the south of the city. There are international flights to **Lisbon**, **London** Heathrow, **Amsterdam** and **Paris**, as well as national ones to **Madrid**, **Barcelona**, and **Bilbao**.
Buses run regularly from Puerta Real to the airport (€1.25). There's also a daily bus (leaving at 1030, T981 257 082) from the **Hotel Atlántico**, Jardines Méndez Núñez, to the international airport at **Santiago**.

Bicycle hire
There's a municipal bike rental shed on Paseo de la Dársena by the leisure harbour. Open 0900-2100 summer; 0900-1400, 1600-2100 winter. A 2-hr rental is €6; a whole day is €21. **Eco-Lógica**, C Cantábrico 2, T981 904 040, are open daily and rent cheap fold-up bikes, better 'slim' bikes and Segways.

Bus
The bus station is to the south of town, on C de Caballeros. Frequent buses (No 1) connect it with the city centre. Within Galicia, **Ourense** is served 8 times daily, **Lugo** 11 times, **Santiago** hourly (via motorway 45 mins, via road 1 hr 20 mins), **Pontevedra** and **Vigo** 9 times, **Betanzos** 6 times, and **Ferrol** hourly. 5 buses daily go down the **Costa da Morte** to **Camariñas**.

Long-distance destinations include **Gijón/Oviedo** (4 a day, 5-6 hrs, €24), **Bilbao** (2 daily, 11 hrs, €49) via **Santander** and **Madrid** (6-7 daily, 7 hrs, €45).

Train

The train station is just across the main road, and up the hill from the bus station. **Santiago** (45 mins, from €4.90) and **Vigo** (2 hrs, from €14) are serviced roughly hourly. There are also trains to **Lugo** (2 daily, 1 hr 30 mins, from €17), **Ourense** (4 daily, 2 hrs 15 mins, €24), **Madrid** (2 daily, 8 hrs, €52.40), and **Barcelona** (1-2 daily, 14½ hrs, from €73).

Costa da Morte p459
Bus

Bus services run by 3 different companies cover the Costa da Morte thoroughly. There are at least 5 buses daily to every destination mentioned on this stretch of coastline. Services run from these towns in both directions, ie to both **A Coruña** and **Santiago**.

❶ Directory

A Coruña p453, map p454

Internet and telephone Locutorio Unicornio, C Estrella 24, T981 210 639, has cheap internet and phone calls; Xebre 2, C San Andrés 138, T881 927 178, another central choice for internet and phone; Plaza@Net, C San Juan 5, internet only. **Laundry** Clean and Clean, C Juan Florez; Self Service, Paseo Marítimo s/n, where the big glass control tower is. **Medical services** Hospital Juan Canalejo, T981 178 000. **Post office** The main post office is on Av de la Marina opposite the tourist office.

Rías Baixas

→ *Colour map 1, B1/2.*

The Rías Baixas are a succession of large and beautiful inlets extending down the west coast of Galicia almost as far as Portugal. The sheltered waters are used to farm much of Spain's supply of shellfish, and the towns still harbour important fishing fleets. It's one of Galicia's prime visitor destinations, a fact which has spawned a few myths that are worth clearing up. Firstly, the rías are not 'fjord-like' – the coast is mostly low hills, and the inlets mostly fairly shallow, retreating over mudflats at low tide. Secondly, while there are some decent beaches here, they are generally not as good as those of the Costa da Morte or north coast. Lastly, they are not remote; much of the coast is a continuous ribbon of strip development. That said, there are many spots worth visiting and much good wine and seafood to be consumed. There are also several villages and peaceful spots that merit exploration; Muros and Cambados are the most appealing bases. The region's cities, Vigo and Pontevedra, are contrasting and highly appealing centres. ▸▸ *For listings, see pages 472-475.*

Muros → *Colour map 1, B1.*

The small town of Muros sits on the north coast of the northernmost *ría* of the Rías Baixas, which is named after it and Noia, its counterpart across the water. Muros has considerable charm, with a small but atmospheric old town stocked with lovely sandstone buildings, and a large fishing harbour. The Gothic church contains a Christ crucified that has a head of real hair; there's a picturesque market reached by a double staircase, and a curious stone reptile slithering over a fountain. Apart from that, it's just strolling the seafront and watching boats come and go; very pleasant indeed. There's **a tourist kiosk** on the waterfront promenade. If you fancy getting out on the water, **Costa Viva** ① *T686 192 031, www.cruceroscostaviva.com*, run cruises in a boat with some underwater visibility. Tapas and Galician wine are put on as part of the ride.

There are a few nice beaches on the Muros and Noia ría between the two towns. The blue-flag beach of **Parameán**, in the village of **Esteiro**, is one of the nicest, with clean, fine, white sand. Around **Abelleira** are another handful of good strands, with **Bornalle** one of the most inviting.

Noia and around → *For listings, see pages 472-475. Colour map 1, B2.*

On the other side and further up the estuary, Noia isn't as attractive a place as Muros, being a busier centre for the area. It's claimed that the town's name derives from that of Noah, because this was the spot where the dove found the olive branch; the ark came to rest on a nearby hill. Folk here believe it too, and the event even features on the coat of arms of the town. The Gothic **Iglesia de San Martín** is the town's highlight. Fronted by a fine *cruceiro*, it's got an excellent carved portal featuring the Apostles, and the Elders of the Apocalypse, and a beautiful rose window above. Another church, the **Iglesia de Santa María** ① *Mon-Sat 1000-1400, 1800-2000*, is full of the tombstones that were salvaged from a recent clean up of the graveyard. Rough slabs of granite dating from the 10th to 17th centuries, they are carved with simple symbols and figures that seem to fall into four distinct types: marks of profession, rebuses of family names, heraldic motifs and full figures of the deceased. It's a fascinating collection. Noia's **tourist kiosk** ① *T981 842 100, Mon-Fri 1030-1300, Sat and Sun 1200-1300 (extended opening in Jul and Aug)*, is opposite the town hall, built around a small, attractive atrium.

Cela vida

Camilo José Cela was a hard-living author who was known in Spain as much for his flamboyant lifestyle as for his novels. Awarded the Nobel prize in 1989, Cela was a friend of Hemingway and the two shared a robust masculine approach to both life and literature.

Cela's first novel *La Familia de Pascual Duarte* (The Family of Pascual Duarte) had to be published in Argentina in 1942 because its was considered too violent and crude for Spain. The story of a murderer, its uncompromising language was unlike anything else in contemporary Spanish literature. The book inspired many imitations and was said to be the most popular Spanish novel since Cervantes. Cela published over 70 works including *La Colmena* (The Hive), a novel about the denizens of 1950s Madrid cafés and their lives and loves. The Nobel citation praised his work for its "rich and intensive prose" and its "restrained compassion."

Although he fought for the nationalists in the Civil war, Cela later published an anti-Franco magazine that became a forum for opposition to the Spanish dictator. His success as an author enabled him to pursue a lifestyle which, among other things, saw him touring his native land in a vintage Rolls Royce. He died in 2002.

South of Noia

Continuing south, the coast is a pretty one, with some decent, if sometimes wild-watered, beaches. One of the better ones is **Ornanda**, just short of the decent village of **Portosín**. At **Baroña** there is a Celtic *castro*, a fort/village well situated on an exposed point. A couple of kilometres from the town of Axeitos down a peaceful country lane is one of the nicer of Galicia's many **dolmens**; it sits in a dappled glade among pine cones. Near here a winding road leads up to a mirador, **La Curota**. If the day is good, the view is absolutely breathtaking, taking in all the *rías*, with their shellfish platforms looking like squadrons of U-boats in harbour. You can see north to Finisterre and south to Baiona, just short of Portugal.

Santa Uxía de Ribeira (usually just called Ribeira or Riveira) is the main town in this region, an important fishing port and popular tourist destination. There are fabulous views over the wide bay with its rocky islets; what's left of the old town clusters behind the fishing harbour, but the major attraction is the fine deep sheltered beach, Playa Coroso, a short walk from the centre. This is the beginning of the next inlet, the **Ría de Arousa**, the largest of this coast. **Cambados** is the most attractive place to stay on this *ría*.

Padrón → *For listings, see pages 472-475. Colour map 1, B2.*

A busy road junction, Padrón at first glance seems unappealing, but it has several interesting associations. It was a Roman town, and tradition has it that the followers of Saint James landed here after bringing his body back from Palestine. The parish church by the bridge over the river displays the *el pedrón* (mooring-stone) under the altar. The small but picturesque old town is a relief to stroll in, away from the busy road.

Padrón is also famous for its peppers, which have DO (*denominación de origen*) status; the small, green *pimientos de Padrón* are mild, slightly sweet and are seen all over Spain. They are typically cooked in hot oil. Although most are harmless, the odd one is famously fiery; the Spaniards have a saying: '*O los pimientos de Padrón: unos pican, y otros no*' (Oh, the peppers of Padrón: some of them bite and some of them don't).

Padrón also has a strong literary connection. It was the long-time home of Galicia's favourite poet, Rosalía de Castro (see box, page 523). Her pretty gardened house has been turned into a museum, the **Casa Museo de Rosalía** ① *Tue-Sat 1000-1330, 1600-1900 (closes 1400 and 2000 in summer), Sun 1000-1330, €1.50*, opposite the station. In it are various personal possessions and biographical notes. Padrón's other writer, the Nobel prize-winning novelist Camilo José Cela (see page 469) was born on the town's outskirts. A former **canon's residence** has been turned into a museum displaying various manuscripts of his work and personal possessions, including a yellowing newspaper collection. Across the road is the collegiate **Iglesia de Santa María de Iria Flavia**, where the writer was baptized; it claims to have been the first church dedicated to Mary in the world (and therefore marks the beginning of Spanish polytheism). There's a small **tourist kiosk** on the main road.

Villagarcía de Arousa and around → *For listings, see pages 472-475. Colour map 1, B2.*

Villagarcía de Arousa is one of the wealthier towns on this stretch of coast, with its fair share of urbanizations and brash modern villas. It's an important fishing port, but the cash here wasn't just the result of a bumper prawn harvest; seafood of a more lucrative, Colombian variety has traditionally found its way ashore around here in notable quantities.

It's an easygoing, uncomplicated sort of town, filled with holidaymakers in summer, and doesn't make a bad base for a relaxed exploration of the coast. There's a **tourist office** ① *T986 501 008, turismo@vilagarcia.es, Mon-Sat 1000-1300, 1630-1830 (2000 summer), Sun summer only 1000-1400*, on the waterfront promenade where the buses stop.

A quieter and more appealing option can be found just to the north in **O Carril**, a pretty fishing harbour with several top-quality restaurants; there's also an excellent beach nearby, **Praia Compostela**, although you won't have it to yourself in summer.

Illa de Arousa
South of Vilagarcía, Illa de Arousa is an island linked to the mainland by a long modern bridge. It's relatively unspoiled, although not especially scenic. The main town, Illa de Arousa, is a small fishing port. The beaches are sheltered and pleasant enough, although they're not blessed with acres of white sand. The southern half of the island also preserves some important waterbird habitats.

Cambados and around → *For listings, see pages 472-475. Colour map 1, B2.*

Cambados
This noble old town is by far the nicest place to stay on this *ría*, and indeed perhaps on the whole of the Rías Baixas. The highlight is the huge granite-paved square, flanked by impressive buildings and an archway, and only slightly marred by the cars zipping across it. Other attractive houses line the narrow lanes of the town. The crumbling **Iglesia de Santa Mariña de Dozo** is now used as a cemetery; its 12th-century ruins are an atmospheric place.

Cambados is also the centre of the Rías Baixas wine region, which has DO (*denominación de origen*) status. Most of the land under vines is given over to the Albariño grape, which produces highly aromatic whites, fruity and flowery but crisp-finished, reminiscent of dry German wines; indeed, one theory of the variety's origin is that Benedictine monks brought it to the region from the Rhine. It tends to be made in small quantities, and is comparatively pricey but a great match with the region's shellfish. You can learn all about it in the **Museo Etnográfico del Vino** ① *Av Pastora 104, T986 526 119, Tue-Sun 1000-1400, 1630-1900, €3,* a wine museum divided between two connected buildings near the Santa Mariña de Dozo church. Entry includes admission to a couple of other museums in town, including a small display of wine routes. Of several bodegas in the area, one of the finest is **Martín Códax** ① *5 km east of town, T986 524 499, www.martincodax.com; it's open for visits by prior appointment Mon-Fri 1100-1300, 1600-2000.* In the centre of town, behind a narrow park. **Expo Salnés** ① *T986 521 008, Mon-Fri 1000-1400, 1700-2000,* is a tourist board-style exhibition about this area of the Rías Baixas and also functions as the town's tourist office.

O Grove and A Toxa

The resort town of O Grove enjoys an excellent natural setting at the tip of a peninsula at the southern mouth of the *ría*. No doubt it was once a charming fishing port, but it is fairly developed these days. Still, it's a cheerful and likeable place and could make a good venue for a relaxed waterside family holiday, with its large number of hotels, outdoor activities and seafood eateries. There are numerous fine beaches within a short drive from town. There's a **tourist information kiosk** ① *T986 731 415,* near the fish *lonja* by the water in the heart of town. Next to it is a large statue of a shell-fishing couple, one of dozens of public sculptures that decorate the town centre.

The most interesting sight in the area is **Acquariumgalicia** ① *T986 731 515, www. acquariumgalicia.com, Tue-Sun 1100-1400, 1630-1930, €10, kids €6.50,* 5 km to the west near the village of **Reboredo**. It's a large and excellent display; of most interest for its detailed coverage of the sealife of the *rías* and North Atlantic, although perennial favourites, such as piranhas and angelfish, are also to be seen. There are some 15,000 creatures among the 20 large tanks. From here, you can also sally forth in a glass-bottomed boat to see fish and shellfish at liberty, although the visibility can be a little murky.

The area around O Grove is also good for watching waterbirds; many species can be seen patrolling the muddy edges of the *ría*. The main focus for life in the town is the waterfront promenade. **Acquavisión** ① *T986 731 246, www.acquavision.com,* and **Pelegrín** ① *T986 730 032, www.crucerospelegrin.com,* among several other boats, run hourly glass-bottomed boat excursions from here in summer. The trips take about 1½ hours and cost around €13 per head. There's most to be seen on and around the shellfish-breeding platforms, and the trip includes a tasting.

It's a sobering thought that A Toxa was described by Georges Pillement in 1964 as "an earthly paradise". A lover of getting off the beaten track, the French travel writer would be appalled at his little island now. It's linked to O Grove by a short bridge, and although it's still attractively wooded, most of the atmosphere has been removed by the construction of several no-holds-barred luxury spa hotels (the thermal waters here are said to be beneficial), ugly apartments and a casino. If you can dodge the old women selling seashells, stroll around the western half of the island, which is still fragrant with pine. Otherwise, while the hotels lack no comforts, the island is an overpriced disappointment.

Praia A Lanzada

The best beach around this region is Praia A Lanzada, on the seaward side of the narrow neck of the peninsula. Its an excellent sandy stretch whose waters are said to boost female fertility. There's a small chapel at the southern end of the beach; a prayer and a dip are the traditional alternative to IVF in these parts. It's most effective on the night of the 23 June, with the moon shining. The swim must last exactly nine waves.

Sanxenxo

The resort of Sanxenxo lies on the northern edge of the Ría de Pontevedra and is something of a focus for the area's nightlife. The nicest bit of it is its high headland, while the waterfront is packed with cafés and bars. It's also a watersports centre, and makes a cheerful seaside base conveniently close to the cities of Pontevedra and Vigo. There's a boat service from Sanxenxo to the beautiful island of Ons (see Pontevedra to Vigo, 478).

⊙ Rías Baixas listings

For Sleeping and Eating price codes and other relevant information, see Essentials pages 31-39.

● Sleeping

Muros *p468*

There are several options on the waterfront road, which is often still referred to as Av Calvo Sotelo.

C Hotel A Muradana, Av Castelao 99, T981 826 885, hotelmuradana@ctv.es. The town's smartest option is unremarkable but decent. The rooms are spacious with TV and phone; some are equipped for disabled travellers. Try for one with a sea view. There's also a restaurant and free Wi-Fi.

C Hotel Punta Uía, T981 855 005, www.hotelpuntauia.com. Perched above the main road halfway between Muros and Noia, near the village of Esteiro, this attractive rural hotel offers wonderful sea views from its rooms and garden. It's a good base for hanging out on the beaches around this part of the *ría*. You pay €15 extra for a room with a balcony, but it's worth it if the weather's clement.

D Ría de Muros, Av Castelao 53, T981 826 056. The most likeable place in town with a guest lounge facing the water. The best bedroom, also at the front, has a curious bedroom/bathroom annexe and is worth nabbing. Good value off season.

E Hospedería A Vianda, Av Castelao 49, T981 826 322. Cheap but serviceable rooms above a café/bar, which is also a great place for a cheap *ración* or *menú del día*.

Noia *p468*

B La Pesquería del Tambre, Central do Tambre, Santa María de Roo, T981 051 620,

www.pesqueriadeltambre.com. Northeast of Noia, along a winding road off the Santiago highway, this former hydroelectric station has been transformed into a sensational rustic hotel. It's a secluded spot, with rooms spread out among different buildings in a picturesque riverside location. There's a pool and restaurant, and utter relaxation. Stay a few days. Recommended.

D Elisardo, Costa do Ferrador 15, T981 820 130. Near the shallows of the *ría* with good, clean rooms with bathroom. It's modern in feel and welcoming in style and offers decent value, even in summer, when you should book as there are only a handful of rooms.

Padrón *p469*

D Hotel Jardín, Rúa Salgado Araujo 3, T981 810 950. This is a great little spot to stay, which offers excellent value in a big 18th-century stone house shaded by palm trees and by the **Jardín Botánico**. There's some traffic noise from the main road.

Vilagarcía de Arousa and around *p470*

A Pazo O Rial, El Rial 1, T986 507 011, www.pazorial.com. Just south of Vilagarcía, on the shoulder of a ridge, this hillside *pazo* (country mansion) in a walled garden off the main road is one of the best places on this coast. It's well priced with attentive service and atmosphere, and it's even got a long *hórreo* and its own *cruceiro*. Recommended.

C Playa Compostela, Av Rosalía de Castro 134, O Carril, T986 504 010, pcompostela@galinor.com. A modern hotel replete with facilities. Rooms are bright and clean, and it's not bad value year round. Free Wi-Fi access.

Illa da Arousa *p470*

E Hotel Benalúa, Rúa Méndez Núñez s/n, T986 551 332. The only hotel on the island, this is a good-value option, with very acceptable rooms with en suite.

Camping
Salinas, T986 527 444. Open Jun-Sep. The campsite with the most facilities.

Cambados *p470*
AL Parador de Cambados, Paseo de Cervantes s/n, T986 542 250, www.parador.es. In the heart of town, this fine place set in a traditional Galician *pazo* (country mansion) has a good garden and recently renovated rooms. There's a pool, tennis court, and pretty patio.

D Casa Mariñeira Lourdes, Av Pastora 95, T986 543 985, www.cmlourdes.net. The nicest of several *casas rurales*, this one has big very homely bedrooms and offers more than decent value. Some rooms share a bathroom and are significantly cheaper. The owners also have rental apartments in the village.

E Hostal Pazos Feijóo, Rúa Curros Enríquez 1, T986 542 810. A decent and centrally located *hostal* in the southern part of town, with a friendly owner. Rooms are simple but spacious, with spotless en suite bathrooms.

O Grove and A Toxa *p471*
There are so many hotels that getting a room is never a problem, even in summer, although finding a bargain is trickier.

LL Gran Hotel La Toja, Isla de la Toxa, T986 730 025, www.granhotellatoja.com. The top hotel in the area, on the secluded enclave of A Toxa. It's got the lot, including a golf course, swimming pools, gym and sauna, and anything else you care to name.

B Hotel Maruxia, C Luis Casais 14, T986 732 795, www.hotelmaruxia.com. This is a reasonable choice and open all year-round – out of season its clean and proper double rooms come down substantially in value, but it's not badly priced for the zone in summer.

D Hostal María Aguiño, Rúa de Pablo Iglesias 26, T986 733 007. A friendly option offering good value, a couple of streets from the waterfront, right in the heart of things.

Praia A Lanzada *p471*
B Hotel Nuevo La Lanzada, T986 743 232, www.hoteleslanzada.com. Open Mar-Oct. This is a more than decent beachfront hotel with fine clean and bright rooms, some with balcony and views; there's also a restaurant. The sister hotel here is a little older but still decent; the prices are the same and it has a restaurant. Minimum 3-night stay in high summer.

Camping
Cachadelos, T986 745 592, www.camping cachadelos.com. Open Apr-Sep. The best equipped of 3 summer campsites, with a pool and wooden bungalows.

Sanxenxo *p472*
There are dozens of hotels here and along this stretch of coast.

L Gran Talaso Hotel Sanxenxo, Paseo de Silgar 3, T986 691 111, www.hotelsanxenxo.com. This large spa hotel has excellent facilities, and pleasing rooms, most with sea views (these cost a little more). There are good off-season rates, and various packages combining your stay with meals, spa treatments, etc. There's also an outdoor pool. A minimum stay applies in summer.

A Antiga Casa de Reis, Reis 39, T986 690 550, www.antigacasadereis.com. In the hills just behind Sanxenxo, this luxurious *casa rural* is one of the best of its kind in this part of the world. The thoughtfully decorated rooms have various artfully chosen curios and noble rustic furnishings, but are spacious and uncluttered. The breakfasts are delicious, and the hosts helpful and charming. Recommended.

D Casa Román, Rúa Carlos Casas 2, T986 720 031, www.casaroman.com. A moderately priced option in Sanxenxo itself, with comfortably simple en suite rooms that are pretty good value for this coastline. Breakfast is included.

D Casa Zulema, Arra/Playa Montalvo s/n, T986 691 991, www.casazulema.com. A reader-recommended spot about 1 km from the beach in Portonovo, west of Sanxenxo, this has correct and clean rooms at a reasonable price, and no-frills but tasty traditional dishes in the bar-restaurant.

🍴 Eating

Muros *p468*

🍴 Don Bodegón, Rúa de Rosalía de Castro 22, T981 827 802. This reliable choice has a good range of seafood and a good atmosphere. It's definitely worth booking in summer. They also do a good charcoal-grilled steak.

🍴 A Dársena, Av Castelao 11, T981 826 864, is a bright and friendly spot that does decent pizzas and good *raciones* of *pulpo*.

Cafés

Café Theatre, in the old Mercedes theatre on the plaza. A decent café and bar.

Camelot, C del Castillo s/n. Built cave-like into bedrock and with comfy seats to enjoy a drink.

Noia *p468*

🍴 Mesón Senra, Rúa Escultor Ferreiro 18, T981 820 084. A characterful restaurant that relies on its typically cosy Galician decor of stone and wood, and sterling service and food. The excellent *zamburiñas* (mini scallops) will satisfy parts other seafoods don't reach, while the sardines (*xoubas* in Galicia) are also bursting with flavour. There are appealing outdoor tables under the stone arches.

Padrón *p469*

🍴 A Casa dos Martínez, Plaza Baltar 7, T981 810 577. In the heart of the picturesque old part of town, this discreet, upmarket place offers imaginatively prepared and presented modern takes on traditional Galician cuisine and politely formal service. The local

peppers (*pimientos de Padrón*) are delicious. The *menú* for €27 includes a decent choice of wines.

🍴 Chef Rivera, Enlace Parque 7, T981 810 523, www.chefrivera.com. The finest spot in town. Sitting under the hotel of the same name, this uses the best of Galician ingredients. The lampreys are great, the octopus sublime and the wine list mighty impressive. Prices are very fair.

🍴 Os Carrisos, C Calvo Sotelo 27. On the main road through town, this excellent traditional *pulpería* has an airy front dining area and a rustic bar where you can drink ribeiro wine and enjoy delicious *raciones* of octopus.

Vilagarcía de Arousa and around *p470*

🍴 Loliña, Praza Muelle s/n, O Carril, T986 501 281. The best place to eat hereabouts, this restaurant is a superb ivy-swathed place with characterful Gallego decor. The house speciality is *rape* (monkfish/anglerfish).

🍴 Casa Bóveda, Paseo La Mariña 2, O Carril, T986 511 204. This is similarly good They do a delicious *arroz con bogavante*, a rice dish sizzling away with pieces of lobster on top.

Cambados *p470*

🍴 María José, Paseo de Cervantes s/n, T986 542 281. A loveable 1st-floor restaurant opposite the parador – the quality of the food is above and beyond what you'd expect for this price; just go with the staff recommendations. Recommended.

🍴 Posta do Sol, Ribeira de Fefiñans 22, T986 542 285. A good seafood restaurant housed in a traditional former bar.

O Grove and A Toxa *p471*

The waterfront in O Grove bristles with seafood restaurants, nearly all of which range from good to excellent. It's difficult to go wrong here, but be careful ordering things by weight, as bills can add up fast.

🍴 Posada del Mar, Av Castelao 202, T986 730 106. Polite service and tasty fresh fish are the hallmarks of this genteel restaurant near the bridge across to A Toxa.

₸₸ Beiramar, Paseo Marítimo 28, T986 731 081. Closed Nov. Another of the best-established of the fishy eating choices, this has excellent presentation and acceptable service in a comfortably attractive dining room.

₸₸ Finisterre, Praza Corgo 2, T986 730 748. Closed Feb. This place treats its fish (and therefore its customers) with all the respect their freshness deserves.

Sanxenxo *p472*

As we went to press, news came out that one of Galicia's foremost chefs, Toñi Vicente, is opening a restaurant near Praia La Lanzada. Called **Laurel**, it will be at Revolta 47, T986 745 801. If it's anything like as good as her former restaurant in Santiago, it'll be a real treat.

₸₸ O Forno, Seixalvo 25, T618 372 603. It's worth seeking out this restaurant on the hill behind town for its excellent Galician cuisine at generous prices.

⊖ Transport

Muros *p468*
Bus There are 3 daily buses to **A Coruña**. From just by the tourist office, buses leave almost hourly for **Santiago via Noia**.

Noia *p468*
Bus Hourly buses to **Santiago** and **Muros**.

Padrón *p469*
Bus and train Regular connections with **Santiago**.

Vilagarcía de Arousa and around *p470*
Bus Hourly buses from **Santiago** and **Pontevedra** to Vilagarcía de Arousa.

Illa da Arousa *p470*
Bus Buses from **Pontevedra** visit the island a couple of times a day, otherwise it's not too far to walk across to the mainland, where buses along the main road are frequent.

Pontevedra, Vigo and south to Portugal

→ *Phone code: 986.*

It's hard to imagine two more contrasting cities than Pontevedra and Vigo, yet both are enchanting. The former is a petite, genteel sort of place, with a picturesque old town studded with gorgeous plazas, while the latter is a big heart-on-sleeve blue-collar sprawl, a fishing city par excellence, situated on a spectacular bay. South of here, Baiona is one of Galicia's most appealing seaside towns, and the Celtic settlement above A Guarda stares across the Miño at Portugal, stone foundations still growling defiantly. ▸▸ *For listings, see pages 482-487.*

Pontevedra and around → For listings, see pages 482-487. Colour map 1, B2. Population: 81,576.

In contrast to its overxdeveloped *ría*, Pontevedra is a charming place; its beautiful old town and relaxed street life make it a top town to visit. It's the most attractive spot in which to base yourself to explore the Rías Baixas; its good bus and train connections make day trips an easy prospect. Its only downside is the occasionally nostril-searing odour from the massive paper mill a couple of kilometres down the *ría*.

Ins and outs

Getting there and around Pontevedra's bus station is a 20-minute walk southeast of the town centre on Rúa da Peregrina. There are frequent connections within Galicia and regular long-distance services. The train station is next door. ▸▸ *See Transport, page 486.*

Tourist information There are three tourist offices in Pontevedra. The Galician regional **tourist office** ⓘ *Rúa Xeneral Gutiérrez Mellado 3, T986 850 814, oficina.turismo.pontevedra@ xunta.es, winter Mon-Fri 1000-1400, 1600-1800, Sat 1000-1230, summer Mon-Fri 1000-1400, 1630-1930, Sat 1000-1400, 1630-1930, Sun 1000-1400,* is just outside the old town. The municipal **information office** ⓘ *Pr da Verdura s/n, T986 090 890, www.visit-pontevedra. com, daily 0900-1330, 1600-1930,* is in the heart of the old town. The third is a **Rías Baixas office** ⓘ *Pr de Santa María s/n, T986 211 700, www.riasbaixas.depo.es, summer Mon-Fri 0900-2100, Sat-Sun 1000-1430, 1630-2000, earlier closing winter,* which has information on this section of coastline and the offshore islands.

Background

Like several inland Galician towns, Pontevedra was formerly an important seaport but was left stranded by its river, which deposited large quantities of silt into the *ría*, handing Vigo the initiative for maritime activity. It's said that Pontevedra was founded by Trojan colonists that left the Mediterranean after the defeat by the Greeks; though there's little evidence, it doesn't even come close to being the tallest of the tall stories along this coast. Pontevedra declined in the 17th and 18th centuries, but on being appointed capital of this economically important Galician province a measure of wealth returned, and it's now a fairly prosperous administrative centre. Its proximity to Vigo means that many people commute between the two cities.

Sights

Pontevedra's endearing old town is built mostly of granite, and preserves a real medieval feel around its network of postcard-pretty plazas and stone colonnades. Perhaps the nicest of the squares is the small, irregular **Praza da Leña**, ringed by attractive houses. Like many of the plazas, it contains a *cruceiro*. The bigger **Praza da Verdura** nearby is another good space with arcades and coats of arms on some of the grander buildings.

Around the large, social **Praza da Ferrería** are two churches, the curiously rounded, domed **Santuario de la Virgen Peregrina**, where pilgrims on their way to Santiago on the *Camino Portugués* traditionally drop in; and the larger **Igrexa de San Francisco**, with some attractive stained glass, carved tombs of goggle-eyed nobles and a fine rose window, as well as an array of saints, pleasingly including some of the less-commonly venerated stalwarts of the church.

Pontevedra

Sleeping 🛏	Eating 🍴	La Casona 3	Bars & clubs 🍸
Casa Maruja 2	Adega dos Avós 5	La Navarra 7	Doctor Livingstone,
Comercio 6	A Taberna do	Loaira 6	Supongo? 12
Parador de	Pincho 4	Mesón Bar Premio 9	
Pontevedra 4	Carabela 1	Os Maristas 13	
Rúas 5	Eirado da Leña 2	Perita 10	
	La Alquería Mudéjar 8		

The **Basílica de Santa María a Maior** ① *daily 1000-1300, 1730-2000, free*, is Pontevedra's finest church, which looks especially attractive when bathed in the evening sun. Dating mostly from the 16th century, it has particularly elaborate ribbed vaulting, late Gothic arches, a dark *retablo* that predates the church, and a sloping floor. The fine Plateresque façade is the work of a Flemish master and depicts scenes from the life of the Virgin Mary. In the gardens on the old town side of the church is a stone marking the location of the old Jewish cemetery.

The **Museo de Pontevedra** ① *winter Tue-Sat 1000-1400, 1600-1900, Sun 1100-1400, summer Tue-Sat 1000-1415, 1700-2045, free to EU passport holders, otherwise €1.20 (they don't tend to check)*, covers five separate buildings, with the main one on Praza da Leña. It's one of the better such museums in Spain's north; the Celtic jewellery is a definite highlight; there's also a large 19th-century silverware collection and a replica of a 19th-century Spanish frigate admiral's onboard quarters. Some good paintings are present, including works by Goya and Zurbarán among many Galician, Aragonese and Catalan artists. One of the museum's buildings is the atmospheric, ruined **Iglesia de Santo Domingo** by the Alameda; it contains a number of tombstones from different historical periods.

Pontevedra to Vigo

Moving southwards along the coast from Pontevedra, the reeking paper mill makes the first few kilometres unattractive, although the cheery maritime murals on the factory are at least a token effort. There's a large naval academy at the small port of **Marín**, and near Mogor are some important Celtic stone carvings. Both Marín and the nearby town of **Bueu** are points of departure for summer excursions to the beautiful and peaceful **Isla de Ons**, one of four island groups that make up the national park of Islas Atlánticas de Galicia, in a glass-bottomed catamaran (**Naviera Illa de Ons**, T986 320 048, www.isladeons.net). The boats make the crossing daily from July to September; aboard you can get a voucher for the island's campsite. There's also a hotel and restaurant on the island, whose details are on the same website; it pays to reserve rooms well in advance. It's a rugged, rustic place, so don't expect luxury: electricity is limited to lunchtimes and evenings.

One of the nicest places on this stretch is the village of **Hío**, on the headland that divides the *rías* of Pontevedra and Vigo; it's 1 km from the main road. Its church has a Romanesque portal, but the highlight is its *cruceiro* out the front, an intricate work carved almost wholly from a single block of granite. At the top is a Crucifixion of some emotion, below is a scene of Mary helping sinners in Purgatory, while Adam and Eve stand bashfully underneath. An angel watches the scenes from another pillar nearby. It's one of the finest *cruceiros* of Galicia, although certainly not the oldest, being sculpted in 1872. There's a small tourist information kiosk nearby. The village itself is a pleasant spot, and there are some very good beaches around the headland.

Cangas is a busy little seaside resort and satellite of Vigo, with some good bars on the waterfront as well as a pretty little chapel. There's a regular ferry across to Vigo used by commuters; it's the smart option, as the traffic between here and there is terrible. Cangas was a hotbed of witchcraft in the 17th century, at least according to those loveable chaps of the Inquisition. Much of the unorthodox behaviour that caused concern could perhaps be attributed to post-traumatic symptoms; the town was viciously sacked by Barbary corsairs shortly before, leaving much of the population dead. If you prefer to stay here to Vigo, see Sleeping, page 482. Moaña, a little closer to Vigo, also has a ferry service, and is a bit quieter.

Vigo → *For listings, see pages 482-487. Colour map 1, C2. Phone code: 986. Population: 297,332.*

Vigo is Galicia's largest city (the fourth largest in Northern Spain), and the world's second largest fishing port by volume (after Toyko), supplying huge quantities of sardines, among other things, to the whole of Europe. With a beautiful location spread along its wide bay, it's a curiously divided place. The old part of town is a working port and wholly down-to-earth. Traffic problems, urban decay and poverty are all present and evident, but it still recalls its golden days as an important steamer port bustling with passengers bound for London, Portugal and South America. Faded but proud old buildings line the streets descending to the harbour, and the fresh seafood on offer here is as good as anywhere in Europe. By contrast, the newer zone around the marina is full of trendy cafés and waterfront promenades. If you're looking for a quiet, restful stop you may hate Vigo; if you're the sort of person who finds busy ports and earthy sailors' bars a little romantic it's an intriguing and likeable place.

Ins and outs

Getting there Vigo's airport is east of the centre and connected with the city by bus. There are daily flights to several Spanish cities, one to Paris, and a budget flight to Brussels. The bus station is a good distance south of the city centre, serviced by city buses from

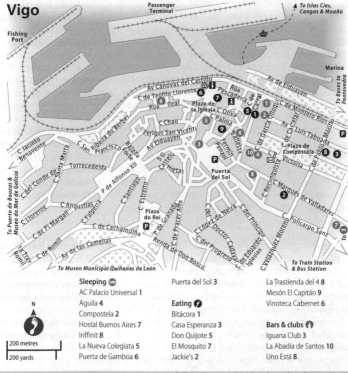

Vigo

Sleeping
AC Palacio Universal 1
Aguila 4
Compostela 2
Hostal Buenos Aires 7
Inffinit 8
La Nueva Colegiata 5
Puerta de Gamboa 6

Puerta del Sol 3

Eating
Bitácora 1
Casa Esperanza 3
Don Quijote 5
El Mosquito 7
Jackie's 2

La Trastienda del 4 8
Mesón El Capitán 9
Vinoteca Cabernet 6

Bars & clubs
Iguana Club 3
La Abadía de Santos 10
Uno Está 8

200 metres
200 yards

Praza Puerta del Sol (No 9A). There are dozens of local buses within Galicia and regular connections to cities throughout Spain. Some buses to Pontevedra arrive and leave from the Arenal, which is much more convenient for the centre. Vigo's train station at the eastern end of town and is well served. ▸▸ *See Transport, page 486.*

Tourist information Vigo's **tourist office** ⓘ *Rúa Cánovas del Castillo 22, T986 430 577, oficina.turismo.vigo@xunta.es, Mon-Fri 0930-1400, 1630-1830, Sat 1000-1330, 1630-1830, open until 1930 summer,* is opposite the passenger terminal at the heart of the waterfront. There's another office on Calle Pescadería nearby.

Background
Vigo's top natural harbour was used by the Phoenicians and Celts before the city as we know it was founded by the Romans, who named it Vicus Spacorum. Vigo's curse was often its pretty offshore islands, the Islas Cíes, which were used throughout history as cover and a supply base for a series of swashbucklers, raiders and pirates, including Vikings, Corsairs and Britons; Sir Francis Drake spent a couple of years menacing Vigo on a regular basis. In 1702 a passing British fleet of only 25 ships heard that the treasure fleet from South America was in the port with a French escort. Their surprise attack was a success; they sank 20 and captured 11 of the fleet. The gold and silver was still on board because at that time only Cádiz had official permission to unload bullion from the colonies. Rumour has it that most of it was dumped into the sea; numerous diving expeditions have been mounted over the last couple of centuries, but no success had been reported. In the late 19th century, as the golden age of the steamer began, Vigo grew massively and became prosperous on the back of this and increasingly efficient fishing methods; nearly all its public buildings date from 1860 to 1890. Decline set in in the 20th century, particularly during the stultifying Franco years, when Spain lagged far behind other European powers, but more recently large manufacturing plants, such as the huge Peugeot-Citröen operation, have brought much employment to the city. Pontevedra's status as provincial capital continues to annoy Vigo (until the new standardized numberplates came in, locals used to travel to far-away Vitoria so their car would bear the 'VI'); there has never been much love lost between the two cities, and locals feel their city doesn't get a fair slice of the pie from the provincial administration. Nevertheless, the local administration is making a big effort at urban renewal, including rehabilitation of the central barrios and the installing of a fine series of modern sculpture all around town, and little by little Vigo is beginning to recover the sparkle that its superb natural setting deserves.

Sights
Vigo's main sight is its busy **waterfront**. There are kilometres of it to wander if you're so inclined, and even the commercial docks are mostly easily accessible. Right in the centre is the passenger terminal where steamers used to dock; next to it is where the ferries leave for the ports of **Cangas** and **Moaña** across the bay, as well as the **Islas Cíes** in summer. The terminal still gets the odd cruise ship in, and lots of yachts still put in at the marina just east of here, which is backed with all manner of trendy bars and restaurants.

To the west of the passenger terminal, it's worth having a look at the fishing port, where boats of all sizes and nationalities drop in on their way to and from the Atlantic fisheries. Further round are repair docks and shipwrecking yards, and the **Puerto de Bouzas** beyond is the customs-bonded dock where commercial goods are unloaded. When the fishing boats come in at dawn, *marisqueiras* (typically the wives of the fishermen) still sell fresh shellfish (the oysters are delicious) around the streets; particularly on the covered **Rúa da Pescadería** near the marina, popularly known as Calle de las Ostras, or Oyster Street.

The main attraction in the town itself is the elegant architecture on the streets leading back from the passenger terminal, very faded but a poignant reminder of golden days. Just to the west, the narrow streets are the oldest part of the town; it's known as **Berbés**, and is full of little watering-holes and eateries. It has its vaguely seedy side but is on the up again, with boutiques, trendy bars and worthwhile fish restaurants.

The **Museo do Mar de Galicia** ① *Av Atlántida 160, T986 247 750, www.museodomar. com, mid-Jun to mid-Sep Tue-Fri 1100-1400, 1700-2000, Sat-Sun 1100-2100, mid-Sep to mid-Jun Tue-Fri 1000-1400, Sat-Sun 1100-1900, €3,* is a modern museum on the waterfront a fair way west of the centre. It's an interesting display of Spanish maritime history and includes an exhibition on the treasure fleet disaster of 1702 and the importance of trade with the New World colonies. There's also an aquarium focusing on the local marine ecosystem.

The **Museo Municipal Quiñones de León** ① *Tue-Fri 1000-1330, 1700-2000, open all day Wed, Sat 1700-2000, Sun 1000-1330,* is a museum in an old Galician mansion in the Parque de Castrelos south of the centre; it has period furniture and a decent collection of Galician paintings and makes a peaceful retreat from Vigo's working centre. In an adjacent annex is a reasonable archaeological collection.

In summer, an open-top **tourist bus** ① *www.vitrasa.es,* does a circuit of the town, including stops at the two museums above and other attractions. A day's hop-on hop-off ticket is €7.50.

The offshore **Islas Cíes** are a complete contrast to Vigo and the overdeveloped *rías*; an unspoilt (though much-visited) natural paradise, uninhabited and only visitable in summer. The area is comprised of three main islands (two of which are connected), rocky and rugged, and harbouring quiet coves with wonderfully romantic white sand beaches once the haunt of pirates. It is one of the archipelagos that make up the newly designated Islas Atlánticas National Park. In summer (mid-June to mid-September), ferries run to the islands from the passenger dock; you'll have to return the same day unless you simultaneously purchase a voucher for the **campsite** ① *T986 438 358, T986 225 582 in winter, www.campingislascies.com,* which has a shop and bar/restaurant. There are four boats a day, and a return ticket is €18.50. There are also boats here from Baiona. Timetables and tickets are on the websites www.mardeons.es and www.crucerosriasbaixas.com; it's worth buying them in advance at busy times. There's not a lot of shade on the islands, so take sunscreen; the breezy westerlies can be deceptive.

South of Vigo → *For listings, see pages 482-487.*

Baiona and around → *Colour map 1, B2.*
Heading south, the elegant port and resort of Baiona is the main destination of interest. On the way, **Playa América** is a long, narrow, popular and adequate beach with a well-equipped campsite (see Sleeping, page 484).

Baiona is a beautiful spot, built behind a large, walled fort on the headland, now a parador (an admission charge of €1 is haphazardly levied). It was mostly built by the counts of Andrade, who bossed most of Galicia in their day, but before that the headland was inhabited by Celts, Phoenicians and Romans. Take the 3-km stroll around the impressive walls, reinforced with cannon, and have a drink at the terraced bar; it's a superb spot, even if you're not staying in the parador itself.

Baiona was agog in 1493, when the *Pinta*, of Columbus's small fleet, appeared at the port entrance with confirmation that the Atlantic could be, and just had been, crossed. There's a replica of the staggeringly small **Pinta** ⓘ *Wed-Mon 1000-1930, daily 1000-2100 in summer, €2*, in the port here, enlivened by a dummy crew.

On the hill above town is a giant and tasteless statue of the Virgin; you can, however, climb it for good views of the town and coast. Baiona has a small but colourful **tourist office** ⓘ *T986 687 067, turismo@baiona.org, winter 1000-1400, 1500-1900, summer 1000-1500, 1600-2100*, which is located by the entrance to the parador.

South of Baiona, the tiny village of **Oia** is a fairly untouched little fishing port. The licheny baroque monastery is in a poor way. The monks here knew about Oliver Cromwell's apocryphal advice to "put your trust in God but keep your powder dry"; they once repelled a Turkish pirate fleet with a volley of cannon fire. If you want to stay in this peaceful place, see Sleeping, below.

A Guarda

The last Spanish town on the Atlantic coast is A Guarda, a fairly uninspiring spot but worth visiting for the **Monte Santa Trega** ⓘ *€1*, high above town. Occupying the headland between the sea and the mouth of the Miño that marks the border with Portugal, it's a long but worthwhile climb (or drive). As well as great views over the town, river mouth and out to sea, you can pace the impossibly narrow streets of the ruins of a large Celtic town. One of the round stone dwellings has been reconstructed; the *palloza*, its direct descendant, was still a feature of many Galician villages until fairly recently. At the top, there's a chapel and a small museum with some finds from the site.

◉ Pontevedra, Vigo and south to Portugal listings

For Sleeping and Eating price codes and other relevant information, see Essentials pages 31-39.

◉ Sleeping

Pontevedra *p476, map p477*
AL Parador de Pontevedra, Rúa Barón 19, T986 855 800, www.parador.es. This lovely parador is in the heart of the old town, set in a *palacio* on a pretty square. There's a beautiful garden and terrace, and the rooms are decorated with style and comfort.
C-D Hotel Rúas, C Figueroa 35, T986 846 416, www.hotelruas.net. You can't beat the location of this hotel, in the liveliest area of the beautiful centre, set right between 2 of the prettiest plazas. The rooms have large comfortable beds and are very good for the price; the showers are gloriously powerful. There's a café downstairs and a warm welcome. It's much cheaper off season. Recommended.

D Hotel Comercio, Rúa González Besada 3, T986 851 217, www.hcomercio.com. This smart modern hotel isn't going to win any design awards but is fairly central, in the new town not far from Praza Herrerías. The rooms have a/c and good bathrooms.
E Casa Maruja, Av Santa María 2, T986 854 901. Good, cheap, if slightly claustrophobic rooms, clean and with TV; some en suite. It's very well located in the old town.

Pontevedra to Vigo *p478*
C Hotel Airiños, Rúa da Marina s/n, Cangas, T986 340 000, www.airinos.com. A decent option on the boulevard. Rooms are comfortably spacious if darkish. It's worth paying a little extra for larger ones with a sea view and lounge area. It's **E** off-season. Free internet.
D Hotel Playa, Av de Ourense 78, Cangas. T986 303 674, www.hotel-playa.com. Slightly cheaper than the Airiños and a short

way east of the main bustle but right on the beach and a good choice for families. Rooms are clean and bright.

Vigo p479, map p479
There's plenty of accommodation for all budgets in Vigo, including a wide choice of chain business hotels.

AL AC Palacio Universal, C Cánovas del Castillo 28, T986 449 250, www.ac-hotels. com. This noble waterfront building in the heart of town is a stylish modern hotel, with spacious rooms, and excellent facilities. Many of the rooms have great views over the port and the sea. You can pull up at the door, but get good instructions about how to use the automated car park opposite if you don't speak Spanish. There are often good offers for this hotel online.

A Hotel Inffinit, C Marqués de Valladares 8, T986 442 224, www.inffinit.com. Glisteningly new, and with eye-catching modern design, this hotel has a fine central location and really comfortable, luxurious rooms with great bathrooms. The suites (**LL**) are really something to behold.

C Compostela, Rúa García Olloqui 5, T986 225 528, www.hcompostela.com. A quality mid-range hotel near the harbour, spruce and comfortable. It's got underground parking, important in Vigo, and there's friendly service and free Wi-Fi.

C Hotel Puerta de Gamboa, C Gamboa 12, T986 228 674, www.hotelpuerta gamboa. com. Right in the heart of old Vigo, handy for port, oyster street, and fish taverns, this new small hotel is a beautiful conversion of a noble old building, with the combination of modern style and original features working well. Free Wi-Fi and cordial service, but no parking. Breakfast included. Recommended.

C Hotel Puerta del Sol, Puerta del Sol 14, T986 222 364, www.alojamientosvigo. com. There's a bit of traffic noise, but this well-kept spot has plenty of character in its comfortable rooms, a good location at the top of the old town, and an underground car park right alongside. They've also got

apartments at competitive prices, located opposite. It's **D** outside of high summer.

E Hostal Buenos Aires, C Rosalía de Castro 6, T986 433 924, hostalbuenosaires@terra.es. A short stroll from the leisure harbour, this has large, spotless rooms with plenty of light and stylish modern bathrooms decked out with slate tiles. It's immaculate, and only the squeaky floorboards can be faulted. Great value year-round.

E Hotel Aguila, C Victoria 6, T986 431 398, www.hotelaguila.com. Central and friendly, this old hotel looks a little dilapidated at first glance, but the rooms – high-ceilinged and full of character – are spotless and have real charm. Prices are excellent for this location, and a simple breakfast is included, as is free Wi-Fi. A tip: turn off the air freshener before you go to sleep.

F La Nueva Colegiata, Plaza de la Iglesia 3, T986 220 952. A decent, cheap option in the old town with modernized facilities and more than adequate heated rooms that are a snip at this price.

Baiona and around p481
LL Parador de Baiona, Monterreal s/n, Baiona, T986 355 000, www.parador.es. One of the chain's finest, superbly set in grassy gardens within the impressively walled fort on the headland. Comfortable rooms; many have great views out to sea. Recommended.

A-B Pazo de Mendoza, C Elduayen 1, Baiona, T986 385 014, www.pazodemendoza.com. In the old dean's house in the centre of town, this is a classy option and very good value for money. Rooms are equipped with modern conveniences but haven't lost the charm of this noble old edifice.

C-D Casa Puertas, Rúa Vicente López 7, Oia, T986 362 144, www.toprural.com. A charming *casa rural* in a stone house in the narrow streets near the monastery. Rooms are simply furnished but comfortable, and offer great value in this peaceful village.

E Hotel Caís, Rúa Alférez Barreiro 3, Baiona, T986 355 643. This friendliest of places is an unbeatable budget hangout. Right by the water, it has spacious rooms with TV and phone, and even a small swimming pool.

F Hospedaje Kin, Rúa Ventura Misa 27, Baiona, T986 355 695. Small rooms in a good location on the main pedestrian street, focus for tapas and restaurants.

Camping

Camping Baiona Playa, Praia Ladeira, T986 350 035, www.campingbayona.com. A year-round campsite with cabins, a pool and all the trimmings on a long beach east of the town.

Playa América, Playa América, T986 365 404, www.campingplayaamerica.com. Open mid-Mar to mid-Oct. Campsite with bungalows and a swimming pool.

A Guarda *p482*

B-C Convento de San Benito, Praza San Benito s/n, T986 611 166, www. hotelsanbenito.es. This is an enchanting and peaceful place to stay, in a lovingly restored monastery with a pretty cloister. Have a look at a few rooms, as they are all quite different and have distinct charms; some are more expensive (**A**) and have hydromassage showers. Recommended.

🍴 Eating

Pontevedra *p476, map p477*

There are characterful, traditional tapas and wine bars along C Isabel II and C Princesa in the old centre. Numerous terraces to eat on crowd the plazas in summer.

🍴🍴🍴 **Casa Solla**, Av Sineiro 7, San Salvador de Poyo, T986 873 198, www.nove.biz/ga/solla. An excellent Galician restaurant with innovative dishes, 5 km west of Pontevedra on the way to Sanxenxo. It's often considered to offer the region's best modern Spanish cuisine, best sampled on the exquisite 12-course degustation menu. The setting, in a noble mansion surrounded by garden, matches the high quality of the food.

🍴🍴🍴 **Eirado da Leña**, Praza da Leña 1, T986 860 225. On Pontevedra's prettiest square, this has a coolly elegant interior and a sunny terrace for convivial lunching among the combined chatter of competing alfresco eateries. Well-prepared fish dishes are the signature here, and there are several set menu options allowing you to try a range of morsels.

🍴🍴 **Adega dos Avós**, C Gutiérrez Mellado 6, T986 896 228. A fairly traditional scene at this spacious and busy café, bar and restaurant apart from the dishes on offer, which include kangaroo, ostrich and zebra.

🍴🍴 **La Casona**, Rúa Tetúan 10, T986 847 038, www.lacasonadepontevedra.com. A friendly, stylish restaurant that makes an excellent choice. The food is generally traditional Galician fare prepared with flair; the *lenguado al albariño* is a good dish of sole cooked in the aromatic local white wine. There's a decent *menú* for €10.

🍴🍴 **Loaira**, Praza da Leña 2, T986 858 815. Run by an enthusiastic young couple, this tiny corner place expands on to the square outside in summer. Good fresh salads and other brightly presented *raciones* are on offer, and there's a reasonably priced lunch *menú*.

🍴🍴 **Mesón Bar Premio**, Rúa da Peregrina 29, T986 103 528. This atmospheric spot is a godsend if you are lugging heavy bags from the bus station into the old town on a hot day. A tapa of the delicious ham and a glass of something cold and you'll be on your way again with renewed vigour. It's also a great spot to sit down and eat and decorated in the traditional manner with venerable wine bottles and hanging *charcutería*.

🍴 **A Taberna do Pincho**, Praza Méndez Núñez 15, T986 857 840. A popular meeting point in the heart of Pontevedra. You'll get a small free snack with your drink, and there's also a wide choice of nibbles or more substantial fare such as *revueltos*, which you can eat at the downstairs tables. There's a lunchtime *menú* for €8.50.

🍴 **Bar os Maristas**, Praza da Verdura 5, T986 844 075. Another old-fashioned place, this is as authentic as it comes, with old men drinking their pre-lunch wines out of traditional white ceramic crucibles. There are cheap *raciones* of very tasty traditional Galician fare and a terrace in summer.

¶ La Alquería Mudéjar, Rúa Churruchaos 2, T986 851 258. With wooden tables, yellow lighting and a convivial buzz, this is a place to lift the spirits. There's a fine selection of wines and plenty of simple *raciones* and dishes. The *tortilla* is great, as are the brochettes; this is a real enclave of genuine hospitality. Recommended.

¶ La Navarra, C Princesa 13, T986 851 254. Traditional with a capital T, this no-frills bar and wine shop serves up wine and traditional Galician fare in a great atmosphere. It's one of several old-time bars worth exploring on this street and Isabel II, which intersects it.

Cafés

Carabela, Praza da Estrela 1, T986 851 215. A famous café with a relaxing outdoor terrace on the largest square, where you can watch Pontevedra's children feeding or chasing the pigeons.

Perita, corner of Av Santa María and C Churruchaos. Serving as both café and night-time bar, this stylish venue is squeezed into an attractive stone space and given a modern feel with its underlit shelves, sleek bar and contemporary art exhibited on the walls. The coffee is excellent and comes with a little pastry; the *copas* are also well poured.

Vigo *p479, map p479*

There are several good restaurants in Berbés around C de Carral, opposite the passenger terminal, and the nearby streets. Seafood terraces line C Pescadeira here. More upmarket choices are clustered in the streets behind the marina; C Taboada is a good place to start. C Olloqui, back from the Universal hotel, is another fertile tapas zone.

¶¶¶ El Mosquito, Praza da Pedra 2, T986 224 411. This upmarket but down-to-earth and cheery restaurant in the old-town streets above the port has a deserved reputation for its seafood. Whatever you choose here is bound to be good; the octopus has an excellent reputation, as do the oysters and the *lenguado* (sole).

¶¶¶ Casa Esperanza, Rúa Luís Taboada 28, T986 228 615. Warmly decorated and with a cordial welcome, this split-level place near the marina is a Vigo classic for the freshness of its seafood. Fish bursting with flavour and great shellfish make this a sound choice.

¶¶ La Trastienda del 4, C Pablo Morillo 4, T986 115 881, www.latrastiendadelcuatro. com. A couple of streets behind the marina, this sophisticated wine bar and restaurant has a colourful summer terrace and an appealing interior reminiscent of an old-time French grocers. The cuisine is innovative and imaginative, fusing styles and ingredients from around the world with success.

¶¶ Mesón El Capitán, C Triunfo 5, T986 220 940. There's plenty of atmosphere and no nonsense at this excellent seafood eatery on one of the old town's major arteries. Whether you eat in the attractive upstairs *comedor* or downstairs by the kitchen, you'll enjoy top-notch *chipirones* on a bed of potato and onion, and a great *jarrete* (stewed lamb thigh), the house speciality.

¶¶ Restaurante Bitácora, Rúa Carral 26. Good *raciones* of seafood in this smartish tapas bar and restaurant. You'll struggle to pass by without entering, the sizzling smells are so enticing. The *zamburiñas* in garlic are especially tasty. They also do a great seafood paella and decent *mariscada* for 2.

¶ Restaurante Don Quijote, C Laxe 4, T986 229 346. This restaurant on a steep street above the passenger terminal is excellent, particularly its wooden outdoor tables. There's a full restaurant menu or excellent *raciones* and tapas; the *mejillones* (mussels) are particularly good, the *chipirones* are juicy and come with Padrón peppers, and the octopus is difficult to beat. Recommended.

¶ Vinoteca Cabernet, Teófilo Llorente 29, T986 227 429. The best feature of this wonderful wine bar is its splendid vine-shaded flagstone terrace in the curious patio area, and it's a great discovery indeed in the middle of old Vigo. Excellent wines, good cured meats and other tapas, and polite service. Recommended.

Cafés
Jackie's, Marqúes de Valladares 14, T986 433 500. One of Vigo's most popular breakfast spots, this busy café serves up strong coffee with a little wedge of madeira cake at its low bar, and also does tapas and has a cheap *menú del día*.

Baiona and around *p481*
Pazo de Mendoza and Casa Puertas mentioned in Sleeping, above, are also reliably good eating places, as is the pricier parador.

¶¶ **Jaqueyvi**, Rúa Xogo da Bola 1, T986 356 157. The corner bar is a great spot for ham and cheese tapas accompanied by local wine. Attached (or around the corner) is a sit-down restaurant with a good selection of Galician dishes, including excellent rices and *fideuàs* (similar, but made with noodles). There's also a fried fish eatery.

¶¶ **Paco Durán**, C Iglesia 60, Baiña, T986 355 017. Up in the hills about 3 km from Baiona, this romantic spot has stupendous views over the bay and the Islas Cíes. There's great baked and grilled fish and very friendly service.

🍸 Bars and clubs

Pontevedra *p476, map p477*
Praza del Teucro is the old-town centre for evening drinking. After hours the *marcha* moves out a little; many people head for Sanxenxo in summer, or the town of Arcade, 5 km south, which has, as well as a number of *marisquerías*, several bars and *discotecas* along its main street, C Castelao.

Doctor Livingstone, Supongo?, Rúa Alta 4. A rhino and an elephant stare you down as you approach the door of this café and bar that's fast become a Pontevedra favourite for *copas*.

Vigo *p479, map p479*
The bars of Berbés around Rúa Real get going at weekends. The classier joints around the

marina see more mid-week action, but are very pricey, particularly on the terrace. Most *discotecas* are near the train station.

Iguana Club, C Churruca 14, www. laiguanaclub.com. One of the legendary live music venues of Northern Spain, with local and international rock bands on regularly. It's also a good spot for a drink, with 2 levels and a warehouse-like feel.

La Abadía de Santos, off C Victoria. A bar with an outdoor terrace located in a side alley that's the entrance to a church. Serves good beer.

Uno Está, Rúa Real 14. Open 2200-late Tue-Sat. This solid stone building in old Vigo is occupied by this intriguing bar that is a light, airy space for a *copa* or professionally mixed cocktail, and frequently has live jazz or fusion bands, or DJs playing hip hop or electronica. Check their page www.myspace. com/unoesta for upcoming events.

🎭 Entertainment

Pontevedra *p476, map p477*
Pontevedra has a good cultural programme; look out for the monthly guide in the tourist office.
Teatro Principal, Rúa Charino 6, T986 851 932.

🎯 Activities and tours

Vigo *p479, map p479*
Vigo's have-a-go football team, **Celta**, T986 214 585, www.celtavigo.net, are currently in the *Segunda* but still very well supported. They don their sky-blue tops at Balaidos, to the southwest of town, normally on a Sun evening. Tickets are available at the stadium for a couple of days before; the booth is also open a couple of hours before the game.

🚌 Transport

Pontevedra *p476, map p477*
Bus
Local **Ourense** is served 8 times a day, **A Coruña** about 10 times, and **Santiago**

(50 mins) even more frequently. There are hourly buses to **O Grove**, and even more to **Sanxenxo**. 10 per day go to **Cangas** and buses leave every 30 mins or so for **Vigo** (some to the bus station, some to the waterfront, 25 mins). 2 a day go to **Padrón** and **Noia**, and 4 to **Tui** and **Valença** (Portugal). Hourly buses head north to **Vilagarcía**, some taking in the island of **Illa Arousa**, and 8 go to **Cambados**. 6 buses cross Galicia to **Lugo** every day.

Long distance 2 to **Madrid**, 2 to **Bilbao** via Oviedo or Burgos, 1 or 2 to **Barcelona** and **Zaragoza**, 1 to **Salamanca**, **Gijón**, and **Valladolid**. There are many more routes from nearby Vigo.

Train
There are frequent connections to **Vigo** (33 mins, €3) and **A Coruña** (1½ hrs, €12.90) via **Santiago**.

Vigo p4/9, map p479
Air
There are daily flights to several Spanish cities, mostly operated by **Spanair** and **Iberia**. Air France fly direct to **Paris**, and Vueling fly direct to **Brussels**.

Bus
Local There are frequent buses to **Pontevedra**, leaving both from the bus station and also from C Arenal 52 (25 mins). Buses to **Santiago** leave every 30 mins, and there are about 10 daily to **Ourense**. Buses leave ½-hourly for **Baiona** and for **Tui** and **A Guarda**. There are about 5 daily buses to **Lugo** (4 hrs).

Long distance Among many long-distance interurban services, there are 6 buses to **Madrid**, 2 to **Bilbao**, 1 or 2 to **Barcelona** and **Zaragoza**, 1 to **Salamanca**, **Gijón**, and **Valladolid**. 4 buses Mon-Fri and 1 on Sat and Sun head to **Porto**. Check www.autna.com for times.

Ferry
Vigo's days as a passenger port are just about over, but there are still hourly ferries

to **Moaña** and ½-hourly to **Cangas**, across the bay. In summer boats go to the **Islas Cíes**, see page 482.

Train
Galician destinations include **A Coruña** almost hourly (2 hrs, from €15), **Ourense** 7 times daily (2 hrs from €16.80), and **Santiago** (1 hr 20 mins, from €9.10) via Pontevedra about 15 times a day. There are good long-distance connections. There is a Barcelona sleeper, a day train to **San Sebastián** and the French border, and a day and night train to **Madrid**. There are 2 trains daily to **Porto** (Portugal), and 4 a day to **León**.

Baiona and around p481
Bus
Buses run to/from **Vigo** every 30 mins. There are boats to the **Islas Cíes** in summer.

A Guarda p482
Bus
Buses leave for **Vigo** and **Tui** ½-hourly (fewer at weekends). There's a ferry across the Miño to **Portugal** and another crossing further east in Golán. The first bridge is at Tui.

⊕ Directory

Pontevedra p476, map p477
Internet Cybercafé Pasaje, Rúa dos Soportais 6. Coin-op machines 40 mins/ €1. **Medical services** The Clínica San Sebastián is a medical centre on Rúa Benito Corbal 24, T986 867 890, with 24-hr attendance. **Telephone** There are cheap *locutorios* on the edge of the old town at C Marqués de Riestra 21.

Vigo p479, map p479
Internet There's an internet and cheap call centre at Rúa Cánovas del Castillo 24, just along from the tourist office. The Hotel Princesa, C Fermín Penzol 14, also has a cybercafé. **Post office** The central post office is on Rúa da Victoria.

Miño Valley

Rising northeast of Lugo, the Miño sweeps through much of Galicia in a southwesterly direction and forms part of the border between Spain and Portugal before it meets the Atlantic near A Guarda. Its lower sections run through a little-explored region of vineyards, monasteries and hidden valleys, watering the pleasant provincial capital of Ourense on the way. ›› *For listings, see pages 493-496.*

Tui/Tuy → *For listings, see pages 493-496. Colour map 1, C2.*

Perched on a rocky hill high above the north bank of the Miño, Tui doesn't have the scurvy feel of most border settlements. It's an attractive, ancient Galician town that has exchanged growls through history with its counterpart fortress town Valença, across the water in Portugal. A former Celtic settlement, it was inhabited by Romans, then Sueves and Visigoths, briefly serving as capital of the boy-king Wittiza in the early eighth century. It was mentioned by Ptolemy, who named it Toudai and attributed its founding to Diomedes, son of Tydeus.

Sights

Tui has a solid assembly of attractive historical buildings, of which the highlight is the **cathedral**, which doubled as a fortress for so long. This function influenced the building's architecture, which has a military simplicity. It was started in the early 12th century and has both Romanesque and later Gothic features. There's a door of each type; the Romanesque portal has a simple geometric pattern, while the Gothic door and porch features an excellent sculptured Adoration, an early work with traces of colour remaining. It's flanked by later statues of the Elders of the Apocalypse. Inside are striking wooden beams; the church has a lean and has had to be reinforced over the years, especially after the 1755 Lisbon earthquake. The tomb of San Pedro González is here; he was a local Dominican who lived in the 13th century and cared for sick sailors, who dubbed him San Telmo after their patron. There's also an attractive cloister with a walkway above it that gives excellent views, as does the tower. There's a small **museum** ① *0930-1330, 1600-2000, only weekends in winter; cloister, tower and museum €3.*

There are several other churches in town and plenty of narrow lanes and fine old houses. It's a popular place with visiting Portuguese, and the town is well stocked with bars. There's a narrow, attractive road bridge from Spain to Portugal 1 km below the town; it was built by Gustave Eiffel in 1884. Although there's a depressing little border-bargain shopping area nearby, the town of **Valença** itself has several pretty corners, well worth ducking across to see.

Ourense/Orense → *For listings, see pages 493-496. Colour map 1, C3. Phone code: 988. Population: 107,742.*

Little-visited Ourense is the capital of Galicia's inland province, a rural zone crisscrossed by rocky hills and pastured valleys where much wheat is farmed and cheese and wine are made. The town itself is a prosperous centre with active streetlife. Once you get away from the busy roads and into the pedestrianized old town, it's a pleasant place indeed, with several beautiful plazas, and well worth a visit. A series of thermal springs make it a great spot to banish chills too.

Ins and outs

Getting there and around The train station is across the river to the north of town (20 minutes' walk); from Parque San Lázaro dozens of city buses go in this direction. The bus station is further in the same direction; buses No 6 and No 12 make it out there.

Tourist information There are two useful tourist offices in Ourense. The **regional office** ① *T988 372 020, oficina.turismo.ourense@xunta.es, winter Mon-Fri 0900-1400, 1630-1830, summer Mon-Fri 0900-1400, 1600-2000, Sat 1000-1400, 1600-2000, Sun 1000-1400, 1700-1900,* is at the southern (city) end of the Ponte Maior Roman bridge, quite a walk from the centre of town. The **municipal office** ① *Rúa Cruz Vermella s/n, T988 366 064, turismo@ourense.es, Mon-Fri 0900-1400, 1500-2000, Sat 1100-1400, also Sun 1100-1400 in summer,* is more central; there's also a friendly office with the same hours by the As Burgas hot springs at Rúa As Burgas 12.

Background

Although tradition claims that the city's name derives from *ouro*, meaning gold, it actually comes from the hot springs; the Roman town was named *Aquae Urentes* (warm waters). It was later an important city of the Suevish kingdom, and later of the Visigoths. As an important linking point between Galicia and the rest of Spain, Ourense flourished after its repopulation during the Reconquista. Following the decline that seemed to affect almost every city in Spain at some point, it is now a prosperous place, thriving as capital of this significant agricultural province.

Sights

The **Catedral de San Martiño** ① *daily 1130-1330, 1600-1930, Sun in afternoon only, free,* was started in the 12th century; most of its features are Transitional in style (ie late Romanesque/ early Gothic). The most impressive of the portals is intricately carved with scalloping and 12 good apostles below a headless Christ. The interior is long and gloomy, with many tombs of prelates carved into the walls; the attractive galleried cupola is a later early Renaissance work. There's an impressive version of Santiago's *Pórtico de la Gloria*, preserving much of its bright paintwork. The chief object of veneration is the *Santísimo Cristo*, a similar spooky Christ to the one in Burgos' cathedral. Made of fabric, the figure has real hair and a purple and gold skirt. It's located in a chapel that's an amazingly bright baroque fantasy in gold. Off the cloister is the **cathedral museum** ① *Mon-Fri 1200-1300, 1630-1900, Sat 1200-1300, 1630-1930, €2.*

The **Praza Maior** is just by here, a very appealing arcaded space. It's overlooked by the **Museo Arqueolóxico** ① *T988 223 884, Tue-Sat 0930-1430, 1600-2100, Sun 0930-1430, free,* the provincial museum, very attractively set in the former bishops' palace. It contains many Roman and Celtic finds as well as some sculpture and paintings from churches in the province. However, it was closed for restoration at time of research.

The pretty, linked **Praza da Magdalena** is off the main square and has beautiful overhanging buildings and roses. It's dominated by the cathedral and the **Iglesia de Santa María Madre**, an attractive baroque church built from the ruins of the 11th-century original; some Romanesque columns and capitals are preserved.

The main pedestrian streets to stroll down of an evening are the **Calle Santo Domingo** and the **Rúa do Paseo**. Fans of cream and brown should check out the latter; at No 30 the **Edificio Viacambre** looks like a Chinese puzzle box gone horribly wrong. The cloister of **Iglesia de San Francisco** is a beautifully harmonious Transitional piece of stonework, although each side has a different number of arches. The double columns are carved with capitals, many vegetal, but some featuring an array of strange beasts.

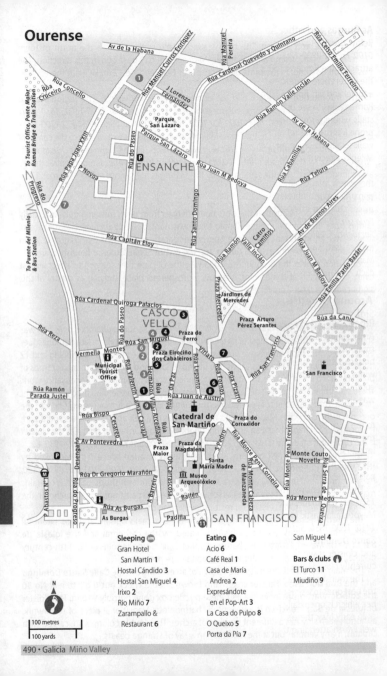

Ourense

Sleeping
Gran Hotel
 San Martín **1**
Hostal Cándido **3**
Hostal San Miguel **4**
Irixo **2**
Rio Miño **7**
Zarampallo &
 Restaurant **6**

Eating
Acio **6**
Café Real **1**
Casa de María
 Andrea **2**
Expresándote
 en el Pop-Art **3**
La Casa do Pulpo **8**
O Queixo **5**
Porta da Pía **7**

San Miguel **4**

Bars & clubs
El Turco **11**
Miudiño **9**

As Burgas and other hot springs

Below the old town, **As Burgas** ① *Tue-Wed 0900-1200, 1800-2300, Thu 0900-1200, 1800-0100, Fri-Sat 0900-1200, 1900-0200, Sun 0900-1200, 1800-0100; €3*, is the hot spring that attracted the Romans. The water streams out at a healthy 65°C. You can bathe open-air in the waters here, a great experience if the stares of passing tourists doesn't put you off. Take a towel and flip-flops. By the time you read this, there should be a visitor centre and some Roman ruins to see here too. Nearby is the traditional food market, with plenty of outdoor stalls where farmers sell their produce. The Romans built a high bridge over the flood-prone Miño; it was rebuilt in medieval times and is still in use (Ponte Maior); it's worth the walk to see its elegant lines. Further along the river is the writhing metallic Puente del Milenio, a recent construction that's particularly impressive when floodlit.

There are several other hot springs along the river nearby, where you can bathe in the waters, particularly nice in the evenings for a relaxing soak under the stars. Some are upmarket spa complexes, others just pools in the ground. The temperatures vary, and some places charge a small admission charge. One of the best is **Chavasqueira** ① *Mercado de la Feria s/n, T988 214 721, www.termaschavasqueira.com, Tue-Sun 0900-2330, to 0300 on Fri and Sat nights, €3.50*, which has free pools outside as well as a pay-to-enter complex. The nicest (and easiest) way to get to the springs is on the Tren das Termas, a 'train' that leaves the Praza Maior at 1000, 1200, 1600, 1800 and 2000 and stops at all the major springs, costing €0.75 each way. The tourist office has a good map/brochure with the springs marked.

Around Ourense → *For listings, see pages 493-496.*

Ribadavia → *Colour map 1, B3.*

An excellent day trip from Ourense is to head down the Miño to Ribadavia, an attractive small riverside town that is the centre of the **Ribeiro wine region**. Ribeiro wines come both in a crisp white and a slightly effervescent red; both resemble northern Portuguese wines and are produced from the same grape varieties. The white *ribeiro* is the most common and is drunk all over Galicia out of distinctive white ceramic crucibles. The area was also notable for having been a profitable tin-mining zone.

Ribadavia is famous for having maintained a sizeable Jewish population from the 12th to the 16th century, even after the expulsion order of 1492. There are still some traces of the **Jewish quarter**; the old synagogue preserves many features despite its conversion into a church and the narrow streets remain, although nearly all the buildings postdate the era. A few Hebrew inscriptions and a Jewish pastry shop evince the town's pride in this part of their history.

The 12th-century **Iglesia de San Xuán** ① *Mon-Sat 0930-1430, 1600-1830, Sun 1030-1500*, has a Romanesque apse and curious portal of Mozarabic influence. The nearby Plaza Mayor is a fantastic long space, which harbours the helpful **tourist office** ① *Mon-Fri 0930-1430, 1600-1830, Sat 1030-1430, 1600-1830, Sun 1030-1430*. The massive **Convento de Santo Domingo** ① *1000-1300, 1700-2000*, was once lived in by kings; the Gothic church and cloister is worth a look. The crumbly castle at the top of town is picturesque, but currently closed for running repairs.

The tourist office can furnish you with a guide to the region's *adegas* (bodegas) – one of the best ones to visit is pretty **Adega Casal de Armán** ① *T699 060 464, www.casaldearman. net*, which is open daily and has a restaurant and accommodation.

In early May, there's a wine festival in Ribadavia, and on the last Saturday in August, it's well worth attending the **Fiesta de la Historia**. The townsfolk are all dressed in medieval costume, and among other events there's a re-enacted battle and a real wedding in a medieval Jewish manner. Shortly afterwards, in early September, are the town fiestas.

North of Ourense

The **Monasterio de Santa María la Real de Oseira** ① *www.mosteirodeoseira.org, Mon-Sat 1000-1200, 1530-1730 (1830 summer), Sun 1230 and 1530-1730 (1830 summer), €2, guided tour only*, is often dubbed the 'Escorial de Galicia' for its immense size and harmonious Renaissance lines. Sitting solitary in a valley, it was founded in the 12th century and still houses a community of Cistercian monks in architectural splendour. The façade, from the early 18th century, is of monumental Churrigueresque style; the Virgin Mary occupies pride of place under- neath a figure of Hope. Below is Saint Bernard, founder of the Cistercian order. The most interesting thing inside is the Claustro de los Medallones, carved with quirky depictions of historical figures. The austere church belies its baroque façade and is of little joy apart from some colourful 17th-century wallpaintings. Worth the journey on its own, however, is the Sala Capitular, with beautiful vaulting flamboyantly issuing from the twisted barbers-pole columns; it's like a fireworks display in stone.

East of Ourense

Off the main road east of Ourense is a beautiful gorge, the **Gargantas do Sil**, running up a tributary of the Miño. It's worth exploring by car or on foot; viney terraces soon give way to rocky slopes dropping steeply into the river.

The **Monasterio de Santo Estevo de Ribas de Sil** stands out like a beacon with its pale walls and brick-red roof against the wooded valley. Apart from the setting, the monastery isn't especially interesting, although there are three cloisters, one of them huge; another still preserves some Romanesque arching.

From near the monastery, the **GR56 long-distance trail** is a good way to explore some remote areas of Ourense province. It heads along the gorge and takes in another couple of monasteries along its 100-km route, before finally ascending steeply to the mountain village of **Manzaneda**, a small ski resort.

The N120 continues León-wards and bids farewell to the Miño just before the town of **Monforte de Lemos**. It's worth making a return train journey from Ourense to here, as the route is spectacular, running along the river and cutting into the Sil gorge for a short while. Monforte is dominated by a hilltop monastery (now a parador) and medieval tower that used to be part of a castle.

Near Monforte are the amusingly named wine towns **Sober** and **Canabal**. This is part of the Ribeira Sacra DO region, and produces both red and white wines, some of high quality. Beyond Monforte, there are several ruinous castles in the valley, including the **Castelo de Torrenovaes** looming over the road near **Quiroga**. There's a Roman tunnel near the road at Monferado. The last major settlement in Galicia is **O Barco**, a friendly but uninteresting town whose primary industry is the manufacture of *orujo*, a grape spirit better flavoured or in coffee than neat.

South of Ourense

South of Ourense, the towns of **Allariz** and **Celanova** are well worth a visit. Allariz flows down the side of a rocky *peña* that once housed a Celtic castro. The beautifully restored old town with its hilly flagstoned streets is picturesque and ideal for strolling. In the heart of it, the late 11th-century **Igrexa de Santiago** is a Romanesque church much modified in later centuries but conserving some interesting carved capitals around its apsidal windows.

Other notable buildings included the **Convento de Santa Clara**, a muscular building by the central car parking space; it was founded in the 13th century but was extensively rebuilt after a fire in the 18th century. Across from it is the baroque church of **San Benito**. There's a little tourist office by the bridge at the entrance to town.

Celanova is known as the 'hidden city' for the reticence of its inhabitants, it's only a village really, dominated by the **Monasterio de San Salvador** ① *Mon-Sat 1100, 1200, 1300, 1700, 1800 (also 1000, 1600, 1900 in summer), €1.20, guided tour only*, on a huge square. While the façade could be called over-ornate, the cloisters are a gem, dating from the 16th century. The Gothic wooden choir is also attractive. Around the back of the monastery is a Mozarabic chapel, **San Miguel**, a well-preserved 10th-century structure.

Some 25 km further south, the Visigothic church of **Santa Comba de Bande** is set above a long *embalse* (reservoir). It's a noble little structure with a small tower and square apse.

East of here, **Verín** makes a good place to explore and stay. It's an attractive walled winemaking town set in a valley, with an attractive church, and featuring a castle complex in the neighbouring village of **Monterrei** that was used in aggressions and defences against the Portuguese. There's a parador next to it.

ⓦ Miño Valley listings

For Sleeping and Eating price codes and other relevant information, see Essentials pages 31-39.

⬤ Sleeping

Tui *p488*
AL Parador de San Telmo, Av de Portugal s/n, T986 600 309, www.parador.es. Below the town, in a modern replica of a Galician *pazo* (mansion), the San Telmo offers good views of the town and river. It's a good place to relax, with a pool and tennis court among its conveniences.
F Hostal Generosa, Av Calvo Sotelo 37, T986 600 055. A simple choice; shared bathrooms, clean, comfortable but without luxury.

Ourense *p488, map p490*
Ourense's accommodations mostly offer exceptional value.
L Gran Hotel San Martín, Curros Enríquez 1, T988 371 811, www.gh-hoteles.com. Looming over the park, this huge hotel may seem like some 1970s airport horror from the outside, but is much better within, although it still feels a bit old-fashioned and in need of a facelift. It has comfortable and well-equipped rooms, many of them with good views of the town.

D Hotel Irixo, C Hermanos Villar 15, T988 254 620, www.hotelirixo.es. This brand new hotel is ideal for those who want a base in the heart of tapas territory. It's decorated in a modern minimalist way, with lots of black and white. The rooms are correct and comfortable; those at the front get inevitable noise from the square, but it's great to be able to look out on the life below.
E Hostal Cándido, Rúa Hermanos Villar 25, T988 229 607. This has a good central location on a quiet square. The en suite rooms are large and have big windows and balconies; the furnishings are modest but comfortable enough. Good value.
E Hotel Río Miño, Rúa Juan XXIII 4, T988 217 594. This curious place offers remarkably good value. Despite the price, rooms are hotel standard, with small but modern bathrooms, telephones and TVs. The exterior rooms are a little lighter but have some noise. If there's nobody at reception, ask in the café.
E Hotel Zarampallo, R San Miguel 9, T988 220 053, www.zarampallo.com. An attractive, central option above a good restaurant. The rooms are well equipped; there's a small price difference between those with a shower and those with a bathtub.

F Hostal San Miguel, Rúa San Miguel 14, T988 239 203. Set above a good restaurant (see below), this offers cheap but adequate rooms with or without small bathroom. It's right in the heart of things, in a quiet corner of the old town.

Ribadavia *p491*
There are a couple of spa hotels within 5 mins' drive of Ribadavia but few choices in the centre itself.
E Hostal Plaza, Praza Maior 15, T988 470 576, www.hostalplazaribadavia.com. By far the nicest place to stay in Ribadavia, this *hostal* is a clean, modern choice right on the beautiful main square, which some of the en suite rooms overlook. Recommended.

South of Ourense *p492*
A Parador de Verín, Verín, T988 410 075, www.parador.es. Opposite the castle in Monterrei, which more or less merges with Verín itself, this parador occupies a well-restored traditional rural Galician *pazo*. It's a good place for families, with plenty of space, gardens, a swimming pool and a lovely rose-edged patio. The rooms are excellent, and several boast super views over the fertile valley.
D Hotel O Portelo, Rúa Portelo 20, Allariz, T988 440 740, www.hoteloportelorural.com. On one of pretty Allariz's hilly streets, this excellent welcoming spot has very pretty rooms decorated in rustic style and taking advantage of the building's beautiful stone. There are modern facilities too, and a good breakfast available for a little extra.

❶ Eating

Tui *p488*
♥♥ O Cabalo Furado, Praza do Concello 3, T986 601 215, www.cabalofurado.com. One of the better restaurants, with cheerful and generous Galician *cocina de siempre*. The lampreys from the river are delicious when in season; there are also decent (**D**) en suite rooms.

Ourense *p488, map p490*
The Casco Vello is the centre for tapas-going and restaurants, particularly around Praza do Ferro, Rúa San Miguel, Rúa Viriato, Rúa Lepanto and Rúa Fornos.
♥♥♥ Porta da Pía, Rúa da Lúa 3, T988 251 882. Closed Mon. This attractive place occupies a noble old building in the old quarter that's blessed with a beautiful garden terrace. Accessible from either of 2 sides, it specializes in high-quality seafood, which can be eaten by the large windows. Specials change daily, but favourites include *arroz con bogavante* (rice with lobster), or *zarzuela de pescado* (spicy fish stew). Service is very good and there's a *menú del día* for €12.
♥♥♥ San Miguel, Rúa San Miguel 12, T988 221 245, www.restaurantesanmiguel.com. An excellent choice for seafood, with superb sardines and a good wine list. They often have locally caught things from the Miño too, such as *lampreas* (lampreys) or the fearsomely expensive *angulas* (elvers). In the café, a *menú del día* is served for €10.
♥♥ Acio, Rúa dos Fornos 1, T988 101 810. You have to see the display of bartop snacks to believe it at this place. Gourmet creations cascade over each other in a devilishly tempting array, and there are good wines to accompany them.
♥♥ Casa de María Andrea, Praza Eirociño dos Cabaleiros 1, T988 227 045. An excellent option with a great location overlooking a pretty little square. The interior is modern and stylish; the upstairs dining area is arrayed around the central atrium and there's an excellent *menú del día* for €10.50, as well as filling *raciones* (€5-13) and a range of daily specials. Recommended.
♥♥ O Queixo, Pr Eironciño dos Cabaleiros 3, T988 227 045. Colourful original paintings and other objets d'art line this wood-beamed, stone-walled redoubt of comfort. A glass of wine comes with the bar's namesake tapa, a creamy soft local cheese. You can also sit down and eat cheese, ham and sausage at tables.

Zarampallo, R San Miguel 9, T988 220 053. One of Ourense's better choices for a meal, with smart Galician fish and stews and a set *menú del día* for €10. Attractively modern interior.

La Casa do Pulpo, Rúa Don Juan de Austria 15, T988 221 005. This friendly eatery is tucked away behind the cathedral. As the name suggests, its speciality is octopus, which can be eaten out the back. The bar has a selection of *pinchos* and little rolls; the calamari ones are particularly tasty. There's also a good selection of Galician wine.

Cafés

Café Real, Rúa Coronel Ceano Vivas 3, T988 239 221. An elegant, old-style café, very spruce and traditional with its polished wood and seriously impressive glass chandelier. 2 levels of seating and occasional live jazz.

Expresándote en el Pop-Art, C Santo Domingo 15, T988 255 756. The name means 'expressing yourself through pop-art'. It's a flamboyant but relaxed café/bar popular with students, right in the centre of Ourense.

East of Ourense *p492*

O Grelo, Rúa Chantada 16, Monforte de Lemos, T982 404 701. An excellent spot with traditional food cooked with a sure touch.

South of Ourense *p492*

Casa Fandiño, Rúa da Cárcel 7, Allariz, T988 442 216. Just up from the church of Santiago in the heart of old Allariz, this is a great place to eat, a traditional restaurant serving up delicious Galician dishes like an *empanada de zamburiñas* (small scallop pie) or hake baked with peas, potatoes and onion. There's a *menú* for €15.

Mesón O Candil, Estrada 31, T988 411 120, in the hamlet of Pazos, on the road between the parador in Monterrei and the town of Verín. An excellent choice for lunch or dinner. It's simple in style, with a range of *parrilladas* (mixed grills of meat or fish), all of which are delicious, especially when washed down with the house red, which they make themselves. There's a pleasant veranda to eat on in good weather.

Restaurante Brasil, Av Castilla 7, Verín, T988 410 249. This traditional-type hotel-restaurant hasn't updated its decor in a few years, but is an excellent place to go for big portions of quality fish and seafood at a more-than-fair price.

Bars and clubs

Ourense *p488, map p490*
Most of the bar action is around Rúa Viriato, Rúa Pizarro, La Unión, Praza do Correxidor and the Jardines de Mercedes.

El Turco, C Hernán Cortés 24. Set up the back of Ourense's old town, away from most of its kind, this pub is situated on a quiet, pretty square, which you can contemplate with good mixed drinks from its summer terrace. Inside, it's classic 1980s music and regular live bands.

Miudiño, Rúa Arcediagos 13, T988 245 536. This harmonious and low-lit stone and wood pub is just down the hill from the back of the cathedral. It's a very popular place for the first *copa* of the evening, and has Guinness on tap.

Entertainment

Ourense *p488, map p490*
Teatro Principal, Rúa da Paz 11, has regular theatre and occasional arthouse cinema. Tickets are cheap.

Festivals and events

Ribadavia *p491*
Last Sat in Aug Fiesta de la Historia, see page 491.
Early Sep Town fiesta.

⊝ Transport

Tui *p488*
Bus
There are ½-hourly buses to **Vigo** and **A Guarda**, and some across the river to **Valença**. From A Guarda, the road follows the north bank of the Miño to Tui, and the first bridge into Portugal.

Train
The station, north of the centre, has 2 trains a day to **Vigo** and to **Porto**; it's easier to cross to **Valença**, where there are more trains into Portugal. Guillarei station, 30 mins to the east, has connections inland to **Ribadavia** and **Ourense**; a lovely trip.

Ourense *p488, map p490*
Bus
Ourense's bus station, T988 216 027, is beyond the train station across the Miño from the old town (see Ins and outs, page 489). From Rúa Progreso, buses No 6 and No 12 go there. There are 6-7 daily services to all the Galician cities: **Lugo**, **A Coruña**, **Santiago**, **Pontevedra**, and about 10 services to **Vigo**.

Around Ourense *p491*
Bus
Buses run very regularly to **Ribadavia** (20 mins) and 2 daily to **Celanova**. There are several buses to **Verín** and the Portuguese border at **Feces**, and 1 daily to **Porto**.

Buses run eastwards to **León** via **Ponferrada**, **Burgos**, **Madrid** 5-6 times (6 hrs 20 mins, €32), **Zamora** and **Salamanca**, as well as other cities.

Train
A few trains daily head east to **León** (3 daily, 4 hrs, €25-30), **Madrid** (2 daily, 5½-7 hrs, €43.70), and more distant destinations. 5 go to **Vigo** (7 daily, 2 hrs, from €16.90) via Ribadavia and **A Coruña** (4 daily, 2½ hrs, €22) via Santiago. These trains tend to be inconveniently timetabled; the bus is a better bet.

Ribadavia *p491*
Bus and train
There are frequent buses and trains to and from **Ourense** (20 mins).

East of Ourense *p492*
Bus and train
There are 3 daily trains on the spectacular ride between Monforte de Lemos and Ourense (40 mins, €12-22). There are also regular buses on this route.

South of Ourense *p492*
Bus
There are buses between Ourense and Allariz more than hourly (30 mins). From Verín, several buses a day head north to Ourense and south to the Portuguese border. Buses running between **Vigo** and **Madrid** also pull in here.

⊙ Directory

Ourense *p488, map p490*
Internet CiberNetrix, C Mercado 54, €1.85 per hr, Mon-Thu 0900-2400, Fri and Sat 0900-0200, Sun 1100-2400.
Laundry Lava Express, Rúa Marañón 17.

Contents

Footprint features

Background

History

Hominids

While Northern Spain was a stamping ground for dinosaurs (literally; footprints are found all over the region), it was a species of hominid, *Homo antecessor*, who first walked upright in the region. Recent finds at Atapuerca, a valley just east of Burgos, have yielded remains of this prehistoric human that date to 1.3 million years ago. These are the oldest known hominid remains in Western Europe. Nearby, several fossilized remains of Homo heidelbergensis, a johnny-come-lately at around half a million years of age, have been discovered. Heidelbergensis is thought to be a distant forebear of the Neanderthals, of whom extensive remains have been found. Many caves in the north of Spain bear evidence of their presence; tools and remains of occupation stretching back around 60,000 years until their extinction around 27,000 years ago.

The Upper Palaeolithic period

Some of the same caves and others, particularly in Cantabria and Asturias, have produced the first signs of *homo sapiens sapiens* in the peninsula. Dating from the Upper Palaeolithic (18,000 BC onwards), these hunter-gatherers produced fairly sophisticated stone and bone tools including arrows and spears. They also experimented with art, and found it to their liking; primitive whittling of deer bones and outlines of hands on cave walls suddenly gave way to the sensitive, imaginative and colourful bison, deer and horses found in several locations but most famously at Altamira in Cantabria, where the work is of amazing artistic quality. This so-called Magdalenian culture seemed to extend across Northern Spain and into southern France, where related paintings have been found at places such as Lascaux.

A more settled existence probably began to emerge around 4000 BC. The most striking archaeological remnants are a great number of dolmens, large stone burial chambers, common across much of northern Europe at the time. These are mostly found along the north coast, particularly in the Basque lands and Galicia. There are also other remnants, such as standing stones and more simple pit burials.

Early inhabitants

The principal inhabitants of the region are known as Iberians by default, but little is known of their origins apart from the fact that they spoke languages that are not from the Indo-European group that unites the vast majority of European and western Asian languages under its umbrella. The Basques, too, seem to have been around in those days. Their language isn't Indo-European either, but no convincing evidence has been found that can link them and the Iberians (or anyone else for that matter). Certain genetic peculiarities in the Basque population have led to theories that they are directly descended from the Palaeolithic inhabitants of the region. This ties in nicely with their own opinion that they are a very old people; they like to say God created Adam from old bones he found in a Basque cemetery.

The third important group were the Celts, who descended from the north in waves in the early to mid first millennium BC. They spoke an Indo-European tongue and settled mostly in the north and west of the peninsula. Their influence is very apparent in place names, language and culture. There are still very close parallels between European areas settled by Celts; sitting over a cider while listening to bagpipes in Asturias you might want to ponder just how old these traditions are. The principal architectural remnant of the early Celts is the *castro*, a fortified hilltop fort and trading compound of which there are very many in Asturias and Galicia.

Celtiberians

While the mountainous terrain of the north meant that distinct groups developed separately in remote valleys, the flatter lands of the centre encouraged contact. The Celts and Iberians seemed to mingle in the centre of Northern Spain and form a single culture, rather unimaginatively labelled Celtiberian. This was a time of much cultural interaction; the Phoenicians, master sailors and merchants from the ports of the Near East, set up many trading stations. These were mostly on the southern coasts of Spain, but they had plenty of contact with the north, and may have established a few ports on the Atlantic coast. There was also cultural contact with the Greeks.

The Phoenicians and Carthaginians

The heirs and descendants of the Phoenicians, the Carthaginians, came to Spain in the third century BC and settled widely in the south. While there was contact with the north, and Hannibal campaigned in western Castilla, the biggest effect was a direct consequence of his disputes with Rome. Bent on ending Carthaginian power in the Mediterranean, the Romans accurately realized that Spain was a 'second Carthage', and set out to change that. Once they realized the potential wealth in the peninsula, they resolved to conquer it entirely.

The Roman conquest

The Romans were given a tough time in the north, which it took them two centuries to subdue. The Celtiberian towns resisted the legions in a very spirited manner. Numancia, near Soria, held out against Roman sieges for many years, and was the centre of resistance that lost Rome tens of thousands of troops. Problems with the Cantabrians and Asturians lasted until Augustus and Agrippa finally defeated them in the late years of the first century BC. The Romans gave up trying to impose their culture on the northern fringes; the Basques and Galicians were very resistant to it, and a 'live and let live' stance was eventually adopted in those areas.

While the south of Spain became a real Roman heartland, the north was always viewed as borderland of a sort. Though vast quantities of gold and silver were mined in the northwest, and wine and oil poured from the Ebro and Duero valleys, few towns were founded in the north, and few wealthy Romans seemed to settle here; a handful of noble villas notwithstanding.

Christianity spread comparatively rapidly into Spain. The diocese of Zaragoza was perhaps founded as early as the first century AD, while León and Burgo de Osma were other important early Christian centres. Christianity was certainly spread out to fit over existing religious frameworks; the Basques had few problems with the Virgin Mary considering their own earthmother figure was named Mari, and here as elsewhere the Christian calendar was moulded around pagan festivals.

 It was the Romans who first created the idea of Spain, Hispania, as a single geographical entity.

The Visigoths

As the Roman order tottered, the barbarian hordes streamed across the Pyrenees and created havoc. Alans, Vandals and Sueves capitalized on the lack of control in the early fifth century AD to such an extent that the Romans enlisted the Visigoths to restore order on their behalf. This they succeeded in doing, but the Sueves hung around and established

San Isidoro

"No one can gain a full understanding of Spain without a knowledge of Saint Isidore." Richard Ford.

Born in AD 560, Isidoro succeeded his brother Leandro as Bishop of Sevilla. Without doubt one of the most important intellectual figures of he Middle Ages, his prolific writings cover all subjects and were still popular at the time of the Renaissance. His *Etymologiae* was one of the first secular books in print when it appeared in AD 1472. The first encyclopedia written in the Christian west, it was the primary source for the 154 classical authors that Isidoro quoted. He also wrote on music, law, history and jurisprudence as well as doctrinal matters.

Isidoro is also recognized as an important church reformer and was responsible for the production of the so-called *Mozarabic rite* which is still practised in Toledo Cathedral today. His writings were an attempt to restore vigour and direction to a church that was in decline following the Visigothic invasions. His emphasis on educational reforms was to put the church in Spain on foundations that were to last centuries. This was recognized by contemporaries when the Council of Toledo in AD653 called him "the extraordinary doctor, the most learned man of the latter ages, always to be named with reverence, Isidore".

Another important element to Isidoro's writings was his prophecies, which were based both on the Bible and classical references. These writings appealed greatly to later generations living in the shadow of the Muslim conquests and were the source of many stories and legends, as well as expectations of a Christian deliverance; they were an important factor in the Reconquista. Following the expulsion of the Moors it seemed to some that an ancient prophecy was about to be fulfilled: Fernando was the hidden king of legend that was to save Christendom. The Ponce de León wrote in 1486: "There will be nothing able to resist his might because God has reserved total victory and all glory to the rod, that is to say the Bat, because Fernando is the *encubierto* (hidden one) ... he will be Monarch of all the world".

Isidoro died in Sevilla in AD 636 and his writings continued to inspire Spain for the next 900 years. His body is now in León, moved there by Fernando I of Castilla who repatriated it from Muslim control around 1060. This act of national piety was carried out with the help of a mystic whose skill revealed the previously lost location of the saint's remains.

themselves in the northwest of the peninsula, with a capital at Astorga. It wasn't to last; the Visigoths came back as they lost control of their French territories and finally put an end to the small Suevish kingdom. After a period of much destruction and chaos, a fairly tenuous Visigothic control ensued. A beacon amidst the maelstrom was San Isidoro, writing in Sevilla, see box, above. Comparatively little is known about the couple of centuries that followed. A handful of Visigothic churches still exist in Northern Spain; these draw on Roman architectural models but add local features, and iconography from the Visigoths' German roots. Visigothic rulers were beset by civil strife, and they never really gained control over the northern reaches of the peninsula.

The Moors

Arriving across the Straits of Gibraltar in AD 711, the Moors had taken most of Spain before the prophet had been dead for a century. Under Arab leadership, most of the invaders were native North African Berbers, but there was a substantial mercenary element, many of them from eastern Europe. The state created was named *Al-Andalus*, and the Moors swept on into France, where they were eventually stopped by the Franks at Poitiers in AD 732.

Geography breaks Spain into distinct regions, which have tended to persist through time, and it was one of these, Asturias, the Moors had some trouble with. They were defeated in what was presumably a minor skirmish at Covadonga, in the far northern mountains, in AD 717. While they weren't too bothered by this at the time, Spain views it today as an event of immense significance, a victory against all odds and a sort of mystical event where God proved himself to be on the Christian side. It was hardly a crippling blow to the Moors, who were on the *autoroutes* of southern France before too long, but it probably sowed the seeds of what became the Asturian monarchy.

A curious development in many ways, this line of kings emerged unconquered from the shadowy northern hills and forests. Whether they were a last bastion of Visigothic resistance, or whether they were just local folk ready to defend their lands, they established an organized monarchy of sorts with a capital that shifted about but settled on Oviedo in AD 808. Their most lasting legacy has been a number of churches and royal halls; beautifully proportioned stone buildings that show some Visigothic characteristics but are also very original in style – far more graceful than the name it has been saddled with, Asturian Pre-Romanesque.

Although turned back in France, they Moors remained strong enough to repulse Charlemagne in northeast Spain in AD 778. After failing to take Zaragoza, he returned huffily to France but had his rearguard ambushed by Basques in the Navarran pass of Roncesvalles. The Basques were infuriated that he'd taken down the walls of Pamplona on his way through; the defeat suffered in the pass became the basis for the fanciful epic poem *Chanson de Roland*, which attributes the attack to Muslims.

Although the southern portion of *Al-Andalus* was a flourishing cultural centre, the Moors couldn't establish complete control in the northlands, and several cities changed hands numerous times in skirmishing and raids in the ninth century. Life in Muslim Spain was relatively good for Christians and Jews, though. Many converted to Islam; those Christians that didn't became known as *mozárabes*.

Though the Covadonga defeat was insignificant, the Asturian kingdom began to grow in strength and the long process of the Reconquista, the Christian reconquest of the peninsula, began. The northmen took advantage of cultural interchange with the south, which remained significant throughout the period despite the militarized zone in between, and were soon strong enough to begin pushing back. The loose Moorish authority in these lands certainly helped; the northern zone was more or less administered by warlords who were only partially controlled by the amirs in Córdoba (who called themselves caliphs as of AD 929). Galicia and much of the north coast was reclaimed and in by the early 10th century King Alfonso III had reconquered León; his son Ordoño II and his successors ruled from there, and the line of kings took on the name of that city.

Asturias/León wasn't the only Christian power to develop during this period. The Basques had been quietly pushing outwards, and the small mountain kingdom of Navarra emerged and grew rapidly. Aragón emerged too, and gained power and size via a dynastic union with Catalunya. The entity that came to dominate Spain, Castilla, was also born at this time. In the middle of the 10th century a Burgos noble, Fernán González, declared independence from the Kingdom of León and began to rally disparate Christian groups in the region. He was so successful in this endeavour that it wasn't too long before his successors labelled themselves kings.

Al-Manzur in Northern Spain

Mohammed ibn-Abi al Ma'afari was born to a poor family near Algeciras around AD 938. Known to latter generations as Al-Manzur or 'the conqueror', he is one of the most remarkable figures of the Middle Ages, representing both the strength of Muslim Spain and its ultimate failure. A lawyer, he succeeded in reforming the administration of the Caliphate and in modernizing its army. Nominally a regent, he was content to let formal power reside with the Sultan, but by AD 996 had assumed the title King.

With his power consolidated, he launched a series of raids across the north of Spain. His army of mercenary Slavs, Christian renegades and North African Berbers sacked Zamora and Simancas in AD 981, Barcelona in AD 985 and León in AD 987. The Leonese king Bermudo had broken an agreement to pay tribute and had to flee to the Asturian mountains. The only opposition to a total takeover of Spain now lay in Asturias and Galicia.

In AD 997 he embarked on his final campaign to extinguish Christian opposition. He took Coruña and the holy city of Santiago, from where he removed the bells of the cathedral to the mosque of Córdoba. On encountering a lone priest protecting the shrine of St James, he is said to have ordered his men to spare him and to leave the holy relics untouched.

While his military exploits were undoubtedly one of the period's great feats of generalship, Al-Manzur was no bloodthirsty tyrant. Under his guidance a university was established in Córdoba and he was a great patron of the arts and science. On his many military campaigns he took a library of books. It was under Al-Manzur that the final expansion of the Mezquita took place.

After an inconclusive battle in 1002 at Calatañazor in Castilla, Al-Manzur died of natural causes. The relief to the Christians was immense. A commentator wrote "In 1002 died Al-Manzur, and was buried in Hell". With his death the Caliphate soon fragmented to a number of small warring states, allowing the Christians to regroup. Never again were the Moors to be so united; his death marked a significant turning point in the history of Spain.

The Moors weren't finished by any means. The formidable **Al-Manzur** managed to sack almost every Christian city in Northern Spain within a couple of decades; surely one of the greater opportunistic military feats of the Middle Ages. Both sides were made painfully aware of their vulnerability and constructed a series of massive fortresses that faced each other across the central plains. The Muslim fortresses were particularly formidable; high eyries with commanding positions, accurately named the 'front teeth' of *Al-Andalus*. There are around 3000 fortresses and castles in various states of repair in Spain; a huge number of them are to be found in this area. The constant violence and the famines that resulted from the Moorish raids, plus the approaching millennium, led many to feel that the end of the world was nigh. Monasteries developed an obsession with the apocalypse and, increasingly, people looked to saints and the Church as their only salvation from impending doom.

It was just after Al-Manzur's death that things began to go wrong for the Moors, as kinstrife and civil war over succession fatally weakened the Caliphate while the Christian kingdoms were gaining strength and unity. The king of Navarra Sancho III (the Great) managed to unite almost the whole of Northern Spain in the early 11th century; although this inevitably dissolved, the rival kingdoms at least had a common goal. The caliphate disintegrated in 1031, to be replaced by a series of city-states, or *taifas*. Pitted against each other as well as the northern kingdoms, they were in no state to resist, and were forced to pay protection money to the Christian armies, enriching the new kingdoms. The big beneficiary was Castilla; King Alfonso VI, with the help of his on-off mercenary **El Cid**, see box, page 239, conquered swathes of Muslim territory, reaching Toledo in 1085.

Alfonso must have dreamed of reconquering the whole peninsula at that point, but he was stopped by the Almoravids, a by-the-book Islamic dynasty that quickly crossed from Morocco to re-establish the caliphate along stricter lines. They soon lapsed into softer ways though, and much of modern Andalucía was lost before a similar group, the Almohads, crossed the straits and took a degree of control back.

The Holy War

The nature of the Reconquista was very similar to that of the Crusades; a holy war against the enemies of the faith that also conveniently offered numerous opportunities for pillage, plunder and seizure of land. Younger sons, not in line for any inheritance under local customs, could fight for the glory of God and appropriate lands and wealth for themselves at the same time. Knightly orders similar to those of the Crusades were founded; the Knights of Calatrava, Alcántara and Santiago.

Santiago (Saint James), although already dead for a millennium or so, also played a major role in the Reconquista. The spurious discovery of his tomb at Compostela in the ninth century had sparked ongoing pilgrimage; it effectively replaced the inaccessible Holy Land as a destination for the devout and the penitent. The discovery came in time to resemble some sort of sign from God, and Saint James took on the role of *Matamoros*, Moor-slayer, and is depicted crunching hapless *Andalusi* under the hooves of his white charger in countless sculptures and paintings – quite a career-change for the first-century fisherman. With an apostle risen from the dead onside, it's little wonder that Christians flocked to the Reconquista banners.

By the mid-12th century Northern Spain was effectively secured under Christian rule. For largely geographical reasons, it had been the fledgling kingdom of Castilla that ended up with the biggest slice of the pie, and Spain's most powerful political entity. It had already been frequently united with the Leonese kingdom by dynastic marriages and this was confirmed in 1230, when Fernando (Ferdinand) III inherited both crowns (a fact still lamented by separatists in León).

While Navarra was still going, up in the mountains, it was Aragón that was the other main beneficiary from the reconquest. Uniting with Catalunya in 1150, it began looking eastwards to that great trading forum, the Mediterranean. After the famous battle of the **Navas de Tolosa** in 1212, the Moors lost Córdoba in 1236 and Seville in 1248 and were reduced to an area around their third great city, Granada, where they held out for another 250 years.

The 13th-15th centuries

With the flush of war fading, the north settled down to a period of prosperity. Castilla became a significant producer of wool and wheat, and the towns of the north coast established important trading links with northern Europe to distribute it. In 1296 the **Hermandad de las Marismas**, an export alliance of four major ports (A Coruña, Santander, Laredo and San Sebastián) was formed to consolidate this. The Basques were doing very well at this time. Demand for Vizcayan iron was high, and Basque sailors explored the whole Atlantic, almost certainly reaching north America a century or more before Columbus sailed.

Places like Burgos and Medina del Campo became powerful centres controlling the distribution of goods to the coastal ports. Guilds and societies became more and more important in the flourishing urban centres. Meanwhile the Castilian kings still pursued military aims. Becoming an increasing anachronism in an increasingly urban society, these crusading kings came to rely heavily on the towns for political and financial support. In order to keep them onside, they began to grant *fueros*, or exemptions from certain taxation and conscription duties, and proto-democratic assemblies, the *cortes*, began to assemble to keep the kings honest.

Towns spent vast sums in constructing soaring cathedrals, symbols of faith in new architectural principles as well as in Christianity. But already in Castilla's time of prosperity the seeds of decline were sprouting. Cities that had forged the Reconquista, Oviedo and León, became insignificant country towns as populations moved southwards in the war's wake. The massive numbers of sheep being grazed in migratory patterns across the land caused large-scale degradation and erosion of the soil; in many ways, the 'war on trees' was to prove as significant as any that had been waged against Moors. The barren landscapes of today's Castilla are a direct result of these post-reconquest years. The *fueros* that were so indiscriminately handed out meant that later kings were barely able to govern the towns, which understandably were reluctant to concede their privileges. The glory of the soldiering years rubbed off on Castilian attitudes too. Sons of minor nobles (*hidalgos*, from *hijos d'algo*, 'sons of something') yearned for the smell of battle, and scorned the dull attractions of work and education, an attitude that has cost Spain dear over the centuries and was memorably satirized in Cervantes' *Don Quijote*. The church, too, was in a poor state. Bled of funds by successive crusading kings, it developed a hoarding mentality and was in no condition to act as a moral light for the young Christian kingdoms. Furthermore, it was far from being a peaceful pastoral and urban golden age. The nuggety walled towns of the Reconquista battle lines provided perfect bases for power-hungry nobles; civil strife was exacerbated by the fact that most kings openly kept mistresses outside their arranged dynastic marriages, and illegitimate children were a dime-a-dozen.

Spain was drawn into the **Hundred Years War** as the bastard Henry of Trastámara waged war with French help on his English-backed brother Pedro I (the Cruel). After Pedro was murdered, his son-in-law John of Gaunt, Duke of Lancaster, claimed the Castilian throne. Landing in Galicia, he waged an inconclusive war with Henry before agreeing to marry his daughter to the king's son. He returned to England happy enough with this outcome and with a substantial retirement package from Castilian funds.

Such conjugal ties were of vital political importance, and one, in 1469, was to have a massive impact throughout the world. The heir to the Aragonese throne, Fernando, married Isabel, heiress of Castilla, in a top-secret ceremony in Valladolid. The implications were enormous. Aragón was still a power in the Mediterranean (Fernando was also king of Sicily), and Castilla's domain covered much of the peninsula. The unification under the *Reyes Católicos*, as the monarchs became known, marked the beginnings of Spain as we know it today. Things didn't go smoothly at first, however. There were plenty of opponents to the union and forces in support of Juana la Beltraneja, Isabel's elder (but assumed illegitimate) sister waged wars across Castilla.

Religious persecution

The reign of the Catholic Monarchs was full of incident, particularly in the year 1492, when Columbus sailed the Atlantic under their patronage, they completed the Reconquista by taking Granada, and thought they would celebrate the triumph by kicking the Jews out of Spain. Spain's Jewish population had been hugely significant since the 12th century, heavily involved in commerce, shipping and literature throughout the peninsula, but hatred against them had begun to grow in the 14th century and there had been frequent pogroms. Many converted during these years to escape the murderous climate; they became known as *conversos*. The decision to expel those who hadn't converted was far more that of the pious Isabel than the pragmatic Fernando and has to be seen in the light of the paranoid Christianizing climate. The Jews were given four months to leave the kingdom, and even the *conversos* soon found themselves under the Inquisition's iron hammer (see box, page 303). The kingdom's Muslim population was tolerated for another decade, when they too were given the choice of baptism or expulsion. The ridiculous doctrine of *limpieza de sangre* (purity of blood) became all-important; the enduring popularity of ham and pig meat surely owes something to these days, when openly eating these foods proved that one wasn't a pork-eschewing Muslim or Jew. But the lack of cultural diversity led to long-term stagnation and the area has arguably still not wholly recovered.

Conquest of the Americas

The treaty of Tordesillas in 1494 partitioned the Atlantic between Spain and Portugal, and led to the era of Spanish colonization of the Americas. In many ways, this was an extension of the Reconquista as young men hardened on the Castilian *meseta* crossed the seas with zeal for conquest, riches and land.

Under the Habsburg monarchy, Carlos V and Felipe II relied on the income from the colonies to pursue wars (often unwillingly) on several European fronts. It couldn't last; Spain's Golden Age has been likened by Spanish historian Felipe Fernández-Armesto to a dog walking on hind legs. Although over the centuries many *indianos* returned from the colonies to their native Navarra, Galicia and Asturias with newfound wealth, the American expansion sounded a grim bell for northern Castilla. The sheer weight of administration required forced the previously itinerant monarchy to choose a capital, and Felipe II set himself up in Madrid. With Sevilla and Cádiz now the focus for the all-important trade with the colonies, Castilla had turned southwards, and its northern provinces rapidly declined, hastened by a drain of their citizens to the New World across the sea.

Regional discontent

The *comunero* revolt of the early 16th century expressed the frustrations of a region that was once the focus of optimistic Christian conquest and agricultural wealth, but had now become peripheral to the designs of a 'foreign' monarchy. Resentment was exacerbated by the fact that the king still found it difficult to extract taxes from the *cortes* of Aragón or Catalunya, so Castilla bankrolled a disproportionate amount of the crippling costs of the day-to-day running of a worldwide empire. A plague in the early 17th century didn't help matters, wiping out about a tenth of the Castilian population. Burgos' population in the middle of that century was a quarter of what it had been at the beginning of it; the same was true throughout the region.

Meanwhile, as an important focus of Spanish naval and maritime power, the north coast continued in a better vein. Much of the shipbuilding for exploration, trade and war took place here, and many of the ships were crewed by Basques and Galicians. **Elkano**, a Basque from Getaria, and his crew, became the first to circumnavigate the world after the death of the expedition's leader, Magellan, half-way round. The ill-fated Spanish Armada sailed from Galicia in 130 ships built on this coast.

A cavalier visit

In the year 1623, a surprising visitor crossed the Pyrenees into Northern Spain. Calling himself Mr Smith and disguised as a travelling salesman, it was actually the Prince of Wales, the future Charles I. This was no regular visit; Charles wanted to travel incognito as he was searching for a bride. His target was the Infanta of Spain and Charles had the idea to size up his potential wife first rather than enter a marriage with someone known only from a flattering portrait.

After arriving at the house of an astonished British Ambassador it soon became apparent that the prince's noble intentions could not be realized without the risk of a major diplomatic incident, poisoning relations between the two counties to the point of war. In view of the breach of normal protocol, it was therefore agreed that a 'surprise' meeting should take place the next day when the prince would fortuitously bump into Felipe IV, King of Spain in the Royal Park. The two were then formally introduced and an official meeting with the princess arranged. However, it became obvious that *realpolitik* would put an end to the prince's romantic dreams. Hell was likely to freeze over before the king of Spain would allow his daughter to marry a Protestant heretic.

Nevertheless there was still the formality of mutual back-slapping and one-upmanship to go through, with an exchange of gifts designed to show the status of both host and guest. Charles, a well known lover of the arts, was delighted to receive paintings by Titian, three sedan chairs, some Barbary horses, a collection of weapons and a golden basin so heavy that it required two men to carry it. In addition, the Spanish monarch, perhaps as a chastisement to Charles, gifted him 18 wildcats with no instructions on how to care for the beasts.

Thoughtfully, however, he provided an elephant as a means to transport the gifts up to the Cantabrian port of Laredo and back to England. The elephant and its four keepers did come with instructions; it was to receive a gallon of wine daily from April to September. In October it was believed to go for a very long sleep.

On returning to England from his disastrous visit Charles was met by a rejoicing populace. Tables were set out in the streets groaning under all manner of food with whole hogsheads of wine and butts of sack whilst every street corner had its bonfire. As a contemporary poet aptly observed, "even the elements rejoiced". It rained for nine hours.

Aragón, meanwhile, had become a backwater since civil strife in the 15th century had deprived it of Catalunya and, thereby, of most of its Mediterranean trade. Above all regions, it suffered most from the loss of the Muslims and Jews; many of its cities had thrived on the cultural mixture. The union with Castilla had eventually deprived it of political significance too, and it retreated behind its *fueros*, stubbornly avoiding taxes and conscriptions, and maintaining a largely feudal system of land ownership, with all-powerful lords free to do as they pleased. This situation was changed partly after Felipe II put down a revolt in the late 16th century, but the province continued to be a minor player, especially compared to its thriving Catalan neighbour. After supporting the wrong side in the war of Spanish succession in the early 18th century Aragón was deprived of its *fueros* and laws and brought to heel, a minor region now in peninsular life. Navarra, meanwhile, had been conquered by Fernando earlier in the century and this, as well as the Basque lands, were under Castilian control.

The decline of the empire

The struggle of the Spanish monarchy to control the spread of Protestantism was a major factor in the decline of the empire. Felipe II fought expensive and ultimately unwinnable wars in defence of Catholicism in Flanders that bankrupted the state; meanwhile, within the country, the absolute ban on the works of 'heretical' philosophers, scientists and theologists left Spain intellectually behind in Renaissance Europe. In the 18th century, for example, the so-called 'Age of Enlightenment' in western Europe, theologists at the noble old University of Salamanca debated what language the angels spoke; that Castilian was proposed as an answer is certain. The decline of the monarchy paralleled a physical decline in the monarchs, as the inbred Habsburgs became more and more deformed and weak; the last of them, Carlos II – a tragic victim of contorted genetics – died childless and plunged the nation into a war of succession. "*Castilla has made Spain, and Castilla has destroyed it*", commented early 20th century essayist José Ortega y Gasset. Despite these misfortunes, the 17th century had been a time of much inspiration in the arts; Spanish baroque was a cheerful façade on a gloomy building, and painters such as Velásquez, Zurbarán and Murillo hit the heights of expression.

The war of the Spanish succession didn't have a massive impact on the north, apart from in Aragón (see above), but the headlong decline continued throughout the 18th century. The Catholic church was in a poor state intellectually, and came to rely more and more on cults and *fiestas* to keep up the interest of the populace; a tradition that is still very strong today. The Jesuits, an order that had its origins with the Basques, and a more enlightened lot than most, were expelled in 1767. They were allowed to take with them only their religious clothing and a supply of chocolate, a commodity that was extraordinarily popular at this time in Spain. After decentralization of trade with the New World, it was the Basques who established a monopoly over the import of the stuff, and for a brief time brought prosperity to their lands as a result.

Napoleon took advantage of the weak King Carlos IV's domestic problems to install his own brother Joseph (known among Spaniards as *Pepe Botellas* or 'Joe Bottles' because of his heavy drinking) on the throne. Spain revolted against this arrogant gesture, and Napoleon sent in the troops in late 1808. The ensuing few years are known in Spain as the *Guerra de Independencia* (War of Independence). Combined Spanish, British and Portuguese forces clashed with the French all across the north, firstly disastrously as General Moore was forced to retreat across Galicia to a Dunkirk-like embarkation at A Coruña, then more successfully as the Duke of Wellington won important battles at Ciudad Rodrigo, Vitoria and San Sebastián. The behaviour of both sides was brutal both on the battlefield and off. Marshal Soult's long retreat across the region saw him loot town after town; his men robbed tombs and burned priceless archives. The allied forces were no better; the men Wellington had referred to as being comprised of the 'scum of the earth' sacked the towns they conquered with similar destructiveness.

Significant numbers of Spaniards had been in favour of the French invasion, and were opposed to the liberal republican movements that sprang up in its wake. The 19th century was to see clash after clash of liberals against conservatives, progressive cities against reactionary countryside, restrictive centre against outward-looking periphery. Spain finally lost its empire, as the strife-torn homeland could do little against the independence movements of Latin America. In 1823 the French put down a democratic revolution and restored the king (Fernando VII) to the throne. When he died, another war of succession broke out between supporters of his brother Don Carlos and his infant daughter Isabella.

Jovellanos

Gaspar Melchor de Jovellanos (1744-1811) was a true product of the Enlightenment who combined careers in politics, social reform and the law. In addition he was a major literary figure who made important contributions to educational theory.

Born in Asturias in 1744, he initially trained as a priest but moved to the law and started a his career as a magistrate in Sevilla. His multi-faceted personality allowed him to develop a variety of writing styles and literary works published under the name Jovino have secured his place in the history of Spanish letters. His best-known work *Epistola de Fabio a Anfriso* (letter from Fabio to Anfriso) is a fairly philosophical reflection on life, while his play *El si de las niñas* introduced melodrama to the Spanish stage.

Jovellanos's interests brought him to the attention of Carlos III who, unusually for a Spanish monarch, saw Spain's forward progress as a practical matter rather than one to be based on a renewal of faith. He was commissioned to report on the condition of agricultural workers and on prisons. Both these works are considered models of their type and were the inspiration for other social reformers. His concern was the application of Enlightenment principles of reason and justice as part of a strategy for bringing Spain into the modern age.

His first political career ended with the death of Carlos in 1788 and the increasing reaction which followed the French Revolution forced him to return to Asturias where he investigated conditions in the coalmining industry. This was where he started keeping his famous diary and founded the **Real Instituto Asturiano**, an important carrier of the Enlightenment message to this industrial part of Spain. Much to his surprise he was appointed Minister of Justice in 1797, a post he held until 1799 when the changing political climate saw him removed from office.

In 1802 he was arrested on the instigation of the Inquisition – by now a diminished force but still one to be reckoned with – and held in Mallorca until 1808. While in exile he continued writing and was especially concerned with education. In 1808 with the French invasion he found himself once again in the field of action as a member of the Supreme National Junta, leading resistance against Napoleon. He was declared a *Padre de la Patria* by the Cortes of Cádiz as the French were closing in. Forced to flee by ship to his native Asturias he became ill during the voyage and died shortly after landing at Puerto de Vega.

The so-called Carlist Wars of 1833 to 1839, 1847 to 1849 (although this is often not officially counted as a 'Carlist War') and 1872 to 1876 were politically complex. Don Carlos represented conservatism, and his support was drawn from a number of different sources. Wealthy landowners, the church and the reactionary peasantry, with significant French support, lined up against the loyalist army, the liberals and the urban middle and working classes. The Carlist stronghold was Navarra and the rural Basque region; liberal reforms were threatening the two pillars of Basque country life: the church and their age-old *fueros*. In between and during the wars, a series of *pronunciamientos* (coups d'état) plagued the monarchy. During the third Carlist War, the king abdicated and the short-lived First Spanish Republic was proclaimed, ended by a military-led restoration a year later. The Carlists were defeated but remained strong, and played a prominent part in the Spanish Civil War. There's still a Carlist party in Navarra and various nominal pretenders to the Spanish throne.

Despite all the troubles, industrialization finally began to reach Spain, and several of the ports of the north coast thrived. Vigo, A Coruña and Santander all flourished; Bilbao, on the back of its iron ore exports, grew into a major industrial and banking centre, and Asturias mined large quantities of coal. Basque nationalism as it is known today was born in the late 19th century. Spain lost its last overseas possessions, Cuba, Puerto Rico and the Phillippines, in the 'Disaster' of 1898. The introspective turmoil caused by this event gave the name to the '**Generación de 98**', a forward thinking movement of artists, philosophers and poets, among whom were the Basques Miguel de Unamuno and Ignacio Zuloaga and the poet Antonio Machado. It was a time of discontent and strikes began to occur more and more regularly in the towns and cities of the north, particularly in Asturias, although Spanish industry profited from its neutrality in the First World War.

After the Second Republic had been established in 1931, a series of petty struggles between conservatives, liberals and socialists undermined the potential value of the democratic process. Unlike the rest of the left, the Asturian miners were fairly united, with anarchists, socialists and trade unionists prepared to cooperate; they went on strike in protest against the entry of the right-wing CEDA into the vacillating centrist government. Proclaiming a socialist republic, they seized the civil buildings of the province. The arms factories worked 24-hour shifts to arm the workers; the army and Civil Guard were still holding out in Oviedo. The government response was harsh. Sending in the feared Foreign Legion and Moroccan troops under Generals Goded and a certain Franco, they swiftly relieved the garrison, defeated the insurrection and embarked on a brutal spree of retribution for which they are rightly unforgiven in Asturias.

The Spanish Civil War

In July 1936 a military conspiracy saw garrisons throughout Spain rise against the government and try to seize control of their towns and provinces. Within a few days battlelines were clearly drawn between the Republican (government) and the Nationalists, a coalition of military, Carlists, fascists and the Christian right. Most of Northern Spain was rapidly under Nationalist control, although frightening numbers of civilians were shot 'behind the lines' after control had been established. The major resistance in the north was in Asturias – where the miners came out fighting once again – Cantabria and the Basque provinces. These latter were in a difficult position; the Basques were democratic in outlook but very Catholic, and the Catholic church was on the Nationalist side for its own protection from the anticlerical Republic and through innate conservatism: a 1927 catechism had claimed that it was a mortal sin for a Catholic to vote for a liberal candidate. Carlist-oriented Navarra sided with the Nationalists, as did Alava, but the majority of Euskadi came out fighting on the side of democracy.

There was long fighting on fronts in Aragón, but the prize, Zaragoza, stayed in rebel hands throughout the war. Meanwhile, the Republican government approved a statute of autonomy for the Basques, and a Basque government was sworn in under the oak tree in **Gernika**, long a symbol of Basque government and *fueros*. The young and able leader, **José María Aguirre**, assured the Republic that "until Fascism is defeated, Basque nationalism will remain at its post". It did, with Basques fighting Nazi forces right through the Second World War, but the government was forced into exile when Bilbao fell in June 1937. This came in the wake of the appalling civilian bombings of Durango and Gernika, when German and Italian planes rained bombs on the defenceless country towns, killing almost 2000. Franco claimed that the devastation of Gernika and Durango was perpetrated by the Basques as a publicity gesture.

Franco's junta, after being formed at Salamanca, had set up base appropriately in deeply conservative Burgos; Castilla was a heartland for Nationalist support and the venue for many brutal reprisals against civilians perceived as leftist, unionist, democratic or owning a fertile little piece of land on the edge of the village. Republican atrocities were equally appalling, but an important distinction is that they were rarely sanctioned or perpetrated by the government.

Separated from the rest of the Republic, Asturian and Cantabrian resistance was whittled away; Santander fell in August 1937, Asturias in October. Franco never forgave the Basques or Asturians, and the regions were treated harshly during his oppressive rule. Development was curtailed and use of the Euskara language was banned (as was Gallego, although Franco himself was Galician). Navarra and Castilla, on the other hand, were rewarded for their roles, if being blessed with a series of concrete crimes against architecture can be called a reward.

The Basques held out high hopes as the Second World War reached its end. Their government-in-exile was officially recognized by the Allies, and many hoped that Franco would soon be deposed and an independent Basque state be established. Their hopes were dashed when the USA decided that the new enemy was communism. If Franco was anything, he was anti-communist, and the Americans under Eisenhower granted Spain a massive aid package and resumed diplomatic relations. This betrayal of the Basques, followed by that of Britain and France, was a bitter pill to swallow.

Transition to democracy

The dollars were dirty, but the country made the most of them; Spain boomed in the 1960s as industry finally took off and the flood of tourism began in earnest. But dictatorship was no longer fashionable in western Europe and Spain was regarded as a slightly embarassing cousin. It was not invited to join the European Economic Community (EEC) and it seemed as if nothing was going to really change until Franco died.

ETA, had their most popular moment when they assassinated Franco's right-hand man, Admiral Carrero Blanco, in 1973. The aging dictator died two years later and his appointed successor, King Juan Carlos II, supervised a return to democracy; La Transición. Northern Spain has largely flowered since the first elections in 1977. Autonomous status was granted to Euskadi and Galicia, and then to Asturias, Cantabria, Navarra, La Rioja, Aragón and Castilla y León, which operate with significant freedom from central government. However, the new constitution specified that no further devolution could occur; Spain was 'indissoluble'.

In 1982, the Socialist government of Felipe González was elected. They held power for 14 years and oversaw Spain's entry into the EEC (now EU), from which it has benefited immeasurably, although some rural areas remain poor by western European standards. González was disgraced, however, when he was implicated in having commissioned 'death squads' with the aim of terrorizing the Basques into renouncing terrorism, which few of them supported in any case. In 1996 the rightist PP (Partido Popular) formed a government under young ex-tax inspector José María Aznar, who was re-elected in 2000. Economically conservative, Aznar strengthened Spain's ties with Europe and set a platform for strong financial performance.

Political repression and cultural rejuvenation

Aznar then turned to ETA, using the prevailing international climate to take strong action. In 2002, the democratically elected party, Batasuna, widely seen as linked to the terrorist group, were banned by the courts after a purpose-built bill was resoundingly passed in parliament. The governing Basque Nationalist Party (PNV), wholly against terrorism, denounced the move the move against their political opponents as 'undemocratic' and 'authoritarian', which it undoubtedly was. Nevertheless, things quietened down and the move, backed by a massive police operation resulting in many arrests, seemed to have paid off. See also box, page 512.

However, Aznar's heavy-handed and undemocratic methods appalled international observers and stirred the ghosts of Francoism in Spain. Then, the *Prestige* disaster (see box, page 458) seemed to reflect the government's refusal to see the bigger picture, and Aznar took the country to war in Iraq against the wishes of a massive majority of the population. On 11 March 2004, three days before the general election, a series of 10 bombs exploded in four commuter trains approaching Madrid's Atocha station; nearly 200 people were killed. The government was quick to blame ETA for the attack despite that group's denial and substantial evidence for involvement by Islamic extremists. The electorate was angered at what was perceived as a vote-minded cover-up and punished Aznar's hand-picked successor, Mariano Rajoy, at the election. Far adrift in the polling only a few days before, the PSOE were elected to government and the new prime minister, 43-year-old José Luis Rodríguez Zapatero, from León, immediately pledged to withdraw Spanish troops from Iraq and re-align the country with 'old Europe'.

Zapatero's government pursued a decidedly liberal course. Spain's religious right were outraged by the legalization of same-sex marriage, and when Zapatero agreed to pass a statute granting the Catalan government more autonomy (approved in a local referendum in Catalunya) the PP, who maintain the ideal that Spain is indissoluble, were furious. Zapatero has also pursued peaceful solutions to the Gibraltar question and initially favoured dialogue with ETA, despite the right's condemnation of "dealing with terrorists". ETA declared a ceasefire in March 2006, but broke it, and stepped up their bombings and assassinations in 2008 in response to a major government crackdown that saw several of their leaders arrested. Zapatero was, however, re-elected in 2008, and has come under increasing criticism for his uncertain handling of 'la crisis', the economic downturn that severely affected Spain, with the key industries of construction and tourism suffering significant reverses, and unemployment skyrocketing to 20%. A failure to reform employment law and encourage private enterprise cost the PSOE dear, and a hastily concocted reform package designed to placate the EU and the moneymasters led to widespread indignation in 2010 as people perceived they were being forced to tighten their belts while the banks and corporations continued on their merry way.

The region is still divided along political lines. The Basques have their PNV, and rural Asturias remains firmly leftist in orientation. On the other side, Navarra is still conservative, Galicia hasn't shaken off its Francoist tendencies, and one suspects plenty in parts of Castilla y León would vote for the man himself if he were still alive (and in democratic mood). The Franco era is rarely discussed; neither is the Civil War, which remains a sensitive issue, with perpetrators of dark deeds still alive and sipping wine in the corner of local bars. No judicial investigation of events of the war or the dictatorship has ever been undertaken; there's a sort of consensus to let sleeping dogs lie: understandable, given the turbulent history of the 19th and 20th centuries.

Most cities of Northern Spain have shaken off the torpor of the Franco era and the preceding centuries of decline and are today bustling, attractive places. EU funding has helped to rejuvenate their architectural heritage, and the lively social life is a marvel of European society. In most urban areas, Francoist street names have been changed and statues pulled down. In some rural areas, though, particularly Castilla and Galicia, depopulation is a serious issue. Many villages are inhabited only by pensioners, if at all, as the young seek employment and fulfilment in urban centres.

ETA and Basque nationalism

Although many Spaniards refuse to distinguish between the two, Basque nationalism and ETA are two very different things. The vast majority of Basque nationalists, ie those who want more autonomy for the region, are firmly committed to a peaceful and democratic path. ETA, on the other hand, have traditionally been pessimistic about the possibility of achieving these aims in this manner, and have sought by planned violent action to force the issue.

To probe the wrongs, rights and history of the issue would require volumes. Viewed in the context of the changing Europe, Basques have a strong case for independence, being culturally and ethnically distinct to Spaniards. The issue is muddied by the large number of Spaniards in the region, but the real sticking point is that Spain has no intention of giving up such a profitable part of the nation. Economics don't permit it, old-fashioned Spanish honour doesn't permit it and, cleverly, the constitution doesn't permit it. It isn't going to happen, and most Basques know it. From this frustration a small percentage of extremism has developed.

The nationalist movement as we know it today was born in the late 19th century, fathered by Sabino Arana, a perceptive but unpleasant bigot who was a master of propaganda. He devised the *ikurriña* (the Basque flag), coined terms such as *Euskadi*, and published manifestos for independence, peppered with dubious historical interpretations.

The tragically short-lived breakthrough came with the Civil War. The sundered Republic granted the Basques extensive self-government, and José Antonio Aguirre was installed as *lehendakari* (leader) at Gernika on 7 October 1936. A young, intelligent and noble figure, Aguirre pledged Basque support to the struggle against Fascism. The government was forced into exile a few months later when the Nationalists took Bilbao, but Basques fought on in Spain and later in France against the Nazis.

The birth of ETA can be directly linked to the betrayal of the Basque government by the western democracies. At the end of the Second World War, supporters of the Republic had hoped that a liberating invasion of Spain might ensue. It didn't, but Franco's government was ostracized by the USA and Europe. The Basque government in exile was recognized as legitimate by the western powers. However, with the Cold War chilling up, the USA began to see the value of the anti-communist Franco, and granted a massive aid package to him. Following suit, France and Britain shamefully recognized the fascist government and withdrew support from the horrified Basques, as well as from the Republican government-in-exile.

ETA was founded by angry Basque youth shortly after this sordid political turnabout. Its original goal was simply to promote Basque culture in repressive Spain, but it soon took on a violent edge. In 1959 it adopted the name, which stands for *Euskadi Ta Askatasuna*, The Basque Country and Freedom. They conducted their first assassination in 1968, and since then have been

On a more positive note, the years since the return to democracy have seen a remarkable and accelerated reflowering of regional culture. The banned languages Gallego and Euskara are ever-more in use, and local artists, writers and poets are being keenly promoted by the regional governments. Museums are mostly free, not so much to responsible for over 800 deaths, mostly planned targets such as right-wing politicians, Basque 'collaborators' and police. The organization is primarily youthful, and uses extortion and donations to fund its activities. Their main demands are autonomy for the Basque region and the union of Navarra with the region, as well as hopefully the French Basque region. Their logo features a snake, representing politics, wrapped around an axe, representing violence, with the motto *Bietan jarrai* (Keep up on both).

Despite the slogans, there's nothing noble or honourable about ETA's normal modus operandi. In many cases it seems that the central leadership has little control over its trigger-happy thugs, and many targets have been people with families with little or no power within the regime. The attitude of the international public has turned against ETA since their glory days; in 1973, when Franco's right-hand man Admiral Carrero Blanco was sent sky-high by an ETA bomb, the terrorist group were liberationist heroes to many.

For many years, the government and police were in a vicious and self-defeating cycle of violence with ETA. Whenever the terrorist group struck, their support dropped dramatically in Euskadi. A few days later, when a mystery retaliatory killing of Basques occurred, anti-government feeling would rise again.

The escalationist attitude of the Madrid government continued in 2002, when the parliament overwhelmingly passed legislation specifically designed to ban Batasuna, the political party often (and probably accurately) linked with ETA. The party was then banned by the courts, outraging Basques and their governing PNV (no friends of Batasuna) as well as many international observers. During the same period, the police embarked on a massive operation, with many high-profile arrests and discovery of arms caches. This significantly impacted the group, as did changing attitudes in the wake of 9/11 and the Madrid train bombings. The 2004 election promised much, as José Luis Rodríguez Zapatero initially favoured dialogue with ETA, despite the right's condemnation of "dealing with terrorists". ETA declared a ceasefire in March 2006, but broke it, and stepped up their bombings and assassinations in 2008 in response to a major government crackdown that saw several of their leaders arrested. A continuing 'judicial offensive', with several Basque organizations and political parties banned by the courts, has dovetailed with the police operations and has left ETA, whose support within the Basque lands has dramatically dwindled over the last few years, looking rather weak. The Basque region has a high degree of autonomy, and a high standard of living, and many Basques are heartily sick of the group's mafia-like extortion, feeling that this has now become ETA's end rather than the means to continue the fight. Although they continue to operate, hopes for a permanent ceasefire and lasting peace are higher than they have ever been.

lure tourists away from the beaches of the south as to encourage their own population to visit and learn. Salamanca, that great university town of the Middle Ages, is a flourishing example; whether the angels speak Castilian or Euskara these days is of little importance.

Economy

Though at time of writing 'la crisis' had plunged the country into dire economic circumstances, the feeling that over the last couple of decades Spain has finally arrived at the table of major economic powers is unlikely to disappear. Nevertheless, with unemployment rates at 20% and the bottom well and truly out of the construction market, it could be a long and painful crawl back to solvency. Despite the long boom, Spain's salary levels remain low, and the rapid rise in property prices over the early years of the 21st century has led to major difficulties in debt repayments for many people.

Spain's main products are textiles, machinery and automobiles, while tourism remains a vital sector; Spain receives more annual visitors than any other European country. The story in the north is a mixed one. Euskadi, an industrial powerhouse, is prosperous by any European standards, while Aragón is also strong, at least in urban areas. Galicia and Asturias are poorer; Galicia's GDP per head isn't much more than half that of Euskadi.

The north still has a very important fishing industry, while the wine trade is also significant among agricultural products. Manufacturing, particularly in the Basque lands, is strong and there's still a shipbuilding industry, although declining. Euskadi and Asturias still produce steel and coal respectively, but the boom years are long gone in that sector. Bilbao and Santander continue to be important banking centres.

One interesting case in Euskadi is the Mondragón cooperative, based in a small town near San Sebastián. Formed by five workers in the 1950s, who were influenced by the social teachings of the local priest, the MCC is now one of Spain's leading companies, with over 20,000 members involved in many types of manufacturing. It's Spain's leader in the production of domestic appliances and also runs a major supermarket chain. Easily the world's most successful attempt at this enlightened form of business, the MCC has served as a model for much sociological study. One of the keys to the cooperative's success was the creation of their own bank, the **Caja Laboral**, with branches throughout the region.

Culture

Architecture

Throughout Northern Spain, the pattern of rapid growth in the wake of the Reconquista was followed by a long decline. Although not an ideal situation for a region to be in, it has had a good effect. The building sprees of the Middle Ages were succeeded by periods where there was hardly any money to fund new construction; the result is a land which has an incredibly rich architectural heritage. Nowhere in Europe has such a wealth of Romanesque and Gothic churches, while the relationships with Islamic civilization spawned some fascinating styles unique to Spain. Today, Spain has shaken off the ponderous monumentalism of the Franco era and become a powerhouse of modern architecture, with exceptional new buildings turning heads all over the country.

Neolithic period
There are some very early stone structures in the peninsula, with the greatest concentration in Alava and in Galicia. Dolmens, *menhirs* and standing stone circles are the most common

remnants of the Neolithic (late Stone Age) era. The first two mostly had a funerary function, while the latter are the subject of numerous theories; some sort of religious/astrological purpose seems likely, but an accurate explanation is unlikely to emerge. The dwellings of the period were less permanent structures, of which little evidence remains.

First millennium BC

The first millennium BC saw the construction of sturdier settlements, usually on hilltops. The sizeable Iberian town of Numancia, though razed after a Roman siege, remains an interesting example and many of the cities of Northern Spain were originally founded during this period. The Celts, too, favoured hilly locations for the construction of *castros*. These fort/villages were typically walled compounds containing a large building, presumably the residence of the chieftain and hall for administration and trading, surrounded by smaller, circular houses and narrow lanes. These dwellings were probably built from mudbrick/adobe on a stone foundation with a thatched roof. The Galician *palloza*, still widely seen in villages well into the 20th century, had probably changed little since these times. There are many well-preserved *castros* in Northern Spain, principally in Galicia and western Asturias.

Phoenician and Carthaginian remains are few in Northern Spain. The Carthaginians were based mostly in the south; their ancestors, the Phoenicians, were so adept at spotting natural harbours that nearly all have been in continual use ever since, leaving only the odd foundations or breakwaters. Greek presence has left a similarly scant architectural legacy in the north.

Roman legacy

The Roman occupation of Hispania was largely administered from the south and east and the majority of architectural remains are in that region. Nevertheless, the Roman legacy is of great interest in the north also. They founded and took over a great number of towns; most of the provincial capitals of the region sit on Roman foundations. Zaragoza, Pamplona, Palencia and Lugo were all important Roman centres, while the abandoned settlements of Clunia and Numancia have extensive, if unspectacular remains. Other settlements are dotted across Castilla y León.

The Roman remains near Palencia are the finest villas of the north; something of an exception, as the presence in this region seems to have been largely of a military/exploitative nature. The Seventh Legion was based at León to administer the mines of the Bierzo region, while the Duero and Ebro valleys produced large quantities of wine; but the majority of the peninsula's wealthy Roman settlements were further south. Although shored up over the years, the walls of Lugo are an impressive sight indeed.

Visigoths

Although the post-Roman period is often characterized as a time of lawless barbarism, the Visigoths added Germanic elements to Roman and local traditions and built widely; in particular the kings of the period commissioned many churches. Most of these were heavily modified or destroyed in succeeding periods, but a few excellent examples remain; the best are San Juan de Baños (near Palencia), Quintanilla de las Viñas (near Burgos) and San Pedro de la Nave (near Zamora). All these date from the seventh century and are broadly similar. Sturdy yet not inelegant, these churches are built around a triple nave with short transepts and square apses. Friezes on the outside depict birds, fruit and flowers with some skill. The interiors are particularly attractive, with treble arches, frequently horseshoe-shaped, and altarstones. These altarstones are found incorporated into many other churches of later date and are interesting for their iconography; early Christian symbols that borrowed heavily from pagan traditions. Depictions of the sun, moon and crops are often accompanied by Celtic-like circles with arched spokes.

Pre-Romanesque

In the eighth century, the style known as pre-Romanesque emerged in the Christian redoubt of Asturias. While there are clear similarities to the Visigothic style, the Asturians added some elements and created a series of buildings of striking beauty, many of which are well preserved today. The style progressed considerably in a fairly short period. There are both churches and royal halls extant. The buildings are generally tripartite, with triple naves (or nave and two aisles) and arches (some exterior) resting on elegantly carved pillars. The small windows reflect this in miniature, often divided by a small column. The floor plan is rectangular or in the shape of a cross, with wide transepts; the altar area is often raised and backed by three small apses, divided from the rest of the interior by a triple arch. Small domes were used in later examples. Narrow exterior buttresses line up with the interior arches. Mural painting is well preserved in many of the buildings; the Asturian (Latin) cross is a frequent motif. The capitals of the pillars are in some cases finely carved, often with motifs presumably influenced by contact with Moorish and Byzantine civilization: palm leaves, flowers and curious beasts.

Mozarabic

During the Muslim occupation of Northern Spain a distinctly Moorish style was used by Christian masons, particularly in church construction. These traditions persisted even after reconquest and were strengthened by the arrival of Christians who had lived in the Muslim south. Known as Mozarabic, it is characterized above all by its horseshoe arches but in some cases also by exuberant fan vaulting and ornate ribbed ceilings; some of the churches feel far more Muslim than Christian. The style persisted, and even some of the most sober of later cathedrals and churches have the odd arch or two that bends a little further in. Fresco-work is present in some Mozarabic buildings too, and in some cases, such as the *Ermita de San Baudelio* (*Berlanga de Duero*), presents a fusion of scenes; some from orthodox Christian iconography and some influenced by time spent in Moorish company, with elephants, camels and palm trees.

Romanesque

The style that spread across the whole of Northern Spain in the 11th and 12th centuries and is most dear to many visitors' hearts is the Romanesque or *románico*. Although there are some examples of the 'Catalan' style, derived from contact with Italy, and of which the Lombard arch (exterior blind-arch decoration in the shape of fingers) is a primary characteristic, most of Northern Spain's Romanesque can be traced back to French influences. Many monks from France arrived in the north of the peninsula in the 11th century and built monasteries along the same lines as the ones of their home country, but the biggest single factor in the spread of the style was the Santiago pilgrimage. News of what was being built in the rest of Europe was spread across Northern Spain and it is fitting that the portal of the cathedral at Santiago is widely considered to be the pinnacle of Spanish Romanesque.

The typical features of Romanesque churches are barrel-vaulted ceilings (stone roofs reduced the number of churches that burned down) with semicircular arches; these also appear on the door and window openings. The apse is also round. Geometric decoration is common, such as the chessboard patterning known as *ajedrezado jaqués*, named for the Pyrenean town of Jaca, from where it spread along the length of the Pilgrim Route. Fine carvings, once painted, are often present on capitals and portals; the cloisters of Santo Domingo de Silos and San Juan de la Peña as well as the church of San Martín in Frómista are excellent examples. The carvings depict a huge variety of subjects: biblical scenes are present and vegetal motifs recurring, but scenes of everyday life from the sublime to the ridiculous, the mundane to the erotic, are common (and often dryly labelled 'allegorical' in church pamphlets), as are strange beasts and scenes from mythology. This is part of the style's charm, as is the beautifully homely appearance of the buildings, often built from golden stone. Some of the towns with an excellent assembly of the Romanesque are Soria and Zamora, as well as those all along the Camino de Santiago. The purest examples are often in the middle of nowhere; places where someone had the money to build a stone church in the 11th century, and no one's had the cash to meddle with it since. Castilla y León in general has numerous churches and chapels of this kind.

Gothic
Austerity in monastic life ushered in the change to elegant remote purity. The whimsical carved capitals disappeared, and the voluptuous curves were squared off as the church authorities began to exert more control over buildings within their dioceses. It seems unbelievable that the word Gothic was originally a pejorative term, applied to the pointed style during the baroque period to mean 'barbarous'. Spanish Gothic architecture also owed much to French influence, although German masons and master builders did much work, particularly in and around Burgos. Advances in engineering allowed lighter, higher structures than their Romanesque forebears, and the wealth and optimism of the rapidly progressing *Reconquista* saw ever more imaginative structures raised. The cathedrals of León and Burgos are soaringly beautiful examples of this.

The basic unit of Gothic is the pointed arch, symbolic of the general enthusiasm for 'more space, less stone' that pervaded the whole endeavour. The same desire was behind the flying buttress, an elegant means of supporting the building from the exterior, thus reducing the amount of interior masonry. Large windows increased the amount of light; the rose window is a characteristic feature of many Gothic façades, while the amount of stained glass in the León cathedral seems to defy physics (to the ongoing concern of engineers). Elaborate vaulting graced the ceilings. The groundplan was often borrowed from French churches; as the style progressed more and more side chapels were added, particularly around the ambulatory.

A feature of many Spanish Gothic churches, and unique to the country, is the enclosed *coro* (choir, or chancel) in the middle of the nave, a seemingly self-defeating placement that robs the building of much of the sense of space and light otherwise striven for. Nevertheless, the choirstalls are often one of the finest features of Gothic architecture, superbly carved in wood. Ornate carved decoration is common on the exteriors of Gothic buildings too. Narrow pinnacles sprout like stone shoots, and the façades are often topped by gables. Portals often feature piers and tympanums carved with biblical figures and scenes, circled by elaborate archivolts.

Mudéjar
As the Reconquista took town after town from the Muslims, Moorish architects and those who worked with them began to meld their Islamic tradition with the northern influences

of Romanesque and Gothic. The result is distinctive and pleasing, typified by the decorative use of brick and coloured tiles, with the tall elegant belltowers a particular highlight. The style became popular nationwide; in certain areas, *mudéjar* remained a constant feature for over 500 years of building. Aragón, which had a strong Moorish population, has a fine collection of *mudéjar* architecture; the Duero Valley and Sahagún are also well stocked. See also the box on page 178.

Plateresque

The 16th century was a high point in Spanish power and wealth, when it expanded across the Atlantic, tapping riches that must have seemed limitless for a while. Spanish Renaissance architecture reflected this, leading from the ornate 'Isabelline' late Gothic style into the elaborate peninsular style known as Plateresque. Although the style originally relied heavily on Italian models, it soon took on specifically Spanish features. The word refers particularly to the façades of civil and religious buildings, characterized by decoration of shields and other heraldic motifs, as well as geometric and naturalistic patterns such as shells. The term comes from the word for silversmith, *platero*, as the level of intricacy of the stonework approached that of jewellery. Arches went back to being rounded, and columns and piers became a riot of foliage and 'grotesque' scenes. The massive façade of San Marcos in León is an excellent example of the style, as is the university at Salamanca.

A classical revival put an end to much of the elaboration, as Renaissance architects concentrated on purity. Classical Greek features such as fluted columns and pediments were added to by large Italianate cupolas and domes. Spanish architects were apprenticed to Italian masters and returned with their ideas. Elegant interior patios in *palacios* are an attractive feature of the style, found across the north, particularly in Salamanca, as well as Valladolid and smaller places such as Medina del Campo.

Spanish baroque

The fairly pure lines of this Renaissance classicism soon moved into a new style: Spanish baroque, and its most extreme form, Churrigueresque. Perhaps the finest baroque structures in Northern Spain are to be found in Galicia, where masons had to contend with granite and hence dedicated themselves to overall appearances rather than intricacy. The façade of the cathedral at Santiago, with its soaring lines, is one of the best of many examples. Compared to granite, sandstone can be carved very easily, and architects in the rest of Northern Spain playfully explored the reaches of their imaginations; a strong reaction against the sober preceding style. Churches became ever larger – in part to justify the huge façades – and nobles indulged in one-upmanship, building ever-grander *palacios*. The façades themselves are typified by such features as pilasters (narrow piers descending to a point) and niches to hold statues. On a private residence, large sculptured coats-of-arms were de rigueur.

Churrigueresque

Named after the Churriguera brothers who took Spanish baroque to an extreme of ornamentation in the late 17th and early 18th centuries, the result of this style can be hideously overelaborate, but on occasion transcendentally beautiful, like Salamanca's superb Plaza Mayor. Vine tendrils decorate the façades, which seem intent on breaking every classical norm, twisting here, upside-down there, treading a fine line between levity and conceit.

Neoclassicism

Neoclassicism again resorted to the cleaner lines of antiquity, which were used this time for public spaces as well as civic and religious buildings. Many plazas and town halls in the north of Spain are in this style, which tended to flourish in the cities that were thriving in the late 18th and 19th centuries, such as Bilbao and A Coruña. The best examples use symmetry to achieve beauty and elegance.

Modernismo

The late 19th century saw Catalán *modernista* architecture break the moulds in a startling way. Apart from a small enclave in Comillas on the Cantabrian coast, there are few examples of the school in Northern Spain, but more restrained fin de siècle architecture can be seen in the fashionable towns of San Sebastián, Santander and A Coruña, as well as the industrial powerhouses of Gijón and Bilbao.

Art nouveau and art deco

At roughly the same time, and equally a break with the academicism of the 19th century, art nouveau aimed to bring art back to life and back to the everyday. Using a variety of naturalistic motifs to create whimsical façades and *objets*, the best art nouveau works manage to combine elegance with fancy. Art deco developed between the World Wars and was based on geometric forms, using new materials and colour combinations to create a recognizable and popular style. San Sebastián is almost a temple to art nouveau, while both it and Bilbao have many good examples of deco, as do many other cities, particularly in old cinemas and theatres.

Avant-garde and modern

Elegance and whimsy never seemed to play much part in Fascist architecture, and during the Franco era Spain was subjected to an series of ponderous concrete monoliths, all in the name of progress. A few avant-garde buildings managed to escape the drudgery from the 1950s on – the Basque monastery of Arantzazu is a spectacular example. The Guggenheim museum is the obvious example of the flowering that has taken place in the last few years in Northern Spain, but it is only one of many. San Sebastián's Kursaal and Vitoria's shining Artium are both excellent examples of modern Spanish works, while the much-admired Valencian, Santiago Calatrava, has done much work in the region too. Zamora is also noteworthy as a city that has managed to combine sensitive modern design with the Romanesque heritage of its old town, but in many parts of the region modern architecture is functional. Vast suburbs of unimaginative apartment blocks gird every city in the region, and in coastal areas, the concrete curse strikes wherever lax planning laws are taken full advantage of.

Regional traditions

Other architectural traditions worth mentioning are in Euskadi, where *baserriak* are large stone farmhouses with sloping roofs, built to last by the heads of families; many are very old. Their presence in the green Basque hills gives the place a distinctly non-Spanish air. The square wooden *hórreos* of Asturias and their elongated stone counterparts in Galicia are trademarks of the region and have been used over the centuries as granaries and drying sheds, although those in Galicia are of a less practical design and were to some extent status symbols also. *Cruceiros* in Galicia are large stone crosses, most frequently carved with a scene of the Crucifixion. Mostly made from the 17th to the 19th centuries, they stand outside churches and along roads.

Arts and crafts

Spain's artistic traditions go back a long way; right to the Palaeolithic, when cave artists along the north coast produced art that ranged from simple outlines of hands to the beautiful and sophisticated bison herds of Altamira.

The Iberians and the Celts produced fine jewellery from gold and silver, and some good sculpture. The Romans' artistic legacy was not as strong in Spain's north as in the south, although there are some notable pieces, including mosaic floors. Ornate bronze, silver and gold pieces are also known from the period of the Visigoths.

Monks of the Middle Ages produced some illustrated manuscripts of stunning beauty, particularly copies of the works of **Beatus of Liébana**. Wallpaintings in Asturian pre-Romanesque and in Mozarabic churches are also early examples of medieval art.

Most of Spanish sculpture through the centuries has been in the religious sphere. The Romanesque master masons responsible for such gems as the cloisters of San Juan de la Peña and Santo Domingo de Silos are not known by name, but arguably the finest of them all is **Master Mateo**, whose tour de force was the Pórtico de la Gloria entrance to the Cathedral of Santiago.

The Gothic period

The ornate development of the Gothic style culminated in the superlative technical mastery of the works of the northern Europeans resident in Castilla, Simón de **Colonia** and Gil and Diego de Siloé, whose stunning *retablos* and tombs are mostly in and around Burgos. Damián Forment was a busy late Gothic sculptor who left his native Aragón to train in Italy, then returned and executed a fine series of *retablos* in his homeland. Saints and Virgins in polychrome (ie with applied colour) wood continued to be popular, and there are some fine examples from the period.

As well as sculptors, there were many foreign painters working in the Gothic period in Northern Spain. As well as *retablos*, painted panels on gold backgrounds were popular, often in the form of triptychs. Frequently illustrating the lives of saints, many of these are excellent pieces, combining well-rendered expression with a lively imagination, particularly when depicting demons, subjects where the artist had a freer rein. Some of the better painters from this period are Fernando Gallego, whose paintings grace Salamanca, **Jorge Inglés**, resident in Valladolid and presumably an Englishman named George, **Juan de Flandes** (Salamanca; Flanders), and **Nicolás Francés** (León; France). These painters drew on influences from the Italian and Flemish schools of the time, but created a distinctive and entertaining Spanish style.

The Renaissance

The transitional painter **Pedro Berruguete** hailed from near Palencia and studied in Italy. His works are executed in the Gothic manner but have a Renaissance fluidity that was mastered by his son, Alonso, who learned under Michelangelo and was court painter to Carlos V. His finest work is sculptural; he created saints of remarkable power and expression in marble and in wood. Juan de Juni, who lived in Valladolid, is also notable for his sensitive sculptures of religious themes.

As the Renaissance progressed, naturalism in painting increased, culminating in the portraits of **Velásquez** and the religious scenes of Murillo in the 17th century.

This was the finest period of Spanish painting; one of its early figures was the 16th-century Riojan painter **Juan Fernández Navarrete**, many of whose works are in the Escorial. He studied in Venice and his style earned him the nickname of 'The Spanish Titian'; his paintings have a grace of expression denied him in speech by his dumbness. A fine portraitist, overshadowed by his contemporary Velásquez, was the Asturian noble **Juan Carreño de Miranda** (1614-1685). Late in life he became court painter and is noted for his depictions of the unfortunate inbred King Carlos II. Although not from the region, several works by the remarkable **Francisco de Zurbarán** hang in Northern Spain; his idiosyncratic style often focuses on superbly rendered white garments on a dark, brooding background, a metaphor for the subjects themselves, who were frequently priests. The religious atmosphere of imperial Spain continued to dominate in art; landscapes and *joie de vivre* are in comparatively short supply.

Gregorio Hernández was a fine naturalistic sculptor working in Valladolid at this time. *Retablos* became more ornate, commissioned by nobles to gain favour with the church and improve their chances in the afterlife. As baroque progressed, this was taken to extremes. Some of the altarpieces and canopies (baldachins) are immense and overgilded, clashing with the Gothic lines of the churches they were placed in; while supremely competent in execution, they can seem gaudy and ostentatious to modern eyes.

The 18th and 19th centuries
The early 18th century saw fairly characterless art produced under the new dynasty of Bourbon kings. Tapestry production increased markedly but never scaled the heights of the earlier Flemish masterpieces, many of which can be seen in Northern Spain. The appropriately enough named Francisco Bayeu produced pictures for tapestries ('cartoons'), as did the master of 19th-century art, **Francisco Goya**. Goya, see box, page 171, was a remarkable figure whose finest works included both paintings and etchings; his fresco work in northern Spanish churches never scaled these heights. His depiction of the vain Bourbon royals is brutally accurate; he was no fan of the royal family, and as court painter got away with murder. His etchings of the horrors of the Napoleonic Wars are another facet of his uncompromising depictions.

After Goya, the 19th century produced few works of note as Northern Spain tore itself apart in a series of brutal wars and conflicts. The rebirth came at the end of the period with the '1898 Generation', see Literature, below. One of their number was the Basque painter **Ignacio Zuloaga** (1870-1945), a likeable painter with a love of Spain and a clear eye for its tragic aspects. His best work is portraiture, often set against a brooding Castilian landscape.

The 20th century
Figures such as **Picasso**, **Miró** and **Dalí** raised the art of the peninsula to worldwide heights in the 20th century, but the Civil War was to have a serious effect, as a majority of artists sided with the Republic and fled Spain with its defeat. Franco was far from being an enlightened patron of the arts, and his occupancy was a monotonous time. The main light in this period came from the Basque lands in the 1950s. Painters such as Nestor Barretxea, and the sculptors **Eduardo Chillida** and **Jorge Oteiza** (see box, page 62) were part of a revival; all three are represented at the tradition-defying monastery of Arantzazu. Chillida (who died in 2002) and Oteiza (2004) continued to be at the forefront of modern sculpture, and their works are widespread through Northern Spain and Europe. Other sculptors – such as the Zaragozans **Pablo Serrano** and **Pablo Gargallo**, the Zamoran **Baltasar Lobo** and the figure and portrait sculptor **Víctor Ochoa** – are also prominent. The provincial governments of Northern Spain are extremely supportive of local artists these days, and the museums in each provincial capital usually have a good collection of modern works, among which female artists are finally being adequately represented; even more than in other nations, the history of Spanish art is a male one.

Literature

The peninsula's earliest known writers lived under the Roman occupation. Martial was born near modern Calatayud and wrote of his native land, while the poet Prudentius was from Calahorra in the Rioja region. After the Roman period, San Isidoro was a significant figure in Spain's literary history, see box, page 500.

In the 10th century a monk made notes in Castilian in the margins of a text at San Millán, in La Rioja; this is the earliest known appearance of the language in writing. Tucked away in his monastery in the Picos de Europa, the monk **Beatus de Liébana** wrote commentaries on the Apocalypse which became a popular monkish staple for centuries, see box, page 371. In the 12th century, *El Cantar de Mío Cid* was an anonymous epic poem recounting the glorious deeds of the northern Spanish mercenary annd strongman, **El Cid**; it's the earliest known work in Castilian. Another early author was the Riojan poet **Gonzalo de Berceo**, who wrote popular religious verses.

An important 13th-century figure was King Alfonso X. Dubbed *El Sabio* (The Wise), he changed the official language of the kingdom from Latin (much bastardized by this time) to Castilian. He was also a poet, and wrote verses in *Galego* (Galician). It wasn't unusual for the nobility to take up the pen and the 15th century saw the **Marqués de Santillana** dashing off verse, including the first Spanish sonnets. The popular form of the period was the romantic ballad, dealing in damsels and knights, Christians and Moors.

One of the finest Spanish poets of any period was the theologian **Fray Luis de León**, see box, page 331, whose 16th-century works include moving personal reflections on religion; the poems *A Cristo Crucificado* and *En la Ascensión* are noteworthy. *Lazarillo de Tormes*, an anonymous work, appeared in 1554. One of the first of the genre known as picaresque (after the Spanish *pícaro*, a rogue), it dealt with a journey across Northern Spain by a blind man's guide. It's frequently described as the first Spanish novel. The extraordinary life of **Miguel de Cervantes** (1547-1616) marks the start of a rich period of Spanish literature. *Don Quijote* came out in serial form in 1606 and is rightly considered one of the finest novels ever written; it's certainly the widest-read Spanish work. Cervantes spent a portion of his eventful life in Valladolid. The royal archives are another frequently overlooked source of interest, particularly those of Felipe II. A fascinating glimpse of the period can be had from reading his tenderly written letters to family as well as his policy decisions that affected half the world.

The opening of public theatres in the 17th century saw the rise of the great dramatists **Lope de Vega** and **Calderón de la Barca** (who was expelled from Salamanca University for defaulting on his college fees). In the 18th century the Basque **Felix María Samaniego** penned popular childlike fables. Meanwhile the Galician priest **Benito Feijóo**, a major Enlightenment figure, wrote important essays from his Oviedo base, and the later Asturian Gaspar Melchior de Jovellanos wrote significant historical-political and sociological works; both were pestered by the Inquisition for their liberal outlook.

Several of the 19th century's major writers emerged from the north. Born in Valladolid, **José Zorrilla** spent much of his life in Mexico; he is famous for his poems and a play about Don Juan, *Don Juan Tenorio*. The playwright José de Echegaray was of Basque descent, while **Leopoldo Alas**, known as *Clarín*, set his novel *La Regenta* in the fictional city of Vetusta, clearly his native Oviedo. It's a fantastic depiction of Spanish provincial life of the time, seen through the eyes of its heroine. At the same time, Galicia's favourite poet, **Rosalía de Castro**, was writing her soulful verses in Spanish and Gallego (see box, page 523).

A watershed in Basque writing came in the late 19th century with the fiery works of **Sabino Arana**. Littered with inaccuracies and untruths, much of his writing reads more

Rosalía de Castro (1837-1885)

"I do not know what I am seeking, but it is something that I lost I know not when". Born in Santiago, poet and novelist Rosalía de Castro grew up in Padrón. Although officially an orphan her mother was, in fact, an unmarried Galician aristocrat and her father a priest. The publication of her *Cantres Gallegos* (*Galician songs*) in 1863 is seen as the high-water mark of the Galician *rexurdimento* (renewal) movement that sought to express liberal ideas through the medium of the Galician language.

Her marriage in 1858 to historian and Galician nationalist Manuel Murgula brought her into contact with other writers who were using the Galician language to express political ideas. Her main achievement was to express traditional Galician tales through complex, innovative metre and in her refreshing use of pastoral imagery. Many of her poems are redolent with *morriña*, a particularly Galician word that refers to a melancholy longing; a feature common to several Celtic cultures.

Her marriage was not a happy one and for the last years of her life she struggled with chronic illness. Her ability to find a distinctive voice against such a difficult background has meant a new interest in her work from feminist critics. She continues to be a source of inspiration to many Spanish authors and in Galicia she is a national hero. Her works have been translated into many languages and are widely available in English.

like propaganda than literature or non-fiction, but it created modern Basque nationalism; since then it has been difficult for Basque writings to avoid the issue.

At the end of the 19th century, Spain lost the last of its colonial possessions after revolts and a war with the USA. This event, known as the 'Disaster', had a profound impact on the nation and its date, 1898, gave its name to a generation of writers and artists who sought to express what Spain was and had been, and achieve new perspectives for the 20th century. One of the foremost was the scholarly Basque **Miguel de Unamuno**, see box, page 96, whose massive corpus of writing ranged from philosophy to poetry and novels, but also included much journalism. His novel *A Tragic Sense of Life* is an anguished an honest attempt to come to terms with his faith and inevitable death. The slightly later novels of **Pío Baroja** often deeply reflect Basque rural life. **Blas de Otero**, who had a complex love for his native Bilbao, spent most of his writing life overseas.

Another of the **Generación de '98** was the poet **Antonio Machado**. His work reflects his profound feelings for the landscape of his homelands of Andalucía and Castilla; he lived for many years in Soria. Along with Federíco García Lorca, he is considered the greatest of Spanish 20th-century poets; Machado and Lorca, Republicans both, were lost in the Civil War. Another notable member was the essayist, historian and critic **José Ortega y Gasset**, who spent time in Bilbao.

Two writers that stand out in post-Civil War Spanish literature are from Northern Spain. **Miguel Delibes** (1920-2010) was from Valladolid and his works range from biting satire to evocative descriptions of the Castilian landscape. His last major novel, *El hereje* (The Heretic), is set in his native city. **Camilo José Cela** (1916-2002), was a Galician realist who won the Nobel Prize for Literature in 1989, see box, page 469. Although the latter fought on the Nationalist side in the Civil War, both battled censors in post-war Spain as editors of anti-Francoist newspapers.

Bernardo Atxaga is the best-known contemporary Basque writer; Julián Ríos is an award-winning Galician writer whose most acclaimed work is the novel *Amores que atan*. Julio Llamazares, a notable Leonese writer, is best known for *La lluvia amarilla* (The Yellow Rain), an elegiac look at vanished ways of Spanish life.

Language

Spanish is, of course, the major language. Known as *español* or *castellano*, the constitution states that all citizens have a duty to know it. Nearly all do, although if you get right off the beaten track in Galicia, Aragón or Asturias you'll find the occasional elderly person who doesn't. Languages and dialects are always thorny political issues, and Northern Spain has its fair share.

Castellano

With Castile playing a major role in the *Reconquista* the language spread rapidly and was adopted as the official one of the kingdom of Alfonso X, which encompassed most of northwest Spain. The fact that it is now spoken as a first language by some 360 million people worldwide is perhaps more than an accident of history; its accessibility and comparatively simple grammar may have aided its spread in the first place. In Spain, the most respected institution dealing with it is the *Real Academia Española*, www.rae.es, a hoary body whose remit is "to purify, clarify, and give splendour" to the language.

There are many regional accents of *castellano*. Many words are purely local; olives are called *aceitunas* in some places and *olivas* in others; ordering buey in Castilla will get you an ox steak, in Galicia a large crab. Similarly, slang differs widely from city to city. One entertaining story about Castilian is that the /th/ sound used for the letters *z* and *c* came about because courtiers were anxious not to offend a lisping Habsburg king. It's almost certainly not true – linguists point to the fact that not all /s/ sounds are converted to /th/ – but it's often used to poke fun at mainland Spain by Latin Americans, who don't do it (neither do Andalucíans).

Gallego

Of the regional languages, the one with the most speakers is *Galego* (Gallego), with some three million in Spain. It's related to Portuguese and the two are mutually intelligible. Although banned under Franco (who was himself Galician), it remained strong and is now taught in schools again. It's similar enough to Castellano not to cause visitors too much concern. ▸▸ *See Footnotes, page 536, for further details of regional dialects.*

Euskara

Although the first known document written in the Basque (Euskara; also known as Euskera) language dates from the same time as Castilian, it's a far older tongue whose origins are as obscure as the Basques themselves. It's a difficult language with no known relatives. Like Finnish, it is agglutinative, meaning roughly that distinct bits are joined on to words for each element of meaning. Some 800,000 people speak Basque in Spain, and the number is rapidly rising. There are actually several Basque dialects, but a standardized version was created in the sixties; this is the teaching language of a significant proportion of schools in the region, with Spanish as a compulsory subject.

Bable

The Asturian tongue, known as Bable, is similar enough to Castilian to be labelled a dialect. In truth, though, it's probably more accurate to put it the other way, as Castilian is thought to be largely derived from the tongue spoken in the Christian mountain kingdom. It's still widely spoken in Asturias, unlike Leonese, which is similar, but spoken by few people in that province (although sporadic efforts are made to revive it).

Aragonese

Aragonese is a word with two meanings; it refers to the version of Castilian spoken in Aragón and also to the native language of the area, more similar to Catalán than anything else and still used, especially in the more remote mountain regions.

Music

Musical traditions

Based on folk traditions the post-Franco years have seen a rapid evolution of traditional forms and their incorporation into the mainstream of musical life. The northwestern regions of Galicia and Asturias derive part of their musical traditions from Celtic origins, and have made much of the fact in recent years; Celtic music festivals, bringing together musicians from Scotland, Ireland, Cornwall, Brittany, and Canada are common across the region. The bagpipes (*gaita*), fiddles, and various whistles are the staple instruments.

In addition, industrial Asturias has a tradition of male voice choirs similar to that of Wales. The unaccompanied choirs sing traditional Asturian songs and of the labour struggles of the 20th century.

Galician groups such as **Leilía** or Habas Verdes explore traditional forms using instruments such as the *pandereta* (tambourine), *caneveira*, a kind of split cane used for making clapping sounds, and the *zanfona*, a Galician hurdy-gurdy.

Galician immigrant history has meant that some musicians have incorporated Latin and other external rhythms into traditional Galician songs. Bagpiper **Carlos Núñez** was probably the first to develop this trend. A veteran of the European circuit, he has collaborated with a variety of musicians, including Ry Cooder. Other recommended Galician bands are **Na Lúa** (In the Moon), **Fia Na Roca** and **Dhais**. For Asturian music **Llan de Cubel** are interesting, while **Hevia** is one of the region's best traditionally based musicians.

Traditional Basque music is an important part of Basque culture and is mostly associated with the accordion, or *trikitrixa*. Musicians associated with this include **Josepa Tapia** and **Kepa Junkera**. The tensions inherent in Basque culture are reflected in both the lyrical content and the forms that are performed. Songs are therefore an important part of Basque musicians' repertoire. On the other hand there is the desire to innovate within the traditional form in order to ensure that it remains a living tradition rather than one of concern only to musicologists.

Benito Lertxundi is the Basques' most revered singer/songwriter and has been an inspiration to musicians for a generation. He was part of the first Basque band, **Ez dok Amairu** (It's Not 13) who were part of the **Kantaldi Garaia** (Its Time To Sing movement). The aim of this movement was to give Basque culture a modern appeal and its effects continue to this day. Independence-minded Basques have frequently found musical expression in anti-establishment hard rock and punk music; some other important bands include Kortatu, Negu Gorriak and Soziedad Alkoholika.

The gaita

Often a surprising sight for visitors who come across it in a procession or festival in Northern Spain, the *gaita* is the Asturian and Galician bagpipe, a related but simpler instrument than its Scottish cousin, normally having only one pipe and the bag, traditionally made from goatskin. The sound produced is clear and slightly cheerier than the Scottish version, and is the basis for much modern Celtic music in the region. The Museo de Gaitas in Gijón is a good exhibition on the history and nature of bagpipes around the world.

Musical genres

By far the most popular form of music is pop, with the reality-TV show *Operación Triunfo* having created a production line of stars who are adored by the younger public. Cantabrian David Bustamante is one of these. Every summer is marked by a handful of *canciones de verano*, modish (and usually awful) hits that are played continuously until autumn comes and then forgotten.

The Spanish passion for dancing is carried out to this and also to the sounds of *bacalao*, light and happy Spanish techno, which is widely popular and an essential background track to any Spanish visit.

Rock music in Spain was a symbol of the *Transición* – the return to democracy, and is still enthusiastically embraced by that and younger generations. Groups of that era, such as León's **Los Cardiacos**, still evoke all the frenetic passion of those years when played in bars. Younger rock groups play to packed houses, particularly in more working-class cities such as Vigo, Gijón, Bilbao or Ponferrada. Big northern Spanish acts include **La Oreja de Van Gogh**, a San Sebastián pop-rock outfit, **Amaral**, a folk-pop duo from Zaragoza, **Café Quijano**, three light-rock brothers from León, **Bunbury**, the idiosyncratic Aragonese singer-songwriter, Celtas Cortos, a Valladolid group incorporating Celtic rhythms into their rock, Oviedo pop-rockers Sueño de Mórfeo, and Asturian indie rocker **Nacho Vegas**.

Jazz, soul and R&B are represented in nearly all of the larger towns, most of which have at least one bar or venue devoted to the style. Live appearances of local musicians are common, while internationally renowned artists mainly play Madrid and Barcelona only, with perhaps a concert in Vigo, Bilbao, Valladolid, Zaragoza, or Gijón thrown in.

Dance

If a broad definition of dance is that it is ritualized movement, then a strong case can be made for saying that dance is at the very core of Spanish society. What else is the *paseo* but an enormous communal dance where each participant has their allotted role and which tradition guides from beginning to end?

Local fiestas and weddings showcase traditional regional dancing, but it is during *la marcha* that Spain's living dance culture comes into its own. Come 0200 the whole of Spain seems to be engaged in an enormous Bacchic celebration of hip-swinging, hand-waving dancing that goes on till the last person leaves.

Although modern in approach, Spain's dance culture has deep roots. In the north, each region has its own traditional dances. Mostly seen at fiestas these dances reflect the historical background of each region. Thus in Galicia and Asturias the dances are Celtic in origin and are similar to Scottish dances, following the basic reel pattern.

Many of the Basque dances are extremely physical as may be judged by their names, such as *Bolant Dantza* (Flying Dance). Perhaps the most famous of all Basque dances are the *Espatas* (Sword dances). Performed using interlocking swords these dances reflect their martial origins although in contemporary Basque culture they are preformed more to impress than intimidate. Less exclusive are the Basque social dances where men and women dance together in a circle linked by either holding hands or handkerchiefs. The dances of the Basque country are more complicated although the difficult parts are usually left to the *dantzari*, or experts.

Northern Spain has a variety of both ballet and modern dance companies that perform all over Spain and abroad. Drawing on local traditions these groups are very much part of the European mainstream and a number of innovative dancers have come from them. They are, however, very much at the top of the dance pecking order. It is much more important to emphasize that dance in Spain is entirely democratic in spirit.

Cinema

After years under the cultural anaesthetic of the fascist dictatorship, Spanish cinema has belatedly made a strong impression on the world stage. With an enthusiastic home audience of cinema-goers, increased funding, and a huge global Spanish-speaking population, it was perhaps only a matter of time.

One of the early pioneers of cinema was the Aragonese film-maker Segundo de Chomón who was hired by the French film company Pathé in order for them to compete against the great Georges Méliès in the late 19th century. He was an innovator in trick photography and made one of the earliest colour films *Le scarabée d'or* (The Golden Beetle). However, it was telling that he had to work outside his homeland. A shortage of capital and an underdeveloped home market meant that it was very difficult to develop any indigenous production facilities. As public awareness slowly mounted, the demand was mostly met by imported American films.

One of the greatest figures in the history of cinema was also Aragonese, coming from a small town in the underdeveloped province of Teruel. Luis Buñuel sprang to prominence in France, where he collaborated with Salvador Dalí in the late 1920s, pioneering surrealism on the screen. Buñuel was sure that the critics were going to hate their first film, *Un chien andalou*, so he took some stones along to the première to lob at any that voiced their disapproval. Luckily, it went down a treat, and they followed it up with the successful *L'Age d'Or*; both produced images that are still iconic. Along with a whole generation of talented artists, Buñuel left Spain with the onset of fascism but did return shortly before his death to work on a number of collaborations. His work has influenced generations of directors.

The beginnings of a native Spanish film industry came during the 1930s with the help of the Republican Government. Locally produced films such as *La Verbena de la Paloma* (Paloma Fair) (1935) and *Morena Clara* (Clara the Brunette) (1936) proved to be immensely popular and produced the first Spanish-language star, the unlikely named Imperio Argentina. Another important development in this period was the move to dub imported films into Spanish, a practice which continues to this day.

The Civil War and its lead-up saw numerous propaganda films made, then the establishment of the Franco dictatorship saw the end of progress and development in the Spanish film industry. For the next 40 years the film industry was to be made subservient to the goals of the state, all film production had to be approved and censorship was strict. The emphasis was on films with a unifying message. Glorified histories, inoffensive comedies and chaste romances were the order of the day. Regional differences were not encouraged and the use of Catalan, Euskara and Gallego was forbidden.

Despite this, some film-makers managed to put their message across. The most important was Antonio Bardem. His films, especially *Death of a Cyclist* (1956) suggested that it was possible to introduce some elements of criticism into film-making. He founded the magazine *Objectivo* in 1953 which, for the 15 issues that it was allowed to operate, became a rallying point for critics of the Franco regime. However, Bardem was arrested on numerous occasions and it became increasingly difficult for him to produce in Spain. Luis Berlanga was another who risked persecution to satirize the state.

Huesca-born Carlos Saura was the stand-out figure of Spanish cinema in the 1960s and 1970s. Films such as *La Caza* (The Hunt, 1965) and *Ana y los lobos* (Ana and the Wolves, 1973) managed to employ symbolism to attack the institutions of the dictatorship, which had become somewhat freer by these times. A similar approach was taken by Victor Erice and his *El espíritu de la colmena* (Spirit of the Beehive, 1973), a film of haunting beauty set in post-war Castilla.

Since the abolition of censorship after Franco's death, things have changed. Spanish cinema has witnessed the transformation mirrored in many aspects of life in the peninsula. Without a doubt, the best-known post-Franco director has been Pedro Almodóvar. Films such as *Atame* (Tie Me Up, Tie Me Down), *Mujeres al borde de un ataque de nervios* (Women on the Edge of a Nervous Breakdown) and the Oscar-winning *Todo sobre mi madre* (All About my Mother) explore the themes of desire and obsession in Madrid that have made Almodóvar one of the world's most popular and prominent directors. His films have propelled actors Antonio Banderas and Penélope Cruz to international stardom.

Another Oscar-winning director is Fernando Trueba, whose *Belle Epoque* (1993) is a romantic comedy set in the pre-Civil War republic, also starring Cruz. Bigas Luna explores the strange worlds of sex, the unconscious and food in films such as *Jamón Jamón* and *La Teta y la Luna*. Basque director Alex de la Iglesia's latest film, *The Oxford Murders*, starring Elijah Wood, was based on the award-winning novel by the Argentine writer Guillermo Martínez. Another prominent director is José Luis Garcí, whose 2008 release *Sangre de Mayo* tells of the Spanish resistance against the French occupation in the early 1800s. Alejandro Amenábar, though born in Chile, was raised in Spain and has achieved great critical success, most recently with Agora, the historical drama set in Roman Alexandria.

Carlos Saura is still directing; his *Carmen* (1983) was highly acclaimed and he has made several quirky films inspired by the world of art and music. Fernando León is another talented writer and director whose 2002 socially aware comedy *Los Lunes al Sol* (Mondays in the Sun) focused on a group of unemployed friends in a north-coast fishing town. It starred Javier Bardem, one of Spain's most talented cinematic actors, nephew of the great Antonio. Bardem, who won an Oscar in 2008 for his role as Anton Chigger in *No Country for Old Men*, is perhaps Spain's finest actor He had previously captured the world's attention in 2004, starring in Amenábar-directed *Mar Adentro* (The Sea Inside), a moving story of a man crippled and bedridden by an accident. Other recent works involving Northern Spain have been *Los Girasoles Ciegos* (The Blind Sunflowers, 2008), which partly takes place in the north, and *La Buena Nueva*, about a young priest's experiences in northern Navarra during the Civil War. Woody Allen is an honorary citizen of Oviedo these days, and part of *Vicky Cristina Barcelona* was filmed there.

At the end of September each year, the film world turns its attention to San Sebastián and over 200,000 visitors come to view the enormous number of both Spanish and international films on offer. As well as awarding internationally prestigious prizes the festival focuses attention on regional Spanish cinema and tries to ensure that it is seen outside the limited area of its production. Spain's other main film event is the awarding of the Goya prizes, which are presented at the end of January.

Recently there has been a recognition that although there is a basic production infrastructure in the North of Spain, especially in the Basque country, there is a need to develop skills in marketing and promotion. The establishment of a national film school in Ponferrada, and the recent successes of Galician-set films indicate that progress is being made.

Religion

The history of Spain and the history of the Spanish Catholic church are barely separable but, in 1978, Article 16 of the new constitution declared that Spain was now a nation without an official religion, less than a decade after Franco's right hand man, Admiral Luis Carrero Blanco, had declared that "Spain is Catholic or she is nothing".

From the sixth-century writings of San Isidoro (see box, page 500) onwards, the destiny of Spain was a specifically Catholic one. The Reconquista was a territorial war inspired by holy zeal, Jews and Moors were expelled in the quest for pure Catholic blood, the Inquisition demonstrated the young nation's religious insecurities and paranoias and Felipe II bled Spain dry pursuing futile wars in a vain attempt to protect his beloved Church from the spread of Protestantism. Much of the strife of the 1800s was caused by groups attempting to end or defend the power of the church, while in the 20th century the fall of the Second Republic and the Civil War was engendered to a large extent by the provocatively anticlerical actions of the leftists.

Although regular church-going is increasingly confined to an aged (mostly female) segment of society, and seminaries struggle to produce enough priests, it's not the whole picture. Romerías (religious processions to rural chapels) and religious fiestas are well attended, and places of popular pilgrimage such as Santiago, Zaragoza, Loiola and Covadonga are flooded with Spanish visitors during the summer. Very few weddings are conducted away from the Church's bosom, and at Easter a sizeable percentage of the male population of some towns participates in solemn processions of religious *cofradías* (brotherhoods). Although not involved to the same degree in education as it once was, the Church and affiliated organizations run some 15% of Spanish schools and several universities. The Church and the right wing remain closely connected in Spain; the opposition Partido Popular is implicitly a largely Catholic party, and allegations of Opus Dei involvement are frequent (see box, page 187).

One curious aspect of Spanish Catholicism is its Marian aspect. Worship and veneration of the Virgin seem to far outstrip that of Christ himself, who is often relegated to a side chapel; María is still by far the most common name in Spain (even being used for boys in combination with another name, eg José María), and the majority of girls are named after one incarnation of the Virgin or another (eg Carmen, Pilar, Mercedes, Esperanza, Concepción, Begoña).

The practice of Catholicism in Spain is far more devotional than liturgical. The devotions of the *Via Crucis*, or Stations of the Cross (which arose in the 17th century), the *Sacred Heart* (which became popular in the 16th), and the *Rosary* are the focus of a sentimental rather than robust approach to the religion; the Bible itself has historically not been widely available to, or read by, the people. Encouraging the performance of these ritualistic elements was a way for the church to keep a superstitious populace in regular attendance;

indulgences were traditionally offered as a carrot. The number of fiestas in Spain, which are nearly all religious in origin, historically had a similar aim. Faced with a recent census form, a massive 94% of Spaniards claim to be Catholics, but less than a third cut regular figures in their parish church.

Land and environment

Geography

Spain's area of 500,000 sq km makes it the fourth largest country in Europe and second largest in the EU after France. It's also high; the average altitude is second only to Switzerland (ok, and Liechenstein). Geographically, Spain is divided into very distinct areas; to a large degree these have corresponded with cultural and political boundaries over time.

Although if you arrive over the Pyrenees it may not seem it, Spain's central plateau, the *meseta*, is high, with an average elevation of some 600-700 m. It covers most of Castilla y León as well as extending further to the south. It's bounded by mountains; the Pyrenees to the northeast, the Cordillera Cantábrica to the north and the Montes de León in the northwest. In itself, it's not particularly flat either.

While Spain's highest peak is in the south, in the Sierra Nevada, it's the Pyrenees that are its biggest and most rugged mountain chain, straddling the northern border. The highest summit of the Pyrenees is **Aneto** (3404 m), one of many that tops the 3000-m mark. The Cantábrica is basically a westwards extension of it, and includes the Picos de Europa in its run along the coast. Further west still, at the corner of Spain, Galicia is fairly hilly with a coast indented with sheltered inlets (*rías*).

The two great rivers of Northern Spain are the **Ebro**, rising in Cantabria and flowing eastwards to its Mediterranean destiny, and the **Duero**, flowing west right across the *meseta* and into Portugal, where it becomes the **Douro**. Galicia's **Miño** is another major river; it forms a long section of the border with Portugal. The scarcity of water on the *meseta* has dictated settlement patterns; most towns and villages are on or near rivers.

Climate

The green hills of the north coast are that way for a reason: it rains a hell of a lot. Parts of Galicia get 2 m of rain a year, more than 10 times the precipitation of some towns in Castilla. It's a typically maritime climate, with mild summers and winters, and the rain fairly constant through the year; up to 150 rainy days per annum.

The high *meseta* has a continental climate with very low rainfall, scorching summers and freezing winters. Adding to the winter discomfort is the biting wind, which 'can kill a man but can't blow out a candle' according to locals. The climate in places like Burgos and León is popularly characterized as *nueve meses de invierno, tres meses de infierno* (nine months of winter, three months of hell).

The mountains, too, receive high rainfall, particularly the coastal Cordillera Cantábrica. Snow is usually there to stay from January on, and many of the higher passes can still be snowbound as late as June.

Storks

One of Castilla's most distinctive summer sights is a squadron of graceful white storks, *cigueñas*, circling their massive nests in the setting evening sun. Most of them arrive in June from Africa and southern Spain and busy themselves with spring-cleaning their nests, feeding on insects and fish from around the *meseta*'s wetlands and raising young. Their distinctive clacking call is an eerie sound when it comes from high in the eaves of a deserted rural church.

Their sheer numbers can be something of a problem, often overwhelming small villages entirely. Councils have taken to moving their nests in some places, as churches and cathedrals struggled to withstand the impact of a hundred or so of the heavy birds. The diminishing natural wetlands of Castilla have meant that the storks have to forage elsewhere for food; they are often to be seen on the edges of town looking for morsels in rubbish dumps or scouring farmers' fields. They normally leave Castilla in late August, although increasing numbers are spending the whole year in Northern Spain as the human presence provides them with a year-round source of food.

Wildlife

The best havens for wildlife in the peninsula are the mountainous parts of Asturias and the Pyrenees, where conservation is most advanced and the habitats less accessible. While the *meseta* can be good for birdwatching, deforestation and the Spanish passion for hunting have made most four-legged creatures larger than a mouse fairly scarce.

In the mountains, a common sight are chamois or isard (*rebeco* or *sarrío*), a type of agile antelope that like the high altitudes. Also common are *jabalí* (wild boar), but being nocturnal, they're harder to see. Extensively hunted, they tend to be extra-wary when people are about. Still present, but in smaller numbers, are brown bears, subject to an Asturian conservation programme, which will hopefully ensure their survival in the wild, and wolves, which still howl in the Galician and Castilian hills. Several varieties of deer are present both in the mountains and on the plains, where their heads make popular trophies.

Smaller mammals include the stoat/ermine, which changes colour in winter, the fox, pine marten, red squirrels and several species of bat. Wildcats are also present, although interbreeding with feral domestic cats has created a debased population.

Other creatures you might spot are salamanders, brightly coloured in yellow and black, and many species of lizard and snake in the dustier lands of Castilla. Few of the snakes are poisonous, although there are a couple of species of viper. Frogs can create deafening noise around some of Castilla's rivers.

Northern Spain is a popular destination for watching flocks of migrating bird species, with plentiful birdlife. Largest of all are the numerous storks of Castilla in the summer months, see box, above. One of the most dramatic species is the lammergeyer, or bearded vulture. Known as 'bone-breaker' (*quebrantahuesos*) in Spanish for its habit of dropping bones on rocks to shatter them and get at the marrow, it's a superb sight, drifting up valleys on its massive wings. Smaller but far more common is the endemic common or griffon vulture (*buitre*), while the fluffy white Egyptian vulture (*alimoche*) can be seen in hilly regions. Golden eagles (*águila real*) can also be spotted in the Pyrenees. Numerous other birds of prey are common sights both in the mountains or circling the the endless horizons of the *meseta*. The rivers of Northern Spain have always been full of trout and salmon, yet overfishing and hydroelectric projects have reduced their numbers in many areas.

Rare sights in the mountains include capercaillie (*urogallo*) and wallcreepers; woodpeckers, choughs and owls are more common. On the plains, larks, doves and grouse are common sights, as are two species of bustard. Coastal areas are home to a wide variety of waterbirds, as are some inland lakes; Galicia, Navarra and La Rioja are good areas for these species. There are many species of interesting butterflies and moths; clouds of them grace the Pyrenees and the Picos in early summer.

Vegetation

The war on trees conducted in Castilla through the centuries is over, with the sinister trunked creatures successfully eliminated. Most of the arid plains of the *meseta* were once covered with Mediterranean forest, but systematic deforestation, combined with over-grazing and war, have left it barren and bare; some of it barely able to support the sparse, scrubby *matorral* that covers the land deemed unfit for agriculture.

Reforestation schemes in Castilla have primarily been for logging purposes, and the region needs a more enlightened environmental programme such as that of Asturias, which preserves some superb stretches of ancient forest. Indeed, Spain's relatively high overall forest cover owes much to its northern provinces.

The forest cover of the northern Spanish coast and mountains is impressive in many parts, with chestnut, beech and holm oak at lower levels, and Scots pine and silver fir higher up, among other species. South of Burgos, one of Castilla's few forested areas is Europe's largest expanse of juniper trees.

In spring, the wildflowers of the Pyrenees and the Cordillera Cantábrica are superb, with myriad colourful species. The *meseta*, too, can be attractive at this time, with fields of poppies and cultivated sunflowers bright under the big sky.

National parks

Spain has several *parques nacionales* (national parks); the first, established in 1918, were Covadonga (now part of the Parque Nacional Picos de Europa) and Ordesa, in the Aragonese Pyrenees. These, along with the offshore islands incorporated into the Parque Nacional Islas Atlánticas de Galicia, are the three in the region covered by this book. Far more numerous, and covering a larger area, are *parques naturales* (natural parks) administered by the autonomous communities. Although protection for the species within these areas in some cases isn't absolute, it is significant, and crucial in many cases for survival. Asturias has the best-administered parks, with several in its forested hills and valleys: Muniellos and Somiedo are two of the finest; those in Galicia and the Pyrenees are also especially worth noting. *Reservas de caza* are protected areas that also have significant coverage but for less noble reasons; so that there'll be plenty of animals to shoot when the hunting season comes around.

Books

Food and drink

Barlow, J, *Everything But the Squeal* (2008), Farrar, Straus & Giroux. Entertaining culinary ramble around Galicia, trying all manner of pork products and finding a few weird old traditions along the way.

Barrenechea, T, *The Basque Table* (1998), Harvard Common Press. A cookbook with traditional Basque recipes.

Casas, Penelope, *The Foods and Wines of Spain* (1982), Knopf. Considered by many as the definitive book on Spanish cooking, the author is married to a Madrileño and covers regional cuisine as well as tapas and traditional desserts.

Ortega, Simone and Inés, *The Book of Tapas* (2010), Phaidon. From the authors of a classic Spanish cookbook, *1080 Recipes*, this is a comprehensive guide to tapas, both traditional and avant-garde.

Radford, J, *The New Spain: A Complete Guide to Contemporary Spanish Wine* (2006), Mitchell Beazley. A comprehensive guide to Spain's wines and wineries.

History and politics

Beevor, A, *The Battle for Spain* (2007), Phoenix. This prolific war historian's take on the conflict. Detailed but readable, it's not perhaps as good as Hugh Thomas's, but it's shorter and benefits from recent research.

Brenan, G, *The Spanish Labyrinth* (1943), Billings & Sons. A good explanation of the background to the Spanish Civil War.

Carr, R (ed), *Spain: A History* (2000), Oxford University Press. An interesting compilation of writing on Spanish history, with entertaining and myth- dispelling contributions from leading academics.

Elliott, J, *Imperial Spain* (1963), Edward Arnold. History as it should be, precise, sympathetic and very readable.

Gibson, I, *Ligero de Equipaje* (2006). A moving biography of poet Antonio Machado by excellent Spanish-based Irishman Ian Gibson. Hopefully it will appear in English soon.

Kurlansky, M, *The Basque History of the World* (1999), Vintage Press. A likeable introduction to what makes the Basques tick, what they eat, what they've done and what they're like.

Rankin, N, *Telegram from Guernica* (2003), Faber & Faber. This biography of the fascinating war correspondent George Steer has more on his Ethiopian experiences than the Guernica events, but is still a decent read that evokes the frenzy of the Civil War.

Steer, G, *The Tree of Guernica* (1938), Hodder & Stoughton. Written by a pro-Republican reporter who was an eyewitness to the atrocity of the bombing, this is of most interest for an evocative description of the event itself.

Thomas, H, *The Spanish Civil War* (1961/1977), Penguin. The first unbiased account of the war read by many Spaniards in the censored Franco years, this is large but always readable. A superbly researched work.

Tremlett, G, *Ghosts of Spain* (2008), Walker. Covering both the history and contemporary changes in Spanish society, this journalist's book is entertaining and informative.

Zulaika, J, *Basque Violence: Metaphor and Sacrament* (2000), University of Nevada Press. An academic but intriguing exploration of the roots of Basque nationalist feeling, and the progression to violence.

Literature, art and reportage

Alas, L (Clarín), *La Regenta* (1885). Good novel about small-town prejudices, set in mythical Vetusta, heavily based on Oviedo.

Atxaga, B, *Obabakoak* (1994), VintageBooks. A dreamlike series of anecdotes making up a novel by a well-respected contemporary Basque author. Drawn from Basque heritage rather than about Basque culture. Individual and profound.

Baroja, P, *The Tree of Knowledge* (1911). While mostly set in Madrid and Valencia, this is the best introduction to this powerful Basque novelist.

Burns, J, *Spain: A Literary Companion* (1995); John Murray. Anthology of Spanish writers.

Cela, C, *La Familia de Pascual Duarte* (1942). Nobel-prize-winning writer's first and best novel, a grimly realistic novel about post-war Spain. *La Colmena* is another good one that has been translated into English.

Cervantes Saavedra, M de, *Don Quijote* (1605/1615). Don Quixote is an obvious choice and a superbly entertaining read.

Cohen, J (ed), *The Penguin Book of Spanish Verse* (1988), Penguin. Excellent collection of Spanish poetry through the ages, with original versions and translations.

Delibes, M, *The Heretic* (2006), Overlook. One of the last works of this great Valladolid writer, it deals with a man's struggles with the Inquisition in his home town in the 16th century.

Hemingway, E, *Death in the Afternoon* (1939), Jonathan Cape. Superb book on bullfighting by a man who fell heavily for it.

Hemingway, E, *Fiesta/The Sun Also Rises* (1927), Jonathan Cape. One of Hemingway's greatest works, an fine description of the Pamplona fiestas and trout-fishing in the Pyrenees.

Orwell, G, *Homage to Catalonia* (1938), Secker & Warburg. About Orwell's experience of the Spanish Civil War, and characteristically incisive and poignant.

Unamuno, M, *Tragic Sense of Life* (1913), Dover Publications (1990). The anguished and heroically honest attempt by the great Basque and Salamantine philosopher to come to terms with faith and death.

Travelogues

Borrow, G, *The Bible in Spain* (1842), John Murray Press. Amusing account of another remarkable 19th-century traveller who

travelled widely through Spain trying to distribute Bibles during the first Carlist War.

Brenan, G, *The Face of Spain* (1950), Turnstile Press. Although set in the south, this is worth a read for Brenan's insights into the people he lived among for many years.

Ford, R, *A Hand-Book for Travellers in Spain* (1845), John Murray Press. Difficult to get hold of (there have been several editions) but worth it; comprehensive and entertaining guide written by a 19th-century British gentleman who spent 5 years in Spain.

Ford, R, *Gatherings from Spain* (1846), John Murray Press. Superb and sweeping overview of Spanish culture and customs; Richard Ford was something of a genius and has been surpassed by few if any travel writers since.

Jacobs, M, *The Road to Santiago*, Pallas Athene Publishers. One of the best guides to the architecture of the Pilgrim Route, full of knowledgeable insight but happily piety-free.

Lee, L, *As I Walked Out One Midsummer Morning* (1969), Penguin. A poignant account of a romantic walk across pre-Civil War Spain.

Nooteboom, C, *Roads to Santiago* (1992), The Harvill Press. An offbeat travelogue that never fails to entertain. One of the best travel books around, soulful, literary and moving, by a Dutch writer with a deep love of Romanesque architecture. Highly recommended.

Pillement, G, *Unknown Spain* (1964), Johnson Press. Likeable and useful (if not hugely entertaining) book describing various routes discovering the architecture of Northern Spain.

Other

Arias Páramo, L, *Guía del Arte Prerrománico Asturiano* (1994), Trea. The best book around on Asturian pre-Romanesque architecture. Spanish, but with an English summary.

Ball, P, *¡Morbo!* (2001). Excellent overview of Spanish football and its rivalries.

Farino, T and Grunfeld, F, *Wild Spain*, Sheldrake Press. Knowledgeable book on Spain's wildlife and the quiet corners where you find it.

Contents

Footnotes

Basic Spanish for travellers

Learning Spanish is a useful part of the preparation for a trip to Spain and no volumes of dictionaries, phrase books or word lists will provide the same enjoyment as being able to communicate directly with the people of the country you are visiting. It is a good idea to make an effort to grasp the basics before you go. As you travel you will pick up more of the language and the more you know, the more you will benefit from your stay.

Vowels

a   as in English cat
e   as in English best
i   as the ee in English feet
o   as in English shop
u   as the oo in English food
ai   as the i in English ride
ei   as ey in English they
oi   as oy in English toy

Consonants

Most consonants can be pronounced more or less as they are in English. The exceptions are:

g   before e or i is the same as j
h   is always silent (except in ch as in chair)
j   as the ch in Scottish loch
ll   as the y in yellow
ñ   as the ni in English onion
rr   trilled much more than in English
x   depending on its location, pronounced
     x, s, sh or j

Spanish words and phrases

Greetings, courtesies

hello	*hola*	I speak a little Spanish	*hablo un poco de español*
good morning	*buenos días*		
good afternoon/evening	*buenas tardes/ noches*	I don't speak Spanish	*no hablo español*
		do you speak English?	*¿hablas inglés?*
goodbye	*adiós/hasta luego*	I don't understand	*no entiendo*
pleased to meet you	*encantado/a*	please speak slowly	*habla despacio por favor*
how are you?	*¿cómo estás?*		
I'm called ...	*me llamo ...*	I am very sorry	*lo siento mucho/ discúlpame*
what is your name?	*¿cómo te llamas?*		
I'm fine, thanks	*muy bien, gracias*	what do you want?	*¿qué quieres?*
yes/no	*sí/no*	I want/would like	*quiero/quería*
please	*por favor*	I don't want it	*no lo quiero*
thank you (very much)	*(muchas) gracias*	good/bad	*bueno/malo*

Basic questions and requests

have you got a room for two people?	*¿tienes una habitación para dos personas?*
how do I get to_?	*¿cómo llego a_?*
how much does it cost?	*¿cuánto cuesta? ¿cuánto es?*
is VAT included?	*¿el IVA está incluido?*
when does the bus leave (arrive)?	*¿a qué hora sale (llega) el autobús?*
when?	*¿cuándo?*
where is_?	*¿dónde está_?*
where can I buy?	*¿dónde puedo comprar...?*
where is the nearest petrol station?	*¿dónde está la gasolinera más cercana?*
why?	*¿por qué?*

Basic words and phrases

bank	*el banco*	market	*el mercado*
bathroom/toilet	*el baño*	note/coin	*el billete/la moneda*
to be	*ser, estar*	police (policeman)	*la policía (el policía)*
bill	*la factura/la cuenta*	post office	*el correo*
cash	*efectivo*	public telephone	*el teléfono público*
cheap	*barato/a*	shop	*la tienda*
credit card	*la tarjeta de crédito*	supermarket	*el supermercado*
exchange rate	*el tipo de cambio*	there is/are	*hay*
expensive	*caro/a*	there isn't/aren't	*no hay*
to go	*ir*	ticket office	*la taquilla*
to have	*tener, haber*	traveller's cheques	*los cheques de viaje*

Getting around

aeroplane	*el avión*	luggage	*el equipaje*
airport	*el aeropuerto*	motorway, freeway	*el autopista/*
arrival/departure	*la llegada/salida*		*autovía*
avenue	*la avenida*	north/south/	*el norte, el sur,*
border	*la frontera*	west/east	*el oeste, el este*
bus station	*la estación de*	oil	*el aceite*
	autobuses	to park	*aparcar*
bus	*el bus/el autobús/*	passport	*el pasaporte*
	el camión	petrol/gasoline	*la gasolina*
corner	*la esquina*	puncture	*el pinchazo*
customs	*la aduana*	street	*la calle*
left/right	*izquierda/derecha*	that way	*por allí*
ticket	*el billete*	this way	*por aquí*
empty/full	*vacío/lleno*	tyre	*el neumático*
highway, main road	*la carretera*	unleaded	*sin plomo*
insurance	*el seguro*	waiting room	*la sala de espera*
insured person	*el asegurado/la*	to walk	*caminar/andar*
	asegurada		

Accommodation

air conditioning	*el aire*	pillows	*las almohadas*
	acondicionado	restaurant	*el restaurante*
all-inclusive	*todo incluido*	room/bedroom	*la habitación*
bathroom, private	*el baño privado*	sheets	*las sábanas*
bed, double	*la cama*	shower	*la ducha*
	matrimonial	soap	*el jabón*
blankets	*las mantas*	toilet	*el inódoro*
to clean	*limpiar*	toilet paper	*el papel higiénico*
dining room	*el comedor*	towels, clean/dirty	*las toallas limpias/*
hotel	*el hotel*		*sucias*
noisy	*ruidoso*	water, hot/cold	*el agua caliente/fría*

Health

aspirin	*la aspirina*	diarrhoea	*la diarrea*
blood	*la sangre*	doctor	*el médico*
chemist	*la farmacia*	fever/sweat	*la fiebre/el sudor*
condoms	*los preservativos,*	pain	*el dolor*
	los condones	head	*la cabeza*
contact lenses	*los lentes de*	period	*la regla*
	contacto	sanitary towels	*las toallas*
contraceptives	*los anticonceptivos*		*femininas*
contraceptive pill	*la píldora*	stomach	*el estómago*
	anticonceptiva		

Family

family	*la familia*	boyfriend/girlfriend	*el novio/la novia*
brother/sister	*el hermano/la*	friend	*el amigo/la amiga*
	hermana	married	*casado/a*
daughter/son	*la hija/el hijo*	single/unmarried	*soltero/a*
father/mother	*el padre/la madre*		
husband/wife	*el esposo (marido)/*		
	la mujer		

Months, days and time

January	*enero*	July	*julio*
February	*febrero*	August	*agosto*
March	*marzo*	September	*septiembre*
April	*abril*	October	*octubre*
May	*mayo*	November	*noviembre*
June	*junio*	December	*diciembre*

Monday	*lunes*		*cuarto*
Tuesday	*martes*	it's one o'clock	*es la una*
Wednesday	*miércoles*	it's seven o'clock	*son las siete*
Thursday	*jueves*	it's six twenty	*son las seis y veinte*
Friday	*viernes*	it's five to nine	*son las nueve*
Saturday	*sábado*		*menos cinco*
Sunday	*domingo*	in ten minutes	*en diez minutos*
at one o'clock	*a la una*	five hours	*cinco horas*
at half past two	*a las dos y media*	does it take long?	*¿tarda mucho?*
at a quarter to three	*a las tres menos*		

Numbers

one	*uno*	eight	*ocho*
two	*dos*	nine	*nueve*
three	*tres*	ten	*diez*
four	*cuatro*	eleven	*once*
five	*cinco*	twelve	*doce*
six	*seis*	thirteen	*trece*
seven	*siete*	fourteen	*catorce*

fifteen	*quince*	forty	*cuarenta*
sixteen	*dieciséis*	fifty	*cincuenta*
seventeen	*diecisiete*	sixty	*sesenta*
eighteen	*dieciocho*	seventy	*setenta*
nineteen	*diecinueve*	eighty	*ochenta*
twenty	*veinte*	ninety	*noventa*
twenty-one	*veintiuno*	hundred	*cien/ciento*
thirty	*treinta*	thousand	*mil*

Regional languages

El País Vasco Spanish is the main language of the Basque lands, and spoken by everyone. The Basque language, Euskara/Euskera, is an ancient and difficult language with no known relatives. After decades of hiding under Franco, the Euskara has come back with a bang. An ever-growing number of people are learning and using it. You'll see it everywhere: on road signs, in bars, on posters. Place names are often written in both Euskara and Spanish. Some of the regional towns use only Euskara. In some cases the Basque version is more common (eg Hondarribia over Fuenterrabia), in others the Spanish takes precedence (Bilbao/Bilbo). A regularly used compromise is to use both in a double-barrelled arrangement, thus Vitoria-Gasteiz. Basque words you'll hear regularly are *eskerrik asko* (thank you) and *agur* (goodbye).

Asturias Bable is broadly very similar to Spanish. The main difference you'll notice is that words tend to end in *u* where they would end in *o* in Spanish, thus *Asturianu*. You'll see many signposts where Gijón has been changed to Xixón with spraypaint.

Galicia *Galego* (Gallego) is the language of *Galiza* (Galicia). It is more similar to Portuguese than Spanish. Though most people in cities use *castellano* in everyday speech, *Galego* is commonly heard in rural areas and seen on signs. *Galego* place names have mostly replaced their Spanish counterparts, and are used in this text. ▸▸ *See also Language, pages 47 and 524.*

Food glossary

It is impossible to be definitive about terms used; different regions often have variants.

For meats, *poco hecho* is rare, *al punto* is medium rare, *regular* is medium, *muy hecho* is well-done.

A

aceite oil; *aceite de oliva* is olive oil
aceitunas olives, also sometimes called *olivas*; the best kind are *manzanilla*, particularly when stuffed with anchovy, *rellenas con anchoas*
agua water
aguacate avocado
ahumado smoked; *tabla de ahumados* is a mixed plate of smoked fish
ajo garlic, *ajetes* are young garlic shoots
ajo arriero a simple sauce of garlic, paprika and parsley
albóndigas meatballs
alcachofa artichoke
alcaparras capers
alioli a sauce made from raw garlic blended with oil and egg yolk; also called *ajoaceite*
almejas name applied to various species of small clam
alubias beans
anchoa preserved anchovy
angulas baby eels, a delicacy that has become scarce and expensive; far more common are *gulas*, false *angulas* made from putting processed fish through a spaghetti machine; squid ink is used to apply authentic colouring
añejo aged (of cheeses, rums, etc)
anís aniseed, commonly used to flavour biscuits and liqueurs
arroz rice; *arroz con leche* is a sweet rice pudding
asado roast; an *asador* is a restaurant specializing in charcoal-roasted meat and fish

atún blue-fin tuna
azúcar sugar

B

bacalao salted cod, an emblematic Basque food; an acquired taste, it is worth trying *al pil-pil* (a light yellow sauce made from oil garlic, and the natural gelatin of the cod, very difficult to make, and Bilbao's trademark dish); *al ajo arriero* is mashed with garlic, parsley, and paprika
berberechos cockles
berenjena aubergine/eggplant
besugo red bream
bistek cheap steak
bizcocho sponge cake or biscuit
bocadillo/bocata a crusty filled roll
bogavante lobster
bonito Atlantic bonito, a small tuna fish
boquerones fresh anchovies, often served filleted in garlic and oil
botella bottle
brasa (a la) cooked on a griddle over coals, sometimes you do it yourself at the table
buey ox, or in Galicia, a large crab

C

cabracho scorpionfish
cabrales a delicious Asturian cheese similar to Roquefort
cabrito young goat, usually roasted (*asado*)
cacahuetes peanuts
cachelos boiled young potatoes, traditionally served with *pulpo* (octopus) in Galicia
café coffee; *solo* is black, served espresso-style; *cortado* adds a dash of milk, *con leche* more; *americano* is a long black
calamares squid
caldereta a stew of meat or fish; the broth may be served separate, like with a *cocido*

caldo a thickish soup

callos tripe

caña a draught beer

cangrejo crab; occasionally river crayfish

caramelos sweets

carne meat

carta menu

castañas chestnuts

cava sparkling wine, mostly produced in Catalunya

cazuela a stew, often of fish or seafood

cebolla onion

cecina cured beef like a leathery ham; a speciality of León province

cena dinner

centollo spider crab

cerdo pork

cerveza beer; *caña* is draught beer

champiñon mushroom

chipirones small squid, often served *en su tinta*, in its own ink, deliciously mixed with butter and garlic

chocolate a popular afternoon drink

chorizo a red sausage, versatile and not too hot

chuleta/chuletilla chop

chuletón massive T-bone steak, often sold by weight

churrasco barbecued meat, often ribs with a spicy sauce

churro a fried dough-stick usually eaten with hot chocolate (*chocolate con churros*)

cigalas The 4WD of the prawn world, with pincers; Dublin Bay prawns in English

cochinillo/lechón/tostón suckling pig

cocido a heavy stew, usually of meat and chickpeas/beans, typical of the mountains; *sopa de cocido* is the broth

codorniz quail

cogollo lettuce heart

comida lunch

conejo rabbit

congrio conger-eel

cordero lamb

costillas ribs

crema catalana a lemony *crème brûlée*

croquetas deep-fried crumbed balls of meat, béchamel, seafood, or vegetables

cuajada junket, a thin natural yoghurt eaten with honey

cuchara spoon

cuchillo knife

cuenta (la) the bill

D

desayuno breakfast

dorada a species of bream (gilthead)

dulce sweet

E

embutido any salami-type sausage

empanada a savoury pie, either pasty-like or in large flat tins and sold by the slice; *bonito* is a common filling, as is ham, mince or seafood

ensalada salad; *mixta* is usually a large serve of a bit of everything; excellent option

ensaladilla rusa Russian salad, potato, peas and carrots in mayonnaise

entrecot A juicy, fatty cut of steak, often from ox

erizos/ericios sea urchins; definitely an acquired taste, but strangely addictive

escabeche pickled in wine and vinegar

espárragos asparagus, white and usually canned

estofado braised, often in stew form

F

fabada the most famous of Asturian dishes, a hearty stew of beans, chorizo, and *morcilla*

fideuá a bit like a *paella* but with noodles

filete a cheap cut of steak

flan the ubiquitous *crème caramel*, great when home-made (*casero*), awful out of a plastic cup

foie rich goose or duck liver from force-fattened birds.

frambuesas raspberries

fresas strawberries

frito/a fried

fruta fruit

G

galletas biscuits
gambas prawns
garbanzo chickpea
granizado popular summer drink, like a frappé fruit milkshake
guisado stewed, or a stew
guisantes peas

H

habas broad beans
harina flour
helado icecream
hígado liver
hojaldre puff pastry
horno (al) oven (baked)
huevo egg

I

ibérico See *jamón*; the term can also refer to other pork products
idiazábal the Basque sheepmilk cheese, a speciality that sometimes comes smoked

J

jabalí wild boar, usually found in autumn
jamón ham; *jamón de York* is cooked British-style ham, but much better is the cured *serrano*; *ibérico* refers to ham from a breed of pigs that graze wild in western Spain and are fed partly on acorns (*bellotas*) Particular regions and villages are known for their hams, which can get mighty expensive
judías verdes green beans

K

kokotxas pieces of hake cheek and throat, cooked in a rich sauce; usually delicious, if a little fatty

L

lacón con grelos Galician stew of pork and potatoes
langosta crayfish
langostinos king prawns
lechazo milk-fed lamb
leche milk
lechuga lettuce
lenguado sole
lentejas lentils
limón lemon
lomo loin, usually sliced pork
longaniza long sausage; an Aragón speciality
lubina sea bass

M

macedonia de frutas fruit salad, usually tinned
magret de pato fattened duck breast
manchego Spain's national cheese; hard, whitish, and made from ewe's milk
mantequilla butter
manzana apple
manzanilla a word referring to the nicest type of olive; also camomile; and a dry wine similar to sherry
marisco shellfish
matanza (la) early Nov is pig-killing time, with much feasting and many pork products
mejillones mussels
melocotón peach, usually canned and served in *almibar* (syrup)
membrillo quince jelly, usually eaten with cheese
menestra a vegetable stew, usually served like a minestrone without the liquid; vegetarians will be annoyed to find that it's often seeded with ham and bits of pork
menú a set meal, usually consisting of three or more courses, bread and wine or water
merluza hake is to Spain as rice is to southeast Asia
miel honey
mollejas sweetbreads; ie the pancreas or neck glands of a calf or lamb

migas breadcrumbs, fried and often mixed with lard and meat to form a delicious peasant dish of the same name

morcilla blood sausage, either solid or semi-liquid; a speciality of León and Burgos

morro cheek, pork or lamb

mostaza mustard

mosto grape juice, a common option in bars

N

naranja orange

nata sweet whipped cream

navajas razor-shells

natillas rich custard dessert

nécora small sea crab, sometimes called a velvet crab

nueces walnuts

O

orejas ears, usually of a pig

orujo a fiery grape spirit, often brought to add to coffee if the waiter likes you

ostra oyster

P

pan bread

parrilla grill; a *parrillada* is a mixed grill

pastel cake/pastry

patatas potatoes; often chips (*patatas fritas*); *bravas* are with spicy sauce; *a la Riojana* is with paprika and chorizo

pato duck

patxarán the sloe-berry, but usually the liqueur made from it, often flavoured with *anis*; some are fairly medicinal, most light, fruity and delicious

pechuga breast (usually chicken)

perdiz partridge

percebes goose-neck barnacles, a curious speciality of Galicia; salty and tasty, but tough to open

pescado fish

picadillo a dish of spicy mincemeat

picante spicy hot

pichón squab

pimienta pepper

pimientos peppers; there are many kinds; *piquillos* are the trademark thin Basque red pepper; Padrón produces sweet green mini ones; Bierzo loves theirs stuffed *rellenos*

pintxo/pincho the reason you put on weight in the Basque country; bartop snack

pipas sunflower seeds, a common snack

plancha (a la) grilled on a hot iron

plátano banana

pochas young haricot beans, a Riojan speciality

pollo chicken

postre dessert

puerros leeks

pulga a colloquial word for the tiny submarine-shaped rolls that feature atop bars in the Basque lands; the word actually means 'flea'

pulpo octopus, particularly delicious *a la gallega*, boiled Galician style and garnished with olive oil, salt, and paprika

Q

queimada a potent Galician ritual drink of *orujo* mixed with coffee and then heated over a fire

queso cheese

R

rabas crumbed calamari strips, often eaten at weekends

rabo de buey oxtail

ración a portion of food served in cafés and bars; check the size and order a half (*media*) if you want less

rana frog; *ancas de rana* is frogs' legs

rape monkfish/anglerfish

relleno/a stuffed

reserva, gran reserva, crianza, cosechero terms relating to the age of wines; see page 37

revuelto scrambled eggs, usually with mushrooms or seafood; often a speciality

riñones kidneys
rodaballo turbot; pricey and delicious
romana (*a la*) fried in batter

S

sagardotegi cider house in the Basque country
sal salt
salchichón a salami-like sausage
salmón salmon
salpicón a seafood salad with plenty of onion and vinegar
San Jacobo a steak cooked with ham and cheese
sardiñas sardines, delicious grilled
seco dry
sepia cuttlefish
serrano see *jamón*
setas wild mushrooms, often superb
sidra cider
solomillo beef fillet steak cut from the sirloin bone
sopa soup

T

tarta tart or cake
té tea
tenedor fork
ternera veal or young beef
tocino pork fat; *tocinillo del cielo* is an excellent caramelized egg dessert
tomate tomato
tortilla a Spanish omelette, with potato, egg, olive oil and optional onion
trucha trout; *a la Navarra* comes with bacon or ham
toro a traditional Basque fish stew or soup

txaka/chaka a mixture of mayonnaise and chopped seafood, featuring heavily in *pintxos*
txakolí slightly effervescent Basque wine produced from underripe grapes
txangurro spider crab, superb

U

uva grape

V

vaso glass
verduras vegetables
vermut vermouth; delicious when it's the bar's own. Traditionally drunk at weekends before lunch – *la hora de vermut*.
vieiras scallops, also called *veneras*
vino wine; *blanco* is white, *rosado* or *clarete* is rosé, *tinto* is red
vizcaína (a la) in the style of Vizcaya, Bilbao's province; usually based on onions and dried peppers

X

xoubas sardines in Galicia

Z

zamburiñas a type of small scallop
zanahoria carrot
zumo fruit juice, usually bottled and pricey
zurito a short beer in the Basque country, useful for tapas-hopping; varies in size from a splash to a quarter-pint

Index → *Entries in bold refer to maps.*

Andy Symington

A freelance writer hailing from Australia, Andy has spent the last decade living in Northern Spain and is the author and co-author of several Footprint handbooks, including *Andalucía*.

Acknowledgements

As always, this guide is a collaborative effort. Hugh O'Keefe and Ruth Nieto Huerta were excellent companions on research trips, and I owe thanks once again to Richard Prowse for providing transport and for tireless joint restaurant research. Particular thanks are due also to many other friends whose recommendations and advice about the region have been most helpful. There are more than I could list, but I especially thank in no particular order: Samuel Prowse Pérez, Mark Hayward, Julieta García, Juancho López, José Vicente Revilla, Silvia González, Gelo Rodríguez, Javier de Celis, Lourdes Villa, Rocío Villa, Chema Montes, Laura Rodríguez Álvarez, Lucía Rodríguez Álvarez, Jon Warren, Nicole Oakley, David Jackson, Constan Chao, Begoña García, Jo Williams, Carmen Hevia, Pelayo González, José Carlos González, Maika Montes, Mike Burren and Fátima Carrasco. Thanks too to my family for constant support; many others, including the helpful staff at tourist offices across the region, considerably eased my path around the north of Spain, and it has been a pleasure as always to work with the excellent team at Footprint.

Credits

Footprint credits

Project editor: Felicitiy Laughton
Layout and production: Angus Dawson
Cover and colour section: Pepi Bluck
Maps: Kevin Feeney
Proofreader: Jen Haddington

Managing Director: Andy Riddle
Commercial Director: Patrick Dawson
Publisher: Alan Murphy
Publishing Managers: Felicity Laughton, Nicola Gibbs.
Digital Managers: Jo Williams, Jen Haddington
Marketing and PR: Liz Harper
Advertising: Renu Sibal, Elizabeth Taylor
Finance and Administration: Elizabeth Taylor

Photography credits

Front cover: Guggenheim Museum, Bilbao; Jose Antonio Jimenez/photolibrary.com.
Back cover: Castillo de Gormaz, Castilla y León; Juan José Pascual/agefotostock.
P1 René Mattes/hemis.fr. **P2-3** Juan Carlos Cantero/photolibrary.com. **P6** Vvp / Dreamstime.com; Kevin George/agefotostock; Alex Segre/Alamy; Andy Symington. **P7** Gonzalo Azumendi/agefotostock; Romain Cintract/hemis.fr. **P8** Bjorn Svensson/ agefotostock. **P9** Javier Larrea/agefotostock; Kevin George/agefotostock; Carles Zamorano Cabello/Alamy; Nick Fraser; PRISMA ARCHIVO/ Alamy. **P10-11** Pecold/Shutterstock. **P12** Alain Felix/hemis.fr.

Footprint feedback

We try as hard as we can to make each Footprint guide as up to date as possible but, of course, things always change. If you want to let us know about your experiences – good, bad or ugly – then don't delay, go to www.footprinttravelguides.com and send in your comments.

Publishing information

Footprint Northern Spain 5th edition
© Footprint Handbooks Ltd
March 2011

ISBN: 978 1 907263 35 4
CIP DATA: A catalogue record for this book is available from the British Library

® Footprint Handbooks and the Footprint mark are a registered trademark of Footprint Handbooks Ltd

Published by Footprint
6 Riverside Court
Lower Bristol Road
Bath BA2 3DZ, UK
T +44 (0)1225 469141
F +44 (0)1225 469461
www.footprinttravelguides.com

Distributed in the USA by Globe Pequot Press, Guilford, Connecticut

Printed in India by Nutech Print Services
Pulp from sustainable forests

Every effort has been made to ensure that the facts in this guidebook are accurate. However, travellers should still obtain advice from consulates, airlines, etc about travel and visa requirements before travelling. The authors and publishers cannot accept responsibility for any loss, injury or inconvenience however caused.

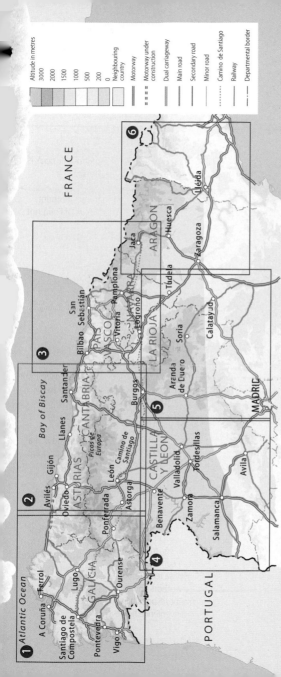

Footprint Mini Atlas
Northern Spain

N

50 km
50 miles

Altitude in metres

3000
2000
1500
1000
500
200
0

Neighbouring country

Motorway
Motorway under construction
Dual carriageway
Main road
Secondary road
Minor road
Camino de Santiago
Railway
Departmental border

FRANCE

PORTUGAL

Atlantic Ocean

Bay of Biscay

Mediterranean Sea

A Coruña
Ferrol
Santiago de Compostela
Pontevedra
Vigo
Ourense
Lugo
GALICIA

Gijón
Avilés
Oviedo
ASTURIAS
Ponferrada
Astorga
León
CANTABRIA
Santander
Llanes
Picos de Europa
Camino de Santiago

PAÍS VASCO
Bilbao
San Sebastián
Vitoria
Pamplona
NAVARRA
Logroño
LA RIOJA
Burgos

ARAGÓN
Jaca
Huesca
Zaragoza
Tudela
Calatayud
Soria
Aranda de Duero
Lérida

CASTILLA Y LEÓN
Benavente
Zamora
Salamanca
Valladolid
Tordesillas
Avila
MADRID

1
2
3
4
5
6

Map 1

Map 2

Bay of Biscay

A

N

10 km
10 miles

Costa Montanesa

Llanes
Puertas
San Vicente de Barquera
Santillana del Mar
Suances
Cabo Mayor
Santander
Arnuero
Noja
ierra de Cuera
arreña
Arenas de Cabrales
Unquera
Comillas
E70
Torrelavega
E67
Parbayon
Gama
Santoña
Laredo
Castro Urdiales
Panes
Celis
N634
Lahezón de la Sal
Varqas
Sarón
A8 E70
Ampuero
ebos
tres
La Hermida
Puentenansa
Cabuérniga
Puente Viesgo
Arredondo
Ramales
B Bil
Castro
San Vicente
Villacarriedo
Lanestosa
Sopuerta
Carranza
Balmaseda
Sodu
Zalla
Potes
La Lastra
N611
A67
Cotillo
N623
CANTABRIA
Espinosa de los Monteros
Artziniega
Espinama
Puerto San Glorio
La Vega de Liébana
Pesaguero
Pico de Tres Mares (2175m)
Espinilla
Pesquerao
Cordillera Cantábrica
Villasante
Cueva
Hadeo de Angulo
Menagaray
Amurri
Orduña
Triollo
San Salvador
Santa María
Reinosa
Embalse del Ebro
Arija
Cilleruelo
Las Rozas
Arija
Sanfelices
Soncillo
Villarcayo
San Pantaleón
amporredondo
Barruela de Santullán
Cubillos
Incinillas
Medina de Pomar
Criales
Velilla de Taril
Cervera de Pisuerga
Cillamayor
Villanueva de la Nia
Ruerrero
Valdenoceda
Pesquera
Puente Arenas
Pedrosa
Quintana Martino Galindez
Cantoral
Nestar
Valdelateja
Escalada
Trespaderne
Frias
Sai
de A
Congosta
La Puebla
Olleros
N611
San Andres de Arroyo
Alar del Rey
Basconcillos
Tubilla del Agua
Villalta
Pesadas de Burgos
Oña
Encio
Pancorbo
Ameyu
aldaña
Renedo
Villaeles
Herrera de Pisuerge
Sotresgudo
Coculina
Masa
Poza
Cornudilla
Cubo de Bureba
A1
E5/80
C
CASTILLA Y LEON
Ventosa
Villadiego
Quintanilla
N623
Briviesca
Castil de Pegas
N1
Carrión de los Condes
120
Osorno
Villamayor
Sasamón
N120
Quintanaortuño
Sotopalacios
Alcocero de Mola
Castildelgado
Monte de Oca
Santo Dom
de la Calz
Villalcázar de Sirga
Marcilla
Castrillo
5
Vivar del Cid
Burgos
San Juan de Ortega
Rubona
Belorado
Pradoluengo
Ezcaray
Frómista
Pedrosa
Castrojeriz
E80
Estépar
N620
4
5
Buniel
Sarracin
Ibeas
Arlanzón
Villamorico
Urquiza
6
Fresneda de la s
Astudillo
Amusco
Pampliega
Sierra de la

Map 3

Bay of Biscay

A

Noja
Gama · Santoña
Laredo
8 · E70
redondo   Cabo Billano
Ramales · Ampuero   Castro-Urdiales   Plencia   Bakio   Bermeo
Carranza   Santura   Mundaka   Elantxobe
nosa de.   Lanestosa   Sopuerta   Portugalete   Getxo   Mungia   Arteaga   Lekeitio
        Balmaseda   Zalla   Sodupe   Basauri   Ondarroa
onteros   Artziniega   Bilbao   Markina-   Deba   Zumaia   San Sebastián/
        Villasante   Hadeo de   Menagaray   Galdakao   Gernika   Xemein   Getaria   Zarautz   Donostia   Pasa
B   tabrica   Angulo   Amurrio   Amorebieta   Berriz   Eibar   Azpeitia   Zestoa   Pasa
rcayo   San   Orduña   Castillo y   Elorrio   Bergara   Loiola   Errezil   Villabona   Andoain
edina   Pantaleón   Criales   Elejabeitia   Durango   Arrasate-   Legazoi   Zumárraga   Tolosa   Goizueta
Pomar   Berberana   Murgia   Mondragon   Bessain   Lizartza
        Osma   Corbesa   Legutiano   Oñati   Betelu
Pedrosa   Espejo   Salinas   N240   Arantzazu   PAIS VASCO   Lecunberri
    Trespaderne   Quintana   de Añana   E5/80   Zalduondo   Altsasu-   Écharri-   A15
Frias   Martino   Bergüenda   /804   Salvatierra   Aranaz   Irurzún
    Oña   Galindez   N1   Equilaz   Olazagutia   Huarte-
        Cornudilla   Vitoria/Gasteiz   Gaceo   Larraona   Araquil   Echa
a   Cubo de Bureba   Encío   Pancorbo   Arraia   Abarzuza   Puente
C   E5/80   Ameyugo   Miranda   Briñas   Maeztu   Santa Kurutze   Estella   la Reina
    Briviesca   Altable   de Ebro   Peñacerrada   Kanzepu   Acado   (Lizarra)   Graqui   Maneru
        Casalarreina   Haro   Bernedo   Monasterio   Mendigorria
Castil de   Castildelgado   Elvillar   de Iracha   Oteiza
Peones   Belorado   Santo Domingo   Laguardia   Los Arcos   Allo   Larraga
Montes de O   de la Calzada   San Asensio   (Biazteri)   Torres del Río   Larraga
Pradoluengo   Elciego   Oyon   Viana   Miranda
Urquiza   Ezcaray   5   Nájera   Cenicero   Logroño   Sesma   Lerin   de Arga
rón   Fresneda   Baños   Nizo   Navarrete   Mendavia   Lodosa   Cárcar   Falces
de la Sierra   Ezcaray   San Millán   Río Tobía   Islallana   Ribaflecha   Andosilla
badillo   Pineda de la   de la Cogolla   LA RIOJA   Ausejo   Persalta
    Sierra Tirón   Anguiano   Torrecilla   El Villar   Calahorra
Barbadillo   Canales   San Lorenzo   Embalse de   en Cameros   San Román   Arnedillo   Arnedo
de Pez   Barbadillo   (2271m)   Glacara   de Cameros   Aldeaunueva
Hotiguela   de Herreros   Mansilla   Autol
badillo   Salas de   Neila   Villavelay   1   2   Enciso   3   Turruncun   Baños de
    los Infantes   Montenegro   Pajares   Yanguas

LA RIOJA

2

Cárcar
Falces
Andosilla
Persalta
Calahorra

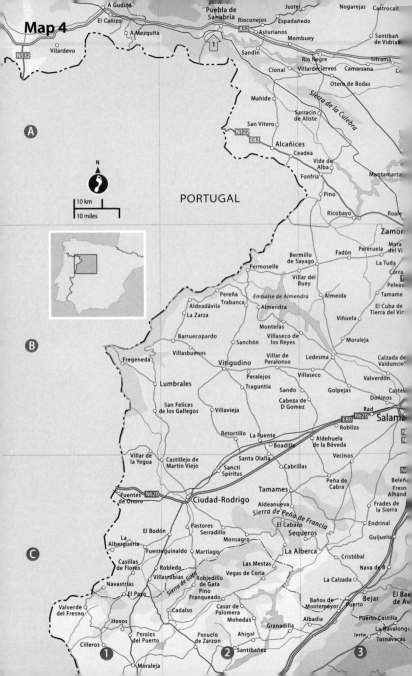

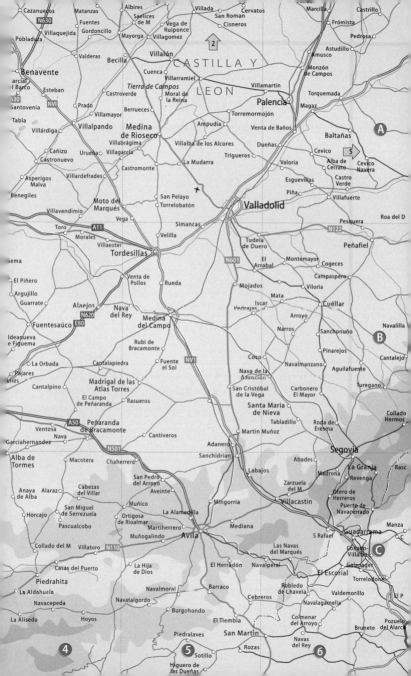

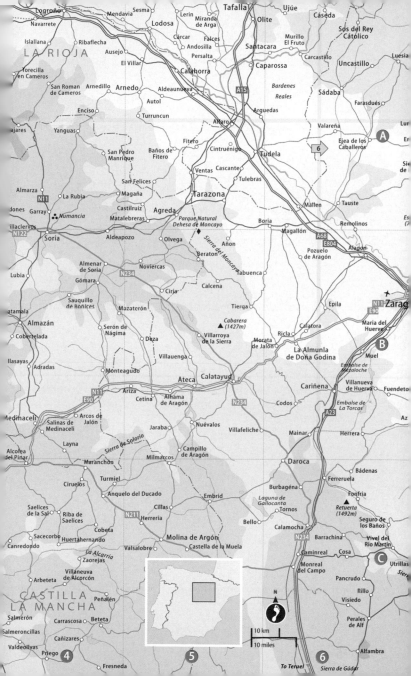

Index